DICTIONARY OF
TWENTIETH-CENTURY BRITISH
CARTOONISTS AND CARICATURISTS

Also by Mark Bryant

Dictionary of British Cartoonists and Caricaturists, 1730–1980
(with S. Heneage)

Dictionary of Riddles

Private Lives: Curious Facts about the Famous and Infamous

World War II in Cartoons

Literary Hymns

The Complete Colonel Blimp

The Comic Cruikshank

Dictionary of Twentieth-Century British Cartoonists and Caricaturists

Mark Bryant

ASHGATE

To John, Moira and the family with warmest wishes from Sandy

Cawdor November 2001

(page 233!)

Published by
Ashgate Publishing Limited
Gower House
Croft Road
Aldershot
Hants GU11 3HR
England

Ashgate Publishing Company
Old Post Road
Brookfield
Vermont 05036–9704
USA

British Library Cataloguing-in-Publication data
Mark Bryant, 1953–
   Dictionary of twentieth century British cartoonists and caricaturists
   1. Cartoonists – Great Britain – Biography – Dictionaries
   I. Title II. Twentieth century British cartoonists and caricaturists
741.5.′092241

Library of Congress Cataloging-in-Publication data
Bryant, Mark, 1953–
   Dictionary of twentieth century cartoonists and caricaturists / Mark Bryant
      p. cm
   Includes bibliographical references
   1. Cartoonists—Great Britain—Biography—Dictionaries. I. Title.

   NC1476 .B79 2000
   741.5′092′241–dc21
   [B] 99–045326

ISBN 1 84014 286 3

Printed on acid-free paper
Copy-edited and typeset by The Running Head Limited,
www.therunninghead.com
Printed in Great Britain at the University Press, Cambridge

Contents

Preface

This is the first ever biographical dictionary specifically devoted to British cartoonists and caricaturists of the 20th century. It derives in part from an earlier volume, *Dictionary of British Cartoonists and Caricaturists, 1730–1980* – which dated itself from the first satirical works of William Hogarth (generally acknowledged as the father of British cartoons and caricature) – but goes far beyond that book in its coverage of the last 100 years. A considerable number of new names have been added and, in the light of new research, many entries have been entirely rewritten and others revised and updated.

The dictionary focuses primarily on British press cartoonists and caricaturists who have worked as full-time professionals for national newspapers and magazines over the last century and whose reputations were established by 1995. Artists who either retired or who ceased to work in this field around 1900 have not been included in detail but have been listed and cross-referenced to the *Dictionary of British Cartoonists and Caricaturists, 1730–1980* for interested readers.

The work of the cartoonist is, by its very nature, ephemeral and, as Sir Osbert Lancaster once said: 'A professional preoccupation with the topical is the surest passport to oblivion.' The hard proof of this has been the considerable amount of detective work that has been required to track down details of deceased artists' lives for this volume, especially those working in the first half of the 20th century. Unlike those of previous generations, very few cartoonists and caricaturists of this period received obituaries in the press or warranted interviews in magazines or other publications. Added to which only a small number ever published collections of their own work, and biographies and autobiographies are extremely rare.

Another difficulty, having decided on producing roughly 500 entries with 100 illustrations, was choosing which artists to include, which to leave out and which to illustrate. The result is, hopefully, a reasonably balanced representation of prominent cartoonists and caricaturists from each decade of the century, with the pictures also giving as varied a selection of styles and techniques as possible within the limitations of black-and-white reproduction and copyright availablility. The emphasis has been on political, editorial, pocket, sports and joke cartoonists, and caricaturists – strip cartoonists, comic artists, animators, 'lightning' caricaturists and humorous book illustrators have generally been omitted (except where they have also worked as one of the above), as these have usually been covered in other publications. Some foreign-born artists whose work appeared regularly in British newspapers and magazines have been included, but otherwise all were either born in Britain or became naturalized British citizens.

Where an artist mentioned in the text has his or her own entry elsewhere in the book their name has been highlighted in capitals on its first occurrence and all pseudonyms, as well the more important cartoon characters, have been cross-referenced. However, owing to the limitations of space, the lists of exhibitions (EXH), books published (PUB) and illustrated (ILL), works held in public collections (COLL) and literature on the artists (LIT) are representative rather than definitive.

A lot has changed in 100 years. When the century opened most cartoonists and caricaturists had usually been to art school and received a training in classical draughtsmanship, many of them also working as illustrators for books, magazines and newspapers. As a result, cartoon drawings would be filled with detail and cross-hatching and were visually very similar to an artist's illustration work. In consequence the caption – often quite long – was critical. Indeed, according to the *Punch* historian R. G. G. Price, when Owen Seaman took over as the magazine's first new Editor of the century in 1906, he asked for pictures to be submitted for his approval with just the caption visible. Their suitability for the paper was judged on this alone before the covering was removed to see how well the joke had been illustrated. By the end of the century, in contrast, many cartoonists were self-taught, and a much looser, simpler style of drawing became the norm, with captions reduced to a single short sentence, sometimes set in speech balloons.

Developments in technology also affected the production process. In 1900, after completing a joke drawing (originally sketched in pencil and then finished in pen, brush and indian ink on paper or board) the artist would deliver it to the publishers to be photographed and printed (in black-and-white) in line or half-tone by hot-metal presses either installed in their offices or in premises nearby. A hundred years later the cartoon or caricature, increasingly drawn in fibretip pen on paper (though steel nibs, brush and indian ink on board are still used), can be faxed from the artist's studio into the newspaper office or scanned by a computer and sent via the Internet for printing anywhere in the world, in colour or monochrome. Alternatively, using a special software package, it can be drawn directly onto the computer screen itself using an electronic pen and sketchpad.

The content of the cartoon changed as well. In the early 1900s, as with the second half of the 19th century, personal attacks on royalty were taboo and satires on public figures generally were considerably restrained. In the words of Sir David Low, these turn-of-the-century artists were still 'wearing lavender vests and dipping their rapiers in lemonade'. Even Sir Francis Carruthers Gould – who in the late 1880s had become the first ever staff political cartoonist on a daily newspaper and continued working until 1914 – said that 'I etch with vinegar, not vitriol'. However, in contrast, by the end of the 20th century, graphic satirists such as Gerald Scarfe and Ralph Steadman – not to mention the creators of television's *Spitting Image* puppet series – had mercilessly lampooned all and sundry (including the House of Windsor), in no-holds-barred assaults which frequently featured grotesque and degrading images. Indeed, Steve Bell's *Maggie's Farm* cartoon series attacking Prime Minister Margaret Thatcher was denounced in the House of Lords as 'an almost obscene series of caricatures'.

The public image of cartoonists and caricaturists has also varied over the course of 100 years. At the beginning of the century, in an age before television, cinema and radio, they were held in high regard – as social commentators and witty graphic journalists they were seen as important members of the media and suitably rewarded by their employers. In 1912 Will Dyson's political cartoons occupied the whole front page of the *Daily Herald* and in the 1920s and '30s such was the competition in Fleet Street for top cartoonists that artists like Strube and Tom Webster were paid record fees for their work. And during World War II the continuing power of cartoons ensured that they still appeared regularly even when the shortage of newsprint meant that many national daily newspapers were reduced to only a few pages.

The advent of the new media, especially the arrival of television in the 1950s, had a considerable impact on Fleet Street in general and the press cartoon in particular as the public became increasingly accustomed to receiving its news and entertainment from sources other than newspapers. However, the end of the century saw a reawakening of interest in the art form. The 1960s heralded the beginnings of the so-called 'Satire Boom', the launch of *Private Eye* and the employment (for the first time) of cartoonists and caricaturists on such upmarket broadsheet newspapers as *The Times* and *Daily Telegraph*. This period also saw the founding of specialist professional societies such as the Cartoonists' Club of Great Britain and the British Cartoonists' Association. And the installation of a new gravestone to the great 18th-century cartoonist James Gillray in 1961 was followed over the next three decades by the unveiling of official commemorative Blue Plaques to honour such 20th-century masters as Bairnsfather, Shepard, Bateman, Low and Vicky.

At the beginning of the 1970s, Britain's first major retrospective exhibition of cartoons and caricatures from Hogarth until modern times, 'Drawn & Quartered', was held at the National Portrait Gallery and shortly afterwards the Centre for the Study of Cartoons & Caricature was set up at the University of Kent. The end of the 1980s witnessed the launch of the Cartoon Art Trust to establish a permanent Museum of Cartoon Art in Britain – thereby answering a clarion call made by H. M. Bateman to the Royal Society of Arts in 1949. And in the last years of the century the British Cartoon Centre opened in London.

British cartoonists and caricaturists have made an important contribution to the nation's artistic heritage in the 20th century and can claim a distinguished pedigree that stretches back more than three hundred years and includes such eminent figures as Hogarth, Gillray, Rowlandson and Cruikshank. They can also count amongst their number some of the world's finest exponents in this field in modern times and yet little information has been generally available on their lives and works. This book, it is hoped, will help redress the balance and perhaps also go some way to giving these artists the recognition they deserve.

Mark Bryant
London, 2000

Acknowledgements

In helping with the preparation of this book thanks must go in the first instance to all the many cartoonists and caricaturists, as well as relatives and friends of deceased artists, who have spared the time to provide biographical information and to discuss details of their work and publications. Grateful acknowledgement is also made to all those whose works appear in the Bibliography and in particular to those individuals whose scholarship and pioneering research in this field have proved invaluable, notably: Dorothy George, Simon Houfe, M. H. Spielmann, R. G. G. Price, William Feaver, B. Peppin and L. Micklethwaite, Keith Mackenzie and Maurice Horn.

Thanks too to the helpful staff of the Advertising Association Library, British Cartoon Centre, British Cartoonists' Association, British Film Institute, British Library, British Museum Prints & Drawings Department, British Newspaper Library, Cartoon Art Trust, Cartoon Gallery, Cartoonists' Club of Great Britain, Fine Art Society, Illustrated London News Library, Imaginative Book Illustration Society, Imperial War Museum Library and Department of Art, Jack Duncan Gallery, Karikatur & Cartoon Museum Basel, London Cartoon Gallery, London Sketch Club, New Zealand Cartoon Archive Trust, London Press Club, Punch Library, Rae-Smith Gallery, St Bride Printing Library, Savage Club, University of Kent Centre for the Study of Cartoons & Caricature, University of London Senate House Library, Victoria & Albert Museum Department of Prints & Drawings and the Westminster Central Reference Library.

In addition, the publishers and author would like to thank the following for their kind permission in allowing illustrations to be reproduced: *Boston Globe*, Chambers Harrap Publishers, *Daily Express*, *Daily Mail*, *Daily Mirror*, *Daily Telegraph*, *Economist*, *Evening Standard*, *Guardian*, John Murray, Laurence Pollinger (estate of Mrs J. C. Robinson), *Listener*, *Nebelspalter*, *Oldie*, *Private Eye*, Solo Syndication & Literary Agency, *Spectator*, *Sun*, *Sunday Telegraph*, *Sunday Times* and *Woman Magazine*.

Particular thanks must also go to Jim Baker, Geoffrey and Geraldine Beare, Syd Brown, the late Mel Calman, Les Coleman, Bill Connelly, David Cuppleditch, Dr Paul Goldman, Paul Gravett, Geoff Hassell, Simon Heneage, Bill Hewison, Pat Huntley, the late David Linton, Alan Mumford, Jane Newton, Terry Parker, John and Felicity Rae-Smith, Bryan Reading, Ian Scott, Professor

ACKNOWLEDGEMENTS

Colin Seymour-Ure, Francis and Pam Wilford-Smith, Dougal Wood and Jenny Wood for invaluable information about cartoonists, and in some cases for allowing access to their personal libraries and archives. Finally, thanks to all at Ashgate Publishing, especially Nigel Farrow for having confidence in this project, as in the earlier dictionary, and to editors Pamela Edwardes and Susan Moore – as well as all at The Running Head Limited – for producing such a handsome volume. Last, but by no means least, the author would especially like to thank the Authors' Foundation and the Society of Authors without whose financial support this book would have been nigh impossible.

While every effort has been made to make this dictionary as authoritative as possible and to trace all artists, relatives and copyright holders, any further information would be most welcome, and will be added to future editions.

Abbreviations

A	Ashmolean Museum, Oxford
AA	Architectural Association
AB	Aberdeen Art Gallery
AC	Arts Council of Great Britain
AG	Abbey Gallery
AI	Association of Illustrators' Gallery
AIA	Artists' International Association
AR	Arnolfini Gallery, Bristol
B	Birmingham City Museum & Art Gallery
BAG	Bluecoat Art Gallery, Liverpool
BAR	Barber Institute, Birmingham
BC	Barbican Centre
BCO	British Council
BED	Cecil Higgins Gallery, Bedford
BEL	Belfast Museum & Art Gallery
BFI	British Film Institute
BG	Baillie Gallery
BGM	Bethnal Green Museum
BI	British Institution
BIB	Bibliothèque Nationale, Paris
BL	British Library
BM	British Museum
BN	Royal Pavilion Art Gallery & Museum, Brighton
BOD	Bodleian Library, Oxford
BR	City of Bristol Museum & Art Gallery
BRU	Bruton Galleries
BSG	Brook Street Gallery
BUR	Burlington Gallery
C	Courtauld Institute
CA	National Museum of Wales, Cardiff
CAC	Camden Arts Centre

CAS	Contemporary Arts Society
CAT	Cartoon Art Trust
CB	CEMA Gallery, Belfast
CBG	Chris Beetles Gallery
CCGB	Cartoonists' Club of Great Britain
CG	Cartoon Gallery (formerly The Workshop)
CHG	Chenil/New Chenil Galleries
CHR	Christie's
CI	Commonwealth Institute
COO	Cooling Gallery
CP	British Communist Party Library
CS	Charterhouse School
D	Derby City Art Gallery
DG	Dudley Gallery
DOW	Dowdeswell Galleries
DUL	Dulwich College
DUN	Dundee Museum & Art Gallery
E	Scottish National Gallery of Modern Art, Edinburgh
EU	Essex University
F	Fitzwilliam Museum, Cambridge
FAS	Fine Art Society
FR	Frost & Reed
FS	Folio Society
G	Glasgow Art Gallery
GC	Garrick Club
GG	Grosvenor Galleries
GI	Glasgow Institute of Fine Arts
GM	Geffrye Museum
GOU	Goupil Gallery
H	Hastings Art Gallery
HAM	Hamilton Galleries
HC	Hampton Court
HCL	House of Commons Library
HLL	House of Lords Library
HU	Hull University
HUN	Hunterian Museum, Glasgow
ICA	Institute of Contemporary Arts
IWM	Imperial War Museum

JDG	Jack Duncan Gallery
KH	Kenwood House, Hampstead
KN	Knokke-Heist Museum, Belgium
L	Walker Art Gallery, Liverpool
LAN	Langton Gallery
LC	Library of Congress, USA
LCG	London Cartoon Gallery
LE	Leeds City Art Gallery
LEG	Leger Gallery
LEI	Leicestershire Museums & Art Galleries
LG	Leicester Galleries
LH	Leighton House
LM	Museum of London
LON	London Group
LTM	London Transport Museum
M	Manchester City Art Gallery
MAD	Musée des Arts Décoratifs, Paris
MAM	Musée d'Art Moderne, Paris
MAN	Manchester Gallery of Modern Art
MCO	Merton College, Oxford
MET	Metropolitan Museum of Modern Art, New York
MG	Mayor Gallery
MIN	Minories, Colchester
MOCA	Museum of Cartoon Art, New York
MOMA	Museum of Modern Art, Oxford
MOMI	Museum of the Moving Image
MT	Mermaid Theatre
N	Nottingham Castle Museum
NAD	National Academy of Design, New York
NBL	National Book League
NEAC	New English Art Club
NEC	National Exhibition Centre, Birmingham
NG	National Gallery
NGG	New Grafton Gallery
NGI	National Gallery of Ireland, Dublin
NGS	National Gallery of Scotland, Edinburgh
NIG	Nigel Greenwood Gallery
NLI	National Library of Ireland
NOR	Norwich Art Gallery

NPG	National Portrait Gallery
NPGS	National Portrait Gallery of Scotland
NT	National Theatre
NWS	New Watercolour Society
NYPL	New York Public Library
OHG	Orleans House Gallery, Twickenham
OWS	Old Watercolour Society
PAG	Patersons Gallery
PG	Piccadilly Gallery
RA	Royal Academy
RAF	RAF Museum
RAH	Royal Albert Hall
RAM	Royal Albert Museum, Exeter
RBA	Royal Society of British Artists
RCA	Royal College of Art
RE	Royal Society of Etchers & Engravers
RFH	Royal Festival Hall
RG	Redfern Gallery
RHA	Royal Hibernian Academy
RI	Royal Institute of Painters in Watercolour
RIBA	Royal Institute of British Architects
RL	Royal Library, Windsor
RMS	Royal Miniature Society
ROH	Royal Opera House
ROI	Royal Institute of Oil Painters
RP	Royal Society of Portrait Painters
RSA	Royal Scottish Academy
RSAB	Royal Society of Artists, Birmingham
RSMA	Royal Society of Marine Artists
RSW	Royal Scottish Society of Painters in Watercolour
RWA	Royal West of England Academy
RWS	Royal Society of Painters in Watercolour
S	Sheffield City Art Galleries
SA	Society of Artists
SAM	Sammlung Karikaturen & Cartoons, Basel
SBA	Society of British Artists
SBC	South Bank Centre
SC	Savage Club
SGG	St George's Gallery

SI	Smithsonian Institute, USA
SIM	Simavi Foundation Cartoon Museum, Istanbul
SM	Science Museum
SWA	Society of Women Artists
T	Tate Gallery
TG	The Gallery
THG	Townley Hall Gallery, Burnley
TM	Theatre Museum
TOW	Towner Art Gallery, Eastbourne
TRY	Tryon Gallery
UAA	Ulster Academy of Arts
UKCC	University of Kent Cartoon Centre
UM	Ulster Museum
US	University of Surrey
UW	University of Wales
V&A	Victoria & Albert Museum
W	Whitechapel Art Gallery
WA	Wakefield Art Gallery & Museum, Yorkshire
WAC	Welsh Arts Council
WAD	Waddington Galleries
WAG	Whitworth Art Galleries, Manchester
WBM	Wilhelm Busch Museum, Hanover
WD	William Drummond Gallery
WG	Walker's Gallery
Y	York City Art Gallery
Z	Zwemmer's Gallery

A

ABRAHAM, Abu (b. 1924). Political and pocket cartoonist, journalist and politician. Abu Abraham was born in Tiruvalla, Kerala, India, on 11 June 1924, the son of A. M. Matthew Abraham, a lawyer. He studied French, mathematics and English at the Travancore University, Kerala, where he was also tennis champion. He graduated in 1945 and was a reporter on the *Bombay Chronicle* (1946–9), drawing cartoons in his spare time. He then moved to the New Delhi satirical journal, *Shankar's Weekly*, in 1951 as staff cartoonist. Abu came to the UK in 1953 and contributed to *Punch, Everybody's, London Opinion, Daily Sketch*, etc., before becoming the *Observer's* first-ever staff political cartoonist in 1956. After ten years he moved to the *Guardian* and drew a regular pocket cartoon there for three years until 1969. He later returned to India and worked for *Indian Express* (1969–81). In addition he was a member of the Rajya Sabha or Upper House of the Indian parliament (1972–8). Described by the *Guardian* as 'the conscience of the Left and the pea under the princess's mattress', he also drew (as 'Abraham') for *Tribune* (1956–7, 1966–9), and received a Special Award from the BFI for his animated film, *No Arks*. He was one of the founder members of the British Cartoonists' Association in 1966.
PUB: (ed.) *Verdicts on Vietnam* (1968), *Abu on Bangladesh* (1972), *Games of Emergency* (1977), *Arrivals and Departures* (1983), (ed.) *The Penguin Book of Indian Cartoons* (1988)
ILL: R. Thapar, *Indian Tales* (1991)

ABU – *see* Abraham, Abu

ACANTHUS – *see* Hoar, Harold Frank

ADAM, David (fl. 1930s). Joke cartoonist. David Adam is best known as the artist who drew the cartoon of a heavyweight man getting into a cab and saying to the driver 'Royal School of Needlework – and drive like mad.' It was published in *Punch* on 28 June 1939 and has often been mistakenly attributed to EMETT, though the style is very different.

ADAMSON, George Worsley RE MSIA MCSD (b. 1913). Freelance designer, illustrator and hu-morist. George Adamson was born in New York City on 7 February 1913, the son of George William Adamson, an engineer. He studied art at Wigan Art School under L. T. Howells ARCA and then at Liverpool City Art School under Geoffrey Wedgwood RE, where he specialized in aquatint and drypoint. Between 1940 and 1946 he served in the RAFVR as a navigator in 210 Coastal Command, flying Catalinas and Liberators, and was for a short while Official War Artist to Coastal Command. He was a lecturer in engraving and illustration at Exeter School of Art (1946–53) before turning freelance. Since then he has contributed 180 cartoons to the *Daily Telegraph's* 'Peterborough' column and supplied drawings and decorations as well as 34 covers for *Punch* (1939–92), commencing under FOUGASSE's editorship. Other freelance work has been for *Nursing Times, The Countryman, New Scientist, Young Elizabethan, Country Fair, Time & Tide, Illustrated London News, Listener, Sketch, Tatler, Radio Times* and *Private Eye*. A Member of the Chartered Society of Designers since 1954, he was elected a Fellow of the Royal Society of Painter-Printmakers in 1987. Influenced by classical artists such as Velázquez, Rembrandt, Goya and Hokusai, he works on paper, gesso surfaces and scraperboard, and uses ink, wash, charcoal, chalk and other media.
PUB: *A Finding Alphabet* (1965), *Widdecombe Fair* (1966), *Finding 1 to 10* (1968), *Rome Done Lightly* (1969)
ILL: 84 books including *The Faber Book of Nursery Verse* (1958); T. Hughes, *Meet My Folks!* (1961), *The Iron Man* (1968); R. Carpenter, *Catweazle* (1970); N. Hunter's 'Professor Branestawm' books (1966–77); F. Waters, *The Day the Village Blushed* (1977); first five volumes of *Private Eye's* 'Dear Bill' books (1980–84); P. G. Wodehouse, *Short Stories* (1983)
EXHIB: RAM; RA; L; American Institute of Graphic Arts, New York
COLL: [drawings/prints] RAM; IWM; UM; [prints] BM; V&A; RE Gallery; NYPL; Wigan Library; RAM; RAF

AJAY – *see* Jackson, Arthur

ALBERT – *see* Rusling, Albert

ALDIN, Cecil Charles Windsor RBA (1870–1935). Joke cartoonist, sporting artist, illustrator, painter and playwright. Born on 28 April 1870 in Slough, Berkshire, the son of a builder, Cecil Aldin was educated at Eastbourne College and Solihull Grammar School. He trained under Albert Moore and then studied anatomy at the South Kensington Schools (fellow students included the future architect Sir Edward Lutyens) and animal painting under Frank W. Calderon. His first commission was for an illustration in *Building News* (1890) for which he was paid 10s. His first drawing (of a dog show at the Agricultural Hall, London) was published in the *Graphic* in 1891 and he was a major contributor to *Illustrated London News* (1892–1911) and *English Illustrated Magazine* (1893–7). He also illustrated Kipling's 'Jungle Stories' for *Pall Mall Budget* and contributed to *Sporting & Dramatic News* (from 1891), *Gentlewoman*, *Queen*, *Black & White*, *Good Words*, *Boys' Own Paper*, *Ludgate*, *Pall Mall Magazine*, *Windsor*, *Pearson's*, *London Opinion*, *Punch*, *Sketch*, *Pick-Me-Up* and others. A specialist in dogs, horses, hunting and coaching scenes and historic buildings, he was elected a member of the RBA (1898), and was a co-founder (with PHIL MAY, TOM BROWNE, LANCE THACKERAY and DUDLEY HARDY) of the London Sketch Club (1898), becoming its President in 1905. Aldin was Master of the South Berkshire Foxhounds (1914) and his bull-terrier 'Cracker' became so famous through his portraits that his death, nearly three years after Aldin's, was announced on BBC radio and led to an obituary in *The Times*. During World War I he was Purchasing Officer for a Remount Depot in Purley, with the rank of Captain. Aldin also drew advertisements for Bovril, Nestlé, Player's, Abdullah and others, produced posters (e.g. for Cadbury's Cocoa and Colman's Starch – his first poster was for Colman's washing blue, 1899), and designed toys, sporting prints (his first-ever series, 'The Fallowfield Hunt', 1899, is one of the most reproduced sets of prints ever published), greetings cards, postcards (e.g. for Lawrence & Jellicoe, Savory, Hills, Moss, Valentines, Voisey and Tuck's 'Celebrated Posters' series) and wallpaper (including nursery friezes) for Liberty and Sanderson's. Aldin dogs also appeared as crockery designs for Doulton and Burgess & Leigh. Elected RBA (1897), he was a member of the Chelsea Arts Club. Influenced by Leech and Caldecott, he never humanized his animals' features and

worked in pen, ink, chalk and crayon, using pastel and watercolour for his sports subjects. He also produced etchings. In addition to his art work he wrote plays (Noel Coward starred in one, *The Happy Family*). Cecil Aldin retired to Palma, Majorca, in 1930 and died in the London Clinic, after suffering a heart attack on the boat returning to the UK, on 6 January 1935. After his death Lord Rosebery led a public appeal which resulted in annual Cecil Aldin Prizes for students of the Royal Veterinary College.

PUB: Many books including [with J. HASSALL] *The Happy Annual* (1907), *The Black Puppy Book* (1909), *Old Inns* (1921), *Old Manor Houses* (1923), *Cathedral and Abbey Churches of England* (1924), *Ratcatcher to Scarlet* (1926), *Dogs of Character* (1927), *An Artist's Models* (1930), *Scarlet to MFH* (1933), [with J. B. Morton] *Who's Who at the Zoo* (1933), *How to Draw Dogs* (1935), *Hunting Scenes* (1936)

ILL: Many books including W. M. Praed, *Everyday Characters* (1896); W. Emanuel, *A Dog Day, or the Angel in the House* (1902); W. Irving, *Christmas Day*; C. Dickens, *Pickwick Papers* (1910); R. S. Surtees, *Handley Cross* (1911); N. Heiberg, *White Ear and Peter* (1912); A. Sewell, *Black Beauty* (1912); J. Masefield, *Right Royal* (1922)

EXHIB: FAS (1935); BUR; L; RA; RBA; RMS; AG

COLL: IWM; V&A; THG

LIT: [autobiography] *Time I Was Dead* (1934); R. Heron, *Cecil Aldin: The Story of a Sporting Artist* (1981), *The Sporting Art of Cecil Aldin* (1990)

ALEC – *see* Wiles, Alec E.

'Alex' – *see* Peattie, Charles William Davidson

'Ally Sloper' – *see* Owen, William and Thomas, William Fletcher

ALPHA – *see* Fitton, James

ANDERSON, Martin 'Cynicus' (1854–1932). Joke cartoonist, designer, illustrator, painter and publisher of satirical postcards, greetings cards, calendars and books. Martin Anderson was born on 14 April 1854 at Leuchars near St Andrews. His father William Anderson was a stationmaster and he had relatives who were shareholders in the Leuchars–St Andrews railway. He was educated at Leuchars School and Madras College, St Andrews, and studied briefly at Glasgow Art College (1868). Apprenticed at first as a designer at Arthur's Calico Printers in Glasgow, he was a staff artist on the *Dundee Advertiser* (1880–88) while also illustrating books for J. Leng and contributing sketches (and covers) for *Quiz* magazine (1881–3). At first he signed himself 'MA' then changed this to 'Cynicus' in 1888 when he gave up working for the *Advertiser*. The name (for him) meant, not 'dog in a manger', but 'the onlooker of the passing show, who puts it down just as he sees it'. He moved to London in 1889 and began designing postcards for Blum & Degen and others. He then set up the Cynicus Publishing Company (1889) from which he issued his hand-coloured caricatures – often with rhyming couplets beneath – in print and book form, later being commissioned to produce possibly the first comic postcards in Britain. He also produced many seaside postcards, especially 'The Last Train to . . .' series, with the name of the town overprinted for each resort. Meanwhile he contributed illustrations to the *Idler, Ariel* and *Echo* and turned down the job of Lobby Artist on the *St James' Gazette* (1893). In 1898 he left London for good and moved to Tayport, Fife, where his sister and others had been hand-colouring his work for the rapidly expanding postcard market. Here he was elected to the town council (1900) and set up the Cynicus Publishing Company Ltd (1902) which produced *c.* 5000 card designs with an annual turnover of *c.* £10,000. The business went into voluntary liquidation in 1911 but was re-formed in 1914 as the Cynicus Art Publishing Company in Leeds. However, when war broke out it closed and he briefly set up a studio in Edinburgh in 1915. Founder of the St Mungo Art Club, and Secretary and Treasurer of the Dundee Art Club, he died at his home, Castle Cynicus, in Tayport, on 14 April 1932. His motto was 'Truth the Lyre'. For his mass-produced cards Anderson first drew a soft outline, then a team of workers would copy the original and add colour with a soft camel-hair brush, and finally he would re-touch each and put his signature on it.

PUB: *Miss Magdalen Green's Grand Tour* (1886), *Miss Magdalen Green's Xmas* (1886), *The Satires of Cynicus* (1890), *The Humours of Cynicus* (1891), *The Fatal Smile* (1892), *Symbols and Metaphors* (1892), *Cartoons Social and Political* (1893), *Cynicus, His Humour and Satire* (1896), *Selections from Cynicus* (1909), *Briton or Norman, Who Shall Rule?* (1911), *Satires of Cynicus* (1911), *The Great Bank Fraud* (*c.* 1916), *Through Wisdom's Glasses* (n.d.)

ILL: J. Timewell, *The Blue Button* (1896)
EXHIB: RSA; Crawford Centre for the Arts, University of St Andrews

'Andy Capp' – *see* Smythe, Reginald

ANGRAVE, Bruce FSIA (1912–83). Joke cartoonist, writer, illustrator and paper sculptor. Bruce Angrave was born in Leicester on 6 December 1912, the son of Charles Angrave, a graphic designer and photographer, and a cousin of Trafford-Smith, Lieutenant-Governor of Malta and later British Ambassador to Burma. He attended the Chiswick, Ealing, Central and Reimann (Westminster) Schools of Art and then worked as Art Director of the London Press Exchange advertising agency. During a trip to the World's Fair in New York in 1939 he saw paper sculptures for the first time in the Polish Pavilion and on his return began producing paper-sculpture caricatures (using Whatman Watercolour Paper) for advertisements, exhibitions and a film. During World War II he produced propaganda illustrations on waste, the blackout, etc., for the Ministry of Information, wrote and illustrated two children's books telling moral tales about 'the essential logic of machinery' and made models for the 'Britain at War' Exhibition in Chicago. He also produced paper sculptures for the Festival of Britain (1951), Expo 70 in Japan and the Ideal Home Exhibition (1971), and for advertising campaigns for London Transport, *Financial Times*, Pathé Pictures, Lever Bros, Yorkshire Relish, Letraset, Trumans Beer, Marley Tiles, Mappin & Webb and others. As a cartoonist he contributed regularly to *Lilliput, London Opinion* (including covers), *Radio Times, Time & Tide, Woman's Realm, Aeronautics, Woman* (a weekly cartoon for 35 years) and *Punch* (often signing 'BA'). In addition he designed for TV (BAFTA Award, 1953) and produced posters and fashion and advertising drawings. His work was influenced by R. Taylor of the *New Yorker* and poster designers Eckersley, Lewitt-Him and Games. He drew on Whatman Board, Winsor & Newton Fashion Plate Board, card and paper and also signed himself 'Bruce' and 'Ruan'. 'His figures, nearly always energetically in motion, are arrested at precisely that moment which reveals their characters and their weaknesses as individuals' (BRADSHAW). Bruce Angrave died at St Peter's Hospital, Covent Garden, on 8 July 1983.

Bruce Angrave, *Woman Magazine, c.* 1965

PUB: *Lord Dragline the Dragon* (1944), *The New English Fictionary* (1953), *The Mechanical Emperor* (1954), *Sculpture in Paper* (1957), *CATalogue* (1976), *MagnifiCAT* (1977), *TripliCAT* (1978), *Angrave's Amazing Autos* (1980), *Paper into Sculpture* (1981)
ILL: J. K. Cross, *The Other Passenger* (1944); S. MacFarlane, *Lucy Maroon* (1944); A. Huxley, *Caught in the Act* (1953); C. Munnion, *Pineapple in Candyland* (1957); [as 'Bruce'] *Tales of Mystery and Adventure* (n.d.)
EXHIB: [paper sculpture] Reed House, Piccadilly

'Animal Crackers' – *see* Spencer, William

ANTHONY – *see* Hutchings, Anthony

ANTON – *see* Thompson, Harold Underwood and Yeoman, Beryl Antonia

APFR – *see* Ritchie, Alick P. F.

APICELLA, Vincenzo FCSD (b. 1922). Joke and political cartoonist, illustrator, designer, photographer and painter. Enzo Apicella was born in Naples, Italy, on 26 June 1922, the son of Salvatore Apicella, a local councillor. He stud-ied languages at the Instituto Orientale, Naples (1941–2) and while serving in the Italian Air Force (1942–3) began contributing articles to *Le Vie dell'Aria* and *Ali di Guerra*. After studying briefly at the film school in Rome (1947) he took up freelance design work, illustration and print journalism before co-founding *Melodramma*, an opera magazine, in Venice (1953). When this folded he came to England (1954) and began designing posters for Schweppes (1956) and sets for TV (e.g. ABC TV's 'Bid for Fame'), as well as producing cartoon films. Self-taught, his cartoons have been published in *Corriere della Sera, La Stampa, Ici Paris, Krokodil, Boz* (including covers), *Observer, Guardian, Punch* (including covers), *Economist, Private Eye, Manifesto* (journalism and political cartoons), *Liberazione* (political cartoons) and *Harpers & Queen*. He has also worked as an interior designer for more than 140 restaurants, notably 70 for the Pizza Express chain (for which he also designed the corporate identity), and has produced murals (e.g. with Misha Black at the Research Design Unit). In addition he was a co-founder of the Arethusa club and Meridiana Restaurant in London and co-owner of Condotti Restaurant in Mayfair. 'One of the creators of the Swinging Sixties in

London' (Bevis Hillier, *Vogue*), Apicella draws with a fine line and a subtle use of colour. 'His cartoons are a major talent displaying an economy of line and the exploitation of space which put him, in my view, into the same class as our mutual friend, the late MARK BOXER' (George Melly). Apart from his political cartoons he is particularly at home with sophisticated caption-less jokes about the world of food, restaurants and chefs. A life-size seated waxwork dummy of him was created by ex-Madame Tussaud's sculptor Lynn Kramer for the Meridiana Restaurant (1974).

PUB: *Non Parlare Baciami* (1967), *Memorie di Uno Smemorato* (1983), *Don't Talk, Kiss* (1988), *Mouthfool* (1993)
ILL: *The Pizza Express Cookbook* (1976); F. Lagattolla, *The Recipes That Made a Million* (1978); J. Routh, *The Good Loo Guide* (1985); L. Grossman, *The Harpers & Queen Guide to Restaurants* (1987); R. Pazzaglia, *Il Guarracino* (1992)
EXHIB: Zarach Gallery; D. M. Gallery; Galeria 'Zapiecek' Desa, Warsaw (1976); Galeria 'Zapiecek' Desa, Cracow (1977); CG; D. Studio
COLL: UKCC

APP – *see* Appleby, Barry

APPLEBY, Barry Ernest (1909–96). Joke and strip cartoonist. Born in Birmingham on 30 August 1909, the son of Ernest James Appleby, Editor of *Autocar*, Barry Appleby won a prize from the Royal Drawing Society at the age of nine. He moved with his family to Kingston, Surrey, as a teenager and studied art at Epsom Art School (1934), Heatherley's (1935), Central School of Art (1936) and the Royal Academy Schools (1936), and cartooning through the PERCY BRADSHAW Press Art School. He began his career as a journalist, freelancing for trade magazines and boys' papers and was later a sports sub-editor on the *Daily Express*. He also worked as a joke cartoonist under the name 'App' and contributed joke drawings to the *Star, Daily Sketch, Daily Mail, Autocar, Reveille, Answers, London Opinion* and other publications (his first *Punch* cartoon, 'Hush, Perkins, the customer is always right', appeared on 14 July 1937). He joined the Auxiliary Fire Service in 1938 and during World War II served in the National Fire Service while drawing instructional and promotional cartoons and posters for the NFS, Ministry of Aircraft Production, RAF, Merchant Navy and National Safety First Association.

Appleby was best known for the internationally syndicated strip 'The Gambols', produced in association with his wife Dobs (Doris). Originally gamblers (horseracing), the suburban, middle-class, never-ageing couple George and Gaye Gambol first appeared on the sports page of the *Daily Express* on 16 March 1950 as a single panel. They turned into a strip on 4 June 1951 and by 1956 were featured in the *Sunday Express* as well. The series ran for 46 years and was syndicated to 47 countries. Barry drew most of the strips, with Dobs adding backgrounds, etc., but ideas for the gags were a joint effort. Barry continued to produce the Gambols alone after his wife's death in 1985. Appleby himself died in hospital near Castle Cary, Somerset, on 11 March 1996, five days before he would have celebrated the 46th anniversary of the strip's first appearance.

PUB: [with D. Appleby] *Have a Care There!* (RoSPA booklet); 45 'Gambols' annuals (from 1952)

APPLEBY, Steven (b. 1956). Joke cartoonist, illustrator, scriptwriter and animator. Steven Appleby was born on 27 January 1956 in Newcastle upon Tyne, the son of Walter Appleby, stone-quarry owner. Educated in York, he studied at Manchester Polytechnic (Foundation course in art) and took a degree in graphic design at Newcastle Polytechnic and an MA in illustration at the Royal College of Art. He then joined the design company Assorted Images, working on merchandising for pop groups, before becoming a professional cartoonist. His work has appeared in numerous publications including *Observer, Punch, Daily Mirror, Cartoonist, Squib, Tatler, Time Out, Esquire, Evening News, New Musical Express, Die Zeit, Reader's Digest, New Statesman, Daily Express, GQ, Company, Guardian, The Times, Daily* and *Sunday Telegraph, Oldie* (including covers), *The Times Magazine* (strip 'Small Birds Singing') and *Harpers & Queen*. In addition he has created and written scripts for the *Captain Star* animated cartoon series for ITV, based on his own strip cartoon (originally entitled 'Rockets Passing Overhead') that first appeared in *New Musical Express* (1986–8), then the *Observer* (1988–90) and *Die Zeit*. Winner of the Max and Moritz Prize in Germany (1994), the animated version features the voices of Richard E. Grant (Captain Star) and Adrian Edmondson as 'Limbs' Jones (who has nine heads and six arms). He has also drawn advertisements for Mercury Communications, Wessex Water and others, produced animated commercials and programme titles (with Pete Bishop) for LWT and MTV and designed a range of greetings cards. He cites his influences as being Edward Gorey, RONALD SEARLE and Oliver Postgate's animated series *Noggin the Nog*, amongst others.

PUB: [with G. Moule] *No, Honestly, It Was Simply Delicious But I Couldn't Eat Another Mouthful* (1984), *Rockets – A Way of Life* (1988), [with K. Poskitt] *99 Dont's* (1992), [with K. Poskitt] *122 Turnoffs* (1993), *Normal Sex* (1993), *Men – the Truth* (1994), [with K. Poskitt] *113 *@!K-UPS* (1995), *Miserable Families* (1995), *A Box of Secret Thoughts* (1996), *ANTMEN Carry Away My Thoughts As Soon As I Think Them . . .* (1997), *Alien Invasion* (1998)

ILL: 'Beachcomber', *Cram Me With Eels* (1994); A. MacFarlane and A. McPherson, *Fresher Pressure* (1994); L. MacRae, *You Canny Shove Yer Granny Off a Bus* (1995); M. Barfield, *Dictionary for Our Time* (1996); M. Killen, *How to Live With Your Husband* (1996)

EXHIB: Diorama Gallery; Creaser Gallery; Barbican; Sue Williams Gallery; JDG; LCG

COLL: V&A

ARDIZZONE, Edward Jeffrey Irving CBE RA (1900–79) – *see* Bryant & Heneage

ARMENGOL, Mariano Hubert (1909–95). Designer, painter, sculptor and political cartoonist. Born in San Juan de Abadesas, Catalonia, Spain, on 17 December 1909, the son of Benito Armengol, a textile manufacturer, Mario Armengol studied in Terrassa, Barcelona, Madrid and Paris before arriving in the UK via Narvik in 1940. During World War II he was a political cartoonist and graphic designer attached to the Ministry of Information, producing advisory booklets and pamphlets, and contributing cartoons to *Message* (a Belgian review), *France* (Free French) as well as propaganda cartoons for neutral countries. These cartoons he drew on large Whatman paper using a brush, ink and lithographic pencil. He also worked as 'Mario', producing smaller drawings in pen and ink only, with no tone. After the war he designed posters for British Rail, drew advertisements for Hammerton Beer, British Drug Houses Laboratory Chemicals, etc., and spent 20 years as a designer for ICI (*c.* 1951–71). In addition he drew illustrations for the

Ministry of Food magazine *Food & Nutrition* (1949), contributed work to the Festival of Britain in 1952–3, produced murals for Westminster Hall and the Science Museum, London, and designed the 'BBC 50' exhibition marking the anniversary of the TV channel. His design of the Industrial Pavilion at Expo Brussels was awarded a gold medal (1958) and he won joint first prize in an international furniture competition in 1968. He also designed a section of the British pavilion at Expo 67 in Montreal, featuring ten of his own 21-foot-high aluminium figures called 'The Brotherhood of Mankind' (these now stand in front of the Calgary Education Centre, Alberta). An admirer of Picasso and the cartoons of DAVID LOW he also painted in oils and produced collages and 3D paper-animal-sculpture greetings cards (for Gallery Five). He died in Nottingham on 27 November 1995.

PUB: *Those Three* (1942), *According to Plan* (1943)

ILL: *Spanish Fairy Stories* (*c.* 1944)

COLL: UKCC

ARMITAGE, Joshua Charles 'Ionicus' (1913–98). Joke cartoonist, illustrator and painter. Jos Armitage was born on 26 September 1913 in Hoylake, Cheshire, the son of a fisherman. He won a Cheshire County Art Scholarship to study at Liverpool City School of Art (1929–35) and later (1936–50) taught art at various colleges including Wallasey School of Art. During World War II he served in the Royal Navy on minesweepers and as a gunnery instructor. His first published work appeared in *Punch* on 29 March 1944 (his pen-name came from a set of Ionic columns on a concert hall in the background of his first cartoon for the magazine), an association that lasted 44 years and included more than 350 drawings. He also contributed to *Lilliput, Medical News, Financial Times, Daily Sketch, Countryman, Dalesman* (covers for 17 years), *Amateur Gardening* and *Tatler*, amongst others. A full-time freelance cartoonist, book and magazine illustrator since 1950 (with particularly long associations with publishers Chatto & Windus, William Kimber, Penguin Books, Hodder & Stoughton, Macmillan, Dent and Oxford University Press), he also worked as a painter (oils and watercolour), and was commissioned to provide 12 watercolours for the United Oxford & Cambridge Club in London. Very interested in architecture, his 'beautifully crafted and detailed drawings . . . contrasted sharply with the over-simplified style of a newer generation . . .

'Originally they made their money in bookends.'

Ionicus (J. C. Armitage), *Squib*, December 1992

His cartoons are somewhere between ACAN-THUS, who also drew architecture, and the political cartoonist NORMAN MANSBRIDGE' (DAVID LANGDON). FOUGASSE also said he had 'a static style that is capable of getting more out of a dynamic subject by sheer force of contrast than most dynamic styles could achieve'. A member of the Royal Liverpool Golf Club, he was also President of the Deeside Art Group. Ionicus died in Hoylake on 29 January 1998.

ILL: Nearly 400 books including covers for 58 titles by P. G. Wodehouse; C. Collodi, *The Adventures of Pinocchio* (1960); R. G. G. Price, *How to Become Headmaster* (1960), *Survive with Me* (1962); E. Blishen, *Town Story* (1964); O. Nash, *A Boy and His Room* (1964), *The Untold Adventures of Santa Claus* (1965); A. Lawrence, *Tom Ass* (1972), *The Good Little Devil* (1978); D. Kossoff, *Sweet Nutcracker* (1985)

COLL: BM; V&A; UKCC

ARMOUR, George Denholm OBE (1864–1949). Joke cartoonist, illustrator and painter. G. D. Armour was born in Waterside, Lanarkshire, on 30 January 1864, the son of Robert Armour, a cotton broker, and was educated at Glasgow Academy and Madras College, St Andrew's. He studied art at the Edinburgh School of Art and the Royal Scottish Academy (*c.* 1880–88), where he was encouraged by Robert Alexander RSA, whom he accompanied on trips to Tangier (from 1887), meeting there the animal painter Joseph Crawhall RWS NEAC, who was also a great influence. He later moved to London to work as a painter and illustrator (sharing a studio with PHIL MAY). In World War I he commanded a cavalry remount squadron, eventually reaching the rank of lieutenant-colonel with the British Salonika Force (1917). He was awarded an OBE in 1919. His first drawings were published in the *Graphic* (1890). As well as producing some 1500 sporting drawings for *Punch* (1894–1941) – becoming the magazine's best-known sporting and equestrian artist after the death of G. H. JALLAND – he also contributed to *Pick-Me-Up, Windsor Magazine, Judge, Field, Passing Show, Sporting & Dramatic News, Pall Mall Gazette, New Budget, Unicorn, Longbow, Butterfly, English Illustrated Magazine, Pall Mall Magazine, Country Life* (from 1912), *Humorist, London Opinion, Sketch, Tatler* and others. In addition he produced advertisements for Eno's, Erasmic Shaving Stick and others. For his illustration work he used mostly pen, brush, ink and watercolour, but also sometimes chalk. He also painted equestrian portraits of the Dowager Duchess of Beaufort and other society figures. Price has described him as 'no mean descendant of Leech . . . a sporting artist whose horses gave readers the pleasure of recognition, rather as RUSSELL BROCKBANK did later with his motorcars'. He was a member of the Savage Club. G. D. Armour died on 17 February 1949.

PUB: *The Humours of Sport* (1904), *Pastime with Good Company* (1914), *Humour in the Hunting Field* (1928), *A Hunting Alphabet* (1929), *Sport and There's the Humour of It* (1935)

ILL: R. S. Surtees (six titles, 1908–29); I. Bell, *Foxiana* (1929); J. Masefield, *Reynard the Fox* (1921); 'B. B.', *The Sportsman's Bedside Book* (1937) and others

EXHIB: FAS (1924); LG; RSA; RWA; GI; L; RSAB; RP; RA; RSW; New Gallery

COLL: V&A

LIT: [autobiography] *Bridle and Brush* (1937)

ARTZ, Sally (b. 1935). Joke and strip cartoonist and illustrator. Born in London on 14 March 1935, the daughter of Benjamin Artz, a painter, Sally Artz studied graphic design at St Martin's School of Art (1951–3). She worked as a commercial artist and with Halas & Batchelor animation studios before selling her first cartoon to *Weekend Mail* in 1955. Since then she has produced strips for *Sunday People* ('Libby – the Adventures of a Liberated Wife', 1971–81); 'Cath's Caff', 1988–91), *Tit-Bits* ('Our Gran', 1978–81) and *Chat* ('The Wright Shower', 1985–95), produced a widely syndicated cartoon feature for the *Daily Mirror* ('Why . . .', 1981–5) and also drew regularly for the paper's business page ('Funny Money', 1990–93). She has also contributed cartoons to *Reader's Digest, Penthouse* (USA), *Weekend, Oui, Bella* ('Suzy Says', 1988–94), *Private Eye, Spectator, Oldie, Mail on Sunday, She, Radio Times, Daily Sketch* and *Punch*, and has designed greetings cards for Accord and Camden Graphics. In addition she has written scripts for 'The Smurfs', produced animated cartoons for TV advertisements (Unichem, 1987) and produced illustrations for educational publishers such as Heinemann and Cambridge University Press. Winner of the Humor Gag section at the International Salon of Cartoons in Montreal (1981), she was Vice-President (with PETER MADDOCKS) of the British Cartoonists' Association (1991–3). Influenced at first by Disney and the American 'funnies' and later by

Nicolas Bentley and the *New Yorker* cartoonist Chon Day, Sally Artz uses a Rotring Art pen and sketches in 3B pencil, using Wiggins Teape Hi-Speed card. For colour work she uses Ecoline inks.

PUB: *Why, Oh Why . . .?* (1989)
ILL: J. Pearce, *Kids Work Out* (1987); A. Wadeley, A. Birch and A. Malin, 'Perspectives in Psychology' series (eight titles from 1992); M. Stoppard, *Sex Ed.* (1997)
COLL: MOCA; UKCC

ATCHISON, Michael (b. 1933). Joke and strip cartoonist and caricaturist. Michael Atchison was born in Victoria, Australia, in 1933 and came to England in 1960, contributing to *Punch* (including covers) and other magazines and newspapers. In 1967 he returned to Australia and worked for the *Sydney Daily Mirror* (1968) before joining the *Adelaide Advertiser* as Political Cartoonist later the same year. He also produces a daily strip, 'Word for Word', dealing with the origin of English words and phrases, which is published in newspapers in the USA, UK, Australia, Canada, South Africa and Papua New Guinea.
COLL: UKCC

ATTWELL, Mabel Lucie SWA (1879–1964). Joke cartoonist, illustrator and writer. Mabel Lucie Attwell was born on 4 June 1879 in Mile End, London, the daughter of a butcher. She attended the Cooper's Company School, then studied painting and drawing at the Regent Street Polytechnic Art School and Heatherley's but did not finish either course. Her first published drawings appeared in *Tatler, Little Folks, Pearson's* and other magazines. This led to commissions for illustrating series of children's books for Chambers and Hodder & Stoughton and Raphael Tuck's 'Raphael House Library of Gift Books', as well as postcards for Valentine & Sons (from *c.* 1914). Specializing in sentimental children's pictures, she also designed dolls, textiles, china (e.g. Shelley Potteries *c.* 1926) and posters (including one of the first for London Underground), produced comic strips and worked in advertising (for companies such as Boots, Erasmic Soap, Hovis, Sunlight Soap and Osman Towels). Perhaps her most famous creations were Diddums, which became a bestselling doll, and The Boo-Boos baby gnomes. She married the illustrator Harold C. Earnshaw in 1908 and her immensely successful children's annual first

appeared in 1922. Elected a member of the Society of Women Artists in 1925, she also wrote children's stories and verse. She was influenced by Hilda Cowham, John Hassall, and Charles and William Heath Robinson. Mabel Lucie Attwell died in Cornwall on 5 November 1964.

PUB: Many books including *The Lucie Attwell Annual* (1922–74), *The Boo-Boos* (1921–2), *Baby's Book* (1922), *Lucie Attwell's Fairy Book* (1932), *Lucie Attwell's Happy-Day Tales* (1932), *Lucie Attwell's Quiet Time Tales* (1932), *The Great Big Midget Book* (1934–5), *Lucie Attwell's Story Book* (1943, 1945, 1953), *Lucie Attwell's Jolly Book* (1953)
ILL: Many books including M. Baldwin, *That Little Lamb* (1905); L. Carroll, *Alice's Adventures in Wonderland* (1910); C. Kingsley, *The Water Babies* (1915); Queen Marie of Romania, *Peeping Pansy* (1919), *The Lost Princess* (1924); A. Marshall, *Wooden* (1920); J. M. Barrie, *Peter Pan and Wendy* (1921); L. Carroll, *Alice in Wonderland* (1922)
EXHIB: SWA 1924; BN (centenary exhibition, 1979); CBG (1984)
COLL: THG
LIT: C. Beetles, *Mabel Lucie Attwell* (1988)

ATTWELL, Michael 'Zoke' (b. 1943). Actor, political cartoonist and caricaturist. Michael Attwell was born in Watford, Hertfordshire, on 16 January 1943. A self-taught artist, he began work as an illustrator for IPC and D. C. Thomson children's comics such as *Bunty, Buster, Whizzer & Chips* and *Hotspur*. He transferred to newspaper cartoons as deputy to Franklin on the *Sun* and joined the *Sunday People* as Political Cartoonist in 1982, later moving to the *News of the World* (1984–8). Also a popular TV actor (he starred as Razor Eddie in *Turtle's Progress* and Kenny in *Eastenders*), his cartooning pseudonym comes from the names of his children – Zoe and Jake.

'Augusta' – *see* Poelsma, Dominic

AULD, Patrick Samuel Manson (1915–89). Joke cartoonist and landscape painter. Pat Auld was born in Reading on 24 February 1915, the second son of Samuel J. M. Auld, Professor of Agricultural Chemistry at University College (later the University of Reading). Educated at Reading School, he was a self-taught artist and first drew (unsigned) a weekly series of strips 'Do You Know Your Reading?' for the *Berkshire*

Chronicle in the 1930s before moving into advertising. During World War II he served briefly in the Grenadier Guards before being invalided out. After the war he rose to become Art Director of Royds advertising agency. His cartoons, mainly in pencil or pen and ink and often on cartridge paper, were published in *Punch*, *Men Only*, *Tatler*, *John Bull*, *Blighty* and *Lilliput* amongst others, and later in life he painted landscapes of Scotland, Spain and elsewhere. He died at his home in Dunragit, Wigtownshire, Scotland, on 18 November 1989.

AUSTIN, David (b. 1935). Pocket and strip cartoonist and illustrator. David Austin was born on 29 March 1935 in Chelmsford, Essex, and worked at first as an industrial chemist and later as a schoolteacher. A self-taught artist, his first drawings were published in a caravan trade magazine in the 1960s and he became a full-time cartoonist in 1976. He has produced a daily pocket cartoon for the *Guardian* since 1990 and his 'Hom. Sap.' strip set in Ancient Rome has appeared in *Private Eye* since 1970. In addition he has worked for *Spectator*, *Field*, *New Scientist*, *Mail on Sunday*, *Today*, *Daily Telegraph* and various other publications. He has a loose drawing style and hand-letters his captions, drawn without speech balloons for 'Hom. Sap', and inside oblong bubbles hanging from the top of the frame in his pocket cartoons.
PUB: *The Book of Love* (1970), *Private Eye David Austin* (1984), [with N. NEWMAN and K.

David Austin, *Guardian*, 9 June 1992

WILLIAMS] *Far From the Madding Cow!* (1990), *Annual Austin* (since 1993)
EXHIB: CG; TG
COLL: BM

AWFLY WEIRDLY – *see* Robinson, Charles

B

BA – *see* Angrave, Bruce

BAB – *see* Gilbert, Sir William Schwenck

BAGHOT-DE-LA-BERE, Stephen RI (1877–1927). Painter, illustrator and joke cartoonist. Stephen Baghot-de-la-Bere was born at Burbage Hall, Leicestershire, in December 1877, the son of Kinard Baghot-de-la-Bere. He was educated at Ilkley College, Yorkshire, and, moving to London in about 1900, studied at Westminster School of Art. He then began to contribute illustrations and cartoons to the *Bystander*,

Illustrated London News, *London Opinion*, *Pears' Annual* and the *Sketch*, while also painting expressionist watercolours. During World War I he moved to Cranleigh, Surrey, where he was a neighbour and friend of DULAC and LAWSON WOOD, and he later served in France as a second lieutenant in the Royal Garrison Artillery (1917). His early cartoons show the influence of JOHN HASSALL but his later style had more in common with the artists of the German magazine *Simplicissimus*. A member of the London Sketch Club, he was elected RI in 1907. Baghot-de-la-Bere died on 29 July 1927.

ILL: J. Swift, *Gulliver's Travels* (1904); M. de Cervantes, *The Adventures of Don Quixote* (1905); A. R. Hope, *The Adventures of Punch* (1905); 'anon.,' *The Life and Times of Lazarillo de Tormes* (1908)
EXHIB: RA; RI; RWA; FAS (1912)
COLL: THG

BAGNALL, Brian (b. 1921). Joke cartoonist and illustrator. Brian Bagnall was born in Manchester on 22 April 1921, the son of Vincent Bagnall, a businessman working in the Lancashire cotton industry. He studied at Xaverian College in the city and at Liverpool University School of Architecture (1946–52). During World War II he served with the Duke of Lancaster's Own Yeomanry (1939–41) and the Royal Artillery (1941–6, POW in Germany 1944–5). Formerly a professional architect, he turned full-time cartoonist in 1980, working in black and white using an Elysée pen on Caslon paper but occasionally also in pen and wash. His drawings have appeared in *Private Eye, History Today, Boz, Spectator, Punch, Oldie, Observer* and elsewhere. Influences have been eclectic but he has always admired the work of Beardsley, BENTLEY and SEARLE.
ILL: H. Cox, *Pressure Cookery* (1954); B. J. Ford, *101 Questions About Science* (1983), *Another 101 Questions About Science* (1984); S. Allison, *I Can't Cook* (1984); *Private Eye* 'Dear Bill' series (1985–90); R. Dobereiner (ed.) *Dobereiner on Golf* (1998) and various books on architecture and law for Blackwells and Penguin
EXHIB: Arts Club; Shalford Mill, Surrey

BAIRNSFATHER, Charles Bruce (1887–1959). Joke cartoonist, artist and journalist. Bruce Bairnsfather was born at Strawberry Bank Cottage, Murree, India (now in Pakistan), on 9 July 1887, the eldest son of Lieutenant (later Major) Thomas Henry Bairnsfather, a Scottish officer in the Indian Army, and Amelia Jane Eliza Every, daughter of a former Deputy Lieutenant of Derbyshire and herself a talented amateur painter. Both of his parents were descended from a common grandfather, Sir Edward Every, 8th Baronet. Bairnsfather was brought to England in 1895 and attended the United Services College, Westward Ho!, Devon (1898–1904). Then he attended an army crammer, Trinity College, Stratford-upon-Avon, while also taking evening classes in art at Stratford Technical College. He sold his first drawing (an advertisement for Player's Navy Mixture) at the age

Bruce Bairnsfather, [Old Bill], in T. and V. Holt, *In Search of the Better 'Ole*, 1985

of 17 for two guineas. Failing the Sandhurst and Woolwich army entrance exams he eventually gained a commission in his father's old regiment, the Cheshires, but resigned to study art at JOHN HASSALL's Art School in Earls Court (1907). Unsuccessful as a professional poster artist he returned to the family home in Warwickshire. He then worked as an electrical engineer for a Stratford-upon-Avon firm specializing in country-house lighting until war broke out in August 1914. Introduced to the 'tea king', Sir Thomas Lipton, by Stratford novelist Marie Corelli, he subsequently drew advertisements for Liptons, Keene's Mustard and Beechams and won a poster competition organized by an opera company. During World War I he served as a machine-gun officer with the 1st Battalion, Royal Warwickshire Regiment, achieving the rank of captain (1915). While stationed near Armentières he drew the first of his famous 'Fragments from France' cartoons ('Where did that one go to?', *Bystander*, January 1915). The cartoons were immensely popular with the troops at the Front (even the Germans appreciated the humour), but the Establishment objected to them and questions were asked in

Parliament about 'these vulgar caricatures of our heroes'. None the less, his work so improved morale ('If you knows of a better 'ole, go to it!', *Bystander*, 24 November 1915, is one of the most famous war cartoons of all time) that he was promoted 'officer-cartoonist' and transferred to the Intelligence Department of the War Office to draw similar cartoons for the French, Italian and American Forces. His most famous character, the 'dim, dull and honest' pipe-smoking, walrus-moustached Midlands Tommy 'Old Bill' Busby, first appeared in 'When the 'ell is it going to be strawberry?' (*Bystander*, 15 September 1915) and became so popular that he appeared in books (250,000 copies were sold of the first anthology of the 'Fragments' cartoons in 1916 alone), plays, musicals, two feature films and comic strips (*Daily Graphic, Passing Show, Illustrated* and *Judge*). In addition he was reproduced on pottery, playing cards, jigsaw puzzles, postcards and other merchandise. An Old Bill waxwork was produced by Madame Tussaud's (1930) and a bus named after him now resides in the Imperial War Museum (complete with 'Old Bill' radiator mascot). Yet, surprisingly, Old Bill was not used in government poster campaigns until World War II. General Sir Ian Hamilton said of the artist: 'The creator of Old Bill has rendered great service to his Country, both as a soldier and as one who has done much to lighten the darkest hour.' Though Bairnsfather repeatedly denied that Old Bill was based on a single person ('he was simply a hieroglyphic for a most prevalent type'), many suggestions have been made regarding his original model. Bairnsfather also contributed cartoons and illustrated articles to *Tatler, Life, New Yorker, Judge* and other publications and went on numerous lecture tours in the UK, USA and Canada. He also edited his own weekly magazine for the *Bystander* group, *Fragments* (1919–20). In World War II he was Official War Cartoonist attached to the USAAF (1942–4), contributing to *Stars & Stripes* and *Yank* and drawing nose-art on US bombers. After the war he continued to work as a lecturer and artist but was never able to break away from 'Old Bill'. The character, along with his younger friends Bert and Alf, had considerable influence on the work of other cartoonists, notably (during World War II) the American Bill Mauldin ('Willie & Joe') and the Welshman W. J. P. JONES ('The Two Types'); Low's 'Colonel Blimp' attracted similar censure by the mili-

tary and government authorities. Bairnsfather disliked calling his work 'cartoons', preferring 'pictures' or 'drawings'. He died of acute renal failure after treatment for cancer of the bladder in Worcester Royal Infirmary on 29 September 1959. His memorial plaque at Cheltenham Crematorium mistakenly gives his age as 71 (he was 72).
PUB: *The Bystander's Fragments from France* (8 volumes, 1916–19), *Bullets and Billets* (1916), *From Mud to Mufti* (1919), *Carry on Sergeant!* (1927), *The Collected Drawings of Bruce Bairnsfather* (1931), *Laughing Through the Orient* (1933), *Old Bill Looks at Europe* (1935), *Old Bill Stands By* (1939), *Old Bill Does it Again!* (1940), [with I. M. Dalrymple] *Old Bill & Son* (1940), *Jeeps and Jests* (1943), *No Kiddin'* (1944)
ILL: Anon., *A Temporary Gentleman in France* (1916); A. J. Dawson, *Somme Battle Stories* (1916), *Back to Blighty* (1917), *For France* (1917)
COLL: IWM
LIT: V. Carter, *Bairnsfather: A Few Fragments from his Life* (1918); W. A. Mutch, *The Bairnsfather Case* (1920); [autobiography] *Wide Canvas* (1939); T. & V. Holt, *The Best of 'Fragments From France'* (1978), *In Search of the Better 'Ole* (1985)

BAKER, Alfred Leslie John (1911–83). Joke cartoonist and watercolourist. Born in Durban, South Africa, on 2 July 1911 of British parents, Leslie Baker was the son of Fred Baker, a manufacturer's agent who was a cousin of FRED PEGRAM. He spent his early childhood in Durban but later came to England and was educated at Belmont and Mill Hill School. He then studied at Chelsea School of Art (1928–32) where his contemporaries were Henry Moore, Graham Sutherland, BRIAN ROBB, RUSSELL BROCKBANK and typographic designer Peter Hatch. He joined Streets Advertising as a visualizer/artist (1932–40) and began producing cartoons from about 1935 for publications such as *Punch, Night & Day, Evening Standard, Titbits, Tatler & Bystander, Lilliput, Blighty, Strand Magazine, London Opinion, Evening News, Everybody's* and Kemsley Newspapers (e.g. the 'Wartime Humour' series in the *Daily Dispatch*). During World War II he served in the Auxiliary Fire Service (stationed at South Ealing and Greenford), exhibited paintings of the Blitz and designed Home Front posters. After the war he returned to advertising, first at John Tate & Partners (1946–c. 1960), then Pemberton's (c. 1960–69) where he was Art Director and later

Director, retiring in 1969 to paint landscapes and birds. He married an art teacher and former Chelsea Art School colleague, Marjorie Bridson (1938) and they had one son, cartoonist NICK BAKER. An admirer of Feliks Topolski, ANTON and PONT as well as English watercolour artists such as Cotman and Bonnington, he worked on Bristol Board or cartridge paper in pen and indian ink, sometimes with grey tone washes. Leslie Baker died on 30 August 1983.

ILL: *Atlas of Breeding Birds in Britain and Ireland* (1976) and many drawings for the RSPB
COLL: IWM

BAKER, Nicholas Bridson (b. 1940). Joke cartoonist and illustrator. The son of LESLIE BAKER, Nick Baker was born on 31 May 1940 in Strawberry Hill, Twickenham, Middlesex. He attended Mill Hill School (1951–6), Ealing Art School (1956–8), the London School of Printing (1958–60) under Tom Eckersley and studied life drawing at evening classes at St Martin's School of Art. He worked for typographic designer Peter Hatch (1960–62) before becoming a visualizer/art director in advertising agencies (1962–73). His first cartoon was published in the *Evening Standard* in August 1966 and he became a full-time freelance in November 1973, contributing to *Punch, Private Eye, Oldie, Financial Times, Time Out, Guardian, Daily Mirror, Erotic Revue, Desire, Daily Express, European, Spectator, Mayfair, Reader's Digest, Town, King, Mail on Sunday* and *Tit-Bits*. He also drew the 'Smiler' page for IPC's *Whoopee!* children's comic (1973–81) and was the *Financial Times*'s court artist at the Guinness trial (1990). He uses a Hughes Spoonpoint pen with Rotring ink on smooth white Excelda Board. Nick Baker cites his main influence as being his parents and he also sometimes signs his work 'Bridson'. He is a former committee member of the Cartoonists' Club of Great Britain.

PUB: *The Naughty Bath Book* (1976), *Songs to Sing in the Bath* (1976), *The One-Eyed Lion* (1983), *The Wonderful One-Eyed Lion* (1984), *Graham the Gorilla* (1985), [with B. Busselle] *Bad Losers* (1985), [with B. Busselle] *Bad Manners* (1986), [with J. Monch] *Second Time Round* (1985)
ILL: R. Clifford's 'The Doctor' series of six books (c. 1975–80); J. Baldwinson, *Plonk and Superplonk* (1975); G. Thaw, *Ha! ha! ha!* (1976); R. Stark, *The Loaves and Fishes Miracle Cookbook* (1976); A. Sampson, *Cabinet Secrets* (1987); R. Griffiths, *Gorilla Number Games* (1988)

EXHIB: Waterman's Art Centre, Brentford, Middlesex; Riverside Gallery, Richmond; Mercury Theatre Gallery, Colchester

BANKS, Jeremy 'Banx' (b. 1959). Joke, strip and pocket cartoonist. Jeremy Banks was born on 10 May 1959 and studied at Hounslow Borough College and Maidstone College of Art. His first cartoon was published in the *Evening Standard* in 1980 and he has since contributed to *Oink!*, Marvel Comics, *She, UK Press Gazette, You, Punch, Private Eye* and *Financial Times*. A strip 'Cecil' also appeared in the *Daily Express*.

PUB: *Cubes* (1982); [with HUSBAND, I. Jackson [and LOWRY] *100 Things to Do With a Black Lace Record* (1990)
ILL: M. Harding, *You Can See the Angel's Bum, Miss Worswick!* (1985); and books by C. Tarrant
COLL: Bradford Museum

BANX – *see* Banks, Jeremy

'Barry Mackenzie' – *see* Garland, Nicholas Withycombe

BARTON, Leslie Alfred (b. 1923). Joke cartoonist, comic artist, illustrator and caricaturist. Les Barton was born on 8 December 1923 in Wareham, Dorset. A self-taught artist, he started work at the age of 14 as a telegraph clerk. His first published cartoon appeared in the *Militant Miner* in 1944. During World War II he served as a draughtsman in the Royal Signals and War Office Signals and produced his first regular cartoons for *WAM* (*West African Magazine*) when stationed in Lagos in 1946. After working as a photographic retouching artist and commercial artist in advertising and drawing strips for IPC and D. C. Thomson children's comics, including 'Billy Bunter', 'I Spy' and 'Harry's Haunted House', he became a regular contributor to *Punch* (from 1954), *Reveille, Private Eye, Spectator, Oldie, Daily Mirror* and the *Daily Sketch*, drew political cartoons and caricatures for *The Statist* (1963) and was staff war artist on the *Sun* during the Falklands War (1982). He has also designed humorous greetings cards for Camden Graphics, Rainbow Cards and Cardtoons, and drawn on-the-spot caricatures at business functions, etc. A founder member of the Cartoonists' Club of Great Britain, he was the organization's Treasurer (1972–93). Les Barton draws with a sketchy, uneven line and his figures have distinctive staring circular eyes with the pupils dead centre.

13

His signature, in letterspaced capitals, is often written in a wave pattern (he also used to sign his work 'Lezz').
PUB: *Miles of Smiles* (1946), *The Best of Barton* (1960), *Just Joking!* (1997)
ILL: J. Rothman, *The World's Best Monster Joke Book* (1983), *The Most Awful Monster Book Ever* (1985); *Billy Bunter* (1972); *The Goodies* (1974)

BATEMAN, Henry Mayo (1887–1970). Cartoonist and caricaturist. H. M. Bateman was born, the son of Henry Charles Bateman, an English export packer and shipper, in Sutton Forest, New South Wales, Australia on 15 February 1887. The family returned to England in 1889 and he attended Forest Hill House School, London. Encouraged by PHIL MAY he left school at 16 to study drawing and painting at Westminster School of Art (1903) and Goldsmiths' Institute (New Cross, London) and later, on the recommendation of JOHN HASSALL, attended Charles van Havermaet's studio (1904–7). Influenced at first by *Comic Cuts* and *Ally Sloper's Half Holiday*, his first humorous drawings were published in *Scraps* (1903), then *Tatler* (1904). He later produced regular full-page theatre caricatures for the *Sketch* while also submitting work to *Rions* (1908), *La Baionnette, Passing Show, London Magazine, Radio Times, Punch* (from 1916), *Bystander, Strand, Life, London Opinion, Field* (sporting cartoons, 1935–7), etc. He joined the London Regiment in World War I but was invalided out with rheumatic fever in 1915. Bateman was one of the highest paid cartoonists of his day and produced a considerable amount of work for advertising (e.g. for Lucky Strike, Wills Tobacco, Moss Bros, Guinness, Erasmic Soap, Shell and Kensitas cigarettes). He also designed posters, and his World War II series for the Ministry of Health, 'Coughs and Sneezes Spread Diseases', was very popular. His most famous drawings, 'The Man Who . . .' series of social gaffes, first appeared in 1912 in the *Tatler* ('The Missed Putt'). He detested modern art (especially Matisse, Picasso and the Cubists) but was a great admirer of OSPOVAT and the Russian-born French cartoonist Emmanuel Poiré, 'Caran D'Ache' (indeed DAVID Low described him as 'the British inheritor of Caran D'Ache'). He worked in pencil, pen, ink and watercolour on Canson paper. Master of the cartoon story without words (he once covered four whole pages of *Punch* with a single cartoon sequence), he 'probably did more than

anyone to bring home to the reader that individual pen and ink lines could be immensely expressive of and by themselves' (Price). In a paper delivered to the Royal Society of Arts in 1949 he first promoted the idea of a permanent museum of cartoon art in Britain, a dream that his daughter Diana Willis (wife of the marine artist Richard Willis) has done much to realize. He was a member of the Savage Club and (proposed by FRANK HART in 1910) the Chelsea Arts Club, for which he produced designs for balls, at one of which he met his future wife, Brenda Collison Weir, a relative of the artist Harry Collison. H. M. Bateman gave up cartooning in 1939 to concentrate on painting and died in Gozo on 11 February 1970.
PUB: *Burlesques* (1916), *A Book of Drawings* (1921), *Suburbia* (1922), *More Drawings* (1922), *Adventures at Golf* (1923), *A Mixture* (1924), *Colonels* (1925), *The Art of Drawing* (1926), *Rebound* (1927), *Brought Forward* (1931), *Considered Trifles* (1934), *The Art of Caricature* (1936), *The Evening Rise* (1960), *The Boy Who Breathed on the Glass at the British Museum* (1964), *The Best of H. M. Bateman: the Tatler Cartoons 1922–26* (1987) and others
ILL: G. Robey, *After Dinner Stories* (1920), *Thereby Hangs a Tale* (1921); L. Reed, *The Complete Limerick Book* (1924), *Nonsense Verses* (1925); D. Coke, *Our Modern Youth* (1924); L. Carroll, *Further Nonsense Verse and Prose* (1926); D. Clarke, *Bateman and I in Filmland* (1926); W. Caine, *What a Scream!* (1927); J. Gordon, *Art Ain't All Paint* (1944); G. Brennard, *Walton's Delight* (1953)
EXHIB: BSG; RA; FAS (1962); LG; LAN; RFH/ NT (centenary exhibition 1987); CGH; Northcote Theatre, Exeter
COLL: Annabels; CAT; V&A; BM; UKCC; A; NPG; SNPG
LIT: *H. M. Bateman by Himself* (1937); M. Bateman, *The Man Who Drew the 20th Century* (1969); J. Jensen (ed.), *The Man Who . . . and Other Drawings* (1975); A. Anderson, *The Man Who Was H. M. Bateman* (1982)

BAUMER, Lewis Christopher Edward RI (1870–1963). Painter, illustrator, joke cartoonist and writer. Lewis Baumer was born on 8 August 1870 in St John's Wood, London. After studying under A. A. Calderon at St John's Wood Art School (1887; fellow students included JOHN BYAM SHAW and Rex Vicat Cole), the RA Schools and the RCA, he began

BREAKFAST – THE DIFFICULT MEAL

H. M. Bateman, *Suburbia*, 1922

contributing illustrations to *Pall Mall Magazine* (1893). He later drew cartoons and illustrations for *Bystander, Cassell's, Graphic* (Christmas Numbers), *Humorist, Idler, Illustrated Bits, London Magazine, London Opinion, Minster, New Budget, Pall Mall Budget, Pears' Annual, Pearson's, Pick-Me-Up, Printer's Pie, Queen, Royal, New Budget, St James's Budget, Sketch, Strand, To-Day, Unicorn* and *Tatler* (notably his portraits of women, known as 'the Baumer girl'). His first cartoon was published in *Punch* in 1897 and he remained with the magazine for 50 years (a record equalled only by Tenniel, STAMPA and SHEPARD), specializing in genteel scenes, tea dances and tennis parties in the tradition of Du Maurier ('his strongest point is the delineation of aristocratic young persons of both sexes . . . No one can better suggest the perfect type of English girl' [Ellwood]). A member of the Langham Sketching Club, Arts Club and Chelsea Arts Club, he was elected RI in 1921. He also drew posters for *Cassell's Magazine* and OK Sauce ('Saucy but quite OK'), advertisements for Erasmic Soap, Abdullah Cigarettes, Kodak and others, designed pottery for Eagle Transfer Co and John Sayer, and some of his *Punch* cartoons were produced as postcards by Raphael Tuck in their 'Good Jokes from *Punch*' series. He worked in oils, watercolour, pen and ink, was an accomplished etcher, and in later life concentrated on painting and drawing portraits, especially of children. For his *Punch* work he sketched first on cartridge paper then pinned thin, semi-transparent smooth-surfaced handmade 'studio paper' over this and worked with a Gillott No. 291 mapping pen and Higgins Waterproof Indian Ink: 'I never work on card; I like the feel of paper; I like to be able to hold it to the light and see my drawing reversed (a wonderful way to discover faults in drawing) . . .' (*Artist*, June 1935). Lewis Baumer died on 25 October 1963.

PUB: *Jumbles* (1897), *Did You Ever?* (1903), *Bright Young Things* (1928)

ILL: More than 25 books including Mrs Molesworth, *Hoodie* (1897); H. Graham, *Deportmental Ditties* (1909), *The Perfect Gentleman* (1912), *The Complete Sportsman* (1914), *Happy Families* (1934); I. Hay, *The Lighter Side of School Life* (1914), *The Shallow End* (1924); E. Blyton, *Silver and Gold* (1925); R. Arkell, *Winter Sportings* (1929); J. B. Emtage, *Ski Fever* (1936)

EXHIB: RA; RI; RP; FAS (1913, 1924)

COLL: V&A; NPG; THG

BAWDEN, Edward CBE RA (1903–89) – *see* Bryant & Heneage

BAXTER, Glen (b. 1944). Joke cartoonist, illustrator and writer. Glen Baxter was born in Leeds on 4 March 1944, the son of Charles Baxter, a welder, and attended Leeds College of Art (1960–65). He taught at the V&A (1967–74) and was a part-time lecturer in fine art at Goldsmith's College (1974–86). His poems and short stories were first published in New York in *Juillard* (1968) and in the magazine *Adventures in Poetry* (1970), and he had his first solo exhibition of art in the city's Gotham Book Mart Gallery (1970). His work has appeared in numerous newspapers and journals throughout the world including *New Yorker, Vogue, Elle, Humo, Observer, Het Parool* and *Globe Hebdo*, and his drawings are widely available as greetings cards. Glen Baxter's cartoons are influenced by old-style boy's adventure books and comic strips and often feature heroes like Biggles but with wildly inappropriate caption lines, producing a rather surreal effect. An admirer of Krazy Kat, he cites Raymond Rousel and Tom Mix as influences on his work.

PUB: *The Falls Tracer* (1970), *The Khaki* (1973), *Fruits of the World in Danger* (1974), *Atlas* (1979), *The Impending Gleam* (1981), *Glen Baxter: His Life* (1983), *Jodhpurs in the Quantocks* (1986), *The Billiard Table Murders* (1990), *Glen Baxter Returns to Normal* (1992), *The Collected Blurtings of Glen Baxter* (1993), *The Wonder Book of Sex* (1995), *Glen Baxter's Gourmet Guide* (1997), *Blizzards of Tweed* (1999)

ILL: W. and B. Kennedy, *Charlie Malarkey and the Belly-Button Machine* (1986); J. Williams, *Quote, Unquote* (1989)

EXHIB: Gotham Book Mart, New York; Anthony Stokes Gallery; NIG; ICA; RFH; Galerie Martine & Thibault de la Châtre, Paris; Adelaide Festival; Ginza Art Space, Tokyo; Artothèque de Caen; Michael Nagy Fine Art, Sydney; Anthony Wilkinson Fine Art; CBG; Modernism Gallery, San Francisco and others

COLL: AC; NYPL: V&A; Southampton University; T; Centre Georges Pompidou, Paris; Fondation Nationale d'Art Contemporain, Paris and others

BEARD, Albert Edgar (1902–91). Joke cartoonist, political and strip cartoonist, and watercolourist. A. E. Beard was born in Birmingham on 16 January 1902. He studied at the Birmingham

I WAS BEGINNING TO SUSPECT THAT THE JOB INTERVIEW WAS NOT GOING AT ALL WELL

Glen Baxter, *Blizzards of Tweed*, 1999

School of Art and with PERCY BRADSHAW. During World War II he served in the Intelligence Corps, interpreting aerial photographs. He contributed to such publications as *Punch* (50 years from 1927), *Answers*, *John Bull*, *Everybody's*, *Daily Mirror*, *Illustrated*, *Recorder* ('Brave New World' series, *c.* 1946), *London Opinion*, *Reveille*, *Tit-Bits*, *Evening Standard*, *Blighty*, *Daily Graphic*, *Humorist*, *Passing Show*, *Daily Sketch*, *New Scientist* and *Procurement Weekly* (ten years). In addition he was Political Cartoonist on the *Sunday Chronicle* and created a popular strip about a family of TV addicts, 'The Gaisby-Knights' (1958–60).

He also drew under the name 'Harvey' and designed advertisements for Standard Fireworks, Oxo, Madame Tussaud's, Pelmanism and others. A. E. Beard died on 3 May 1991.
ILL: R. L. Clarke, *Lighter Engineering* (1973)
EXHIB: RSAB
COLL: UKCC

BEATON, Sir Cecil Walter Hardy (1904–80). Photographer, stage designer, illustrator, author and caricaturist. Cecil Beaton was born on 14 January 1904 in Hampstead, London. He was educated at Harrow School and St John's

College, Cambridge, and contributed theatre caricatures to *Granta* while a student. Best known as a photographer, he also wrote a number of books (which he illustrated himself), contributed drawings to *Vogue* and was an accomplished caricaturist, particularly of stage and screen celebrities and High Society figures. He later returned to art school (aged 50) and studied at the Slade School of Art. He received the Légion d'Honneur (1950) and CBE (1957) and was knighted in 1972. Cecil Beaton died in Wiltshire on 18 January 1980.

PUB: *The Book of Beauty* (1930), *Cecil Beaton's Scrap Book* (1937), *Cecil Beaton's New York* (1938), *History under Fire* (1941), *Near East* (1943), *Ballet* (1951), *The Glass of Fashion* (1954), *The Face of the World* (1957) and others
ILL: P. Louys, *The Twilight of the Nymphs* (1928); M. Arlen, *A Young Man Comes to Town* (1932); R. B. Sheridan, *The School for Scandal* (1939) and others
EXHIB: COO; RG; BC; NPG; Museum of the City of New York; Lefevre Gallery
COLL: NPG; TM; University of Texas
LIT: C. Beaton, *Photobiography* (1951); J. Danziger, *Beaton* (1980); H. Vickers, *Cecil Beaton* (1985)

BEERBOHM, Sir Henry Maximilian NEAC (1872–1956). Caricaturist, journalist and author. Max Beerbohm was born in Kensington, London, on 24 August 1872, the son of Julius Ewald Beerbohm, a grain-merchant of mixed German, Dutch and Lithuanian extraction, and his second wife Eliza Draper. He was the half-brother of Sir Herbert Beerbohm Tree, the actor-manager. Educated at Charterhouse School, his first caricatures (signed 'H. M. B.') were published in the school magazine, *Greyfriar*, when he was aged 15. He studied at Merton College, Oxford, graduating in 1895, and began contributing caricatures (e.g. 'Club Types') to *Strand Magazine* (1893) and *Pick-Me-Up* (1894) while still a student. During the same period, having been introduced into the circle of Oscar Wilde and Aubrey Beardsley by the painter Sir William Rothenstein, he contributed an article 'A Defence of Cosmetics' to the first issue of the *Yellow Book* (1894). After graduating he drew the first of his nine caricatures for *Vanity Fair* (1896–1905) – published under the pseudonyms 'Ruth', 'Max' and 'Bulbo' – and contributed to various other journals, including *John Bull*, *Savoy* and *Daily Mail*. He published a collection of essays in 1896 and in 1898 succeeded George Bernard

Shaw as theatre critic for the *Saturday Review* edited by Frank Harris, resigning in 1910. In addition he wrote some plays, notably *The Happy Hypocrite* (produced by Mrs Patrick Campbell at the Royalty Theatre, 1900). His first solo exhibition was held in 1904 and after his marriage to the American actress Florence Kahn he moved to Rapallo, Italy (1910). The following year his most famous book, the fantasy novel *Zuleika Dobson*, was published. He returned to Britain during the two World Wars (1915–19 and 1939–47) but otherwise lived mostly in Italy until his death. Self-taught as an artist, he admired the work of the *Vanity Fair* caricaturist 'Ape' (Carlo Pellegrini) – to whom he dedicated his first cartoon collection, *Caricatures of Twenty-Five Gentlemen* (1896) – and the political cartoonist and caricaturist Alfred Bryan who later taught J. A. SHEPHERD. He was himself admired by Oscar Wilde, Aubrey Beardsley and RAVEN HILL ('Since "Ape" there has been no one with such an awful instinct for the principal parts of a man's appearance'), and SICKERT drew his portrait for *Vanity Fair* (1897). Beerbohm held that 'The most perfect caricature is that which, on a small surface, with the simplest means, most accurately exaggerates, to the highest point, the peculiarities of a human being, at his most characteristic moment, in the most beautiful manner.' FOUGASSE called him 'the first caricaturist with an acute literary sense and the first, in consequence, to make truly psychological caricatures. He wasted no time in attempting academic draughtsmanship . . . but, fortified in his literary equipment, went straight to the point by the quickest road.' He worked in pencil, ink and watercolour in sometimes remarkably pale washes (e.g. his pale pink and blue portrait of Winston Churchill). A member of the Athenaeum Club and the Savage Club, he was knighted in 1939. He also broadcast on radio (from 1935). Max Beerbohm died at his home Villino Chiaro, Rapallo, Italy, on 20 May 1956.

PUB: Many books including [essays] *The World of Max Beerbohm* (1896), *Caricatures of Twenty-Five Gentlemen* (1896), [play] *The Happy Hypocrite* (1897), *More* (1899), *The Poets' Corner* (1904), *A Book of Caricatures* (1907), *Yet Again* (1909), [novel] *Zuleika Dobson* (1911), [cartoons] *The Second Childhood of John Bull* (1911), *A Christmas Garland* (1912), *Fifty Caricatures* (1913), *A Survey* (1921), *Rossetti and his Circle* (1922), *Things New and Old* (1923), *Observations* (1925), *Heroes and Heroines of Bitter Sweet* (1931), *Max's Nineties* (1958)

EXHIB: Carfax; LG: GGG; PG (1996); NEAC
COLL: T; V&A; NPG; A; MCO; CAT; Princeton; Harvard; Chicago; Huntingdon Library; BM; University of Texas; Yale
LIT: Lord David Cecil, *Max* (1972); R. Hart-Davis, *Catalogue of the Caricatures of Max Beerbohm* (1972), *The Letters of Max Beerbohm* (1988); J. G. Riewald, *Beerbohm's Literary Caricatures* (1977); N. J. Hall (ed.) *Max Beerbohm Caricatures* (1997)

BELCHER, George Frederick Arthur RA (1875–1947). Joke cartoonist, illustrator, etcher and painter. George Belcher was born in London on

NO INTERFERING WITH NATURE
VISITOR. *'A lonely sort of spot to live in, this. What do you do for a doctor if you are ill?'*
NATIVE. *'We don't much bother about doctors in these parts. We mostly dies natural deaths.'*

George Belcher, *Taken from Life*, 1929

19 September 1875, the son of Dr Joseph Belcher. He was educated at King Edward VI School, Berkhamsted, Hertfordshire, and studied at Gloucester School of Art. He began contributing to *Punch* in 1906 and produced more than 1000 drawings for the magazine before he retired in May 1941. He also contributed to *Tatler*, *Cosmopolitan*, *Vanity Fair* and others. Influenced at first by PHIL MAY (FOUGASSE called him 'Phil May in chalk'), particularly in his drawings of Cockney charladies and rustic characters, he differed from May in that 'He drew the poor as a kindly gentleman who paid them to come and be drawn by him, not, like Phil May, as somebody sketching the neighbours' (Price). A fine draughtsman, he worked in black chalk with 'simple but beautifully observed linework to which the chalk gave richness and fullness' (FOUGASSE). He was also 'one of the few Punch draughtsmen of the period to reveal humour in character or to have a line humorous in itself' (Price). However, he preferred to have his jokes provided for him. In addition he illustrated books, designed posters and comic postcards (e.g. for Raphael Tuck), painted sporting pictures, etched and produced coloured aquatints. Proposed by his friend Sir Alfred Munnings he was elected ARA (1931) and later RA (1945), the first cartoonist to be so honoured. He was a member of the Savage Club and Chelsea Arts Club. George Belcher died at Chiddingfold, Surrey, on 3 October 1947.
PUB: *Characters* (1922), *By George Belcher* (1926), *Taken from Life* (1929), *Potted Char* (1933)
ILL: F. F. Moore, *The Lighter Side of English Life* (1913); S. Aumonier, *Odd Fish* (1923); J. Ferguson, *The Table in a Roar* (1933)
EXHIB: RA; RSA; LG; FAS (1924); LAN
COLL: T; V&A; CAT; BM: THG; Royal College of Surgeons

BELCHER, William FCSD (b. 1923). Joke cartoonist, designer, illustrator, journalist and painter. Bill Belcher was born in Wells-next-the-Sea, Norfolk, on 2 June 1923 and after service with the Royal Signals in North Africa, Sicily and Italy (1941–6) attended Worthing School of Art (1947–50) and studied at the Royal College of Art's School of Textiles (1950–54). The winner of an RSA travelling bursary, he visited Switzerland, Scandinavia and France before becoming a full-time freelance designer, humorous illustrator, cartoonist and painter in 1954. His first cartoons appeared in the newly

launched *She* in 1955 and he continued to work for the magazine until 1985. He has also contributed to *Best* (1985–91), *Investors Chronicle* (including covers), *Oldie* (including covers), *Good Housekeeping*, *Designer* (including covers and book reviews), *House and Garden*, *Which?*, *Observer*, *Punch*, *Sunday Times*, *Radio Times*, *Evening Standard*, *Economic Affairs* and others. He has also worked for BBC2 TV, for design groups with clients such as IBM, Unilever, BP, CBI and Grant Thornton, devised and illustrated games and puzzles for Galt Toys, contributed to the Friends of the Earth playing-card set and designed more than 100 book jackets. A former Fellow of the Chartered Society of Designers, he cites his main influences as BAWDEN, Steig, Ungerer and Klee. Belcher works mainly in pen and ink and watercolour but has also painted in oils and mixed media. He is married to the designer and artist Colleen Farr.
PUB: *Boondoggles* (1998)
ILL: K. Whitehorn, *How to Survive Children* (1975); M. Speight, *Murdo* (1983); G. Jones, *Forked Tongues Annual* (1985), *Political Insults* (1987); T. Hinde and C. Chitty, *Just Chicken* (1985); P. Murray, *The Commercial Touch* (1986); R. Lederer, *Crazy English* (1992)
EXHIB: [Oil paintings] RA; Gimpel Fils; England & Co; AIA Galleries

BELL, Steve (b. 1951). Editorial/political cartoonist and strip cartoonist. Steve Bell was born in Walthamstow, London, on 26 February 1951 and educated at Slough Grammar School, Teeside College of Art (Middlesbrough), and Leeds University, graduating in fine art in 1974. After taking a teaching certificate at Exeter University he taught art at a secondary school in Birmingham before becoming a freelance cartoonist in 1977. His first regular paid work was for *Whoopee!* comic in 1978. Editorial/Political Cartoonist on the *Guardian* since 1990 (succeeding GIBBARD), he has also contributed to *Cheeky*, *Jackpot*, *Private Eye* (colour covers for Christmas issues from 1992), *New Statesman*, *New Society*, *Leveller* ('Lord God Almighty' strip), *Social Work Today*, *NME*, *Journalist*, *Time Out* and *City Limits*. He created the popular 'If . . .' political strip cartoon series for the *Guardian* in 1981 and an earlier *Time Out* (later *City Limits*) series, 'Maggie's Farm' (begun 1979) was described in the House of Lords (March 1987) as 'an almost obscene series of caricatures'. He has also made animation shorts (with Bob Godfrey) for Chan-

Steve Bell, [Major, Thatcher, Frost], *Bell's Eye*, 1999

nel 4 and BBC TV. He has been voted CCGB
Humorous Strip Cartoonist of the Year (1984,
1985), *What the Papers Say* Cartoonist of the Year
(1993), CAT Political Cartoonist of the Year
(1995, 1997) and CAT Strip Cartoonist of the
Year (1996, 1997, 1998). Steve Bell draws his
cartoons to reproduction size and works on card
or watercolour paper using John Heath's Tele-
phone Pen (Fine), brush and indian ink.
PUB: *Maggie's Farm* (1981), *Further Down on
Maggie's Farm* (1982), *Maggie's Farm the Last
Roundup* (1987), the 'If . . .' series (13 titles since
1983), [with B. Homer] *Waiting for the Upturn*
(1986), [with R. Woddis] *Funny Old World* (1991),
For Whom Bell Tolls (1994), [with S. Hoggart]
Live Briefs (1996), *Bell's Eye* (1999)
EXHIB: BC; CG; Oxford Gallery, Oxford;
Gardner Arts Centre, University of Sussex; LCG
COLL: BM; V&A; UKCC

BELLEW, Hon. Patrick Herbert (1905–84). Joke
cartoonist and commercial artist. Paddy Bellew
was born on 2 April 1905 in Dunleer, Co. Louth,
Ireland, the younger son of the Hon. Richard
E. Bellew and the half-brother (by a previous
marriage) of the 5th Baron Bellew. He may
also have been a distant relative of the pioneer
American cartoonist (of British descent) Frank
Henry Temple Bellew. Largely self-taught as an
artist, his cartoons were published regularly in

magazines such as the *Bystander*, *Tatler* and *Men
Only* during the 1930s and he also produced
advertisements for Scrubb's Ammonia, Oxo
and others. In addition he drew a large drawing (24 × 5 feet) entitled 'The Ruthless Hunt'
which covered three walls of Punch's Club in
London. During World War II, Bellew served
at first in the RNVR but later moved to the
USA and from 1942 served in the US Army,
producing training films and cartoons while stationed in New York. After the war he remained
in New York, working in advertising for companies such as McCann Ericksson and producing freelance cartoons for Esso and others.
Normally right-handed, Bellew (who signed
himself 'PHB' or 'P. Bellew') drew cartoons and
produced watercolours left-handed. He worked
in pen, brush and ink, wash, pencil and crayon
in a style that showed the influence of H. M.
BATEMAN and *New Yorker* artists such as Peter
Arno. Bellew did very little cartoon work after
1960 and died in Litchfield, Connecticut, in 1984.
PUB: *Point of View* (1935), *Private View* (1937)
ILL: 'Sabretache', *Stand To Your Horses* (1932);
H. J. C. Graham, *The Biffin Papers* (1933); *Punt-
ers Pie* (1938); J. Swift, *Gulliver's Travels* (1945)

BELSKY, Margaret Constance [née Owen]
(1919–89). Pocket cartoonist and illustrator.
Margaret Belsky was born in Dorset on 20 June

'With this model we allow a special reduction for police costs.'

Margaret Belsky, *Sun*, 1964

1919. Known as 'Cooee' (she had an Australian/Irish father), she attended Bournemouth School of Art, won a *Punch* competition and went on to study illustration and engraving at the Royal College of Art. She began cartooning when her Czech soldier-fiancé (later her husband Franta Belsky ARCA FRBS, President of the Society of Portrait Sculptors) showed her work to the editor of *Lilliput*. The first woman to draw a daily front-page cartoon for a national newspaper, she drew pocket cartoons for the *Daily Herald* (later the *Sun*) for 19 years (from 1951), producing more than 6000 cartoons for this paper alone. She also worked for *Punch, Guardian, Sunday Graphic, John Bull, New Statesman, Financial Weekly* and the *People*. In addition she illustrated children's books and designed jackets for Penguin Books. Regarding herself modestly as 'the poor man's OSBERT LANCASTER' her jokes

often made fun of dogs and Tory ladies and she described her politics as 'pinkish'. She died on 26 January 1989.
ILL: Eight titles by A. Oates; R. Brown, *Chubb on the Trail* (1976); E. Ramsbottom and J. Redmayne, *Colour* (1978); P. Arnold and P. Scott-Kay, *The Gay Way Workbook* (1980)
COLL: UKCC

'Bengo' – *see* Timyn, William

BENNETT, David Neil 'NB' (b. 1941). Joke and strip cartoonist and illustrator. Born in Warsop, Nottinghamshire, on 13 January 1941, the son of Stanley Bennett, a headmaster, Neil Bennett ('NB') gained an O-level in art at Brunts Grammar School, Mansfield, but is otherwise self-taught. After reading English at King's College, London (1959–62), he taught English for 23 years, mainly at the North Notts College of Further Education, Worksop, before resigning to become a full-time freelance cartoonist at the age of 46. His first cartoon was published in the *Cricketer* magazine in the 1960s and since then his work has appeared in *Private Eye, The Times, Spectator, Law Society Gazette, Punch, Independent Saturday Magazine, Esquire* ('Jekyll and Heidi' strip), *Cricketer, Gramophone, Museums Journal, ECOS, Economic Affairs, Oldie, New Statesman* and *Men Only*. Happiest drawing in black and white and in line, he rarely uses washes or colour. An admirer of Tom & Jerry, Laurel & Hardy, Monty Python and 'The Bash Street Kids' ('a real work of genius') in the *Beano*, his cartoons frequently feature death and old people. He draws quickly using fibre-tipped pens on bank paper.
COLL: BM; V&A

BENTLEY, Nicolas Clerihew FSIA FRSA (1907–78). Joke, political and pocket cartoonist, caricaturist, illustrator, commercial artist, actor and author. Nicolas (originally Nicholas) Bentley was born on 14 June 1907 in Hampstead, London, the son of the writer, journalist and amateur artist (and inventor of the 'clerihew') E. Clerihew Bentley. His godfather was G. K. CHESTERTON. Educated at University College School, London, he studied at Heatherley's School of Art for 18 months (1924–5) and then worked briefly as a circus clown and as a film extra (1925). He was then employed as a junior in the W. S. Crawford advertising agency, where he met the poster artist Horace Taylor with

Neil Bennett, unpublished

whom he subsequently worked (1927–8). He was a 'space salesman' on the *Daily Telegraph* in 1929 and illustrated his first book, *New Cautionary Tales* by Hilaire Belloc (a friend of his father), in 1930. The same year he joined Shell-Mex's publicity office, where he employed WALTER GOETZ and John Reynolds (son of FRANK REYNOLDS) as artists, leaving in 1932 to become a freelance illustrator and commercial artist. His first successful advertising cartoon series was 'Mr Can and Mr Can't' for Eno's Fruit Salt (1933) and he subsequently drew for Pan Yan Pickle, Sankey-Sheldon Steel and others. He also contributed cartoons to *Bystander, Lilliput, Men Only, Daily Express, Sunday Express, Night & Day, Punch* and *Radio Times*. During World War II he worked in the Ministry of Information and served as a fireman. He later worked for the *News Chronicle* (1955–7), was one of the founders of the book publishers André Deutsch (the three arrows in the company's logo represent himself, Deutsch and the third direc-

tor, Diana Athill) and worked as an editor for Mitchell Beazley, Sunday Times Publications (1962–3) and Thomas Nelson (1963–7). In addition he drew topical pocket cartoons for the *Daily Mail* ('Watch My Line', 1958–62) and *Sunday Telegraph* (1972–4) and cartoons and caricatures for *Sunday Times, Punch, Private Eye* (notably illustrating 'Auberon Waugh's Diary' from its inception in 1972) and others. He also wrote novels and continued to illustrate books. Influenced by Caran D'Ache and the *New Yorker* cartoonist Ralph Barton (he even dropped the 'h' in his Christian name so that his signature could appear symmetrically in two lines like Barton's), his style 'owed something to RIDGEWELL and SHERWOOD, and something also to the smart magazine and advertising type of artist like FISH' (Price). He also admired Steinlen, Doré, Léandre, Gulbransson, William Nicholson, George Price, MERVYN PEAKE and Lewitt-Him. Bentley often drew figures without background or setting, making much use of solid blacks and only rarely working in colour. After making a detailed pencil rough he used a Gillott 303 pen and indian ink (using a brush for large areas of black), working 'half-up' in size and employing reducing and magnifying glasses as required. He occasionally also worked in chalk. Elected FSIA in 1946 he was a member of the Garrick Club and one of the founder members of the British Cartoonists' Association in 1966. He sometimes signed his work 'NB'. Nicolas Bentley died in Somerset on 14 August 1978.

PUB: *All Fall Down!* (1932), *The Beastly Birthday Book* (1934), *Die? I Thought I'd Laugh!* (1936), *The Time of My Life* (1937), *Ballet-Hoo* (1937), *Le Sport* (1939), *Animal, Vegetable and South Kensington* (1940), *How Can You Bear to be Human?* (1957), *Nicolas Bentley's Book of Birds* (1965)

ILL: 75 books including H. Belloc, *New Cautionary Tales* (1930), *Ladies and Gentlemen* (1932); J. B. Morton, *By the Way* (1931), *1933 and Still Going Wrong!* (1932); T. Benson and B. Askwith, *Foreigners* (1935), *Muddling Through* (1936); E. C. Bentley, *More Biography* (1929), *Baseless Biography* (1939); T. S. Eliot, *Old Possum's Book of Practical Cats* (1940); G. Mikes, *How to be an Alien* (1946); *The Duke of Bedford's Book of Snobs* (1965)

COLL: UKCC; BM; NPG; CAT

LIT: N. Bentley, *A Version of the Truth* (1960); R. McLean, *Nicolas Bentley Drew the Pictures* (1990)

'Canon – you're fired!'

Nicolas Bentley, *Die? I Thought I'd Laugh!*, 1936

BERGER, Oscar (b. 1901). Caricaturist. Born in Presov, Eperjes, Czechoslovakia, on 12 May 1901, the son of Henry Berger, Oscar Berger won a scholarship to Berlin Art School (1920) and later joined the staff of the city's largest daily paper as artist. When Hitler came to power he left the country, travelling to Prague, Paris and Budapest before arriving in London in 1935, and remained in England throughout the war years. He wrote and illustrated a popular series, 'World Adventures with a Sketch-Book', for the *Evening News*, drew a series of celebrity caricatures for *Sunday Dispatch* called 'Star Signs' and regularly produced work for *Daily Sketch*, *Referee*, *Daily Telegraph* (for whom he covered the signing of the United Nations Charter in San Francisco in 1945), *Lilliput*, *London Opinion*, *Courier*, *News of the World*, *Le Figaro*, *Illustrated*, *Saturday Review*, *New York Times*, *Life*, *New York Herald-Tribune*, *This Week*, *Look* and *Picture Post*. In addition he produced posters for the theatre and worked in advertising for the Post Office, Shell, London Passenger Transport Board, Wolsey Socks, Gillette and others. Berger was held in such high esteem that many celebrities

Oscar Berger, [Churchill], *Famous Faces*, 1950

(including Roosevelt, Churchill, Garbo, Pavlova, Chaplin, Dietrich, King Victor Emmanuel) actually sat to have their caricatures drawn. After World War II he moved to the USA and became a naturalized US citizen in 1955. He is a member of the National Press Club (USA). He has a flamboyant, fluid line.
PUB: *Tip & Top* (1933), *A la Carte* (1948), *Aesop's Foibles* (1949), *Famous Faces* (1950), *My Victims* (1952), *I Love You . . .* (1960), *The Presidents* (1968)
ILL: H. H. Ewers, *Die Traurige Geschichte meiner Trockenlegung* (1927)
COLL: NPG; Library of Congress; Metropolitan Museum, New York

BERRYMAN – *see* Ullyett, Royden

BESTALL, Alfred Edmeades MBE (1892–1986). Illustrator, joke and strip cartoonist, commercial artist and painter. Alfred Bestall was born in Mandalay, Burma, on 14 December 1892, the son of the Rev. Arthur H. Bestall, a Methodist missionary. He was educated at Rydal School, Colwyn Bay (1904–11), and won a scholarship to Birmingham Central School of Art (1912–14) where he studied under Catterson Smith. During World War I he served in the Royal Army Service Corps in Flanders and began contributing cartoons to *Blighty* magazine. After the war he studied illustration under A. S. Hartrick at the Central School of Art, London (1919–22) and began contributing cartoons and illustrations to the *Bystander*, *Eve*, *Gaiety*, *London Opinion*, *Passing Show*, *Piccadilly*, *Punch* (from 1922) and *Tatler* (including more than 40 full-colour plates). In 1935 he took over the 'Rupert Bear' strip cartoon in the *Daily Express* from Mary Tourtel (1897–1940), wife of its writer H. B. Tourtel (a sub-editor on the paper), whose eyesight had begun to fail after 14 years on the strip, which had been introduced in 1921 to rival Charles Folkard's 'Teddy Tail' in the *Daily Mirror*. Bestall introduced a 'surreal quality with action and humour replacing Tourtel's gentler depiction of suspense' (Whalley & Chester) and continued to draw the strip for three decades, contributing to the 'Rupert' annuals up to his 90th year. As well as writing and illustrating more than 300 stories (1935–65) he created the characters Tigerlily, Willie Mouse, Pong-Ping, Sailor Sam and the Old Professor. He also painted in oils and watercolour and, himself an origami artist, was President of the British Origami Society. He was appointed MBE in 1985. Alfred Bestall

died in Porthmadoc, Gwynedd, Wales, on 15 January 1986, aged 93.
PUB: All 'Rupert' books 1935–65
ILL: More than 50 books including E. Blyton, *The Play's the Thing!* (1927), *Plays for Older Children* (1941), *The Boy Next Door* (1944); A. Frome, *The Disappearing Trick* (1933); D. Glass, *The Spanish Goldfish* (1934); M. Inchfawn, *Salute to the Village* (1943); E. Jones, *Folk Tales of Wales* (1947); A. Dumas, *The Three Musketeers* (1950)
EXHIB: RA; RBA
LIT: C. and A. Bott, 'Alfred Edmeades Bestall' (Exhibition Catalogue, Rake Court, Godalming, Surrey, 1988)

BEUTTLER, Edward Gerald Oakley (1880–1964). Joke cartoonist. E. G. O. Beuttler was the eldest son of Thomas Bream Beuttler, later one of the Directors of Education of Western Australia. He first went to sea in 1896 and joined the RNVR in 1898 as a midshipman, rising to the rank of lieutenant (1914) and later wing-commander. He was also Superintendent of Akbar Nautical School in Heswall, Cheshire (*c.* 1907). Before and during World War I he contributed cartoons, many with a nautical flavour, to the *Bystander* (from 1915), *Punch*, *Sketch* and *Winter's Pie*. He was also a regular contributor to the *Tatler* (1916–1942). He is most commonly seen in pen and wash, occasionally in colour, and his animated style owes a good deal to H. M. BATEMAN. Some of his cartoons were also produced as sets of postcards by The Syren & Shipping Ltd. The *Daily Sketch* said of him: 'Beuttler is to the Navy what BAIRNSFATHER is to the Army.' He married the actress Isabel May Roddick of F. R. Benson's company in 1908. E. G. O. Beuttler died in Bovey Tracey, Devon, on 29 January 1964, aged 84.
PUB: *Humours of the Merchant Marine* (1912), *Humour in the Navy* (1916), *The Merry Mariners* (1917), *Humour Afloat* (1919)
COLL: Newton Abbott Golf Club, Devon

BINDER, Pearl [Lady Elwyn Jones] (1904–90). Illustrator, painter, author, broadcaster and caricaturist. Pearl Binder was born on 28 June 1904 in Fenton, Staffordshire, the daughter of a Jewish tailor, and spent her childhood in Lancashire. She studied at Manchester School of Art, and moved to London in 1925 where she began to contribute to the *Sketch* the same year. In 1926 she spent a year in Paris studying at the Académie Colarossi, drawing for *Le Rire* to supplement her income, and returned to London in 1927. Her first humorous book illustrations were published in Coralie Hobson's *Bed and Breakfast* in 1926. She later studied lithography under A. S. Hartrick at the Central School of Art, London (1928), fellow students including JAMES BOSWELL and JAMES FITTON. Primarily a book illustrator and designer, she also contributed cartoons and illustrations to *Fantasio* (1926), *Left Review*, *New Masses*, *New Coterie*, *Harper's Bazaar*, *Lilliput*, *Observer*, *Vogue* and *Tatler* amongst others. In addition she designed for the theatre and drew caricatures. In 1933 she was a founder member (with Boswell, Fitton, ARDIZZONE and others) of the left-wing Artists' International Association. The same year her first book as author was published (*Odd Jobs*) and she visited Moscow where she later had an exhibition of her lithographs. She also drew for BBC TV in 1939 (one of the first artists to do so), broadcast on radio, and in World War II worked for the Government's Press Information Service. Her preferred medium was lithography but she also designed 22 stained-glass windows in the House of Lords commemorating former Lord Chancellors. She cited her influences as PHIL MAY, FISH, Beardsley, Steinlen, Daumier, Covarrubias, El Greco, Holbein and Picasso. In 1937 she married the barrister and political writer Frederick Elwyn Jones QC (later a Labour MP, Attorney-General and Lord Chancellor). She was a Fellow of the Royal Anthropological Institute. Pearl Binder (Polly Elwyn Jones) died in Brighton on 26 January 1990.
PUB: *Odd Jobs: Stories and Drawings* (1933), *Misha and Masha* (1936), *Misha Learns English* (1942), *Russian Families* (1942), *Muffs and Morals* (1953), *The Peacock's Tail* (1958), *The English Inside Out* (1961), *Magic Symbols of the World* (1972)
ILL: Many books including C. Hobson, *Bed and Breakfast* (1926); L. de G. Sieveking, *All Children Must be Paid For* (1927); J. Austen, *Persuasion* (1928); J. Driberg, *People of the Small Arrow* (1930); G. de Nerval, *Aurelia* (1932); T. Burke, *The Real East End* (1932); P. Godfrey, *Back Stage* (1933); L. Golding, *The Dance Goes On* (1937); A. Lomax, *Harriet and her Harmonium* (1955); J. Gladstone, *Stories from Ladder Street* (1979)
EXHIB: Moffat Gallery (1928); BN (1968); MT (1973)
COLL: V&A; BN; BM; Moscow Museum of Modern Western Art

BIRD, Cyril Kenneth 'Fougasse' CBE (1887–1965). Joke and strip cartoonist, illustrator, writer and editor. Kenneth Bird was born on 17 December 1887 in Cheltenham, the son of iron merchant and cricketer Arthur Bird. He attended Farnborough Park School, Hampshire (1898–1902), Cheltenham College (1902–4) and King's College, London, where he trained as an engineer. He also took evening art classes at Regent Street Polytechnic and the Bolt Court School of Photo-Engraving. A machine-gun instructor in the Artists' Rifles (1904–8) and employed at the Rosyth naval base (1909–14), he served in the Royal Engineers in World War I, achieving the rank of lieutenant, but was invalided out when shot in the spine at Gallipoli (1915). As 'Bird' was already in use as JACK YEATS' pseudonym, he began drawing cartoons as 'Fougasse' (the name given to a small anti-personnel mine: 'its effectiveness is not always reliable and its aim uncertain'), studying with PERCY BRADSHAW's Press Art School. At first he drew like BERT THOMAS but gradually developed his own style (motoring and radio being frequent subjects), contributing to *Tit-Bits*, *Punch* (1916–52), *Bystander*, *Graphic*, *London Opinion*, *Sketch* and *Tatler* and succeeded GEORGE MORROW as Art Editor of *Punch* in 1937. He became Editor in 1949 (the only cartoonist ever to hold the post), was a member of the *Punch* Table (1937), and regularly illustrated the magazine's 'Charivaria' page until DOUGLAS ENGLAND took over. In addition he produced a number of drawings for advertising (Guinness, Austin Reed, Vyella socks, Abdulla cigarettes, Pyramid handkerchiefs, etc.). An air-raid warden in World War II, perhaps his most memorable cartoons from this period are the posters he designed for government departments, such as the red-bordered 'Careless Talk Costs Lives' series (originally entitled 'Careless Talk May Cost Us All Dear') for the Ministry of Information. A pioneer of the idea that humour is more important than art – 'It is really better to have a good idea with a bad drawing than a bad idea with a good drawing' – he also lectured on cartooning on radio (he was a member of the BBC 'Brains Trust') and elsewhere. His distinctive, strikingly economical style, often using only a few lines but expressing great dynamism, is immediately recognizable and has influenced many artists. 'Clarity and speed were everything in his work and he was constantly trying to simplify . . . he rapidly developed a personal style that was perhaps the first introduction of contemporary advertising technique to the editorial pages of *Punch* . . . the decorative element was thrown out with the linear padding' (Price). Elected a Fellow of King's College, London (1936), he was created CBE in 1946. A member of the Athenaeum Club and the Arts Club, he retired in 1953. He was married to the

'That reminds me, dear – did you remember the sandwiches?'

Fougasse (Kenneth Bird), *Punch*, 27 June 1951

watercolour artist Mary Holden Bird (née Caldwell). Kenneth Bird died on 11 June 1965.
PUB: *A Gallery of Games* (1921), *Drawn at a Venture* (1922), *PTO* (1926), *E and OE* (1928), [with W. D. H. MacCullough] *Aces Made Easy* (1934), *Fun Fair* (1934), *The Luck of the Draw* (1936), [with W. D. H. MacCullough] *You Have Been Warned* (1935), *Drawing the Line Somewhere* (1937), *Stop or Go* (1938), *Jotsam* (1939), *The Changing Face of Britain* (1940), . . . *and the Gatepost* (1940), *Running Commentary* (1941), *Sorry – No Rubber* (1942), *The Fougasse Painting Book* (1942), [with A. W. Bird] *Just a Few Lines* (1943), *Family Group* (1944), *Home Circle* (1945), *A School of Purposes* (1946), *You and Me* (1948), *Us* (1951), *The Neighbours* (1954), *The Good-Tempered Pencil* (1956), *Between the Lines* (1958)
ILL: Many books including H. L. Wilson, *So This is Golf* (1923); H. J. C. Graham, *The World's Workers* (1928); G. Reed, *The Little Less* (1941)
EXHIB: FAS (1924, 1926, 1929, 1933; Memorial, 1966); RSA
COLL: IWM
LIT: B. Hillier (ed.), *Fougasse* (1977)

BIRD, W. – *see* Yeats, Jack Butler

BIRDSALL, Timothy (1936–63). Political, strip and pocket cartoonist, illustrator and broadcaster. Timothy Birdsall was born on 10 May 1936 in Cambridge and attended Cambridge University where he was a contemporary and friend of Bamber Gascoigne and Michael Frayn. A talented artist as a student (he illustrated *Granta* while at Cambridge), his early professional cartoon work included a regular strip for *Variety* (1957–8). He later joined the *Sunday Times* (1960–62) to produce a series of front-page pocket cartoons, 'Little Cartoons by Timothy', and from 1962 until his death drew political cartoons and caricatures for the *Spectator* and cartoons for *Private Eye*. However, his biggest audience was as resident cartoonist drawing live on Ned Sherrin and David Frost's satirical BBC TV show *That Was the Week That Was* (1963). Influenced by EMETT, SEARLE and FFOLKES, he was working on a book, *This Book is Good for You*, when he died of leukaemia on 10 June 1963. A tribute, *Timothy*, reproduced many of his cartoons. A highly inventive cartoonist, he was a fine draughtsman with a love of detail. 'Timothy didn't construct abstract cartoons out of created symbols which needed naming. He preferred to find some genuine context which

'I said the Labour Party are looking pretty silly.'

Timothy Birdsall, *Sunday Times, c.* 1960

fitted his intentions and he went further afield than most cartoonists in his search for these contexts' (Bamber Gascoigne).
PUB: [M. Frayn and B. Gascoigne eds] *Timothy* (1964)
ILL: R. Brook, *Really, Nurse!* (1960), *Wake up, Nurse!* (1963); J. Harborne, *The World in My House* (1960); R. Mander and J. Mitchenson, *The Theatres of London* (1961); M. Frayn, *The Day of the Dog* (1962); A. Elliot-Cannon and N. Adams, *Travelling Light* (1962); D. Frost and N. Sherrin (eds), *That Was the Week That Was* (1963)
EXHIB: William Ware Gallery

BLAKE, Quentin Saxby OBE RDI FSIAD (b. 1932). Joke cartoonist, illustrator and writer. Quentin Blake was born in Sidcup, Kent, on 16 December 1932, the son of a civil servant. He was educated at Chislehurst & Sidcup Grammar School, read English at Downing College, Cambridge (1953–6), and took teacher training at the Institute of Education, University of London (1956–7). He also attended life classes part-time at Chelsea School of Art and studied anatomical sculpture at Camberwell School of Art. During his National Service (1951–3) he taught English at Aldershot and illustrated a book for teaching illiterate soldiers to read. He contributed his first cartoon to *Punch* at the age of 16 and has worked as a freelance illustrator and teacher since 1957. He has taught English (part-time) at the Lycée Français, London, and was Tutor (1965–78) then Head of the Department of Illustration at the Royal College of Art (1978–86), succeeding BRIAN ROBB. He is particularly well-known for his jackets and illustrations for children's books. He has also designed covers for *Punch*, contributed to the *Spectator* (including covers) and *Soldier*, and drawn advertisements for Guinness and others. In 1979 he was joint winner of the Whitbread Award and in 1981 won the Kate Greenaway Medal for *Mr Magnolia*. He was appointed the first-ever 'Children's Laureate' in 1999. Blake's scratchy style and zany humour have been strongly influenced by ANDRÉ FRANÇOIS, whom he greatly admires. He works most frequently with indian ink and watercolour on Arches or Canson paper.

PUB: *Patrick* (1968), *A Band of Angels* (1969), *Jack and Nancy* (1969), *Angelo* (1970), *Snuff* (1973), *Lester and the Unusual Pet* (1975), *Lester at the Seaside* (1975), *The Adventures of Lester* (1977), *Mr Magnolia* (1981), *Quentin Blake's Nursery Rhyme Book* (1983), *Quentin Blake's ABC* (1989), *The Green Ship* (1998), *Zagazoo* (1998)

ILL: Many books including E. Blance and A. Cook's 'Monster' series; J. P. Martin's 'Uncle' series; J. Aitken's 'Mortimer' series; R. Dahl's books beginning with *The Enormous Crocodile* (1978); Aristophanes, *The Birds* (1971); C. Freud, *Grimble* (1974); L. Carroll, *The Hunting of the Snark* (1976); and books by S. Gibbons, R. Hoban, E. Bowen, O. Nash, P. Campbell (seven titles)

EXHIB: CG; NT; CBG; AI

COLL: BM; V&A

BLAM – *see* Blampied, Edmund

BLAMPIED, Edmund RE RBA (1886–1966). Printmaker, painter, joke cartoonist and illustrator. Edmund Blampied was born in Jersey, Channel Islands, on 30 March 1886, the son of John Blampied, a farmer who died shortly before he was born. He was probably also related

to the St Helier artist Clifford George Blampied. Educated at Trinity School, Jersey, he studied under Philip Connard CVO RA RWS and Thomas McKeggie at the Lambeth School of Art (1903–4) and was awarded a scholarship to study etching under Walter Seymour at the LCC Art School at Bolt Court (1905–13). He also studied lithography with Sir Malcolm Osborne CBE RA PRE RBC before returning to the Channel Islands. He began as a book illustrator, producing drawings for two volumes by Edith Nesbit while still a student and continuing during World War I with works by J. J. Farnol and others and contributions to French magazines such as *Fantasio* (1916–19) and *Le Rire* (1917). He later drew cartoons and illustrations for the *Bystander*, *Apple*, *Men Only*, *Graphic*, *Hutchinson's* (e.g. illustrations to stories by E. F. Benson), *News Chronicle*, *Illustrated London News*, *Strand*, *Sketch* and *Tatler* amongst others. Best known as an etcher and lithographer, he was elected ARE (1920), RE (1921) and a member of the Senefelder Club for lithographers (1923). He won a Gold Medal for lithography at the Paris International Exhibition (1925) and by 1926 his fame was such that a complete catalogue of his etchings and drypoints was published. As a cartoonist his London exhibition, 'Nonsense Show' (1931), was widely praised and his book of cartoons, *Bottled Trout and Polo* (1936), has echoes of PAUL CRUM. Referring to his illustration work, Hodnett called him 'technically the equal of the colour-plate masters Arthur Rackham, William Russell Flint and EDMUND DULAC'. In World War II Blampied remained in the Channel Islands during the German occupation (1940–44) and designed the Islands' Occupation and Liberation stamps. Elected RBA in 1938, he was also a member of the Chelsea Arts Club. He drew in ink and pencil and also painted in watercolours and oil and modelled in clay. In addition he designed advertisements for Pears Soap and others. He signed some of his cartoons 'Blam'. He was married to Marianne van Abbé. Edmund Blampied died in Jersey on 26 August 1966.

PUB: *Hot Dogs* (1934), *Bottled Trout and Polo* (1936)

ILL: Many books including E. Nesbit, *The Phoenix and the Carpet* (1903), *The House of Arden* (1908); W. T. Titterton, *Me as a Model* (1914); J. J. Farnol, *The Money Moon* (1914), *The Chronicle of the Imp* (1915); E. Dell, *The Way of an Eagle* (1916); R. L. Stevenson, *Travels with a Donkey* (1931);

J. B. Priestley, *Albert Goes Through* (1934); H. C. Hunt, *Hand-Picked Howlers* (1937), *More Hand-Picked Howlers* (1938), *Ripe Howlers* (1939), *Hand-Picked Proverbs* (1940); J. M. Barrie, *The Blampied Edition of Peter Pan* (1939)
EXHIB: RA; RE; LG; RSA; Bull & Saunders; Salon des Humoristes, Paris; Guernsey Museum & Art Gallery (1986); Senefelder Club
COLL: BM; V&A; Société Jersiaise; Boston Public Library; Cleveland Museum of Art (USA); L; THG
LIT: C. Dodgson, *A Complete Catalogue of the Etchings and Dry-Points of Edmund Blampied* (1926); M. Syvnet, *Edmund Blampied* (1986)

'Bleep and Booster' – *see* Timyn, William

BLOWER, Patrick (b. 1959). Editorial/political and pocket cartoonist. Patrick Blower was born on 10 January 1959 in Brussels, the son of Michael Blower, an English architect. He studied English literature at University College, London (1978–81), and then spent two years in New York (1982–4) working in a variety of jobs including painter and decorator, art-gallery attendant, plasterer and snack-bar worker. His first cartoon was published in the *New York East*

Village Eye in 1983. He moved back to London in 1984 and worked in advertising sales, TV production and as a painter before turning freelance cartoonist in 1986, contributing to trade magazines such as *Local Government Chronicle* and *British Baker*. He contributed his first pocket cartoons to the *Independent* (1992) and has been Pocket Cartoonist on the *Mail on Sunday* (since 1994) and *Evening Standard* (since December 1996). He succeeded JAK as the *Evening Standard*'s Political Cartoonist in July 1997 and has also worked for *Daily Express* ('On This Day', daily cartoon, 1993–5), *Total Football*, *Punch* and *Spectator*. Influenced by Brueghel, Sempé, Hergé and Franquin, he works in most media from pen and ink to computer.
PUB: *Get Stuffed* (1992)

BOND, Simon Patrick Everett (b. 1947). Joke cartoonist, illustrator, writer and publisher. Simon Bond was born on 19 August 1947 in New York, the son of Terence R. Bond, a diplomat and civil servant. He attended West Sussex College of Art and Design (1965–8) and was a paste-up artist on *Tatler* (1969–70) and manager of a jewellery shop before returning to the USA on health grounds in 1970. For more than a

Simon Bond, *Odd Visions and Bizarre Sights*, 1983

decade he lived in Phoenix, Arizona, working in a variety of jobs – including dealing in anti-quarian prints and pictures and performing stand-up comedy in clubs – and contributing cartoons to *Saturday Evening Post, Esquire, National Lampoon, New Yorker, Men Only* and *Vole*. He returned to the UK in 1982 and has since produced freelance cartoons for *Punch* and *Private Eye*. Best known for his bestselling book, *101 Uses of a Dead Cat* (1981), he was also publisher and co-editor of *Squib* magazine (1992–3). He draws roughs with a 2H pencil on A4 cartridge paper and works up the cartoons with a fine Edding needlepoint nylon-tip pen. He tends to draw actual size for bookwork and 9¹/₂ × 11¹/₂ in. for *Punch* and *New Yorker* and never uses washes, tints or cross-hatching, preferring to draw up-and-down lines for shadows. For colour work he prefers coloured pencils.

PUB: Many books including *Real Funny* (1976), *101 Uses of a Dead Cat* (1981), *Unspeakable Acts* (1982), *101 More Uses of a Dead Cat* (1982), *Odd Visions and Bizarre Sights* (1983), *Success and How to Be One* (1984), *Teddy* (1985), (ed.) *Sherriffs at the Cinema* (1985), *Tough Ted and Desmond Dougall* (1986), *Uniformity* (1986), *Have a Nice Day* (1986), *Stroked Through the Covers* (1987), *A Bruise of Bouncers* (1987), *Totally US* (1988), *Odd Dogs* (1989), *Tough Ted and the Tale of the Tattered Ear* (1989), *Holy Unacceptable* (1990), *Dubious Practices* (1991), *Uses of a Dead Cat in History* (1992), *Commuted to Life* (1992), *Everybody's Doing It* (1993)
ILL: P. Richter, *Don't Get Mad, Get Even* (1983), *How to Thrive on Rejection* (1985), *Richter's Legal Nuggets* (1987)
EXHIB: NT; CG; CBG; Atlanta, Georgia USA

'Bonzo' – *see* Studdy, George Ernest

'Boo-Boos, The' – *see* Attwell, Mabel Lucie

BOSWELL, James E. ARCA (1906–71). Painter, illustrator, cartoonist and writer. James Boswell was born on 9 June 1906 in Westport, New Zealand, the son of E. B. Boswell, a school-teacher of Scottish descent. In 1917 the family moved to Auckland where he attended Auckland Grammar School and Elam School of Art (1924) before leaving to study at the Royal College of Art in London (1925–9). He also studied in the studio of Frederick J. Porter and worked first as a landscape painter and lithographer, but by 1932 had given up painting, joined the Communist Party and taken to illustration and graphic design. In 1933 he was a founder member (later Chairman, 1944) of the Artists' International Association (with Misha Black, PEARL BINDER, JAMES FITTON, James Holland and Clifford Rowe). He was Art Director of the publicity department of Asiatic (later Shell) Petroleum (1936–47) and illustrator for *Left Review* from its launch (1934–8) while also contributing anti-fascist drawings to the *Daily Worker* as 'Buchan'. He also drew for *Poetry and the People, Current Affairs, Our Time, Sunday Telegraph, Radio Times* and *Punch*. After service in the Royal Army Medical Corps as a radiographer in Iraq and the Middle East (1941–5) he joined *Lilliput* as Art Editor (1947–50). He then turned freelance and in 1951 Basil Spence commissioned him to paint a 20ft × 50ft mural for the Sea and Ships pavilion in the Festival of Britain. The same year he became Editor (a post he retained until his death) of J. Sainsbury's house journal, *JS Journal*, and wrote the history of the firm. Designer and director of Topic Records, he also designed the Labour Party's posters and overall publicity campaign for the 1964 general election, as well as numerous book jackets. He was influenced by George Grosz. James Boswell died in London on 15 April 1971.
PUB: *Painter and Public* (1950), [with R. Bennett] *Cat Meets Dog* (1951)
ILL: 16 books including J. Pudney, *Low Life* (1947); W. Mankowicz, *A Kid for Two Farthings* (1953); J. Symonds, *Dapplegray* (1962), *Conversation with Gerald* (1974); C. Mackenzie, *Little Cat Lost* (1965)
EXHIB: RCA; ICA; LON; Senefelder Club; Charlotte Street Centre; RA (1947); Wolf Mankowicz Gallery; Paris Salon; John Moore Gallery, Liverpool; Drian Gallery; County Town Gallery, Eastbourne; Heal's Gallery; New Vision Centre; CI
COLL: BM; V&A; T; New Zealand NG (Wellington NZ); IWM; TOW
LIT: [autobiography] *The Artist's Dilemma* (1947); W. Feaver, *Boswell's London* (1978)

BOTTERILL, H. – *see* Thompson, Harold Underwood

BOTZARITCH [or BOTZARIS, originally BOCARIC], Anastas Sava (1896–after 1941). Caricaturist, painter and sculptor. Anastas Bocaric Sava was born in Belgrade, Serbia, on 24 May 1896, the son of Cavaliere Anastas

Sava Botzaritch, [Austen Chamberlain], n.d.

Bocaric Sava, a historical painter who was also a professor at the National Serbian School of High Art and Court Painter to King Peter of Serbia. He worked at first for his father, travelling widely and learning ten languages. Then, intended for the diplomatic service, he was posted to the Serbian Embassy in Rome but after meeting the sculptor Ivan Mestrovic in Athens decided to become an artist. He then studied in Zagreb, Rome, Florence, Naples (under the sculptor Pellegrini), Prague and at the École des Beaux-Arts in Paris, and won an Italian award for portraiture. During World War I he served as an interpreter for the Allies and after the war returned to Belgrade to work with Mestrovic. Promoted by George Bernard Shaw in the UK and USA, he settled in England in 1922 and worked as a caricaturist while also painting portraits and producing sculpture busts in bronze and copper of celebrities and High Society figures such as Shaw, Viscountess Curzon, Philip Guedalla and others. He moved to Venezuela in 1941.

PUB: *25 Caricatures* (1926), *Sculpture by Sava Botzaris* (1929)

EXHIB: [sculpture] French Gallery (1929); LG (1938)

COLL: [bronze] Brooklyn Museum, New York; Henry Ranson Research Center, University of Texas, Austin, Texas

BOUCHER, William Henry ARE (fl. 1868– d.1906) – *see* Bryant & Heneage

BOVEY, A. J. (1900–after 1945). Joke cartoonist, caricaturist, illustrator and writer. Bovey's cartoon career began when his first submitted drawing (to *Pan*) was accepted when he was 19. He worked in a shipping office, then in the Bank of England and while there collaborated with Sheridan Bickers on *Theatre World*, for which he drew many covers and caricatures. He left the Bank in 1926 to work in a succession of advertising agencies: Dorlands, Crawfords and Bensons – where he was part of the team that produced the famous Guinness and Bovril advertisements. During World War II he drew propaganda cartoons for the Ministry of Information and served in the Home Guard. He also illustrated children's books, wrote light verse (e.g. 'Lottie the Land Girl' [1942] and 'Zero Hour' [1945] in the *Strand*), produced a regular full-page feature 'Delirious Dialogues' for the *Bystander* and contributed to *Passing Show, Men Only* and *London Opinion*.

BOXER, Charles Mark Edward 'Marc' (1931– 88). Pocket and strip cartoonist, caricaturist and publisher. Mark Boxer was born on 19 May 1931 in Berkhamsted, Hertfordshire, the son of Steven Boxer, an army officer. He was educated at Berkhamsted School and King's College, Cambridge (1950–53), where he was Editor of *Granta* (1952–3) and was briefly sent down for publishing a blasphemous poem. His first cartoons were published in *Granta* and *Punch*. He then worked as a freelance cartoonist for *Ambassador, Lilliput, Vogue, House & Garden* and *Punch* before becoming Art Director of *Queen* (1957– 61). He was the first Editor of the *Sunday Times Magazine* (1962–5), a director of the *Sunday Times* (1964–6), Editorial Director of *London Life* (1965), Assistant Editor of *Sunday Times* (1966–79), a director of the book publishers Weidenfeld & Nicolson (1980–83), Editor of *Tatler* (1983–7), Editorial Director of Condé Nast Publications (1986–8) and Editor-in-Chief of *Vogue* and *Tatler* (1987–8). As a cartoonist he worked for *The Times* (diary illustrations) and *Sunday Times*

Mark Boxer, [Enoch Powell], in M. Amory (ed.), *The Collected and Recollected Marc*, 1993

(Atticus, 1969–83), *New Statesman* (caricatures, 1970–78), *Guardian* (1983–6), *Observer* (caricatures, 1983–8), *Daily Telegraph* (1986–8), *Sunday Telegraph* (caricatures, 1987–8) and *New Yorker* (caricatures). His most popular creations were Simon and Joanna String-Along – an awful upper-middle-class trendy couple from London's NW1 district based on characters from Alan Bennett's BBC series *On the Margin*. They first appeared in the strip 'Life and Times in NW1' in the *Listener* in August 1967 and from 1969 featured as a pocket cartoon in *The Times*. A variant of the series continued in colour in *Nova* as 'Tinderbox Green: An Everyday Story of Estate Living', written by Peter Preston. Boxer also drew for advertising, notably Smirnoff Vodka, and produced all 12 jackets for the Penguin edition of Anthony Powell's *A Dance to the Music of Time*. He admired Low, VICKY, PONT, LANCASTER and Steinberg, was voted Granada TV's *What the Papers Say* Cartoonist of the Year (1972) and received the Glen Grant Social and Political Cartoonist Award (1981). Mark Boxer used a dip pen with a Gillott 404

nib and calligraphic ink on A4 Croxley Script, drawing with a No. 3 or No. 4 brush for thick lines. His captions were typed on an old Remington typewriter with a large typeface that used to belong to the short-sighted Lord Thomson of Fleet. Each caption was typed using fresh carbon paper cut into strips 3 × 4 in. long. HEWISON has commented that he possessed 'the best qualities of the untrained amateur drawing at the peak of his ability . . . That, coupled with a sharp sense of observation, can sometimes make a Marc caricature particularly devastating.' He died of cancer on 20 July 1988 at his home in Brentford, Middlesex.
PUB: *The Trendy Ape* (1968), *The Times We Live In* (1978), *Marc Time* (1984) *People Like Us* (1986), *Paint Pots* (1988)
ILL: R. Ingrams (ed.), *Private Eye Book of Pseuds* (1973); C. James, *Felicity Fark* (1975), *Britannia Bright* (1976), *Charles Charming* (1981); A. Barrow, *The Great Book of Small Talk* (1987)
EXHIB: CG; Parkin Gallery; LAN
COLL: NPG; V&A; BM
LIT: M. Amory (ed.), *The Collected and Recollected Marc* (1993)

BOYD, Alexander Stuart RSW (1854–1930). Illustrator, joke cartoonist, journalist, writer and painter. A. S. Boyd was born in Glasgow on 7 February 1854, the son of Alexander Boyd, a muslin manufacturer. His father died when Boyd was ten and he studied briefly at the Glasgow School of Art aged 12. He worked at first as a clerk in the Royal Bank of Scotland (1873–9), painting in his spare time, and exhibiting his works in Scottish galleries from 1877 onwards. He turned full-time artist in 1879, illustrating a serial for *Good Words* magazine that year amongst other work. He then studied at Heatherley's in London (1880) before returning to Glasgow to work as a cartoonist for newly launched weekly *Quiz* (1881–8) under the pseudonym 'Twym'. Meanwhile, he continued to paint, being elected a member of the Royal Scottish Society of Painters in Watercolour (RSW) in 1885 and a member of the Glasgow Art Club. He began work as a book illustrator in 1884 and wrote his first book, *Sweet Briar*, in 1886. He then joined the *Baillie* as a cartoonist (still as 'Twym') in 1888 and became Glasgow Correspondent for the newly launched *Daily Graphic* (1890). Moving to London in 1891 he began to contribute cartoons and illustrations under his own name to the *Graphic* (from 1893), *Punch*

(from 1894), *Good Words, Black & White, Idler, Sunday Magazine, Pall Mall Magazine* and others. He emigrated to New Zealand in 1912 and eventually became President of the Auckland Society of Artists. As well as working in his 'angular style of pen drawing' (THORPE), he painted in watercolour and oils. His wife, Mary, was a travel writer and he also illustrated some of her books. A. S. Boyd died in Auckland, New Zealand, on 21 August 1930.
PUB: *Sweet Briar* (1886), *The Gailes of 89* (1889), *When We Were Laddies at the Scule* (1902), *Glasgow Men and Women* (1905)
ILL: Many books including C. Blatherwick, *Peter Stonnor* (1884); W. Roberts, *The Birthday Book of Solomon Grundy* (1884); I. Zangwill, *Ghetto Tragedies* (1884); I. Maclaren, *The Days of Auld Lang Syne* (1898); R. L. Stevenson, *A Lowden Sabbath Morn* (1898), *A Cotter's Saturday Night* (n.d.); M. Boyd, *Our Stolen Summer* (1900), *A Versailles Christmas-Tide* (1901), *The Fortunate Isles* (1911)
EXHIB: RA; RSA; RSW; GI
COLL: V&A; G

BRADSHAW, Percy Venner 'PVB' (1877–1965). Joke cartoonist, illustrator, writer and art teacher. Percy Bradshaw was born in Hackney, London, on 27 November 1877 the son of William Bradshaw, a warehouseman and later a commercial traveller for a hosiery company. Educated at Haberdashers' Aske's School, Hatcham, London, he left school at the age of 14 to work as a clerk in an advertising agency while studying art at evening classes at Goldsmith's and Birkbeck College. Having sold his first drawing to *Boy's Own Paper* aged 15 he transferred to the agency's art department. He turned full-time freelance cartoonist at the age of 18, contributing to *Boy's Own Paper, Home Chat* and *Sunday Companion*, and won first prize in a cartoon competition run by *Artist* magazine (he drew a jester's head). He then briefly worked on the art staff of the *Daily Mail* before freelancing again for *Tatler, Sketch, Bystander* and *Windsor Magazine*. In addition he wrote articles for the *Daily Graphic* and a series 'Black and White Drawing as a Profession' for *Boy's Own Paper* which prompted so many letters that he decided to found the Press Art School correspondence course in 1905. His first pupil was LEO CHENEY, later to design the most famous version of the Johnnie Walker whisky trademark figure created by TOM BROWNE. Other cele-

brated pupils included RIDGEWELL, D'EGVILLE, FOUGASSE, A. E. BEARD, Ern Shaw, Honor Appleton, JOE LEE, DAVID GHILCHIK, PETER FRASER, CHARLES GRAVE, G. S. DIXON, NORMAN PETT, STAN TERRY, BERTRAM PRANCE and RALPH STEADMAN. The school (of which he was principal for more than 50 years) was run at first from his home, but later moved to Tudor Hall in Forest Hill, London (once the home of Baroness Burdett Coutts), where he had his own presses, and from 1914 produced 20 issues in portfolio form of *The Art of the Illustrator*. By 1916 Bradshaw was enrolling 3000 students a year and employed more than 20 staff, and by 1943 more than 4000 drawings by his pupils had appeared in *Punch* alone. His consultant staff included BERT THOMAS, HEATH ROBINSON, FRED PEGRAM, HARRY ROUNTREE and Leo Cheney. During World War I he served as a Special Constable and after the war produced hundreds of postcards for companies such as Raphael Tuck, Moss, Wrench and Misch, worked part-time for Royds advertising agency (1930) and from 1933 was London sales organizer for the printer Sun Engravings of Watford. A special six-month supplement to his course, 'Caricature and Humorous Drawing', was published in 1936. During World War II he served as a firewatcher and wrote humorous verse for Allied Newspapers and a popular series of articles about cartoonists ('They Make Us Smile') for *London Opinion*. He often signed his work 'PVB' and was a great admirer of PHIL MAY. He was a member of the London Sketch Club and a committee member of the Savage Club (he wrote its official history in 1958). Percy Bradshaw died in Hither Green Hospital, Lewisham, London on 13 October 1965.
PUB: *The Art of the Illustrator* (1918), *Art in Advertising* (1925), *Fashion Drawing and Designing* (1936), *I Wish I Could Draw* (1941), *They Make Us Smile* (1942), *Marching On* (1943), *Drawn from Memory* (1943), *Nice People to Know* (1944), *I Wish I Could Paint* (1945), *Lines of Laughter* (1946), *Seen in Perspective* (1946), *The Magic of Line* (1949), *Water-Colour Painting* (1949), *Water-Colour* (1952), *Sketching and Painting Indoors* (1956), *Brother Savages and Guests* (1958)

BREEZE, Hector (b. 1928). Joke cartoonist, commercial artist and illustrator. Hector Breeze was born on 17 November 1928 in London and educated at Dartford Technical College. He was first employed in a government drawing office and

'Why don't you ever dress up as Albert Schweitzer?'

Hector Breeze, *Private Eye*, 16 April 1965

studied art at evening classes before selling his first drawing to *Melody Maker* in 1957. He has since worked in advertising and produced cartoons for *Private Eye, Punch, Evening Standard, Daily Mirror, Daily Sketch* and *Guardian* (letters page). He has been the Pocket Cartoonist on the *Daily Express* since 1982. Voted CCGB Feature Cartoonist of the Year (1984, 1985) he also practises letter-carving in stone but is best known for his drawings featuring impoverished gentry with characteristic chinless faces and tiny dot eyes. 'His happy stamping ground is Royalty on the blink and fly-blown Beckettian tramps . . . his people look as if they have been standing too close to the fire and have melted a little' (HEWISON).
PUB: *Private Eye Hector Breeze* (1973)
ILL: T. Wogan, *The Day Job* (1981)
EXHIB: (with NICK NEWMAN) JDG
COLL: UKCC; V&A; BM

BRIAN – *see* ffolkes, Michael

'Briggs the Butler' – *see* Graham, Alexander Steel

BRIGGS, Raymond Redvers DFA FSIAD (b. 1934). Illustrator and caricaturist. Raymond Briggs was born in Wimbledon, London, on 18

January 1934, the son of a milkman. He was educated at Rutlish School, Merton, and studied at Wimbledon School of Art (1949–53) and, after National Service, at the Slade (1955–7). He has been a freelance illustrator since 1957 – working for clients such as the BBC, Condé Nast magazines, Oxford University Press and Penguin Books – and has taught illustration part-time at Brighton Polytechnic (1961–87). Best known for his children's books such as *Father Christmas, Fungus the Bogeyman* and *The Snowman* (made into a successful animated film in 1982), he has also produced work for the *Guardian*. In addition he wrote and illustrated a satirical picture-book, *The Tin-Pot Foreign General and the Old Iron Woman*, following the Falklands War and featuring caricatures of British Prime Minister Margaret Thatcher and Argentinian leader General Galtieri. He won the Kate Greenaway Medal for *The Mother Goose Treasury* (1966) – featuring more than 800 illustrations – and *Father Christmas* (1973). He works in line and watercolour, gouache, pencil and crayons.
PUB: Many books including *The Strange House* (1961), *Midnight Adventure* (1961), *Ring-a-Ring O' Roses* (1962), *Sledges to the Rescue* (1963), *Mother Goose Treasury* (1966), *Father Christmas* (1973), *Fungus the Bogeyman* (1977), *The Snowman* (1978), *Gentleman Jim* (1980), *When the Wind Blows* (1982), *Fungus the Bogeyman Plop-Up Book* (1982), *The Tin-Pot Foreign General and the Old Iron Woman* (1984), *Unlucky Wally Twenty Years On* (1989), *The Man* (1992), *The Bear* (1994), *Ethel & Ernest* (1998)
ILL: R. M. Sanders, *Peter and the Piskies* (1958); E. Vipont, *The Elephant and the Bad Baby* (1969); I. Serrailler, *The Tale of Three Landlubbers* (1970); V. Haviland, *The Fairy Tale Treasury* (1972)
COLL: V&A

BRIGHTWELL, Leonard Robert FZS (1889–1983). Joke and strip cartoonist, illustrator and etcher. Leonard Brightwell was born in London on 17 May 1889 and attended Alleyn's School and the Latymer School, Hammersmith, before studying at Lambeth School of Art. He began drawing animals at the age of six and sold his first drawing to *Boy's Own Paper* for 7s 6d when aged 16. From 16 until the age of 40 he contributed cartoons to many papers and magazines including *Bystander, Chums, Joy Street, Quiver, London Opinion, Graphic, Happy Days, Humorist, Little Folks, Pall Mall, Pearson's, Puck, Royal, Sketch, Tatler* and *Punch* (1905–29).

A specialist in animal drawing (ALDIN was best known for dogs, Brightwell for monkeys), he studied animal anatomy at the London Zoo and became a Fellow of the Zoological Society of London (1906) and of the New York Zoo (1922). During World War I he served in the army on the Western Front and in World War II was an air-raid warden. Very interested in fish, in 1922 he joined the Marine Biological Association and took part in many expeditions on scientific and commercial deep-sea trawlers. In addition he was involved with restorations of extinct animals for the British Museum and produced humorous and educational animated cartoons. He was President of the London Sketch Club (1928). Best known for his black-and-white pen drawings he also worked in colour, and said that 'From the beginning I have been an ardent admirer of Landseer, Breton Riviere, Cecil Aldin, J. A. SHEPHERD, HARRY ROUNTREE, Barie Kano and such Americans as Charles Knight, Bruce Horsfall, Fuertes, Livingston Bull and Paul Bransom.'
PUB: 19 books including *A Cartoonist Among Animals* (1921), *The Tiger in the Town* (1930), *Zoo Calendar* (1934), *The Zoo You Knew* (1936), *The Zoo Story* (1952)
ILL: E. H. Barker, *A British Dog in France* (1913); E. Davies, *Our Friends at the Farm* (1920); C. Evans, *Reynard the Fox* (1921); L. Mainland, *Zoo Saints and Sinners* (1925); E. Boulanger, *A Naturalist at the Zoo* (1926); H. Chesterman, *The Odd Spot* (1928); M. Swannell, *Animal Geography* (1930); Sister Margaret, *Zoo Guy'd* (1935); O. Bowen, *Taddy Tadpole* (1946)
EXHIB: Abbey Gallery; Arlington Gallery; Brook Street Art Gallery; Connell & Sons Gallery (1926, 1938); L

'Bristow' – *see* Dickens, Frank William Huline

BROCK, Charles Edmund RI (1870–1938). Illustrator, portrait painter and joke cartoonist. C. E. Brock was born in Holloway, London, on 5 February 1870, the son of Edmund Brock, a specialist reader in oriental languages for Cambridge University Press. He was the eldest of four brothers, who included H. M. BROCK and the landscape artist and illustrator Richard Henry Brock. In addition, he was a cousin of FRED PEGRAM. He attended St Barnabas School and Paradise Street Higher Grade School, Cambridge, and his sole art training consisted of working in the studio of the Cambridge sculp-

tor Henry Wiles. His first published works were book illustrations for *The Parachute and Other Bad Shots* by J. R. Johnson (father of actress Celia and literary agent John), but he soon became a regular contributor to *Punch* (1901–10), *Good Words* (1895–6), *Illustrated London News, Fun, Graphic, Captain, Chums, Little Folks, Quiver, Strand, Pearson's Magazine, Windsor Magazine* and other publications. He also illustrated Macmillan's 'Standard Novels' series and many other books. In addition, Raphael Tuck published some of his *Punch* drawings as postcards. He shared a studio and worked closely with his younger brother, sketching on paper, then using Goodall's Bristol Board and Bradauers 518 and 515 nibs, ink and watercolour. In addition he worked in charcoal and painted portraits in oils. Influenced at first by the illustrator Hugh Thomson (as was his brother), Charles once substituted for Thomson (on *Pride and Prejudice*) in Macmillan's 'Thomson edition' of Jane Austen's novels. He often used models and the many antiques and props collected by both brothers often turn up in their drawings. He was elected RI in 1908. C. E. Brock died on 28 February 1938.
ILL: Many books including J. R. Johnson, *The Parachute and Other Bad Shots* (1891); T. Hood, *Humorous Poems* (1893); J. Swift, *Gulliver's Travels* (1894); W. Scott, *Ivanhoe* (1900); R. Kipling, *Rewards and Fairies* (1910); F. H. Burnett, *Little Lord Fauntleroy* (1925); Mrs Molesworth, *The Cuckoo Clock* (1931); T. W. Wilson, *Through the Bible* (1938), plus Dent's 'English Idylls' series and titles by J. Austen, C. Lamb, O. Goldsmith, D. Defoe
EXHIB: L; RA; RI; GI; ROI; RSA
COLL: THG
LIT: C. M. Kelly, *The Brocks* (1975)

BROCK, Henry Matthew RI (1875–1960). Illustrator, landscape painter and joke cartoonist. H. M. Brock was born in Cambridge on 11 July 1875, the son of Edmund Brock, a specialist reader in oriental languages for Cambridge University Press. In addition he was a cousin of FRED PEGRAM (whose sister Doris Joan Pegram he later married). He was the youngest of four brothers who included C. E. BROCK and the landscape artist and illustrator Richard Henry Brock. He attended St Barnabas School and Paradise Street Higher Grade School, Cambridge, and later studied at Cambridge School of Art. Like his eldest brother (with whom he shared a studio), he worked mostly as a book illustrator (his first drawing was published in 1893 when he was 18), notably on Macmillan's 'Standard Novels' and other series – especially adventure stories. However, he also contributed to *Punch* (1905–40), *Graphic, Holly Leaves, Strand Magazine, Chums, Boy's Own Paper, Quiver, Cassell's, Country Life* (including the George V Coronation cover, 22 June 1911), *Fun, Humorist, Little Folks, Pearson's Magazine, Windsor Magazine, Sphere, Sketch, Captain* (1911–24), *Sparkler* and others. In addition he worked in advertising, producing drawings for Ronuk Polish, Johnnie Walker Whisky, Erasmic Soap, Player's Airman Tobacco, etc. During the 1920s he produced posters for D'Oyly Carte, and drew 100 watercolour illustrations of Gilbert and Sullivan characters and 50 characters from fiction for Player's cigarette cards. He worked closely with his eldest brother, sketching on paper, then using Goodall's Bristol Board and Bradauers 518 and 515 nibs, ink and watercolour. In addition he worked in charcoal and watercolour and painted portraits in oils. Influenced at first by the illustrator Hugh Thomson (as was his brother Charles), Henry had a stronger line than his brother and had 'a flexible technique which is the direct result of infinite study from nature. If it is more workmanlike than artistic, it still has the power to charm in its unfailing dexterity' (Ellwood). He often used models and the many antiques and props collected by both brothers often turn up in their drawings. He was elected an RI in 1906. H. M. Brock died on 21 July 1960.

ILL: Many books including F. Marryat, *Japhet in Search of a Father* (1895); W. M. Thackeray, *Ballads and Songs* (1896); J. F. Cooper, *The Last of the Mohicans* (1900); C. Kingsley, *Westward Ho!* (1903); T. Hughes, *Tom Brown's Schooldays* (1911); *The Book of Fairy Tales* (1914); R. L. Stevenson, *Treasure Island* (1928); *The Book of Nursery Tales* (1934); D. M. Stuart, *The Young Clavengers* (1947) and titles by Scott, Defoe, Cervantes, Dickens and Goldsmith
EXHIB: B; L; RA; RI; RSAB; GI; RSA
COLL: V&A; THG; Reading University Library
LIT: C. M. Kelly, *The Brocks* (1975)

BROCKBANK, Russell Partridge (1913–79). Joke and strip cartoonist and art editor. Russell Brockbank was born on 15 April 1913 in Niagara Falls, Canada, the son of an Englishman,

Russell Brockbank, *The Brockbank Omnibus*, 1957

Clarence Brockbank FCIC AMIE, who owned an industrial ceramics factory. Educated at Ridley College, Ontario, he studied at Buffalo School of Art, New York, and, when he went to England in 1929, Chelsea School of Art under Harold Williamson. He worked at first in his father's factory (becoming manager at the age of 19), but then began contributing to *Speed* magazine (1935–9) and by the age of 24 had become a professional artist. He served as a lieutenant with the Royal Navy Volunteer Reserve during World War II (on northern convoys and in the Pacific). A specialist in motoring and aviation cartoons, he first drew for *Punch* in 1939 and was the magazine's Art Editor from 1949 to 1960. He also contributed to *Motor* (especially the famous 'Major Upsett' strip), *Commercial Motor, Light Car, Cadet Journal, Lilliput, Aeroplane, Road & Track, Automobile Jahr, Car Graphic* and other publications. Obsessed by cars ('I once got a D-type Jag up to 148 mph . . . near Godalming'), he most enjoyed drawing classic Alfa Romeos, Bugattis and Mercedes. His drawings were always completely accurate in detail and he discovered at an early age that 'you must make cars lean forward a bit and get their wheels off the ground if you want to give an impression of speed'. He used Cie Française fine nibs on Bristol board and sometimes used scraperboard. He was a member of the Savage Club and the BARC. Russell Brockbank died on 14 May 1979.

PUB: *Round the Bend* (1948), *Up the Straight* (1953), *Over the Line* (1955), [with R. Collier] *Bees Under My Bonnet* (1955), *The Brockbank Omnibus* (1957), *Manifold Pressures* (1958), *Move Over!* (1962), *The Penguin Brockbank* (1963), (ed.) *Motoring Through Punch* (1970), *Brockbank's Grand Prix* (1973), *The Best of Brockbank* (1975)
ILL: J. B. Boothroyd, *Motor if You Must* (1960); *The Dashboard Revolution* (1970)
EXHIB: SGA
COLL: UKCC

BROOK, Ricardo (fl. 1913–32). Political and joke cartoonist and poster designer. Ricardo Brook began work aged 16 as a junior in the chambers of a barrister MP in the Temple. His first humorous drawings were published in the comic papers at this time and he was then apprenticed to a firm of lithographers. A poster he designed for one of PHIL MAY's lecture-tours impressed the great cartoonist and later Brook worked for various art printers and advertising companies designing posters, etc. He also drew political cartoons for *Morning Leader* and the *Star* and the first joke cartoon he sent in to *Punch* was accepted for publication. He also contributed to *Humorist, Passing Show, London Opinion* and other magazines.

BROOKES, Harris – *see* Stampa, Giorgio Loraine

BROOKES, Peter (b. 1943). Political cartoonist, caricaturist and illustrator. Born in Liverpool on 28 September 1943, the son of RAF Squadron Leader G. H. Brookes, Peter Brookes trained as a pilot in the RAF (1962–5) while reading for a London University degree. He then attended Manchester College of Art (1965–6) and the Central School of Art, London (1966–9), and was a lecturer at the Central School (1976–8) and RCA (1979–90). His first published cartoon was a cover for *New Society* in 1968. He succeeded RANAN LURIE as Political Cartoonist and illustrator for *The Times* (1982) and was cover artist (with GARLAND) of the *Spectator* (1986–98). In addition he has contributed to *Time* magazine, *Radio Times* (including covers), *New Society, New Statesman* (covers), *L'Expansion, Marie Claire, Cosmopolitan, Listener* (covers), *The Week* (covers), *Sunday Times* and *Times Literary Supplement* (caricatures), produced illustrations for The Folio Society, Royal Mail stamps and Glyndebourne Opera, and designed book jackets for Macmillan, Penguin Books and others. In addition he has produced advertisements for JWT, Pentagram, The Partners and O & M. Elected to membership of the Alliance Graphique Internationale (1988) he has also won the Designers' & Art Directors' Silver Award (1985), the W. H. Smith Award for Illustration (1989) and The Macallan Best Political Cartoon Award (1997), and was voted CAT Political Cartoonist of the Year in 1996 and 1998. He uses a dip pen with Gillott 404, 303 or 1950 nibs and Pelikan black ink on T. H. Saunders paper but also likes to work with watercolour and gouache.

PUB: *Nature Notes* (1997); *Nature Notes 2* (1999)
ILL: J. Verne, *Around the World in Eighty Days* (1982); J. Pool, *Lid Off a Daffodil* (1982); A. G. MacDonell, *England, Their England* (1986); G. Chaucer, *Troilus and Criseyde* (1990); A. Trollope, *Sir Harry Hotspur* (1992), *The Bertrams* (1993)
EXHIB: CG; RCA; CBG
COLL: IWM; UKCC; A

BROOKES, Richard 'Brook' (b. 1948). Political/editorial, pocket and strip cartoonist, caricaturist and illustrator. Born in Bangor, Wales, on 16 June 1948, the son of an electrician, Rick Brookes studied art at Manchester School of Art (L. S. Lowry's old college) and worked at first as an assistant art editor for *Mirabelle* magazine and then as a graphic artist and designer for IPC magazines such as *Woman's Own*, *Woman's Realm* and *Ideal Home*. He was then an illustrator and staff cartoonist at the *Evening Standard* (1977–95), where he deputized for JAK. He took over from TOM JOHNSTON on the *Sun* (1996) and then on the death of CARL GILES became Editorial Cartoonist on the *Daily Express* (1996–7). In addition he has contributed to *Mail on Sunday*, *The American* and *Punch* and worked on the Allied Lyons advertising campaign for Saatchi & Saatchi. Greatly influenced by Giles, Low and JAK, Brookes also admires Oliphant, MATT and MAC. He uses a Swan fountain pen with a flexible nib, and used to hide a rook in his drawings 'because there is a rook hidden in "Brookes" '.

BROWN, David (b. 1957). Political and sports cartoonist, caricaturist and illustrator. Dave Brown was born in Barnehurst, Kent, on 4 December 1957 the son of Arthur Leslie Brown, a teacher. He studied fine art at Leeds University (1976–80). He worked at first as an art teacher at Strathcoma Social Education Centre, Wembley, and was a painter, freelance graphic designer, stage designer and motorcycle courier (1980–83) before winning the *Sunday Times* Political Cartoon Competition in 1989. His first cartoon was published in the *Sunday Times* on 11 June 1989, and he has been a full-time cartoonist ever since. Political Cartoonist on the *Independent* (1996–7 and since October 1998) he has also been a contributor to *Daily Express* (sports cartoons), *Guardian*, *New Statesman*, *Daily Mail* (sports cartoons), *Prospect* and *Financial Times*. He prefers to work with a dip pen and

THE UNRAVELLING OF THE EURO DREAM

Dave Brown, [Kohl, Chirac, Blair], *Sunday Times*, 1 June 1997 indian ink, sometimes also with watercolour, on Bristol board, though he also works on paper.

ILL: S. Reeve and C. McGhee, *The Millennium Bomb* (1996)

COLL: Bank of England Museum

BROWN, Francis (fl. 1900s–20s). Political cartoonist. Francis Brown worked for *Westminster Gazette* (fl. 1905–6) and *Daily Herald* (1920s). His books *The Doings of Arthur* (1905) and *Political Parables* (1906) collect together his weekly drawings for the *Westminster Gazette* and feature the exploits of Conservative Prime Minister Arthur Balfour during his three years in office (1902–5) as written (in a childish hand) by the imaginary 'office boy' of the newspaper. During World War I Brown drew caricatures of the Kaiser for the postcard publisher A. M. Davis (in the series 'Nothing to Laugh At').

PUB: *The Doings of Arthur* (1905), *Political Parables* (1906)

BROWN, Frank Hilton 'Eccles' (1926–86). Political, pocket and joke cartoonist. Frank Brown was born on 8 May 1926 in Forest Gate, London, the son of Sidney Brown, a toolmaker, and educated at the Beal Modern School, Ilford, Essex. He began cartooning during World War II while serving as a cartographer with the Royal Engineers in Ceylon, drawing for *SEAC Radio Times* (1945) and *Indian Listener*. After the war he qualified as an architect at the Regent Street Polytechnic (1947–53) and worked for the LCC Housing Department (from 1953), but continued to submit cartoons, jointly with his twin brother Sidney, to a number of papers (including the *Daily Mirror*), and trade union journals (such as *TGWU Record* and *ASTMS Journal*), under the name 'Hilton'. A former Secretary of the British Cartoonists' Association, he is best remembered for his work as 'Eccles' over more than three decades on the *Daily Worker/Morning Star* which he joined in 1952, at first drawing pocket cartoons and later taking over from GABRIEL as staff cartoonist in 1956. Frank Brown died in London on 18 September 1986.

BROWNE, Gordon Frederick RI RBA (1858–1932). Illustrator, painter, joke cartoonist and writer. Gordon Browne was born in Banstead, Surrey, on 15 April 1858, the son of the cartoonist and celebrated Dickens illustrator Hablot Knight Browne ('Phiz'), who also drew the second cover design for *Punch* (1842). He studied at Heatherley's and the South Kensington Schools and his first job was illustrating Ascott R. Hope's book *The Day After the Holidays* in 1875 when he was only 17. He then contributed to *Aunt Judy's Magazine* and began to work regularly for journals after being invited to finish a commission to illustrate Talbot Baines Reed's serial 'The Adventure of a Three-Guinea Watch' in *Boys' Own Paper* (1880) which his brother had been unable to complete. He later contributed joke cartoons and illustrations to many magazines and journals including *Punch* (from 1896), *Chums* (notably the original cover drawing), *Captain, Quiver, Black & White, Good Words, New Budget, Lika Joko, Holly Leaves, Illustrated London News, Girls' Own Paper, Strand, Cassell's Magazine, Boys' Own Paper, Cassell's Saturday Journal, Pall Mall Magazine, English Illustrated Magazine* and *Graphic*. In addition, after illustrating James Cook's *The Voyages* for Routledge (1882) he became a prolific book illustrator, notably producing 550 drawings for Henry Irving and Frank Marshall's eight-volume edition of the *Works of William Shakespeare* (1888–90). He also wrote and illustrated three books of nonsense rhymes for children under the pseudonym 'A Nobody' (1895–1900) and drew a series of postcards for John Walker & Co. on the newly introduced game of Ping Pong (this game was very fashionable for five years [1899–1904] and only returned into vogue in the 1920s, when it was renamed Table Tennis). An admirer of Edwin Abbey, George Soper and HARRY ROUNTREE, he was elected RBA (1894) and RI (1896). He used an 'F' nib and Stephens' Ebony Stain on Turnbull drawing boards. As well as working in pen and ink and watercolour (he especially liked drawing Roundheads and Cavaliers) he also exhibited oil paintings at the Royal Academy (from 1886). Thorpe admired his industry but called him a 'competent but uninspired draughtsman', adding that 'If he failed to achieve greatness it was because of a monotonous sameness in many of his illustrations, particularly in facial character.' G. F. Browne died at his home at 474 Upper Richmond Rd, Richmond, Surrey, on 27 May 1932.

PUB: [with L. Richards] *Gordon Browne's Old Fairy Tales* (1886–7), *A Apple Pie* (1890), *Nonsense for Somebody, Anybody and Everybody, Particularly the Baby-Body* (1895), *Some More Nonsense for the Same Bodies as Before* (1896), *A Nobody's Scrapbook* (1900)

ILL: Many books including J. Cook, *The Voyages* (1882); D. Defoe, *The Life and Surprising Adventures of Robinson Crusoe* (1885); H. Irving and F. Marshall (eds), *Works of William Shakespeare* (1888–90); [with LEWIS BAUMER] E. Nesbit, *The Story of the Treasure Seekers* (1899); H. C. Andersen, *Fairy Tales* (1901); W. M. Thackeray, *The Rose and the Ring* (1909); C. Reade, *The Cloister and the Hearth* (1912); E. A. Browne, *The Queen of Hearts* (1919); M. de Cervantes, *Don Quixote* (1920)
EXHIB: RA; RI; RBA; RWA; L; ROI; M; B; London Salon; GI
COLL: BM; V&A; THG

BROWNE, Thomas Arthur RI RBA RMS (1870–1910). Joke and strip cartoonist, illustrator, painter and commercial artist. Tom Browne was born in Nottingham on 8 December 1870, the son of Francis Browne. Educated at St Mary's National School, Nottingham, he left aged 11 to work as an errand boy in a milliner's shop and in the local lace market before becoming apprenticed to a lithographic printer (1884–91). His first drawing (an eight-panel strip 'He Knew How to Do It' for which he was paid 30s.) was published in *Scraps* on 27 April 1889. After finishing his apprenticeship he studied at an art school in Nottingham for three months and began to draw for *Chums* (1893–5) and others, his first magazine work appearing in *Lady's Realm*. In 1895 he moved to London where he created his most famous characters, the two tramps Weary Willy and Tired Tim, who first appeared (as Weary Waddles and Tired Timmy in the strip 'Innocents on the River') in the newly launched *Illustrated Chips* on 16 May 1896. Modelled on Don Quixote and Sancho Panza, they were the first true comic-strip heroes and ran for 63 years until *Chips* folded in 1953 (though Browne himself had ceased drawing them *c.* 1900). In 1897 he began to contribute to *Punch*, exhibited for the first time at the Royal Academy and the same year set up his own colour printing company, Tom Browne & Co. (printing his own poster designs and showcards) in Nottingham. In 1904 he visited the USA and drew 'Boston Types' for *Commercial Tribune*, later returning (with LANCE THACKERAY) as a special artist for the *Tatler* covering the St Louis Exhibition, and then later still to work as a cartoonist on the *Chicago Tribune* for four months (1906). He also worked for the *Weekly Telegraph* (e.g. the series 'In Other

People's Shoes' in which celebrities were drawn in odd clothing), *Black & White, Captain, Cassell's, Eureka, Graphic, London, Odd Volume, Cycling, Wheel, Cycle Magazine, Illustrated Sporting & Dramatic News, Pearson's, Pick-Me-Up, Printer's Pie, Moonshine, Royal, Sketch, Strand* and *To-Day*. In addition he designed many advertisements. e.g. for Johnnie Walker Whisky (creating in 1910 the first version of the famous striding beaver-hatted Regency Buck, later more familiar in the version by LEO CHENEY), Sunlight Soap, Fry's (e.g. 'See Their Eyes, As She Buys Fry's'), Beechams and Raleigh Bicycles (including posters). He also designed postcards for Davidson Brothers, Collins, Hartmann, Valentines and Tuck, and painted in oils and watercolour (particularly Dutch scenes). An admirer and friend of PHIL MAY and DUDLEY HARDY, both artists greatly influenced his style, as did JOHN HASSALL. Elected RBA (1898), RMS (1900) and RI (1901) he was a member of the Savage, Yorick and Langham Sketch Clubs, and was a founder member (with Hardy, May, ALDIN and Thackeray) of the London Sketch Club, becoming its President in 1907. His motto (based on Zola's) was 'No day without its sketch'. Tom Browne died of throat cancer at his home in Blackheath, London, on 16 March 1910 aged 39. As a member of the Army Service Corps Territorials or 'Rough Riders' he was buried with military honours at Shooter's Hill Cemetery, London.
PUB: *Tom Browne's Annuals* (1899–1905), *Cycle Sketch Book* (n.d.), *The Night Side of London* (n.d.)
ILL: H. Keble, *The 'Chicot' Papers* (1901), *Letters to Dolly* (1902); B. Pain, *The One Before* (1902); F. Richardson, *The Man who Lost his Past* (1903); L. Larkin, *Larks and Levities* (1903)
EXHIB: RA; RI; RBA; RMS; FAS; London Sketch Club (161 works displayed in 1914); Brighton (1996)
COLL: V&A; THG
LIT: A. E. Johnson, *Tom Browne RI* (1909); *The Postcards of Tom Browne* (1978)

BRUCE – *see* Angrave, Bruce

BUCHAN – *see* Boswell, James E.

BUCHANAN, Frederick [originally Friend] Charles 'FB' (1879–1941). Joke cartoonist, caricaturist and illustrator. Fred Buchanan was born in Woolwich, London, on 14 June 1879, the son of Friend Charles Buchanan. Educated at Roan

School, Greenwich, he was self-taught as an artist. During World War I he served in the Artists' Rifles. His work, which was influenced by that of JOHN HASSALL, appeared in *Punch* (from *c.* 1904), *Strand* (e.g. story illustrations *c.* 1900), *Cartoon, Passing Show, Bystander, Captain, London Illustrated Weekly, Humorist, Magpie, London Opinion, Pall Mall Gazette, Fun, Graphic, John Bull* and elsewhere in the 1920s and 30s. He also produced advertisements for Bovril and others and drew comic postcards for Woolstone Brothers and Raphael Tuck. In addition he wrote one of the courses for the London School of Cartooning (as did E. T. REED, ARTHUR FERRIER and others). He became President of the London Sketch Club in 1935, succeeding HARRY RILEY, and was also a member of the Strand Club and the Ilford Dramatic Society.
ILL: C. E. Hughes, *Sport in a Nutshell* (1921)

BUCHANAN, P. R. G. 'The Tout' (1870–1950). Sports cartoonist and caricaturist. The Tout worked as a sports cartoonist and caricaturist for the *News of the World* and *Tatler* in the 1930s and exhibited 128 drawings at Walker's Gallery, London, in 1931.
EXHIB: WG (1931)

BULBO – *see* Beerbohm, Sir Henry Maximilian

BULL, René (1872–1942). Joke and strip cartoonist, illustrator and war artist. René Bull was born in Dublin of an English father and a French mother on 11 December 1872. Educated at Clangowes School, he studied engineering in Paris (*c.* 1890) and aged 19 was offered a job on the building of the Suez Canal by Ferdinand de Lesseps. However, he turned it down and instead took drawing lessons from the Russian-born French cartoonist 'Caran D'Ache' (Emmanuel Poiré). Returning to Ireland, his first drawings were published in the Dublin journal *Freeman's Weekly*. He then contributed to *Illustrated Bits* before meeting the editor of the newly launched *Pick-Me-Up*, for which he drew wordless strip cartoons in the style of Poiré from 1893. In 1896 he was appointed 'special artist' for *Black & White* and travelled in Europe, reporting on the Armenian massacres, the Graeco-Turkish war, the recapture of Khartoum, the Battle of Omdurman and other major news items. He also drew cartoons for the magazine and for many others including *Bystander, Le Rire, Les Annales, Rions, Lika Joko, Ludgate, Cassell's,*

Chums, English Illustrated Magazine, Lady's Realm, London, London Opinion, New Budget, Pall Mall Budget, Pearson's, Printer's Pie, Royal, Strand, Tatler and *Sketch* (notably humorous 'inventions' which predate those of HEATH ROBINSON). In addition he drew advertisements for Erasmic Soap, Connolly Leather and others, illustrated Gift Books and designed comic postcards for Davidson (e.g. 'Illustrated Limericks'), Faulkner, Landeker & Brown and Charles Voisey. During World War I he served in the RNVR (1916), achieving the rank of lieutenant, and in the RAF (1917), becoming a major. He later worked in the Air Ministry. In addition to his art work, Bull was very skilled at making model locomotives. He was Honorary Secretary of the London Sketch Club. René Bull died on 13 April 1942.
ILL: *Black & White War Albums* (1899); J. de la Fontaine, *La Fontaine's Fables* (1905); J. C. Harris, *Uncle Remus* (1906); *The Arabian Nights* (1912); *The Rubaiyat of Omar Khayyam* (1913); A. E. Johnson, *The Russian Ballet* (1913); P. Mérimée, *Carmen* (1916); R. Fyleman, *A Garden of Roses* (1928) and others
EXHIB: BRU
COLL: V&A

BUNBURY – *see* Lancaster, Sir Osbert

BURGIN, Eric (1926–66). Joke and strip cartoonist. Eric Burgin was born in Maidenhead on 3 February 1926 and educated at Gordon Road School in the town, leaving at 14 to become an engineering apprentice in a local machine shop. He joined the RAF as an air-gunner in 1943, serving in Singapore and the Far East and later returning to Maidenhead to work in an aircraft components factory. He became a full-time freelance cartoonist in 1954 and produced 'Anagrins' (illustrated anagrams) for the *Evening News* and 'The Niteleys' strip (about a family of TV fanatics) for the *Daily Sketch* as well as numerous contributions to *Punch* (including covers), *Daily Mirror* and other publications. One of the founder members (and a committee member) of the Cartoonists' Club of Great Britain, he was voted CCGB Humorous Cartoonist of the Year three times (1962, 1963 and 1964). An influential cartoonist, FOUGASSE said that his ideas had 'a touch of Thurber and [his] drawings would have also, if they hadn't learnt about perspective' and in his *Evening News* obituary JOE LEE called him 'the most brilliant of our younger men'. Price saw him as 'a fertile inventor of the fantastic' in the tradition of PAUL CRUM: 'With the blazing imaginations of MAHOOD and Burgin this particular tradition has developed as far as it can . . . [and] Burgin scored in that the shapes in his drawings were themselves often funny, like some of the Miró shapes.' Eric Burgin died of a heart attack, aged 40, on 5 March 1966.

BURKE, Christopher (b. 1955). Illustrator and caricaturist. Chris Burke was born in London on 4 October 1955, went to St Martin's School of Art (1974–5) and studied graphic design at Canterbury College of Art (1975–8). He worked for five years as an art director in small advertising agencies before becoming a freelance illustrator and caricaturist. His first cartoon was published in *Radio Times* in March 1984 and his first caricature for the same magazine a week later. He has also contributed to *Sunday Times*, *Guardian*, *Sunday Telegraph*, *Evening Standard*, *Punch* (including covers), *Observer* and the *Listener*. He has also produced advertising work for the Irish Tourist Board, Air India and posters for Welsh National Opera, COI and London Underground. In addition he has designed stamps, written and illustrated children's books and designed promotional material for Wine Cellar and Ottakars Bookshops. He uses a dip pen, watercolours, concentrated watercolour inks, and wax pencil on smooth watercolour paper or thick cartridge. For his illustration work for the Save the Childen Fund he was awarded a Creative Circle Gold Medal (1989). He cites Daumier as his greatest influence.
PUB: *Rain and Shine* (1987), *Not Your Average GI Joe* (1989), *Who's Afraid Now?* (1991), *Scaredy Cat* (1993)
ILL: L. Henry, *Charlie and the Big Chill* (1995), *Charlie, Queen of the Desert* (1996)
EXHIB: Roughs Gallery; McGrath Gallery, Richmond; TG; Trinity Arts, Tunbridge Wells
COLL: V&A; LTM

BURNETT, Hugh 'Phelix' (b. 1924). TV producer and broadcaster, cartoonist, writer and illustrator. Born in Sheffield on 21 July 1924, the son of a former Editor of the *Methodist Recorder*, Hugh Burnett was educated at Latymer School, Hornsey School of Art and the London School of Economics. During World War II he served in the Intelligence Corps and was posted to the Burma frontier (airport security), where

his cartoons in *Soldier* magazine and other Forces periodicals led to a transfer to Radio SEAC in Ceylon and promotion to the rank of captain. After the war he worked in the War Office, joining the BBC Overseas Broadcasting Service in 1950. In addition he worked as a freelance cartoonist under the name of 'Phelix', contributing to *Daily Mail*, *Daily Herald*, *Sunday Dispatch*, *Daily Express*, *John O' London's Weekly*, *Tit-Bits*, *Modern Woman*, *News on Sunday*, *Evening News*, *Sunday Pictorial*, *Christmas Pie*, *Evening Standard*, *Gibraltar Chronicle*, *Everybody's*, *London Opinion*, *Men Only*, *Time*, *Life*, *New Statesman*, *Punch*, *Private Eye*, *She* and *Oldie*. He has also worked as a producer and presenter of TV documentaries (22 for the BBC to date), was the creator of the series *Face to Face* and his drawings have appeared in four Video Arts films. He is particularly well known for his cartoons featuring monks, which were VICKY's favourite cartoon characters and one of which Augustus John hung on his bedroom wall. Hugh Burnett prefers to draw with a felt-tip pen and on any paper that is to hand. As his main founts of inspiration he cites a meeting with Picasso in Antibes, the work of PONT, Peter Arno and Steinberg and 'the delightful insanity which surrounds us all'.
PUB: *Top Sacred* (1960), *Sacred and Confidential* (1961), *Nothing Sacred* (1962), *Adam and Eve* (1963), [with F. Topolski] *Face to Face* (1964), *Beware of the Abbot* (1965), *Book of the Monk* (1966)
ILL: B. Campbell-Kemp, *Come Live With Me* (1974); F. Pagden, *The Acts of St Lynas* (1996)

BUTTERWORTH, George Goodwin (1905–88). Political, strip and sports cartoonist, and illustrator. George Butterworth was born in Woodsmoor, Stockport, Cheshire, on 5 January 1905 and after studying at Stockport Art School won a scholarship to Manchester College of Art where he was a contemporary of PEARL BINDER. At the age of 17 he was employed as a caricaturist and sports cartoonist on the *County Express* (Stockport) and five years later joined Kemsley Newspapers as a staff artist, working (from 1932) as 'Gee Bee' on the *Daily Dispatch* (sports cartoons) and was (from 1939) Political Cartoonist on various papers within the group (*Evening Chronicle*, *Empire News* and *Sunday Chronicle*) but mainly the *Daily Dispatch* (1939–52). He briefly joined the RAF in 1939 but returned to political cartooning as a service to his country, and it was his cartoon 'Maltese Cross' in the *Daily Dispatch* which led to the island receiving that award in reality in April 1942. In 1952 he introduced a regular strip, 'The Daily Dees' (featuring the Dee family), in the *Daily Dispatch*, and continued to work for the *News Chronicle*, when it absorbed the *Dispatch* in 1958, and the *Daily Mail*, when it in turn absorbed the *Chronicle*, until he retired in 1968. In addition, his drawings appeared in the *New York Times*, *Chicago Tribune*, *New Zealand Truth*, *Malta Times* and the 1943 *Encyclopaedia Britannica Year-*

book, and he illustrated Manchester United Football Club programmes for 20 years (1933–52). Butterworth worked in pen and ink and also used brushes, charcoal and scraperboard. In 1979 he turned to landscape painting in oils. He died in Haslemere, Surrey, on 17 October 1988.
PUB: *Hitler and His Crazy Gang* (1941)
EXHIB: City Hall, Manchester; [oil paintings] Guildhall, Winchester
COLL: UKCC

C

CALDWELL, William (b. 1946). Political/editorial and pocket cartoonist and commercial artist. Bill Caldwell was born in Glasgow on 30 September 1946, the son of William McComish, an opera singer and musical director. At the age of 12 he changed his name to Caldwell (his mother's name). Educated at Vale of Leven Academy, Alexandria, Dumbartonshire, he began work at Hambro's merchant bank (1967) but left after a year to study graphics at Stockport College of Technology. He worked at first in advertising but shortly after selling his first joke cartoon to the *Daily Sketch* in 1971 turned full-time freelance cartoonist. For seven years he successfully syndicated nine weekly strips to 90 provincial and overseas papers via P.A. Features and Advance Features. A topical pocket cartoon brought him to the attention of Express Newspapers who hired him as pocket cartoonist for their new title, the *Daily Star*, when it was launched on 2 November 1978. After a year he moved from a single column to five columns as the paper's first-ever staff Editorial/Political Cartoonist and continued in this position until December 1998. He was also Editorial Cartoonist on the short-lived *Sunday Scot* and has been Editorial Cartoonist of the Scottish *Sunday Mail* since 1990. He has also worked in advertising for BUPA, Parcelforce and others and has occasionally drawn as 'Bill McComish'. Bill Caldwell draws in the realistic manner of GILES, MAC and JAK and worked at first in pen and indian ink on watercolour paper. However, since 1992 he has mostly used a Pilot Lettering pen on A4 photocopy paper

and sometimes also draws on an Apple Mac computer with Photoshop software.
PUB: *Self-Servicing Your Car* (1975), [with A. Prosser and U. Geller] *1001 Amazing Facts and Mysteries* (1982), *The Daily Star Caldwell Cartoon Book* (1985), *The Star Caldwell Cartoon Book Two* (1987); *Bill Caldwell Cartoons* (1990), *Bill Caldwell Cartoons* (1991), *Bill Caldwell Cartoons* (1993)
COLL: Museum of Berlin

CALMAN, Mel FRSA FSIA AGI (1931–94). Pocket cartoonist, illustrator and writer. Mel Calman was born in Hackney, London, on 19 May 1931, the son of a timber merchant from Odessa. He was educated at the Perse School, Cambridge, and studied illustration at Borough Polytechnic (1949–51), St Martin's School of Art (1951–3) and Goldsmith's College (1954–5). He was cartoonist on the *Daily Express* (1957–63), *Sunday Telegraph* (1964–5), *Observer* (1965–6), *Sunday Times* (1969–84) and *The Times* (1979–94). He also contributed to numerous magazines, including *Cosmopolitan* and *House & Garden*, and founded The Cartoon Gallery (formerly The Workshop), a gallery devoted to cartoon art, in 1970. In addition he made an animated cartoon, *The Arrow*, for the BFI and contributed illustrations to many books and periodicals. Cofounder (with Simon Heneage) of the Cartoon Art Trust, he was its Chairman from 1993 to 1994. He also worked in advertising for Shell, Guinness and others, was resident cartoonist on BBC TV's *Tonight* programme (1963–4), and wrote four plays for BBC Radio. His cartoons, which regularly featured a naïf-style 'little man'

Mel Calman, *It's Only You That's Incompatible!*, 1984

character, were usually drawn in pencil, using 4B or 5B for the main illustration and 4B for lettering. He often drew at twice reproduction size on Croxley Script paper. Influenced by Thurber, he said his 'little man' was '*not* autobiographical. At least not totally.' STEADMAN has called him 'A champion of the considered understatement and an artist who has written the human condition in a nutshell.' He was always encouraging to new artists (it was through his advice that POSY SIMMONDS had her first cartoons published) and the British Cartoonists' Association (sponsored by *The Times*) founded the annual Mel Calman Awards for young cartoonists in his honour in 1995. He died in the Odeon Cinema, Leicester Square, London, on 10 February 1994.

PUB: *Through the Telephone Directory* (1962), *Bed-Sit* (1963), *Boxes* (1964), *Calman & Women* (1967), *The Penguin Calman* (1968), *My God* (1970), *Couples* (1972), *This Pestered Isle* (1973), *The New Penguin Calman* (1977), *But It's My Turn to Leave You* (1980), *How About a Little Quarrel Before Bed?* (1981), *Help!* (1982), *It's Only You That's Incompatible!* (1984), *Modern Times* (1988), *Merrie England plc* (1990), *Calman at the Movies* (1990), *Calman at the Royal Opera House* (1990), *Calman's Savoy Sketchbook* (1994), *A Little Light Worrying* (1996)

ILL: J. de Manio, *To Auntie With Love* (1967); K. Whitehorn, *Whitehorn's Social Survival* (1968); B. Parsons, *The Expectant Father* (1975); B. James, *1001 Money Saving Tips* (1976); B. Redhead and K. McLeish (eds), *Pieces of Hate* (1982)
LIT: [autobiography] *What Else Do You Do?* (1986)
EXHIB: CG
COLL: BM; V&A; CAT

CANE, Arthur Reginald (1885–1951). Joke cartoonist and commercial artist. The great grandson of the painter and engraver Robert Pollard and great-great-grandson of James Pollard, painter of hunting and coaching scenes, Arthur Cane was born on 24 December 1885 in Battle, Sussex, the son of Thomas Cane, a schoolmaster. He left school at 16 and became Assistant Master at a Poor Law institution in the Midlands. In 1905 he enlisted in a Lancer Regiment, travelling with the army to South Africa (1907). During World War I he served with the cavalry, infantry and mounted police, was wounded three times and had his left leg amputated a fortnight before the Armistice. He later studied at Chelsea School of Art and worked in a number of advertising agencies while contributing freelance cartoons to *Punch* (from 1927), *London Opinion*, *Razzle*, *Men Only*, *Tatler*, *Sketch*, *Illustrated*, *Passing Show* and others. He greatly admired and was influenced by GILBERT WILKINSON and worked in pen and ink plus watercolour. Arthur Cane died in the Connaught Hospital, London, on 19 July 1951.

'Captain Pugwash' – *see* Ryan, John Gerald Christopher

CAR – *see* Churchill, Robert Frederick Goodwin

CASALI, Kim [née Marilyn Judith Grove] (1941–97). Joke cartoonist. Kim Casali was born in Auckland, New Zealand, on 9 September 1941 and at the age of 19 travelled to Europe and the USA. A self-taught artist, her illustrated messages to Italian computer engineer Roberto Casali (whom she met at a ski club in Los Angeles in 1967) were the original vehicle for the 'Love is . . .' cartoons for which she was best known. The first drawing, which served as a thumbnail signature to a domestic note, featured Kim herself with freckles and long hair (a male figure, representing Roberto, came later). After she had produced a booklet of 100 of these drawings while working for a design company, a friend suggested she showed them to a contact on the *Los Angeles Times*, in which they were first published on 9 January 1970. From there the cartoons were quickly syndicated worldwide, appearing in the UK originally in the *Daily Sketch* in April the same year and continuing in the *Daily Mail* when it took over the *Sketch*. The Casalis were married in 1971 and moved to England in 1972. Kim Casali (who signed herself 'Kim') had her work reproduced on T-shirts, watches, jewellery, underwear, etc., worldwide. Kim Casali died in Weybridge, Surrey, on 15 June 1997. Her eldest son Stefano took over the drawing of the 'Love is . . .' series on her death. PUB: More than 25 'Love is . . .' collections (since 1972)

'Celeb' – *see* Peattie, Charles William Davidson

CG – *see* Gould, Sir Francis Carruthers

CHAD – *see* Chatterton, George Edward

CHASEMORE, Archibald (fl. 1867–1902) – *see* Bryant & Heneage

CHAT – *see* Chatterton, George Edward

CHATTERTON, George Edward 'CHAT' FRSA FIAL (b. 1911). Joke and strip cartoonist, photographer, writer and artist. George Chatterton was born in Kidderminster, Hereford, on 15 July 1911 and studied at Kidderminster School of Art and Farnborough School of Photography. He served with the RAF as artist-photographer (1938–50) but began drawing for magazines and newspapers in 1932, contributing to *Blighty*, *Weekend*, *Weekly News*, *RAF Review*, *Boy's Own Paper*, *Daily Mirror*, *Daily Sketch*, *Everybody's*, *Leader*, *London Opinion*, *Picturegoer*, *Weekend Mail* and others. Though he also produced the strips 'Sherriff Shucks' and 'Leo CV', he is best known for creating the character 'Chad' (sometimes mistakenly ascribed to JACK GREENALL) in the strip cartoon 'Chad by Chat' in 1938. Chad was immensely popular during World War II and was featured looking over a wall in a series 'Wot! No . . .?'. He has also written and illustrated (in black and white) a collection of adventure stories of the French Foreign Legion, *Tattered Tricolor*. Chatterton is a member of the Artists' League of Great Britain.
PUB: [stories] *Tattered Tricolor* (1937)

CHEERO – *see* Studdy, George Ernest

CHEN, Jack [real name Ch'en I-fan] (b. 1908). Political cartoonist, caricaturist, illustrator and writer. Born in China, Jack Chen was self-taught as a cartoonist. He began to draw cartoons for the Chinese press in 1926 and then moved to Moscow where he studied under Pavel Novitsky at the Polygraphic Faculty of VKhUTEMAS (Higher Art and Technical Workshops) for three years (1927–30), where he was a near-contemporary of the three cartoonists who became the famous 'Kukryniksi' group. While a student he became Moscow Charleston Champion and his work placements included the Soviet Mint, *Pravda* (his student photo of Lenin's widow, Krupskaya, was used on the front page and later made into a montage poster by the cartoonist Deni) and the Ogonyok Publishing House which shortly thereafter launched a new paper, *Moscow News*, staffed by English and American journalists. Chen joined the paper after graduating and later became its chief cartoonist and Art Editor while also drawing book and magazine illustrations and posters. He eventually left the paper and became a freelance artist and critic. Chen came to Britain in the 1930s and worked for *Tribune*, *Our Time* and *Daily Worker* and during World War II drew the last cartoon published by the latter paper before it was closed down for 19 months by the government. This cartoon, 'Their Gallant Allies', was drawn in a style reminiscent of DAVID Low and published on 20 January 1941. It shows Churchill and a colleague inspecting a line-up that consists of figures labelled: 'Dictator Salazar', 'Dictator Metaxas', 'Fascist Staremberg', 'Dictator [Indian] Princes' amongst others, with Polish Prime Minister Sikorski holding a flag that reads 'War on USSR, Peace with Italy'. Chen has also produced fine charcoal portraits and illustrations for *Seven* magazine and has written on art for *The Studio* and *Art & Industry*. He was influenced at first by the American cartoonist Fred Ellis, whom he met when they were both working for *Pravda* during Chen's student days.
PUB: *Japan and the Pacific Theatre of War* (1942), *Soviet Art and Artists* (1944), *The Chinese Theatre* (1949), *Russian Painting of the 18th and 19th Centuries* (1948), *New Earth* (1957), *A Year in Upper Felicity* (1973), *Inside the Cultural Revolution* (1976), *The Sinkiang Story* (1977)

CHENEY, Leopold Alfred (1878–1928). Sports, joke and political cartoonist, caricaturist and illustrator. Leo Cheney was a bank clerk in Accrington, Lancashire, who became the first-ever pupil of PERCY BRADSHAW's cartoon correspondence course. Bradshaw subsequently helped him sell drawings to *Boys' Own Paper*, *Bystander* and other publications (he later joined Bradshaw's Press Art School as a staff member). He sold his first sporting illustrations to the *Manchester Evening News* in 1907 and subsequently became staff sports cartoonist and caricaturist on the paper and then for *Passing Show* in London. In addition he deputized as Political Cartoonist during POY's absence from the *Daily Mail* in 1920–21. He is perhaps best remembered as the creator of the most famous version of the 'Johnnie Walker' character for John Walker & Sons' Whisky (earlier versions had been drawn by TOM BROWNE, BERNARD PARTRIDGE, RAVEN HILL and H. M. BROCK). He also drew advertisements for Chairman Tobacco, Comfort Soap and others. Bradshaw thought he was sometimes too generous with his blacks but commended his 'painter-like breadth and variety of touch . . . the vigour and vivacity of his pen strokes . . . the dexterous use he makes of white spaces, the variety of his pliable, alert line'. He was a member of the Manchester Sketch Club and the Savage Club. Leo Cheney died on 29 September 1928.
ILL: J. B. Nichols, *The Valet as Historian* (*c.* 1934)

MR RAMSAY MACDONALD AND THE RAGAMUFFIN

Leo Cheney, [Ramsay MacDonald], n.d.

CHESTERTON, Gilbert Keith (1874–1936). Author, journalist, caricaturist and illustrator. G. K. Chesterton was born in Kensington, London, on 29 May 1874, the son of Edward Chesterton, head of Chesterton's Estate Agency, and himself an amateur artist. His mother, Marie-Louise Grosjean, was French. He was educated at St Paul's School (1887–92) with E. C. Bentley (father of NICOLAS BENTLEY) and then studied at the Slade School of Art before working in book publishing and journalism. In 1918, after the death of his younger brother, Cecil Chesterton, journalist and editor of *New Witness*, he took over the publication and later began his own newspaper, *GK's Weekly* (1925–38), which he also illustrated. Perhaps best known for his 'Father Brown' stories (from 1911) and such novels as *The Napoleon of Notting Hill* (1904), he also illustrated three of his own books as well as many by Hilaire Belloc (George Bernard Shaw dubbed the two friends 'Chesterbelloc'). He rarely signed his caricatures and usually worked in pen and ink but also drew with coloured chalks on brown paper. G. K. Chesterton died at his home in Beaconsfield on 14 June 1936.
PUB: [with illustrations by the author] *Greybeards at Play* (1900), *The Club of Queer Trades* (1905), *The Coloured Lands* (1938)
ILL: E. C. Bentley, *Biography for Beginners* (1905), *More Biography* (1929); H. Belloc, *The Green Overcoat* (1912), *Mr Petrie* (1925), *The Emerald* (1926), *The Haunted House* (1927), *But Soft – We Are Observed* (1928), *The Missing Masterpiece* (1929), *The Man Who Made Gold* (1930), *The Postmaster-General* (1932), *The Hedge and the Horse* (1936)
EXHIB: NBL, 'G. K. Chesterton. A Centenary Exhibition' (May 1974)
COLL: BL
LIT: A. S. Dale, *The Art of G. K. Chesterton* (1985)

CHESTERTON, Raymond Wilson 'Ray' (b. 1912). Joke cartoonist, illustrator, writer and designer. Ray Chesterton was born in Ashford, Kent, on 22 February 1912, the son of the Rev. Ridley Chesterton, a Baptist minister. He

worked at first as a journalist for the *Worthing Gazette* and, a self-taught artist, had his first cartoons published in *London Opinion* in 1941 while he was serving in a Coast Defence Battery. He later contributed to *Lilliput, Tatler, Punch, Men Only, Daily Sketch, Light Car, Answers, Soldier* and other journals and regularly illustrated BERNARD HOLLOWOOD's 'Family Money-Go-Round' column in the *Daily Telegraph* and his wife Joyce Chesterton's 'Family Affair' column in the *Daily Mirror*. In addition he has designed annual reports and educational material. He is an admirer of LANCASTER, Peter Arno and ANTON. BRADSHAW has said of him: 'Ray has a technique of child-like simplicity which gives an air of artlessness to very sophisticated and grown-up jokes.' He draws with a dip pen and indian ink, usually on A5 paper.
ILL: R. G. G. Anderson, *Heard in the Slips* (1967), *Heard in the Line-Out* (1969), *Heard in the Scrum* (1964), *Heard at the Helm* (1968)
COLL: UKCC

CHIC – *see* Jacob, Cyril Alfred

CHRISTOPHER – *see* Wren, Ernest Alfred

CHRYS – *see* Chrystal, George Fraser

CHRYSTAL, George Fraser 'Chrys' (1921–72). Political, pocket and sports cartoonist. George Chrystal was born in Aberdeen. After war service in the RAF as a pilot-instructor, he attended Gray's School of Art, Aberdeen. He later worked for Aberdeen Journals Ltd, and produced sporting cartoons for the *Scottish Daily Mail* before joining the *Daily Mail* and *News of the World* (1960) as Political Cartoonist. He also contributed to *Punch, Power News* and other magazines and drew regularly for *Farmer & Stockbreeder* and its successor *British Farmer & Stockbreeder* from the 1950s to his sudden death on 1 December 1972 in Guildford, Surrey. His work bore considerable similarity to that of GILES.
PUB: *The Best of Chrys* (c. 1973)

CHURCHILL, Robert Frederick Goodwin (b. 1910). Joke cartoonist, illustrator and painter. Robert Churchill was born in Liverpool on 28 October 1910, the son of a pioneer motor-car designer and manufacturer. He attended the Liverpool Institute (former pupils had included Arthur Askey and Tommy Handley) and started work as a trainee in the Dunlop Rubber Company while studying in the evenings at Liverpool School of Art. He later moved to the company's headquarters in London where he continued his studies at Hornsey Art School and the London School of Process Engraving. His first drawings were published in technical magazines, *Practical Mechanics* and *Practical Motorist*, before he met art agent Percy Lisby, after which he worked for *London Opinion, Men Only, Humorist, Punch* and others. In 1939 he joined the Auxiliary Fire Service and was a fire officer in World War II, attaining the rank of captain. He also produced a daily current affairs cartoon for the *Evening Standard* (1943–6) and – under the pseudonym 'Car' – a weekly strip, 'Saturday News Reel' (1945–6). In 1946 he moved to *Sunday Pictorial* where he continued the weekly strip (this time under his own name, with the title 'Sunday Newsreel') and a feature cartoon under the pseudonym 'Goodwin'. Emigrating to Montreal, Canada, in 1948, he contributed to *Saturday Evening Post, New Yorker* and other publications before returning to the UK in 1955. By then his work as an international marketing and advertising executive had taken over and he ceased to draw cartoons. He retired in 1973 and now paints professionally, exhibits regularly, and is an active member of the council of the London Sketch Club.
PUB: *The Cartoonist's Bible* (1980)

CLEAVER, Thomas Reginald (fl. 1887–d.1954). Pictorial journalist, illustrator, joke cartoonist and writer. Reginald Cleaver first started contributing illustrations to the *Graphic c.* 1887. In 1890 he joined the newly launched *Daily Graphic* (the first illustrated daily newspaper), and with A. C. CORBOULD quickly established a new school of pictorial news reporting. He also contributed to *Pearson's, Strand, Punch* (1891–1937) and others. A specialist in parliamentary scenes for his illustration work on the *Daily Graphic*, his cartoons were mostly of a social nature. He worked in pen, pencil and wash, and developed a style of shading using parallel lines in place of cross-hatching which was very influential. THORPE called him 'an accurate draughtsman with great mastery of the pen, a clean, sure, open line, a great gift of portraiture and a sense of humour'. His brother Ralph Cleaver also drew for *Punch, Illustrated London News, Illustrated Sporting & Dramatic News, St James's Budget, Gentlewoman, Penny Illustrated, Strand,*

Graphic and *Daily Graphic*. He is not to be confused with the children's-story writer Hylton Reginald Cleaver (1891–1961). Reginald Cleaver died on 5 December 1954.
PUB: *A Winter Sport Book* (1911), *Included in the Trip* (1921), *Alpine Sport: A Sketch Book* (1922)
ILL: *Parliamentary Pictures & Personalities*, *'Graphic' Illustrations of Parliament, 1890–1893* (1893); R. Kipling, *Humorous Tales from Rudyard Kipling* (1931)
COLL: V&A; NPG

'The Cloggies' – *see* Tidy, William Edward

CLUFF – *see* Longstaff, John

COIA, Emilio (1911–97). Caricaturist and art critic. Emilio Coia was born in Glasgow on 13 April 1911, the son of Giovanni Coia, an Italian émigré who owned ice-cream shops and cafés in the city. Educated at St Mungo's Academy, Glasgow, he began studying at the Glasgow School of Art under MAURICE GREIFFENHAGEN at the age of 16. While a student he drew for *GUM* (Glasgow University Magazine) and was the first artist to cover the General Assembly of the Church of Scotland (for the *Scots Observer*). After five years at art school he moved to London and sold his first caricatures to the *Sunday Chronicle*, while also contributing to *Everybody's*, *Bookman*, *Daily Express*, *Tatler*, *Sketch*, *Passing Show*, *Sunday Referee*, *Week-end Review*, *News Chronicle* and others. A long association with the *Sunday Chronicle* came to a sudden end when the paper's most influential columnist, Beverley Nichols, objected strongly to Coia's drawing of his friend the novelist Ethel Mannin and demanded that it be removed from the artist's first one-man show at the Reid & Lefebre Gallery, London (1932). When Coia refused he was sacked by the *Chronicle*'s Editor James Drawbell. He then worked as assistant advertising manager and later personnel manager at a heavy engineering firm which during the war years produced anti-aircraft shells and winches for the Admiralty. After the war he returned to advertising, working for the Dolcis Shoe Company and later for Saxone in Kilmarnock, before turning full-time freelance once more. He worked at first mostly for the *Glasgow Evening Times* and was Art Adviser to the newly formed Scottish Television (for which he also produced live TV sketches). When Roy Thomson bought the *Scotsman* in the 1950s Coia was taken on by Editor Sir Alastair Dunnett as the paper's first caricaturist (including, from 1956, daily drawings during the annual Edinburgh Festival) and, later, art critic. He also drew for and contributed art criticism to *Scottish Field* and lectured on art and caricature for the Scottish Arts Council and others. Yehudi Menuhin described him as 'every musician's favourite caricaturist' and added that 'a good caricaturist needs more than a brilliant sense of humour, tragedy and concern. Emilio Coia has all these qualities in addition to his wonderful draughtsmanship.' Elected President of the Glasgow Arts Club three times, he was a Fellow of the Royal Society of Edinburgh. He was also awarded an Honorary Doctorate in Arts from the University of Strathclyde (1986) and received an Honorary Fringe First from the Edinburgh International Festival (1995). Many celebrities sat for their caricatures, including Augustus John, G. B. Shaw, Dame Edith Sitwell, W. H. Auden, Yehudi Menuhin, Shostakovich, Rostropovich, DAVID LOW, Sir Thomas Beecham and Dame Rebecca West. An admirer of MAX BEERBOHM, he drew in ink and pencil. His early angular style of drawing earned him the title of 'the first Cubist caricaturist'. His wife Marie (a fellow Glasgow School of Art student) was also a respected artist and one-time President of the Scottish Society of Women Artists. Emilio Coia died on 17 June 1997.
EXHIB: Reid and Lefebre Gallery (1932); Edinburgh International Festival (Retrospective, 1991)

COLE, Richard Anthony (b. 1942). Editorial cartoonist, caricaturist, illustrator, painter and sculptor. Richard Cole was born on 19 August 1942 in Wimbledon, London, the son of Archibald George Cole, an ecclesiastical wood-carver. He began illustrating covers for *Audio Record Review* (later *Hi-Fi News*) in 1957 when still at school and later attended Wimbledon School of Art (1960–63) and Brighton College of Art (1964). Between 1965 and 1970 he taught art at France Hill Comprehensive School, Camberley, Surrey, and Woking Grammar School and his first political caricatures appeared in *Kingston Borough News* in 1970. Full-time freelance work followed with profiles and political cartoons for *The Times* (1973–87), daily TV caricatures for the *Daily Express* (1978–80), caricatures and illustrations for the book pages

Richard Cole, [Thatcher, Clark *et al.*], *Guardian*, 27 January 1997

of the *Daily Telegraph* (from 1988) and editorial and political cartoons, caricatures and general illustrations for the *Sunday Times* (1973–95). Since 1995 he has also drawn for the *Sunday Telegraph* and the *Guardian*. Other work has included illustrations for BBC TV's *Tonight* and *Panorama* programmes and Channel 4 News. In addition he has been CBS News Contract Artist since 1983, covering parliamentary debates, criminal trials, etc. At first influenced by the German Expressionists and DAVID LOW, in the 1980s he began a series of woodcuts, the discipline of this technique having a dramatic effect on his work. He abandoned the use of steel nib and cross-hatching and developed a much simpler linear style with a sable brush and indian ink on 'Bread and Butter' paper. Cole also works in black conté crayon and watercolour.

ILL: D. Atkins, *George Brown's Rules for Vintage Golfers* (1997); D. Bogarde, *For the Time Being* (1998)

EXHIB: Heffers Gallery, Cambridge; Edwin Pollard Gallery; Anna Mei Chadwick Gallery; Château de Longpra, France

COLL: BM; Bank of England Museum; SAM

COLLINS, Clive Hugh Austin (b. 1942). Editorial cartoonist, caricaturist, illustrator and comic artist. Born in Weston-Super-Mare, Somerset,

on 6 February 1942, Clive Collins studied graphic design at Kingston School of Art (1958) and worked in marine insurance and as a film extra, before helping to run a film studio. He then repped for a small artwork studio before becoming Editorial and Political Cartoonist – together with PAUL RIGBY – on the *Sun* (1969). He left in 1970 to become the first-ever Political Cartoonist on the *People*, returning to the *Sun* in 1971 on the death of GORDON HOGG to become 'Lucky Jim', a cartoon racing-tipster (1971–85). During the same period he also became stand-in cartoonist for FRANKLIN on the *Sun* and JAK on the *Evening Standard* (adopting the pseudonym 'Ollie' for the latter work during the Falkands War). He was Deputy Editorial Cartoonist (under GRIFFIN) on the *Daily Mirror* from 1985 until Griffin's departure to the *Express* in 1996 and was sports illustrator for the paper's Mike Langley column (1991–6). In addition he has illustrated the *Reader's Digest* 'Buy-Lines' advertising feature since 1985, and has freelanced for *Punch* (1964–92, and since its relaunch in 1996), Shell UK house magazine, *Daily Mirror*, *Oui*, *Mad*, *Odds On*, *Sporting Life*, *Squib* and *Playboy* (USA). Other work has included occasional copywriting, scriptwriting, audio-visual work, greetings card designs, live and studio caricature work, and animation

Clive Collins, *c.* 1990

storyboards, etc. Chairman of the Cartoonists' Club of Great Britain (1990–94), and Editor of the Club's newsletter (1987–94), he has won numerous awards including first prize at international cartoon competitions in the UK (Glen Grant Cartoonist of the Year, 1979); Knokke Heist, Belgium (1982); Montreal (1985); Skopje, Macedonia (1986); Amstelveen, Netherlands (1987) and nine medals for the annual Japanese *Yomiuri Shimbun* competition since 1980. He was voted CCGB Cartoonist of the Year in 1984, 1985 and 1987, and has been on the judging panels of many international competitions including being elected President of the International Salon Jury in Montreal in 1985. Influenced by GILES, STARKE, George Price, Charles Addams, R. B. Wilson and George Booth, he is a particular admirer of CHARLES GRAVE. Clive Collins draws roughs in pencil, then works with a 0.3 Pilot Marqueur à Dessin, using a Speedball A5 pen to 'heavy' the lines if required. For expansive line work he uses a 00 sable brush, gouache colours or inks, and Rotring black.
PUB: *Montreal Cartoonist of the Year* (1985), *Handbook on Sailing and Watersports* (1989)
ILL: G. Bel, *The Joys of Moving Home* (1989); J. McCulloch, *Sir Edward and Nimrod* (1989); J. Pascoe, *The Idiot's Guide to Sex* (1991), *1992 and All That* (1991); E. Laine, *A Hard Man is Good to Find* (1988); P. Hancock, *Is That What You Mean?* (1990), *Is That What You Mean Too?* (1992); 'Funny Book of . . .' series for Hodder Headline (1996)
EXHIB: Central Library, Margate; BC; CG; Montreal; Zagreb

'Colonel Pewter' – *see* Horner, Arthur Wakefield

COLVIN, Neville (1918–91). Political, strip and sports cartoonist, and illustrator. Neville Colvin was born in Dunedin, New Zealand, the son of an accountant. He attended Otago Boys' High School and, intending to become a teacher, studied for an arts degree at Otago University. However, World War II intervened and he served with the Second New Zealand Expeditionary Force in the Middle East, drawing maps. It was for the Army's newspaper *NZEF Times* that he created the popular soldier character 'Fred Clueless' (he once described him as 'the most stupid little sod you could imagine') which began his cartoon career. After the war he joined the *Wellington Evening Post* (1946) as Political and Sports Cartoonist but resigned over the paper's censorship of his anti-(Conservative) government drawings. He moved to the UK in 1956 and after a period working for the *Daily Sketch* he turned freelance, working for *News Chronicle*, *Daily Telegraph*, *News of the World*, *Evening Standard*, *Daily Express* and *Sunday Express*. He is perhaps best known for drawing the 'Modesty Blaise' continuity strip (a kind of James Bond spoof created by Peter O'Donnell), for nine years – ending in 1986 when he resigned aged 68. The strip was immensely popular (it continues to this day in the *Evening Standard*, drawn by Romero), was syndicated internationally and has been made into two films. Colvin was greatly influenced by DAVID LOW, who also came from Dunedin and who had lived in the same part of London. He died in Hampstead, London, in the first week of November 1991.
ILL: L. Hobbs, *Kiwi Down the Strada* (1963)
COLL: NPG

COOKSON, Bernard (b. 1937). Editorial cartoonist and illustrator. Born in Manchester on 3 January 1937, the son of Richard Cookson, an engineer, Bernard Cookson attended Manchester Art School (1953–6) and was a visualizer in an advertising agency before doing his National Service as a Photographic Interpreter with the RAF in Cyprus. His first cartoon was published in the *Daily Mirror c.* 1965. He became a freelance cartoonist in 1967, succeeded DAVID MYERS on the *Evening News* as Social/Political Cartoonist (1969–76), and took over the TV strip 'The Niteleys' from ERIC BURGIN on the *Daily*

Sketch. Influenced by Eric Burgin, he has also contributed to *Punch, Spectator, Daily Express, Sporting Life, Today* and the *Sun* and draws with a Pentel pen on cartridge paper. He is also a former committee member of the Cartoonists' Club of Great Britain.
PUB: *Till Divorce Us Do Part* (1976), *Cookson's Wine Lovers* (1993)
ILL: H. Vickers and C. McCullough, *Great Country House Disasters* (1982); J. Timpson, *The Lighter Side of Today* (1983); W. Donaldson, *Great Disasters of the Stage* (1984); S. Tumin, *Great Legal Fiascos* (1985); M. Perry, *Knightsbridge Woman* (1995)
COLL: UKCC

COOP, J. Wallace 'Wal' (fl. 1908–1940s). Political cartoonist and caricaturist. Wal Coop lived in Birkenhead and Liverpool and worked at first as a caricaturist on the *Liverpool Courier* (c. 1908) for whom he produced a book of 89 pen-and-ink caricatures of the members of the Liverpool Cotton Exchange (Liverpool then being the leading cotton port in the UK), including one of the book's compiler, Seymour Taylor. He was later Political Cartoonist on *News of the World* in the 1930s and during World War II, signing himself 'WAL' or 'Wal Coop'.
PUB: [with S. Taylor] *Bulls and Bears* (1908)
EXHIB: L (1911–13)

CORAM, Robert S. E. 'Maroc' (fl. 1930s–after 1970). Joke and pocket cartoonist and caricaturist. Robert Coram was the son of Sydney Coram, a prominent advertising man, and attended St Dunstan's School, Catford, London. He studied at Goldsmith's College in the evening while working for a papermaking firm, then moved into advertisement canvassing before selling his first cartoon in 1936. He served in the National Fire Service in World War II with the cartoonist Betts and organized an exhibition of art by firemen at the Central School of Art and then at the Royal Academy (1941). Maroc contributed regularly to *Punch* (from 1938), *London Opinion, Answers, Lilliput, Blighty, Inky Way Annual, Weekend Mail, Passing Show, Sunday Chronicle, Daily Dispatch, Children's Own Favourite, Men Only, Strand, Sunday Telegraph* and *Razzle* (especially the 4–6-page 'Reggie' series), and drew pocket cartoons for the *Evening Standard*. His comic strips included 'Prairie Pete and Pronto', 'Ann Howe', 'Bob and Tanner', 'Wibble and Wobble'

and his pocket cartoon series included 'Wartime Humour' and 'To-Day's Smile'.
ILL: A. E. Morley, *Recipe for Laughter* (1945); [with T. Speer] E. Glen (ed.) *Stand Easy* (n.d.)

CORBOULD, Alfred Chantrey RBA (1852–1920). Joke cartoonist, graphic journalist and painter. A. C. Corbould was born in Kensington on 13 July 1852, the son of the portrait painter Alfred Hitchens Corbould and Charles Keene's sister. He was also the grandson of Henry Corbould FSA, designer of Queen Victoria's portrait for the first-ever postage stamps in 1840, and the nephew of Edward Henry Corbould RI, drawing master to Victoria and Albert's children. He was named after Keene's godfather, Sir Francis Chantrey RA. His first drawings were published in *Illustrated Police News* and *Fun* and, introduced by his uncle Charles Keene, he became a regular contributor of hunting and countryside cartoons to *Punch* (from 1871) and also drew for *Harper's Magazine* (from 1885). In 1890 he joined the newly launched *Daily Graphic* as a pictorial journalist (covering the Russo-Turkish War and other events), and with REGINALD CLEAVER established a new school of graphic reportage. He also contributed cartoons, mostly on sporting themes, and illustrations to *Black & White, Cornhill, London Society, New Budget, Pick-Me-Up, Lika Joko, Strand, St James's Budget, Illustrated London News* and *St Paul's*. A close friend of PHIL MAY and admired by LOUIS WAIN, he was a member of the Savage Club and was elected RBA (1893). His brother, Aster Richard Chantrey Corbould, also drew for *Punch* after being introduced to the magazine by his uncle.
PUB: *The Corbould Sporting Alphabet* (1900)
ILL: E. O'Reilly, *Dinglefield* (1883), *Kingie* (1886); *Kitty's Adventures* (1886); N. O'Donoghue, *The Common Sense of Riding: Riding for Ladies* (1887); H. S. Pearse, *The 'Comet' Coach* (1895)
COLL: V&A

COWHAM, Hilda Gertrude SGA (1873–1964). Illustrator, joke cartoonist, poster and postcard designer, painter and writer. Hilda Cowham was born in Westminster, London, the daughter of Joseph Henry Cowham, a Professor of Education, and was the grand-daughter of Tinsley Cowham. While still at school she won a drawing competition in the *Studio* magazine.

She then studied at Wimbledon Art School (under Alfred Drury ARA), Lambeth School of Art and the RCA. While a student she contributed cartoons to *Pick-Me-Up* and the *Sketch*. Her work later appeared in *Moonshine* (from 1896), *Girl's Realm*, *Strand*, *Graphic*, *Sphere*, *Little Folks*, *Pearson's*, *Printer's Pie*, *Queen*, *Tatler*, *Windsor Magazine* and *Punch*. Often mistakenly believed to have been the first woman to draw for *Punch* (this was in fact Helen Hopper Coode in 1859), her drawings often featured children and she famously created the 'Cowham Kid'. She also designed postcards for Inter-Art, Valentines and others, drew posters and advertisements (e.g. for Wilkinson's Liquorice Allsorts, Fry's Cocoa), wrote and illustrated children's books, painted watercolours and etched. In addition she designed crockery for Shelley Pottery and produced dolls. She was a member of the Society of Graphic Artists and the Three Arts Club. Her decorative style shows the influence of Forain, Art Nouveau and Japanese prints and her work in turn influenced MABEL LUCIE ATTWELL and others. She usually drew with a brush. She was married to the book illustrator and watercolour painter Edgar Lander. Hilda Cowham died on 28 September 1964.
PUB: *Fiddlesticks* (1900), *Peter Pickle and His Dog Fido* (1906), *Blacklegs* (1911), *The Funny Bunny ABC* (1912), *Curly Heads and Long Legs* (1914)
ILL: E. Player, *'Our Generals'* (1903); A. Golsworthy, *Ping Pong People* (c. 1905); J. Lea, *Willie Wimple's Adventures* (1908); R. Jacoberns, *The Record Term* (c. 1910); *Good Old Nursery Rhymes* (1916); P. Morris, *The Adventures of Willy and Nilly* (1921)
EXHIB: RA; RI; WG; SWA; L; London Salon
COLL: V&A; THG

CRANE, Walter RWS ROI (1845–1915) – *see* Bryant & Heneage

CROMBIE, Charles Edward (1885–1967). Joke cartoonist, illustrator and commercial artist. Charles Crombie is best known for his sporting cartoons, especially a series of coloured lithographs he drew for Perrier (1905) featuring Puritans playing golf in Jacobean clothes. He also produced two similar series, on cricket and motoring. All of these later appeared in the 'Crombie Series' of comic postcards for Valentines and some were transfer-printed on to Royal Doulton pottery. Influenced by the style of JOHN HASSALL, his drawings also appeared in *Illustrated London News*, *Bystander*, *Graphic*, *Holly Leaves*, *Humorist*, *Passing Show*, *London Magazine*, *Pearson's*, *Printer's Pie*, *Royal Magazine*, *Sketch*, *Golf Illustrated*, *Rions* (1908–9) and *Le Rire* (1910). He also illustrated P. G. Wodehouse stories in the *Strand Magazine*.
PUB: *Some Classic Rules of Golf* (1905), *The Laws of Cricket* (1906), *Motoritis* (1906), *Simple Simon and his Friends* (1906)
ILL: J. Sherratt, *The Goblin Gobblers* (1910); W. M. Thackeray, *Vanity Fair* (1924); J. Allan, *The Canny Scot* (1932)
EXHIB: BUR
COLL: THG

CRUM, Paul – *see* Pettiward, Roger

CUMBERWORTH, F. H. (fl. 1930s). Political and sports cartoonist. F. H. Cumberworth was born in New Zealand and worked for local papers before joining the *Sydney Evening News*. He then moved to the UK where he worked on the *News Chronicle*, at first as a daily sporting cartoonist but by 1934 was established as the paper's Political Cartoonist. He used a brush and indian ink.

CUMMINGS, Arthur Stuart Michael OBE (1919–97). Editorial/political cartoonist and caricaturist. Michael Cummings was born in Leeds on 1 June 1919, the son of A. J. Cummings, Political Editor of the *News Chronicle*. Educated at The Hall, Hampstead, and Gresham's School, Holt, he later studied at Chelsea School of Art (1945–8), where he was taught by Graham Sutherland and specialized in etching. He then taught art for a short while at St Albans Girls' Grammar School. Though later a strong Conservative, Cummings drew his first cartoon for the left-wing *Tribune* (edited by future Labour Party leader Michael Foot) in 1939 and he became Political Cartoonist on the paper in 1948. He then succeeded STRUBE as Political Cartoonist on the *Daily Express* (1949–90), working alternately with the paper's Social Cartoonist GILES, and later took on the *Sunday Express* (1958–96) as well. He also worked for *Punch* (1943–80, signing himself at first 'A. S. M. Cummings', but later taking over the 'Essence

Study of a typical French family having its morning hate . . .

Michael Cummings, [De Gaulle], *Daily Express*, 19 February 1969

of Parliament' illustrations from A. W. LLOYD (1953). In addition he contributed to the *Daily Mail* (from 1990), *The Times* (from 1995), *Oldie* (from 1992), *Paris-Match*, *L'Aurore* and *Candide*. At first he drew with a fine line for *Tribune*, etc., but later changed to his familiar bold style – described by ACANTHUS as 'an unusual staccato line' with a lot of solid black areas – to suit the design of the *Express*. Cummings roughed out his cartoons in pencil on A3 layout paper (usually six drawings from which the editor chose one) and used a dip pen and brush with Pelikan black ink on Daler board (half imperial size) for the finished work. Like MAC he used to conceal an image of his wife in his early cartoons. The Rt Hon. Michael Heseltine when Deputy Leader of the Conservative Party described being caricatured by him as 'Death by a thousand strokes . . . But at least I die laughing.' Cummings was the favourite cartoonist of Winston Churchill, who said in a letter to Arthur Christiansen, Editor of the *Express*, in December 1949: 'Cummings may well become one of

the greatest cartoonists of our time.' He also claimed to have been the only political cartoonist to have drawn every British Prime Minister from Churchill to Blair. However, his cartoons could also be controversial: a 1960s cartoon showing a boatload of golliwogs arriving in the UK caused complaints and print unions prevented publication of the Scottish edition of the *Express* containing a drawing of Soviet President Brezhnev dressed as a Roman Catholic priest with a consignment of tanks marked 'IRA'. One of the founder members of the British Cartoonists' Association in 1966, Cummings was awarded an OBE in 1983. He died in London on 9 October 1997.

PUB: *These Uproarious Years* (1954), [with M. C. Hollis] *The Ayes and the Noes* (1957), *How to Become an MP* (1959), *On the Point of My Pen* (1985) ILL: T. Arthur, *Ninety-five Per Cent is Crap* (1975) EXHIB: GG; HAM; JDG COLL: UKCC

CYNICUS – *see* Anderson, Martin

D

DARLING, Philip Michael (b. 1923). Joke cartoonist. Mike Darling was born in Kennington, London, on 24 July 1923, the son of Robert Michael Darling, a civil servant. After service as a pilot in the RAF during World War II (1941–6) he studied painting at Harrow School of Art (1947–50) and the Royal Academy Schools (1950–54). He has also taught drawing and lectured in Art History at Harrow School, Bideford School of Art and North Devon College. His first cartoon was published in the *Daily Express* in 1952 and since then his work has appeared in numerous publications including the *Listener, New Statesman, Spectator, Punch* and *Oldie*. Influenced by FRANÇOIS, SEARLE and STEADMAN, he draws in pen and ink with watercolour.
EXHIB: Burton Gallery, Bideford, Devon

DAVEY, George (1882–1944). Joke cartoonist, illustrator, painter, etcher and journalist. George Davey drew daily cartoons for *Westminster Gazette* and also contributed to magazines and comics such as *Fun, Jester & Wonder, Lot o' Fun* (where he created the character 'Dreamy Daniel' in 1906), *Comic Life, Scraps, Chums, Ally Sloper's Half Holiday, Big Budget, Puck, English Illustrated, Punch, Penny Wonder, Passing Show* and others, signing his work 'Geo Davey'. In addition he produced humorous drawings for postcard, Christmas card and calendar companies such as Henderson & Sons, Valentines, Misch & Stock and J. Mandel & Co, and painted landscapes in oil and watercolour. He was a member of the London Press Club.

DAVIDSON, Lilli Ursula Barbara Victoria [née Commichau] FSIA (b. 1915). Humorous illustrator and cartoonist. 'Victoria' (as she signs her work) was born in Munich, Bavaria, on 8 January 1915, the daughter of the painter Armin Commichau, and originally intended to be a dancer. She studied fashion art at the Lette Haus in Berlin under Siebert-Wernekink (1930–33) and worked at first as a fashion designer and as an illustrator and layout artist for magazine publishers in Berlin before coming to the UK in her twenties to marry an English scientist. Her first cartoon was published in *Lilliput* in 1937 and she was a regular contributor of cartoons and illustrations to the magazine (including covers and 'Gulliver's Diary'), as well as to *Picture Post* (readers' letters, 1937–57) and *Radio Times* (1947–62). She has also contributed to the *Daily Sketch, The Bureau of Current Affairs, COI, Die Neue Auslese* and *Süd-Deutsche Zeitung*. In addition she has drawn for advertising campaigns for Stock Brandy, Nestlé, Guinness (e.g. the poster of a girl playing the Guinness harp), Turog Brown Bread, Kelloggs, Persil and the GPO, amongst others, and has designed posters for London Transport. In the 1960s she produced three-dimensional fabric collages in the spirit of Victorian decoration. She sometimes also signs her work with just a 'v'.
PUB: *A Number Book* (1938), *Life and Adventures of Timothy Turnip* (1943), [with R. Ferguson] *Memoirs of a Fir-Tree* (1946)
ILL: *Latham's Nonsense Verses* (1948)
COLL: Museum of Modern Art, New York

DAVIEN, Geoffrey (fl. 1940s). Caricaturist and sculptor. Geoffrey Davien is best known for creating three-dimensional 'Sculptoons' which were photographed and used as illustrations for film reviews, etc., in the *Sunday Graphic* from 1946. The figures, of Hollywood stars, sports celebrities, politicians and so forth (e.g. Rita Hayworth, footballer Stanley Matthews and boxer Bruce Woodcock), were made of painted clay modelled on a wire skeleton about a foot high. They were featured on BBC TV's *Picture Page* programme in September 1946 along with 'Mum' cartoons drawn live by IAN DICKSON who had also begun work for the *Sunday Graphic* that year. The caricature style of Davien's sculptoons anticipated that of the SPITTING IMAGE studio of the 1980s.
COLL: NPG ('Sculptoons' of Bertrand Russell, Macmillan, Manny Shinwell, 1st Earl of Wootton; plaster bust of Hugh Dalton; caricature of Ernest Bevin); BFI

DAVIES, Robert Russell (b. 1946). Journalist, broadcaster, actor and caricaturist. Russell Davies was born on 5 April 1946 in Barmouth, Merionethshire, the son of John Gwilym Davies. He was educated at Manchester Grammar School and St John's College, Cambridge. He has been a freelance journalist and broadcaster since 1970. His work for the BBC has included presenting the TV arts programme *Saturday Review* as well as BBC2 jazz programmes and writing and presenting a history of radio comedy for Radio 4. He has also been Acting Editor of *Punch* and worked for *Observer* and other newspapers and magazines. Russell Davies has been cartoonist on *Liberal News* (1971) and resident caricaturist on the *Times Literary Supplement* (1972–4).

PUB: [with L. Ottaway] *Vicky* (1987), *Ronald Searle* (1990), (ed.) *The Diaries of Kenneth Williams*, (ed.) *The Kenneth Williams Letters*

ILL: C. James, *Peregrine Prykke's Pilgrimage* (1976)

DAVIS, Roy (b. 1921). Joke and strip cartoonist and scriptwriter. Roy Davis was born in London on 9 October 1921 and attended West Kensington Central School. He trained in shorthand, typing and bookkeeping, intending to pursue a clerical career, but his first job was as a wallpaper designer with A. Sanderson's Studio (from 1938) and he had his first cartoon published in *Answers* in 1939. He joined the RAF in 1940 and was commissioned in the RAF Regiment in 1944, serving in France, Holland, Germany, India and Java. After the war he rejoined Sanderson's briefly, leaving to join GB Animation in Cookham as a storyman (1946–50). On the company's demise he became a freelance cartoonist, his work appearing in *Tatler, Punch, Tit-Bits, Daily Sketch, Daily Mirror* and *Sporting Record*. During this period he also wrote and drew strips for juvenile publications such as *Mickey Mouse Weekly, Sun, Comet* and *Sunny Stories* and in 1964 he joined the staff of IPC Magazines, writing scripts for *Whizzer & Chips, Shiver & Shake, Knockout, Princess Tina, Buster* and others. He left IPC in 1974 but continued to produce scripts on a freelance basis for the company until 1992. A founder member of the Cartoonists' Club of Great Britain, he was voted Top Scriptwriter (1979) by the Society of Strip Illustrators. Influenced by HEATH ROBINSON and EMETT, he works mainly in pen and ink (though his scrapmetal sculptures appeared twice on BBC TV's *Vision On* programme).

D'EGVILLE, Alan Hervey FRGS FCI (1891–1951). Joke cartoonist, political caricaturist, illustrator and writer. Alan d'Egville was born on 21 May 1891, the son of Louis d'Egville of the Academy of Dramatic Art who taught dancing and deportment to royalty, and maternal grandson of the painter John Dawson Watson RWS. He

was most probably also related to the drawing master and pupil of Pugin, James T. Hervé D'Egville NWS, who taught H. B. Brabazon amongst others. Educated in Berkhamsted (Hertfordshire) and in France, Germany and Spain, he studied motoring at Daimler, Paris (1912) and taught the tango at his father's academy before working as private secretary to the chairman of Rolls-Royce. Meanwhile, he had subscribed to PERCY BRADSHAW's Press Art School and was studying for the Indian Civil Service when World War I broke out. Enlisting as an interpreter, he transferred to the Intelligence Department, where he was mentioned in despatches and became Chief Intelligence Officer, 4th Corps. After the war he spent six weeks at St John's Wood School of Art, was a tour guide in the Near East for Arnold Lunn Travel, and wrote and illustrated travel articles for *Britannia & Eve*. He also contributed political caricatures to *Bystander*, theatrical cartoons to *Pan* and humorous drawings to *Sketch, Passing Show, Men Only, London Opinion, Tatler, Le Rire, Humorist, Punch* (from 1935) and others. He briefly took over from HASELDEN on the *Daily Mirror* before a period of travel and travel writing, two years as a cartoonist in New York and Hollywood, and two years as a humorous columnist on *Daily Sketch*. In World War II he served in the Security Service, attaining the rank of major. After the war he contributed to *Life* and *Judge*, wrote scripts for Fox Films, and worked in advertising (producing advertisements for e.g. Hector Powe). Co-founder of the Kandahar Ski-racing Club, he was an expert award-winning skiier (he taught King Albert of Belgium) and often drew on this subject. He died on 15 May 1951.

PUB: *S'No Fun* (1925), *Modern Ski-ing* (1927), *Slalom* (1934), [with G. D'Egville] *Darts with the Lid Off* (1938), *The Game of Ski-ing* (1938), [with K. R. G. Browne] *Huntin', Shootin' and Fishin'* (1939), *Brass Tacks for Britain* (1945), *Calling All Fly-Fishers* (1946), [with D. Rooke] *Call Me Mister!* (1946), *A Touch of the Sun* (1947), *Rude Health* (1948), *Let's Be Broad-Minded* (1948), *Calling All Coarse Fishers* (1949), *Calling All Sea Fishers* (1950); *Ski-ing* (1947), *Money for Jam* (1947)

LIT: *Adventures in Safety – an Autobiography* (1937)

DE LA BERE – *see* Baghot-de-la-Bere, Stephen

DE LA NOUGEREDE, Alan Nightingale (b. 1932). Editorial cartoonist, strip cartoonist

and caricaturist. Born in Nowgong, India, on 12 December 1932, the son of Louis Joseph de la Nougerede, the Forest Officer for Assam in the Indian Civil Service and one of six brothers (Cedric Nightingale is a Sussex watercolourist), Alan de la Nougerede came to England on 27 March 1947. Self-taught in drawing, he studied oil painting with St John Earp and Cynthia Weller, sharing a studio with them (*c.* 1957–65). He was an accountant in the City and the provinces when his first cartoon was published in the *Evening Standard* on 4 January 1968. He became a professional artist and cartoonist in 1971 (continuing as an accountant part-time until 1986). Editorial Cartoonist on the *People* (1986–8) he has also worked in advertising for Star Computers and Moores Rowland chartered accountants, amongst others, and freelanced as a strip cartoonist for the *Daily Express, Evening News* and *Post* and as a joke cartoonist for the *Sun, Daily Mirror, Daily Sketch, Daily Star, Mayfair, Fiesta, Penthouse* (USA), *Playboy, The Director, Certified Accountant, Accountants' Weekly, Listener, The Cartoonist, Weekend, Squib, Punch* (from 1970), *Private Eye, Oldie, Printing Industries, Ariel* (BBC staff magazine) and others. In addition he has drawn numerous caricatures on commission and at social functions. Working mostly with Rotring indian ink and a Gillott 1290 nib, and occasional watercolour (his early magazine work was drawn in coloured inks), he cites BILL TIDY as being the biggest influence on his humour and MIKE WILLIAMS and QUENTIN BLAKE on his art.
ILL: 'Septimus', *Newby Revisited* (1980), L. Hopkins, *Business Ratios* (*c.* 1980), *Credit Rating Reports* (1988)
EXHIB: [watercolours] Ebury St Gallery; Bayswater Rd; JDG
COLL: UKCC

DE MORGAN, William Frend (1839–1917) – *see* Bryant & Heneage

DENIM – *see* Joss, Frederick

DENNYS, Isabelle Dorothy Joyce (1893–1991). Joke cartoonist, illustrator, writer and playwright. Joyce Dennys was born in Murree, India (now Pakistan) on 14 August 1893, the fourth child of Captain (later Colonel) Charles Dennys, an Indian Army officer. In addition, she was the sister of General Lance Dennys, a cousin of the poet (and assistant to Gordon Craig) Richard Dennys, and as a child was a bridesmaid at the wedding of the poet Harold Munro. Returning to England, she attended Eastbourne Ladies' College, Sussex, then aged 13 went to boarding school at Princess Helena College, Ealing. She studied at Exeter Art School and her first cartoon was published *c.* 1911. She contributed to *Punch* (from 1932), *Sketch, Printer's Pie, Harper's Bazaar* and other publications, drew advertisements for Abdullah Cigarettes and others, and in 1914 designed recruitment posters for the WRNS and VAD (Voluntary Aid Detachment). In addition she wrote a number of plays (including the 1950s West End musical *Kookaburra*), illustrated children's books and wrote and illustrated a humorous series of books about doctors (her husband Tom Evans was a doctor). During World War I she served in the VAD. She is particularly well known for her series of humorous letters between 'Henrietta' and 'Robert' in the *Sketch* (from 1939), describing life in a small coastal town in Devon during World War II (the Dennys family lived in Budleigh Salterton, Devon). The series featured Joyce Dennys herself as Henrietta; her husband Tom (who won a DSO and bar in World War I) as 'Charles'; Linnet, their daughter, and Perry, their dog – all other characters were entirely fictitious. When it was published in book form in the 1980s Henrietta was described as 'A 1940s Adrian Mole' (*The Times*). Joyce Dennys died in London on 23 February 1991.
PUB: *Mrs Dose the Doctor's Wife* (1930), *Repeated Doses* (1931), *The Over-Dose* (1933); [with R. Bennett] *Puffin, Twink and Waggle at Home* (1943), *Puffin, Twink and Waggle at the Zoo* (1943), *Puffin, Twink and Waggle at the Fair* (1944), *Puffin, Twink and Waggle at the Seaside* (1944); [plays] *The Bells Ring* (1947), *Art With a Capital 'A'* (1953), *At the Turn of the Tide* (1961); *Henrietta's War* (1985), *Henrietta Sees it Through* (1986)
ILL: H. C. Gordon and M. C. Tindall, *Our Hospital ABC* (1916); H. C. Gordon, *Our Girls in War Time* (1917), *Rhymes of the Red Triangle* (1918); 'Evoe' [E. V. Knox], *A Winter Sports Alphabet* (1926); M. M. Bruce, *The Peregrinations of Penelope* (1930); B. Nicholls, *For Adults Only* (1932)
EXHIB: Exeter [oil paintings, 1983]
COLL: IWM [recruitment posters]

DERRICK, Thomas ARCA (1885–1954). Illustrator, painter, art-teacher and joke cartoonist.

NEWS

Thomas Derrick, *Punch*, 4 May 1938

Thomas Derrick was born in Bristol and educated in Didcot, Berkshire. He studied at the Royal College of Art and during World War I was Art Adviser to the government's Foreign Propaganda Department. After the war he taught at the Institute of Decorative Painting at the RCA for five years, lectured on art at the London Day Training College, produced illustrations for St Dominics Press and other publishers, and designed book jackets and bindings for Chatto & Windus. From 1932 he contributed to *Punch*, notably charcoal sketches and full-page drawings: 'What were important were his full-page compositions in which time and space became plastic, as in a Disney Silly Symphony' (Price). His work also appeared in the *Bookman*, *GK's Weekly*, *London Mercury*, *Sunday Express*, *Joy Street*, *Everyman*, *Week-End Review* (political cartoons), *Time & Tide* (political cartoons) and elsewhere. In addition, he produced advertisements for Shell and others, painted murals, designed stained glass, and produced woodcuts (e.g. illustrating Ambrose Bierce's *Battle Sketches*). An admirer of the works of Randolph Caldecott and Walter Crane, he thought Tenniel's *Alice in Wonderland* the most perfect children's book ever produced. His style influenced the caricaturist R. S. SHERRIFFS. He was married to the daughter of Sir George Clausen RA. Thomas Derrick died on 18 November 1954.

PUB: *Everyman* (1927), *The Prodigal Son and Other Parables* (1931), *The Muses* (1933)

ILL: Many books including J. de la Fontaine, *Les Fables* (1910); G. Boccaccio, *The Decameron* (1920); A. Bierce, *Battle Sketches* (1930); G. K. Chesterton, *The Turkey and the Turk* (1930); H. Belloc, *Nine Nines* (1931); C. Alington, *Cautionary Catches* (1931); R. Dark, *Shakespeare – and That Crush* (1931); S. L. Robertson, *The Shropshire Racket* (1937); Rev. A. Tooth, *The Pagan Man* (n.d.)

EXHIB: RA; NEAC; FAS; RE; RI

COLL: Brooklyn Museum, New York; BM

LIT: H. R. Westwood, *Modern Caricaturists* (1932)

DICKENS, Frank William Huline (b. 1932). Strip cartoonist, illustrator and writer. Frank Dickens was born in Hornsey, North London, on 2 February 1932, the son of a painter and decorator. He went to Stationer's School, left at 16, and was a buying clerk in an engineering firm in Tottenham, North London, for three months before becoming a racing cyclist (1946–

Frank Dickens, [Bristow], *Bristow* (title page detail), 1970

70). A self-taught artist, he moved to Paris after National Service in Air–Sea Rescue and began selling cycling cartoons to *Paris-Match* and *L'Equipe* in 1959, followed by *Evening Standard*, *Daily Sketch* and *Daily Mirror*. He had his first strip – about a crook called Oddbod – accepted by the *Sunday Times* in 1960. Five times voted CCGB's Strip Cartoonist of the Year (1962, 1963, 1964, 1965, 1989), he is best known as the creator of Bristow, the bowler-hatted 'ineffectual rebel' with a toothbrush moustache who works in the offices of R. L. Chester-Perry Co. Ltd. ('Pendennis' in the *Sunday Times* has described Bristow as 'The Good Soldier Schwejk of the white-collar workers'.) Originally developed from a character in his book, *What the Dickens* (1961), the strip first appeared in the *Preston Journal* and other regional papers before being taken up by the *Evening Standard* on 6 March 1962. It has since been widely syndicated internationally and even produced on stage (ICA, 1971, starring Freddie Jones). Dickens' work has also appeared in the *Daily Mail*, *Daily Express*, *Sunday Express*, *Sunday Times*, *Punch*, *Today* and *TV Times*, and he has worked in advertising for companies such as British Telecom, London Transport, Haig Whisky, Peugeot and Mercedes-Benz. In addition he has written two thrillers and a number of children's books. He used to work (without roughs) on cs10 Fashion Board with a dip pen, a No. 8 Rapidograph and Pelikan ink, though nowadays he uses felt-tip pen, usually on paper. He also paints in watercolours and oils. Frank Dickens was one of the founder members of the British Cartoonists' Association in 1966.

PUB: *What the Dickens* (1961), [R. STEADMAN ill.] *Fly Away Peter . . .* (1964), *The Great Boffo* (1972), *Boffo: the Great Air Race* (1976), *Boffo: the Motor Cycle Race* (1976), *Albert and the Space Rocket* (1978), *Albert Herbert Hawkins, the Naughtiest Boy in the World* (1980), *Albert and the Olympics* (1980), [novel] *A Curl Up and Die Day* (1980), *Teddy Pig* (1980), *Teddy Pig and Julia's Birthday* (1981), *The Naughty World of Albert Herbert Hawkins* (1990) plus 7 Bristow books from *Bristow* (1966)

ILL: C. Ward, *How to Complain* (1974); M. Parkin, *Molly Parkin's Purple Passages* (1979); N. Charles and J. James, *The Rights of Woman* (1990)

EXHIB: Belgrave Gallery

DICKINSON, Geoffrey Samuel (1933–88). Joke and pocket cartoonist, illustrator, painter and art editor. Geoffrey Dickinson was born in Liverpool on 5 May 1933, the son of Albert Dickinson, a master coach-painter, and was educated at Southport School of Art (1950–53) and the Royal Academy Schools (1953–7). Originally intending to be a professional landscape painter, he taught art full-time at Tavistock Boys' School, Croydon (1957–8), and part-time at Selhurst Grammar School, Croydon (1958–67) – where pupils included MARTIN HONEYSETT – while freelancing for BBC TV, producing graphics and animation. A contributor to *Punch* (including covers) since 1963, he won first prize at the International Federation of Periodical Publishers Congress in Rome in 1965 for his cover for the magazine and later joined the staff as Deputy Art Editor (1967) under BILL HEWISON, becoming a member of the *Punch* Table in 1969. In addition, he drew two covers for *Time* magazine (1966 and 1969) and contributed to *Reader's Digest*, *Which?*, *Esquire*, *Soldier*, *High Life*, *Daily Mirror*, *Daily Telegraph*, *Times Educational Supplement*, *Evening Standard*, *Primary Health Care*, *British Journal of Hospital Medicine* (1984–8), Hallmark Cards and others. He left *Punch* in 1984 and joined the *Financial Times*, drawing daily pocket cartoons as well as humorous illustrations for the weekend supplement. Dickinson was a jury member at international cartoon festivals in Piracicaba, Brazil (1976) and Cordoba, Argentina (1979). An admirer of Cézanne, Japanese printmakers, FRANÇOIS, Keene and Low, he worked mostly in pen and ink but also used gouache, acrylics, watercolour, coloured inks, scraperboard, wood-engraving,

etching and oils. He was married to the illustrator and cartoonist Jackie Sinnott. Geoffrey Dickinson died at King's College Hospital, London, on 21 March 1988.

PUB: *There's a Lot of It About* (1985), *Probably Just a Virus* (1986)

ILL: S. Oram, *Starters Places – England* (1972); D. Barlow, *Sexually Transmitted Diseases* (1979); R. Morley, *Book of Bricks* (1978), *Book of Worries* (1979); H. Davies, *Father's Day* (1981); E. Prosser and A. O'Brien, *Learning to Drive with Hannah Gordon* (1975); R. Gordon, *Fifty Years a Cricketer* (1986), *Gordon in the Garden* (1987)

EXHIB: RA; RSBA; RE; CG

COLL: V&A; UKCC

DICKSON, Ian (1905–87). Joke and strip cartoonist and illustrator. Ian Dickson was born in Dunedin, New Zealand, on 15 January 1905 and moved to Melbourne when he was aged eight. Largely self-taught as an artist, he later moved to Adelaide to work on the *Adelaide Register News Pictorial* as cartoonist and illustrator for a year before it folded. Moving again, he became staff artist on *Brisbane Telegraph* and produced illustrations for Queensland Government tourist brochures. He then emigrated to England where he sold work to *Razzle* in the 1930s and drew illustrations for film companies. Then followed a period in Ceylon working for the *Times of Ceylon* and *Ceylon Observer* and then back to Britain and regular contributions to *Punch*, *London Opinion*, *Daily Sketch*, *Daily Mirror*, *Weekend*, *Men Only* and *Blighty*. He also drew the 'Mum' weekly strip in *Sunday Graphic* for 15 years until the paper folded. During World War II he served in the RAF. Renowned for his pictures of glamour girls, he was influenced by the style of *Esquire* artists and particularly admired the work of John Held Jr and Russell Patterson. His daughter is the illustrator Kate Aldous. Ian Dickson died on 21 July 1987.

'Diddums' – *see* Attwell, Mabel Lucie

'Dilly and Dally' – *see* Fearon, Percy Hutton

DIXON, George Scholefield (1890–1960). Joke cartoonist, illustrator, portrait painter and commercial artist. G. S. Dixon was born in Leeds, Yorkshire, on 20 April 1890, the son of George Dixon, a newspaper manager. He was educated at Bede College, Whitley Bay, and Mill Hill House School, Leicester. After studying at Leeds Art School he moved to London in the 1920s

and began contributing cartoons to *Punch* (1920s and 30s), *Passing Show*, *Tatler* and *Bystander* amongst other publications. He was a member of the Savage Club, London Sketch Club (becoming its President in 1938) and the Arts Theatre Club. G. S. Dixon died on 5 July 1960.
EXHIB: RA; L

DODD, Maurice Stanley (b. 1922). Joke and strip cartoonist, illustrator, scriptwriter and author. Maurice Dodd was born in Hackney, London, on 25 October 1922. Leaving school at 15 he volunteered for the RAF in World War II and served as an engine fitter with the Servicing Commando in North Africa, the Mediterranean, the Netherlands and Germany. He sold his first cartoon (as 'Mog') to *Seven* magazine in 1945. On demobilization he attended Hammersmith School of Arts & Crafts (1946–50) and in 1952 joined Halas & Batchelor to work on the UK's first full-length animated feature film, *Animal Farm*. He subsequently worked for a number of advertising agencies as writer and artist – including creating Young & Rubicam's 'Clunk Click' seatbelt campaign and other road-safety campaigns which won 13 international awards. In 1959 he went into partnership with Dennis Collins, taking over the scriptwriting and ideas for 'The Perishers' cartoon strip in the *Daily Mirror*, and taking over the drawing as well in 1983 when Collins retired. In 1992 he again went into partnership, enlisting the aid of Bill Mevin to produce the finished drawings for the strip. He has also storyboarded 20 animated versions of the strip for BBC TV and created the non-Perisher characters Gernommy, Churchmouse, Cellmate (for the charity Prisoners Abroad) and Merrymole. In addition he has produced cartoons and illustrations for *John Bull*, *Motorsport*, *Morning Advertiser*, *Sunday Mirror*, *Daily Record*, *MG Enthusiast*, *Young Elizabethan* (also stories), *Dogs Today* (also stories), *The Universe*, *Union Jack* (political cartoons), *Catholic Worker* (political cartoons) and *Direct Action* (political cartoons). Maurice Dodd cites his influences as Al Capp's 'Li'l Abner', Segar's 'Popeye', Bernard Graddon's 'Just Jake' and Walt Kelly's 'Pogo'.
PUB: [with D. Collins] 'The Perishers' books from 1963; *The Perishers' Dotty Dictionary* (1977), *The Perishers' Very Big for Its Size Story Book* (1979), *The Perishers' Rather Big Little Book* (1979), *The Tale of a Tail* (1981), *Merrymole the Magnificent* (1982), *Merrymole the Intrepid* (1984)

ILL: J. Phelan, *Wagon Wheels* (1951); M. Ende, *Jim Button and Luke the Engine-Driver* (1963)
EXHIB: [paintings] RA
COLL: UKCC

DONEGAN, John (b. 1926). Joke cartoonist and illustrator. Born in London, John Donegan first began work as an art director in advertising and became a full-time cartoonist in 1975. His work has appeared in *Punch* (including covers) and many other magazines. His advertising work has included drawings for Volkswagen (Germany), American Express (Germany), British Airways, BT and others. He won the Designers & Art Directors Award (1964) for his posters for the *Sunday Times*.
PUB: *Dog Almighty!* (1986), *Dog Help Us!* (1987), *For Dog's Sake!* (1990)

DONNISON, T. E. (fl. 1882–1903). Joke cartoonist and illustrator. T. E. Donnison was born in Ireland and educated at Rugby School. After studying law he practised as a solicitor for 15 years while taking art lessons in his spare time. He eventually became a full-time cartoonist and illustrator, contributing to *Boy's Own Paper*, *Fun*, *Longbow* and *Moonshine*. His 'pre-history' cartoons in *To-Day* echo those of E. T. REED and GEORGE MORROW in *Punch*. Donnison usually worked in pen and ink.
PUB: *The Jaw-Cracking Jingles* (1899), *Odds and Ends and Old Friends* (1902), *'Pure Fun' for Boys of All Sizes* (1903)
EXHIB: L

'Dot and Carrie' – *see* Horrabin, James Francis

DOUGLAS – *see* England, Thomas Douglas

DOWD, James Henry (1884–1956). Joke cartoonist, painter and etcher. The brother of the Fleet Street artist Leo (Leonard P.) Dowd and the *Daily Herald*'s Joseph Dowd, J. H. Dowd was a regular contributor to *Punch* for over 40 years (1906–48). He was also the magazine's first illustrator of film criticism, continuing in this post for more than three decades (he was succeeded by SHERRIFFS in 1948), and also drew theatre caricatures (with WHITELAW). In addition he worked for *Graphic*, *Strand* and *Bystander*, designed posters for London General Omnibus Company, London Underground Electric Railways and others and was a member of Chelsea Arts Club. Particularly noted for his drawings

of children – 'J. H. Dowd was the ARMOUR of the nursery' (Price) – stylistically he was 'one of the early pioneers of the vital expressive line that seems to be part of the subject, instead of merely illustrating it' (*Punch* obituary). J. H. Dowd died in Epsom, Surrey, on 16 March 1956.
PUB: *The Doings of Donovan In and Out of Hospital* (1918); [with texts by B. E. Spender] *Important People* (1930), *People of Importance* (1934), *Serious Business* (1937)
ILL: J. Drinkwater, *Robinson of England* (1937)
EXHIB: G; L; RA; RMS; RSA; AG; GI; International Society; RP; COO; Arts & Dramatic Club
COLL: BM; [posters] IWM; V&A

DRAWL – *see* Ward, Sir Leslie Matthew

DREDGE, Peter (b. 1952). Joke and strip cartoonist. Pete Dredge was born in Nottingham on 20 September 1952, the son of Frank Dredge, a sales representative for Distillers Ltd. He studied art and graphic design at Trent Polytechnic, Nottingham (1971–5). After selling his first cartoon to *Punch* in 1976 he turned full-time cartoonist. Since then he has also contributed to *Private Eye* (including the strip 'The Directors' from February 1995), *Radio Times*, *Spectator*, *Listener*, *Daily Star*, *Oldie*, *Penthouse*, *Men Only*, *Times Educational Supplement*, *Times Magazine*, *Ariel*, *National Lampoon*, *Risqué*, *New Statesman*, *Cartoonist*, *Squib*, *Maxim*, *Daily Express*, *Mayfair*, *Sun*, *Daily Mirror*, *Fiesta* and *Knave*. In addition he has worked in advertising for such clients as Boots, Legal & General, Allied Domecq, Grant Thornton, Bass, Fisons, Pretty Polly and IT & T, and produced greetings card designs for Hallmark, Athena, Paperhouse and Statics. He was also a gag-writer for BBC TV's *Not the Nine O'Clock News* (c. 1980). In addition he has been Senior Tutor for the cartoonist and illustrator correspondence course at the Morris College of Journalism since 1995 and is a director of the College of Cartoon Art. Influenced by HARRY HARGREAVES, MIKE WILLIAMS, ALBERT RUSLING and Frank Bellamy, he was voted CCGB Joke Cartoonist of the Year (1986) and Provincial Press Cartoonist of the Year (1987). He uses a Gillott nib and indian ink on 100 gsm laser print paper.
EXHIB: Nottingham Playhouse; BC

DRENNAN, Patricia (b. 1933). Joke and strip cartoonist and illustrator. Pat Drennan was born in Belfast on 16 May 1933 and studied at Belfast College of Art (1950–54) and the Accademia delle Belle Arti, Palermo (1957–8). She has had cartoons published in the *Daily Mirror*, *Daily Star*, *Sun*, *News of the World*, *Mail on Sunday*, *Medical Digest*, *Punch*, *Reader's Digest* and elsewhere. She also drew a regular strip cartoon for the *Evening News*, has worked in advertising for Fortnum & Mason, Radio Rentals, Chivas Regal and others, and has designed charity Christmas cards and illustrated books. In addition she has taught art in Belfast and London, and won first prize in the Waddington's Cartoon Awards in 1988. Influenced by the artists of the *New Yorker* and *Saturday Evening Post*, she uses a Gillott 303 nib with Higgins ink or fibretips but also likes working in pencil, coloured pencil, coloured inks and watercolour (especially seaside scenes).
ILL: D. George, *Mimoon and the Jug* (1977); A. Loudan, *Dear Sir Anthony* (1987); P. Hichens and J. Wilkerson, *Marriage Around the Clock* (1989); M. Stacey, *Superscrooge* (1991), *Superscrooge 2* (1992)

DULAC, Edmund (1882–1953). Illustrator, designer, painter and caricaturist. Edmund Dulac (an Anglophile, he changed his name from Edmond) was born in Toulouse, France, on 22 October 1882, the son of a commercial traveller for a textile company. His father was also a dealer in paintings and his uncle imported Japanese prints. Intending to enter the diplomatic service, he studied law at Toulouse University, then changed his mind and studied art at Toulouse Art School and (for three weeks) the Académie Julian in Paris. Impressed by the work of Beardsley and Morris he decided that his real interest was in book illustration and moved to England in 1904, becoming a naturalized British citizen in 1912. He began work for J. M. Dent, producing 60 watercolour illustrations for a new edition of the Brontë sisters' novels (1905) at the age of 22. He then drew illustrations and caricatures for *Pall Mall Magazine* (including covers) and became famous three years later when he illustrated Hodder & Stoughton's *Stories from the Arabian Nights* retold by Laurence Housman (1907). Subsequently (with Arthur Rackham) one of the leading 'Gift Book' illustrators (1907–14), he won two gold medals at the Barcelona International Exhibition (1911). In 1908 he published the comic collection

Lyrics Pathetic and Humorous from A to Z, and later exhibited caricatures at the International Society and the Leicester Galleries (1914). In 1919–20 he drew a series of 59 pen and ink caricatures of figures in politics and the arts for the weekly *Outlook*, and from 1923 produced colour covers for *American Weekly*. In addition he contributed to *L'Illustration, Comoedia Illustré* (1911–21), *Tout-Paris, La Gazette du Bon Ton, Les Annales* (1925–6), *Byblis* and others. He also designed the King's Poetry Medal (1933) and the classic profiles of George VI (1937) and later Elizabeth II (1952) used on British stamps and coins, as well as banknotes for Poland, Czechoslovakia, Italy, Spain, Turkey and Ceylon. During World War II he designed banknotes and stamps for the Free French (1940). In addition he painted portraits (e.g. the wife of the Chinese ambassador), designed sets and costumes for the theatre (as well as the Cathay Lounge of the ocean liner *The Empress of Britain*, 1930) and made wax-doll caricature models. In the 1940s he continued to illustrate books (especially for the Limited Editions Club in the USA) and designed wallpaper, playing cards and chocolate boxes for Cadbury's. He was a friend of W. B. Yeats (brother of the painter and cartoonist JACK YEATS) and the poet dedicated his collection *The Winding Stair* (1933) to him. Dulac in turn designed Yeats' gravestone (1939). Influenced by Vuillard, Corot, Burne-Jones, Beardsley, Morris, Walter Crane, Rackham, Persian miniatures and Japanese prints, he worked in a wide variety of media, including watercolour, gouache and linocut, and often used hot-pressed Whatman Board and handmade papers for his drawings. 'Dulac was both a fastidious draftsman and a fecund visualizer . . . One characteristic that separates [him] from many other illustrators is the intelligence in the faces of his characters' (Hodnett). Co-founder and later Chairman (1926) of the Film Society, he was also a member of the London Sketch Club. Edmund Dulac died of a heart attack while demonstrating flamenco dancing in Dorset on 25 May 1953.
PUB: *Lyrics Pathetic and Humorous from A to Z* (1908), *Edmund Dulac's Picture Book for the French Red Cross* (1915), *Edmund Dulac's Fairy Book* (1916)
ILL: *Stories from the Arabian Nights* (1907); W. Shakespeare, *The Tempest* (1908); *The Rubaiyat of Omar Khayyam* (1909); *The Sleeping Beauty and Other Fairy Tales* (1910); *Stories from Hans*

Andersen (1911); E. A. Poe, *The Bells* (1912); *Princess Badoura* (1913); *Sinbad the Sailor and Other Stories from the Arabian Nights* (1914); H. Beauclerk, *The Green Lacqueur Pavilion* (1926); R. L. Stevenson, *Treasure Island* (1927); M. Cary, *The Daughter of the Stars* (1939) and others
EXHIB: LG (Memorial 1953); Mappin Art Gallery, Sheffield; International Society; BR; GM; RI; L; FAS; Ridley Art Club; Hartnoll & Eyre
COLL: BM; V&A; IWM; LM [wax statuette of Sir Thomas Beecham]; NYPL; Texas University; CAT; BN; F
LIT: C. White, *Edmund Dulac* (1976)

DUNCAN, Riana (b. 1950). Joke cartoonist, illustrator and writer. Riana Duncan was born in Paisley, Scotland, on 2 July 1950 and studied graphics under Georg Hadeler and Nol Kroes at the Free Academy of Fine Arts, The Hague (1968–71). She spent several years exhibiting graphics and textiles before turning to writing and illustrating children's books, and took up cartooning in 1979. Her work has appeared in *Guardian, Punch, Men Only, Weekend, Spectator, Observer, Nieuwe Revu* and *She*. She draws in ink using Rotring pens with a minimal line, rarely crosshatching, and also uses watercolours applied with a very fine brush.
PUB: *A Tale of Ten Town Mice* (1978), *A Nutcracker in a Tree* (1980), *History and Her Story* (1986), *Not Tonight* (1987), *If You Were a Bird* (1987), *The Mating Game* (1988), *Emily's Paintbox* (1988), *When Emily Woke Up Angry* (1989), *The ABC of Sex* (1989), *Monogamy* (1990), *Emily's Bed* (1990)
ILL: M. Rogers, *Cindy and the Silver Enchantress* (1978); S. Cline and D. Spender, *Reflecting Men* (1987); M. Rosen, *Rude Rhymes* (1989), *Dirty Ditties* (1990), *Who Drew On the Baby's Head?* (1991), *Vulgar Verses* (1991)

DUNN, Sheila (fl. 1920s–after 1950). Joke cartoonist and illustrator. Sheila Dunn studied at St John's Wood School of Art and contributed fashion drawings to *Vogue* and cartoons to *Punch* and elsewhere. She was Art Editor of a children's magazine and in addition drew advertisements for Quality Street and Cadbury's Chocolates, Morley Silk Stockings and others.
ILL: C. Mackenzie, *Unpleasant Visitors* (1928); F. Salton [author of *Bambi*], *Fifteen Rabbits* (1943), *Reni the Rescuer* (1944)

'Dux and Drakes' – *see* Fearon, Percy Hutton

'That's an excellent suggestion, Miss Triggs. Perhaps one of the men here would like to make it.'

Riana Duncan, *Punch*, 8 January 1988

DYSON, William Henry (1880–1938). Political cartoonist, caricaturist and etcher. Will Dyson was born in Ballarat, Australia, on 3 September 1880, the younger brother of Edward Dyson, writer and *Sydney Bulletin* journalist, and Ambrose Dyson, cartoonist of the *Sydney Bulletin* and *Adelaide Critic*. Educated in Melbourne, Dyson was a self-taught artist and his work was first published in the *Sydney Bulletin* and *Lone Hand* when he was 17. In 1903 he took over from his brother on the *Adelaide Critic*, producing Australia's first cartoons printed in colour, and later worked for *Gadfly* (1906) and drew colour caricatures for covers of *Clarion* (1908). He moved to England in 1909 and married Ruby Lindsay, the sister of cartoonist, writer and painter Norman Lindsay, in 1910 (Ruby herself was a successful illustrator who later drew covers for *The Suffragette*). In London he worked first for *New Age* and later (from 23 September 1912) was the first-ever cartoonist on the Labour Party paper, the *Daily Herald*. During World War I he produced a series of anti-Kaiser drawings, 'Kultur Cartoons', which were published as a book, and in 1915 he was sent to the Front as official war artist to the Australian Imperial Forces and was twice wounded. He also contributed to *Weekly Dispatch*, *World* (colour caricatures in the *Vanity Fair* style signed 'Emu'), *Daily Chronicle*, *British Australian*, *New English Weekly*, *Daily Sketch*, *London Mercury*, *Pearson's Magazine*, *Reveille* and *Odd Volume*. After the war he produced perhaps his best-known drawing for the *Daily Herald* (13 May 1919), 'Curious, I seem to hear a child weeping', predicting the cause of World War II. Returning to Australia in 1925 (being replaced on the *Herald* by WILL HOPE), he was staff cartoonist on the *Melbourne Herald*, and also worked for *Melbourne Punch* and *Table-Talk*. He later went back to England to produce front-page cartoons for the *Daily Herald* in August 1931 (taking over from Gordge), and a cartoon he drew in June 1935 led to the paper being banned in Italy. A passionate Socialist and a very influential artist, he was much praised by DAVID LOW who none the less felt that he had a tendency to overcaricature – his capitalists were too bloated, working men

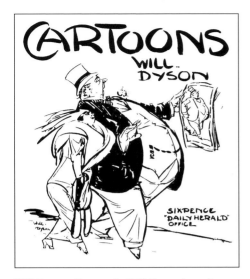

Will Dyson, *Cartoons by Will Dyson* (cover), 1913

too idealized, etc. – and the *Herald* itself tried to limit the number of devils that crept into his drawings. JOHN JENSEN has said of his work: 'Stylistically Dyson had few imitators – his work was too complex – but the power of his ideas brought back to British cartooning the strong flavour and impact of a Gillray after years of Victorian politeness.' G. K. CHESTERTON called him 'the most original and penetrating artist of our time'. He worked at great speed, using mostly brush and ink but also pen and litho crayon or conté crayon on cartridge paper. President of the Chelsea Arts Club (1933), he introduced Aneurin Bevin to the Club and drew colour caricatures of its members. Will Dyson died of a heart attack at his home, 8 Netherton Grove, London SW10, on 21 January 1938.
PUB: *Cartoons* (1913), *More Cartoons* (1914), *Kultur Cartoons* (1915), *Conscript 'Em* (1915), *Will Dyson's War Cartoons* (1916), [drawings] *Australia at War* (1918), *Old King Coalition* (1918), *Poems: In Memory of a Wife* (1919), (ed.) *The Drawings of Ruby Lind* (1919), *Mister Asquith* (1920), *Collected Drawings* (1920), *Artist Among the Bankers* (1933)
ILL: E. Dyson, *Fact'ry 'Ands* (1906), *Spats' Fact'ry: More Fact'ry 'Ands* (1914); E. Pataud and E. Pouget, *Syndicalism and the Co-operative Commonwealth* (1913); G. Gould, *Lady Adela* (1920)
EXHIB: Melbourne (1909); LG; RHA; RSA; CHG (1916); Ferargil Galleries, New York; Gumps Gallery, San Francisco; SGG; CG; Australia House, London
COLL: V&A; Australian War Memorial; NG of NSW; NG of Victoria; UKCC; IWM; [lithographs] BM; Chanteau Collection
LIT: R. McMullin, *Will Dyson* (1984); J. Jensen, *Will Dyson* (1996)

E

ECCLES – *see* Brown, Frank Hilton

ECKHARDT, Oscar RBA (fl. 1892–1902) – *see* Bryant & Heneage

EDGELL, David (b. 1930). Editorial and advertising cartoonist, actor and photographer. David Edgell was born in Leicester on 29 June 1930 and attended Leicester School of Art (1946–9). Staff cartoonist in the Features Department of the *Daily Express* (1962–86), he has also worked for the *Sunday Times* and *Observer* and produced a considerable amount of advertising work for clients such as Shell, British Airways, Egg Marketing Board, Air Canada, American Express, Abbey National Building Society, Woolwich Building Society, *Financial Times*, BP and British Rail. He has also lectured at Hornsey College of Art (1982–3), been Food Photographer for *Vogue*, *Queen* and *Sunday Times* and is a professional actor holding an Equity card. In addition, he was one of the founder members of the British Cartoonists' Association in 1966.
PUB: *A Book of Melancholy* (1981)

ef – *see* Fraser, Eric George

EGAN, Beresford Patrick (b. 1905). Sports cartoonist, caricaturist, illustrator and writer. Beresford Egan was born in England but educated in

South Africa. He worked at first as a bank clerk for six months but later became sports cartoonist on the *Rand Daily Mail*, Johannesburg. He returned to the UK in July 1926 and contributed drawings to *London Mystery Magazine, London Opinion, Pearson's Magazine, Clarion, Preface, Everybody's, Razzle, Royal Magazine, Man About Town* and *Time & Tide*. In addition he wrote and illustrated a number of books, including *The Sink of Solitude* (1928), a satire on Radclyffe Hall's *The Well of Loneliness*, and *Policeman of the Lord* (1928), an attack on Home Secretary Sir William Joynson-Hicks. He dedicated his novel *No Sense in Form* (1933) to the *Bystander* cartoonist Leslie Butler. A talented actor himself (he played Svengali, Dracula and Rasputin), he also wrote and illustrated his own monthly theatre reviews for *Courier* (1956–9). In addition he worked in advertising for companies such as High Duty Alloys (published in *The Aeroplane*, 1935–9) and Floris Bakeries. He worked mostly in pen or brush and ink but also used oils, watercolour, chalk, scraperboard, gouache, coloured inks and pencil. Until 1943 he usually employed just a No. 3 sable hair brush but thereafter was more flexible: 'the singing line, as tensile and vibrant as a violin, was my objective technically speaking'. His style showed the influence of Beardsley in its use of solid blacks.

PUB: [with B. de Shane] *De Sade* (1929), *Pollen* (1933), *No Sense in Form* (1933), *But the Sinners Triumph* (1934), *Epitaph* (1943), *Epilogue* (1943) ILL: P. Loys, *Aphrodite* (1927), *Cyprian Masques* (1929), *The Adventure of King Pausole* (1930); P. R. Stephenson, *Policeman of the Lord* (1928), *The Sink of Solitude* (1928); C. Baudelaire, *Les Fleurs du Mal* (1929); N. Balchin, *Income and Outcome* (1936) and others

EMETT, Frederick Rowland OBE (1906–90). Joke cartoonist, illustrator, theatrical designer, commercial artist and inventor. Rowland Emett was born in New Southgate, Middlesex, on 22 October 1906, the son of Arthur Emett, part-time inventor and owner of an advertising company, and Alice Veale. He was the grandson of William Henry Emett, lithographer and Court Engraver to Queen Victoria. Educated at Waverley Grammar School, Birmingham, he studied briefly at the Birmingham School of Arts & Crafts. He then worked for an advertising agency as a commercial artist while also painting landscapes, exhibiting at the Royal Acad-

emy in 1931. During World War II he worked as a draughtsman for the Air Ministry. His first cartoon was published in *Punch* on 10 December 1939 and he later contributed to *Lilliput, Life* and other magazines, drew advertisements for Shell, Guinness, Patons & Baldwins Wool, Yardley, Fisons, etc., produced Christmas cards for Ward Gallery and designed stage sets (e.g. *A Penny for a Song* at the Haymarket Theatre in 1951). However, it was his work for *Punch* (1939–51) that made his reputation. Here he drew fantastic locomotives, trams, old-fashioned pleasure-steamers and spindly figures in bizarre cartoons which normally occupied half a page of the magazine. 'The poet laureate in line of rococo engineering' (Eric Keown), his imaginative, delicate and highly decorative style showed the influence of Richard Doyle and HEATH ROBINSON and he usually drew in pen and ink but sometimes also worked with washes, gouache and watercolour. In 1951 his 'Far Twittering to Oyster Creek Branch Line Railway', which had begun life in *Punch* in March 1944, was turned into a reality and, featuring the engines 'Nellie', 'Neptune' and 'Wild Goose' fitted out in brass and mahogany, became one of the most popular items of the Festival of Britain, attracting two million passengers. After the success of this he left *Punch* and largely gave up drawing to concentrate on his inventions. These included the Astroterramare, 'an amphibious monster propelled by a rocket and vaguely held up by sails, balloons and an umbrella' (*Daily Telegraph* obituary) for Shell Oil; eight machines for the United Artists' film *Chitty Chitty Bang Bang* (1968); the 23-foot-high Rhythmical Time Fountain for the Victoria Centre, Nottingham (1974); the elephant-shaped Forget-Me-Not Computer for Honeywell Computers; and other installations in Britain and North America (for example at the Ontario Science Centre in Toronto, the Smithsonian Institute in Washington, The Museum of Science & Industry in Chicago and elsewhere). He was appointed OBE in 1978. Rowland Emett died in a nursing home in Hassocks, Sussex, on 13 November 1990.

PUB: *Engines, Aunties and Others* (1943), [with M. Emett] *Anthony and Antimacassar* (1943), *Sidings and Suchlike* (1946), *Home Rails Preferred* (1947), *Saturday Slow* (1948), *Buffers End* (1949), *Far Twittering* (1949), *High Tea* (1950), *The Forgotten Tramcar* (1952), *A New World For Nellie* (1952), *Nellie Come Home* (1952), *Hobby Horses* (Guinness, 1958), *The Early Morning Milk Train*

'Thank GOODNESS the kids have finally gone back to school . . .!'

Rowland Emett, *The Early Morning Milk Train*, 1976

(1976), *Alarms and Excursions* (1977), *Emett's Ministry of Transport* (1981)
ILL: W. de la Mare, *Peacock Pie* (1941), *Bells and Grass* (1941)
EXHIB: CBG (1988)
COLL: V&A; T; CAT; Ontario Science Centre, Toronto; Smithsonian Institute, Washington DC; Museum of Science & Industry, Chicago; Victoria Centre, Nottingham; Eastgate Shopping Mall, Basildon

EMMWOOD – *see* Musgrave-Wood, John Bertram

EMU – *see* Dyson, William Henry

EN – *see* Norfield, Edgar George

ENDER, Peter (fl. 1930s–60s). Joke and strip cartoonist, journalist, writer and illustrator.

Peter Ender won a number of drawing prizes at school but otherwise had no art training. He worked at first in the men's wear department of a celebrated London department store for three years where he also drew for the house magazine. A keen football fan and admirer of the work of TOM WEBSTER, his first published cartoons (in the style of Webster) appeared in the *Southend Standard*. Later he also contributed to *Punch*, *Passing Show*, *Sunday Dispatch*, *Winner*, Allied Newspapers, *Guide & Ideas*, *Tatler & Bystander*, *Answers*, *Topical Times*, *Daily Express*, *London Opinion*, *Men Only*, *Daily Sketch*, *Leader*, *Star*, *Illustrated*, *Lilliput*, *Blighty*, *Soldier* and *Razzle*. He also produced a strip cartoon for *Winner* and 'Illustrated Idioms' and 'Have You Seen Oscar?' for the *Star*. Other strips have included 'Mugli, the Mischievous Moor', 'Spic,

Span and Soccer', 'City Snips' and 'Dart Art'. During World War II Sergeant Ender served as a driver in the RASC in Persia, was appointed Official Cartoonist for the Public Relations Department of the Persia and Iraq Forces and was Art Editor of *Soldier*. In addition he was wartime film critic for the army papers *Basrah Times*, *Iraq Times* and *Trunk Call*, designed sets for the PAI Players company at the Baghdad Theatre and drew propaganda posters for the government such as 'Keep it Under Your Hat'. His signature was, like GILBERT WILKINSON's, very hard to read.

PUB: *Back at the Front* (1942), *Up the Garden Path* (1944)

ENGLAND, Thomas Douglas (1891–1971). Joke and strip cartoonist and commercial artist. Douglas England was born on 7 January 1891 and worked in a bank before serving in France in World War I. He later lived in East Africa, returning to England to study at the Royal Academy Schools. He then worked as a commercial artist, designing advertisements for Moss Bros, Schweppes, Guinness, Nescafé, Crosville Buses and others and contributed regularly to *Punch*, producing cartoons in colour and black-and-white and sharing the 'Charivaria' illustrations with FOUGASSE (and later taking over from him). Signing his drawings 'Douglas' he worked in brush and indian ink. 'Often his pictures burlesqued the glossy hats, the stylish prance of advertisement characters. He was fertile in jokes that depended on this contrast between the smart and the tripped-up' (Price). He died in March 1971.

ESPOIR, G. – *see* Hope, William

EVANS, Powys Arthur Lenthall 'Quiz' (1899–1981). Caricaturist and painter. Powys Evans was born on 2 February 1899 in London, the son of William Evans, County Court Judge for Mid-Wales, and the younger brother of the artist Gwen Evans. He studied under Spencer Gore NEAC (1910) and Robert Bevan NEAC LG, with SICKERT and Sylvia Gosse RBA RE SWA at Sickert's School in Rowlandson House (1912–13), was taught lithography by Ernest Jackson ARA and later attended the Westminster School of Art and the Slade under Henry Tonks NEAC (1915–17). During World War I he served in the Welsh Guards on the Western Front. He sold his first drawing to *Pan* in 1919 and then drew for *Tatler*. However, he first made his name in 1922 when (drawing as 'Powys Evans') he exhibited and later published (as a portfolio) a collection of 10 caricatures of the actors from Sir Nigel Playfair's production of John Gay's *The Beggar's Opera* at the Lyric Theatre, Hammersmith. Playfair himself (who was also manager of the theatre), conductor Frederick Austin, designer Claude Lovat Fraser and John Gay were also caricatured. In April 1922 he began a regular series of portraits of poets, artists and writers in the *London Mercury* which lasted nine years and in July the same year he also started work for the *Saturday Review*, drawing celebrity caricatures for the weekly for four years under the pseudonym 'Quiz'. He also contributed to *Everyman's*, *Bookman*, *GK's Weekly*, *The Golden Hind*, *John O'London's* and *Time & Tide*. Admired by MAX BEERBOHM, who wrote an introduction to the catalogue of Evans' solo exhibition at the Leicester Galleries, London (1924), his pen, brush and ink style used a lot of solid blacks in the manner of Beardsley. As well as caricatures, he also drew portraits and painted topographical scenes and fantasies in watercolour. He moved to Dolgellau, Wales, in the 1930s and thereafter concentrated on painting. He was a member of the Savile Club. He is not to be confused with Sir John Paget Mellor Bt (1862–1929), who worked for *Punch* and drew seven caricatures for *Vanity Fair* (1889–98), also under the pseudonym 'Quiz'.

PUB: *Eighty-Eight Cartoons* (1926), *Fifty Heads* (1928)
ILL: J. Gay, *The Beggars' Opera* (1922)
EXHIB: NEAC; LG; GOU; Bumpus (1931); COO; LAN (retrospective 1975)
COLL: NPG; BM; V&A; National Library of Wales

EVANS, Treyer Meredith (1889–after 1958). Joke cartoonist and illustrator. Treyer Evans was born on 6 June 1889 in Chichester, Sussex, the son of Price James Evans, a dentist, and educated at Grosvenor House School, Bognor. He worked at first as an illustrator for Pearson and Hulton magazines (1909–10) and later drew cartoons and illustrations for *Punch*, *Little Folks*, *Nash's*, *London Magazine*, *Girl's Realm*, *Scout*, *Royal Magazine*, *Sketch*, *Tatler*, *Humorist* (including covers), *Strand Magazine* (notably drawings for stories by P. G. Wodehouse) and *London Opinion* (especially the 'We Discover

Quiz (Powys Evans), [Professor Henry Tonks], *Eighty-Eight Cartoons*, 1926

England' humorous series in 1947 with Anthony Armstrong, later published in book form). He was a member of the Savage Club.

PUB: *Pull-Out Painting Books* (1957)

ILL: Many books including A. Brazil, *A Fortunate Term* (1921); F. Inchfawn, *Will You Come As Well?* (1931), *The Verse Book of a Garden* (1932); A. Armstrong, *England Our England* (1948);

G. Trease, *The Hills of Varna* (1948); E. Blyton, *The Christmas Book* (1944), *The Mystery of the Vanished Prince* (1951), *The Mystery of the Strange Bundle* (1952), *The Mystery of Holly Lane* (1953), *The Mystery of Tally-Ho Cottage* (1954); M. E. Proctor, *Three Wise Men* (1958)

'Eve' – *see* Fish, Anne Harriet

F

FALCONER, Pearl FSIA (fl. 1930s–after 1975). Joke cartoonist, painter, costume designer and illustrator. Pearl Falconer was born in Dundee and studied at St Martin's School of Art and at Central School of Arts & Crafts. She began as a fashion artist drawing for *New York Times* and *New York Herald-Tribune* and her work later appeared in *Harper's Bazaar, Housewife, Listener* and *Radio Times* amongst others. She also designed murals for three pavilions in the Festival of Britain (1951). Pearl Falconer was married (1938–47) to RICHARD WINNINGTON.

ILL: H. Phillips, *Ask Me Another* (1945), *Something to Think About* (1958); B. Aldiss, *The Brightfount Diaries* (1955); N. Savage Carson, *The Happy Orpheline* (1960), *The Orphelines in the Enchanted Castle* (1963), *A Pet for the Orphelines* (1963); P. Farmer, *The China People* (1960); M. Treadgold, *The Winter Princess* (1962) and others

COLL: V&A

FANTONI, Barry Ernest (b. 1940). Joke and pocket cartoonist, novelist, broadcaster and jazz musician. Barry Fantoni was born in London on 28 February 1940, the son of the artist Peter Fantoni. Educated at Archbishop Temple School, London, he studied at Camberwell School of Arts & Crafts (1954–8). While working as a painter (1958–63) he had his first cartoon published in *Private Eye* (1963). He has been on the editorial staff of *Private Eye* since 1963 (co-writer with Richard Ingrams of 'Sylvie Krin', 'E. J. Thribb' and 'Old Jewett' columns). Editor of *St Martin's Review* (1969–74) he was Diary cartoonist of *The Times* (1983–91). He has also drawn for *The Listener* (1968–89) and *Radio Times* and has been art critic of *The Times* (1973–7) and

record reviewer for *Punch* (1976–7). In addition he has appeared as a film and TV actor, written scripts for the satirical 1960s TV show *That Was the Week That Was* and detective novels featuring 'Mike Dime', created a one-man show 'From

'It seems they moved "Red Container with Hose" five times before discovering it was a fire extinguisher.'

Barry Fantoni, *The Best of Barry Fantoni*, 1990

the Dragon's Mouth' and in 1990 formed Barry Fantoni's Jazz Circus. His first play, *Modigliani, My Love*, opened in Paris in 1999. As well as his familiar spiky, kindergarten-style pocket cartoons, he is also known for his pop-art caricatures. 'An accomplished painter of neorealist portraits and a fine draughtsman [he] opts for the Faux-naif style in his cartooning and because he *can* draw well he has to push his cartoon method to the opposite extreme' (HEWISON). He was President of the Chelsea Arts Club (1978).

PUB: [with R. Ingrams] *The Bible for Motorists* (1970), *Private Eye Barry Fantoni* (1975), *The Times Diary Cartoons* (1984), *Barry Fantoni's Chinese Horoscopes* (1985), *Barry Fantoni Cartoons* (1987), *The Best of Barry Fantoni* (1990)

ILL: D. Greenbaum, *How to be a Jewish Mother* (1966); *The BP Festivals and Events in Britain* (1966); G. Melly, *The Media Mob* (1980)
EXHIB: [as 'Stuart Harris' with W. Rushton] RA (1963); [as Barry Fantoni] RA (1964, 1975, 1978); Woodstock Gallery; Comara Gallery, Los Angeles; Brunel University; [with P. Fantoni] LAN; Annexe Gallery; Katherine House Gallery; Fulford Cartoon Gallery; NGG; Arts Club; Old Town Books, Clapham; Gillian Jason Gallery
COLL: UKCC; V&A; BM

FAWKES, Walter Ernest 'Trog' (b. 1924). Caricaturist, political cartoonist, pocket cartoonist, strip cartoonist, writer and jazz musician. Born in Vancouver, Canada, on 21 June 1924, Wally Fawkes came to England in 1931 and left school

Trog (Wally Fawkes), [Britannia, Blair], *Sunday Telegraph*, 5 April 1998

at 14 to study art at Sidcup Art School and under John Minton at Camberwell (where he was a contemporary of HUMPHREY LYTTELTON and SMILBY). During World War II he drew maps and painted camouflage and in 1945 was 'discovered' in an art competition run by the *Daily Mail*'s Political Cartoonist, LESLIE ILLINGWORTH, and offered a job on the paper, eventually taking over from Illingworth (1968–71). His work has also been published in *Punch* (especially covers, since 1971), *Spectator* (since 1959), *New Statesman* (since 1965), *Today*, *London Daily News* and *Private Eye*, and his well-known series 'Flook' (originally a children's strip 'Rufus and Flook' created by Douglas Mount on 25 April 1949) ran for 35 years (1949–84) on the *Daily Mail*, with writers Humphrey Lyttelton, George Melly (1956–71), Barry Norman, Barry Took and Compton Mackenzie as well as himself. It moved to the *Mirror* (where it was written by Keith Waterhouse) in 1984. The strip was at first called just 'Rufus' after the red-headed boy who featured in it, and Flook was so-named because originally the magical creature could only make that sound (Trog's own pseudonym comes from the name of one of his early jazz bands, the Troglodytes). Fawkes also succeeded ABU as Political Cartoonist and Caricaturist on the *Observer* (1965–96), for which he also produced a regular pocket cartoon 'Mini-Trog', and *Sunday Telegraph* (since 1996) and has produced covers for *The Week* since 1997. Twice winner of Granada TV's *What the Papers Say* Cartoonist of the Year Award, he also won the US Cartoonists' & Writers' Syndicate World Award (1976) and was voted International Political Cartoonist of the Year (1976) by the International Salon of Cartoons, CCGB Humorous Strip Cartoonist of the Year (1981), CAT Caricaturist of the Year (1997) and was presented with the CAT Lifetime Achievement Award in 1997. An admirer of DAVID LEVINE ('the best caricaturist in the world'), he uses either Truline or Bristol board, Higgins black ink and a dip pen with Gillott 291 nib and a brush (he also does his roughs with a brush), though he has also worked in scraperboard. An accomplished clarinettist, Wally Fawkes was a co-founder of Humphrey Lyttelton's jazz band (1948). A firm believer that making a political cartoon is like condensing the action, conflict and character development of a play into a single line, Fawkes also sees it as uniquely dependent on caricature. At first influenced by Illingworth, he introduced a

grisaille tonal style using gouache on the *Mail* and has since employed a variety of techniques, notable successes being his striking colour caricature covers for *Punch*. 'There is an astonishingly sharp focus . . . particularly in the caricature, which makes the characters seem larger than life, as if seen under a brilliant light and a powerful lens . . . his blacks seeem to be blacker than black . . .' (RAYMOND BRIGGS). He was one of the founder members of the British Cartoonists' Association in 1966.

PUB: [with D. Mount] *Rufus and Flook v. Moses Maggot* (1950), [with R. Raymond] *Rufus and Flook at School* (1951), [with G. Melly] *Flook* (1958), [with G. Melly] *I, Flook* (1962), *A Flook's Eye View of the Sixties* (1970), [with G. Melly] *Flook by Trog* (1970), [with B. Took] *Flook and the Peasants' Revolt* (1975), *The World of Trog* (1977), *Trog Shots* (1984)

ILL: R. Eckersley, *Some Nonsense* (1946); M. L. Norcott, *Out and About with Undertakers* (1946), *Our Dogs* (1948); G. Melly, *Owning-Up* (1965), *Mellymobile: 1970–81* (1982); B. Took (ed.), *The Max Miller Blue Book* (1975)

EXHIB: CG; Cambridge (1980); JDG

COLL: BM; IWM; UKCC; V&A

LIT: F. Whitford, *Trog: 40 Graphic Years* (1987)

FCG – *see* Gould, Sir Francis Carruthers

FEARON, Percy Hutton 'Poy' (1874–1948). Political/editorial cartoonist. Percy Fearon was born in Shanghai, China, on 6 September 1874, the son of Robert Inglis Fearon. He studied at the Art Students' League and Chase School of Art in New York and subsequently under Hubert Herkomer in Bushey, Hertfordshire. He began as principal cartoonist on *Judy* (1897–8) and later joined the *Manchester Evening Chronicle* (1905–7), *Daily Dispatch* and *Sunday Chronicle* (1907–13) before moving to London to work on the *Evening News* (1913–35) – his deputy was LEO CHENEY – and *Daily Mail* (1935–8). His most famous creations were John Citizen, Cuthbert the World War I conscientious objector, Dilly and Dally, Dux and Drakes, Government Gus and Dora (personifying the Defence of the Realm Act, 1914). His pseudonym is said to originate from the American pronunciation of his name – Poycee – while he was in New York. Philip Connard RA once described him as 'the prettiest draughtsman of all cartoonists'. He was a member of the Savage Club. Poy retired in 1938, being succeeded at the *Daily Mail* by

Poy (Percy Fearon), [Dilly and Dally], n.d.

Leslie Illingworth, and died in Putney on 5 November 1948.
PUB: *Poy's War Cartoons* (1915), [with W. McCartney] *Dilly and Dally in Pictures and Words* (1919), *100 Poy Cartoons* (1920), *How to Draw Newspaper Cartoons* (1936)
COLL: UKCC

FENNING, George Wilson (1882–after 1934). Joke cartoonist. Wilson Fenning was born on 6 June 1882 in Cheltenham, Gloucestershire, the son of George Fenning, a schoolmaster. He was educated at Cheltenham Grammar School and studied at Cheltenham School of Art. His cartoons appeared in *Punch* (from 1922), *Humorist, Sketch, Passing Show, London Opinion* and elsewhere.

FENWICK, Ian (*c.* 1909–1944). Joke cartoonist, illustrator and painter. Ian Fenwick was educated at Winchester College. During the 1930s and '40s he contributed to the *Bystander, Humorist, London Opinion, Men Only, Strand* (notably the 'Ranks and Regiments' series from July 1943–April 1944), *Bulldozer, News Chronicle, Sunday Dispatch* and the *Tatler*. In World War II he served in the 1st Special Air Service Regiment, achieving the rank of major before being killed in Normandy in August 1944. Influenced by Peter Arno and artists of the *New Yorker,* he also invented a cartoon character called 'Trubshaw' who features in the collection *Enter Trubshaw.*

The fictional character was reputedly based on Michael Trubshawe, a colourful and eccentric army officer who served during the war in the Highland Light Infantry with Fenwick's childhood friend, the actor David Niven. (Trubshawe was later Niven's best man and became an actor himself, appearing in *The Guns of Navarone* and other films.) Fenwick also painted London scenes in watercolours.
PUB: *The Bed Book* (1935), *I'm Telling You When and Where to Winter Sport* (1937), *Drawing Without Tears* (1938), *Start Early* (1939), *Enter Trubshaw* (1944), [with J. Barrington], *Lord Haw-Haw of Zeesen* (n.d.)
ILL: 'A. N. Other', *Pick-me-up* (1933); P. Barrington, *Songs of a Sub-Man* (1934); J. Barrington, *Lord Haw-Haw of Zeesen* (1939); J. C. Squire, *Weepings and Wailings* (1935); A. Clitheroe, *Car Canny* (1939)

FERRIER, Arthur (1891–1973). Joke cartoonist, caricaturist, illustrator and painter. Arthur Ferrier was born in Glasgow, the son of an organist. He studied analytical chemistry at Glasgow Technical College and sent his first cartoons to George Whitelaw, then cartoonist on the *Glasgow Evening News*. With Whitelaw's encouragement he began selling material to the *Glasgow Daily Record* (*c.* 1917). When the paper's editor (William McWhirter, father of the *Guinness Book of Records* twins) moved to London to edit the *Sunday Pictorial*, Ferrier followed in 1919, still working as a chemist and submitting cartoons to the paper in his spare time. He eventually took over from the *Pictorial*'s ageing staff artist G. M. Payne (brother of A. B. Payne who created the famous *Daily Mirror* strip 'Pip, Squeak and Wilfred') and made his mark with the 'Our Dumb Blonde' feature which ran for seven years (from 1939) in the paper. This was succeeded by 'Spotlight on Sally' (with Jane Hamilton as model) in *News of the World* (from 1945), 'Film Fannie' in two colours for *Everybody's* and 'Eve' (with a script by George Webb) in the *Daily Sketch* (1953–6). He also drew theatre cartoons and caricatures for *News of the World* (1923–59) and a series 'Ferrier's World Searchlight', and contributed to *Punch* (from April 1918), *Razzle, London Opinion, Parade, Everybody's, Escort, Passing Show, Strand* and *Blighty.* Best known for his pin-up pictures and cartoons featuring leggy blondes (Keith Mackenzie described him as 'the Charles Dana Gibson of his day'), his work was very popular with the troops in World War II. In addition he worked in advertising (e.g. covers and fashion plates for Hector Powe the tailors' house journal, *POW*, Bear Brand Hose, J. Lyons, Gillott & Sons and others), painted portraits in oils of society figures and stage stars such as Jack Hulbert, and owned a pet monkey. He also wrote one of the courses for the London School of Cartooning (as did FRED BUCHANAN and E. T. REED). His dictum was 'There's no better medicine than laughter.' Ferrier used Gillott 290 and 659 pens and also worked in pastels, gouache, oils, watercolour, pencil and felt-tip. He was a member of the Savage Club and the London Sketch Club. Arthur Ferrier died in the Royal Marsden Hospital, London, on 27 May 1973 at the age of 82. PUB: *Arthur Ferrier's Lovelies Brought to Life by Roye* (1941), *Beauty at Butlin's* (1946), *Arthur Ferrier's Dumb Blonde* (1946)

ffOLKES, Michael [real name Brian Davis] FCSD FSIA (1925–88). Joke cartoonist, caricaturist and illustrator. Michael ffolkes was born in London on 6 June 1925, the son of the graphic artist Walter Lawrence Davis MSIA, and Elaine Rachel Bostock. He attended Leigh Hall College, Essex, then studied art at St Martin's School of Art (1941–3) under wood-engraver John Farleigh CBE RBA RE SWE. After working in various commercial art studios he joined the Royal Navy (1943–6) and then studied painting at Chelsea School of Art (1946–9). He turned professional cartoonist soon afterwards, adopting the name of 'Michael ffolkes' after flipping through *Burke's Peerage*. His work appeared primarily in *Punch* from 1946 – he had his first drawing accepted (as 'brian') in 1942 at the age of 17 – for which he also drew regular film-star caricatures (1961–72 and 1978–88), numerous covers and illustrated David Taylor's 'Passing Through' column. He also contributed to *Strand Magazine, Leader, Lilliput, Daily Telegraph, Country Fair, Daily Sketch, Spectator, Sunday Telegraph, Playboy, Private Eye, New Yorker, Connoisseur, Reader's Digest, Basler Zeitung, Krokodil, Esquire* and *Pardon* (Germany). In addition he illustrated 'The Way of the World' column (written by Michael Wharton) in the *Daily Telegraph* from 1955 until his death, featuring such characters as Peter Simple, Dr Spaceley-Trellis, Dr Heinz Kiosk and others. ffolkes' drawings were elegant, stylish and flamboyant and often featured mythological and historical subjects, frequently adorned with large sexy ladies ('ffolkes

draws the most stylish nudes in the business' [HEWISON]). Influenced by Disney, PONT, EMETT, RONALD SEARLE, ANDRÉ FRANÇOIS, Rubens and Saul Steinberg, he worked in pen and ink and wash but was particularly adept with watercolours. Of his *Playboy* cartoons a perceptive American admirer said they were 'a mixture of buttercups and gin'. He used Daler board or Daler Langton watercolour paper and Higgins black ink or Dr Martin's coloured inks with a dip pen and a Perry Durabrite No. 16 nib, though he did sometimes also use Pentel pens and pastels. He was elected FSIA in 1968, a member of the *Punch* Table in 1978, was Vice-President of the British Cartoonists' Association and a member of the Savage and Toby Clubs. He also designed clothes for Anya Scott as 'ffanya'. Michael ffolkes died in London on 18 October 1988 at the age of 63. PUB: *ffanfare!* (1953), [with B. A. Young] *Tooth and Claw* (1958), *Hic!* (1962), *How to Draw Cartoons* (1963), *ffolkes' Companion to Sex* (1965), *ffolkes' Companion to Matrimony* (1966), *ffolkes' Companion to the Pop Scene* (1967), *Mini Art* (1968), *I'm Out of Pink* (1972), *Private Eye ffolkes* (1976), *ffolkes' ffauna* (1977), *ffolkes' Companion to Mythology* (1978), *Rude As You Please* (1981), *Ruder If You Please* (1982), *Draw Cartoons* (1982) ILL: More than 50 books including P. Roberts, *Tinpanalley* (1958); A. Russell, *The Anna Russell Song Book* (1960); M. Wharton, *The Best of Peter Simple* (1963); *The Stretchford Chronicles* (1980); M. Pyke, *Butter Side Up!* (1976); S. Raven, *The Fortunes of Fingel* (1976); N. Rees, *Quote . . . Unquote* (1978); G. Greer, *Rose Blight, the Revolting Garden* (1979); H. Vickers, *Great Operatic Disasters* (1979); A. Loos, *Gentlemen Prefer Blondes* (1985) EXHIB: RA; LG; Arthur Jeffress Gallery; CG; NFT; Palace Theatre COLL: V&A; BM; T; SAM; BFI; CAT; UKCC LIT: [autobiography] *ffundamental ffolkes* (1985)

FIDDY, Roland John (1931–99). Joke and strip cartoonist, illustrator and artist. Born in Plymouth, Devon, on 17 April 1931, the son of Eric Fiddy, a sailor in the Royal Navy and later a Police Inspector in the Naval Dockyard, Plymouth, Roland Fiddy attended Devonport High School. He studied illustration at Plymouth College of Art (1946–9) and – after National Service in the RAF (1949–51) – at the Royal West of England College of Art, Bristol (1952–3). He worked as an art teacher in Bristol for two years before turning professional cartoonist, selling his first cartoons to *Lilliput* (July 1949) and *Punch* (1952) and later contributing to the *Daily Mail, Daily* and *Sunday Express, Eagle* (e.g. writing and illustrating the 'Sir Percy Vere' strip, 1960–63), *News Chronicle, Reveille, Boys' World, Girl, Look & Learn, Everybody's, Daily Mirror, Evening Standard, Politiken, Sofia News, De Tijd, Weekend, She, Harper's Bazaar, Woman's Realm* and others. Advertising work included Thorn EMI, Kodak, American Express, Royal Bank of Scotland and Chivas Regal. In addition, he designed the logo for the Federation of European Cartoonists' Organizations. Strip cartoons by Roland Fiddy included 'Tramps' for the *Daily* and *Sunday Express* (1976–85), 'Him Indoors' for the *People* (1986–90) and 'Paying Guest' for the *Sunday Express* (1985–6). His work was syndicated by the Cartoonists' & Writers' Syndicate of the USA from 1988 and he won numerous awards for his work, including first prize at international competitions in Knokke-Heist, Belgium (1990), Netherlands International Cartoon Festival (1985, 1986), Beringen Festival, Belgium (1984, 1986), Sofia Festival (1986) and São Paolo, Brazil (1987) and medals at the Japanese Yomiuri Shimbun contest (1984–6, 1988–9 and 1991–3). Married to the Danish artist Signe Kolding he admired the work of ANDRÉ FRANÇOIS, EMETT, SEARLE, Sempé, Steig and Steinberg. He preferred to draw captionless cartoons and used a Rotring Art pen or a dip pen and indian ink, and sometimes also watercolour on handmade paper. Roland Fiddy died of cancer in Hastings on 3 July 1999.

PUB: *The Best of Fiddy* (1966), [with I. Reid] *Tramps in the Kingdom* (1979), *For Better, For Worse* (1988), *Crazy World of Love* (1988), *Crazy World of the Handyman* (1988), *Fanatic's Guides* (series of 12 books, 1989–95), *Victim's Guides* (series of 7 books, 1993–5), *That's My Cat* (1997), *I Love You* (1997), *Missing You* (1997), *An Uplifting Story* (1997)
EXHIB: [paintings and illustration] RA; Odense Art Gallery, Denmark; Hastings Museum & Art Gallery; Horsham Arts Centre, Sussex
COLL: UKCC

FIELD, John – *see* Friell, James

FISH, Anne Harriet (1890–1964). Caricaturist, joke and strip cartoonist, illustrator, painter and designer. Anne Fish was born in Brynland Avenue, Horfield, Bristol on 27 March 1890,

Most women live for the present, and the handsomer the present, the better they live.

Anne Fish, in S. Tremayne, *Tatlings*, 1922

the daughter of Benjamin Fish, an accountant. The family then moved to Ealing, West London, and she was educated at home before studying art under C. M. Q. Orchardson and GEORGE BELCHER, and at the JOHN HASSALL School of Art (then called the New School of Art). She began work as a book illustrator for John Lane (possibly introduced by Hassall), her first title being *Behind the Beyond* (1913) by the Canadian humorist Stephen Leacock. She also contributed to US magazines such as *Vogue* and *Vanity Fair* (including covers) before, recommended by Hassall, she met the editor of the *Sketch* and began contributing to the magazine (1914). This led to a commission from the *Tatler* to illustrate a new satirical 'society' feature, 'The Letters of Eve' (written by Mrs Maitland Davies), which first appeared on 20 May 1914 and for which she is best known. The original series spawned three 'Eve' books (1916–19), 'drawn by Fish and written by "Fowl"' (the *Tatler*'s Editor, Edward Huskinson), an exhibition at the Fine Art Society (1916) and 12 silent two-reel comedy films produced by Gaumont (1918). In addition Fish contributed humorous illustrations, caricatures and joke cartoons to *Eve, Punch, London Calling, Vanity Fair, Vogue, Harper's Bazaar, Cosmopolitan* and others. She also painted in oils and watercolour, etched, created textile designs for her husband Walter Sefton (a Belfast linen manufacturer), and drew advertisements for Abdulla Cigarettes, Eno's Salts, Erasmic, cosmetic companies and others. The original 'Eve' feature was not limited to the usual single- or multi-panel format but often spread over a complete page. A spoof on social butterflies and heroic-looking but ultimately helpless Edwardian men, it was a great success, as much for its decorative fashion-style drawing as for its satire on a society that the war and universal suffrage would change for ever. The eponymous heroine herself (a Bright Young Thing) had an oval face, no nose and a tiny dot for a mouth with a single curl of her otherwise bobbed black hair showing in the centre of her forehead. Very slim and always fashionably dressed, she was depicted attending country-house parties, visiting crusty relations and doing her bit for the war effort as a nurse, postal worker, police auxiliary, etc., in a world peopled with caricatured social types such as Lady Amelia Frump and Reggie Nutt-Slacker. She also had two almost identical sisters, Evelyn and Evelinda, a Pekinese lap-dog, Tou-Tou, and an army officer husband, Adam. Such was her popularity that there was even spin-off merchandising such as one-inch-high Eve figurine jewellery charms, a Tou-Tou stuffed toy and an 'Eve' waltz. Anne Fish continued to illustrate Mrs Davies' text until 1920 when the series was transferred to *Pan*, where it was illustrated by Jo White and then Dolly Tree. Fish drew in pencil, pen and ink, and watercolour and in her lavishly produced edition of Fitzgerald's *Rubaiyat of Omar Khayyam* also used gold and solid colours. An admirer of Burne-Jones and Beardsley, her preference for solid blacks and fine lines echoes the work of the latter (who was also published by John Lane) in some degree though not consciously so, as she 'only saw Beardsley's work some time after I was told I copied his style' (*Drawing & Design*, September 1923). Her most familiar drawings often have no backgrounds and the figures no shadows, with long-line shading mostly being used rather than cross-hatching or wash and fine dotted lines to show pleats, folds, furs, steam, etc. A member of the Arts Theatre Club, the Penwith Society of Artists,

the Newlyn Society of Artists and the St Ives Old Society of Artists, she retired to St Ives in Cornwall in the late 1940s and thereafter concentrated on painting, mostly landscapes and cats. Anne Fish died in St Ives on 10 October 1964.
PUB: [with 'Fowl'] *The Eve Book* (1916), *The New Eve Book* (1917), *The Third Eve Book* (1919); [with M. Lavington] *The Noah's Ark Book* (1918); [with D. Parker *et al.*], *High Society* (1920), *Awful Weekends – and Guests* (1938), *All's Well that Ends Swell* (1939)
ILL: S. Leacock, *Behind the Beyond* (1913), *The Marionettes' Calendar 1916* (1915), *Further Foolishness* (1917); G. Frankau, *One of Us* (1917); three books by Lady K. Vincent (1925–7); E. Fitzgerald, *The Rubaiyat of Omar Khayyam* (1922); R. Holmes, *Clock and Cockatoo* (1922); S. Tremayne, *Tatlings* (1922); H. J. C. Graham, *The World We Laugh In* (1924)
EXHIB: FAS (1916); RA; Dulwich (1987); London Salon
COLL: V&A
LIT: W. Connelly, 'A Pretty Kettle of Fish', *Journal of the Decorative Arts Society*, Autumn 1999

FITTON, James RA FSIA (1899–82). Painter, graphic designer, illustrator and joke cartoonist. James Fitton was born in Oldham, Lancashire, on 11 February 1899, the son of James Fitton, an engineer. He attended Watersheddings Board School, Oldham (1904–13), and left aged 14 to to become apprenticed to a calico print designer. At the suggestion of Suffragette leader Christabel Pankhurst he sent some of his cartoons to Britain's first Labour newspaper, the *Daily Citizen* in Manchester (where TOM WEBSTER was sports cartoonist), which published them and employed him as an office boy in its circulation department (1915) until the paper closed later the same year. He then worked for a textile merchant (1915–21) while taking evening classes at Manchester School of Art, where he was a contemporary and close friend of L. S. Lowry. He moved to London *c.* 1920 and was a studio assistant with Johnson Riddell Printers before turning freelance illustrator and designer, working for British Gas Association, Lasky Films, etc., producing cartoons for the *Daily Worker* as 'Alpha' and studying at the Central School of Art under A. S. Hartrick in the evenings. In 1933 he taught lithography at the Central School (pupils included his friends PEARL BINDER, JAMES BOSWELL and

EDWARD ARDIZZONE), and in the same year was a founder member, with James Boswell, of the left-wing Artists' International Association. He, Boswell and James Holland – all committed socialist illustrators – were known as the 'Three Jameses'. During World War II he produced posters for the Ministry of Information and Ministry of Food (1939–45) and was later Art Director of C. Vernon & Sons advertising agency and Chief Assessor to the Ministry of Education National Diploma of Design (1940–65). He also designed posters for London Transport, Abbey National, Shell and Ealing Studios films such as *Kind Hearts and Coronets*. Elected ARA in 1944 and RA in 1954, he contributed humorous illustrations and joke cartoons to *Lilliput*, *Left Review*, *Everyman*, *Our Time*, *Leader*, *John Bull*, *Guardian*, *Daily Express*, *Evening Standard*, *Strand Magazine* and *Time & Tide*. Influenced by George Grosz, Fitton's cartoons were drawn in ink, watercolour, wash and crayon (sometimes also including newspaper cuttings). Regarded as one of the finest graphic designers of the 1930s, he also painted in oils and watercolours, produced lithographs and designed stage sets (he was also co-designer, with John Minton, of the Chelsea Arts Ball in 1953). Fitton was also a member of the Art Panel of the Arts Council, a Trustee of the British Museum (1969–75) and a member of the Senefelder Club and painted a mural for the Festival of Britain in 1951. He was married to the painter and illustrator Margaret Cook. James Fitton died in Dulwich, London, on 2 May 1982.
PUB: [with H. F. Hutchinson] *The First Six Months Are the Worst* (1939), [with S. Pearce] *Hyacinth Pink* (1947)
EXHIB: Arthur Tooth Gallery; RSAB; GI; L; LG; NEAC; RA; RG; COO; Zwemmers; Manchester Academy of Fine Arts; W; LON
COLL: CAS; T; V&A; BM; IWM; CA; Museum of Western Art, Moscow

FIX – *see* Kelly, Felix Runcie

FLAM – *see* Mendoza, Philip

FLATTER, Joseph Otto (1894–1988). Political cartoonist, painter and illustrator. Joseph Flatter was born in Brigittenau, Vienna, on 26 May 1894 and was a student at the Royal Academy of Fine Art in the city when World War I broke out. He served in the Austrian Imperial Army

and after the war earned a living as a portrait painter and art lecturer. He came to England in 1934 to research English art for a lecture tour of Czechoslovakia but in 1936, aware of the growing power of the Nazis, decided to stay. In 1940 he was arrested and interned on the Isle of Wight, despite being classified as a 'harmless alien'. However, after he had spent three months as camp cook the Ministry of Information – at the suggestion of DAVID LOW and others – procured his release to work on anti-Nazi cartoons for its Overseas Department. He also drew for the Belgian Refugee Government, a Free French newspaper, *Die Zeitung* (a German paper published in London), *Sunday Dispatch* and the *Sketch*. In addition he produced a series of illustrations satirizing Hitler's *Mein Kampf*, which were exhibited around the country and in 1946 he was sent to Nuremberg to draw the defendants in the Nazi War Crimes Trials. Before 1937 he worked in oils and charcoal; during World War II he used pens, brushes and ink, heightened with colour; and after the war he used gouache. Flatter wrote an unpublished autobiography, 'A Painter's Monologue'.
EXHIB: Künstlerhaus, Vienna (1981); RP; Wiener Library
COLL: Vorarlberger Landesarchiv, Bregenz, Austria; Dokumentationszentrum des Österreichischen Widerstandes, Vienna; IWM; V&A

'Flook' – *see* Fawkes, Walter Ernest

FLUCK, Peter (b. 1941). Political cartoonist, caricaturist, animator and writer. Peter Fluck was born on 7 April 1941 in Cambridge, the son of Herbert William Fluck, a gardener, and attended Cambridge Art School (1957–62) where he met ROGER LAW. He was later paste-up artist on *Private Eye*, artist-reporter on *New Statesman* and produced political cartoons for *Labour Weekly* (1971–81). In addition, he has produced models for covers of the *Economist*, illustrations for *Radio Times* and other work for the *New York Times*, *Der Spiegel*, *Panorama* (Netherlands), *National Lampoon* and Penguin Books. (For details of the 'Luck and Flaw' partnership and 'Spitting Image' see entry for Roger Law.) Other work has included caricature animation and robotics and he is currently creating abstract kinetic sculptures. For his caricature work he used pen, plasticine and clay. With Roger Law he was given the CAT Lifetime Achievement Award in 1998.

PUB: [as Spitting Image] *The Appallingly Disrespectful Spitting Image Book* (1985), *Spitting Images* (1987), *The Appallingly Disrespectful Spitting Image Giant Komic Book* (1988), *Goodbye* (1992), *Thatcha – The Real Maggie Memoirs* (1993)
ILL: [as Luck & Flaw] C. Dickens, *A Christmas Carol* (1979), R. L. Stevenson, *Treasure Island* (1986); L. Chester, *Tooth & Claw – The Inside Story of Spitting Image* (1986)
EXHIB: [as Spitting Image] CG

FORD, Frank (fl. 1930–51). Joke cartoonist and illustrator. Frank Ford worked at first in business and for a well-known London publishing company before becoming a freelance artist, contributing to *London Opinion, Strand, Night & Day, Men Only, Passing Show, Punch, Lilliput, Razzle, Pie, Tatler* and the *Bystander*. In addition he drew advertisements for Grey's Cigarettes and others. He worked in pen and ink, pencil, crayon and wash and his style shows the influence of *New Yorker* artists such as Whitney Darrow and Peter Arno.
PUB: *You Needn't Laugh!* (1935), [with G. Ford] *Digby's Holiday* (1951)
ILL: D. Fiske, *Why Should Penguins Fly?* (1937)

FORD, Noel (b. 1942). Editorial and joke cartoonist and author/illustrator of children's books. Noel Ford was born on 22 December 1942 in Nuneaton, Warwickshire, the son of Thomas Joseph Ford, company fireman at Courtaulds, and was educated at King Edward VI Grammar School, Nuneaton, and Birmingham College of Arts & Crafts (1958). He was lead guitarist in a travelling rock band (appearing on TV's *New Faces* talent show), a furniture salesman, lab technician, clerk and screenprinter before drawing political cartoons for electoral reform author John Creasey. His first cartoon was published in the *Nuneaton Evening Tribune* in 1968. He then dabbled in short-story writing for magazines and BBC Radio, turning full-time cartoonist in February 1975. Deputy Editorial Cartoonist to BILL CALDWELL on the *Daily Star* (1979–92), he has also been Editorial Cartoonist on the *Church Times* since September 1989. In addition he has contributed to *Private Eye, Punch* (from 1976 and including over 30 cover illustrations), *Weekend, Truck & Driver, The Golfer* and others. In addition he has worked in advertising for companies such as Coopers & Lybrand (also illustrating their annual calendar 1991–8), Thomas Cook, Digital, Guinness,

British Telecom, Mercury, Mercedes Benz, Legal & General, Hamlet Cigars, etc., and has designed greetings cards (one of which was voted Best Humorous Greetings Card 1989/90). The awards which he has won for his work have included medals in the Yomiuri Shimbun contests, United Nations Cartoonists Against Drug Abuse Exhibition and others. He was also voted Dog Cartoonist of the Year by the National Canine Defence League/Spillers Bonio (1990). Noel Ford was a founder member of the Cartoonists' Guild and was a founder and is currently a Course Director of the College of Cartoon Art. He uses Pelikan and Lamy fountain pens on laser-printer paper. However, in recent years all his colour work has been produced on a Macintosh G3 computer using a Wacom graphics tablet and stylus.
PUB: *Deadly Humorous* (1984), *Golf Widows* (1988), *Cricket Widows* (1989), *Business Widows* (1990), *Nuts* (1991), *Limeroons* (1991), *The Lost Wag* (1993), *An Earful of Aliens* (1993), *Diary of an Alien* (1994), *The Greedy Ghost* (1996)
ILL: Many books including A. Davidson's 'Catfoot' series; J. Hunter's 'Harry, Mari & Squib' series; J. Rothman, *The Cannibal Cookbook* (1982)
EXHIB: Nuneaton Art Gallery; Belgrade Theatre, Coventry; BC
COLL: MOCA

'The Fosdyke Saga' – *see* Tidy, William Edward

FOTIS, Fotis (b. 1933). Political and joke cartoonist, caricaturist, painter and sculptor. Fotis was born in Athens, Greece, on 18 October 1933 and studied at the Academy of Fine Arts in Athens, in Munich and at the London School of Printing. In the 1950s he freelanced for various Greek newspapers and magazines as well as *Die Wochen Presse, Stern, La Presse, Münchner Illustrierte*, etc. He then moved to the USA and joined the staff of the *New York Herald-Tribune* (joke cartoons, 1963) and produced graphic designs for advertising agencies and book publishers. He was Political Cartoonist on *Nation* magazine (1964–5) and returned to Greece in 1978 where he was Media and Communication Adviser to the Minister of Communications (1978–80). He then became Political Cartoonist on the national daily *Mesimvrini* (1980–86). In addition he has contributed to the *Daily Mirror, Daily Sketch, Punch, Evening Standard, Birmingham Evening Dispatch, Saturday Review, True, Post,*

This Week and others and has produced sculpture and paintings for private commissions from 1964 until the present day. His son Evan Fotis is also a cartoonist and caricaturist.

EXHIB: Fotis Art Centre, Athens

FOUGASSE – *see* Bird, Cyril Kenneth

'Fragments from France' – *see* Bairnsfather, Charles Bruce

FRANCIS, Clive (b. 1946). Actor and caricaturist. Best known as a theatre, TV and film actor, Clive Francis was born on 26 June 1946 in Eastbourne, Sussex, the great-nephew of the landscape painter Donald Towner and the son of the actor Raymond Francis. He attended Ratton Secondary Modern School and studied at the local art school on Saturday mornings but gave up at the age of 13. He later joined RADA and after several years in repertory made his first West End appearance in *There's a Girl in My Soup* (1966). Since then he has made more than 100 TV appearances and performed with the RSC, National and Chichester theatre groups. It was Towner who first introduced him to Beardsley and the posters of Toulouse-Lautrec, both of whom were an early influence on his style. Later artists he has admired are BEER-BOHM, BENTLEY, NERMAN, SHERRIFFS, SEARLE, Covarrubias and Hirschfeld. He began caricaturing professionally in 1983 (creating a series of theatrical greetings cards) and has designed posters for productions at the London Palladium and National Theatre as well as covers for many books. Of his work he has written: 'Caricature is in a way rather akin to plastic surgery. As bits are taken away so bits are added on. The only difference being that the caricaturist reveals, mercilessly, warts, tucks and all . . . I would define my work as tongue-in-cheek portraiture.' Clive Francis works in ink and gouache and uses a brush. He is married to the actress Natalie Ogle.

PUB: *Laugh Lines* (1989), *Sir John: The Many Faces of Gielgud* (1994), *There is Nothing Like a Dane* (1998)

ILL: J. Gielgud, *Stage Directions* (1987), *Early Stages* (1987); A. Guinness, *Blessings in Disguise* (1985); M. Denison, *Double Act* (1985); C. Freud, *Clement Freud's Book of Hangovers* (1986); G. Smith, *Stephane Grappelli* (1987); Kestelman and Penhaligon, *A Two Hander* (1996); R. Briers, *Coward and Company* (1999)

EXHIB: IML Gallery; Snow Goose Gallery, Brighton; Lyric Theatre; NT (1988, 1989, 1994); Norwich Playhouse; RSG; Vaudeville Theatre

FRANÇOIS, André [real name Andre Farkas] (b. 1915). Joke cartoonist, illustrator, designer, painter and sculptor. André François was born in Timisoara, Romania, on 9 November 1915, the son of Albert Farkas, and studied at the Budapest School of Fine Arts before moving to France in 1934. There he studied with poster artist A. M. Cassandre (1935–6) before beginning to draw cartoons under the name 'André François' in 1944. Influenced at first by the French cartoonists Jean Effel and Raymond Peynet, he has contributed to *La Tribune des Nations* (1953–60), *Holiday*, *Sports Illustrated*, *Femina*, *Lilliput*, *Vogue* (France), *Life*, *Punch* (including covers), *New Yorker*, *Esquire* and *Fortune* (including covers for these last four) and others. He has also worked in advertising for Kodak, Olivetti, Wilmot Breeden car components, Citroën, Pirelli and Esso and produced animated TV ads for Jack-in-the-Box restaurants and the American Gas Association. In addition he has designed stage sets for Roland Petit's ballet company (1956), Peter Hall's *The Merry Wives of Windsor* (1958) and Gene Kelly's *Pas de*

André François (Andre Farkas), *André François' Double Bedside Book*, 1952

79

Dieux (1960). He feels his work is more a defence against what goes on in the world around him than an attack upon it. Since 1960 he has concentrated mostly on painting. He is a Chevalier de la Légion d'Honneur and is an Honorary Doctor of the University of London (RCA). François' deceptively rough-hewn, scratchy line and child-like style has been much admired by artists such as RONALD SEARLE and QUENTIN BLAKE. The latter said of his work: 'Part of the charm is that the drawings don't appear to have gone through a process of preparation; it is as though they had just been scratched down on the paper at the moment they were thought of. And yet they are instinct with a sense of drawing.'
PUB: *Issy-les-Brioches* (1946), [with Chaval and Mose] *Magnigances* (1952), *Andre Francois' Double Bedside Book* (1952), *The Tattooed Sailor* (1953), *Mit Gesträubten Federn* (1955), *The Half-Naked Knight* (1958), *The Biting Eye* (1960), *Penguin André François* (1964), *You are Ri-di-cu-lous* (1970), *André François* (1976), *Sirènades* (1998)
ILL: Diderot, *Jacques le Fataliste* (1947); J. Symonds, *William Waste* (1947); Balzac, *Contes Drôlatiques* (1957); A. Jarry, *Ubu-Roi* (1958); J. le Marchand, *The Adventures of Ulysses* (1960); J. Prévert, *Lettre des Îles Baladar* (1952); R. McGough, *Mr Noselighter* (1976); Queneau, *Si Tu Imagines* (1979); B. Vian, *L'Arrache-Cœur* (1982) and many children's books
EXHIB: New York; Galerie Delpire, Paris; Stedelijk Museum, Amsterdam; MAD; Chicago Arts Club; Palais des Papes, Avignon; Musée Saint-George, Liège; Musée Tavet, Pontoise; Galerie Bartsch-Chariau, Munich; MAM (retrospective, 1986); Château-Musée, Dieppe; Mitsukoshi Museum, Tokyo (retrospective, 1995); Rupertinum, Salzburg

FRANKLIN, Stanley Arthur (b. 1930). Editorial/political and strip cartoonist and caricaturist. Born on 30 October 1930 in Bow, London, Stanley Franklin studied lithography at Mornington Crescent Working Men's College (1946–8) and life drawing at Hammersmith School of Arts & Crafts (1948–51). His staff cartoon work began with the 'Mr Farthing' strip on the *Daily Herald* (1954–5) and he later became Political Cartoonist for the *Daily Mirror* (May 1959–70). He was then Editorial Cartoonist on the *Sun* (1974–98) – taking over from RIGBY. He has also freelanced as a political cartoonist for the *New Statesman* (1974) and produced cartoon graphics

for BBC TV comedy shows (1971–3) such as *The Marty Feldman Show, Them* and *Lame Ducks*. Other work has included 'relief painting' and making pottery figurines (including six London characters for the Royal Adderley Pottery, Stoke-on-Trent in 1971). Voted CCGB Cartoonist of the Year as well as Social and Political Cartoonist of the Year (1981), Franklin was also awarded a Victor Silvester gold medal for ballroom-dancing (1958). He works with a mapping pen and brush and draws a third up on Bristol board. Franklin's mascot is the little man with a big nose called Raspberry (so called because of his spotty nose) who appears looking on in all his cartoons (a pigeon was added when he joined the *Sun*). He was one of the founder members of the British Cartoonists' Association in 1966.
ILL: J. Speight, *The Thoughts of Chairman Alf* (1973), *Alf Garnett Scripts* (1973); *Dick Emery in Character* (1973)
EXHIB: [relief paintings, pottery and drawings] Daily Mirror Building; Treadwell Gallery; Richmond Art Gallery, Surrey
COLL: NPG; [Falklands War cartoons] IWM; [Silver Jubilee Cartoons] Buckingham Palace; [relief paintings] Dunedin Art Gallery, New Zealand

FRASER, Eric George FSIA (1902–83). Illustrator, painter, commercial artist, art teacher and joke cartoonist. Eric Fraser was born at 39 Vincent St, Westminster, on 11 June 1902, the son of a solicitor's clerk. He was educated at Westminster City School (1913–19), attended SICKERT's evening classes at Westminster School of Art while still at school, and won a scholarship to study at Goldsmith's College of Art (1919–24) under E. J. SULLIVAN and Clive Gardiner. He received his first commission from his agent, R. P. Gossop, in 1923 and the following year his etching 'The Glass House' was exhibited at the Royal Academy. Thereafter he contributed illustrations and joke cartoons to numerous publications including *Radio Times* (from 1926), *Harper's Bazaar* (from 1929), *Britannia & Eve, Bystander, Leader, Lilliput, Listener, Nash's, Night & Day, Men Only* (covers), *Vogue, Art & Industry, Studio, London Mystery Magazine, London Opinion* and *Punch*. At one time he shared a studio with Milner Gray and he also taught graphic design part-time at Camberwell School of Art & Crafts (1928–40) and fashion and figure composition at the Reimann School, Westminster (1938–9). In addition he produced a considerable amount of commercial art (for example, designing Barkers Christmas catalogue, advertisements for Guinness, Goddard's Silver Polishes, etc., and, in 1933, creating the famous 'Mr Therm' character for the Gas, Light & Coke Company). In 1938 he designed a mural for the Ministry of Health and during World War II served as an ARP Warden. He also produced murals for the Festival of Britain's Origin of the Peoples Pavilion (1951) and for the British Pavilion at the Brussels Exposition (1958). One of the first ten people to be elected FSIA (1945) he was also a member of the Art Workers' Guild (1935) and an Honorary Member of the Association of Illustrators (1978). Influenced at first by E. J. Sullivan as an illustrator, Eric Fraser was an extremely versatile artist who also practised etching and lithography, and designed stained-glass windows for the church of St Mary the Virgin, Hampton, Middlesex (1960–63), in which he is buried. His best-known work is in pen-and-ink or scraperboard, notably book illustrations and jackets for the Folio Society (1952–79), Golden Cockerel Press, Everyman Library and others. He sometimes signed his work 'ef'. Eric Fraser died at his home, Penn's Place, 9 Church St, Hampton, Middlesex, on 15 November 1983.

ILL: Many books including H. T. Russell, *Brighter French for Bright Young People Who Already Know Some* (1927); E. V. Knox, *Here's Misery!* (1928); *The Complete Shakespeare* (1951); Tacitus, *The Reign of Nero* (1952); I. Nievo, *The Castle of Fratta* (1954); C. Kingsley, *The Golden Fleece* (1965); Ovid, *The Art of Love* (1971); J. R. R. Tolkien, *The Lord of the Rings* (1977), *The Hobbit* (1979); H. Mitchnik, *Egyptian and Sudanese Folk Tales* (1978); O. Wilde, *Three Fairy Tales* (1983)

EXHIB: Many exhibitions including RA; V&A 'The Art of *Radio Times*' (1981–2); RCA 'Eric Fraser, An Illustrator of Our Time' (1991); Qantas Gallery; Bentall's Gallery, Kingston; Kingston Art Gallery; RFH; Orleans House Gallery, Twickenham (retrospective, 1986); Graves Art Gallery, Sheffield; SSA (1986)

COLL: V&A; BM

LIT: A. Davis, *The Graphic Work of Eric Fraser* (1974); S. Backemeyer, *Eric Fraser: Designer & Illustrator* (1998)

FRASER, Peter (1888–1950). Joke and strip cartoonist and illustrator. Born in the Shetlands on 6 November 1888, Peter Fraser studied at the Central School of Arts & Crafts and via PERCY BRADSHAW's correspondence course. He worked in the City of London (1907–10) and first contributed to *Punch* in 1912, producing nearly 200 illustrations for the magazine up to 1941. He also drew for *Sketch*, *Time & Tide*, *Passing Show*, *Happy Days* (strips 'Jim Crow' and 'Pip the Pup'), *Humorist* and *Tatler*. During World War I he served as a gunner in the Royal Field Artillery and the Royal Garrison Artillery in France for three years. Many of his drawings featured Cockney children whom he met during his work in missions in Old Kent Road and Stepney. He also designed the 'Animal Frolics' pottery series for James Kent Ltd (*c.* 1946). Peter Fraser died on 5 March 1950.

PUB: *Funny Animals* (1921), *Tufty Tales* (1932), *Moving Day* (1945); 10 books with E. Fraser including *Chuffy* (1942), *Duckling to Dance* (1944), *Jack and Jock's Great Discovery* (1944), *Camping Out* (1945) and *Binky the Bear Cub* (1945)

ILL: W. H. Harrison, *Humour in the East End* (1933); S. Rye, *The Blackberry Picnic* (1946), *Bevis and the Giant* (1948)

'Freaky Fables' – *see* Handelsman, John Bernard

'Fred Basset' – *see* Graham, Alexander Steel

FRIELL, James 'Gabriel' (1912–97). Political cartoonist and journalist. James Friell was born in Glasgow on 13 March 1912, the son of James Friell, an actor. Leaving school at 14 he worked at first in a solicitor's office and taught himself to be a cartoonist, freelancing regularly for local papers, especially the *Glasgow Evening Times* (1930–39). He then studied commercial art at Glasgow School of Art (1930) from where he was recruited as a 'graphics man' by the advertising department of Kodak who sent him to London in 1932. Billed as 'Fleet Street's greatest discovery since DAVID LOW', he joined the *Daily Worker* as Political Cartoonist in February 1936 (as 'Gabriel') while also contributing to *World's Press News*. In World War II he served in the Royal Artillery (1940–46) but was kept under observation as a 'Dangerous Red' by the War Office. He helped set up *Soldier* magazine in 1944, working as cartoonist, art editor, layout man and printer liaison, and also contributed to *Seven* (including covers) and *Bulldozer* (including covers), signing himself 'Jas F.', 'Gnr Friell' or 'Jas Friell'. He rejoined the *Daily Worker* in 1946 but left when the Soviet Union invaded

"I COME AS A HERALD OF PEACE" *Herr Hitler*

Gabriel (James Friell), [Goebbels, Hitler], *Daily Worker*, 20 March 1936

Hungary in 1956 and joined the *Evening Standard* (1957–62) under Editor Charles Wintour, drawing as 'Friell' and succeeding EMMWOOD. In 1962 he left the *Standard* and worked freelance for Thames TV and others before joining *New Civil Engineer* as its first cartoonist (1972–88), drawing as 'Field'. He also produced advertisements for Murray's Mellow Mixture Tobacco and others, and was awarded a Bronze Medal at the International Film and TV Festival for his cartoons for the Grand Metropolitan Catering Service. James Friell retired in 1988 aged 75 and died at his home in Ealing, West London, on 4 February 1997.

PUB: *Gabriel Cartoons* (1938), [with Dyad] *Daily Worker Cartoons* (1944), *Gabriel's 1946 Review* (1946)

ILL: [as John Field] D. Gamblin, *Water on the Brain* (1979)

EXHIB: UKCC

COLL: UKCC

FRIERS, Rowel Boyd MBE RUA UWS (1920–98). Painter, illustrator, designer, pocket, strip, political and joke cartoonist. Rowel Friers was born in Belfast, Northern Ireland, on 13 April 1920, the youngest son of William Friers, Cashier for the Irish Distillery, Belfast. He was educated at the Boyd Endowment School, Belfast, and Park Parade School but left at 16 to be apprenticed as a lithographic and letterpress artist with the poster printers S. C. Allen. The same year he won a drawing competition in the *Belfast Telegraph* and in 1937 graduated to poster and showcard design at Allens while studying two afternoons a week and most evenings at the Belfast Municipal College of Art (1935–43). His first cartoon (a strip on the Russo-Finnish War) was published in *Portsmouth Evening News* (1940) after his brother Ian, a sculptor, showed it to a Royal Naval Volunteer Reservist who was a journalist for the paper. In payment he received 10s. 6d. at a time when his weekly

wages were 6s. 6d. When the printers went into liquidation (1940) he studied full-time at the art college and then started a commercial studio. He later contributed to *Dublin Opinion* (from 1943, later becoming its Associate Art Editor), *Reynolds News, News Letter* (from 1990), *Economist, Irish Press, Courier, Everybody's, Belfast Telegraph* ('NewSlant' cartoons), *Irish Times, Punch, Daily Express, London Opinion, Radio Times, Sunday Independent* and *Men Only*. In addition he produced watercolours, oil paintings and murals (for the Ministry of Food during World War II and in Belfast restaurants) and was a member of the Committee and Council of the Royal Ulster Academy. Elected a full Academician of the RUA in 1953, he was later its Vice-President (1960–61) and President (1993–7). He became a member of the Ulster Watercolour Society in 1977, was awarded an MBE in 1977 for his 'contributions to journalism and broadcasting', and received an Honorary MA from the Open University in 1981. A member of the Board of Governors of Belfast College of Art, he was also on the Board of Trustees of the National Self-Portrait Gallery, University of Limerick. An admirer of ILLINGWORTH, EMETT, GEORGE MORROW, SCARFE, SEARLE and STEADMAN, he also designed more than 100 stage sets for theatre and opera, and worked for Ulster TV and the BBC. Regarding the Troubles he said: 'As far as politics is concerned, the only side I am on is sanity. I just make fun of all the madness,' and he liked to quote Bill Beckett ('Maskee') of *Dublin Opinion* who once said 'Humour is the safety valve of a nation.' Rowel Friers died at his home in Holywood, Co. Down, Northern Ireland, on 21 September 1998.
PUB: *Wholly Friers* (1950), *Mainly Spanish* (1951), *Riotous Living* (1971), *Pig in the Parlour* (1972), *The Book of Friers* (1973), *The Revolting Irish* (1974), *On the Borderline* (1982), *Trouble Free!* (1988), *Friers Country* (1992)
ILL: More than 50 books including J. McNeill (nine titles, 1955–70); R. Harbinson, *Tattoo Lily* (1961); W. White, *The Beedy Book* (1965); F. M. McDowell, *Other Days Around Me* (1966); W. B. Yeats (ed.), *Irish Folk Tales* (1973); C. Cusack, *The Humour is On Me* (1980)
EXHIB: CB; Grendor Gallery, Holywood; Davis Gallery, Dublin; Irwin Gallery, Armagh; Seymour Gallery, Lisburn
COLL: UAA; NPG; National Self-Portrait Collection, University of Limerick
LIT: R. Friers, *Drawn from Life* (1994)

'Fred Clueless' – *see* Colvin, Neville

FURNISS, Harry (1854–1925). Caricaturist, joke and political cartoonist, illustrator, author, lecturer and film producer. Harry Furniss was born in Wexford, Ireland, on 26 March 1854, the son of James Furniss, a civil engineer from Yorkshire, by his second wife. His mother was the miniaturist painter Isabella Mackenzie, daughter of the Scottish topographer, printer and newspaper publisher Eneas Mackenzie, who founded the Mechanics' Institution, Newcastle. Educated at the Wesleyan College, Dublin (where he produced *The Schoolboy's Punch*), he studied at the Royal Hibernian Schools and the Hibernian Academy. His first published cartoon appeared in *Zozimus* on 31 August 1870 (signed 'H. Fs'). He worked at first as a clerk to a wood-engraver, who taught him to engrave, and in 1873 moved to England, working at first for *London Society* and then as an illustrator and graphic reporter for the *Illustrated London News* (from 1876) and *Illustrated Sporting & Dramatic News*. He also contributed to *Black & White, Pall Mall Budget, Cassell's, Cornhill, English Illustrated Magazine, Good Words, Graphic, Daily News* (parliamentary illustrations from 1896), *Illustrated Bits, Pall Mall Magazine, Pears Annual, Pearson's, St James's Budget, Sketch, Vanity Fair* and the *Windsor Magazine*. His first cartoons were published in *Punch* on 30 October 1880, and he was made a member of the Table in 1884. For the next three decades (until 1894) he contributed more than 2600 drawings to the magazine, including jokes, illustrations, drama criticism, headings and parliamentary sketches. He is perhaps best known for his drawing of a tramp (who Charles Keene alleged was a portrait of himself) writing a letter: 'I used your soap two years ago; since then I have used no other.' *Punch* later sold the copyright in the cartoon to Pears Soap and it subsequently became a very famous advertisement. In addition, in 1881 he took over from LINLEY SAMBOURNE as the illustrator of the 'Essence of Parliament' feature (being himself succeeded by E. T. REED) and created the image of Gladstone with an enormous winged collar (but believing that in Britain 'we never make capital out of our subjects' deformities', he always drew him with the missing first finger on his left hand intact). He left *Punch* in 1894 and set up the weekly *Lika Joko* (a pseudonym he had first used at *Punch*), which sold 140,000 copies on its first day. Then in 1895

'INTERVIEWED!'

Harry Furniss, [self-portrait, Harry How], in H. How, 'Illustrated Interviews', *Strand Magazine*, Vol. V, 1893

he merged *Lika Joko* with *Pall Mall Budget* to form the short-lived *New Budget* (contributing to it himself under many pseudonyms including A. S. Cribble, A. Newman, J. Owen and W. Kayess). An admirer of Dürer, Rowlandson, Rembrandt, Charles Keene ('the greatest artist in black and white England ever produced') and Maroni (whose *Tailor* he thought the best portrait ever painted), he rarely used an easel but preferred to work standing up at a waist-high desk. He drew in pen and ink but also worked in chalk and painted in watercolours and oils (including 87 canvases lampooning the Royal Academy shows). He was 'not a great draughtsman . . . [but] a very experienced pictorial journalist who could work fast and get a likeness easily. It is said that he would chat to a man and caricature him on a pad held in his pocket' (Price). He could also write backwards well (a skill he learned while reversing his drawings for woodblock engraving) and once sent a cheque to Linley Sambourne signed in this manner (it was accepted by the bank). In addition he was a good mimic and toured Britain (from 1888) with his illustrated lectures on the 'Humours of Parliament' and 'The Frightfulness of Humour'. Highly inventive, he only once accepted a cartoon idea from someone else (Lewis Carroll). He later worked for the Edison Film Company in the USA (1912) and himself wrote and produced animated films, such as *War Cartoons* (1914) and *Peace and Pencillings* (1914). In addition he illustrated Dickens and Thackeray, wrote and illustrated children's books, designed postcards (e.g. the 'Free Trade' political cartoon series for John Walker & Co.) and drew posters for Bovril and others. He was a member of the Savage Club (designing the menu for the 25th anniversary dinner in 1882 at which Edward VII, then Prince of Wales, was present) and the Garrick Club. His daughter Dorothy (who was later herself an illustrator) modelled for many of the girls in his drawings, his son Lawrence was the child in Burton Barber's *Bethgelert* and Furniss himself was the model for John Brown in the portrait commissioned by Queen Victoria from Barber. Harry Furniss died at his home The Mount, High Wickham, Hastings, Sussex, on 14 January 1925.

PUB: More than 20 books including *Pictures at Play* (1881), *A River Holiday* (1883), *Parliamentary News* (1885), *Harry Furniss's Royal Academy* (1887), *MPs in Session* (1889), *Royal Academy Antics* (1890), *Our Joe* (1903), *Harry Furniss at Home* (1904), *How to Draw in Pen and Ink* (1905), *More About How to Draw in Pen and Ink* (1915), *Garrick Gallery Caricatures* (1923), *Some Victorian Women* (1923), *Some Victorian Men* (1924), *The Two Pins Club* (1925), [novel] *Poverty Bay* (1905)

ILL: Many books including G. A. Henty, *Seaside Maiden* (1880); L. Sterne, *Tristram Shandy* (1883); W. Besant, *All in a Garden Fair* (1884); J. Payn, *The Talk of the Town* (1885); G. a'Beckett, *The Comic Blackstone* (1887); F. C. Burnand, *The Incompleat Angler* (1887); L. Carroll, *Sylvie and Bruno* (1889), *Sylvie and Bruno Concluded* (1893); G. E. Farrow, *The Wallypug of Why* (1895), *The Wallypug Book* (1905); *The Charles Dickens Library* (1910); *The Works of Thackeray* (1911)

EXHIB: RA; RHA; FAS (1894, 1898, Memorial 1925); NPG 'Harry Furniss' (1983); Gainsborough Galleries

COLL: NPG; V&A; HCL; H; LC; BM; THG

LIT: H. Furniss, *Confessions of a Caricaturist* (1901), *My Lady Cinema* (1914), *My Bohemian Days* (1919)

G

GABRIEL – *see* Friell, James

GAIS – *see* Gaisford, R. G.

GAISFORD, R. G. 'Gais' DFC (1913–after 1958). Joke cartoonist and writer. A self-taught artist, Gaisford began work in the publicity department of Canadian National Railways. He later worked in an advertising agency while selling ideas, jokes and cartoons to magazines (from 1939) via the art agent Percy Lisby. After his work began to appear in *London Opinion*, *Punch* (from 1939) and *Tatler* he turned full-time freelance. During World War II he served as a wireless operator/air gunner in the RAF, flying in Stirling bombers. He achieved the rank of flight-lieutenant and was awarded the DFC. After the war he wrote and designed advertisements and his cartoons also appeared in *Lilliput*, *Punch*, *Daily Mirror*, *Inky Way Annual*, *Illustrated*, *Night and Day*, *Strand* and *Evening Standard*. An admirer of Thurber and the Marx Brothers, he preferred drawing captionless cartoons. He also illustrated a brochure on Family Allowances published by *The Lancet*.

GALE, George (b. 1929). Editorial/political cartoonist and caricaturist. George Gale was born on 11 June 1929 in Leven, Fife. He was educated in Scotland but has been living in London since the 1950s. After studying as a draughtsman and spending a period as a commercial artist, he began freelancing, selling cartoons to *The Times* (from 1973), *Economist*, *Tribune*, *Financial Times* and other British and European newspapers and journals. He was Editorial/Political Cartoonist of the *Daily Telegraph* (1986–9) and has been Editorial/Political Cartoonist of the parliamentary weekly *The House Magazine* since 1989. Influenced by Gillray, Cruikshank, Low and VICKY, he works mainly in pen and ink, gouache and crayon. His son Iain Gale is a journalist on the *Independent*.

ILL: I. Gale, *The Flying Hammer* (1985)
EXHIB: Leatherhead Theatre; Jacey Galleries; Waterman Gallery
COLL: Florence Nightingale Museum, London; University of Edinburgh; Sussex Yeomanry Museum, Taunton

GAMMIDGE, Ian Berwick TD (b. 1916). Joke and strip cartoonist and scriptwriter. Born in Ashstead, Surrey, on 15 April 1916, the son of F. N. Gammidge, an accountant, Ian Gammidge is a self-taught artist and was an insurance salesman before serving in the Army in World War II (later gaining a Territorial Decoration [1950]). After the war he attended St Martin's School of Art (1946) and sold his first cartoon to *Lilliput* in May 1946 ('Flora was holding the little beast a second ago', about a baby lost during its christening). Freelance since then, his work has appeared in *John Bull*, *Sunday Pictorial*, *Inky Way Annual*, *Everybody's*, *Tatler*, *London Opinion*, *Draper's Record* and elsewhere. He joined the staff of the *Daily Mirror* in May 1947, taking over from Jack Hargreaves as writer of 'The Flutters' strip (drawn by L. G. Gamblin), and then succeeding Brian Cooke as writer of 'The Larks' (drawn by Jack Dunkley) and Bill Connor ('Cassandra') as writer of 'Ruggles' (drawn by S. P. Dowling). He still produces strip cartoons for the paper and has also drawn weekly joke cartoons for *Sunday Pictorial* (later the *Sunday Mirror*) (1947–81) and wrote the last episodes of NORMAN PETT's creation, 'Jane'. Retired since the early 1980s, he drew with a pen using a Perry Iridinoid nib.
PUB: [with Fel] *Little Joe* (1975), [with J. Dunkley] *Mr Digwell's Everyday Gardening Book* (1977), [with J. Dunkley and B. Cooke] *Life with the Larks* (1978), *Gardener's Mirror* (1981)
COLL: UKCC

GARDNER, Norman Gouldney Rodway 'Rire' (1910–93). Joke cartoonist and cartographer. N. R. Gardner was born in Cheltenham, Gloucestershire, on 19 January 1910, the son of Frederick Gardner, a commercial clerk. Educated at Cheltenham Grammar School, he worked at first at Borrow & Co., map and guide publishers, in the city (1927–40) before joining the mapping section of the War Office in 1940 and continued as a professional cartographer until his retirement in 1975. A self-taught artist, after encouragement from ARTHUR FERRIER when he sent some drawings to *The Artist* magazine, he took corre-

spondence courses in drawing for reproduction at the Press Art School run by PERCY BRADSHAW and poster art at the JOHN HASSALL School. His first published humorous drawing was an advertisement for 'Cleano', a window-cleaning product (1929), for which he was paid 7s. 6d. His cartoons were later published in *Punch* – the first being in January 1946 ('Now see what happens if you don't practise') – and one was included in a group of the magazine's drawings exhibited in the Time-Life building, New York (1952). He also contributed to the *Evening News*, *Evening Standard*, *London Opinion*, *Men Only*, *John Bull*, *Lilliput*, *Modern Woman* and others. For his cartoon work he roughed out designs first in pencil and then drew the finished joke in pen and ink on thin card. He used the pseudonym 'Rire' for his more risqué work. N. R. Gardner died in Cheltenham on 15 April 1993.

GARLAND, Nicholas Withycombe OBE (b. 1935). Political cartoonist and strip cartoonist. Nicholas Garland was born on 1 September 1935 in Hampstead, London, the son of Thomas Garland, a doctor, and the sculptor Peggy Garland. He emigrated to New Zealand at the age of 11 (1946–54), returned aged 19, and studied at the Slade School of Fine Art (1954–7). After working for some years as stage manager at the Royal Court Theatre his first drawing (a caricature) was published in *Queen* magazine (c. 1963) after its Editor, MARK BOXER, saw some of his sketches. He then contributed illustrations to the arts pages of the *Spectator* before creating, with writer Barry Humphries, the 'Barry Mackenzie' strip in *Private Eye* (1964–74). 'Barry Mackenzie's chin was taken from Desperate Dan, and his double-breasted suit, striped tie and wide-brimmed hat were inspired by [the outfits of] a group of middle-aged Anzacs I once saw marching down Whitehall during a Remembrance Day parade. The name Mackenzie came from an Australian cricketer and Barry, of course, from Barry Humphries.' Two films were made featuring the character, which caused problems with the censor even in Australia. (In *The Adventures of Barry Mackenzie* [1972], scriptwriter Barry Humphries himself played the part of Mackenzie's aunt Edna Everidge.) Garland was also the first Political Cartoonist on the *Daily Telegraph* (1966–86). He left to join the newly founded *Independent* (1986–91) and returned to the *Telegraph* in 1991. He

Nicholas Garland, [Benn, Garland, Thatcher, Steel, Owen, Heath, Callaghan, Wilson], *Twenty Years of Cartoons by Garland* (title page), 1984

has also drawn weekly political cartoons for the *New Statesman* (1971–6), and contributed to the *Spectator* (including covers, 1971–97), and *Investors Chronicle*. In addition he has designed book jackets and has been twice voted Cartoonist of the Year by Granada TV's *What the Papers Say* Awards (1972, 1987). An admirer of VICKY, who influenced his style, he used to produce roughs on A4 layout paper using 3B pencil before transferring to Daler NOT wash-and-line board and a Sheaffer fountain pen (fine and medium nib) with Sheaffer cartridge ink, using indian ink with a brush for filling in large areas. However, more recently he has concentrated on pen and wash drawing on Aquarelle Arches cold-pressed watercolour paper. One of the founder members of the British Cartoonists' Association in 1966, he was awarded an OBE in 1998.

PUB: [with B. Humphries] *The Wonderful World of Barry Mackenzie* (1968), *Bazza Pulls It Off!* (1972), *The Complete Barry Mackenzie* (1988), *An Indian Journal* (1983), *Twenty Years of Cartoons by Garland* (1984), *Travels With My Sketchbook* (1987), *Not Many Dead* (1990)

ILL: T. B. Macaulay, *Horatius* (1977); J. Fuller, *Come Aboard and Sail Away* (1983); A. McPherson and A. Macfarlane, *Mum – I Feel Funny!* (1982); W. Cope, *The River Girl* (1991)

EXHIB: CG; Vilnius Art Gallery, Lithuania; GG

COLL: V&A; A; UKCC; CAT; IWM; BM

GARY – *see* Smith, Gary James

GAS – *see* Stevens, G. A.

GASKILL, David Thomas (b. 1939). Editorial and strip cartoonist, caricaturist and illustrator. Dave Gaskill was born in Liverpool on 27 May 1939, the son of Ernest Gaskill, an RAF sergeant. He is self-taught apart from two years of evening classes at Stockport College, Cheshire (1962–3). His first cartoon was published in the letters column of the *Manchester Evening*

News in 1971. He worked as an engineering and design draughtsman in Britain, Germany and South Africa (1955–72) before becoming a full-time cartoonist, first in Johannesburg, South Africa (1973–85), where he worked for the *Sunday Express, Citizen, Star, Financial Mail, Sunday Times* and *Rand Daily Mail*; then Australia (1986–7) on the *West Australian* and *Business Daily*; and New Zealand (1987) for the *New Zealand Herald*. Returning to the UK in 1987, he has been Editorial Cartoonist on *Today* (1988–95, succeeding KAL, until its closure), *News of the World* (from 1986), *Mail on Sunday* (1996) and in 1996 succeeded RICK BROOKES as Editorial Cartoonist on the *Sun*. He has also freelanced for *Reader's Digest* (South Africa), *Signature Magazine, Diners Club, Republican Press* and various national and international advertising agencies in South Africa. He received four Standard Bank Special Merit awards for his work in South Africa where he was also resident cartoonist on the TV series *Take My Word*. He works with waterproof, light-fast felt-tip pens on 200g paper and uses mainly gouache and colour inks for colour work.

PUB: *Dave Gaskill's World* (1992)
ILL: D. Taylor, *Man in the Soup* (1980); J. Margolis, *Commuters' Tales* (1992)
EXHIB: BC

GED – *see* Melling, Gerard

GEE BEE – *see* Butterworth, George Goodwin

Geo. M. – *see* Morrow, George

GG – *see* Hogg, Gordon

GHILCHIK, David Louis ROI RWE (1892–1972). Political and joke cartoonist, portrait and landscape painter, commercial artist, caricaturist and illustrator. David Ghilchik was born in Botosani, Romania, and came to England at the age of five, the family settling in Manchester. His father wanted him to become a doctor but agreed to allow him to spend a year at art school before taking up medicine. In the event Ghilchik won an art scholarship and so medicine was dropped. He left school at 16 and while studying at Manchester School of Art under Adolphe Valette (L. S. Lowry was a contemporary student), succeeded the political cartoonist Sid Treeby on the Manchester-based *Labour Leader* (then the official Labour Party newspaper be-

fore the *Daily Herald*) when Treeby returned to Australia in 1908. His first cartoon for the paper was used as a full front page. He also drew political cartoons for the Manchester-based socialist weekly, *Laughter Grim and Gay*, before moving to London to study at the Slade under Henry Tonks and then in Paris, Florence and Venice on a travelling scholarship. He then worked as a commercial artist for Norfolk Studios. In World War I he served first as a driver/mechanic in the Royal Army Service Corps and later in the Intelligence Corps in Italy. His first cartoon for *Punch* was published while he was on active service in France and he later contributed regularly to the magazine (1921–39), drawing largely social and domestic jokes in the tradition of LEWIS BAUMER. He also drew for *Humorist, Bystander, Time & Tide, Blighty, Passing Show, News Chronicle* (daily 'Hector says . . .' feature), *Tobacco* (caricatures), *Christmas Pie, Radio Times* (caricatures) and *Men Only* and was Political Cartoonist on the *Daily Sketch* during World War II. A founder member of the Society of Wood Engravers (1920), he was also President of the London Sketch Club (1942), Vice-President of the United Society of Artists, a member of the Savage Club and was elected ROI *c.* 1960. Ghilchik preferred to draw from life in pen, Biro or fine sable brush on Bristol board (double sheet thickness), Whatman Board or fashion/ivory boards. He used a Mitchell 0299 or Gillott mapping nib (but preferred a lettering nib for his 'Hector' drawings) and lampblack (for washes) and waterproof indian ink. He sometimes also used scraperboard (e.g. for *Radio Times* work). Influenced by Ingres, he thought Augustus John was Britain's greatest living artist. He married the painter Josephine Duddle in 1915 and their daughter Deirdre had a picture hung at the Royal Academy when she was only 16 (another daughter married the opera singer Terence O'Donoghue). David Ghilchik died on 24 November 1972.

PUB: *Drawing Children* (1961)
ILL: J. A. Hammerton, *The Rubaiyat of a Golfer* (1946)
EXHIB: RA; ROI; RI; RBA; NEAC; L; RP
COLL: [Paintings] Guildhall Art Library; IWM

GIBBARD, Leslie David (b. 1945). Editorial/political and pocket cartoonist, caricaturist, film animator and journalist. Les Gibbard was born on 26 October 1945 in Kaiapoi, New Zealand, the son of Ray and Dorothy Gibbard, both teachers.

Les Gibbard, [Heath, Thatcher], *Gibbard's Double Decade Omnibus* (part-title page), 1991

As a schoolboy in Auckland he was tutored in charcoal and pastels by Franz Szirmay. Working at first as a newspaper journalist (1962–7), he also produced cartoons, caricatures and illustrations for the publications he wrote for, namely *Auckland Star*, *New Zealand Weekly News*, *Sunday News* and *Melbourne Herald* as well as *New Zealand Herald* where he was coached and greatly influenced by MINHINNICK. His first published drawing was a caricature of Reginald Maudling for the *Auckland Star* in January 1962.

He came to London on 1 June 1967 and worked as a freelance cartoonist (occasionally under the name of 'Spike') before becoming arts caricaturist and pocket cartoonist for the *Sunday Telegraph* (1967–70) and succeeding BILL PAPAS as Political Cartoonist on the *Guardian* (1969–94). He has also contributed to the *Daily Mirror* (caricatures), *Daily Sketch*, *Daily Telegraph*, *Sunday Mirror*, *Evening Standard*, *Time Out*, *Melody Maker* and others. In addition he has worked as an animator for Richard Williams' studio (1973–5)

89

– where he initially assisted Ken Harris of Warner Bros and attended life classes by Disney animator Art Babbitt – and has produced his own animated political cartoon series *Newshound* for Granada TV's *Reports Politics* (1976–7). He has also key-animated the stories of Beatrix Potter, *Wind in the Willows*, *Famous Fred*, *The Bear* and others for TV. In addition he has drawn weekly political cartoons for BBC TV's *On the Record* (1988–95) and *Newsnight* programmes and Channel 4's *A Week in Politics* (1982–6). Gibbard was voted BISFA Slide/Strip Artist of the Year in 1980 and National Canine Defence League Dog Cartoonist of the Year in 1989. During the Falklands War, when the Argentinian cruiser *General Belgrano* was sunk with a loss of 362 lives, Gibbard drew a pastiche of Zec's famous World War II cartoon, re-captioning it 'The Price of Sovereignty Has Increased – Official'. This caused a brief furore in the tabloid press, with the *Sun*'s leader-writer branding him a traitor. He works in pen and ink using a Gillott 404 nib on cartridge paper, an HB pencil and a No. 4 sable brush. For TV drawings he uses Daler line-and-wash board with a neutral tint wash. He cites his influences as being Low, Minhinnick, Tom Webster, Searle and Disney.

PUB: *Gibbard's Double Decade Omnibus* (1991)
ILL: A. Mitchell, *The Half Gallon Quarter Acre Pavlova Paradise* (1972), *Westminster Man* (1982); F. Keating, *Caught by Keating* (1979)
EXHIB: Holland Gallery; UKCC
COLL: UKCC
LIT: N. Harris, *Flyaway People* (1971)

GILBERT, Sir William Schwenck 'Bab' (1836–1911) – *see* Bryant & Heneage

GILES, Carl Ronald OBE (1916–95). Editorial/political cartoonist, animator and journalist. Carl Giles was born on 29 September 1916 in Islington, London, the son of Albert Giles, a tobacconist, and grandson of Alfred 'Farmer' Giles, a jockey who had ridden for Edward VII. He attended Barnsbury Park School – where he was taught by the severe, skeletal Mr Chalk (his real name) who later featured in his cartoons – and left at the age of 14, working first as an office boy and then as an animator in Wardour Street, London. Moving to Elstree he joined Alexander Korda's studios (1930–35) and was one of the principal animators of Korda's *The Fox Hunt* (artist Anthony Gross), the first British animated

Carl Giles, [Grandma], n.d.

colour cartoon with sound. He also animated Roland Davies' *Sunday Express* strip 'Come on Steve'. On the death of his brother he returned to London to work for *Reynolds News* (1937–43), producing political cartoons and a strip 'Young Ernie'. Invited by Editor John Gordon to join the *Sunday Express* in October 1943 he later also became Deputy Cartoonist to Strube on the *Daily Express* and the paper's war correspondent. He eventually took over from Strube, drawing two cartoons a week for the *Daily Express* (alternating with Cummings), and one for the *Sunday Express*. In addition he also contributed to *Men Only* and other publications. During World War II he produced animated films for the Ministry of Information and his cartoons were reproduced as posters for the Railway Executive Committee and others. In addition he drew advertising cartoons for Guinness, Fisons and others and designed Christmas cards for the RNLI, Royal National Institute for the Deaf and Game Conservancy Research Fund. He was awarded the OBE in 1959 and the Cartoonists' Club of Great Britain Special Award for Distinguished Services to Cartooning in 1992. He also received a Granada TV's *What the Papers Say* Award for his work. One of the founder members of the British Cartoonists' Association in 1966, he was later its President (succeeding Illingworth) until his death. Giles was best known for his *Express* 'family', especially the character Grandma, 'a bleakly menacing figure drawn from his dark subconscious, bird in hat, umbrella in hand and "reeking of bombazine"' (Keith Mackenzie).

An animated version of the series appeared as a TV advertisement for Quick Brew tea with voices supplied by Nigel Stock as Father, Meg Johnson as Mother and Pat Hayes as Grandma. Giles cites his influences as BAIRNSFATHER and PONT ('When he went I felt I had lost a dear friend'), and he has himself directly influenced the style of JAK, MAC and others. Described by VICKY as 'a present-day Hogarth', SEARLE has said of him: 'in his superb understanding of human behaviour no one can touch him' and Lord Beaverbrook called him 'a man of genius ... who takes the solemnity out of the grand occasion and helps the world to keep sane by laughing at its soaring moments'. However, he never succeeded as a political cartoonist: 'I do not think that Giles could possibly compete in Low's field. He is not a political cartoonist. Whenever he tries this line of country, he flops badly' (Arthur Christiansen, Editor of the *Daily Express*, in a letter to Lord Beaverbrook, 30 December 1949). He drew without distortion with his cartoon figures set against elaborately detailed naturalistic backgrounds, often with fascinating 'sub-plots' occurring away from the main focus of the picture. He never submitted roughs ('I can't work that way – I just sit down and draw the thing') and never worked at the *Express*'s office in London but sent his drawings in from his home in Ipswich, Suffolk. Carl Giles left the *Express* in October 1989 and died in hospital in Ipswich, Suffolk, on 27 August 1995.

PUB: Giles annuals (from 1946), *Children* (1955), *Nurse!* (1975)

ILL: W. Tute, *The Grey Top Hat: The Story of Moss Bros of Covent Garden* (1961); Philip, Duke of Edinburgh, *The Wit and Wisdom of Prince Philip* (1965), *More Wit and Wisdom of Prince Philip* (1973)

EXHIB: L; NMCA; CAT (1993)

COLL: CAT; [animated film] IWM; UKCC; V&A

LIT: P. Tory, *Giles: A Life in Cartoons* (1992), *The Giles Family* (1993), *Giles at War* (1994), *The Ultimate Giles* (1995)

GILLETT, Edward Frank RI (1874–1927). Joke cartoonist, illustrator and painter. Frank Gillett was born in Worlingham, Suffolk, on 23 July 1874, the son of the Rev. Jesse Gillett, Vicar of Aldeby, Norfolk. He was educated at Gresham's School, Holt, and worked at first as a clerk at Lloyd's (1890–96) in London. While there he began contributing cartoons to *Fun* (1895) and later joined the staff of the *Daily Graphic* (1898–1908). He also contributed regularly to *Black & White* (1908–11), *Illustrated Sporting and Dramatic News* (1910–23), *Bystander* (notably the 'Topicator' feature), *Idler, Judy, Strand, Little Folks, Ludgate Magazine, Odd Volume* and *Pearson's Magazine*. Best known as a sports cartoonist, especially of equestrian subjects, he usually worked in pen and ink but also used drypoint and painted in oils and watercolour. A member of the Langham Sketch Club, he was elected RI in 1909. Frank Gillett died in Beccles, Suffolk, in May 1927.

EXHIB: RA; RI; G; L; FAS

COLL: THG

GILLIAM, Terry Vance (b. 1940). Joke cartoonist, illustrator, animator and film director. Born in Minneapolis, Minnesota, USA, on 22 November 1940, Terry Gilliam studied political science at Occidental College, Los Angeles (1958–62), where he edited the college humour magazine. Moving to New York he became Associate Editor of *Help!* magazine (1962–5), founded by *Mad*'s Harvey Kurtzman, and after working as a freelance cartoonist and illustrator joined Carson Roberts Advertising Agency as Art Director/Copywriter (1966–7). In 1967 he moved to London, working as a freelance illustrator for *Sunday Times, Nova* and *Queen*, and was Art Director of *The Londoner*. After selling comedy sketches to LWT's *Do Not Adjust Your Set* (1968) he was resident cartoonist on the *We Have Ways of Making You Laugh* TV series for which he also produced an animated cartoon. This led to animation for BBC2's *Marty* series (starring Marty Feldman, 1969) and *Do Not Adjust Your Set*. He was a founder member of the *Monty Python's Flying Circus* team on BBC TV in 1969. Other work includes animated title sequences for *Cry of the Banshees* (1970) and *William* (1972) and animation for TV's *The Marty Feldman Comedy Machine* (1971). Film credits (as animator, co-writer and actor for 'Python' films) include *The Miracle of Flight* (1971), *Monty Python's And Now for Something Completely Different* (1971), *Monty Python and the Holy Grail* (co-director, 1974), *Jabberwocky* (director, 1976), *Monty Python's Life of Brian* (designer, 1978), *Time Bandits* (producer-director 1980), *Monty Python's Meaning of Life* (1983), *Brazil* (co-writer, director 1985), *The Adventures of Baron Munchhausen* (director and co-writer, 1989), *The Fisher King* (director, 1991), *12 Monkeys* (director, 1996),

Fear & Loathing in Las Vegas (director and co-writer, 1998). He was made an Honorary Doctor of Fine Arts by Occidental College, Los Angeles (1987), and by the RCA (1987).

PUB: *Animations of Mortality* (1978), [with M. Palin] *Time Bandits* (1981), [with C. McKeown] *The Adventures of Baron Munchhausen* (1989), *Not the Screenplay of Fear & Loathing in Las Vegas* (1999), *Gilliam on Gilliam* (1999)

ILL: H. Kurtzman, *Harvey Kurtzman's Fun and Games* (1965); [Monty Python team], *Monty Python's Big Red Book* (1971), *The Brand New Monty Python Book* (1973), *Monty Python and the Holy Grail* (1977), *Monty Python's Scrapbook* (1979), *Monty Python's Life of Brian* (1979), *The Complete Works of Shakespeare and Monty Python* (1981), *Monty Python's Meaning of Life* (1983); R. McGough, *Sporting Relations* (1976); A. Yule, *Losing the Light* (1991), *The Fisher King* (1991)

LIT: J. Matthews, *The Battle of Brazil* (1987)

GILROY, John Thomas Young ARCA FRSA (1898–1985). Advertising cartoonist, portrait and landscape painter. John Gilroy was born at Whitley Bay, Newcastle-upon-Tyne, on 30 May 1898, the son of John William Gilroy, a marine landscape painter. He attended Sandyford School and Heaton Park Upper School and studied at the King Edward VII School of Art, Newcastle (1909). From the age of 15 he began drawing theatre cartoons for the *Newcastle Evening Chronicle* and won a scholarship to Armstrong College Art School, University of Durham (1912), but his studies were interrupted by World War I during which he served with the Royal Field Artillery in France, Italy and Palestine. After the war he went to the RCA, London (1919–23), becoming a British Institute Scholar (1921) and an RCA Travelling Scholar (1922). After graduating he stayed on as a teacher at the RCA (1923–5) and also taught life drawing at Camberwell School of Art (1924–6), designing poster advertisements in his spare time. In 1925 he joined the staff of the S. H. Benson (later Ogilvy, Benson & Mather) agency and quickly established himself as a gifted and imaginative artist working on campaigns for Skipper Sardines, Bovril, Macleans and Colman's Mustard and others. Perhaps his best remembered campaign was for Guinness (1928–68), with scripts by Dorothy L. Sayers – notably the girder carrier in 'Guinness for Strength' and the toucan and other zoo animals (the zoo-keeper was a self-portrait). However, he also designed more than 400 greetings cards for Royle's over 35 years (becoming acting Art Director in 1966) and produced illustrations (including covers) for *Radio Times* (from 1932) and 'Headlines' for the *Star*. During World War II he created Ministry of Information posters such as 'Make Do and Mend' and 'Keep it Under Your Hat' but later concentrated on portrait painting. His sitters included Queen Elizabeth and many other members of the Royal Family, as well as Churchill, Heath, Pope John Paul XXIII, and numerous politicians and actors. In 1951 Gilroy moved into PARTRIDGE's old home in Holland Park Rd, London, and while there became Head of the Art Department of T. F. Carrington Van Posting Ltd. Chairman of the Works of Art Committee of the Garrick Club, he received an Honorary MA from Newcastle University in 1975 and was appointed a Freeman of the City of London in 1981. Gilroy died in Guildford on 11 April 1985.

ILL: *Rough Island Story* (1931–5); H. MacLennan (ed.), *McGill, The Story of a University* (1960); D. L. Sayers, *The Recipe Book of the Mustard Club* (n.d.)

EXHIB: Upper Grosvenor Galleries; FAS (1936); RA; ROI; RBA; NEAC; LH; Laing Art Gallery, Newcastle; RCA; Guinness Hopstore, Dublin; Sunderland Public Art Gallery; Austin Reed, London; Cheltenham Art Gallery

COLL: THG; NPG

GIOVANNETTI, Pericle Luigi (b. 1916). Joke and strip cartoonist. Giovannetti was born in Basel, Switzerland, on 22 June 1916, but lived in Monterubbiano, Italy before moving back to Switzerland (Ascona) for good in 1947. His first cartoons were published in *Nebelspalter* and he gave birth to his most famous creation, Max the Hamster, in *Punch* in April 1952. Also published in *Nebelspalter* and *Glamour*, the cartoon was quickly syndicated worldwide and even appeared in Japan as 'Mr Makkusu-san'. Max was also adopted as a mascot on HMS *Birmingham* in 1953 and in 1957 as the motif for Jet Fighter Squadron No. 21 of the Swiss Air Force. Endearing but without the cloying sentimentality of some earlier animal characters, the pot-bellied Max, normally seen squatting face on, is drawn in crisp outline in ink, with occasional use of cross-hatching and solid blacks. Unframed, the multi-picture sequences progress in a variety of geometrical patterns across the page, with sometimes as many as 12 images in

P. L. Giovannetti, *Max* (cover detail), 1954

a story. Price wrote: 'What was enjoyable in Max was that, with him, some of the humours of animal and child returned to *Punch* purged of sentimentality.' Giovannetti also produced a book about Max's great-grandfather, a Syrian hamster named Hamid of Aleppo.
PUB: *Aus Meine Menagerie* (1951), *Gesammelte Zeichnungen* (1948), *Max* (1954), *Max Presents* (1956), *Beware of the Dog* (1958), *Nothing But Max* (1959), *Birds Without Words* (1961), *The Penguin Max* (1962)
ILL: C. King, *Hamid of Aleppo* (1958)
COLL: SAM

GITTINS, Harold (fl. 1930s–after 1950). Sports and pocket cartoonist. Harold Gittins came from Manchester and studied at the Manchester School of Art. In World War I he served in the South Lancashire Regiment and then the Royal Flying Corps, where he was shot down by the 'Red Baron', Manfred von Richthofen, but later attended the German ace's funeral. He drew sports cartoons for the *Evening News* for many years in the journalistic multi-frame style of TOM WEBSTER and produced pocket cartoons for the paper during World War II. In addition he contributed to *Blighty* and others. He used ink and wash on Bryce Smith Fashion Process Board.

PUB: [with ILLINGWORTH, NEB, LEE and MOON] *400 Famous Cartoons* (1944)
COLL: UKCC

GLAN – *see* Williams, Glan

GLASHAN, John [real name John McGlashan] (1927–99). Joke and strip cartoonist, illustrator, writer and painter. John Glashan was born in Glasgow on 24 December 1927, the son of portrait painter Archibald McGlashan RSA (President of the Glasgow Art Club, 1959–61). He was educated at Woodside School and studied painting at Glasgow School of Art. Moving to London in the 1950s, he began as a portrait painter but lack of work led him to drop the 'Mc' from his name and become a cartoonist and illustrator. His first book illustrations appeared in 1959 and his first cartoons were published in *Lilliput* (from 1960) followed by regular features in *Queen* (from 1961). His first joke published in *Punch* – about a man who turned his home into a replica of the House of Commons – was an inspiration for N. F. Simpson's play, *One Way Pendulum*. He also drew for *Holiday*, *Private Eye*, *Daily Telegraph* (from 1963), *Harpers & Queen*, *Tatler*, *Sunday Times* ('Woman' feature), *Evening Standard*, and illustrations for the William Hickey column in the *Daily Express*. In 1978 he took over Jules Feiffer's spot on the *Observer Magazine* and began his 'Genius' strip featuring Anode Enzyme (IQ 12,794) and his patron Lord Doberman, the richest man in the world, drawn as tiny sketchy figures against a huge backdrop of fantastical architecture. This ran until 1983 when he turned to landscape painting, drawing cartoons again for the *Spectator* from 1988. He also worked in advertising for companies such as ICI and Blue Nun and illustrated books. An admirer of ANDRÉ FRANÇOIS, he used A4 typing paper and a dip pen, adding watercolour for extra dimension, and never drew roughs. Another feature was his handwritten captions which tended to appear within the pictures themselves. 'I have discovered that the nearer humour approaches seriousness, the funnier it will be. "Being funny" is not funny. Humour is seriousness in disguise.' The 'Genius' feature won the Glen Grant Strip Cartoon Award (1981). He was one of the founder members of the British Cartoonists' Association in 1966. John Glasham died of cancer in London on 15 June 1999.

PUB: *The Penguin John Glashan* (1967), *The Eye of the Needle* (1961), *Private Eye John Glashan* (1975), *John Glashan's World* (1991) and others
ILL: A. Sampson, *Tonight and Other Nights* (1959); [Private Eye], *The pSecond Book of Pseuds* (1977); C. Logue (ed.), *Sweet and Sour* (1983)
EXHIB: Francis Kyle Gallery; FAS; CG
COLL: BM

GOETZ, Walter (1911–95). Joke and strip cartoonist, illustrator and landscape painter. Walter Goetz was born on 24 November 1911 in Cologne, Germany, the son of Alfred Götz, a German-Jewish silk wholesaler whose father had been a founder of Gebrüder Bing & Söhne, the family firm. His uncle was the art collector Richard Goetz. Brought up at first in Berlin he was sent to Bedales School in England (from 1923) where a fellow pupil and friend was Julian Trevelyan RA. Unable to take up a place to read history and English at Cambridge University through lack of funds, Goetz returned to Germany in 1929 and studied painting in Berlin for two years under Joseph Block. Then, after working briefly as a commercial artist in Cologne, he transferred to Bing's London office and arrived back in Britain in 1931, becoming a naturalized British citizen in 1934. His first cartoon appeared in *Everybody's* in the early 1930s. He also designed book jackets and produced illustrations and worked for his friend NICOLAS BENTLEY at Shell-Mex. He drew 'Colonel Up and Mr Down' (from January 1934) and 'Dab and Flounder' for the *Daily Express* (1934–54) under the name of 'Walter'. During World War II he worked in the Political Warfare Executive in Woburn Abbey, producing aerial leaflets in German, later transferring to the French section where he edited *Cadran* (a magazine modelled on *Picture Post*) for distribution in liberated France. His work appeared in *Punch* (from 1933), *Bystander, Lilliput, Vogue, Harpers, Night & Day, Contact, News Chronicle, France-Soir* and *Paris-Match*. In addition he designed costumes for opera and illustrated a number of books, notably the 'Major Thompson' series written by Pierre Daninos, which led to a wax figure based on his portrait of the Major being exhibited in the Musée Grevin wax museum in Paris. He moved to Paris in 1951, working at first for the US Information Service, and later (1959) became an art dealer and painter and did not return to England permanently until 1980. Goetz worked in pen and ink (also wash) for his cartoons and gouache and watercolour when painting. A member of the Garrick Club, he died in London on 13 September 1995.
ILL: D. Miller, *Who's Who in the Wars* (1940); J. Laver (ed.), *Memorable Balls* (1954); P. Daninos, *Les Carnets du Major Thompson* (1954), *Major Thompson Lives in France* (1955), *Le Secret du Major Thompson* (1956), *Major Thompson and I* (1957)
EXHIB: [landscape paintings] LG; SGG; Galeries Roux & Hentschel, Paris; RG; [costume designs for *The Pearl Fishers*] Music & Theatre Gallery; Lefevre Gallery
COLL: V&A; CAT

GOG – *see* Hogg, Gordon

GOODWIN – *see* Churchill, Robert Frederick Goodwin

GORDON, Gay – *see* Hogg, Gordon

GORDON, Michael (b. 1948). Illustrator, greetings cards designer, joke cartoonist and writer. Mike Gordon was born in Middleton, Lancashire, on 16 March 1948 and spent one year at Rochdale School of Art (1963) before working as a heating engineer, producing cartoons in his spare time. A full-time cartoonist since 1983, his principal freelance work has been for book publishers such as HarperCollins, Headline, Ladybird, Longman, Puffin, Random Century, Reed International and Simon & Schuster. Since 1982 he has also produced over 300 greetings cards for Hanson White/Accord, Hallmark, Design Concept and Russ Berrie as well as cartoons for advertising and character origination for Alton Towers theme park (1988). He has won a number of awards for his work including Berol Cartoonist of the Year (1988), and cites his influences as Tony Ross, Paul Coker and RALPH STEADMAN. Mike Gordon uses dip-pens, airbrush and water-soluble inks on Scholleshammer paper.
PUB: *Duffer's Guides* (seven titles 1983–8), *Haunted House* (1989), 'Fascinating Facts' series (1989), *Phallic Thimbles* (1990)
ILL: More than 40 titles including 'Lift & Look' series (1985); C. Clarke, *Grub on a Grant* (1985), *Mean Beans* (1993); G. Steddy, *The Adventures of Henry Hound* (1988); N. and T. Morris, 'Practise at Home' series (1990); R. Powell, 'Mini-Boo' series (1990); 'I'm Alive' series (1991–3); M. Butterfield, *Dinosaur Dice Games* (1992)

GOULD, Sir Francis Carruthers (1844–1925). Political cartoonist, caricaturist, illustrator and painter. F. C. Gould was born in Barnstaple, Devon, on 2 December 1844, the son of Richard Gould, an architect. He worked at first in a bank (aged 16) and then, aged 20, as a broker in the London Stock Exchange (1864–88). His first cartoon was published in *Truth* in 1879 and he continued to draw for the journal and illustrate its Christmas issues until 1895. A self-taught caricaturist ('the faculty of personal caricature has simply eaten out through the shell'), he worked at first from photographs but after 1889 preferred to draw from life. He left the Stock Exchange in 1887 to join the *Pall Mall Gazette* as the first-ever staff political cartoonist on a daily newspaper (parliamentary cartoons had appeared in *Punch* and other magazines much earlier). He stayed with the paper for five years until it changed ownership when he moved (being succeeded by HALKETT) to the newly launched *Westminster Gazette* (1893), remaining there until he retired in 1914. In 1894 he also founded his own monthly journal, *Picture Politics*, which ran for 20 years. In addition he contributed to *Vanity Fair* (seven caricatures, 1879–99), *Cassell's Magazine*, *Pall Mall Budget* (weekly cartoons), *Star*, *Westminster Budget*, *Strand* (regular caricatures and illustrations for the 'From Behind the Speaker's Chair' parliamentary series by Henry W. Lucy) and others, and designed political postcards for E. Wrench and others (e.g. the 'Westminster Cartoon Series' from his *Westminster Gazette* cartoons). A committed Liberal himself ('I am an out-and-out Radical'), he was once described by Lord Rosebery as 'one of the most remarkable assets of the Liberal Party', and was knighted after the Liberal victory in 1906. Particularly well known for his caricatures of Liberal Prime Minister Herbert Asquith and the monocled statesman Joseph Chamberlain (who collected his drawings), he was never malicious in his work, claiming that 'I etch with vinegar, not vitriol'. During World War I he designed a series of Toby Jug caricatures of 'Prominent Personages of the Great War' including Woodrow Wilson, Foch, Lloyd George, Haig, Beatty, Jellicoe, French and Joffre. He often signed his drawings simply 'FCG' or 'CG'. His son, the landscape painter Alec Carruthers Gould RBA RWA (1870–1948), also drew cartoons and caricatures. Sir Francis Carruthers Gould died in Porlock, Somerset, on 1 January 1925.

'Dare to stick together –
The Party made of two.'

Francis Carruthers Gould, [Joseph Chamberlain, Lord Salisbury], in Sir W. Lawson, *Cartoons in Rhyme and Line*, 1905

PUB: *Cartoons of the Campaign* (1895), *Froissart's Modern Chronicles* (from 1902), *Political Caricatures* (from 1903), *The Goulden Treasury* (1906)
ILL: *Fairy Tales from Brentano* (1885); [with A. Carruthers Gould] G. Allen, *Michael's Crag* (1893); H. Begbie, *The Political Struwwelpeter* (1899), *The Struwwelpeter Alphabet* (1900); H. H. Munro, *The Westminster Alice* (1902); R. E. Welsh, *The Capture of the Schools* (1903); H. W. Lucy, *Peeps at Parliament* (1903), *Later Peeps at Parliament* (1904); Sir W. Lawson, *Cartoons in Rhyme and Line* (1905)
EXHIB: BSG; WG
COLL: BM; V&A; NPG

GOURSAT, Georges 'Sem' (1863–1934). Caricaturist and portrait painter. Born in Périgueux, Dordogne, southern France, on 23 November 1863, the son of a grocer, Sem worked at first as the manager of a colonial store in Périgueux for 15 years. He moved to Paris in 1900 and caricatured all the leading international celebrities of his day, including most of the crowned heads of Europe. His work first appeared in *L'Entracte Périgourdin* (1886–7) and he later drew for *Le*

Rire (1897–1912), *Le Journal* (1903–28), *La Vie Parisienne* (1905–11), *Le Figaro* (1905–17), *Les Annales* (1905–31), *L'Illustration* (1906–19), *Le Matin* (1909–13), *La Baïonette* (1915–19) and many others. He began his annual 'albums' of racecourse habitués from Paris and Deauville, etc., in 1900 and often visited the UK between 1905 and 1910 to sketch at the Newmarket races and Cowes Regatta. Sem was a close friend of the British king Edward VII, himself a keen sportsman and racehorse-breeder, and when an exhibition of Sem's works was held at the Fine Art Society in London in 1908, the king himself attended and Queen Alexandra bought the entire collection for his birthday (it now resides at Sandringham). An admirer of the work of 'Cham' (he chose his pseudonym in his honour), he once said: 'I never draw from life . . . I watch and I listen and then I go away into solitude gradually to await the crystallization of an impression in my brain.' Sem was particularly well known for his caricatures of the personalities of the horseracing world, as well as royalty, actors, writers and the smart set of Parisian society into which he was introduced by the aesthete Jean Lorrain. He was awarded the Légion d'Honneur in 1973. Sem died at his home in Paris on 27 November 1934.
PUB: Annuals from *Les Sportsmen* (1900); *Un Pékin sur le Front* (1917), *Le Grande Monde à l'Envers* (1919), *La Ronde de Nuit* (1923)
EXHIB: Baillie Gallery (1907); FAS (1908, 1917)

GRAHAM, Alexander Steel (1917–91). Joke and strip cartoonist. Born in Glasgow on 2 March 1917, Alex Graham was educated at Dumfries Academy and Glasgow School of Art (where he won the Newbury Medal). During World War II he served in the Argyll & Sutherland Highlanders and began selling cartoons to *Tatler* while in the Army. In 1944 he sold a strip to the *Glasgow Weekly News* and became a full-time cartoonist in 1945, contributing 'Wee Hughie' (unsigned) to the *Dundee Weekly News*, followed by 'Our Bill' (1946). 'Briggs the Butler' featured in *Tatler & Bystander* from 9 July 1946 until 1963 but perhaps his most famous creation was 'Fred Basset – the Hound That's Almost Human', which began in the *Daily Mail* on 9 July 1963 and continued to run after his death in 1991. Fred the Basset Hound never speaks but his thoughts appear in balloons. The strip was syndicated worldwide to nearly 200 papers (the dog's name changing to Wurzel,

Lorang, Koraskoira and others) and was made into 20 short films for TV from 1976, featuring the voice of Lionel Jefferies. Other examples of Alex Graham's work appeared regularly in the *New Yorker, Men Only, Woman's Journal, Housewife, Reveille, Golfing* and *Sunday Graphic* ('Willy Nilly' strip, 1947). He is also particularly remembered for his *Punch* cartoons, especially the 'Graham's Golf Club' series (a later series with the same name appeared in the *Sunday Telegraph* from 1988) and in HEWISON's view 'has probably got more mileage out of the cocktail party than any other cartoonist'. He died at his home in Sussex on 3 December 1991.
PUB: More than 40 Fred Basset annuals (from 1964), *Please Sir, I've Broken My Arm* (1959), *The Eavesdropper* (1961), *The Doctor and the Eavesdropper* (1961), *Graham's Golf Club* (1965), *Oh Sidney – Not the Walnut Tree* (1966), *To the Office and Back* (1967), *Normally I Never Touch It* (1968), *Daughter in the House* (1969), *I Do Like to Be . . .* (1970), *At Least I'm Practically Alone* (1972), *It's Spring, Arthur, Spring!* (1973), *All the Other Men Have Mellowed* (1974), *Augustus and His Faithful Hound* (1978), *Graham's Golf Club* (1990)
ILL: M. Parkinson, *Football Daft* (1968); W. Loving, *A Lively Retirement* (1975) and others
EXHIB: RSA; FR
COLL: V&A; UKCC; IWM

'Gran'pop' – *see* Wood, Clarence Lawson

GRAVE, Charles (1886–1944). Joke cartoonist, illustrator and commercial artist. Charles Grave was born in Barrow-in-Furness in July 1886, the son of John Grave. He was educated at Tottenham Grammar School, London, and studied with PERCY BRADSHAW's Press Art School. He began contributing to *Punch* in 1912 (continuing until 1939), and was elected to the Table in 1935. A very popular artist, he specialized in naval and maritime humour: 'Charles Graves . . . did for ships and sailors and foreign ports what REYNOLDS did for suburban householders and village cricketers' (Price). He also originated the journalistic sporting cartoon style (later popularized by TOM WEBSTER) in the *Illustrated Sporting & Dramatic News*, and contributed to *Bystander, Daily Chronicle, Daily Graphic, Nash's, Passing Show, Printer's Pie, Sporting Life, Strand* and the *Tatler*. In addition he designed advertisements for Eclipse Razors and others. During World War I he served in the Middlesex Regiment and the Royal Tank Corps. A member of

the London Sketch Club, National Sporting Club and the Press Club, he usually drew in pen and ink but also painted in watercolour. He is not to be confused with Charles L. Graves, brother-in-law of Earl Grey and uncle of Robert Graves, who was Assistant Editor of *Punch* (1928–36).
PUB: *Bluejackets and Others* (1927)
ILL: H. R. Murray, *Kultur and the German Blunder(buss)* (1914); T. C. Wignall, *The Story of Boxing* (1923); Sir W. H. Flower, *A Book* (1925): E. P. Leigh-Bennett, *All at Sea* (Moss Bros, n.d.)

GRAY – *see* Jolliffe, Gray

GRAY, Alfred (fl. 1883–1906) – *see* Bryant & Heneage

GREENALL, Jack (1905–83). Joke and strip cartoonist. Jack Greenall was born in Whitefield, Lancashire. He sold his first cartoon at the age of 15 and his first strip, 'Pa, Ma and the Boy', appeared in *Pictorial Weekly* in 1929. He also contributed to *Ideas*, *Punch* (from 1934), *By-*

Jack Greenall, [Useless Eustace], n.d.

stander, *Passing Show*, *Razzle* and children's comics such as *Sparkler* and *Jolly Comic*. His most famous creation was Useless Eustace – a comical Everyman figure who later appeared in many guises but was originally a bowler-hatted office clerk – which ran in the *Daily Mirror* from 21 January 1935 until Greenall's retirement in 1975, after which it was continued by PETER MADDOCKS. The name Eustace was suggested by the genie in Darlington's book *Alf's Button*, but the character was not modelled on anyone: 'He is a hotch-potch of the many asses who cheerfully go through life doing the wrong thing at the wrong time.' Greenall once accidentally drew him with two left hands. Postcards featuring the character's antics were also published by Raphael Tuck & Sons Ltd. A variant, 'Useless Eunice', appeared in *Woman's Sunday Mirror*. In *Drawing Secrets!* he recommends students use HB pencil, Waverley pen, No. 2 or No. 3 brushes and black ink so there is some evidence that he used these himself. The wartime wall-peeping character 'Chad' ('Wot! No . . . ?'), sometimes mistakenly ascribed to Greenall, was in fact created by CHATTERTON. Jack Greenall died in Lancing, Sussex, in July 1983.
PUB: *Drawing Secrets!* (1944), *Useless Eustace* (1945, 1947), *Drawing's Fun* (1946), *Draw Your Own Christmas Cards* (1947), *Draw My Way* (1948), *Pencil Pranks* (1949)
COLL: UKCC

GREIFFENHAGEN, Maurice William RA NEAC (1862–1931) – *see* Bryant & Heneage

GREN – *see* Jones, Grenfell

GRH – *see* Halkett, George Roland

GRIFFIN, Charles William Langmead (b. 1946). Editorial/political, joke and pocket cartoonist and caricaturist. Charles Griffin was born on 20 May 1946 in Ruislip, Middlesex, the son of Alec Griffin, a furniture manufacturer's agent. Educated at Berkhamsted School, Hertfordshire, he spent two years at the Royal Military Academy, Sandhurst, where he failed to graduate but had some of his first caricatures and cartoons published in its journal, *Wishtream* (1965–8). After working as a hotel barman, furniture salesman and personnel manager he studied at Harrow School of Art (1971), Corsham School of Art and at Bath Academy of Art (1971–3), where he specialized in graphics. He then

'That ginseng you gave me worked a treat, Mr Christie.'

Charles Griffin, [HRH Queen Elizabeth the Queen Mother, Linford Christie], *Sun*, 5 August 1999

worked as a designer and paste-up artist on *The Villager* (1973–4) and in advertising (1974–6). His first caricatures were published in the Chelsea F.C. programme in 1976. He sold his first drawing (a pocket cartoon) to the *Daily Mail* in November the same year and began freelancing for various publications such as *Punch, Tennis World* (1977–81), *New Civil Engineer* (1979–85), *The Times* (1982–3) and *Observer* (1981–3), and he also taught art part-time at Camberwell School of Art (*c.* 1980). In 1983 he joined the *Sunday People* as Political Cartoonist, later taking over from KEITH WAITE at the *Daily Mirror* (1985–96), for both of which papers he has also done freelance cartoon work. He was Editorial / Political Cartoonist on the *Daily Express* from 1996 to 1998, succeeding RICK BROOKES,

and took over from FRANKLIN drawing the Saturday cartoon for the *Sun* (1998). Voted CCGB Social and Political Cartoonist of the Year (1986, 1987, 1988) and Feature Illustrator of the Year (1984), he won the *UK Press Gazette* / British Press Awards 'Image of the Year' prize in 1994 for his work on the *Daily Mirror* and won the CAT Caricaturist of the Year Award in 1998. Griffin also specializes in the study and detailed painting of cavalry uniforms. Influenced by CARL GILES, Mort Drucker and DAVID LEVINE, he used to draw on cartridge paper but found that a dip pen scratched the surface, so now uses a smooth coated paper (Excelda).

ILL: *Test Match Special* (1981); *Test Match Special 2* (1983); J. Archer, *First Among Equals* (1985); D. J. Taylor and M. Berkmann, *Other People* (1990)

GRIMES, Leslie (1898–1983). Political and strip cartoonist, and commercial artist. Leslie Grimes was born on 27 November 1898 in Chertsey, Surrey. He attended an orphanage school, then Kingston Art School where his work came to the attention of Philip de Laszlo who helped him to study in Paris. In World War I he served in the army (1915) then the RFC and later worked as a commercial artist and was a technical illustrator for Douglas Motorcycles. He also designed London Underground posters for LCC Evening Continuation Schools, Ministry of Labour/RoSPA industrial accident warnings ('A Cat Can Afford to Risk a Life or Two – You Keep Away') and others. While in advertising he contributed humorous sketches to *The Motor Cycle*. He joined the *Star* as Political Cartoonist in 1927 (succeeding DAVID Low and later handing over to WYNDHAM ROBINSON) and created the hugely successful 'All My Own Work'

series for the paper in 1938. In addition he drew for *Soldier* and others. He resigned from the *Star* in May 1952 and went to Ibiza to paint. Grimes used to draw with conté chalk, sitting on the floor, and would often use the side of the chalk for shading. For his work on the *Star* he would use a brush and always worked in tone because it was a quicker process than engraving line blocks.
COLL: [posters] IWM
EXHIB: RA (oil painting, 1944)

GRISET, Ernest Henry (1843–1907) – *see* Bryant & Heneage

GROSSMITH, Walter Weedon (1854–1919) – *see* Bryant & Heneage

GUS – *see* Smith, George William

H

HAILSTONE, Harold William (1897–1982). Joke cartoonist and illustrator. Harold Hailstone was born in London on 14 July 1897, the son of William Edward Hailstone, a dentist, and brother of the portrait painter Bernard Hailstone RP. He was educated at the Sir Andrew Judd School, Tonbridge, and joined the army in World War I, later transferring to the RFC (training as a pilot). After the war he attended Goldsmith's College where colleagues included Graham Sutherland. He drew frequently for *Illustrated London News*, *Humorist*, *Pearson's*, *Passing Show*, *Bystander*, *Tatler*, *Sketch*, *Britannia & Eve*, *Strand Magazine* and *Punch*. He was a flight-lieutenant in the RAF (1938–45) and an Official War Artist (1944–5). After World War II he was a staff cartoonist and illustrator for the *Daily Mirror* and retired in the mid-1960s. Hailstone worked in ink, oil and watercolour. He died at his home, Corneys Cottage, Harlow, Kent, on 21 November 1982.
COLL: IWM

HALDANE, David (b. 1954). Joke and strip cartoonist, illustrator and scriptwriter. David Haldane was born on 10 November 1954 in

Blyth, Northumberland, and studied graphic design at Newcastle-upon-Tyne Polytechnic. He began cartooning in 1978 and has contributed to *Punch* (1979–92, including covers), *Guardian* (1989–91), *Sunday Times*, *Mail on Sunday*, *Sun*, *Oink!*, *Spectator*, *Observer*, *Private Eye* and *Daily Mirror*. He has also produced greetings cards for Camden Graphics, drawn illustrations for advertising (e.g. Asda, Pedigree Chum), written scripts for Central TV's 'SPITTING IMAGE' and lectured in graphic design at Northumberland College.
PUB: *The Zoo Goes to France* (1982)

HALKETT, George Roland (1855–1918). Political cartoonist, caricaturist, journalist and illustrator. G. R. Halkett, who had a French mother, was born in Edinburgh on 11 March 1855 and left school aged 15 to work in an insurance office. He studied art in Paris, and after returning to Scotland became art critic of the *Edinburgh Evening News* in 1876. His *New Gleanings from Gladstone*, the first of a series of booklets of political cartoons with a strong anti-Gladstone bias, was published in 1880. In 1885 he succeeded PHIL MAY as cartoonist on the *St Stephen's*

Review when May went to Australia and in 1892 replaced F. C. GOULD as staff caricaturist on the *Pall Mall Gazette*. He was also art critic for the paper and later became Art Editor (1897) and Editor of the *Pall Mall Magazine* (1900–1905). In addition he contributed to *Punch* (from 1897, notably a popular series of caricatures of celebrities as chairs, 'Seats of the Mighty'), *Strand, Butterfly* and *Pall Mall Budget*. He was elected President of the recently founded Society of Illustrators in 1897. Halkett was seen as a better draughtsman than Gould. Ruskin described his caricatures as 'far more powerful and less gross than those of the old English school' and of *The Irish Green Book* Sir George Trevelyan said: 'Nothing more infamous than those caricatures could be produced in any country in the world.' He worked in pen and ink and watercolour and often just signed his drawings 'GRH'. G. R. Halkett died in London on 4 December 1918.

PUB: *New Gleanings from Gladstone* (n.d.), *The Gladstone Almanack* (n.d.), *The Egyptian Red Book* (1885), *The Irish Green Book* (1888), *The C. B. Book* (1906)

ILL: J. and W. Grimm, *Rumplestiltskin* (1882); M. Hunt, *Our Grandmother's Gowns* (1884); *The Elves and the Shoemaker* (n.d.); *Never Again! The History of a Crime* (c. 1918)

EXHIB: RSA; GI; BSG

COLL: V&A; NPG

LIT: J. A. Hammerton, *Humorists of the Pencil* (1905)

HALL, Maurice (1915–after 1940). Joke cartoonist, journalist, textile designer and painter. Maurice Hall studied briefly at art school and began producing comic sketches and articles for magazines while also designing textiles, furnishing fabrics, curtains, etc., for Bond Street shops and elsewhere, and exhibiting and selling original modernist landscapes and still-life paintings (also in Bond Street). He began drawing cartoons at the age of 20 and was fond of American humour. His work appeared in *Men Only, London Opinion, Punch, Illustrated, Razzle, Bystander, Lilliput, Soldier, Christmas Pie* and elsewhere. During World War II he volunteered for the Royal Norfolks and served variously in the Infantry, Signals, Regimental Office and Motor Transport section. 'Hall's work has a liveliness about it that is simply the result of sketching at first-hand. His figures, therefore, do not look as if they have been posed in the same position for the last half-hour. There is nothing special about the technique, except a balanced pattern of black against half tone, and various textures to help the design, but there is primarily, of course, a good deal of thought behind the *idea*' (BRADSHAW).

HAMMOND, Aubrey Lindsay (1893–1940). Caricaturist, theatre and poster designer, illustrator and art teacher. Aubrey Hammond was born in Folkestone, Kent, on 18 September 1893, the son of Lindsay Hammond and grandson of Alfred Elmore RA. He was educated at Bradfield College, Berkshire, and studied at the BYAM SHAW School of Art, the London School of Art and the Académie Julian, Paris. He began work as a designer for the theatre in 1913, and after war service in France with the Royal Fusiliers and Royal Dublin Fusiliers (1914–19) returned to this profession, designing sets and costumes for numerous productions, including the Royal Opera, Covent Garden. In addition he was General Scenic Supervisor to the Shakespeare Memorial Theatre, Stratford, and art director

Aubrey Hammond, [self-portrait], (Savage Club dinner menu card design), 4 March 1933

on a number of films for Grosvenor Films Ltd (from 1936). His caricatures were published in a number of newspapers and magazines during the 1920s and 30s such as *Evening News, Evening Standard, Nash's* and the *Tatler*. He also produced advertisements for Hector Powe, Canadian Club Whisky and others, designed theatre posters and taught Commercial and Theatrical Art at the Westminster School of Art. He was a member of the Royal Automobile Club, the London Sketch Club and the Savage Club. Aubrey Hammond died on 19 March 1940 aged 46.
ILL: L. Melville, *The London Scene* (1926); P. Traill, *Under the Cherry Tree* (1926); D. Greville, *The Diary of Mr Niggs* (1932)
EXHIB: PG; RG; International Theatrical Exhibition, Vienna (1936); British Theatrical Section, Paris Exhibition (1937); International Theatre Exhibition, Ottawa (1938)
COLL: V&A; BN

HANDELSMAN, John Bernard (b. 1922). Joke, strip and pocket cartoonist, illustrator, animator and writer. Bud Handelsman was born on 5 February 1922 in New York City, USA, the son of two teachers, and started drawing cartoons as a child. He attended the Art Students League, New York (1938–42) and served in the US Army Air Corps in World War II. After the war he studied electrical engineering at New York University (1945–6) and worked for various advertising agencies as a commercial artist and typographic designer until 1960 when he turned freelance cartoonist. He came to England in 1963 and began contributing pocket cartoons to the *Evening Standard* and joke cartoons to the *Observer, New Statesman, Punch* (including covers and the popular 'Freaky Fables' series), *New Yorker* (since 1967), *Saturday Review, Saturday Evening Post, Look, Esquire* and *Playboy*. In addition he has written scripts and humorous articles, worked in graphic design, received *Playboy*'s award for Best Black and White Cartoon (1978) and created a ten-minute animated film, *In the Beginning*, based on the Creation and broadcast on BBC TV on Christmas Eve 1992. He returned to the USA in 1981. Handelsman also signs his work 'JBH' and uses a Hunt 107 nib and indian ink and Dr Martin's watercolour on Bristol plate or watercolour paper.
PUB: *You're Not Serious, I Hope* (1971), *Freaky Fables* (1979), *Freaky Fables* (1984), *Further Freaky Fables* (1986)

ILL: A. McGovern, *If You Sailed on the Mayflower* (1969); J. Fritz, *Who's That Stepping on Plymouth Rock?* (1975); R. B. Gross, *A Book About Benjamin Franklin* (1975); A. Hilton (ed.), *This England* (1978); J. Cleese and R. Skynner, *Families and How to Survive Them* (1983), *Life and How to Survive It* (1993); D. Frost and M. Shea, *The Mid-Atlantic Companion* (1986)
COLL: Cincinnati Art Museum, Ohio; UKCC

HARCOURT – *see* Mallett, Harcourt Dennis

HARDING, Leslie Clifford 'Styx' (1914–91). Joke and strip cartoonist. Leslie Harding was born in Stepney, London, on 2 June 1914 and studied at Leyton School of Art. He began cartooning at the age of 18, producing sporting strips for the *Daily Mail*, and later contributed regularly to the *Daily Express, Reveille, Weekend* (10 years), *London Opinion, Shoot!* (15 years), *Sunday Citizen* and children's comics, and illustrated advertising campaigns for British Rail ('Away Day' posters) amongst others. During World War II he served in North Africa with the Tank Corps. Himself a great admirer of BRUCE BAIRNSFATHER, he also taught other artists, including REG SMYTHE the creator of 'Andy Capp', and was Honorary President of the Laurel & Hardy Fan Club. He died in Portsmouth on 11 May 1991.
PUB: *Styx Christmas Fun Book* (1957), *Pick of the Famous Weekend Styx Cartoons* (1957), *Laugh With Styx* (1958), *Styx Holiday Fun Book* (1958), *Weekend Styx Calendar 1959* (1958), *The Best of Styx* (1959), *Styx Again!* (1959), *Weekend Fun Book* (1960), *The Styx Cartoon Show* (1963)

HARDY, Dudley RI RBA ROI RMS (1867–1922). Painter, poster artist, illustrator and joke cartoonist. Dudley Hardy was born in Sheffield on 15 January 1867, the son of the marine painter Thomas Bush Hardy RBA, and the brother of the illustrator F. C. Hardy. He studied successively at Düsseldorf Academy of Art under Crola and Löwenstein (aged 15), in his father's studio, under A. A. Calderon, in Antwerp under Verlat and finally in Paris under Raphael Collin and Carl Rossi. In 1885, aged 18, he exhibited his first picture, an oil painting, at the Royal Academy. His first press work was as a graphic war journalist in the Sudan for *Pictorial World*, but his mother refused to let him go, so he faked his reports from home in Hampstead. He then started contributing illustrations and

cartoons to *Sketch, Pick-Me-Up, Illustrated London News, Le Rire* (1903), *Pall Mall Gazette* (from 1894), *Gentlewoman, Longbow, Illustrated Bits, St Paul's* (in black and red), *Ariel, English Illustrated Magazine, Ludgate, Idler, Minster* and *Punch*. However, he is celebrated as the first successful UK poster artist, famously designing 'The Yellow Girl' for Jerome K. Jerome's magazine *To-Day*, and a series advertising productions at the Savoy Theatre. 'I think you can educate the masses to a great extent by improving the art of the advertisement. By this means you can make the streets the Royal Academy of the masses' (*Strand Magazine*, 1894). In addition he illustrated books and drew comic postcards for Collins, Valentines, Davidson, Faulkner and Tuck (notably in the 'Celebrated Posters' series) and advertisements for Nestlé's Milk, Orient Line Shipping (posters) and others. Influenced by the first great poster artist, the Frenchman Jules Chéret, he worked in pen and ink, pencil, brush and wash and used Michallet paper for his watercolours. He also painted Eastern scenes and studies of Dutch and Breton peasants, and four of his watercolours were hung in the cabin of the First Officer on the *Mauretania*. Elected RBA (1889), RI (1897) and ROI (1898), he was also a member of the Savage Club and, along with TOM BROWNE, LANCE THACKERAY, CECIL ALDIN and PHIL MAY, was a founder member of the London Sketch Club, becoming its President in 1902. Dudley Hardy died on 11 August 1922.
ILL: A. Werner, *The Humour of Holland* (1894); B. Harte, *The Bell Ringer of Angels* (1897); F. E. Weatherley, *Lays for the Little Ones* (1898); E. H. Cooper, *Wyemarke and the Sea-Fairies* (1899); R. Strong, *Sensations of Paris* (1912)
EXHIB: RA; RI; RBA; ROI; RMS; FAS
COLL: LE; NE; THG
LIT: A. E. Johnson, *Dudley Hardy* (1909); P. V. Bradshaw, *The Art of the Illustrator 19* (1918)

HARGREAVES, Harry MSIAD (b. 1922). Joke and strip cartoonist, illustrator, animator and writer. Harry Hargreaves was born in Manchester on 9 February 1922, the son of Harry Hargreaves, a civil servant in the Ministry of Labour, and educated at Chorlton High School, Manchester. A former Manchester Cathedral choirboy (1930–33), he taught himself cartooning from the age of nine, had his first cartoon published in the *Manchester Evening News* on 10 November 1936, aged 14, and at 17 was producing weekly strips for *Beano* and *Dandy*. He

trained as a furniture designer at Manchester School of Art (part-time, 1938) and then as an engineer, working for companies such as Rolls-Royce and Ford (1938–9). During World War II he served in the RAFVR Signals in the Far East (1940–45). After the war he joined J. Arthur Rank's Gaumont British Animation Ltd as a cartoon animator (1946–9). When the Cartoon Unit disbanded he turned freelance for three years, creating and developing strips (e.g. 'Harold Hare') for Amalgamated Press comics such as *Sun, Comet* and *Knockout*, producing advertising work for Rowntrees, Dunlops and Pickerings, and designing toys for Mettoy. He then joined the Toonder Film Studios, Amsterdam, as a Master Cartoonist (1953) and produced a cartoon strip, 'Little Panda' which was syndicated to 150 daily newspapers across Europe, including the London *Evening News*. Returning to the UK in 1954 he continued the strip for eight years (until 1961) while freelancing for publications such as *Illustrated, Lilliput, Blighty, Men Only, Daily Sketch, Daily Graphic, Punch, Daily Telegraph, Tatler, Life, Christian Science Monitor, Countryman, Eureka!* (Italy), *Air Safety, The Cricketer, TV Comic, Daily Mirror, TV Times* (USA), *Animals Magazine* and *Stern*. Perhaps his most celebrated creation is The Bird, a scruffy sparrow which first appeared in *Punch* on 29 October 1958 and has been published worldwide, including in colour (as 'Early Bird', 1985–7) on TV-am. His daily strip, 'Hayseeds', containing British wildlife characters (e.g. Toby the Badger), ran in the *Evening News* (1968–81) and has also been syndicated internationally. In addition, he has had his own TV programme, *Discs-a-Gogo*, on TWW. Advertising clients have included Barclays Bank, Kelloggs, Guinness, Saxo Salt, the Coal Board, Walls and Post Office Telegrams and he has provided illustrations for Army Air Corps and Wildfowl & Wetlands Trust publications, produced greetings cards for Sharpes (1987–8), and been involved in mechanical and soft-toy design. Influenced by Disney, Da Vinci, Rembrandt, Rackham, SHEPHERD and ILLINGWORTH, he works in pencil, pen (Gillott 290, 291, 292 and Hughes 894) and indian ink, watercolours and acrylics on various kinds of board, watercolour and cartridge paper. HEWISON has remarked on his 'outstanding skill at drawing movement. This is not merely technique but a real knowledge of how animals move, fall, skid, collide etcetera – [rather] than an ability to caricature movement.'

Harry Hargreaves, *Daily Telegraph, c.* 1983

PUB: *How's That!* (1959), *Not Out!* (1960), *The Bird* (1961), *The Bird and Others* (1962), *It's a Bird's Life* (1965), *Strictly for the Bird* (1967), *The Bird Set* (1968), *Birds of a Feather* (1969), *Googlies* (1971), *Hayseeds* (1971), *Hayseeds 2* (1972), *Bird for All Seasons* (1973), *Canny Curlew* (1988)
ILL: S. Raven, *Quick Quiz* (1981); K. Grahame, *The Wind in the Willows* (1983); Dennis Henshaw, *Brush Your Teeth with Wine* (1961)

EXHIB: Gloucester Library; Blackwell's Bookshop, Oxford
COLL: Musée des Hommes, Montreal; UKCC

HARO – *see* Hodson, Haro Reginald Victor

HARPUR, Merrily (b. 1948). Joke and strip cartoonist, illustrator and writer. Merrily Harpur was born on 2 April 1948 and educated at

Headington School, Oxford, and Trinity College, Dublin. After a period restoring oil paintings she became a freelance cartoonist and writer working for *Guardian* (from 1978), *Punch*, *The Times*, *Sunday Telegraph* (including the strip 'The Arcadians'), *Listener*, *Field*, *Country Living* and others. She has also produced cartoon backdrops and animated titles for Miles Kington's TV series *Let's Parler Franglais*.
PUB: *The Nightmares of Dream Topping* (1984), *Pig Overboard!* (1984), *Unheard of Ambridge* (1989)
ILL: M. Kington, 'Let's Parler Franglais' series (from 1979)

HARRIS, Herbert H. (fl. 1930s). Advertising cartoonist, poster artist, illustrator and writer. H. H. Harris drew multi-frame story cartoons for *Bystander* in the 1930s and contributed joke cartoons to *Passing Show* and others but is perhaps best known as the creator of the famous 'Pyjama Man' advertisements for Bovril which he created while working for the S. H. Benson agency. The first of these was published in 1920 and showed a smiling shipwrecked man, still wearing his green-striped pyjamas, sitting astride a giant floating jar of Bovril with the slogan 'Bovril prevents that *sinking* feeling'. (The slogan had actually been invented earlier but had been withheld because of the *Titanic* disaster.) Linked advertisements using the same character in different situations continued into the 1930s. Indeed the 1920 cartoon, like the Guinness drawings of GILROY, became so familiar that as late as 1963 NORMAN MANSBRIDGE attacked Macmillan's defence policy in *Punch* in January 1963 by depicting him as the Pyjama Man clinging to Polaris.
PUB: *Jolly Junior's Fairy Tales* (1945), *Junior's Jolly ABC* (1945), *What Fun* (1946)

HARRISON, Charles (*c.* 1860–1943). Joke cartoonist and illustrator. Charles Harrison was born in London into a theatrical family and attended St Thomas's College, Hackney. He began work as a child actor, appearing in *Oliver Twist* (with Henry Irving) amongst other productions. He then worked briefly in the City while taking evening classes in drawing, before returning to the stage. His first illustrations appeared in a suburban London comic paper which he ran himself with a local printer, and he later contributed to Red Lion House publications. Regular commissions for the children's weekly magazines *Funny Folks* and *Scraps* published by James Henderson led to his joining the company's staff. His 'Toy Books' series (1883) showed the influence of CRANE and Caldecott but he later developed a more individual style and was particularly good at parodies of classical Egyptian and Japanese art. In 1893 he left Henderson's to join the staff of *Cassell's Saturday Journal*, for which he drew a page of social cartoons every two weeks which were a precursor of those by HASELDEN in the *Daily Mirror*. In addition he was cartoonist on the *Pall Mall Gazette* under the editorship of W. T. Stead and drew a daily cartoon for the *Daily Express* for six months in 1912 but gave it up because 'the strain was too great'. He also contributed to *London Opinion*, *Chums*, *Evening News*, *Boy's Champion*, *Winter's Pie*, *Passing Show*, *Pearson's*, *Sketch*, *Humorist*, *St Stephen's Review*, *St James' Budget* (theatre drawings), *Pall Mall Budget*, *Punch* (1895–20 December 1934), *Judge* (USA) and *Daily Mail*. In addition he worked in advertising for Attenbury Pastilles and others and created a number of advertisement characters. A great admirer of the work of John Leech, Harrison never used models, just observation and memory, and worked in both colour and black and white. He was a member of the London Sketch Club. Charles Harrison died in November 1943.
PUB: *Rhymes and Jingles* (1883), *The Prince and the Penny* (1883), [with W. K. Haselden] *Accidents Will Happen* (1907), *A Humorous History of England* (1920)
ILL: S. H. Hamer, *Master Charlie* (1899); R. Andom, *Troddles and Us and Others* (1901); H. Rowan, *London Japanned* (1910); F. McAbe, *A Living Machine* (1921)

HART, Frank (1878–1959). Joke cartoonist, illustrator, lecturer and children's writer. Frank Hart was born in Brighton on 1 November 1878 and studied at Heatherley's under John Crompton. His work appeared in the *Humorist*, *Little Folks*, *Odd Volume*, *Printer's Pie*, *John Bull*, *Punch* (1911–29), *Graphic*, *Country Life*, *Field* and *Temple* amongst others. He also lectured on black-and-white art and was a member of the Chelsea Arts Club. Frank Hart died on 23 May 1959.
PUB: *Dolly's Society Book* (1902), *The Best Nursery Rhymes* (1910), *The Animals Do Their Bit in the Great War* (1918), *Andrew, Bogie and Jack* (1919), *One Long Holiday!* (1921), *Everyhorse* (1935)

ILL: M. Fisher, *The Golliwog's Dream and Other Stories for Little Folk* (*c.* 1910)
EXHIB: RA; RI

HARVEY – *see* Beard, Albert Edgar

HASELDEN, William Kerridge (1872–1953). Editorial and strip cartoonist and caricaturist. Born on 3 December 1872 in Seville, Spain, the son of Adolphe Henry Haselden, an English civil engineer, W. K. Haselden was self-taught as an artist. He left school at 16 and worked as an underwriter at Lloyd's for 13 years while freelancing cartoons for *The Sovereign, St James's Gazette* and *Tatler*. He joined the *Daily Mirror* (1904–40) under Hamilton Fyfe as Editorial Cartoonist and also produced regular theatre sketches for *Punch* (1906–36) with G. L. STAMPA. Regarded as the father of the British newspaper strip cartoon, Haselden is also celebrated as the creator of 'The Sad Experiences of Big and Little Willie', lampooning Kaiser Wilhelm of Germany and his son during World War I (it first appeared on 2 October 1914), which the Kaiser himself later admitted to have been 'damnably effective'. Other characters created by Haselden include Miss Joy Flapperton, Colonel Dugout and Burlington Bertie. Admired by BEERBOHM, SICKERT (who called him the 'English Aristophanes') and Paul Nash (who compared him to Leech as 'one of the best draughtsmen we possess'), he was offered a knighthood by Stanley Baldwin but turned it down as he 'didn't want all the fuss'. Haselden worked with a pen and indian ink on board. He died on 25 December 1953.
PUB: *Daily Mirror Reflections* (annuals 1908–37), *The Sad Experiences of Big and Little Willie* (1915)
ILL: C. Harrison, *Accidents Will Happen* (1907), *The Globe 'By the Way' Book* (1908); E. B. Tweedie, *America As I Saw It* (1913), *Women the World Over* (1914)
EXHIB: Dore Gallery; Aldeburgh Festival
COLL: BM; NPG, UKCC: CAT

HASSALL, John RI RMS (1868–1948). Joke cartoonist, illustrator, poster and commercial artist, and painter. John Hassall was born in Walmer, Kent, on 21 May 1868, the son of Lieutenant Christopher Clark Hassall, an officer in the Royal Navy. His father died when Hassall was eight and his stepfather was General Sir William Purvis Wright KCB. Educated at Newton Abbott College, Devon, and Neuenheim College, Heidelberg, he failed to be accepted by the Royal Military Academy, Sandhurst, and moved to Minnedosa in Manitoba, Canada, where he worked as a farmer for three years with his brother Owen. When his first published drawing 'A Surprise Party' appeared in the *Daily Graphic* on 26 February 1890, he returned to the UK, took advice from his friend DUDLEY HARDY and studied in Antwerp and under Bouguereau and Ferrier in Paris. Returning to Britain his first humorous drawing appeared in the *Sketch* on 7 March 1894 and he first exhibited at the Royal Academy the same year. His first commercial commission was from the Belfast printers David Allen, for a black-and-yellow poster advertising the musical comedy *The French Maid*. He continued to work for the company for seven years, producing many theatrical posters as well as advertisements for Vim, Wills Capstan Cigarettes, Osram Lamps, Colman's Mustard, Sunlight Soap, Lux, Fry's, Cadbury's, Bovril, Oxo, Veritas Gas Mantles ('I Bet That's a Veritas'), Andrews Liver Salts (poster 'I Must Have Left It Behind'), London Underground and others. 'King of the Posters' (*The Times* obituary), perhaps his most famous design was 'Skegness is *so* bracing' (1908), featuring the Jolly Fisherman skipping along the beach, and based on an earlier idea he had used for 'There Was an Old Man of Penzance'. In addition, he illustrated books (including designing the covers of the 'Punch Library of Humour') and contributed illustrations and cartoons to *Bibby's Annual, Captain* (including the original cover design), *Cassell's, Comica* (1908–9), *Star, Eureka, Collectors' Magazine* (including covers), *Holly Leaves, To-Day, Idler, Illustrated Bits, Judy, London Opinion, Lika Joko, Moonshine, New Budget, Odd Volume, Pall Mall, Pears Annual, Pick-Me-Up, Printer's Pie, St Paul's, Sketch* and *Tatler*. In 1905 he set up the New Art School and School of Poster Design (later known as the John Hassall School), with his old Antwerp tutor Charles van Havermaet, in Earls Court, London, pupils including BAIRNSFATHER, BERT THOMAS, H. M. BATEMAN, ROUNTREE, Gladys Peto and FISH. In addition he collaborated with CECIL ALDIN on many projects including book illustrations and wallpaper frieze designs. He also designed pottery for Royal Doulton, Atlas China and others and drew some of the earliest postcards (from 1899) for Tuck, Faulkner, Davidson, Baird, Inter-Art and others. In World War I he served as a Special Constable (1916–18), guarding the gates of Buckingham Palace

RAILWAY TRAVEL IN WARTIME

W. K. Haselden, *Daily Mirror*, 29 April 1918

amongst other duties. A friend of Baden-Powell, he designed the first cover for *Scouting for Boys* and the movement's Imperial Jubilee flag (1920). Influenced by Mucha, Dudley Hardy, the *Judge* artist Eugene Zimmerman, and the French poster artist Jules Chéret, he worked in ink, wash, gouache and watercolour and also painted in oils and watercolours. For Hassall a good poster 'should hit the passser-by right in the eye-ball. This is best attained by a huge splash of one colour, which should dominate the whole picture . . . The second essential is simplicity . . . the third essential is that the poster should clearly indicate what it advertises' (*Pearson's Magazine*, 1905). He was elected RI in 1901, and in 1939 was awarded a Civil List pension for 'services to posters'. His last poster design was 'Save Poland' in World War II. Known as Jack to his friends, he lived in the Bedford Park 'Bohemian Quarter' in Chiswick along with Hardy, TOM BROWNE, LANCE THACKERAY and Cecil Aldin. A member of the Strand, Odd Volumes, Knights and Savage Clubs (he designed the Savage's Red Indian logo), he was also one of the founder members (with Aldin, Browne, Thackeray and Hardy) of the London Sketch Club (President 1903). Of his children, his daughter Joan Hassall became a celebrated wood-engraver, Christopher Vernon Hassall was poet, actor and lyricist for Ivor Novello and another son, Ian Dingwall Hassall, also an artist, became the youngest-ever member of the London Sketch Club (from the day he was born). John Hassall died in Kensington, London, on 8 March 1948. He donated his huge collection of Mesolithic flints to the Fitzwilliam Museum, Cambridge, all except one, which he had buried with him, to confuse future archaeologists.

PUB: *Two Well-Worn Shoe-Stories* (1899), *The Book of John Hassall* (1907), *Keep Smiling* (1914), *Ye Berlyn Tapestrie* (1915), *The Hassall ABC* (1918) ILL: Many books including H. A. Spurr, *A Cockney in Arcadia* (1899); P. Montrose, *Oh! My Darling Clementine* (1900); G. C. Bingham, *Six and Twenty Boys and Girls* (1902); W. Emanuel, *People* (1903), *Keep Smiling* (1914); D. Tovey, *The Coronation Picture Book* (1903); G. E. Farrow, *Absurd Ditties* (1903), *Round the World ABC* (1904); S. H. Hamer, *The Princess and the Dragon* (1908); W. C. Jerrold, *Mother Goose's Nursery Rhymes* (1909); C. Perrault, *The Sleeping Beauty* (1912); [with H. Rountree] R. S. S. Baden-Powell, *Now, Then!* (1927); *Blackie's Popular Nursery Stories* (1931) and many books by the children's writer G. A. Henty

EXHIB: RA; RI; FAS; LH 'John Hassall' (1968) COLL: V&A; SC; Essex University Library; THG LIT: A. E. Johnson, *John Hassall* (1907); D. Cuppleditch, *The John Hassall Lifestyle* (1979)

HAWKER, David (b. 1941). Joke cartoonist and illustrator. Born in Earlsfield, London, on 9 October 1941, the son of George Hawker, a head gardener, David Hawker was educated at Midhurst Grammar School, Sussex, and Queen Mary's Grammar School, Basingstoke, Hampshire. He has worked as a salesman, gardener, laundry assistant, cleaner and driving instructor. Self-taught apart from a short correspondence course in art, he sold his first cartoon while working as an architectural draughtsman in 1967 and turned full-time freelance in 1969. His cartoons have appeared in *Punch* (from 1970), *Spectator* and *Private Eye*. Advertising clients include BUPA and Terrys of York (TV commercials). Hawker uses a Waverley nib for a variety of line and is an admirer of the work of *New Yorker* cartoonist Richard Taylor. COLL: UKCC

'Hayseeds' – *see* Hargreaves, Harry

HEATH, Michael John (b. 1935). Political and strip cartoonist. Michael Heath was born on 13 October 1935 in Bloomsbury, London, the son of Amalgamated Press and D. C. Thomson children's comics illustrator George Heath (creator of 'The Falcon' in *Radio Fun*, and the artist credited with introducing the American-style speech-bubble into British cartoons). He studied at Brighton Art College (1952–3) and his first cartoon was published in *Melody Maker* (1954). He worked at first as an animator with Rank (1955) before turning full-time freelance in 1956. Since then he has contributed to *Man About Town*, *Lilliput*, *Mail on Sunday*, *Honey*, *Tatler*, *Men Only*, *Woman's Sunday Mirror*, *Sunday Times*, *Evening Standard* (1976–86), *Evening News*, *Guardian*, *Private Eye* (from June 1962, especially the series 'Great Bores of Today' and 'Heath's Private View'), *Spectator* (from 1957), and *Punch* (1958–92, including covers). He has been Cartoon Editor of *Spectator* since 1991 and was Political Cartoonist on the *Independent* (1990–94). He has been voted CCGB Pocket Cartoonist of the Year (1977), Granada TV's *What the Papers Say* Cartoonist of the Year (1979) and Glen Grant Cartoonist of the Year (1977). Heath draws on layout paper using dip pen and indian ink and never uses pencil. His distinctive

'No ice, thank you.'
ENGLISHMAN IN BAR

Michael Heath, *Welcome to America*, 1985

fine line work, with occasional use of collage, has been widely admired and HEWISON has described him as having 'the best visual memory in the business', being particularly good on dress and interiors.

PUB: *Private Eye Michael Heath* (1973), *Michael Heath's Automata* (1976), *Book of Bores* (1976), *The Punch Cartoons of Heath* (1976), *Love All?* (1982), *The Best of Heath* (1984), *Welcome to America* (1985), *Baby* (1988), *The Complete Heath* (1990)

ILL: Many books including E. G. Hardy (ed.), *Bloomers* (1966); S. Oram, *France* (1972); W. Donaldson, *1992 and All That* (1990)

EXHIB: CG; RFH

COLL: BM; A; UKCC; V&A

HEBBLETHWAITE, Sidney H. (fl. 1898– d. 1914). Joke cartoonist, comic-postcard artist and illustrator. Sidney Hebblethwaite's cartoons were first published in *Pick-Me-Up* in the 1890s. He later contributed to the *Graphic*, *Strand* and the *Tatler*. In addition he drew series of comic postcards for Raphael Tuck such as 'Racing Illustrated' and 'Comic History'. 'His work showed promise of great possibilities which was, however, defeated by his early death' (THORPE).

ILL: 'Dodo', *A Trip to Mars* (1901)

HELLMAN, Louis Mario MBE (b. 1936). Architect, joke cartoonist, caricaturist, illustrator and writer. Born in London on 19 March 1936, the son of Mario Biselli Hellmann [sic], an actor, Louis Hellman attended the Bartlett School of Architecture, London (1955–62), and the École des Beaux-Arts, Paris (1960–61). An architect by profession (he once worked for the GLC but

now has his own practice), his first cartoon was published in the *Evening Standard* in 1955 and he has drawn cartoons for *Architects Journal* since 1967 featuring his 'bearded and bow-tied homunculus architect' (Knevitt) with his eyes at the top of his bald, earless and oblong head. He has also regularly contributed caricatures to *Architectural Review* (since 1984) and cartoons to *Building Design* (since 1987) and *Design Week* (since 1994). Other publications which have featured his work include *Sunday Times, New Statesman, Euromoney, Guardian, Private Eye, Spectator, Observer, Built Environment* and *RIBA Journal*, and he has occasionally deputized on the *Evening Standard* as Editorial/Political Cartoonist. He also made an animated film on architectural history for BBC2 TV (*Boom!*, 1976) and has produced calendars for Hepworth Building Products, lectured on architecture internationally and written extensively on the subject in periodicals. Influenced by Steinberg, Low, Feiffer, FRANÇOIS and VICKY, he uses pen and ink, collage, watercolour and acrylic on smooth board or paper. His work has been described by Sir Hugh Casson as 'blissfully funny. As . . . a sharp observer on our industry he is unrivalled,' and by Nikolaus Pevsner as 'by far the best architectural lampooning known to me'.
PUB: *A is For Architect* (1975), *All Hellman Breaks Loose* (1980), *Architecture for Beginners* (1986)
ILL: Many books including G. Brandreth, *The Big Book of Secrets* (1977); C. Knevitt, *Perspectives* (1986)
EXHIB: AA; NEC; RIBA; Cambridge Architecture Centre
COLL: RIBA
LIT: C. Knevitt, *Seven Ages of the Architect* (1991)

HEWISON, William Coltman (b. 1925). Caricaturist, editorial cartoonist, designer, illustrator and writer. Bill Hewison was born in South Shields, Co. Durham, on 15 May 1925, the son of Ralph Hewison, a signwriter and decorator. Educated at South Shields Art School (1941–3), he was a gunner and wireless operator with the 1st Royal Tank Regiment in World War II and later served in GHQ, Cairo (1945–7). He then attended Regent Street Polytechnic Art School (1947–9) – where he gained a bronze medal for life drawing – and the Institute of Education, London University (1949–50). His first cartoon was published in *Lilliput* in 1949 and more followed in *Punch* in 1950. He joined the editorial staff of the latter in 1956 as Assistant Art Editor,

and was subsequently Art Editor (1960–84), theatre caricaturist (1961–92, succeeding SEARLE), illustrator and occasional political cartoonist as well as art critic (1984–7), book reviewer and feature writer. His work has also appeared in *Truth, Listener, Sunday Times, The Times, Reader's Digest, Spectator, Oldie, High Life, Executive World, Architecture Journal, Classical Music, Europe* and others, and advertising clients have included BP, GPO, the Wine Society and Robeco. Since 1992 he has been regular theatre caricaturist for *The Times*. He has also taught art part-time at Latymer Upper School, Hammersmith (1950–56). Elected a Member of the Society of Industrial Artists in 1953 he joined the *Punch* Table in 1960, and married the artist Elsie Hammond in 1950. Influenced by Ronald Searle and LESLIE ILLINGWORTH, he uses a mapping pen and indian or coloured inks as well as pencil, gouache and watercolour. 'His line has been described as having the power of a rhino whip and the spikiness of barbed wire' (Feaver). Price, however, saw him more as a decorator: 'his humour might be wild but his drawing was realistic, or rather, of reality with its comic aspects heightened'. He sometimes just signs his work 'H'. He was one of the founder members of the British Cartoonists' Association in 1966.
PUB: *Types Behind the Print* (1963), [novel] *Mindfire* (1973), *The Cartoon Connection* (1977), [with R. Thomson] *How to Draw and Sell Cartoons* (1985), and he has edited and introduced 21 *Punch* cartoon collections on various themes (since 1987)
ILL: R. Lewis, *What We Did to Father* (1960); H. F. Ellis, *Mediatrics* (1961), *A. J. Wentworth, B.A. (Retd.)* (1962); K. Amis, *Lucky Jim* (1974); B. Took and M. Feldman, *Round the Horn* (1975); M. Becket, *Economic Alphabet* (1976); P. G. Wodehouse, *The Great Sermon Handicap* (1989)
EXHIB: NT (1980, 1985, 1990, 1995)
COLL: BM; V&A; TM; UKCC; SAM; Princeton University, USA

HEWITT, Harold (1909–after 1950). Joke cartoonist. Harry Hewitt contributed to *Night & Day, Punch, Bystander, Strand* (e.g. Lord Dunsany's 'The Khamseen'), and *Lilliput* and also produced advertisements for Schweppes, Bowaters, Winsor & Newton and others. He worked in pen, brush, Mandarin ink and watercolour on Winsor & Newton's Whatman Board. Harold Hewitt was married for some years to the novelist Kathleen Hewitt, whom he met when she was an artist's model. During World War I he served in the army.

H.Fs – *see* Furniss, Harry

HICKEY – *see* Hickson, George Harvey Forster

HICKLING, P. B. (fl. 1895–1960). Joke cartoonist and illustrator. P. B. Hickling's earliest cartoons appeared in *Fun* (1895) and he later contributed to *Boy's Own Paper*, *Cassell's*, *Girl's Realm*, *Grand*, *Graphic*, *Strand* (e.g. illustrating 'Tetherstones' by Ethel M. Dell), *Humorist*, *Hutchinson's*, *Printer's Pie*, *Magpie*, *Pearson's*, *Royal Magazine*, *Tatler* and *Punch*. He also drew advertisements for Mansion Polish and others. Hickling was a friend of the ROBINSON brothers and a member of their 'Frothfinders Club'. He drew mostly in pen and ink.
ILL: J. Long, *The Three Clerks* (*c.* 1908); J. F. Fraser, *Life's Contrasts* (1908); C. F. Parsons, *All Change Here!* (1916); N. Barr, *The Inquisitive Harvest Mouse* (1949) and many more
COLL: THG

HICKS, Victor (fl. 1913–42). Caricaturist, strip and joke cartoonist, illustrator and commercial artist. Victor Hicks became interested in drawing when suffering from mumps as a child. He contributed to *Everybody's*, *Bystander*, *Razzle*, *The Stage*, *The Artist*, *Illustrated Sporting & Dramatic News*, etc., and designed theatre programmes and posters (e.g. for *The Golden Boy* at the Coliseum, Julian Wylie's *Cinderella* at Drury Lane and *Rio Rita* at the Prince Edward Theatre). In addition he designed book jackets for Cassell & Co. (e.g. Sax Rohmer's *The Bride of Fu Manchu*), Constable and the Reader's Library, drew advertisements for Gaymer's Cider and the 'Eat More Fruit' campaign, and produced showcards for Waddington's playing cards, amongst others.
PUB: *A Modern Drawing Book* (1935), *Modern Playcraft* (1937), *Rainbowland* (1942)
ILL: A. C. Firidon (ed.), *The Ceejay* [Competitors' Journal] *Annual* (1913)

HICKSON, George Harvey Forster 'Hickey' (fl. 1930s–after 1959). Joke cartoonist. Hickey was born in Australia and worked as an accountant before coming to the UK where his cartoons appeared in *Lilliput*, *Razzle*, *Eagle*, *Inky Way Annual*, *Punch* (nearly 200 cartoons, 1946–59) and other publications. FOUGASSE described him as 'a humorist whose drawings, far from

attempting to adapt themselves to the subject, usually seem to be doing their best to play them down as dispassionately as possible, a form of foil-acting which, although it is all against the run of contemporary trends, can be very pleasant'. A professional musician, he married a *Daily Mail* journalist and later moved to Auribeau, near Cannes, France.

HIGH, Graham Douglas (b.1957). Political cartoonist. Graham High was born in Dundee, Scotland, on 27 March 1957. He studied drawing and painting at Edinburgh College of Art (1975–9) and won a travelling scholarship to the USA in 1980. He has been Political Cartoonist on the *Scotsman* since 1987 and has also contributed to *Scottish Business Insider* (covers). Voted Cartoonist of the Year in the Bank of Scotland Press Awards (1998) he was also co-founder of Rogues Gallery, Edinburgh (1996), which exhibited work by many British cartoonists. Graham High is also a keen jazz guitarist and composer, has recorded with Indian fusion group 'Looking East' (1995) and performs regularly in Scotland. He works with a brush and acrylic ink on cartridge paper and admires Daumier, STEADMAN and EMILIO COIA.
EXHIB: Glenkinchie Whisky Distillery, Scotland
COLL: BM; Glenkinchie Whisky Distillery, Scotland

HILL, Leonard Raven (1867–1942). Political and joke cartoonist, caricaturist and illustrator. Leonard Raven Hill was born in Bath on 10 March 1867, the son of William Hill, a law stationer. Educated at Bristol Grammar School and Devon County School, he studied at the Lambeth School of Art under J. Sparkes from 1882 (fellow students included F. H. TOWNSEND and the illustrator Charles Ricketts). While still a student he contributed joke cartoons to *Judy* signed 'Leonard Hill' (1885) and some early drawings also appeared in the *Nutshell*. He then studied at the Académie Julian in Paris under Bouguereau and Aimé Morot (1885–7) and exhibited at the Paris Salon aged 20. On his return to Britain he worked at first as a painter, exhibiting at the Royal Academy (1889). However, he had more success contributing joke cartoons, theatrical caricatures and illustrations to *Black & White*, *Cassell's*, *Daily Chronicle*, *Daily Graphic*, *Idler*, *Ludgate Magazine*, *Minster*, *Pearson's*, *Pears Annual*, *Pall Mall Gazette*, *Printer's Pie*, *Reveille*, *St Paul's*, *Sketch*, *Strand* and the

CARRIER: *'Try zideways, Mrs Jones, try zideways!'*
MRS JONES: *'Lar' bless 'ee, John, I ain't got no zideways!'*

Leonard Raven Hill, *Punch*, 17 October 1900

Windsor Magazine. He was Art Editor of *Pick-Me-Up* (1890), and then became founder and Joint Editor of the weekly *Butterfly* (1893). When this folded after 10 months he worked for *Pall Mall Budget* and then set up the short-lived *Unicorn* in 1895. His first drawing for *Punch* appeared on 28 December 1895 and he continued to work for the magazine for nearly 40 years, being elected to the Table in 1901. In 1910 he succeeded Bernard Partridge as Second Cartoonist, drawing political cartoons until he retired in 1935 (being himself succeeded by Shepard), a notable example being his widely admired World War I cartoon, 'The Return of the Raider', depicting the Kaiser and Admiral Tirpitz. However, he was more at home with social drawings, a famous example from 1900 being of a fat lady trying to get through a bus door with the driver saying 'Try zideways, Mrs Jones, try zideways!' to which she replies 'Lar' bless 'ee, John, I ain't got no zideways!' In addition he drew advertisements for Selfridges and others, and postcards for Jarrold & Sons, Tuck and Wrench. He also produced lithographs and etched. Influenced at first by Charles Keene, he worked in pen and ink and sometimes wash, and had a 'free and hasty technique' (Ellwood). As well as Keene and Linley Sambourne he admired the Swiss-born American joke and political cartoonist 'Zim' (Eugene Zimmerman): 'For absolute comic humour . . . no one has equalled Zimmerman, of the New York *Judge*, in my opinion. Charles Keene is, of course, miles ahead of any other man in quiet humour' (*Strand*, vol 27). He was a member of the Savage Club. His second wife was *Punch*'s advertising manager, Marion Jean Lyon. Leonard Raven Hill died in Ryde, Isle of Wight, on 31 January 1942.

PUB: *The Promenaders* (1894), *Our Battalion* (1902), *An Indian Sketch Book* (1903), *London Sketch Book* (1903), *Raven Hill's London Sketchbook* (1906), *The South Bound Car* (1907)

ILL: R. Kipling, *Stalky and Co.* (1899); T. Coutts, *The Pottle Papers* (1899); Sir W. Besant, *East London* (1901); J. H. Harris, *Cornish Saints and Sinners* (1906); E. V. Lucas, *Slowcoach* (1910); K. Howard, *The Happy Vanners* (1911)

EXHIB: RA; RI; RBA; RSA; FAS

COLL: BM; V&A; B; THG; NPG

HILL, Roland Pretty 'Rip' (*c.* 1866–1949). Caricaturist and illustrator. Rip is best known as the designer of two sets of caricature cigarette cards – on cricketers and footballers – issued by John Player & Sons in 1926. He also drew cricket caricatures for the *Evening News*, *Weekly Dispatch* and the *Cricketer*, and produced illustrations and cartoons for the *Windsor Magazine*, *Truth*, *Sketch*, *Strand*, *Black & White* (political cartoons about South Africa, 1899) and *Daily Mail* amongst others. He worked on Winsor & Newton's Bristol Board. Roland Pretty Hill (not to be confused with the Halifax born artist and illustrator Roland Henry Hill) died in London on 29 December 1949 aged 83 and in his *Wisden* obituary is credited with being 'the first line artist to concentrate on cricket'.

PUB: *Kricket Karicatures from the Evening News* (1896, 1899), *Rip's Cricket Caricatures from the Weekly Dispatch* (1907), (ed.) *The Empire Cricket Album* (1924)

H.M.B. – *see* Bateman, Henry Mayo and Beerbohm, Sir Henry Maximilian

HOAR, Harold Frank 'Acanthus' PhD FRIBA (1909–76). Architect, joke and political cartoonist. Frank Hoar was born in India. He attended Plymouth College and won a scholarship to the Bartlett College of Architecture, London University, at the age of 15. While he was being taught life drawing at the Slade his caricatures of teachers attracted the attention of the art school's head, Professor Tonks, and he was encouraged to caricature the entire tutorial staff. Trained as an architect under Sir Albert Richardson, he was joint winner of an architectural competition for developing Gatwick Airport (1936) and became a greatly respected town-planning consultant. His cartoons were published first in *London Opinion*, then in *Punch*. In World War II he worked in the Rescue Service during the Blitz. Some of his best cartoon work was for *Building* from 1960 and for the *Sunday Telegraph* (political cartoons), but he also contributed to *Men Only*, *Builder* and other publications. An accomplished draughtsman who worked mostly in black and white using Perry 606 or Gillott 303 nibs, Price wrote of his work for *Punch*: 'He could make a building funny in itself, and his precision made a point of rest in the paper when other drawings were less determinate in outline.' Acanthus died on 3 October 1976.

PUB: *Pen and Ink Drawing* (1955), *Ancestral Manners* (1961), *An Introduction to English Architecture* (1963), *European Architecture from Earliest Times to the Present Day* (1967)
ILL: [as Frank Hoar] C. Scott, *Westminster Abbey* (1976)
EXHIB: RA; Arts Club; RWCS
COLL: UKCC

HOBART, Nicholas 'Nick' (b. 1939). Joke and strip cartoonist and writer. Nick Hobart was born in London in June 1939. He worked at first in a bank and after two years' National Service was employed by a farmers' cooperative in Devon. He emigrated to Canada in 1972 and began cartooning in his spare time, turning full-time freelance in 1974 and becoming Cartoon Editor of *Canadian Review* (1975–7). He moved to Florida, USA, in 1978. A self-taught artist who signs his work 'Nick', his cartoons have appeared in *Punch* (including covers), *Spectator*, *Penthouse* (Germany), *Playboy*, *Saturday Evening Post*, *Wall Street Journal* and elsewhere as well as in a number of trade journals. In addition he produced a strip, 'Rev', which was published in South Africa. An admirer of the work of CLIVE COLLINS and PETE DREDGE, he won First Prize in the Gag Cartoon category at the Montreal Cartoon Festival (1982) and Fourth Prize in 1983.

HOD – *see* Hollowood, Albert Bernard

HODSON, Haro Reginald Victor 'Haro' (b. 1923). Joke cartoonist, illustrator, poet and writer. Haro Hodson was born in Glasgow on 9 February 1923, the second son of Canon R. V. Hodson, a hunting parson who was rector of Minchinhampton, Gloucestershire. At 16 he left school to study at Stroud School of Art (1939). During World War II he served in the army and was later attached to GHQ New Delhi as an official war artist. His first published drawing appeared in *Lilliput* in 1941. After the war he read English at Oxford University and spent a year at Corsham Art School (1947). During this period his poems were published in the *Observer* and *Adelphi* and broadcast on the BBC. He joined the staff of the *Observer* as an illustrator (1948–64) and has contributed, freelance, to the *Daily Mail* (and later *Mail on Sunday)* since 1962 and *Daily Telegraph* (since 1997). His drawings have also appeared in *Punch*, *Tatler*, *Time & Tide*, *Harpers & Queen* and *New York Herald-*

Tribune. He has additionally designed posters for West End theatre productions and the Royal College of Nursing, drawn illustrations for Berry Brothers, designed Christmas cards for Gallery 5, been occasional TV critic on the *Daily Mail* (1978–85) and produced book and theatre reviews for the *Observer*, *Daily Mail* and *Glasgow Herald*. He married the writer Elizabeth Mavor in 1953. A great admirer (and friend) of MAX BEERBOHM, he cites other influences as William Blake, the 13th-century 'Master of the Leaping Figure', and PHIL MAY. At the start of his career he worked with pen and indian ink but now uses a variety of Pentels for speed. He draws with a flamboyant, minimal line and owns pug dogs which often feature in his cartoons.

PUB: [poetry] *The Visitor* (1951)
ILL: Many books including eight titles by P. Jennings from *Oddly Enough* (1950); R. C. Robertson Glasgow, *All in the Game* (1952); D. Parsons, *True to Type* (1955); A. Melville, *Myself When Young* (1955); M. Moore, *And What Do You Do?* (1960); A. Adburgham, *A View of Fashion* (1966); C. Freud, *Freud on Food* (1978)

HOFFNUNG, Gerard FSIA (1925–59). Cartoonist, caricaturist, musician and broadcaster. Gerard Hoffnung was born in Berlin on 22 March 1925, the son of Ludwig Hoffnung, a corn merchant. He came to England in 1938, attending Highgate School and the Hornsey School of Art (1942–3). He spent some months after this washing bottles at the Express Dairy Farm near Golders Green, then taught art at Stamford School (1945–6), was staff artist on the *Stamford Mercury* (*c.* 1946) and the *Evening News* (1947) and assistant art master at Harrow School (1948–9). During this period he also freelanced for *Lilliput* (which he had first contributed to aged 15), *Seven*, *Contact*, *Strand Magazine*, *Housewife*, *Tatler* and *Radio Times*. This was followed by a short interval in New York (1950) working for Cowles Magazines (staff cartoonist on *Flair*) after which he returned to England to work for the *Daily Express*, *Punch* (from 1952), *Graphis*, *Saturday Evening Post* and others. A frequent broadcaster on the BBC from 1951, he also created the Hoffnung Music Festivals at the Royal Festival Hall (1956, 1958 and 1959) and produced designs for the Chelsea Arts Ball – including the penultimate one held in the Albert Hall on New Year's Eve 1957 – and a Glyndebourne Opera programme. In addition

THE VIOLON DOUBLE

Gerard Hoffnung, *The Hoffnung Symphony Orchestra*, 1955

he published numerous books, which after his death formed the basis of seven short animated films by Halas & Batchelor, *Tales of Hoffnung* (1964). He also produced advertising work for Guinness, Kia-Ora, Krug Champagne,

Lockwood & Carlisle Piston Rings and others. Hoffnung was an accomplished bass tuba player and music was always a great influence on his work. He mainly drew with a mapping pen and indian ink and also used watercolours and wax crayons. Sometimes he signed himself G. A. Hoffnung, the 'A' being for Adam, but there is no evidence for this being a genuine middle name. He died in London on 28 September 1959.

PUB: *The Maestro* (1953), *The Hoffnung Symphony Orchestra* (1955), [with J. Symonds] *The Isle of Cats* (1955), *The Hoffnung Music Festival* (1956), *The Hoffnung Companion to Music* (1957), *Hoffnung's Musical Chairs* (1958), *Ho Ho Hoffnung* (1959), *Hoffnung's Acoustics* (1959), *Birds, Bees and Storks* (1960), *Hoffnung's Little Ones* (1961), *Hoffnung's Constant Readers* (1962), *The Penguin Hoffnung* (1963), *Hoffnung's Encore* (1968), *Hoffnung's Harlequinade* (1979), *Hoffnung's Humoresque* (1984), *Hoffnung in Harmony* (1985)
ILL: J. Broughton, *The Right Playmate* (1951); Lady Pakenham, *Points for Parents* (1954); P. Cudlipp, *Bouverie Ballads* (1955); Colette, *The Boy and the Magic* (1964)
EXHIB: Many shows including RFH; WAC tour; Berlin Festival; Edinburgh Festival; Japanese tour (1992); Lincoln Center, New York (1970); V&A; OHG
LIT: [various authors], *O Rare Hoffnung* (1960); A. Hoffnung, *Gerard Hoffnung* (1988)

HOGG, Gordon 'Gog' 'GG' (1912–73). Joke and strip cartoonist and caricaturist. Born in London, Gordon Hogg won a London County Art Scholarship at the age of 14 and studied art with Ruskin Spear for three years before becoming a commercial artist. His first cartoon was published in the *Daily Sketch* in 1938. During World War II he was Official War Artist to the Indian Army under Auchinleck. After the war he became chief editorial artist on the *Daily Sketch* and took over the 'Pop' cartoon for 10 years when MILLAR WATT retired in 1949. When the strip eventually folded on 23 January 1960, he worked for children's comics such as *Wham, Sunday Extra* and *Smash*. He also drew a strip 'Miss Muffet' and was 'Gay Gordon', the racing and sports cartoonist on the *Sun*. He died in March 1973 aged 61.
PUB: *Pop at His Best!* (1953)

HOLDER, Trevor 'Holte' (b. 1941). Joke cartoonist and illustrator. Trevor Holder was born

in Birmingham on 5 January 1941 and is a self-taught artist. He left school at 15 and worked as a technical illustrator and graphic designer, producing cartoons in his spare time, before turning freelance cartoonist in 1981. His drawings have appeared in *Punch* (including the magazine's final cover in 1992 before its relaunch some years later), *Listener, Reader's Digest* and elsewhere and he has also produced cartoons for advertising for companies such as Esso. He works in pen and ink, watercolour, gouache and oils.
ILL: R. Breen, *Cambridge Oddfellows and Funny Tales* (1997), *Oxford Oddfellows and Funny Tales* (1997)

HOLLAND, Frank (fl. 1895–after 1933). Political and strip cartoonist, caricaturist and journalist. Art Editor of the weekly comic and story paper *The Gleam*, Frank Holland drew comic strips in the 1890s and early 1900s for *Illustrated Chips, Comic Cuts, Comic Home Journal, Funny Wonder, Halfpenny Comic, Dan Leno's Comic Annual, Big Budget, Jester & Wonder* and *Picture Fun*. He later worked for *Fun* and *Black & White*, and *c.* 1912–19 was Political Cartoonist on the controversial magazine *John Bull*, edited by the very patriotic but essentially devious businessman Horatio Bottomley (who was later imprisoned). He was also Political Cartoonist on *Reynolds News* (*c.* 1911–22), being succeeded by SPI.

HOLLAND, John Anthony (b. 1932). Joke and topical cartoonist and illustrator. Tony Holland was born on 7 August 1932 in Peterborough, Northamptonshire, the son of a schoolmaster. He went to school in Market Bosworth, Leicestershire, and after studying English, history and French at Sheffield University (1950–53) he spent his National Service in the RAF (1953–5). He then taught English, history and maths for three years at schools in Leicestershire and London before becoming a professional freelance artist. A self-taught artist, he sold his first cartoon to the *Daily Sketch* in the 1950s and later drew for the paper a series of long thin cartoons called 'Tall Story' which were printed vertically along the gutter and ran for 18 months. In addition he has been Diary Cartoonist on the *Daily Telegraph* and City Cartoonist on the *Sunday Telegraph* (1963–96), and has contributed to *Punch, Accountancy* (colour cartoons), *Daily Mirror, Time & Tide, Statist, News of the World, New Elizabethan, Spectator, Oldie* and vari-

TAKING THE CAKE
No matter what sort of cake you make,
Or how much care and pains you take,
Or rich or plain doesn't matter a bit,
Somebody'll turn up their nose at it.

Frank Holland, [Lloyd George, Joseph Chamberlain, Churchill], *Reynolds News*, 2 April 1922

ous financial journals. He works in felt-tip pen using Pantone colours on cartridge paper. He was married to the cartoonist Lesley-ann Vernon.
PUB: [with A. E. BEARD and Bax] *Spin-off: A Selection of Cartoons from the New Scientist* (1965) ILL: A. Twort, *A Hole in My Bucket* (1963); N. Buchanan, *Know Your New Pension Rights* (1976); 'Ivanhoe Career Guides' (annually from 1989)

HOLLOWOOD, Albert Bernard 'Hod' FRSA (1910–81). Economist, pocket and joke cartoonist, author, broadcaster and editor. Bernard Hollowood was born in Burslem, Staffordshire, on 3 June 1910, the son of Albert Hollowood, clerk and amateur cricketer, and educated at Hanley High School and St Paul's College, Cheltenham. He studied economics at London University (1934–6) and lectured on the subject at the City School of Commerce, Stoke-on-Trent (1936–41), and Loughborough College (1936–43,

as Head of the Commerce Department). He then joined the staff of the *Economist* (1944–5, becoming Assistant Editor), was Research Officer at the Council of Industrial Design (1946–7) and Editor of *Pottery & Glass* (1944–50). A self-taught artist, he sold his first drawings to *Chambers Journal, Lilliput* and *Men Only* in 1942 and then began contributing to *Punch*, being elected to the *Punch* Table in 1945 and becoming the magazine's Editor (1957–68). He was also pocket cartoonist for the *Sunday Times* (1957–60) and a regular contributor to *The Times, Geographical Magazine, Socialist Commentary, Surrey Advertiser, News Chronicle, Cricketer, London Opinion, New Yorker, Evening Standard, Daily* and *Sunday Telegraph*. An admirer of the work of PONT and PAUL CRUM, he divided joke drawings into two types: the 'immediate' (e.g. those of LANGDON) and the 'continuous performance' (e.g. those of PONT, EMETT, BATEMAN, HEATH ROBINSON) – the latter being a succession of chuckles rather than one quick guffaw. He was never a good draughtsman: 'In a period in which the superiority of drawing to caption has reversed the old order, the limitations of Hollowood's draughtsmanship have distracted some attention from the brilliance of his ideas' (Price). He used a mapping pen and indian ink on Whatman paper. Elected FRSA in 1949, he was awarded the RSA Silver Medal for his lecture on humour in 1962. A member of the Court of Governors of the London School of Economics, he also played cricket for Staffordshire (1930–46). He also wrote and drew as 'Mammon'. Bernard Hollowood died in Guildford, Surrey, on 28 March 1981.

PUB: *Direct Economics* (1943), *Money is No Expense* (1946), *An Innocent at Large* (1947), *Britain Inside Out* (1948), *Scowle and Other Papers* (1948), *Poor Little Rich World* (1948), *Pottery and Glass* (1949), *The Hawksmoor Scandals* (1949), *Cornish Engineers* (1951), *The Story of Morro Velho* (1954), *Money* (1957), *Tory Story* (1964), *Pont* (1969), *Cricket on the Brain* (1970), *Tales of Tommy Barr* (1970), *Funny Money* (1975)

ILL: G. Reynolds, *Organo Pleno* (1970), *Full Swell* (1972)

EXHIB: US; LSE; Staffordshire University; The Studio, Arundel; Boxgrove Priory Church, Chichester

COLL: UKCC

HOLTE – *see* Holder, Trevor

'Hom. Sap' – *see* Austin, David

HONEYSETT, Martin (b. 1943). Joke cartoonist and illustrator. Born in Hereford on 20 May 1943, Martin Honeysett attended Selhurst Grammar School, where he was taught art by GEOFFREY DICKINSON, and Croydon School of Art (1960–61). He then worked briefly in a London animation studio and in a factory in Manchester before emigrating to New Zealand (1962–5), where he had a variety of jobs, from lumberjack to stage hand for the New Zealand Ballet Co. After a further period in Canada (1965–8), he returned to England to work as a bus-driver for London Transport while cartooning in his spare time. He sold his first cartoon to the *Daily Mirror* in May 1969 and turned full-time freelance in 1972, contributing to *Punch* (from 1970, including covers), *Private Eye, Daily*

Martin Honeysett, *Private Eye*, April 1997

Mirror, Evening Standard, TV Times, Radio Times, Observer and *Sunday Telegraph*. He has also won awards for his work at festivals in Eindhoven, Holland and Kyoto, Japan. Honeysett's spidery style of drawing emphasizes his often macabre sense of humour.

PUB: *Private Eye Martin Honeysett* (1974), *Honeysett at Home* (1976), *Martin Honeysett* (1977), *The Motor Show Book of Humour* (1978), *The Not Another Book of Old Photographs Book* (1981), *Microphobia* (1982), *Fit for Nothing* (1983), *The Joy of Headaches* (1984), *Animal Nonsense Rhymes* (1984), *The Best of Honeysett* (1985), *Witch Doctor?* (1985)

ILL: R. Buckman, *Jogging From Memory* (1980); I. Cutler, *Life in a Scotch Sitting Room Vol. 2* (1984), *Gruts* (1986), *Fremsley* (1987), *One-and-a-Quarter* (1987), *Glasgow Dreamer* (1990), *Fly Sandwich* (1992); D. King-Smith, *H. Prince* (1986), *Farmer Bungle Forgets* (1987); S. Townsend, *The Queen and I* (1992)

EXHIB: CG; BC

COLL: V&A; UKCC; BM

HOOPER, William John 'Raff' (1916–96). Joke, political and strip cartoonist, animator, writer and broadcaster. Bill Hooper was born in West London on 21 August 1916. He worked as a laboratory assistant in a medical clinic in Windsor before volunteering for RAF aircrew in 1939, later joining 54 Squadron, Fighter Command HQ and Intelligence. Self-taught as an artist, he is best known as 'Raff' (the name comes from his dog while in the RAF), the creator of Pilot Officer Percy Prune. The name 'Prune' was a schoolboy term for new recruits and PO Prune was a persistently inept pilot who first appeared (unnamed) in *Forget Me Nots for Fighters* (*c.* 1940), a book produced after the Battle of Britain which showed the lessons learned by fighter pilots. The character was then christened and appeared regularly in *TEE EMM* (for *Training Manual*), an aircrew training magazine edited by *Punch* writer Anthony Armstrong from 1 April 1941. Other creations were Aircraftsman Plonk, Prune's mechanic, Prune's girlfriend WAAF Winsum and his mascot dog Binder. Prune variants included a bearded Fleet Air Arm version, Sub-Lt Swingit, the Free French Air Force Aspirant Praline (created for the *Bulletin des Forces*) and a French resistance variant. Like JON's Two Types, Prune and his colleagues were not based on real people, but by mistake his name got into the Air Ministry phone book, his portrait was hung in the National Gallery and the Luftwaffe awarded him an Iron Cross. After the war Hooper was Political Cartoonist on the *Sunday Chronicle* and for 15 years worked as a presenter and animator for BBC TV. For the National Coal Board he created a 'Prunish' miner character called 'Davy Lump' whose misadventures were intended to save lives underground. In addition he worked on a training magazine for an Anglo-US company, and two dog characters from *TEE EMM*, based on his own pets Toro and Willy, were featured in a BBC TV animated film, *Willy the Pup* (*c.* 1946). He also devised, wrote and illustrated the 'Did You Know That?' strip for the *Star* (three years) and for 12 years (until *c.* 1970) worked as a journalist on the *Sunday Pictorial* (later *Sunday Mirror*). The Prune cartoons were originally drawn in cartridge-paper sketchbooks. A collection of mannikins of the Prune characters made by Hooper is on display at the RAF Museum. Bill Hooper died on 14 October 1996. His son John Hooper is a journalist on the *Guardian*.

PUB: [as '977950'] *Forget Me Nots for Fighters* (*c.* 1940), [as Raff] *Behind the Spitfires* (1941), [with A. Armstrong] *Plonk's Party of ATC* (1942), *Prune's Progress* (1942), *Nice Types* (1943), *More Nice Types* (1944), *Whiskers Will Not be Worn* (1945), *Goodbye Nice Types!* (1946); [as Bill Hooper] *The Odd Facts of Life* (1965), *The Passing of Pilot Officer Prune* (1975); [as Bill Hooper with D. Dickinson] *Clangers* (1970), [as K. de Barri] *The Bucks and Bawds of London Town* (1972)
ILL: A. Armstrong, *Sappers at War* (1949); J. H. Coombs, *Bar Service* (1965)
EXHIB: RAF (1991)
COLL: RAF; IWM
LIT: B. Hooper, *Pilot Officer Prune's Picture Parade* (1991); T. Hamilton, *The Life and Times of Pilot Officer Prune* (1991)

HOPE, William 'G. Espoir' (fl. 1910s–after 1963). Political and sports cartoonist. Will Hope was born in New Zealand and worked as Political Cartoonist for *New Zealand Truth* (*c.* 1913) and *New York Globe* (*c.* 1915) before moving to the UK. He was Sports Cartoonist on the back page of the *Daily Herald* after World War I and drew political cartoons (as 'G. Espoir' – his name in French – and 'Will Hope') for the short-lived weekly *The Communist* (1920–23), the official organ of the Young Communist Party edited by Raymond Postgate (later founder of the *Good Food Guide*) and Francis Meynell (later Sir Francis Meynell, a director of the *Daily Herald* and founder of the Nonesuch Press). It was a cartoon by Hope attacking J. H. Thomas, Secretary of the National Union of Railwaymen (and later a Labour Cabinet Minister), that led to a libel action which eventually closed down the paper. He also worked (as 'Espoir') for George Lansbury's *Labour Weekly* and in 1924 (as 'Will Hope') became Political Cartoonist on the *Daily Herald* – by then the official organ of the Labour movement – taking over from WILL DYSON, but was later sacked by Hamilton Fyfe. Failing to get himself reinstated by the powerful print union the London Society of Compositors he was forced to emigrate and moved to Canada. Unfortunately his left-wing politics were also unsuited to Canadian newspapers. Sir Francis Meyell said of him: 'Here's a man who can draw . . . He's got pen-control . . . and his line is like a line of downs – mighty movement stilled . . . He had . . . a swift but sure beauty of touch which Dyson . . . has never in my opinion equalled. "Espoir's" name will live in the record of politics, and in the records of art.' He is not to be confused with the children's story writer, William Edward Stanton Hope (1889–1961) who, though better known as 'Stanton Hope' also worked as 'Will Hope'.

PUB: *Communist Cartoons by 'Espoir' and Others* (1922, reissued 1982)

HOPKINS, Everard (1860–1928). Painter, illustrator and joke cartoonist. Everard Hopkins was born on 5 February 1860 in Hampstead, London, the son of Manley Hopkins, author, journalist and poet and Consul-General for Hawaii in London (1856–96), and Kate Smith, a relative of Gainsborough and Sydney Smith. He was also the brother of the poet Gerard Manley Hopkins (who wrote 'Epithalamion' for Everard's wedding), Arthur Hopkins RWS (1847–1930, who also contributed to *Punch, Graphic* and *Illustrated London News*) and Lionel Hopkins, British Consul-General in Tientsin, China. Educated at Charterhouse School, he studied art at the Slade School (1878) and contributed illustrations and cartoons to *Punch* (from 1891), *Black & White, Quiver, Cassell's, Gentlewoman, Graphic, Illustrated London News* and *Woman's World*. In addition he was Assistant Editor of *Pilot*. Some of his *Punch* drawings were issued as postcards by Raphael Tuck. As well as pen and ink he worked in watercolour and pastel and was a member of the Savile Club. Everard Hopkins died on 17 October 1928.
PUB: [novel] *Lydia* (1910)
ILL: M. Gray, *A Costly Freak* (1894); L. Sterne, *A Sentimental Journey* (1910); A. Tennyson, *The Princess* (1911)
EXHIB: RA; RI; NWS
COLL: V&A

HORNER, Arthur Wakefield (1916–97). Political, pocket, joke and strip cartoonist, caricaturist, illustrator and animator. Arthur Horner was born in Melbourne, Australia, on 10 May 1916, the son of Arthur Horner, a civil servant. When he was 13 his family moved to Sydney where he attended Sydney High School and East Sydney Technical College and began writing and acting in radio plays. As a cartoonist he was a regular contributor to the *Sydney Bulletin* and was on the staff of *Smith's Weekly* and later *ABC Weekly* before serving in the Army in World War II, first as OC of a camouflage unit in New Guinea and later as head of a Military History Field Unit in Borneo. Moving to London in 1946, he studied at the Central School of Arts & Crafts under Ruskin Spear and Bernard Meninsky before drawing regularly for *Lilliput* and becoming Political Cartoonist on *Tribune*. In the early

1950s he was Pocket Cartoonist on the *News Chronicle*, succeeding VICKY as the paper's Political Cartoonist in 1954. While there he created the 'Colonel Pewter' strip which was seen as the *News Chronicle*'s answer to the *Daily Mail*'s 'Flook' by TROG. It ran for 18 years in its different incarnations in the *Chronicle* (1952–60, when the *Chronicle* was taken over by the *Daily Mail*), *Daily Mail* (1960–64) and *Guardian* (where it was the paper's first cartoon strip, 1964–70) and was widely syndicated abroad. The eccentric Colonel Hugo Pewter (Rtd) lived at 'Chukkas' in the English village of Much Overdun with his great-nephew Martin and Sirius the dog (offspring of a local bitch and a visiting space-dog). After retiring the Colonel in 1970, Horner created a daily 'first-person' strip, 'The Thoughts of Citizen Doe', which ran for about two years. He was also Political Cartoonist on *New Statesman* (1966–71), *Times Higher Education Supplement* and *Humanist* and his work featured in *Private Eye, Punch, Truth, Sunday Times* and on BBC TV. Horner returned to Australia in 1976 to produce political cartoons, caricatures and theatre drawings for Melbourne's *The Age*. He was married to the Australian artist Victoria Cowdroy ('Royston'). Horner mostly worked in line (pen and ink, fibre pen or crayon), line and wash, and occasionally line and spirit colours. For early newsprint reproduction he developed a unique way of getting half-tone effects for line-block processing by manipulating textured plates under a drawing while rubbing a crayon on top. He also produced lithographs, etchings, aquatints and seriographs, and experimented with animated film. He cited his influences as OSPOVAT, the artists of *Simplicissimus*, Lautrec, Topolski and BATEMAN. One of the founder members of the British Cartoonists' Association in 1966, he continued to work for the *Melbourne Age* until well into his 70s and only stopped drawing with the onset of Parkinson's Disease. He died in Melbourne in February 1997.
PUB: *Colonel Pewter in Ironicus* (1957), *Dog-Star; and Come Back, Sirius* (1972), *The Penguin Colonel Pewter* (1978), *The Book of Uriel* (1979)
ILL: R. Woddis, *Lot '71* (1971), *Sex Guyed* (1973); T. Kavanagh, *The ITMA Years* (1975); B. Took and M. Feldman, *The Bona Book of Julian & Sandy* (1976); M. Lurie, *Toby's Millions* (1978)
EXHIB: CG; Victorian Ministry of Arts, Australia (1977)

COLL: UKCC; State Library of Victoria; National Museum, Canberra; Mitchell Library, Sydney

HORRABIN, James Francis MSIA (1884–1962). Joke, strip and political cartoonist, journalist, MP and caricaturist. J. F. Horrabin was born in Peterborough, Lincolnshire, on 1 November 1884, the son of James Woodhouse Horrabin, the owner of a silver-plate works, and Mary Pinney. After attending Stamford Grammar School he studied in the evenings at Sheffield Technical School of Art (fellow students included J. H. Dowd and the sculptor David Jagger) while working as a designer in the family business. He was next employed in the Art Department of the *Sheffield Telegraph* (1906–9), working in the style of HASELDEN, and was Art Editor of the *Yorkshire Telegraph & Star* (1909–11) before moving to London in 1911 as Art Editor of the *Daily News*. In addition he lectured on geography at the Central Labour College and edited and drew cartoons for *The Plebs*, the journal of the National Council of Labour. He also contributed to *New Leader*. In World War I he served in the Queen's Westminster Rifles in France (1917–18), later returning to the *Daily News* and starting a popular children's strip 'Japhet and Happy' (originally a single panel called 'Adventures of Noah and Family, including Japhet' before Happy the bear was introduced). Begun in June 1919, the strip ran daily until the end of World War II in the *Daily News* and then the *News Chronicle* (it was later renamed 'The Arkubs'). However, he is perhaps best known for the strip 'Dot and Carrie' which ran for nearly 12,000 episodes in the *Daily News'* sister paper the *Star* (appearing on the same page as the political cartoon by Low) and then the *Evening News*. Begun in 1922 and originally written by his brother-in-law, H. O. Botho, it featured two typists, pretty blonde Dorothy and dark bespectacled Caroline, their grumpy boss Mr Spilliken, the office boy Adolphus and the charlady, Mrs Mopps. The series continued for 40 years, until Horrabin's death. Horrabin was elected Labour MP for Peterborough (1929–31), was Vice-President of the India League and helped found the Fabian Colonial Bureau and was its Chairman (1945–50). He also drew caricatures of his fellow MPs in 'Star Man's Diary'. An accomplished map artist, he produced maps for many books and was admired by H. G.

Wells, who saw him as 'not so much an illustrator as a collaborator' (Preface to *The Outline of History*) and dedicated *The Brothers* to Horrabin. In addition he broadcast on BBC TV about maps (from 1938) and during World War II produced maps for films made by the Ministry of Information. He was elected MSIA in 1946. J. F. Horrabin died on 2 March 1962.
PUB: More than 30 books including *Some Adventures of the Noah Family* (1920), *The Noahs on Holiday* (1921), *Japhet and Fido* (1922), *Mr Noah* (1922), *More About the Noahs – and Tom Tosset* (1922), *Dot and Carrie* (1923), *Dot and Carrie (and Adolphus)* (1924), *Atlas of European History* (1935), *An Atlas-History of the Second World War* (1940–46)
ILL: H. G. Wells, *The Outline of History* (1920); L. Hogben, *Mathematics for the Million* (1936), *Science for the Citizen* (1938), *Principles of Animal Biology* (1940); J. Nehru, *Glimpses of World History* (1939)

HOUGHTON, George William OBE (1905–93). Sports cartoonist, illustrator, painter, commercial artist and writer. George Houghton was born on 9 September 1905, in Perth, Scotland, the son of a barber. He attended Dronfield School, Sheffield, and at the age of 19 began work as an illustrator for an advertising agency, his most famous creation being the Polar Bear image for Fox's Glacier Mints. He then left to travel the world illustrating a series 'Around the World on a Five Pound Note' for the *Daily News*. However, when this failed he produced a strip for the *Daily Graphic* ('Dad and the Boy') while living in France, and in the early 1930s studied at the École des Beaux-Arts in Paris. At about this time he also worked in the Paris office of the *Daily Mail* as a journalist, covering the Spanish Civil War. Houghton returned to England in 1937 and joined the RAF (eventually achieving the rank of group captain), working closely with Air Chief Marshall Lord Tedder and his successor Sir Trafford Lee-Mallory. He was mentioned in dispatches three times and was awarded an OBE by George VI. A play he wrote about his experiences in the Western Desert (*They Flew Through Sand*) became the first play to be televised after the war, and starred Kenneth More. In 1945 he began 'People in the News', a regular celebrity column in *Men Only*, and in 1952, while working as an advertising executive, wrote and illustrated his first golf

book, which was a great success and encouraged him to write more than 40 more and produce an annual Golf Addict's Calendar. For 15 years he was an Associate Editor of *Golf World* and founded and became President of the Golf Addict's Society of Great Britain in the mid-1960s. He died in October 1993 aged 88.
PUB: More than 40 books
ILL: T. Ray, *My Turn Next* (1963)

HUGHES, David (b. 1952). Editorial cartoonist, illustrator and caricaturist. David Hughes was born in Twickenham, Middlesex, on 6 January 1952, the son of William Arthur Hughes, a plumber and decorator, and studied at Twickenham College of Technology (1968–72). His first published cartoon was a zodiac illustration for the *Daily Express* in January 1973. Staff cartoonist on the *Daily Express* (1973–4), he has also been a full-time postman (1975–7), a graphic designer at Granada TV (1980–84) and Lecturer in Illustration at Manchester Polytechnic (1987–90). In addition he illustrated 'A Doctor Writes' in the *Observer* (1990–92), drew covers for *Punch* (1990–92), was the artist for the American Express press advertising campaign (1993–5) and produced opening title drawings for Channel 4 TV's *A Week in Politics* (1989–96). Other clients have included *New Yorker, Today, Time Magazine, Rolling Stone, Premiere, ES, Telegraph Sunday Magazine, Illustrated London News, Creative Review, The Times, Washington Post, Observer Magazine, Radio Times, GQ* (USA), *American Health,* and book publishers Sphere, Transworld, Viking, Faber & Faber, Walker Books and Abacus. He has also won a number of awards for his work including the Mother Goose Award (1990) and Creative Review Humour Award (1991), and designed the sets and costumes for a production of Stravinsky's *The Rake's Progress* at the Spoleto Festival in Italy (1993) and *The Cunning Little Vixen* (1998). At first he drew on smooth board but now uses a Gillott 404 pen on Canson paper or watercolour paper.
PUB: *Black & White* (1986), *Bully* (1993), *Little Robert* (1996)
ILL: E. Morecambe, *Eric Morecambe on Fishing* (1984); C. Martin-Jenkins (ed.), *The Cricketer Book of Cricket Eccentrics* (1985); J. Mark, *Strat and Chatto* (1989); G. Davidson, *What Treasure Did Next* (1997)
EXHIB: John Holden Gallery, Manchester; Association of Illustrators Gallery; Beint & Beint Gallery; Museo Civico, Spoleto, Italy; Assembly Rooms, Edinburgh; Gibbes Museum of Art, Charleston, USA

'Humours of History' – *see* Moreland, Arthur

HUMPH – *see* Lyttelton, Humphrey Richard Adeane

HURST, Hal RI RBA ROI VPRMS (1865–1938) – *see* Bryant & Heneage

HUSBAND, William Anthony (b. 1950). Joke, sports and strip cartoonist, illustrator and scriptwriter. Born in Blackpool, Lancashire on 28 August 1950, Tony Husband is a self-taught artist. He worked on the printing side of an advertising agency and as a window-dresser and jewellery repairer before becoming a cartoonist. His first cartoons were published in *Weekend* and the *Daily Mirror* and he turned full-time freelance in 1984. Co-editor and co-founder of the children's comic *Oink!* (1985–8), he has drawn pop-music cartoons for the *Daily Star* and topical football cartoons for *Shoot!* His work has also appeared in *Punch, Private Eye* (including 'The Yobs' strip since 1985), *Spectator, Oldie, The Times, Sunday Times* ('Mr Clean' strip), *Men Only, Club International, Playboy, Fiesta, BA News, Solicitors Journal, Reader's Digest* and many German publications. In addition he was co-writer and deviser of the award-winning children's TV programme *Round the Bend* (featuring puppets by SPITTING IMAGE) and the successful touring play, *Save the Human,* in which giant cartoons were projected on a screen behind the actors. He has designed numerous greetings cards including a 100-card series 'Rhino's Revenge' for Camden Graphics. Husband was voted CCGB Joke Cartoonist of the Year (1984, 1985, 1987), CCGB Strip Cartoonist of the Year (1988), *The Times* Strip Cartoonist of the Year (1989) and CAT Sports Cartoonist of the Year (1995). Influenced by MIKE WILLIAMS, Sempé, ALEX GRAHAM, BILL TIDY and LARRY, he works very fast using Artline Drawing System 08 pens on cartridge paper and Pantone markers for colour on bleedproof layout paper. He has a loose sketchy style and an often black sense of humour.
PUB: *Use Your Head* (1984), *Bye Bye Cruel World* (1985), *Animal Husbandry* (1986), *The Greatest Story Never Told* (1988), *Yobs and Other Cartoons* (1988), [with D. Day] *True Tales of Environmen-*

tal Madness (1990), *Save the Human* (1990), [with J. Banks, R. Lowry and I. Jackson] *100 Things to Do With a Black Lace Record* (1990), *Dinos* (1993) and six collections published in Germany
ILL: J. Eastwood, *100 Per Cent British* (1989), *100 Per Cent Japanese* (1990), *100 Per Cent Australian* (1990); F. Nelson (ed.), *NSPCC Book of Famous Faux Pas* (1990)
EXHIB: CG; Librays Theatre, Manchester
COLL: BM

HUSTLEBUCK – *see* Wood, Clarence Lawson

HUTCHINGS, Anthony (b. 1946). Joke and strip cartoonist, illustrator and greetings card designer. Tony Hutchings was born in London on 17 August 1946 and studied commercial art at Southend College of Art. A freelance cartoonist, he works mostly for children's comics such as *Whoopee!*, *Buster*, *Whizzer & Chips* and *Roy of the Rovers* but has also had drawings published in *Punch*, *Private Eye*, *Mayfair*, *Daily Mail*, *Sun*, *Daily Mirror*, *Daily Star*, *Club International*, *Men Only*, *Fiesta*, *Knave*, *Accountancy*, *Weekend* and others. In addition he has produced humorous greetings cards for Royle and Otter House and advertising cartoons for ICI. Twice voted CCGB Joke Cartoonist of the Year (1987, 1989), he prefers working in full colour with inks.
PUB: Purnell's 'Word Book' series (from 1977), *Middle Age Sex* (1991), *Bosom Buddies* (1991), *The Very Best of Essex Girl Jokes* (1991), *Keep Fit Sex* (1992), *Laugh at the Olympics* (1992), *Columbus* (1992)
ILL: M. Young's 'SuperTed' series (from 1983) and many titles by A. Gelman

HYNES, Edward Sylvester FRGS (1897–1982). Joke and political cartoonist, caricaturist, illustrator and painter. Edward Hynes was born in Burren, Co. Clare, Ireland, the seventh of eight children of a surgeon, and was brought up in Nottingham. He was a cadet on HMS *Worcester* before serving as a navigator in the Merchant Navy for ten years, leaving to study medicine at Sheffield University for three years. After World War I he returned to the sea for a while but finally abandoned this career in favour of cartoons. Some of his early caricatures appeared in the Fleetway Press publication *Town Topics* (21 September 1923) but Hynes is perhaps best known for his colour caricature covers for *Men Only* (July 1937–June 1956), taking over from

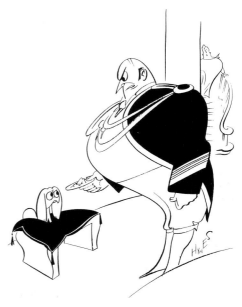

'Not quite to your liking, eh? You little squirt.'

Edward Hynes, in *The Razzle Annual*, 1935

Eric Fraser and being himself succeeded by Sherriffs. He also contributed to the *Daily Sketch*, *Lilliput*, *Gentlewoman*, *Evening News*, *Strand*, *Humorist*, *Razzle* (including covers), *Sunday Express*, *Bystander*, *London Calling*, *Night & Day* and *London Opinion*, drew theatre caricatures for *Illustrated Sporting & Dramatic News* and designed advertisements for Guinness, Player's Tobacco, Wright's Coal Tar Shaving Cream, Mex Petrol, J. Lyons, Erasmic Shaving Stick and others. Hynes disliked the use of photographs in caricature, especially of people he had not met – 'To my mind caricaturing is the very antithesis of photography' – and also did not believe in people formally sitting for him. He preferred to memorize a subject's features from life and retain 'an impression of the way in which they differ from their fellows. Then a week or a fortnight later, I try my hand at the caricature. Only the essential "differences" remain in my memory, and that is exactly what is needed for a caricature.' He was a Fellow of the Royal Geographical Society. Edward Hynes retired to his birthplace in Burren, Co. Clare, Ireland, where he painted in oils and produced charcoal sketches. He died at Bayfield House, Newquay, Burren, on 12 May 1982 and is buried in Corcomroe Abbey.

PUB: *Cocktail Cavalcade* (1937)
COLL: IWM: British & Dominion School of Drawing

I

'**If . . .**' – *see* Bell, Steve

ILLINGWORTH, Leslie Gilbert (1902–79). Political cartoonist and illustrator. Leslie Illingworth was born at 9 Harbour Rd, Barry, Glamorgan, on 2 September 1902, the son of Richard Illingworth, a clerk on the Barry Railway. He was educated at Barry County School (with RONALD NIEBOUR) and won a scholarship to Cardiff Art School when he was 15, drawing for the *Western Mail* while still a student (his first cartoons having been published in the *Football Express*). In 1920 a scholarship to the Royal College of Art (where one of his teachers was THOMAS DERRICK) brought him to London (contemporaries included Barbara Hepworth, Henry Moore, Eric Ravilious, Edward Bawden and JOHN GILROY). Offered the job of Political Cartoonist on the *Western Mail* when STANIFORTH died, he returned to Wales in 1921. He came back to London in 1924 and studied at the Slade while continuing to work for the *Western Mail* (until 1927). He also studied in Paris at the Académie Julian and supported himself by freelancing for *Nash's*, *Passing Show*, *Strand Magazine*, *Good Housekeeping*, *London Opinion*,

THE BUS

Leslie Illingworth, [Hitler, Goering, Neville Chamberlain, Churchill *et al.*], *Daily Mail*, 7 May 1940

Red Magazine, Wills' Magazine, Answers, Tit-Bits and later *Life*. In addition he produced illustrations for advertisements such as 'Beer is Best' and for Winsor & Newton, Grey's Cigarettes, Symington's Soups, Eiffel Tower Lemonade and Wolsey underwear. His first contribution to *Punch* was on 27 May 1931, and he succeeded BERNARD PARTRIDGE as Second Cartoonist opposite E. H. SHEPARD in 1945, becoming a member of the *Punch* Table in 1948 and later taking over from Shepard as Cartoonist, alternating with NORMAN MANSBRIDGE (1949–68). Towards the end of 1939 he submitted drawings to the *Daily Mail*, under the pseudonym 'MacGregor' (his mother's maiden name) and, POY having retired, joined the paper as Political Cartoonist that year. He retired in 1969 and was succeeded by WALLY FAWKES. He later returned to Fleet Street to work as guest cartoonist on the *News of the World* (1974–6). During the war he produced work for the Ministry of Defence and in 1963 drew a cover for *Time* magazine. In addition he wrote a course on 'Political Cartoons' for BRADSHAW's Press Art School. He was voted CCGB Political and Social Cartoonist of the Year in 1962 and received an Honorary D.Litt. from the University of Kent (1975). Illingworth always claimed he was unable to caricature women and preferred to paint them in oils. He used a Gillott 290 pen with Higgins ink on hot-pressed fashion board, roughing out in pencil first, and was one of the first cartoonists to employ scraperboard. His work was widely admired by his fellow cartoonists and his 'classical' style has been likened to the early work of Tenniel. He had a 'faultless pen-and-ink technique, a technique which is essentially naturalistic yet masterly in its variety of textures, arrangement of tones, and subtle atmospheric perspective. It is hardly cartooning . . .' (HEWISON). In his *Guardian* obituary, Malcolm Muggeridge stated his belief that Illingworth's cartoons would last longer than LOW's: 'Illingworth's go deeper, becoming, at their best, satire in the grand style rather than mischievous quips; strategic rather than practical.' One of the founder members of the British Cartoonists' Association in 1966, he was its first President. His uncle, Frank Illingworth, also drew for *Punch*. Leslie Illingworth died on 20 December 1979.
PUB: [with GITTINS, LEE, NEB and MOON] *400 Famous Cartoons* (1944)
ILL: B. Hollowood, *The Hawksmoor Scandals* (1949)

EXHIB: Wiggin Gallery, Boston Public Library, Massachusetts
COLL: UW; UKCC; BM; National Library of Wales
LIT: D. Hill, *Illingworth On Target* (1970)

INCE, Charles Percy RI RBA (1875–1952). Painter, joke cartoonist and illustrator. Charles Ince was born in London on 10 June 1875, the son of Charles Frederick Ince, owner of the printers and publishers Chas. F. Ince & Sons Ltd, Shoe Lane, and later became a director of the company himself. He was educated at Cowper Street School and King's College, London, and studied under the landscape painter Henry George Moon. Ince contributed humorous illustrations and cartoons to *Bystander, Tatler* (1900–1910), *Punch, Sketch, Studio* and *Illustrated London News* amongst others. He worked in black and white and colour and his charcoal drawings show the influence of GEORGE BELCHER. Also known as a landscape painter working in watercolour and oils, he was elected RBA in 1912 and RI in 1927, and was auditor and a council member of the Royal Society of British Artists. Charles Ince died on 8 July 1952.
EXHIB: RA; RI; RBA; RWS; ROI; GI; FAS; GOU

IONICUS – *see* Armitage, Joshua Charles

IRELAND, John (b. 1949). Caricaturist and illustrator. John Ireland was born on 19 March 1949 in Aldershot, Hampshire, the son of John Ireland, a civil servant. After a foundation course at Farnham Art School he studied graphic design at Ravensbourne Art School. His first caricature was published in *Radio Times* in 1975 and since then he has contributed to the *Observer, Punch* (including covers), *Sunday Times* and *Daily Express* amongst other publications. He works in ink with watercolour wash and cites his influences as RONALD SEARLE and the artists of *Beano* and *Dandy* comics.
PUB: *Cricket Characters* (1987), *Racing Characters* (1988), *Golf Characters* (1989), *Snooker Characters* (1989), *Rugby Characters* (1990)
ILL: T. Wogan and T. Fairbairn, *To Horse! To Horse!* (1982); L. Piggott, *Short Heads and Tall Tales* (1986); P. Tinnniswood, *Uncle Mort's North Country* (1986); J. Timpson, *Early Morning Book* (1986); J. Virgo, *Snooker Sideshow* (1987); S. Gallier, *One of the Lads* (1988); B. Grobbelaar, *Bring on the Clown* (1988); S. Lavelle, *Webster, The World's Worst Dog* (1994)

J

JACKSON, Arthur 'Ajay' (1912–after 1968). Joke and strip cartoonist, comics artist and painter. One of three brothers, Arthur Jackson started work aged 14 as a junior artist in a company making cinema signs, earning 6s. a week filling in lettering. He then spent eighteen months as a ladies' underwear salesman, sold his first cartoon to a national daily at the age of 15, and began taking art lessons in the evenings. At the age of 17 he returned to the showcard business until he fell down a cellar and was bedridden for a number of years. He then started drawing for *Beano* (e.g. 'Handy Sandy'), *Dandy* and *Topper* children's comics and after selling his first adult joke cartoon to *Punch* (a sad-looking St Bernard dog with a barrel around its neck labelled 'No Whisky') became a regular contributor to the magazine. He also drew for *Everybody's*, *London Opinion*, *People's Journal*, *Evening Standard* and others. He is not to be confused with the joke cartoonist Alfred Jackson or the illustrator, painter and comics artist Albert Edward Jackson. Arthur Jackson also painted portraits, including one of George Bernard Shaw which the writer owned.

JACKSON, Raymond Allen 'JAK' (1927–97). Editorial/political cartoonist and illustrator. JAK was born in the Middlesex Hospital, London, on 11 March 1927, the son of Maurice Jackson, a tailor. Educated at Clipstone Road School and Lyulph Stanley School, he studied at Willesden School of Art (1941–4) before spending three years in the Army Education Corps teaching conscripts to paint. He then returned to Willesden School of Art to take a National Diploma in Design (1948–50). He then worked for Link House Publishing Group (1950–51) as a staff artist, retouching pubic hair on photos for *Health & Efficiency*, etc., and for Keymers Advertising (1951–2) while also contributing to *Punch*, *Lilliput* and other publications. He joined the *Evening Standard* in 1952, first as an illustrator on the TV page then, after the death of VICKY, as Political Cartoonist (1966–97), while also drawing for the *Daily Express* (then *Mail*) on Saturdays and the *Mail on Sunday*. One of his cartoons, 'Homo-electrical-sapiens Britannicus 1970', nearly resulted in the *Standard*'s closure by industrial action. In addition

he has drawn advertisements for Carling Black Label Beer and others. An admirer of SEARLE, Oliphant, STEADMAN and (the early) GILES (whose detailed and realistic style influenced his greatly), he roughed cartoons out in 2B pencil on A2 layout paper, using CS6 abraded board for finished artwork (17 × 21½ in., reducing to five columns) and Pelikan ink, brush and mapping pen, tints being indicated with pale blue ink. JAK always drew hands with three fingers in the style of Disney animators and signed his name in capitals with 'blob' serifs. Though he was very good at depicting buildings, what he liked drawing best were 'Long-legged, high-bosomed bimbos... He enjoyed doing navvies as well and clubmen deep in leather chairs in vast smoking rooms and tea-ladies, skinheads, drag queens...' (Angus McGill, *Evening Standard* obituary). He claimed to have been the first to break the (post-Victorian) unwritten prohibition on caricaturing the Royal Family. Labour Prime Minister Tony Blair called him 'one of the finest political cartoonists'. A judo blackbelt, his motto was 'Never explain; never complain'. He was voted CCGB Political/Social Cartoonist of the Year (1964, 1965, 1985), British Press Awards Cartoonist of the Year (1981) and Glen Grant Sports & Royal Cartoonist of the Year (1981). He was one of the founder members of the British Cartoonists' Association in 1966. JAK died at his home in Wimbledon, London, on 27 July 1997 following a heart operation.
PUB: 31 annuals from *The Nutty World of JAK* (1966)
ILL: Several books including *Russia Dies Laughing* (1982)
EXHIB: HAM; BM
COLL: V&A; UKCC
LIT: A. McGill and P. McKay, *JAK: His Life and Work* (1997)

JACOB, Cyril Alfred 'Chic' (b. 1926). Joke and strip cartoonist, illustrator and scriptwriter. Born on 25 February 1926 in Dulwich, London, the son of William Charles Jacob, Assistant Publisher of the *Star*, 'Chic' Jacob (a contraction of a childhood pet-name 'Chicabiddy' that stuck) is self-taught. During World War II he was evacuated to Sussex and worked on local farms

before serving as a radar rating in the Royal Navy (1944–7), mostly in SE Asia Command. Thereafter he returned to farm work, then moved to London in 1949, drawing cartoons in his spare time (his first in a national publication was for *Everybody's* in 1950). He later became staff financial cartoonist on the *Daily Express* (1964–73) and then the *Observer* (1973–92). His work has also appeared in *Punch*, *Picturegoer*, *Star*, *Daily Sketch*, *Daily Mirror*, *Sunday Dispatch*, *Accountancy Age*, *Law Society's Gazette*, *Spectator*, *New Statesman*, *Oldie*, *Insider* and *Private Eye*. The second Chairman of the Cartoonists' Club of Great Britain, succeeding IAN SCOTT, he has been Treasurer of the British Cartoonists' Association since 1992. He was voted CCGB Topical Cartoonist of the Year in 1964 and Humorous Strip Cartoonist of the Year in 1966. A freelance scriptwriter for BBC TV's *Vision On* and *Beyond Belief*, he has also written radio scripts for comedians Dick Emery and Roy Hudd. Influenced at first by Chon Day and the cartoonists of the *New Yorker*, as well as by ERIC BURGIN, he works in ink with a flowing line and a subtle use of colour, usually watercolour or gouache. At first he used a Gillott 303 nib and indian ink but now mostly works in felt-tip or artpen.
PUB: *A Boy's Own War* (1990)
ILL: [with J. Mortimer] *Laugh With the Motorist* (1963); M. Harding, *The 14 1/2 lb. Budgie* (1980); D. Hunn, *Aiming High* (1984); A. de Courcy, *A Guide to Modern Manners* (1985)
EXHIB: BC; Umeleska Beseda Gallery, Bratislava
COLL: UKCC

JAK – *see* Jackson, Raymond Allen

JALLAND, George Herbert (fl. 1888–1910). Joke cartoonist, illustrator and journalist. G. H. Jalland wrote articles and drew illustrations for the *Badminton Magazine of Sports & Pastimes* in the 1890s and also drew hunting and sports cartoons for *Punch* (1888–1905) in the tradition of A. C. CORBOULD. In addition he contributed to *Holly Leaves*, *Pall Mall Magazine*, *Graphic*, *Sporting Magazine*, *Fores Sporting Notes & Sketches* and *Illustrated Sporting & Dramatic News*. His work was also included in Raphael Tuck's postcard series 'Motoring Jokes from *Punch*'.
PUB: *The Sporting Adventures of Mr. Popple* (1898)
ILL: T. Smith, *The Life of a Fox* (1896); G. C. G. F. Berkeley, *Reminiscences of a Huntsman* (1897);

P. Beckford, *Thoughts on Hunting* (1899); G. E. Collins, *Tales of Pink and Silk* (1900)
EXHIB: FAS (1901)

'Jane' – *see* Pett, William Norman

JAS – *see* Shepherd, William James Affleck

JAS F. – *see* Friell, James and Sullivan, James Francis

JASSEF – *see* Sullivan, James Francis

JBH – *see* Handelsman, John Bernard

JBP – *see* Partridge, Sir John Bernard

JCW – *see* Walker, J. C.

JENNINGS, Nicola (b. 1958). Caricaturist, political cartoonist and illustrator. Nicola Jennings was born in London on 10 September 1958. Her maternal grandfather was Christopher Hollis MP, a *Punch* contributor (*see also* CUMMINGS). She studied art at Taunton Art School (1976–7) and theatre design at Wimbledon School of Art (1977–80). Most of the 1980s

Nicola Jennings, [Mitterrand], *Guardian*, 26 June 1994

she spent working backstage in the theatre and illustrating books. She began caricature work for the *London Daily News* (1987) and *Daily Mirror* (1987–96). She has also worked for the *Guardian* (since 1991), *Observer* (since 1990) and *Prospect* magazine and TV work has included *A Week in Politics* for Channel 4 (1995–7) and BBC2's *The Midnight Hour* (1994), *Peering Into Europe* (1997), *The Year in 1998* (1998) and Channel 4's *President Blair* (1999). Influenced by Hogarth, Edward Lear, Beardsley and Scarfe, she uses dip pen and ink on paper, and for TV work draws on a computer, the result being transferred to Betacam.
ILL: J. Ebdon, *Ebdon's Iliad* (1982); G. Ewart (ed.), *Other People's Clerihews* (1983), *The Ewart Quarto* (1984); R. Irvine, *A Girl's Guide to the English Public Schoolboy* (1983); R. Taylor, *The Human Cookbook* (1986); F. Bressler, *Beastly Law* (1986)
EXHIB: Groucho Club
COLL: UKCC

JENNIS, Gurnell Charles ARE (1874–1943). Joke cartoonist, caricaturist and etcher. Charles Jennis contributed to *Pick-Me-Up* (caricatures, 1896), *Bystander*, *Graphic* and others. His first *Punch* cartoon was published on 25 September 1912 and his drawings, mostly of country and domestic scenes, appeared in the magazine for 12 years, the last being printed on 15 October 1924. Well-known as an etcher, his *Punch* work 'had much of the quality and distinction of the woodcut' (*Punch* obituary). A member of the Chelsea Arts Club, he was elected ARE in 1914.
EXHIB: RA; RE; NEAC; L
COLL: V&A

JENSEN, John (b. 1930). Political, joke, pocket and strip cartoonist, caricaturist, illustrator and writer. Born in Sydney, Australia, on 8 August 1930, the son of the cartoonist Jack Gibson, John Jensen (he adopted the 'new' surname – his stepfather's – in the 1940s) studied at the Julian Ashton Art School, Sydney (1946–7). His first cartoon was published in the *Sydney Sun* in 1946 and he began freelancing as a cartoonist thereafter for publications such as *Australia National Journal* and *Pertinent*. Emigrating to England in 1950, he became Pocket Cartoonist on the *Birmingham Gazette* (1951–3) and then the *Glasgow Bulletin* (1953–6). He returned to London in 1956 and produced freelance work for *Punch* (from

John Jensen, [Pavarotti], 1989

1953, including covers), *Lilliput*, *Daily Express*, *Evening News*, *New Statesman*, *Sketch*, *Books & Bookmen*, *High Life*, *King*, *Daily Sketch*, *Weekend* and *Sunday Dispatch*. The first-ever Political Cartoonist on the *Sunday Telegraph* (1961–79), he also regularly drew theatre caricatures for *Tatler* (1973–7), social cartoons for *Spectator* (1973–6), a weekly strip for *Now!* magazine (1979–81) and cartoons and illustrations for the *Sunday Correspondent*. A director of the Cartoon Art Trust since 1988 and its Chairman from 1992 to 1993, he was one of the founder members of the British Cartoonists' Association in 1966 and has been its Chairman since 1995. He has also written occasional journalism, mostly on cartoonists and cartoons. Ambidextrous, he is an admirer of BATEMAN, OSPOVAT, Peter Arno, BERT THOMAS, TRIER, Hiroshige, and Olaf Gulbransson, and prefers to watch his caricature subjects on video in addition to studying photographs. He works on paper and draws twice publication size using a dip pen, brush and Kandahar ink. For colour work he uses watercolour paper and Winsor & Newton watercolour and gouache paints. His draughtsmanship and versatility have been widely admired, not least by Frank Keating whose sports column he illustrated in *Punch* for many years: 'his line is so varied. Sometimes it can be brilliantly grotesque, other times it has a lovely smooth flow. He's master of both.'
PUB: (ed.) *The Man Who . . . and Other Drawings* [H. M. BATEMAN] (1975), *The Only Good Bank Manager is . . .* (1991)
ILL: More than 60 books including several of M. Green's 'The Art of . . .' series (from 1960); W. Davis, *The Supersalesman's Handbook* (1986); S. Hoggart, *On the House* (1981), *Back on the House* (1982); K. Waterhouse, *Mrs Pooter's Diary* (1983); D. Moore, *Dudley Moore's Musical Bumps* (1986); J. Booth (ed.), *Creative Spirits* (1997)
EXHIB: CG; NT [with B. HEWISON]; CBG; BC; Muzeum Karykatury, Warsaw
COLL: V&A; CAT: UKCC; TM; A; National Museum of Australia, Canberra; SAM; BM; Muzeum Karykatury, Warsaw

JMS – *see* Staniforth, Joseph Morewood

'John Citizen' – *see* Fearon, Percy Hutton

'Johnnie Walker' – *see* Browne, Thomas Arthur and Cheney, Leopold Alfred

JOHNSTON, Thomas (b. 1953). Political, pocket, strip and joke cartoonist, and musician. Tom Johnston was born in Belfast on 18 May 1953 and attended Leeds Art College (1972–5) and the University of London (1975–6). His first cartoon was published in the *Daily Mirror* in 1976 and he became a full-time freelance the same year. He contributed at first mostly to the music press, appearing in *Melody Maker*, *Sounds* and *Smash Hits*, but later moved to the *Evening News*, then the *Evening Standard*. He joined the *Sun* in 1981 and later succeeded FRANKLIN as Political Cartoonist (1992–6) on the paper, moving to the *Daily Mirror* in 1996 to replace GRIFFIN as Political Cartoonist. His work has also been published in *Today*, *News of the World* ('Short John Silver' strip), *Punch* and *Private Eye* amongst others. In addition he has been a professional bass guitarist in rock bands and was a founder member of the group The The in 1977. An admirer of the French cartoonist Reisir and of MICHAEL HEATH, he works in felt-tip pen on paper.
PUB: *Tom Johnston* (1992)

JOLLIFFE, Gray (b. 1937). Joke and strip cartoonist, commercial artist and illustrator. Gray Jolliffe was born in Cremyll, Cornwall, on 3 June 1937, the son of W. J. Jolliffe, an RAF officer. After National Service in the RAF (1956–8) – his first cartoon was for an RAF blood-transfusion poster in 1957 – he started his career as an advertising copywriter and became creative director of Kirkwoods and then (part-time) of both Chetwynd and Dewe Rogerson. He has also directed commercials. Since the success of his 'Wicked Willie' books featuring a talking penis he has become a full-time cartoonist. A self-taught artist, his cartoons have appeared in the *Sunday Express*, *You*, *Cosmopolitan*, *Hello* ('Jolly Giraffe' strip), *Evening Standard*, *Oldie*, *Men Only*, *Daily Mail* ('Up and Running' strip), *Sunday Times*, *Woman's Journal*, *Marketing Week*, *Business Life*, *Club Pour Hommes* and elsewhere and he has also worked in advertising for Toshiba, Safeway, Shell, Cadbury's, Hewlett Packard, Hamlet Cigars, Perrier, Boodle & Dunthorne, Nicorettes, Ricoh Brobat Bloo Loo, Scottish Widows, Solo Softener, Batchelors Cuppa Soup and others. In addition he has produced greetings cards, 'Wicked Willie' videos and numerous books, and scripted a TV special 'Stainless Steel and the Star Spies'. He was voted CAT Advertising Cartoonist of the Year in 1997.

Jolliffe, who signs his work 'Gray', draws distinctive frog-eyed figures with sausage-shaped noses and works with felt-tip pen and Magic Markers on paper.

PUB: *Christmas Already!* (1978); [with P. Mayle] *The Honeymoon Book* (1983), *Man's Best Friend* (1984), *Twinkle Winkle* (1985), *Wicked Willie's Guide to Women* (1986), *Wicked Willie's Low-Down on Men* (1987), *Dear Willie* (1989), *Wicked Willie Stand-Up Comic* (1990) and *Willie's Leg-Over Handbook* (1991); [with O. Dalton] *The Whole Hog* (1987), [with L. Graham] *Pussy Pie Hits Town* (1988), *The Unadulterated Cat* (1989); *How to be a Happy Cat* (1986); *Christmas Already Again Yet* (1987); *Apathy Made Easy* (1993); *Girl Chasing* (1989); *Man Hunting* (1990)

ILL: G. Search and D. Denison, *Getting in Shape* (1988)

EXHIB: Grosvenor House Gallery; Sloane Club; Groucho Club

COLL: V&A (Christmas cards)

JON – *see* Jones, William John Philpin and Musgrave-Wood, John Bertram

JONES – *see* Jones, Grenfell

JONES, Grenfell 'Gren' MBE (b. 1934). Editorial and strip cartoonist, illustrator and writer. Gren Jones was born in Hengoed, Wales, on 13 June 1934, the son of Harry Jones, a collier. At the age of eight he began drawing pocket cartoons in the style of RONALD NIEBOUR ('Neb was responsible for my first interest in cartoons') and his first published drawing was a joke cartoon for *Spick & Span*. He sold his first news-related cartoon to the *Birmingham Mail* with the help of JON, whom he greatly admired. Employed at first as an engineering designer (1958–63), he was later one of the founder members of what became the Barron Knights satirical pop group and worked as a freelance cartoonist for a number of years before joining the *Western Mail* and *South Wales Echo* in 1968. Apart from his daily news-related cartoon he is best known for his creation (in his *South Wales Echo* strip 'Ponty an' Pop') of the village of Aberflyarff in Scrumcap Valley on the River Efflew, with its colourful characters such as Ponty and Pop and Bromide Lil, the tattooed barmaid of the Golden Dap. In addition, his strip 'Big Deal' has been syndicated for 35 years. He was awarded the MBE in 1990 for his services to the newspaper industry and has been voted CCGB Provincial Cartoonist of the Year four times (1983, 1985, 1986, 1987). He has also produced sporting calendars (golf, cricket and rugby) as well as some with a business theme (notably for Bemrose Publishers for 20 years), and is official 'war artist' for the Welsh Rugby Union. In addition he has sometimes worked as 'Jones'. Gren prefers to work in line and wash.

PUB: *My Wales* (1971), *More of My Wales* (1973), 12 annual volumes of collected cartoons from the *South Wales Echo* (from 1982), 'Duffer's Guide' series (eight titles from 1985), 'A Portrait of . . .' series (three titles from 1987), 'Welshman' series (from 1989), *Gren's Guide to Rugby* (1996), *Ponty an' Pop: The Aberflyarff Story* (1996)

ILL: T. Bellion, '*And the Tanker Spent a Comfortable Night*' (1979); D. Parry-Jones, *Boots, Balls and Banter* (1980); M. Boyce, *I Was There* (1981); R. Noble, *Welsh Nicknames* (1998)

EXHIB: WAC touring exhibition (1985–6); St David's Hall, Cardiff

COLL: Wales Tourist Board; WAC; National Library of Wales, Aberystwyth

JONES, William John Philpin 'JON' MBE (1913–92). Political, sports and pocket cartoonist. Born on 17 August 1913 in Llandrindod Wells, Wales, the son of John Jones, a bookmaker, 'JON the cartoon' first showed a talent for drawing as a boy by winning a prize at the National Eisteddfod and had his first cartoon published in the *Radnor Express* in 1928. After studying at the Birmingham School of Art (1932) he won a scholarship to the RCA in London but did not complete the course, returning to Wales to work as a cartoonist on the *Western Mail*. In 1937 he joined Godbolds advertising agency in London and in World War II served at first in the Welch Regiment. Attached to Princess Patricia's Canadian Light Infantry during the Sicily landings in 1943, he was Assistant Military Landing Officer at Salerno and Anzio. He later joined the British Newspaper Unit under Hugh (later Lord) Cudlipp and contributed cartoons to *Eighth Army News* (where his famous 'Two Types' series first appeared under the title 'Page Two Smile' in July 1944 and as 'The Two Types' on 16 August 1944), *Union Jack, Crusader* ('Philpin' weekly political cartoons) and *Soldier*, which were later syndicated

'It may taste a bit odd. I brewed it in a teapot.'

JON (W. J. P. Jones), *JON's Complete Two Types*, 1991

elsewhere. After the war he followed Cudlipp to the Mirror Group, working on the *Sunday Pictorial* (sports cartoons, May 1946–52) and in 1952 joined Kemsley Newspapers, drawing for the *Daily Graphic, Sunday Graphic, Empire News* and *Sunday Times*. In 1955 he moved to the *News Chronicle*, creating two daily pocket cartoons – 'The Sporting Types' and a political series – and continued to draw for the newspaper when it was absorbed by the *Mail* in 1960. Over the next 21 years he contributed more than 15,000 cartoons on politics, current affairs and sport to the paper, and was elected CCGB Topical & Sports Cartoonist of the Year (1966) and Pocket Cartoonist of the Year (1981). He retired from the *Daily Mail* in 1981 but continued to draw for the new *Mail on Sunday* until 1988 and for the *South Wales Argus* and *Abergavenny Chroni-*

cle until 1990. He was one of the founder members of the British Cartoonists' Association in 1966. JON is perhaps best remembered for his immortal creations, The Two Types, a roguish pair of moustachioed Desert Rat officers who rank with BRUCE BAIRNSFATHER's 'Old Bill', DAVID LOW's 'Colonel Blimp' and NORMAN PETT's 'Jane' as classic British comic characters. Though only some 300 Two Types cartoons appeared between 1943 and 1946, over a million copies of wartime collections of the drawings were published. Their effect on allied morale was tremendous and earned him an MBE from Winston Churchill. JON died in St Joseph's nursing home, near Newport, Wales, on 28 June 1992.

PUB: *The Two Types* (1945), *JON's Two Types in Italy* (1945), *The Two Types* (1960), *Wilson in*

Wonderland (1968), *JON Cartoons* (1978), *Maggie* (1979)
ILL: L. Sellers, *Cooking with Love* (1970); B. Sanctuary, *How to Eat Cheaply and Well* (1970); [with R. Ullyett] *'I'm the Greatest!'* (1975); S. Hull, *Cooking for Baby* (1976)
EXHIB: CG; Austin Reed
COLL: CA; IWM; UKCC; National Library of Wales, Aberystwyth
LIT: *JON's Complete Two Types* (1991)

JOSS, Frederick 'Denim' [real name Fritz Josefowitsch] (*c.* 1909–1967). Political, pocket and strip cartoonist, caricaturist, journalist and writer. Born in Vienna, Fred Joss studied art at the city's Kunstgewerbeschule and then hitchhiked around Europe, working in a variety of jobs in Denmark, Holland, Paris, Spain and Bulgaria. By the age of 19 he was working as a cartoonist in Rio de Janeiro. He then returned to Vienna and worked for an evening newspaper, moving to Britain in 1933. He joined the *Star* as Political Cartoonist in 1934 (succeeding WYNDHAM ROBINSON), sharing an office with sports cartoonist ROY ULLYETT, and stayed with the paper for 21 years. In addition he drew pocket cartoons (in pencil on flimsy paper) for the *Star* ('Joss Stick'), a caricature series ('Types of Men') using newspaper cuttings for tinting, and a popular Saturday strip ('Round-Up'). During World War II he served as a gunner (achieving the rank of sergeant) and also drew cartoons under the name of 'Denim'. In addition he wrote a controversial satirical novel about arms racketeers in the Spanish Civil War, using the pseudonym 'F. J. Joseph'. After the death of his first wife, Clara, and a close friend he felt unable to draw for a while and left the *Star* (1955). He then spent some time travelling and sketching in the Far East, writing and illustrating articles for the *Mainichi Daily News*, *Economist*, *Eastern Horizon*, *Kukje Shin Bo* and others, reporting on the Korean War for the British Press, and holding exhibitions of his drawings. In addition he drew lightning caricatures on television and broadcast on *geisha* in Hong Kong, where he eventually settled. As 'Denim' he drew on small sheets of airmail paper using a fountain pen and blue pencil. He also used pastels, Swan watercolour pencils, wax crayon and ballpoint pen. His style was to draw rough in fountain pen, then place the drawing on a lightbox, cover it with very

Fred Joss, [LESLIE ILLINGWORTH], in A. H. Heighway (ed.), *Inky Way Annual*, 1948

smooth white writing paper, then with a broad dip pen (a 'squeezer') he drew over this in Mandarin ink or black Scribtol, using Chinese white to correct any errors and blue pencil to indicate where tints should appear. 'Blacks are sloshed on with a number eight watercolour brush, real sable if possible – Fenton or Winsor & Newton' (*The Artist*, June 1953). Of his pen-and-ink technique he said: 'I always smudge my right forefinger with some ink from the nib, and use my fingertip as a brush, in addition to the pen work.' Fred Joss died after falling from the roof of the Hong Kong Hilton Hotel in April 1967.
PUB: [as F. J. Joseph] *Amateurs in Arms* [novel] (1938); [as Denim] *200 Cartoons by Denim* (1946), *Another 200 Cartoons* (1946), *Up Against It* (1947); [as Frederick Joss] *Of Geisha & Gangsters* (1962)
ILL: G. R. Tabouis [trs. P. Selver], *Blackmail or War* (1938)
EXHIB: LEG ('Sketches of Tunisia', 1951); 'East of Aden', London (1961)
COLL: UKCC

JWT – *see* Taylor, John Whitfield

K

KAL – *see* Kallaugher, Kevin

KALLAUGHER, Kevin 'KAL' (b. 1955). Political cartoonist and caricaturist. Kevin Kallaugher was born in Norwalk, Connecticut, USA and took a degree in visual and environmental studies at Harvard, where he produced an animated colour film as part of his thesis and drew a weekly strip 'In the Days of Disgustus' in *Harvard Crimson*. After graduating in 1977 he came to England on a bicycle tour and stayed, working first as a semi-professional basketball player before joining the *Economist* as the weekly's first-ever resident caricaturist in March 1978. He has also been Political Cartoonist on the *Oxford Sunday Journal* (1980), *Observer* (1983–6), *Today* (1986–7) and *Sunday Telegraph* (1987–8). He returned to the USA in 1988 to work for the *Baltimore Sun* and continues to draw two cartoons a week for the *Economist* and two for its Web Edition. He is also a regular contributor to the *International Herald-Tribune* (Paris), *Central Europe* (Vienna) and *Mediaweek* (New York). Widely syndicated, his work has appeared in more than 100 papers worldwide. He is an admirer of Oliphant, McNelly and LEVINE. His work for the *Economist* was unsigned (which is magazine policy), but he always included his wife's name in the drawing somewhere. His caricatures of Margaret Thatcher and Neil Kinnock were animated by Richard Williams' studio for use as a TV commercial for *Today* newspaper. KAL has won a number of awards for his work, including CCGB Feature Cartoonist of the Year (1982), Best Editorial Cartoon at the *Witty World* International Cartoon Festival, Budapest (1990) and the Grafica Internazionale Award at the International Festival of Satire in Pisa (1996). A past President of the Association of American Editorial Cartoonists, he has also been British and European editor of *Target* magazine and curator of 'Worth a Thousand Words', an exhibition of cartoons, caricatures, paintings, etc., by 50 artists at the Walters Art Museum, USA.
PUB: *Drawn from the Economist* (1988), *KALtoons* (1992), *KAL Draws a Crowd* (1997)
EXHIB: London, New York, Washington, Baltimore
COLL: UKCC

KAPP, Edmond Xavier (1890–1978). Caricaturist, illustrator, painter and writer. Edmond Kapp was born in Islington, London, on 5 November 1890, the son of Emil B. Kapp and the elder brother of the painter Helen Kapp. He was educated at Owen's School, London, and studied in Paris, at Berlin University and at Christ's College, Cambridge (1910–13). While he was at Cambridge some of his caricatures were published in *Granta*, the *Cambridge Magazine* and *Tatler* and were exhibited in the town (1912). After graduating he contributed to the *Daily News*, *Onlooker* and *News Weekly*. During World War I he served in the Royal Sussex Regiment on the Western Front and later became a Captain in Army Intelligence. In 1919 his exhibition at the Little Art Rooms, Adelphi, London, was praised by MAX BEERBOHM. He then studied at the Slade (1919), in Vienna, at the British Academy in Rome (where he was influenced by the American painter Maurice Sterne) and in Paris. On his return he drew for the *Law Journal* (1924, caricatures of lawyers and judges), *Apple*, *Bystander*, *Onlooker*, *Observer*, *Radio Times*, *Tatler*, *Time & Tide* and others. In 1926 he travelled to Spain and in 1938 visited Antibes where, uniquely, Picasso sat for him and declared that Kapp was 'incapable of making a bad drawing' (Matisse also sat for Kapp). He worked in pencil, lithographic chalk and other media, and disliked the term 'caricature', preferring to describe his works as 'attempts to do portraits or character studies'. During World War II he was an Official War Artist (1940–41, drawing 'Life Under London' for the Imperial War Museum) and later was appointed Official Artist to Unesco (1946–7). Six colour lithographs from a series of ten he drew for Butterworths in 1925 were reproduced as stained-glass windows in Yale Law School Library, USA. From 1960 onwards he concentrated on painting (mostly abstracts and portraits). Kapp also wrote nonsense verse under the name 'Otto Watteau'. He was married to the writer Yvonne Cloud. Edmond Kapp died on 29 October 1978.
PUB: *Personalities* (1919), *Reflections* (1922), *Ten Great Lawyers* (1924), *Minims* (1925), [with Y. Cloud] *Pastiche* (1926)
ILL: L. Housman, *Trimblerigg* (1924)
EXHIB: LG; W (retrospective 1961); Wildenstein Gallery; LM; IWM; BAR

COLL: BM; V&A; NPG; A; B; M; IWM; LM; F; BIB; Art Gallery of Western Australia, Perth; Tel Aviv Art Gallery, Israel; Albright Art Gallery, Buffalo, USA

KAPP, Helen (b. 1901) – *see* Bryant & Heneage

KELLY, Felix Runcie 'Fix' (b. 1916–after 1988). Painter, theatrical designer, joke cartoonist and illustrator. Felix Kelly was born in Auckland, New Zealand, and was a self-taught artist. He taught art at Auckland Art School and came to the UK in 1937, working at first for Unilever. During World War II he served in the RAF and began contributing cartoons to *Lilliput* and elsewhere under the name 'Fix' or 'Fix Kelly'. He later became a set designer (1952–65) for the Haymarket, Phoenix, Sadlers Wells and Old Vic theatres and illustrated books for Longman, Hutchinson, Macmillan, Chatto & Windus and others. He worked in pen and ink, pencil and colour, and was also a distinguished landscape, architectural and fantasy painter (owing something to De Chirico and Dali) in oils and gouache – commissions included 'Cliveden' for Hon. Mrs William Astor, 'Grantley Hall' for Lord Grantley, 'Abbey Hill' for Lennox Berkeley and 'Three Sisters' for Herbert Read.
ILL: H. E. Read, *The Green Child* (1945); E. Burton, *The Elizabethans at Home* (1958), *The Georgians at Home* (1967), *The Jacobeans at Home* (1967), *The Early Victorians at Home* (1972); I. Brown, *London* (1960)
EXHIB: Lefevre Gallery; LG (1950, 1952); Tooth Gallery; Partridge Fine Art; Portraits Inc., New York; Arthur Jeffress Gallery; Kennedy Galleries, New York; Delgado Museum of Art, New Orleans
LIT: Sir H. Read, *Paintings by Felix Kelly* (1946)
COLL: Aberdeen Art Gallery

KEM – *see* Marengo, Kimon Evan

KENT, Capel John (b. 1937). Joke and strip cartoonist, illustrator, writer and painter. John Kent was born on 21 June 1937 in Oamaru, New Zealand, the son of R. C. H. Kent of the New Zealand Justice Department, and came to London in 1959. A self-taught artist, he worked at first as a copywriter and art director in advertising before having his first strip 'Grocer Heath' accepted by *Private Eye* in 1969, closely followed by the controversial 'Varoomshka' for the *Guardian* (1969–79). Varoomshka was inspired by the fashion model Verushka and was originally based on Kent's wife, Nina. He has described the character as 'the permanent link between absurdities. A Miss Everyone who, unlike most people, manages to retain a sense of incredulity at all she encounters.' An innocent blonde beauty asking simple questions of wily politicians in the Wilson/Callaghan era, Kent's character exposed hypocrisy and self-interest in government, and trade-union leader Jack Jones even brought libel proceedings against one attack made in the cartoon. John Kent still works regularly for *Private Eye*, combining political comment and caricature with a strip format, and has also contributed to the *Sunday Times* (1980–83, 1990–94), *Evening Standard* (1982–6), *The Times* (from 1998) and *Daily Mail* (from 1974). In addition, he has lectured at the RIBA and elsewhere. Influenced by the American cartoonist Al Capp (creator of 'L'il Abner'), he works mostly in felt-tip pen on A4 paper.
PUB: *Varoomshka* (1972), *Varoomshka's Bumper Colouring Book Annual* (1975), *John Kent's Venice* (1988), *John Kent's Florence and Siena* (1989)
ILL: R. Michael (ed.), *The ABZ of Pornography* (1972); R. Huggett, *The Wit and Humour of Sex* (1975); B. Norman, *Tales of the Redundance Kid* (1975)
EXHIB: De Marco Gallery, Edinburgh; ICA
COLL: IWM; V&A; UKCC

KIM – *see* Casali, Kim

KING, William Gunning NEAC (1859–1940). Painter, etcher, illustrator and joke cartoonist. William Gunning King was born in South Kensington, London, on 2 September 1859, the son of William Bignell King and the brother of the painter Edward R. King NEAC. He was educated at the Western Grammar School, Kensington, and studied at the South Kensington Schools and the RA Schools where he won a silver medal for drawing. He contributed joke cartoons and illustrations to *Punch* (1905–16), *Cassell's*, *Illustrated London News*, *Illustrated Sporting & Dramatic News*, *Pick-Me-Up*, *Quiver*, *Windsor*, *Graphic*, *English Illustrated Magazine*, *Illustrated London News* (1882–99), *Sketch* and others. Perhaps his most famous drawing was 'Sometimes I sits and thinks; and then again I just sits', published in *Punch* on 24 October 1906. He also designed comic postcards for S. Hildesheimer and Raphael Tuck, and drew advertisements for Joseph Bibby and others. In addition he painted landscapes, portraits and still lifes – exhibiting at the Royal Academy 47 times (from 1881) and winning a gold medal at the International Exhibition at Crystal Palace (1899) – and contributed a watercolour to the Queen's Doll's House. Rather old-fashioned in style for his day (Price called him 'a good mid-Victorian illustrator forty years on'), he was greatly influenced by Charles Keene. Indeed, FOUGASSE held that 'Gunning King may be said to have translated Charles Keene's line into process'. Elected NEAC in 1887, he drew mostly in ink and chalk. William Gunning King died in October 1940 aged 81.

EXHIB: RA; RI; RBA; NEAC; RSA; L; G; GG; ROI
COLL: V&A; Brighton; THG

KRAUZE, Andrzej (b. 1947). Political/editorial cartoonist, illustrator, poster artist and painter. Andrzej Krauze was born in Warsaw on 7 March 1947 and studied painting and illustration at the Academy of Fine Art in the city (1967–73). While still a student he began contributing cartoons to the satirical magazine *Szpilki* (1971–79) and after winning first prize in a poster competition organized by the National Theatre, Warsaw (1971) he began working regularly as a poster-designer for the theatre (1971–3). After graduating (his diploma submission, an animated cartoon film entitled *The Flying Lesson*, was censored by the authorities) he travelled to Paris and London and then returned to Warsaw to work as Political Cartoonist on the important weekly *Kultura* magazine (1974–81) until it was closed when martial law was imposed, after which he drew for the trade union paper *Solidarnosc*. He also worked as a designer and illustrator in book publishing (1974–9) before moving to Amsterdam, where he worked as an illustrator for the newspaper *Handelsblad* (1980) and then Paris, contributing to *L'Express, L'Expansion, Lire* and *L'Alternative*.

After the imposition of martial law in Poland in 1981 he moved to London and has since then contributed to *New Statesman* (political cartoons and illustrations from 1988), *Guardian* (political cartoons and illustrations from 1989), *Sunday Telegraph, New York Times, International Herald-Tribune, Bookseller, Aamulehti* (Finnish daily, political cartoons and illustrations, 1985–95), *The Times, Listener, New Scientist, Campaign, Modern Painters, Independent on Sunday* and others. He was appointed Visiting Lecturer (1985) and External Examiner in the Department of Illustration (1997) at the Royal College of Art. In addition he has won First Prize in the Forte Dei Marmi (Italy) political satire competition (1982) and the Victoria & Albert Museum Award for Illustration (1996). He has also designed posters for the Old Vic Theatre under the directorship of Jonathan Miller (1986–90).

PUB: *Happiness in a Spray Can* (1977), *Mr Krauze's Animals* (1978), *Love Me* (1980), *Andrzej Krauze's Poland* (1981), *A Year of Martial Law* (1982), *Coming Back to the West* (1983), *La Satira Politica di A. Krauze* (1984) and others

ILL: Many books including S. Szechter, *A Stolen Biography* (1985); P. Wright, *On Living in an Old Country* (1985); E. Lehtola, *Pisaratartunta* (1987); M. Rosen (ed.), *Culture Shock* (1990), *Action Replay* (1993); L. Spencer, *Hegel for Beginners* (1996), *The Enlightenment for Beginners* (1997); S. Brenner, *Loose Ends* (1997)

EXHIB: 22 solo shows since 1981 including Polish Cultural Centre; Edinburgh Festival; Galleria Municipale, Padua; Galerie Remont, Berlin; Casino Municipale, Venice; Simon Capstick Gallery; Jablonski Gallery

COLL: [posters] Museum of Modern Art, New York; [posters] Museum of Modern Art, Tokyo; [posters] Museum of Modern Art, Tampere, Finland; [posters] Stedelijk Museum, Amsterdam; [posters] Musée des Arts Décoratifs, Paris

L

'The Lady and the Wimp' – *see* Williams, Christopher Charles

LAIDLER, Gavin Graham 'Pont' ARIBA (1908–40). Joke and strip cartoonist. Graham Laidler

was born on 4 July 1908 in Jesmond, Newcastle upon Tyne, only son of George Gavin Laidler, the proprietor of a distinguished firm of painters and decorators founded in 1823. He was educated at Trinity College, Glenalmond, Perth,

THE BRITISH CHARACTER
IMPORTANCE OF TEA

Pont (Graham Laidler), *Punch*, 30 October 1935

and at the Architectural Association's School of Architecture in London (1926). Soon after qualifying he contracted tuberculosis, and after a major operation in 1932 was unable to pursue an architectural career. While still a student his first cartoon strip, 'The Twiff Family', began to appear in *Woman's Pictorial* (1930–37 when it was taken over by the children's comic illustrator Fred Robinson), and he had his first cartoon accepted by *Punch* in August 1932. The first drawing in his celebrated series 'The British Character' ('Adaptability to Foreign Conditions') appeared in the magazine on 4 April 1934 and when *Night & Day* tried to lure him away *Punch* signed him up for a unique exclusive contract. Pont, whose name arose from a family joke concerning 'Pontifex Maximus' was, with PAUL CRUM (Roger Pettiward), very influential: 'these two, Pont and Pettiward, probably did more during this period to carry the development of modern pictorial humour a whole stage further than any two or twenty others put together' (FOUGASSE). He worked in pen, ink and wash and sometimes watercolour, mainly on Whatman Boards. Pont also produced illustrated Christmas catalogues for W. Glendenning & Sons, Wine Merchants (1931 and 1932). 'Descended from W. BIRD rather than TOWNSEND,' says Price, Pont 'set a fashion for the small single-figure drawing with a single short line of dialogue . . . which epitomized the whole of the situation or the whole of the character'. HEWISON has described his 'easy assurance and wiry delicacy of line . . . in spite of their cross-hatchery and careful composition [his cartoons] are untutored and amateur in the best sense of the word – the work of a natural draughtsman . . . he was able to tackle subjects that would scare the daylight out of most trained artists, and bring them off beautifully.' In describing his work Pont always insisted: 'I do not try to draw funny people . . . I try very hard to draw people exactly as they are.' He died of poliomyelitis in Hillingdon County Hospital, Uxbridge, Middlesex, on 23 November 1940.

PUB: *The British Character* (1938), *The British at Home* (1939), *The British Carry On* (1940), *Pont* (1942), *Most of Us Are Absurd* (1946), *The World of Pont* (1983)

EXHIB: Charterhouse School; LAN; CG

COLL: V&A; CAT; BM

LIT: B. Hollowood, *Pont* (1969); R. Ingrams (ed.) *The British Character and the World of Pont* (1985)

LAMB, Kathryn (b. 1959). Joke and strip cartoonist, illustrator and author. Kathryn Lamb was born in Bahrain on 25 May 1959, the daughter of Sir Archie Lamb, former British Ambassador to Kuwait and Norway. After studying English at Oxford University (1979–81), where she contributed cartoons to student papers, she worked for a variety of publications. Her first cartoon was published in *Private Eye* in May 1979 and the same year she created the strip 'Lord Arthur and His Square Table' (1979) which ran for eight years in the magazine. She currently illustrates 'Pseuds Corner' for *Private Eye*, produces a regular strip 'M'Lud' for the *Oldie* and has contributed to *Punch*, *Spectator*, *Daily Telegraph*, *Big Farm Weekly* and *The Times*. In addition she has drawn greetings cards for businesses and The Alzheimers Society and was commissioned to design a 'get well' card for King Hussein of Jordan. Although most of her work is produced in very fine detailed pen and ink she also uses watercolour washes.

PUB: *Animal Madness* (1989), *Lamb's Tales* (1989), *One Ewe Over the Cuckoo's Nest* (1991), *Help! My Family is Driving Me Crazy* (1997), *Help! My Social Life is a Mess!* (1997), *Help! Let Me Out of Here!* (1998), *Boywatching* (1998), *Girls Are From Saturn, Boys Are From Jupiter* (1999)

ILL: J. Gladstone, *Up Country* (1988); S. Milligan, *Condensed Animals* (1991); T. Dicks, *The Good, the Bad and the Ghastly* (1995); R. Rushton, *Staying Cool, Surviving School* (1993)

EXHIB: CG

COLL: BM

LANCASTER, Sir Osbert CBE ROI (1908–86). Pocket and political cartoonist, illustrator, author, theatre designer and painter. Osbert Lancaster was born in Notting Hill, London, on 4 August 1908, the son of Robert Lancaster, a businessman who was killed at the Battle of the

'How on earth can I pick up my skirt when that ghastly little Viscountess in the row behind kicked my shoes out of reach!'

Osbert Lancaster, *Daily Express*, 1953

Somme in 1916 and who greatly admired PHIL MAY. His grandfather was Sir William Lancaster who had made a fortune in the City in life assurance and was Secretary of the Prudential Assurance Company. His mother was the flower painter Clare Bracebridge Manger, who had been taught by Algernon Talmage ARA RWA, was the last surviving former pupil of G. F. Watts and had exhibited regularly at the Royal Academy. Educated at St Ronan's Preparatory School, Worthing, and Charterhouse, Surrey, he left aged 17 to study at the BYAM SHAW School of Art (1925–6). In 1926 he entered Lincoln College, Oxford (where he was a contemporary and friend of Stephen Spender, Randolph Churchill, James Lees-Milne and John Betjeman) to study English. While a student he contributed caricatures and humorous articles to *Cherwell*.

135

However, gaining only a fourth-class degree (1930) and failing to qualify as a barrister, he studied art at Oxford's Ruskin School (1929–30) and stage design under Vladimir Polunin (formerly Diaghilev's designer) at the Slade (1931–2), where he met and married (1933) his first wife Karen, daughter of Sir Austen Harris, Vice-Chairman of Lloyds Bank. He then worked as a freelance illustrator, designing posters for London Transport and others before becoming, with Betjeman's help, an assistant editor on the *Architectural Review* (1934–9). In 1936 he wrote and illustrated his first book, *Progress at Pelvis Bay*, the first of many satires on architecture and social mores. He was also art critic for the short-lived magazine *Night & Day* (1937) and later for the *Observer* (1942–4). He joined the *Daily Express* in 1938 and the following year, John Rayner, Features Editor of the paper, invited him to draw single-column cartoons on the European model (later known as 'pocket' cartoons, a phrase Lancaster himself coined) for the paper. The first one appeared in Tom Driberg's 'William Hickey' gossip column on 1 January 1939, but they later transferred to the front page and it is estimated that he drew some 10,000 in all between 1939 and 1981. He also drew large political cartoons (as 'Bunbury', in an allusion to the imaginary character in Oscar Wilde's play, *The Importance of Being Earnest*, rather than to the 18th-century caricaturist) for the *Sunday Express*. During World War II he worked for a time at the Ministry of Information News Department (1939) and then the Foreign Office News Department (1940), and in 1944 he was sent by the Foreign Office to the British Embassy in Athens as Press Attaché (Second Secretary) for two years. After the war he continued to draw cartoons (including caricatures for the *Strand Magazine*, covers for *The Ambassador*, and a self-caricature for *Cornhill*), painted murals, produced books and designed advertisements (e.g. for Krug Champagne). In addition he was appointed Sydney Jones Lecturer in Art at Liverpool University (1947) and was a governor of King Edward VII School, King's Lynn. He worked with John Piper on designs for the Festival of Britain (1951) and on Piper's recommendation designed his first stage set for Sadler's Wells (he subsequently designed for many other theatres including Glyndebourne, Royal Opera House and the Bulgarian State Opera). Appointed CBE (1953) he was later knighted (1975), and elected ROI

(1979) and RDI (1979). In his pocket cartoons Lancaster created a cast of strong characters of whom Maudie, Countess of Littlehampton, and her monocled husband Willy are best known but Canon Fontwater, Father O'Bubblegum and Mrs Rajagojollibarmi are also memorable. He worked remarkably fast: 'The cartoons only used to take about five minutes . . . no, maybe we'd better say fifteen – don't want to make it sound too easy!' FOUGASSE saw him as 'of the school of Thurber . . . his real bent is literary and his drawings are only used to make points more easily put into a graphic shorthand than into a hundred words or so.' BRADSHAW said, 'the line with which he draws his shrewdly observed people is almost juvenile in its deliberation and simplicity. But the artlessness of the style only serves to add pungency to the wit of a very grown-up mind.' He was greatly influenced by MAX BEERBOHM and admired GEORGE MORROW, DULAC and Caran D'Ache, but disliked the work of LINLEY SAMBOURNE. Voted CCGB Topical Cartoonist of the Year (1962), he was one of the founder members of the British Cartoonists' Association in 1966. After the death of his first wife he married the journalist and magazine editor Anne Scott-James (1967). Sir Osbert Lancaster died in Chelsea on 27 July 1986.

PUB: Many books including *Progress at Pelvis Bay* (1936), *Our Sovereigns from Alfred to George VI, 1871–1937* (1937), *Pillar to Post* (1938), *Homes Sweet Homes* (1939), *Pocket Cartoons* (1940), *New Pocket Cartoons* (1941), *Further Pocket Cartoons* (1942), *Assorted Sizes* (1944), *Cartoons* (1945), *Classical Landscape with Figures* (1947), *Saracen's Head* (1948), *Drayneflete Revealed* (1949), *Facades and Faces* (1950), *Signs of the Times* (1961), *All Done from Memory* (1963), *With an Eye to the Future* (1967), *Sailing to Byzantium* (1969), *The Littlehampton Bequest* (1973), *Scene Changes* (1978), *The Life and Times of Maudie Littlehampton* (1982)

ILL: Many books including M. Barsley, *Grabberwocky* (1939); V. Graham, *Say Please* (1949); S. Lambert, *London Night and Day* (1951); C. N. Parkinson, *Parkinson's Law for the Pursuit of Progress* (1958), *In-Laws and Outlaws* (1962); N. Mitford, *The Water Beetle* (1962); N. Dennis, *An Essay on Malta* (1972); M. Beerbohm, *Zuleika Dobson* (1975); Saki, *Short Stories* (1976), *The Unbearable Bassington* (1978); A. Scott-James, *The Pleasure Garden* (1977), *Down to Earth* (1971)

EXHIB: NPG (1973); Redfern Gallery (Retrospective 1980); CG

COLL: T; V&A; NPG; ROH; FS; CAT

LIT: E. Lucie Smith (ed.), *The Essential Osbert Lancaster* (1988); R. Boston, *Osbert* (1989)

LANGDON, David OBE FRSA (b. 1914). Topical cartoonist, caricaturist and illustrator. Born in London on 24 February 1914, the son of Bennett Langdon, David Langdon studied art at Davenant Grammar School, London, but otherwise is self-taught. He went on to work in the London County Council Architects Department (1931–9), was an Executive Officer in the London Rescue Service (1939–41) and was a squadron leader in the RAF (1941–6). He was Editor of the *Royal Air Force Journal* (1945–6) and his first cartoons were published in *Punch* and *Time & Tide* in 1937. A regular contributor to *Punch* (1937–92, elected to the Table 1958) and the *Sunday Pictorial/Mirror* (1948–90), his drawings have also appeared in *Lilliput* (from its first volume), *Paris-Match*, *Radio Times*, *Saturday Evening Post*, *Aeroplane*, *Royal Air Force Review*, *Collier's*, *True*, *Spectator* and the *New Yorker*. He has also produced an annual racing calendar for Ladbrokes since 1959, drawn a set of caricatures of lawyers and High Court judges, and produced a considerable amount of advertising work including the famous wartime 'Billy Brown of London Town' series for London Transport as well as drawings for Bovril, Winsor & Newton, Shell, Schweppes and others. Awarded an OBE in 1988 and elected FRSA, he is also official artist for the Centre International de Recherche et des Études at St Ghislain, Belgium. An occasional lecturer and a designer of corporate logos, he works in ink with a brush over a pencil outline drawn half larger than reproduction size on white Bristol board. He cites his influences as Daumier and FOUGASSE. Praised by Price as 'the great master of the topical comic idea', Langdon has an economical style and claims to have introduced the 'open mouth' into humorous art. He considers the idea for a cartoon of primary importance and has coined the phrase 'controlled mind-wandering' to describe his method of getting ideas.
PUB: *Home Front Lines* (1941), *All Buttoned Up!* (1944), [with R. B. Raymond] *Slipstream* (1946), *Meet Me Inside* (1946), *The Way I See It* (1947), *Let's Face It* (1951), [with D. Clayton] *Wake Up and Die* (1952), *Look at You* (1952), *All in Fun* (1953), *Laugh with Me* (1954), *Funnier Still* (1956), *A Banger for a Monkey* (1957), *Langdon at Large* (1958), *I'm Only Joking* (1960), (ed.) *Punch with Wings* (1961), *David Langdon's Casebook* (1969),

How to Talk Golf (1975), (ed.) *Punch in the Air* (1983), *Soccer – It's a Funny Old Game* (1998)
ILL: C. H. W. Jackson, *It's a Piece of Cake* (1943); G. Mikes, *Little Cabbages* (1955), *The Best of Mikes* (1962), *Germany Explored* (1969); D. Rooke, *Camper Beware!* (1965); Sports Council, *Sport For All* (1975); B. Boothroyd, *Let's Move House* (1977); F. Trueman and F. Hardy, *You Nearly Had Him That Time* (1978); J. Goldsmith and V. Powell-Smith, *Against the Law* (1980); Reader's Digest, *You and Your Rights* (1981); P. G. Wodehouse, *The Parrot and Other Poems* (1988); D. Copisarow, *Compliment Slips* (1988); P. Richards, *Living Medicine* (1990)
EXHIB: Various shows in Oxford, Ottawa, New York, London, Lille and elsewhere
COLL: V&A; UKCC; BM

LARRY – *see* Parkes, Terence

LAW, Roger (b. 1941). Caricaturist, strip cartoonist, illustrator, film-maker and writer. Roger Law was born on 6 September 1941 in Littleport, Cambridgeshire, the son of a builder, and attended Littleport Secondary Modern School and (aged 14) Cambridge School of Art (where he met PETER FLUCK and was taught by Paul Hogarth) until expelled in 1959. With his future wife, quilt designer Deirdre Amsden, he art-edited six issues of *Granta* and became an active CND campaigner, designing posters and pamphlets for the cause. He later moved to London, producing illustrations for *Queen*, and was resident artist designing weekly 14-foot murals for Peter Cook's Establishment Club. With Cook he also produced his first national strip 'Almost the End' in the *Observer* (1962) and freelanced for *Private Eye* (from 1962), *Town*, *Topic*, *Sunday Times*, *Nova*, *Men Only*, *Ink* and others. He then joined the *Sunday Times* as journalist and caricaturist (1964–8) and co-designed record covers for Track Records (e.g. 'The Who Sell Out' and Hendrix's 'Axis Bold as Love' – which subsequently became one of the bestselling posters of the 1960s). He won a Designers' & Art Directors' Association Silver Award (1967) for his first published caricature models in *Nova* (1966) and was artist-in-residence at Reed College, Portland, Oregon (1967), where he produced his first puppet film. After working in New York for Bush Bins Studio (1969), *Esquire* and other publications he returned to England and the *Sunday Times Magazine* (1970–75). The 'Luck & Flaw' partnership with Peter Fluck began with work for the *New York Times* (1976) followed by *National Lampoon, Sunday Times, Economist, Men Only, Marxism Today, Der Spiegel, Panorama* (Holland), *Stern* and *Time*. They also produced huge carnival heads of Hitler and others for an Anti-Nazi League rally, Thatcher teapots, etc. The *Spitting Image* TV programme, using Law and Fluck's animated caricature puppets, was first conceived in 1982 and the first pilot was screened in June 1983, produced by John Lloyd and directed by former *Muppet Show* director Philip Casson, for Central TV. Roger Law has also lectured at the RCA, the Central School of Art and Hornsey College of Art and won the Society of Illustrators' Award for Consistent Excellence (1983). In addition he received the CAT Lifetime Achievement Award (1998) with Peter Fluck. He has been influenced by the artists of *L'Assiette au Beurre* and by George Grosz.

PUB: [as Spitting Image] *The Appallingly Disrespectful Spitting Image Book* (1985), *Spitting Images* (1987), *The Appallingly Disrespectful Spitting Image Giant Komic Book* (1988), *Goodbye* (1992), *Thatcha – The Real Maggie Memoirs* (1993)

ILL: [as Luck & Flaw] C. Dickens, *A Christmas Carol* (1979), R. L. Stevenson, *Treasure Island* (1986); L. Chester, *Tooth & Claw – The Inside Story of Spitting Image* (1986)

EXHIB: [ceramics, with J. Tchalenko] V&A; [as Spitting Image] CG

LIT: [autobiography, with L. Chester and A. Evans] *A Nasty Piece of Work* (1992)

LEE, Joseph Booth (1901–74). Joke, political and strip cartoonist and journalist. Joe Lee was born on 16 May 1901 in Burley-in-Wharfedale, Yorkshire, won a scholarship to Leeds Grammar School and learned cartooning via Percy Bradshaw's Press Art School correspondence course. He also attended Leeds School of Art (*c.* 1915–18), where his contemporaries were Henry Moore and Barbara Hepworth, with the intention of becoming an architect. On Christmas Eve 1919 he came to London to take up a scholarship at the RCA but was unable to pay his way. He worked freelance at first (his first cartoon appeared in the *Bystander* in 1920) and the following year, when he was 19, *Strand Magazine* described him as 'the youngest of the men of his craft who have now an established reputation'. He joined the *Pall Mall Gazette* (1920) as daily cartoonist and political writer and when that folded 18 months later moved to the *Liverpool Daily Courier* as cartoonist and Art Editor. Thence he went to the *Sunday Express* from which, as a committed Socialist, he resigned during the General Strike. Then followed work producing a daily political or social cartoon for the *Daily Chronicle* (from 1926), syndicated cartoons for Allied Newspapers, a strip ('Pin-Money Myrtle') for the *Daily Mail* (1933) and freelance work for *Bystander, Tatler, Sketch, London Opinion, Punch* and others. On 14 May 1934 he created the hugely popular 'London Laughs' series of joke drawings with a London background (retitled 'Smiling Through' during World War II) for the *Evening News* (1934–66). These were the first non-political topical cartoons in the UK (there was a brief 'New York Laughs' series in 1946). Nearly 9000 cartoons later, having become the longest running daily cartoonist in history, he retired to Norwich in July 1966 but continued to produce political cartoons three days a week for the local *Eastern Daily Press* and work for children's comics like *Wham!* and *Whizzer & Chips*. In addition he drew advertisements for British Railways and others. In 1963 the CCGB presented him with an award for Special Services to Cartooning. He worked mostly in black and white using a brush and watercolour and was influenced by Rowlandson and Phil May. Lee was particularly good at depicting cricket-loving colonels, chubby and slightly vulgar ladies with sparkling jewellery and dapper City gents, and had 'an enviably perceptive eye for detail, particularly when drawing architecture' (Cookson). His second marriage was to the painter Kathleen Seaman, daughter of the writer and editor H. W. Seaman. He died on 15 March 1974.

PUB: [with Illingworth, Gittins, Moon and Neb] *400 Famous Cartoons* (1944), *London Laughs 1934–51* (1951)

ILL: J. Mardle, *Broad Norfolk* (1973)

EXHIB: IWM; CG

COLL: UKCC; CAT; BM

LEES [real name Peter Lees Walmesley] (*c.* 1908–42). Joke, political and strip cartoonist. Born in Norfolk, the son of the managing director of the Great Yarmouth Gas Company, Lees attended Nelson's old school at North Walsham and Norwich Art School. His first published drawing was of gas appliances on a leaflet for his father's company and he joined Dorlands Advertising Agency in London in 1927, producing illustrations for Bovril and others for six years before turning freelance and contributing strips to London dailies and joke cartoons to *Lilliput, Punch, Strand, Bystander, Night & Day* and elsewhere. His first strip was 'Our Wilhelmina' in the *Daily Express*, followed by 'Hector' the dog in the *Daily Chronicle* (and later *News Chronicle*), and then 'The Kid' in *John Bull*. A gunner in the army during World War II, he continued to contribute drawings to papers, including editorial cartoons for the *Sunday Graphic*. Lees' style shows the influence of Peter Arno's wash and line technique.

LEETE, Alfred Chew (1882–1933). Joke and strip cartoonist and illustrator. Alfred Leete was born on 28 August 1882 in Thorpe Achurch, Northamptonshire, the son of J. A. Leete, a farmer. Educated at Kingsholme School, Weston-super-Mare, and the Weston School of Science & Art, he left at the age of 12 to be an office boy in a Bristol surveyor's office. He worked as a draughtsman in a furniture company and for a lithographer in the city before his first cartoon was accepted by the *Daily Graphic* (which paid him 2s. 6d.) at the age of 16. Self-taught as an artist, he then began to contribute regularly to *Bristol Magpie* and in 1905 moved to London where his drawings began to appear in *Ally Sloper's Half-Holiday, Pall Mall Gazette, Pick-Me-Up* (which ran his series 'Play Titles Travestied' for eight years), *Bystander, Sketch, Passing Show* and *Punch* (1905–33). In 1914 he created the hugely successful 'Schmidt the Spy' strip for *London Opinion* which was later published as a book and was turned into a film in April 1916 by Phoenix Films with Lewis Sydney playing Schmidt. His best-known work is Kitchener's recruiting poster 'Your Country Needs You', which first appeared as a cover of *London Opinion* on 5 September 1914 (with a different caption) and was later copied by James Montgomery Flagg in the USA, with Uncle Sam replacing Kitchener. Leete also produced posters for the Tank Corps ('Let Professor Tank Teach You a Trade'), Underground Electric Railways and others and drew for advertising – clients included Bovril, Ronuk Polish, Pratt's Petrol, Hector Powe, Connolly Leather and Rowntree's Chocolate (for whom he created the character 'Mr York of York, Yorks', who featured in the first British animated commercial with sound). He also created the famous bearded, top-hatted and bespectacled 'Father William' character for the brewers William

Younger & Co., originally introduced with the caption 'Oi be 101 and getting "Younger" every day.' He was a member of the Savage Club and President of the London Sketch Club (1925). Alfred Leete died in London on 17 June 1933.
PUB: *Schmidt the Spy* (1915), *The Worries of Wilhelm* (1916), *A Book of Dragons* (1931), *The Work of a 'Pictorial Comedian'* (1936)
ILL: T. R. Arkell, *All the Rumours* (1916), *The Bosch Book* (1916)
EXHIB: Woodspring Museum, Weston-super-Mare (1982)
COLL: IWM

LEIST, Frederick William ROI RBA (1877–1945). Sports cartoonist, caricaturist, illustrator, art teacher and painter. Fred Leist was born in Sydney and contributed drawings to the *Sydney Bulletin* and *Sydney Mail* before moving to London in 1908. He studied at the Julian Ashton School, London (1908), and contributed to the *Graphic* (1901–10) and *Strand* (illustrating stories by Edgar Jepson and Austin Philips and others 1914–16), and also exhibited landscapes and figure painting in oils. He was elected RBA in 1913 and ROI in 1916. An Official War Artist in France during World War I, he later painted two large murals for the Australian pavilion at the Wembley exhibition which led to commissions in the USA. He returned to Australia in 1926 and became head teacher of painting at East Sydney Technical College. He was a member of the Chelsea Arts Club.
ILL: B. Marchant, *The Gold-Marked Charm* (1919)
EXHIB: L; P; RA; RBA; ROI and elsewhere

LEVINE, David (b. 1926). Caricaturist, illustrator and watercolourist. David Levine was born on 20 December 1926 in Brooklyn, New York, and studied at Tyler School of Fine Arts, Temple University, Philadelphia (1944, 1946–9) and the Hans Hoffman School, New York City (1949). He served with the US Army in 1945–6. His first caricature appeared in *Esquire* in 1958 but he has since become particularly associated with the *New York Review of Books*, which has featured his caricatures and satirical drawings since its inception in 1963. He has also worked for the *Sunday Times* and others and has received numerous awards, including the Gold Medal for Graphics from the American Academy in 1992. Influenced by Doyle, Tenniel, Doré and Daumier, he always works from photographs and draws his caricatures on sheets $13\,^{3}/_{4}$

× 11 in., first in pencil and then in pen and ink. Levine's work is very influential (TROG has called him 'the best caricaturist in the world'). His fine, cross-hatched style has been greatly admired and frequently imitated by a number of contemporary caricaturists worldwide. He received the CAT Lifetime Achievement Award in 1996.

PUB: *A Summer Sketchbook* (1963), *The Man from M.A.L.I.C.E.* (1966), *Pens and Needles* (1969), *Caricatures* (1969), *Identikit* (1969), *No Known Survivors* (1970), *The Arts of David Levine* (1978)

ILL: Many books including E. Kirtland, *Buttons in the Back* (1958); W. Irving, *Rip Van Winkle* (1963); W. Kauff, *The Heart of Stone* (1964); J. P. Wood, *The Snark Was a Boojum* (1966); A. E. Kahn, *Smetana and the Beetles* (1967); *The Fables of Aesop* (1975)

EXHIB: Forum Gallery, New York; Weslyan University; Brooklyn Museum; Princeton University; Galerie Yves Lambert, Paris; Yale University; Hirshhorn Museum, Washington, D. C. (1980); Davis Gallery, New York; SI (1970); Pierpont Morgan Library; A (1987)

COLL: A; Brooklyn Museum, New York; Cleveland Museum of Art, Ohio; NPG; Fogg Art Museum, Harvard; NAD; Princeton University Library, New Jersey

LEWIN, Frederick George RWA (1861–1933). Joke cartoonist, illustrator, journalist and painter. F. G. Lewin was born in Bristol, the son of a sea captain. He was educated in Bristol and worked at first as a reporter on the *Western Daily Press*. A self-taught artist, he contributed to *Punch*, *Zig Zag*, *Magpie*, *London Opinion*, *Bristol Evening Times* and *Bristol Evening Post* amongst other publications. He also designed comic postcards for Inter-Art, W. E. Mack, J. Salmon and E. W. Savory, illustrated books and exhibited watercolours and oil paintings. He was elected RWA in 1906. F. G. Lewin died in Redland, Bristol on 14 October 1933.

PUB: *An ABC Book for Good Boys & Girls* (1911), *Rhymes of Ye Olde Sign Boards* (1911), *Characters from Dickens* (1912)

ILL: A. L. Salmon, *Bristol* (1922)

EXHIB: RWA (more than 60 watercolours, 1903–16)

LEZZ – *see* Barton, Leslie Alfred

LLOYD, Arthur Wynell MC (1883–after 1953). Political cartoonist, caricaturist and illustrator.

A. W. Lloyd was born in Hartley Witney, Hampshire, on 4 April 1883, the son of E. W. M. Lloyd. He was educated at Rugby School and won a classical scholarship to Queen's College, Oxford. While an undergraduate he began drawing caricatures which were seen by Sir Arthur Boscawen, a member of his college, who introduced him to the magazine publisher Sir Arthur Pearson. For Pearson he drew cartoons for the Tariff Reform League (in which Pearson was involved), before moving to South Africa to draw for the *Rand Mail* and *Johannesburg Star*. After eight years in Johannesburg he returned to the UK and began contributing to *Punch* (*c.* 1912). He later went back to South Africa, working for the *Sunday Post* and *Sunday Times* in the Transvaal. During World War I he fought with General Jan Smuts against the Germans in East Africa, attained the rank of captain, was shot in the head in 1917 (severely impairing his hearing) and, invalided out, was awarded a Military Cross. His book, *Jambo, or With Jannie in the Jungle* is a collection of cartoons about the war ('Jambo' means 'good to see you'; Jannie is Jan Smuts). He was later a political cartoonist on *News of the World* for two and a half years (1925–7), but is perhaps best known for his illustrations to *Punch*'s 'Essence of Parliament' column (later renamed 'Impressions of Parliament'), to which he contributed caricatures for more than 40 years, taking over from E. T. REED in 1912 and himself being succeeded by MICHAEL CUMMINGS in 1953. He was a member of the Athenaeum Club and St Stephen's Club.

PUB: *Jambo, or With Jannie in the Jungle* (1917, 1920)

EXHIB: Sporting Gallery, Covent Garden (opened by Rt Hon. Stanley Baldwin, June 1925); Cooling Gallery (1934, 115 drawings)

COLL: BM

'London Laughs' – *see* Lee, Joseph Booth

LONGSTAFF, John 'Cluff' (b. 1949). Joke, pocket and strip cartoonist. Born in Darlington, Co. Durham, on 25 June 1949, John Longstaff studied graphics at Teesside College of Art and worked in local government before becoming a cartoonist in 1982. His work has appeared in *Private Eye*, *Punch*, *Brain Damage*, *Gas*, *Spectator*, *Times Saturday Review*, *Independent Magazine*, *Sunday Telegraph*, *Northern Echo* (pocket cartoons) and *Literary Review*. Influenced by MICHAEL

HEATH, McLACHLAN, MATT PRITCHETT, SEARLE, PAUL CRUM, GLASHAN and HUSBAND, he mostly draws in black and white but sometimes also adds watercolour for strips.
EXHIB: JDG
COLL: BM

LOW, Sir David Alexander Cecil (1891–1963). Political cartoonist, strip cartoonist, caricaturist, illustrator and writer. David Low was born in Dunedin, New Zealand, the son of David Brown Low, a Scottish-born chemist, on 7 April 1891. He was educated at the Boys' High School, Christchurch. Self-taught, apart from a correspondence course with New York School of Caricature (*c.* 1900) and a brief stay at Canterbury School of Art, he was attracted to caricature through reading English comics such as *Chips, Comic Cuts, Larks* and *Ally Sloper's Half*

Holiday. Early influences were *Punch* artists such as TOM BROWNE, Keene, SAMBOURNE and PHIL MAY and caricaturists Gillray, Daumier and Philipon. At the age of 11 his first strip was published in *Big Budget* and a topical cartoon was accepted by the weekly *Christchurch Spectator*. He then began to win drawing competitions in the Australian magazine *New Idea*, and contributed police-court drawings to *New Zealand Truth*. In 1907 he joined the *Sketcher* and in 1908 became the *Spectator*'s Political Cartoonist, later moving to the *Canterbury Times* (1910) and the *Sydney Bulletin* (1911–19). At the *Bulletin* his technique benefited from the influence of WILL DYSON and Norman Lindsay, and his bestselling *The Billy Book* lampooning Austra-lian PM Billy Hughes drew praise from Arnold Bennett (who later said 'Low draws as the fishes swim'), and led to his move to England. His first cartoon to

David Low, [Mussolini, Franco, Stalin, Hitler], *Evening Standard*, 2 May 1940

be published in Britain (a syndicated *Sydney Bulletin* drawing from 20 October 1914) appeared in the *Manchester Guardian* on 4 January 1915. He arrived in London in August 1919 and changed his signature from 'Dave Low' to 'Low' when he began work on the Liberal evening paper the *Star* in 1919. Here he greatly increased the space allocated to his cartoons and some of his drawings were used as election posters by the Liberal Party in 1922 and 1923. He then became the first-ever Political Cartoonist on the Conservative *Evening Standard* in 1927, drawing four cartoons a week. The *Standard* had a smaller British circulation than the *Star* and the *Evening News*, but enabled his cartoons to be syndicated to 170 journals worldwide. After his cartoons were reduced in size he was invited by the Editor Percy Cudlipp to join the pro-Labour *Daily Herald* (1950), succeeding GEORGE WHITELAW, and drawing only three cartoons a week for the same salary (£10,000). In 1953 he moved to the *Manchester Guardian*, becoming the paper's first staff cartoonist (they had previously used syndicated cartoons, including his own work). In addition, he contributed to *Picture Post*, *Ken* (large double-page cartoons), *Graphic*, *Life*, *New Statesman* (of which he later became a director), *Punch*, *Illustrated*, *Colliers*, *Nash's Magazine*, *Pall Mall Magazine* (in which the satirical 'The Modern Rake's Progress', based on Edward VIII, first appeared in September 1934) and others. He received honorary doctorates from the universities of New Brunswick, Canada (1958) and Leicester (1961), and was knighted in 1962. Low has been perhaps the most influential cartoonist and caricaturist of the twentieth century – he produced over 14,000 drawings in a career spanning 50 years and was syndicated worldwide to more than 200 newspapers and magazines. He also created a number of memorable comic characters, including the TUC carthorse, Musso the Pup, the Coalition Ass and the walrus-moustached Colonel Blimp. He drew in pencil for the two famous series of caricatures of politicians and literary figures published in the *New Statesman* in the 1920s and 30s but otherwise worked mainly in ink using a pen and brush. Alternately praised and attacked by Churchill, who called him 'a green-eyed young Antipodean radical' and tried to ban a film based on the character Colonel Blimp, Low always regarded himself as 'a nuisance dedicated to sanity'. While at the *Standard* he worked from his studio in Hampstead and did not submit roughs but drew a single very detailed pencil sketch which he would then transfer to a clean sheet, spending five to eight hours on the finished drawing which would be collected by the paper at 5.30 pm each day. He was a member of the Savage Club and the National Liberal Club. Sir David Low died on 19 September 1963.

PUB: *Low's Annual* (1908), *Caricatures* (1915), *The Billy Book* (1918), *Man, the Lord of Creation* (1920), *Lloyd George & Co.* (1921), [with F. W. Thomas] *Low & I* (1923) and *The Low & I Holiday Book* (1925), *Sketches by Low* (1926), [with 'Lynx' (R. West)] *Lions & Lambs* (1928), *The Best of Low* (1930), [with K. Martin] *Low's Russian Sketchbook* (1932), *Caricatures by Low* (1933), [with H. Thorogood] *Low & Terry* (1934), [with R. West] *The Modern Rake's Progress* (1934), *Ye Madde Designer* (1935), *Low's Political Parade* (1936), *Low Again* (1938), [with Q. Howe] *A Cartoon History of Our Times* (1939), *Europe Since Versailles* (1940), *Europe at War* (1941), *Low's War Cartoons* (1941), *Low on the War* (1941), *The World at War* (1941), *British Cartoonists, Caricaturists and Comic Artists* (1942), *Years of Wrath* (1946), *Low's Company* (1952), *Low Visibility* (1953), *Low's Cartoon History 1945–53* (1953), *The Fearful Fifties* (1960)

ILL: J. Adderley, *Old Seed on New Ground* (1920); H. G. Wells, *The Autocracy of Mr Parham* (1930); P. Fleming, *The Flying Visit* (1940)

EXHIB: London Gallery; National Museum of Canada; Monks Hall Museum, Eccles; Nationalmuseum, Stockholm; Queen Elizabeth the Second Arts Council of New Zealand; LAN; NPG; CG; (touring exhibition in NZ 1997–9)

COLL: UKCC; NPG; New Zealand House; V&A; Victoria State Library, Melbourne; Turnbull Library, Wellington, NZ; LSE (cuttings collections); Yale University (letters and papers); BM; CAT

LIT: [autobiography] *Low's Autobiography* (1956); C. Seymour-Ure and J. Schoff, *David Low* (1985); M. Bryant (ed.), *The Complete Colonel Blimp* (1991)

LOWRY, Raymond (b. 1944). Joke and strip cartoonist, illustrator and journalist. Ray Lowry was born on 28 August 1944 in Cadishead, near Manchester, the son of John Thomas Lowry, a bricklayer. Self-taught as an artist, he started work in an advertising agency in Manchester and his first cartoon was published in the *Manchester Evening News c. 1967*. He turned professional cartoonist in 1969, contributing to *Punch* (including covers), *Private Eye*, *Vox*, *International*

Times, *Oz* and *Guardian*. He is perhaps best known for his work in the music press, notably the strip 'Only Rock 'n' Roll' in the *New Musical Express* (from 1977). In addition he has designed record sleeves (e.g. The Clash's *London Calling* in 1979) and wrote a monthly column for *The Face* magazine for three years. Simon Frith writing in *New Society* has described him as 'a jaded rock 'n' roll fan, a 1950s person, cynical and angry . . . Lowry's real hate-figures aren't businessmen but the *Sunday Times* bourgeois pop person'. His cartoons also often feature the juxtaposition of images from two types of spectacle – war and entertainment – combining, for example, Nazi Germany with Hollywood. He has a distinctive, sketchy pen line and uses a Gillott nib with indian ink and a lot of wash, signing his work 'R. LOWRY'.
PUB: *Only Rock and Roll* (1981), *This Space To Let* (1986), [with I. Jackson, HUSBAND, and BANKS] *100 Things to Do With a Black Lace Record* (1990), *Lowry Ink* (1998)
ILL: C. Heylin (ed.), *The Penguin Book of Rock and Roll Writing* (1992); J. Green and G. Barter, *A Riot of our Own* (1997)
EXHIB: Gallery Downstairs, Burnley; CG; LCG
COLL: V&A; UKCC

LOYE, Charles Auguste 'G. Montbard' (1841–1901) – *see* Bryant & Heneage

LUCK and FLAW – *see* Fluck, Peter and Law, Roger

'Lucky Jim' – *see* Hogg, Gordon and Collins, Clive Hugh Austin

LUDLOW, Henry Stephen (1861–after 1934) – *see* Bryant & Heneage

LUMLEY, Savile (fl. 1895–1949). Joke cartoonist and illustrator. In the 1890s Savile Lumley shared a studio in Abbey Road, St John's Wood, with G. L. STAMPA who was then studying at the Royal Academy Schools with HEATH ROBINSON, LEWIS BAUMER and others so it is likely that Lumley was at the RA at the same time (1895–1900). His first cartoons started appearing in *Sketchy Bits* during this period and he also contributed to *Tatler* and other magazines before World War I. However, he is best known for his famous recruiting poster 'Daddy, what did you do in the Great War?' (*c.* 1915). After the war he illustrated books and comics

for children, including the *Boys' and Girls' Daily Mail*, *Boy's Own Paper*, *Chums*, *Little Folk*, *Young England*, *Nelson Lee*, *Champion Annual*, *Chatterbox*, *Printer's Pie*, *Scout*, *Schoolfriend Annual* and *Schoolgirl's Own Annual* and contributed cartoons to the *Humorist* in the 1920s and 30s. He usually worked in pen and ink.
ILL: E. Everett-Green, *A Disputed Heritage* (1911); C. Howard, *Chappie and Others* (1926); R. L. Stevenson, *The Black Arrow* (1949)
COLL: IWM

LUNT, Wilmot (fl. 1900–after 1934). Joke cartoonist and painter. Wilmot Lunt was born in Warrington, Cheshire, the son of John Lunt, a local merchant. He was educated at the Boteler Grammar School in Warrington, whose art master had previously worked at Warrington Art School and taught Luke Fildes RA, and H. Woods RA. He studied at the Lancashire School of Art, the Royal College of Art and at the École des Beaux-Arts and the Académie Julian in Paris. His first published drawing was for the *Idler* and he later contributed joke cartoons to the *Bystander*, *Cassell's*, *London Opinion*, *Odd Volume*, *Pearson's*, *Printer's Pie*, *Royal Magazine*, *Sketch*, *Tatler* and *Punch* (1908–23). In addition he produced advertisements for Erasmic, King George IV Whisky and others. He was a member of the Chelsea Arts Club.
ILL: E. G. Bulwer-Lytton, *The Caxtons* (1905), *Eugene Aram* (1905)
EXHIB: RA; RI; Paris Salon (oil painting, 1901)

LURIE, Ranan Raymond (b. 1932). Caricaturist, political cartoonist and illustrator. Ranan Lurie was born on 26 May 1932 in Port Said, Egypt, and was educated at Herzelia College, Tel Aviv, and Jerusalem Art College. He started work as a journalist on the *Ma'ariv Daily* (1950–52). He then became Features Editor of the *Hador Daily* (1953–4), Editor-in-Chief of the weekly *Tavel* (1954–5) and Political Cartoonist on the *Yedioth Aharonot Daily* (1955–65). At the invitation of *Life* he emigrated to the USA in 1968, drawing political cartoons for the magazine until 1973. He then moved to *Newsweek* (1974–6) and at the same time was Editor and Political Cartoonist of *Vision Magazine*. A freelance contributor to the *Wall Street Journal*, *New York Times* (since 1970) and *Paris-Match*, he has also been staff Political Cartoonist on the *Honolulu Advertiser* (1979), *Die Welt* (1980–81), *The Times* (1981–3, the paper's first since MAHOOD), *Asahi*

Shimbun (1983–4) and *US News and World Report* (1984–5). In addition he has been Chief Editorial Director of the Editors' Press Syndicate since 1985, has frequently appeared on TV in the USA, Germany and elsewhere, and has taught 'The Philosophy of Political Cartooning' at the University of Hawaii, West Point Academy and Stanford University. Listed by the *Guinness Book of Records* as the world's most widely syndicated political cartoonist, his work appears in 1015 publications in 79 countries with a circulation of 85 million copies (March 1993). He has received numerous awards including the US Headliners Award (1972), Outstanding Editorial Cartoonist from the US National Cartoonists' Society (1972–8), the New York Front Page Award (1972, 1974, 1977) and the John Fischetti Political Cartoon Award (1982) and has been granted the unique honour of a US Senate exhibition of his art. He sees every cartoon as a four-wheeled vehicle: the wheels are the humour, the drawing of the metaphor, the caricature and the facts; the vehicle itself is the message the cartoon has to convey to the reader. 'Lurie – the man they call Van Gogh with a sense of humour' (*Punch*). He draws in ink with fine hatching and a liberal use of solid blacks, but also paints in oils and sculpts.
PUB: *Among the Suns* (1952), *Lurie's Best Cartoons* (1961), *Nixon Rated Cartoons* (1973), *Pardon Me, Mr President* (1974), *Lurie's Worlds 1970–1980* (1980), *So Sieht Es Lurie* (1981), *Lurie's Almanack* (1982, 1983), *Taro's International Politics* (1984), *Lurie's Middle East* (1986), *Lurie's Mideast Almanac* (1986), *Lurie's Fareast Views* (1987)
ILL: Several books
EXHIB: Numerous shows worldwide

LYNCH, John Gilbert Bohun (1884–1928). Author, journalist, illustrator and caricaturist. Bohun Lynch was born in London on 21 May 1884. Of Irish extraction, his maternal grandfather was Captain G. B. Martin CB RN. He was educated at Haileybury and University College, Oxford. Boxing Correspondent for *Field & Sport*, he also wrote for the *Dramatic News* and (under the pen name 'Jackie Bloomer') for *Boy's Friend*

Weekly and others. He contributed to *Home Chat, Quarterly Review, Answers, Chums, Fortnightly Review* and *London Mercury* (caricatures) and one of his drawings is illustrated in the *Studio* publication *Caricature of To-Day* (1928). An authority on old furniture, he also wrote a book on caricature and an article on the subject for the *Encyclopaedia Britannica*. He was a member of the Savage Club. Bohun Lynch died on 2 October 1928.
PUB: Many books including *Oxford Quips* (1908), *Glamour* (1912), [novel] *Cake* (1913), *The Complete Amateur Boxer* (1913), *Prominent Pugilists of Today* (1914), [novel] *Unofficial* (1915), *The Complete Gentleman* (1916), *The Tender Conscience* (1919), *Forgotten Realms* (1920), *Max Beerbohm in Perspective* (1921), *A Perfect Day* (1923), *A Muster of Ghosts* (1924), *The Prize Ring* (1925), *A History of Caricature* (1926), *Respectability* (1927)
ILL: R. Berkeley, *Decorations and Absurdities* (1923), *Unparliamentary Papers and Other Diversions* (1924); H. Wolfe, *Lampoons* (1925); J. Palmer, *Reflections of a Boxing Referee* (1927)

LYTTELTON, Humphrey Richard Adeane 'Humph' (b. 1921). Jazz musician, journalist, broadcaster and joke cartoonist. Humphrey Lyttelton was born in Eton, Buckinghamshire, on 23 May 1921, the son of the Hon. George Lyttelton. He was educated at Sunningdale School and Eton College and trained under John Minton at Camberwell School of Art (where contemporaries included WALLY FAWKES and SMILBY). During World War II he served in the Grenadier Guards (1941–6). Best known as a musician, he produced regular cartoons (as 'Humph') and articles for the *Daily Mail* (1949–53), *Melody Maker* (from 1954), *Reynolds News* (1955–62), *Sunday Citizen* (1962–7) and also contributed to *Bystander, Harper's & Queen, Field, High Life, Punch* and other publications.
PUB: *Second Chorus* (1958), *I Play As I Please* (1954), *Take it From the Top* (1975), *Why No Beethoven?* (1984)
ILL: T. Brooke-Taylor *et al., I'm Sorry I Haven't a Clue* (1980)
COLL: UKCC

M

MA – *see* Anderson, Martin

MAC – *see* McMurtry, Stanley

McALLISTER, Bryan (b. 1945). Pocket and strip cartoonist, and journalist. Bryan McAllister was born in Peterborough but moved to Bath in his early teens and attended Keynsham Grammar School. He started work packing chickens, then spent two years as a clerk in the Ministry of Defence in Bath while contributing cartoons to the local paper. Leaving the civil service for a graphics course at the Royal West of England College of Art, he became daily topical cartoonist for the *Western Daily Press* while still a student (aged 19). He then worked for the London Press Exchange advertising agency as a copywriter for clients such as Cadbury's and Beecham's, leaving to join a TV production company and then Vernon's advertising agency where he was a writer and producer. At this time he also drew a strip for *TV Times* about two philosophical tramps whose only possession was a TV set. However, he is best known for his trenchant pocket cartoons for the *Guardian* ('committed wisecracks' – Brian Redhead), which appeared from the mid-1970s until the radical redesign of the paper in 1989. He was also the original writer of 'The Belchers' strip in *Vole* before illustrator BRYAN READING took over the script himself. A characteristic of McAllister's drawings is that his figures' feet never appear in the picture. His style has influenced that of MATT PRITCHETT. He received Granada TV's *What the Papers Say* Award in 1979.
PUB: *Little Boxes* (1977), *More Little Boxes* (1980), *Look, No Feet!* (1987)

McCORMICK, Malcolm (b. 1943). Caricaturist, political and strip cartoonist and illustrator. Malky McCormick was born in Glasgow on 24 June 1943. His work has appeared in the *Sunday Telegraph*, *Sunday Times*, *Scottish Daily Express*, *Sunday Mail* (especially 'The Big Yin' from 1975), *TV Times*, *Sun*, *Racing Post*, *Kilmarnock Standard*, *Daily Record*, *Evening Times*, *Golf Monthly*, *Daily News* and others. He has also worked on TV and produced posters and greetings cards.

PUB: *McCormick So Far* (1990)
ILL: B. Connolly, *Bring on the Big Yin* (1977)

MACDONALD, Alister K. (fl. 1898–1947). Illustrator and joke cartoonist. A. K. Macdonald's earliest drawings appeared in the *Longbow* (1898), *Pearson's Magazine* (1900) and *Bystander*. He later contributed to *Cassell's*, *Holly Leaves*, *London Opinion*, *Nash's*, *Pears*, *Royal Magazine*, *Moonshine*, *Sketch*, *Strand*, *Tatler*, *Fragments*, *Printer's Pie* and *Illustrated London News*. In addition he produced advertisements for Lux and Pears Soap, menu designs for Cunard Line Shipping, book illustrations for Putnams and others, and postcards for Hendersons and Valentines.
ILL: Lady Cynthia Asquith, *The Silver Ship* (1926), *The Treasure Ship* (1926), *Sails of Gold* (1927), *The Childrens' Cargo* (1930); A. Armstrong, *The Naughty Princess* (1945)

McGILL, Donald Fraser Gould (1875–1962). Joke cartoonist and postcard designer. Donald McGill was born on 25 January 1875 in London, the son of an army captain and a relative of the founder of McGill University, Montreal. He was educated at Blackheath Proprietary School where he lost a foot after a rugby accident at the age of 16. He then attended Blackheath Art School (1891) and worked in the drawing office of Maudleys, a company of naval architects in London (1893–6). Apprenticed to Thames Ironworks, Shipbuilding & Engineering Co. until 1907, he began sending painted postcard cartoons to The Pictorial Postcard Company in 1904 and worked full-time in this profession from 1908. McGill was a partner in the firm of Hutson Bros (1908–10), leaving to work freelance for The Pictorial Postcard Co. (1910–14) and when its owner, Joseph Asher, was interned as an alien during World War I, he moved to Inter-Art Co. (1914–31) and freelanced once more from 1931 to 1936. The years 1936–52 were spent largely working for Asher's new firm D. Constance (1936–52) – where he produced 'The New Donald McGill Comics Series' – and he was later contracted to the company (1952–62), becoming director in charge of postcard design when Asher died. Considerable critical attention was given to McGill's work as an art form with the publication

of George Orwell's essay 'The Art of Donald McGill' in *Horizon* in February 1941 (Orwell described his jokes as 'a chorus of raspberries'), but some were less appreciative. D. Constance were fined under the Obscene Publications Act, 1857, but McGill always claimed he was a 'seaside artist' depicting 'honest vulgarity'. Described as 'King of the Saucy Postcards' in his *Sunday Telegraph* obituary, Donald McGill produced 10,000 designs over a period of 50 years, two of his most famous being 'Please, Lord, excuse me while I kick Fido!' and 'I can't see my little Willie'. During World War I he also produced anti-Kaiser postcards for Inter-Art as well as some attacking US neutrality (e.g. 'Say, I'm neutral an' I don't care a darn who licks the Germans!'). McGill died in St James's Hospital, Balham, London, on 13 October 1962.
EXHIB: Brighton Festival (1967); Cartoon Originals Gallery (1974); LAN; Littlehampton Museum, Sussex
COLL: V&A
LIT: A. Calder-Marshall, *Wish You Were Here* (1966); B. N. Buckland, *The World of Donald McGill* (1976); E. Buckland, *The World of Donald McGill* (1984)

McGLASHAN, John – *see* Glashan, John

MACKAY, Wallis (*c.* 1850–d.1907). Joke cartoonist, illustrator and journalist. Wallis Mackay was the youngest of three sons of a Belfast clergyman. He came to London with his two journalist brothers, William and Joseph, aged about 22 and began contributing drawings to *Punch* (from 1870). He then won a competition to design the heading for the *Illustrated Sporting & Dramatic News* when it was launched and subsequently worked regularly for the magazine, drawing the 'Captious Critic' illustration (later taken over by Alfred Bryan) with text by his brother Joseph, but Wallis later wrote this as well. Chief cartoonist on *Zozimus*, he also worked for the *Illustrated London News* (from 1880), *Fun* (from 1893), *Judy* and *John Bull* and illustrated many books including a children's story, *Father Bunny's Secret*, by his wife Emily Nichols (sister of the comedian Harry Nichols). His book *The Piccadilly Peepshow* is a satire on the 1879 Royal Academy exhibition, while *The Home Rule Pill* uses political cartoons to attack specific sections in Gladstone's controversial Irish Home Rule Bill. Wallis Mackay signed his cartoons 'XX' (in reality W above M), and also

worked under the pseudonym 'Short'. He was a member of the Savage Club. Suffering from financial difficulties, he committed suicide by gas poisoning at his home in Rutland Street, London, on 18 April 1907.
PUB: *The Piccadilly Peep-Show or Round the RA in 20 Minutes* (1879), *The Prisoner of Chloane* (1890), *The Home Rule Pill* (1893), *Wallis Mackay's Dramatic & Pantomimic Scrapbook* (1897), *Wallis Mackay, His Horn Book* (1898)
ILL: Many books including H. G. Churchill, *Puttyput's Protégée* (1872); G. S. Brodie, *Vagrant Verses* (1876); B. L. Farjeon, *The Mystery of Roaring Meg* (1878), *The Bells of Penraven* (1879); [as 'Short'] J. Latey, *The Showman's Panorama* (1880); G. A. MacDonnell, *Chess Life-Pictures* (1883); H. Lennard, *Ye Legende of Dicke Whyttyngton and Hys Catte* (1885); E. Mackay, *Father Bunny's Secret* (1896)

MACKENZIE, Keith (1924–80). Joke cartoonist, caricaturist, journalist, art editor, illustrator and painter. Keith Mackenzie was born in London on 16 July 1924, the son of an East India Company merchant. He was educated at Rugby School and studied at Chepping Wycombe School of Art (1941–3) under J. C. Tarr ARCA and at the Slade under Professor Randolph Schwabe. After winning a *Punch* Scholarship in Humorous Art (1947) he drew cartoons for *Punch, Evening Standard, News Chronicle* and others before becoming Cartoon Editor of the *Daily Sketch* (1970), taking over from JULIAN PHIPPS. He was later Cartoon Editor on the *Evening News*. He also worked in watercolour, lithography and etching. He was married to the wood-engraver Zelma Blakeley RE. Keith Mackenzie died in London in October 1981.
EXHIB: RA; SGA; WAG; Senefelder Club
COLL: UCL; UKCC

McLACHLAN, Edward Rolland (b. 1940). Joke and political cartoonist, writer, illustrator, designer and occasional caricaturist. Born in Humberstone, Leicestershire, on 22 April 1940, Ed McLachlan attended Wyggeston Grammar School and Leicester College of Art (1956–9), and was later a lecturer in graphics at Leicester College of Art (1967–70). As a cartoonist he has been a regular contributor to *Sunday Mirror* (1967–70, political cartoons), *Punch* (from 1961, including covers), *Private Eye* (since 1967), *Daily Mirror* (pocket cartoons, 1972–4) and *Sunday Telegraph*. Other markets have included *Spectator, Mail on Sunday, Investors Chronicle, New*

Edward McLachlan, *Private Eye*, 2 October 1998

Statesman, Stern, Tomorrow (Sweden), *Playboy, Ad Weekly* and various book publishers. He also draws for advertising and has designed and written more than 300 commercial advertising films. He was voted CCGB Advertising Cartoonist of the Year (1981) and Illustrative Cartoonist of the Year (1980) and CAT Gag Cartoonist of the Year (1997). In addition he wrote and designed the ITV series *Simon and the Land of Chalk Drawings* and designed *Bangers & Mash* for the same company. He draws on Oram & Robinson Board or paper and his favoured medium is inks and wash.

PUB: 'Simon' series (1969–74), *The Dragon That Only Blew Smoke* (1971), *The Cartoons of Edward McLachlan* (1973) and others

ILL: More than 200 children's books including P. Groves, 'Bangers & Mash' series (40 books, from 1975); R. Kilroy [G. Brandreth], 'Graffiti' series (1979–81); G. Brandreth, *Cockburn's A–Z of After Dinner Entertainment* (1985).

EXHIB: CG; Rogues Gallery, Edinburgh; LCG

COLL: UKCC, BM, V&A

McLEAN, Talbert (1906–92). Painter and joke cartoonist. Talbert McLean was born in Dundee, Angus, on 15 October 1906, the son of John McLean, a banjo-player, and studied design at the Dundee School of Art (1923–7), later teaching there part-time for five years. He then came to London and painted scenery at the Old Vic and Covent Garden, supplementing this activity with freelance cartoons, often in watercolour, under the name of 'Talbert' for *Men Only* (from its first issue), *London Opinion, Night & Day, Bystander, Everybody's, Pearson's, Strand Magazine, Lilliput, Razzle, Passing Show* and *Tatler*. In 1937 he moved to Liverpool and in World War II served first in Europe with the Royal Tank Regiment as a driver and wireless operator, then with the Royal Engineers in their map repro section in North Africa. He returned to Angus after the war, was appointed Art Master of Arbroath High School in 1948 and later taught at Arbroath Academy. His style was influenced by Peter Arno, *New Yorker* cartoonists and the work of the painter William Scott CBE.

A distinctive trademark was the addition of splashes of line or ovals of tone (usually done with a 'stumpy') around his drawings to 'pull them together'. He died in Ninewells Hospital, Dundee, on 29 May 1992.

EXHIB: Talbot Rice Gallery, University of Edinburgh (retrospective 1992); Cyril Gerber Gallery, Glasgow

COLL: E; G; HUN; DUN

McMURTRY, Stanley 'mac' (b. 1936). Editorial and political, joke and strip cartoonist, animator, illustrator and writer. Born in Edinburgh on 4 May 1936, Stan McMurtry moved to Birmingham at the age of eight, attended Birmingham College of Art (1950–53) and spent his National Service in the Royal Army Ordnance Corps (1954–6). His first cartoon was published in *Today* on 7 January 1961. He was a cartoon film animator at Henley-on-Thames, producing films for ITV (two of which won awards at Cannes Film Festivals) before becoming a freelance cartoonist in 1965. At first he drew strips for *Wham, Buster* and other children's comics while also contributing joke cartoons (as 'Stan McMurtry') to *Punch* (including covers), and elsewhere. He then worked (as 'mac') for the *Daily Sketch* as Political and Social Cartoonist (1969–71) until it was absorbed by the *Daily Mail*, succeeding ILLINGWORTH and alternating at first with EMMWOOD until he retired in 1975. Since then he has drawn four cartoons a week for the paper. In addition he has worked in advertising, book illustration and greetings cards design, written comedy scripts (in collaboration with BERNARD COOKSON) for Dave Allen and Tommy Cooper, and produced a children's book, *The Bunjee Venture*, which was made into a cartoon film by Hanna-Barbera. Twice voted CCGB Social and Political Cartoonist of the Year (1983, 1984) and twice CCGB Cartoonist of the Year (1983, 1988), he has also been voted Man of the Year by RADAR. He roughs out ideas in pencil on transparent A2 layout paper and usually draws the finished cartoon on No. 3 Art Line board (though he

'Oh dear, I thought they'd got rid of the cockroaches . . .'

Mac (Stanley McMurtry), *Daily Mail*, 24 November 1988

sometimes uses A3 paper) in half imperial size using a Gillott 404 nib (and a brush for large black areas) and Pelikan black ink, using blue ink for tone areas. When the drawing is dry he covers it with Kodatrace, going over the tone areas in black ink as a guide for the mechanical tint. A miniature portrait of his blonde second wife Janet has always featured somewhere in his *Mail* cartoons since 1980 – unless the subject is purely political – and he signs his work with a sans-serif, lower-case script ready-made label. His work for the *Mail*, which is realistically drawn with authentic details, shows the stylistic influence of GILES. He is a member of the London Sketch Club and Chelsea Arts Club.

PUB: *MAC's Year* (annuals since 1979), *The Bunjee Venture* (1977)
EXHIB: Bohun Gallery, Henley-on-Thames; HAM
COLL: UKCC
LIT: M. Bryant (ed.), *25 Years of MAC* (1996)

MADDOCKS, Peter (b. 1928). Joke and strip cartoonist, animator and scriptwriter. Born in Birmingham on 1 April 1928, Peter Maddocks was taught by NORMAN PETT at Moseley School of Art, Birmingham (1939–42) but left aged 15 to join the Merchant Navy (1943–9). On his return he set up his own advertising agency, designing cinema posters, and wrote western stories for the Amalgamated Press 'Kit Carson' series. He produced his first cartoons for the *Daily Sketch* (1953–4) and then moved to the *Daily Express* (1955–65) where he created the popular strip 'Four D. Jones' – featuring a cowboy with a 'time hoop' through which he travelled in the fourth dimension – which ran for 10 years, and 'No. 10' for the *Sunday Express* (which ran for 21 years). He was Cartoon Editor of Express Newspapers (1965–6), Special Features Editor of *King* magazine (1968–71) and ran the London School of Cartooning correspondence school in Fleet Street (1977–90). He

'Ten years ago Tarzan would have made that jump without a 'chute!'

Peter Maddocks, in M. Bryant (ed.) *Airborne Free*, 1990

has also contributed to the *Daily Star, Daily Record* ('Cop Shop' strip), *Manchester Evening News, Mail on Sunday, Private Eye, Daily Mirror* (taking over 'Useless Eustace' from JACK GREENALL in 1975), *Daily Telegraph* (from 1977), *Evening Standard* (sports cartoons 1966–70), *Evening News* (1974–7), *Sunday Telegraph* (1971–3), *Mayfair* (1967–84), *Woman's Own* (1976–7) and others. In addition he has produced animated commercials for Halas & Batchelor and created animated films for BBC TV since 1984 (notably *The Family Ness, Jimbo and the Jet Set* and *Penny Crayon*) and GMTV from 1993. A prime mover (with backing from CARL GILES and OSBERT LANCASTER) in the formation of the British Cartoonists' Association in 1966, and its first-ever Hon. Secretary, he is currently its Joint President. He uses a black Parker fibre-tip or No. 6 Rotring pen on cartridge paper or 85 gsm A4 typing paper and Dr Martin's watercolours. His characters tend to be slightly goggle-eyed with splayed-out fingers.
PUB: *No. 10* (1973), *Private Eye Maddocks* (1981), *Peter Maddocks' Animal Antics* (1982), *Men – A Field Guide* (1983), *Speedy-Ness Saves the Day* (1984), *Ferocious-Ness Loses His Roar* (1984), *So You Want to Be a Cartoonist?* (1982), *How to be a Super Cartoonist* (1985), *'Jimbo'* series (from 1986), *Condomania* (1987), *Condomania Through the Ages* (1988), *Caricature and the Cartoonist* (1989), *How to Draw Cartoons* (1991), *Cartooning for Beginners* (1992), *Hard Times* (1993), *The High Fibber Diet* (1995)
ILL: J. Amos, *Spain* (1987), *France* (1987)
COLL: UKCC

'Maggie's Farm' – *see* Bell, Steve

MAHOOD, Kenneth (b. 1930). Political, joke and pocket cartoonist, illustrator and painter. Kenneth Mahood was born in Belfast on 4 February 1930, worked in a solicitor's office and was an apprentice lithographer (1945–9) before becoming a professional painter in 1950, exhibiting in Belfast, London and Dublin and winning a CEMA scholarship to study art in Paris. His first cartoon was accepted by *Punch* when he was 18 and he later became a regular contributor and the magazine's Assistant Art Editor (1960–65) under WILLIAM HEWISON. He was also the first-ever Political Cartoonist on *The Times* (1966–8), and has worked as Pocket Cartoonist on the *Financial Times* (1972–82) and *Daily Mail* (since 1982, succeeding JON). In addition he has contributed drawings to the *New Yorker*, produced a number of books and worked in collage. His work has been admired by Hewison, who has described him as having 'one of the sharpest (and most subtle) minds among the present generation of cartoonists'. One of the founder members of the British Cartoonists' Association in 1966, he was elected to the *Punch* Table in 1978.
PUB: *Not a Word to a Soul* (1958), *Fore!* (1959), *The Laughing Dragon* (1970), *Clanky, the Mechanical Boy* (1971), *Why Are There More Questions Than Answers, Grandad?* (1974), *Losing Willy* (1977), *The Secret Sketchbook of a Bloomsbury Lady* (1982), *The Gospel According to Mahood* (1984), *Name Droppings* (1986), *Star-Crossed Lovers* (1986)
ILL: B. Hollowood, *Tory Story* (1964); S. Oram, *Italy* (1972); R. Benedictus, *Fifty Million Sausages* (1975); Oxfam, *The Crack-a-Joke Book* (1978); W. C. Bindweed, *Not Another Cube Book!* (1981)
EXHIB: [painting] WAD, Dublin and London; RA
COLL: V&A; IWM; UKCC

'Major Thompson' – *see* Goetz, Walter

'Major Upsett' – *see* Brockbank, Russell Partridge

MALLET, Harcourt Dennis MSIAD (1909–88). Joke and strip cartoonist, writer and illustrator. Dennis Mallet was born in Wallington, Surrey, on 23 May 1909 and was educated at Parkside Preparatory School, Tonbridge School and Goldsmith's, London. His first published cartoon appeared in *Novel* magazine in 1930 while he was still a student and from 1932 he contributed regularly to *Punch* (30 years), *Tatler* (35 years, including commissioned illustrations of George VI's Lying in State, 1953), *London Opinion, Sketch, Men Only, Lilliput, Humorist, Sunday Graphic, Countryman* and others, and his children's strips for *Eagle* and *Swift* ran for 400 consecutive weeks during the 1950s. He was particularly fond of combining cartoons with his own verse, as instanced by his long-running series 'My Aunt' in *Tatler & Bystander*. During World War II he served in the RAF (1940–46). An admirer of H. M. BATEMAN, RONALD SEARLE and Peter Arno, Dennis Mallet also designed numerous greetings cards, produced comic postcards for Raphael Tuck, illustrated language courses for Oxford University Press and in the 1970s was commissioned to draw promotional cartoons for Les Ambassadeurs Club in Piccadilly. He died in Amersham, Buckinghamshire, on 23 November 1988. His son, Lyndon, is also a cartoonist and writer.

ILL: L. F. Feaver, *Up Fell, Down Dale* (1937); H. Farjeon, *Herbert Farjeon's Cricket Bag* (1946); L. Brewer, *Vote for Richard* (1948); J. T. Thrower (ed.), *The Spice of Life* (1950); K. Waterhouse and G. Deghy, *How to Avoid Matrimony* (1957); G. Deghy, *Paradise in the Strand* (1958); *The Countryman Book of Humour* (1975); *The Story of Father Christmas*; 12 humour and travel titles by D. Hay; more than 20 educational books for Oxford University Press

MAMMON – *see* Hollowood, Albert Bernard

'Man Who . . ., The' – *see* Bateman, Henry Mayo

MANSBRIDGE, Norman Arthur (1911–93). Political, joke and strip cartoonist, illustrator and writer. Norman Mansbridge was born on 22 July 1911 in Wanstead, Essex, the son of Arthur Mansbridge, an illustrator and writer. He attended Forest School, Essex, and Heatherley's in London. Apprenticed to a commercial art studio, he spent several years in advertising before becoming a freelance cartoonist, contributing his first drawing to *Punch* in 1937. During World War II he served in the Auxiliary Fire Service and was a radio officer in the Merchant Navy, during which time he had a roving commission as a war artist. After the war he returned to London and worked for *News Chronicle, Men Only, Sunday Times, Lilliput, Daily Sketch* and *Birmingham Post* before becoming Political Cartoonist on *Punch*. The only cartoonist to have had eight colour pages in a single issue of *Punch* ('The Pursuit of Happiness'), he later turned to producing strips for IPC and Fleetway children's comics such as *Tiger, Shiver & Shake* and *Whizzer & Chips* (his *Knockout* strip 'Fusspot' ran for 20 years from 1971). In addition he exhibited oil paintings at the Royal Academy and taught art, worked in advertising (e.g. Vantella shirts) and drew covers for books (e.g. Basil Boothroyd's *The Whole Thing's Laughable*, 1964). A member of the Savage Club, he was elected a member of the *Punch* Table in 1958 and was one of the founder members of the British Cartoonists' Association in 1966. Preferring to memorize a subject rather than draw it on the spot, Mansbridge worked first in pencil and then with a fountain pen and black ink. He died on 6 March 1993.

PUB: *The Modern Mariner* (1946), *The Pale Artist* (1947)
ILL: J. Dyrenforth and M. Kester, *Adolf in Blunderland* (1939); L. M. Bates, *Tideway Tactics* (1947); L. Gibb, *The Joneses: How to Keep Up With Them* (1959), *The Higher Joneses* (1961); M. Muggeridge, *Things Past* (1978)
EXHIB: [oil paintings] RA
COLL: V&A; MET; UKCC

MARC – *see* Boxer, Charles Mark Edward

MARCHANT, Leslie Pinney (1897–1988). Joke, political and strip cartoonist. L. P. Marchant was born on 1 October 1897 in Shamley Green, near Guildford, Surrey and studied at the Slade School of Art. He was a frequent contributor to *Punch* from the 1920s onwards and also drew political cartoons for *Evening News* in the 1940s and a strip cartoon for a Scottish newspaper in the 1950s and '60s. In addition he drew for *London Opinion, Daily Mirror, Weekend Mail, Passing Show* and children's comics such as *Dandy* and *Mickey Mouse Weekly*. He worked in pen and ink and pencil but also painted in oils and watercolours for pleasure. Leslie Marchant died in Yeovil, Somerset, in September 1988.

MARENGO, Kimon Evan 'Kem' (1904–88). Political cartoonist and caricaturist. Kem was born in Zifta, Egypt, on 22 January 1904, the son of Evangelos Marangos, a Greek cotton merchant, and grew up in Alexandria. He edited and illustrated the political weekly *Maalesh* (1923–31), and later moved to Paris to study at the École Libre des Sciences Politiques. His cartoons were published in *Le Petit Parisien, John Bull, La Bourse Égyptienne, Cartoon Comment, Men Only, New York Times, Liberal News, Razzle, Daily Herald* and *Daily Telegraph*. During World War II he ran the 'KEM Unit' in the Political Information Department of the Foreign Office, producing propaganda cartoons for the Middle East. Many of his drawings also appeared as postcards and posters. After the war he studied at Exeter College, Oxford, and wrote a thesis on 'The Cartoon as a Political Weapon in England 1784–1832'. When his pseudonym was copied he was forced to litigate up to the House of Lords and the case, 'Marengo v. *Daily Sketch* and *Sunday Graphic* Ltd [1948]', set a precedent for civil litigation. He was awarded the Légion d'Honneur and Croix de Guerre. He usually worked in pen, brush, ink and poster colour on white card. Kem died on 4 November 1988.

PUB: *Oua Riglak!* (1926), *Alexandrie, Reine de la Méditerranée* (1928), *Gare les Pattes!* (1929), *Toy Titans* (1937), *Adolf and His Donkey Benito* (1940), *Lines of Attack* (1944)
ILL: P. Tissier, *I Worked With Laval* (1942)
COLL: UKCC

MARIO – *see* Armengol, Mariano Hubert

MARKSMAN – *see* Walker, J. C.

MAROC – *see* Coram, Robert S. E.

MARTIN, Leonard Bradshaw (1895–after 1950). Joke cartoonist. L. B. Martin was born in Forest Gate, London, on 23 September 1895. He was a regular contributor to *Punch* from *c.* 1918 to 1939 and his work also appeared in *Men Only*, *Lilliput*, *Daily Sketch*, *Passing Show*, *Humorist*, *Tit-Bits*, *Blighty* and other publications. In addition he drew comic postcards.

MARTIN, Sidney William (1919–93). Pocket and political cartoonist, caricaturist and illustrator. Bill Martin was born in Perth, Western Australia, on 28 December 1919, the son of George Martin, a wheat farmer. Educated at Perth Boys School, he left aged 14 to work for an electrical company and then for a process engraver. A self-taught artist, his first caricatures and cartoons appeared in the *Perth Sunday Times* in the late 1930s and he also drew illustrations and wrote articles for *Wings* while serving as an air gunner and later wireless operator in the RAAF (1941–6). After working in advertising in Perth and Melbourne, he came to England in 1953 and joined the *Sunday Express* as cartoonist, illustrator and latterly Art Director, retiring in 1984. He also drew for *Sporting Life* as 'Williams'. He used Parker pens with indian ink and sometimes also Rotring pens. In addition he painted in oils and watercolour. His trademark was a circle above the 'I' in 'Martin' and he sometimes also included himself smoking a pipe in his drawings. Bill Martin died at his home in Westcott, Surrey, on 4 June 1993.
ILL: M. Davidson, *The Sunday Express Weekend Gardening Book* (1976)

MASON, George Finch (1850–1915). Joke cartoonist, sports artist, illustrator and writer. Finch Mason was the son of a teacher at Eton College. Educated at Eton himself (1860–64) he was 'Uncle Toby' of *Sporting Times* for many years and also wrote as 'Fusbos' for *Fores Sporting Notes & Sketches*. He contributed hunting cartoons to *Punch* (1881–3), produced a number of sporting prints for Fores (from 1886) and published two volumes of *Finch Mason's Sporting Annual* (1895, 1896). In addition he wrote a number of books and produced at least two series of comic postcards, 'Sporting Notions', for J. Alderton and a hunting series for F. C. Southwood. Finch Mason died at his home in Chelsea, London, in July 1915.
PUB: Many books including *My Day With the Hounds* (1882), *Flowers of the Hunt* (1889), *Finch Mason's Sporting Annual* (1895, 1896), *The Tame Fox* (1897), *Annals of the Horse-Shoe Club* (1902), *Miniature Sporting Nonsense Rhymes* (1907), *Heroes & Heroines of the Grand National* (1907), [with J. Maunsell Richardson] *Gentleman Riders Past & Present* (1909)
ILL: T. Dykes, *All Round Sport* (1887); H. Garle, *Hunting in the Golden Days* (1896); R. Herbert, *When Diamonds Were Trumps* (1908) and others
COLL: V&A

MATT – *see* Pritchett, Matthew and Sandford, Matthew

MAX – *see* Beerbohm, Sir Henry Maximilian

'Max' – *see* Giovannetti, Pericle Luigi

MAY, Frederick MBE TD (1891–1976). Caricaturist and painter. Fred May was born in Wallasey, Liverpool on 25 January 1891, the son of John Morritt May, a cabinet-maker. His great-uncle was one of PHIL MAY's brothers. He studied at Liscard School of Art, Wallasey, and at Reading University Art School under the ornithological artist A. W. Seaby. At the age of 19 he started work as a cartoonist for the *North Eastern Daily Gazette* (now the *Evening Gazette*) in Middlesbrough (1909) and contributed his first caricatures to the *Tatler* in 1917 while serving as an infantry officer in the 7th Battalion, Green Howards (he was wounded at Arras). He remained with the magazine for 59 years (1917–76) and also contributed to the *Liverpool Daily Post*, *Sketch*, *Graphic*, *News Chronicle*, *Harpers* (USA), *Shooting Times* and *Auckland Gazette* (New Zealand). In World War II he served as a staff officer – achieving the rank of major – at GHQ 21 Army Group and with SHAEF and was Ground Liaison Officer with HQ Fighter Command. He was later awarded the MBE (1939), Légion D'Honneur (1945), Order of St John, Palmes d'Académie, Médaille du Mérite and Territorial Decoration. In addition to newspaper and magazine work he drew book covers. Sir David Murray RA, when President of the Royal Academy, is reported to have said that May had the finest line of any black-and-white artist he knew. He met US actor James Cagney during the war and they became life-long friends (Cagney was godfather to May's grandson). His book *City Lights* is a collection of more than 60 caricatures which were published on the City Page of the *News Chronicle* in 1932, featuring politicians such as Neville Chamberlain and various captains of industry. Fred May worked in brush, pen and indian ink on Bristol board. He died in Odiham, Hampshire, on 31 October 1976. His son is the automobile and aviation artist Phil May.

PUB: *City Lights* (1933)
COLL: RAF; NPG; York City Library; Green Howards Regimental Museum, Richmond, Yorkshire; Liverpool Artists Club

MAY, Philip William RI NEAC (1864–1903). Joke and political cartoonist, caricaturist and illustrator. Phil May was born at 66 Wallace Street, New Wortley, Leeds on 22 April 1864, the seventh child of Philip William May, a commercial traveller who had trained as an engineer under George Stephenson, painted in watercolours and died when May was nine. His grandfather, Charles Hugh May, was a wealthy Derbyshire landowner and amateur caricaturist. His mother was the daughter of Eugene Macarthy, manager of Drury Lane Theatre; his aunt Maria was a famous actress married to Robert William Honner, Manager of Sadlers Wells Theatre; and his elder brother Charles was an illustrator. He was educated at St George's School, Leeds, Oxford Place School and Park Lane Boarding School. He left school at the age of 13 and worked as a barrister's clerk, for an estate agent, in a music store and as a timekeeper in an iron foundry before becoming an assistant scene painter at Leeds Grand Theatre, where he also drew very accomplished caricatures of actors. His first drawings were published in *Yorkshire Gossip* when he was 14. He then became a professional actor and set-designer for a touring theatrical company (1879) and moved to London in 1883. Here, a chance meeting with the actor Lionel Brough (who bought one of his caricatures of Henry Irving and others) led to an introduction to the Editor of *Society*, who published his drawings. Then at the age of 19 he joined the newly launched *St Stephen's Re-*

'By the way, when does your American tour come off?'
'Oh, not for about a year.'
'Well, let's go in here and have a drink before you go.'

Phil May, [self-portrait smoking cigar], *Phil May's Illustrated Annual*, Winter 1901–2

view (1884) where he drew political cartoons with TOM MERRY (and was later, in 1885, joined by caricaturist Matt Morgan). One of the most notable of these was 'Old Gravedigger's Christmas Eve' (27 December 1884), featuring Gladstone, which predicted the death of Gordon at Khartoum the following year. In addition he contributed to *Penny Illustrated* and *Pictorial World* and at one time shared a studio with G. D. ARMOUR. In 1885, having been offered considerably more than his current salary (£10 a week), he left the *St Stephen's Review* (being succeeded by HALKETT) and moved to Australia to work as Political Cartoonist on the *Sydney Bulletin* with Livingstone Hopkins, returning to

Britain (via Italy and Paris) in 1889. He took up his old job at the *Review* in 1890 and in 1891 had great success with his illustrations to *The Parson and the Painter* by William Allison, the Editor of the *Review*, enabling him to buy a house and a horse (called Punch). The following year he began his own magazine, *Phil May's Annual* (1892–1905), and his first *Punch* drawing appeared on 14 October 1893. He joined the staff in 1895 but the story that, a heavy drinker, he signed the Table underneath is untrue (his initials are carved between those of Thackeray and Du Maurier). He also drew for *Pall Mall Budget, Pick-Me-Up* (1891–3), *Graphic, Daily Graphic, Illustrated London News, Sketch, English Illustrated Magazine, Daily Chronicle, Unicorn, Eureka, Savoy, Mascot, Century, Tatler, Penny Illustrated*, etc. In addition he drew advertisements for Player's Navy Cut, Geradel's Pastilles and others, designed postcards for Tuck, Valentine, Davidson, Wrench, etc., and once made a laughing self-portrait plaster sculpture ('If I ever get to ninety'), which now hangs in the London Sketch Club. He was a great admirer of Gillray ('there is nobody today to touch him'), Whistler, Cruikshank, Keene and SAMBOURNE ('All that I know as an artist I learnt from Sammy'). A very fast worker, he used models ('draw from life and keep drawing from life') and was one of the first artists to make full use of the newly invented photographic or 'process' (as opposed to wood-engraved) method of reproduction. For his *Punch* drawings he worked first in pencil and then drew over this in pen and ink. 'May's line at its best may be said to be alive. It is certain that no English draughtsman has ever attained greater vigour or vivacity in black and white' (E. V. Lucas). His uncluttered style had immense influence on later artists: 'He certainly had a greater effect on pictorial humour . . . than any other pictorial humorist of his or the following generation, and he shewed the way for all the free and lively work which followed after him' (FOUGASSE). 'He surely gave more magic to a single line than any draughtsman who ever lived, and he was unquestionably the creator of the simplified technique of modern humorous drawing' (BRADSHAW). 'Black-and-white art is summed up in two words – Phil May' (Whistler). He was a member of the Savage Club and Chelsea Arts Club (from 1891, proposed by Whistler), and was, with CECIL ALDIN, TOM BROWNE, DUDLEY HARDY and LANCE THACKERAY, a founder of the London

Sketch Club (a very good silhouettist, the frieze at the club was partly due to him). He was elected NEAC (1894) and RI (1897). Phil May died of cirrhosis of the liver at his home, 20 Holland Park Road, London, on 5 August 1903, aged 39. He was buried near the *Punch* cartoonist Richard Doyle in Kensal Green Cemetery. A Blue Plaque to his memory was erected at his home in 1976.

PUB: *Phil May Winter and Summer Annuals* (1892–1904), *Phil May's Sketch Book* (1895), *Gutter-Snipes* (1896), *Phil May's Graphic Pictures* (1897), *A. B. C* (1897), *Phil May Album* (1899/1900), *Sketches from 'Punch'* (1903), *Phil May Folio* (1904)

ILL: 'Rev. Joseph Slapkins' [W. Allison], *The Parson and the Painter* (1891); H. Pearse, *The Comet Coach* (1895); A. Patchett, *The Withered Jester* (1895); C. Bertram, *Isn't it Wonderful?* (1896); F. C. Burnand, *Z. Z. G. or Zig Zag Guide* (1897); W. Besant, *East London* (1902); Mrs M. Spielmann, *Littledom Castle* (1903)

EXHIB: FAS (1895); LG (1903, 1908); LE (1913, 1936); RA (1898)

COLL: BM; V&A; NPG; T; G; L; THG

LIT: J. Thorpe, *Phil May, Master Draughtsman and Humorist* (1932)

MAYBANK, Thomas – *see* Webb, Hector Thomas Maybank

MAYS, Douglas Lionel (1900–91). Joke cartoonist, painter and illustrator. D. L. Mays was born on 4 August 1900 in Kingston-upon-Thames, Surrey, and educated at Tiffin School, Kingston. He served in the Rhineland Army of Occupation and then studied illustration under E. J. SULLIVAN and Harold Speed at Goldsmith's College (1920–23), where his contemporaries were Graham Sutherland and ERIC FRASER. He worked for *Beano, Big Budget, Holiday Annual* and *Dandy* before his first drawing for *Punch* was accepted in June 1932 (he continued to work for *Punch* as a cartoonist and illustrator until 1954). A pacifist during World War II, he spent the period as a farmer. Mays' drawings were in the tradition of George du Maurier and often featured the upper middle classes, especially women and children, the models for whom were his wife and four daughters. He also handled architectural, romantic and topographical subjects, drew for *John Bull, Passing Show* and *Tatler*, and designed Christmas cards for Royles. Mays was greatly admired by FOUGASSE, who called him 'a really magnificent pen-draughtsman',

and Price said of him 'Only Mays was really interested in costume. Since BELCHER, hardly anyone had drawn people.' As well as pen and ink he also worked in oils and watercolour. He was a member of the Art Workers' Guild. D. L. Mays died on 19 May 1991.
PUB: *Percy's Progress* (1944)
ILL: Many books including A. Chaffee, *Wandy, the Wild Pony* (1933); N. Streatfeild, *Tennis Shoes* (1937), *The House in Cornwall* (1940), *Curtain Up* (1944); M. Twain, *The Adventures of Tom Sawyer* (1962); A. Buckridge, 11 'Jennings' titles; A. Brazil, *Three Terms at Uplands* (n.d.)
EXHIB: RA; RBA; SGA
COLL: National Gallery of Canada, Ottawa

MECHAM, William 'Tom Merry' (1853–1902) – *see* Bryant & Heneage

MEL – *see* Melhuish, John Barradale

MELHUISH, John Barradale 'Mel' MBE (1893–after 1952). Caricaturist and sports cartoonist. J. B. Melhuish, who also signed his work 'Mel', was born in Exeter, Devon, on 9 January 1893, the son of John Underhill Melhuish, and was educated at Wellington School, Somerset. He produced drawings for a wide variety of markets, including at least two sets of golf caricature cigarette cards for Churchmans and a set of 50 rugby ones for Wills. He also contributed to the *Illustrated Sporting & Dramatic News*, *Evening Standard*, *Sporting Life* (sports cartoons signed 'J. B. Melhuish'), *Sportsman* and *Inky Way Annual*, and drew illustrations for dinner menus (e.g. one depicting comedian and broadcaster Ted Ray for the 20th annual dinner of the Vaudeville Golfing Society in 1949). Awarded an MBE in 1918, he was also a member of the Press Club.

MELLING, Gerard 'GED' (b. 1934). Pocket cartoonist. Ged Melling was born in Stirling, Scotland, the son of William Melling, a coalminer, and left school at 15 to become an apprentice house painter. He studied painting at St Martin's School of Art (1961–4) and his first cartoon was published in *Time Out* in 1967. A professional cartoonist since 1984, he has worked for *The Times* and *Economist* since 1989 and has also contributed to the *Daily* and *Sunday Telegraph*, *Financial Times*, *Spectator*, *Observer*, *Oldie*, *Sporting Life* and *Private Eye*. He uses a Rotring Art Pen on photocopy paper.
PUB: *Guttae* (1974)

ILL: A. James, *Memoirs of a Fen Tiger* (1986); P. Howard, *A Word in Time* (1990)
EXHIB: [drawings and paintings] London, Dublin, Canada

MENDOZA, Philip 'Pip' 'Flam' 'Spike' (*c.* 1899–after 1966). Joke, strip and political cartoonist, poster artist, illustrator and painter. Philip Mendoza was born in Hackney, London, the son of a portrait painter of Spanish origin. Named after the cartoonist PHIL MAY, he was brought up at first in Cannes, France, but later returned with his family to England and was educated in London (*c.* 1907). At the age of 14 he was a pavement artist in Manchester and he later studied at St Martin's School of Art. He then moved to Yorkshire, worked briefly as a poster artist, and became an illustrator for the *Newcastle Evening Chronicle*. He also worked variously in a shipyard, coal mine and glass foundry and was a cinema operator and stage manager. During World War I he served in the King's Own Yorkshire Light Infantry and in the 1920s was working freelance in London for the *Daily Mail* and *Sunday Dispatch* under the names 'Pip', 'Flam' and 'Spike' while also drawing for *Lilliput*, *London Mystery Magazine*, *New Clarion* (political cartoons) and other publications. In addition he designed posters for the Ministry of Labour and a notable series featuring 'Percy Vere' for the Royal Society for the Prevention of Accidents. He also produced strips in the 1950s and 60s for Amalgamated Press children's comics such as *Jack & Jill* and *Captain Vigour*.
ILL: 'Yaffle', *Pity the Poor Rich* (1947)
EXHIB: [portrait of his wife, 1939] RA
COLL: [posters] IWM

MERRY, Tom – *see* Mecham, William

MILLAR, Philip (*c.* 1913–after 1960). Joke and strip cartoonist. Philip Millar contributed regularly to *Razzle* for 21 years (1932–53) and also worked for the *Sunday Chronicle*, *Daily Mirror*, *Punch*, *London Opinion*, *Daily Sketch*, *Answers*, *Blighty*, *Weekend Mail*, *Reveille* and others.

MILLS, Arthur Wallis (1878–1940). Joke cartoonist and illustrator. Wallis Mills was born in Windmill Hill, Sussex, on 21 October 1878, the son of the Rev. Michael Edward Mills, Senior Chaplain of the Bengal Ecclesiastical Establishment and Vicar of Long Bennington and Foston, Lincolnshire. He was educated at Bedford School and studied art at the South Kensington

Schools. His first drawing for *Punch* appeared on 24 December 1898 and he continued to work for the magazine until a year before his death. He also contributed cartoons to *Judy, Ludgate Magazine, Royal Magazine* and *To-Day* before 1900 and later drew for *Bystander, Cassell's, Graphic, Humorist, Printer's Pie, Passing Show, London Opinion, Sketch Book, Strand* and *Tatler*. In addition, he drew advertisements for Kodak and others and designed comic postcards for William Lyon and William Collins ('Prehistoric Sports' series). During World War I he served in France as a gunner for the Royal Garrison Artillery and in the Camouflage Corps (1915–19). He was a member of the Savage Club amongst others. Wallis Mills died at his club in St James's, London, on 4 April 1940.
ILL: A. Williams, *Petrol Peter* (1906); J. Austen, *Works* (1908); A. Lang, *The Red Book of Heroes* (1909)
EXHIB: RA
COLL: BM

MILLS, W. (fl. 1930s–40s). Joke cartoonist, architectural draughtsman, teacher, illustrator and painter. Born in Cheshire, Mills was a teacher of architecture and began drawing cartoons in his spare time for *Punch* and *London Opinion*. He also drew landscapes for *Britannia* and other journals, illustrated magazine stories and painted scenery for local Gilbert and Sullivan productions. PERCY BRADSHAW said of him 'He teaches architecture and draws it beautifully. His landscape drawings . . . are most distinguished examples of decorative penwork. He uses colour with the vigour and sense of selection of a poster artist . . . [in his serious story illustration] he draws graceful women and real men with all the charm and conviction which the most exclusive magazine would demand.' An admirer of the *Radio Times* work of ARTHUR WATTS, Mills himself thought his cartoons 'abominably bad joke drawings – from the drawing point of view'. His favourite shape for cartoons was a long narrow strip and though he was equally at home with pen, charcoal or brush, his cartoons were usually drawn in pen and ink.
EXHIB: [oil painting] Manchester Art Gallery

MINET, Francis 'Pav' (b. 1913). Political and joke cartoonist, stained-glass artist and restorer. Pav was born in Islington, London, on 20 August 1913 and attended St Martin's School of Art (1928–34). A stained-glass artist with Heaton

Butler & Bayne in London (1924–39), he served in the Royal Artillery during World War II, designing camouflage, and was a prisoner of war in Germany (1940–45). After the war he continued working as a stained-glass artist with Goddard & Gibbs Studios, London (1946–78). He also drew political cartoons for left-wing and anti-fascist organizations (1936–9) and contributed cartoons to *Punch* (1957–73, including many covers), *Private Eye, Daily Sketch, Daily Herald, Daily Mirror, Daily Express, Evening Standard, Evening News, Star, Sunday Dispatch, Reynolds News, Everybody's, Weekend, Reveille, Tit-Bits, Portsmouth News* and *Portsmouth Journal*.
EXHIB: [paintings] Hampstead Art Gallery
COLL: UKCC

MINHINNICK, Sir Gordon Edward George KBE OBE (1902–92). Political/editorial cartoonist, strip cartoonist and journalist. Minhinnick was born on 13 June 1902 in Torpoint, Cornwall, the son of a naval engineer, and educated at Kelly College, Tavistock, Devon, intending to enter the navy as a cadet. However, the family moved to New Zealand in 1921 and Minhinnick began work first as a sheep farmer and then as an architectural draughtsman (1923–5) while drawing cartoons in his spare time for the Wellington *Free Lance* whose staff he later joined (1925–6). He then worked for *Christchurch Sun* and *Auckland Sun* (1927–30) – for which he also wrote a regular column – and was Political/Editorial Cartoonist of the *New Zealand Herald* (1930–87). During World War II he created the popular 'Soldier Sam' strip for the *Herald*. In 1950 the *Evening Standard* in London offered him the chair vacated by DAVID LOW but he preferred to stay in New Zealand. Himself influenced by Low, Minhinnick drew his cartoons left-handed with broad brushstrokes and lettered them with a right-handed pen. Seeing his role as being more to amuse than provoke, he once said, 'I don't wave any party banners and I feel that cartoons of approbation are rarely very successful.' He received an OBE (1950) and a KBE (1976) and though he retired from the *Herald* in 1976 he continued to draw for the paper. He died on 19 February 1992. Former New Zealand Prime Minister Sir Robert Muldoon said of Minhinnick's work (which had commented on 13 administrations and 11 prime ministers): 'I never saw better anywhere.'
PUB: *Minhinnick Cartoons* (1938), *Min's Pie* (1952), *Min's Sauce* (1976) and others

ILL: [with F. Alexander] P. A. Lawlor, *Murphy's Moa and Other Christmas Sketches* (1936)

MINNION, John Robert (b. 1949). Caricaturist and illustrator. Born in Guildford, Surrey, on 13 August 1949, John Minnion was largely self-taught apart from a short course on typography and magazine production at the London College of Printing (1976–7). After producing and selling his own versions of Lewis Carroll's *Jabberwocky* (1973) and *The Hunting of the Snark* (1976), he was Political Caricaturist at the *New Statesman* (1978–88). He has also contributed to *Listener*, *The Times*, *Guardian*, *Marxism Today*, *Nursing Times*, *Classic CD*, *Sunday Business*, *On Air*, *Daily Express*, *New Zealand Listener* and other publications. Preferring to work in black and white, he uses a mapping pen and brush with indian ink or coloured inks. He cites his influences as Beardsley and Trog.
PUB: *Maestri* (1983), [with N. Kenyon] *Britannia Rules the Staves* (1988), *Thatcherian Values* (1990), [with J. Beadle and R. Ainsley] *The Sideways Guide to Composers* (1993), *Composing Mortals* (1998)

ILL: L. Carroll, *Jabberwocky* (1973), *The Hunting of the Snark* (1976); N. Sherrin, *Loose Ned* (1990); R. Morley, *Robert Morley's 2nd Book of Bricks* (1981); R. Woddis, *God's Worried* (1982)
EXHIB: Turnstile Gallery; RFH; Fairfield Halls, Croydon; BC; Brighton Festival; Wigmore Hall; St David's Hall, Cardiff; Guildford Book Festival; Royal Academy of Music; Chelmsford Festival
COLL: IWM

'Modesty Blaise' – *see* Colvin, Neville

MOG – *see* Dodd, Maurice Stanley

MONTGOMERY, Evelyn Corrie [née Hands] (1912–75). Caricaturist. Eve Montgomery was born at 260 Caledonian Road, Holloway, London, on 8 February 1912, the daughter of Hugh Hands, a doctor. She began drawing her father's patients in his surgery in Brighton when aged 10 and studied at the Regent Street Polytechnic School of Art (1928), but had to give up her studies when her father died in 1930. While she was working for the War Office in World War II a public relations officer saw her caricatures of colleagues and helped her get a job as a freelance

John Minnion, [Liszt], *Listener*, 3 June 1986

theatre caricaturist for the *Star* (1943–53). She produced nearly 700 drawings for the paper illustrating A. E. Wilson's reviews and also worked for *The Stage* (1952–3) and the *Daily Express* (1946). Montgomery sketched from life in pencil in the theatre itself then finished the drawing in pen and indian ink at her desk. She later took evening classes in oil painting at St Martin's School of Art (1963–5) and became a full-time artist using a palette knife with oil and polymer. Eve Montgomery died in Brighton on 12 September 1975.
EXHIB: [paintings] Bramante Galleries
COLL: CAT

MOON, Sidney (fl. 1930s–after 1948). Political cartoonist. After training by correspondence course, Sid Moon worked on the *Cambridge Daily News* until 1935 (when he was succeeded by RONALD SEARLE) before moving to London to work for the *Sunday Dispatch* and *Daily Worker*. He also contributed to *Inky Way Annual*, *Everybody's* (signed 'SID MOON') and other publications. Moon signed his work with an anthropomorphic crescent moon.
PUB: [with NEB, LEE, GITTINS and ILLING-WORTH] *400 Famous Cartoons* (1944)

MORELAND, Arthur (1867–after 1948). Political and joke cartoonist and caricaturist. Arthur Moreland was born on 12 October 1867 in Higher Ardwick, Manchester, the grandson of an antiquarian bookseller and the son of a domestic property speculator. Through his father Moreland got his first job working for the *Manchester Evening Mail* and then worked as a 'newspaper inspector' overseeing distribution of the *Star* to newsagents in south London. Then after drawing a caricature of Ernest Parke he was transferred to the company's Art Department and drew his first cartoon for the *Star*'s sister paper the *Morning Leader* in April 1896. He remained with the *Leader* for 18 years. Untrained as an artist (Mr Boot, Art Editor of *Strand Magazine*, recognized his natural gift for caricature and advised him against going to art school as he would then lose it), Moreland used to attend the Press Gallery of the House of Commons with F. C. GOULD. Though himself a lifelong Conservative, Moreland drew the celebrated Chinese Labour Cartoon ('an infamous document', said Colonial Office Minister Alfred Lyttelton MP) which was credited with leading to the large Liberal majority in the 1906 election after Lib-

eral candidates pasted more than three million posters of the cartoon all over the country. The drawing shows the ghosts of two British soldiers standing by an open grave and one of them pointing at imported Chinese labourers in chains escorted by armed guards with the caption: 'Look there, Bill, that's what you and I, and 20,000 others, died for.' Moreland was best known, however, for his creation of the popular 'Humours of History' series of cartoons – perhaps the first regular series ever to be published in the UK – which first appeared in the *Morning Leader* in 1898 and continued via the *Daily News* through some 160 cartoons. In these drawings, the first of which was 'Ages, BC: Prehistoric London' amusing parallels are made between historical incidents and the present day. He also contributed to *Punch*, *Strand*, *Boy's Own Paper*, *Passing Show*, and others. In addition he produced a number of series of political postcards for Faulkners (e.g. 'John Bull' and 'Fiscal Speeches') as well as comic cards for Eyre & Spottiswoode taken from the 'Humours of History' cartoons. He disliked drawing from life. Moreland joined the Press Club in 1903 and began a series of caricatures of its members, beginning with Thomas McDonald Rendle, each of which was signed by the victim and hung on the wall. He was later Hon. Secretary of the Club for about 14 years until he resigned in 1929. He was also a member of the Savage Club.
PUB: *Humours of History* (1898, 1903, 1905, 1913, 1915, 1918, 1920, 1921, 1923), *More Humours of History* (1925)
ILL: T. J. Macnamara, *The Gentle Golfer* (1905), *The History of the Hun* (1917), *The Comic History of Sport* (1924); W. R. Hadwen, *The Difficulties of Dr Deguerre* (1926), *Dickens in London* (1928); N. Jackson, *Lays from Lancashire* (1930), *Dickens Landmarks in London* (1931)
COLL: IWM

MORROW, Albert George (1863–1927). Joke cartoonist, poster artist, illustrator and painter. Albert Morrow was born in Comber, Co. Down, Ireland, one of eight sons of George Morrow, a decorator. He was the elder brother of GEORGE MORROW and the brother of EDWIN, Harry (who helped found the Ulster Literary Theatre) and NORMAN MORROW. He studied at the Belfast School of Art and the South Kensington Schools in London. While still a student he came to the notice of Comyns Carr, Editor of *English Illustrated Magazine*, who gave him his first com-

EXPLODED REPUTATIONS
THE SIRENS

George Morrow, *More Morrow*, 1921

mission (illustrating a series on English industries) in 1884. He later contributed to *Punch, Little Folks, Big Budget, Boy's Friend, Cassell's, Good Words, Illustrated Bits, London Magazine, Puck, Boy's Leader, Chums, Ching Ching's Own* and others. He was also well known as a theatrical and commercial poster artist: his first design ('The Stranglers of Paris') was for Clement Smith who had published posters by PHIL MAY (whom Morrow greatly admired). His best-known posters were for the magazines *Illustrated Bits* and *Good Words* and for the play *The New Woman* by Sidney Grundy. In addition he produced many illustrations for children's books, and as a watercolour painter exhibited at the Royal Academy Summer Show seven years in succession. A founder member of the Chelsea Arts Club, he was also a member of the Savage Club. Albert Morrow died in West Hoathly, Sussex, in October 1927. (*See also* SIGGS.)
ILL: F. Wicks, *The Stories of the Broadmoor Patient* (1893), [with H. FURNISS] *My Undiscovered Crime*s (1909); W. Collins, *No Name* (*c.* 1915); E. L. Haverfield, *The Happy Comrade* (1920); C. H. Avery, *Between Two Schools* (*c.* 1923)
EXHIB: RA
COLL: THG; BM; V&A

MORROW, Edwin A. (fl. 1903–after 1929). Joke cartoonist and painter. Edwin Morrow was one of eight sons of George Morrow, a decorator. He was the brother of GEORGE, ALBERT, Harry (who helped found the Ulster Literary Theatre) and NORMAN MORROW. As four of the five artists in the family studied at Belfast School of Art and the South Kensington Schools it is probable that Edwin did. His work was published in *Punch, Passing Show, Bystander, Strand Magazine* and elsewhere. He was a member of the London Sketch Club and the Savage Club.
EXHIB: RA

MORROW, George (1869–1955). Joke cartoonist and illustrator. George Morrow was born in Belfast, one of eight sons of George Morrow, a decorator. He was the younger brother of ALBERT MORROW and the brother of EDWIN, Harry (who helped found the Ulster Literary Theatre) and NORMAN MORROW. Apprenticed at first to a sign-painter, he later studied art at the Belfast School of Art, the South Kensington Schools and in Paris. He began work as a book illustrator, his first commission being for Mary Russell Mitford's *Country Stories* in 1896. The same year he also began to contribute to *Pick-Me-Up, Idler,*

Windsor Magazine and others. After he illustrated a book for *Punch* writer E. V. Lucas his work began to appear in the magazine, his first contribution being an illustration for one of a series of humorous articles by Lucas on 19 September 1906. He remained with the magazine for nearly 50 years (until 1954), being elected to the *Punch* Table in 1923 and taking over from FRANK REYNOLDS as Art Editor (1930–37), being himself succeeded in this role by FOUGASSE. He occasionally deputized for the 'Essence of Parliament' feature illustrated by A. M. LLOYD and drew 24 big political cartoons for the magazine but 'They were certainly not his *métier*' (E. V. Knox, *Punch* obituary). However, what he was best known for were heraldic and historical jokes (of the kind pioneered by E. T. REED), and drew many series of these including 'Forgotten Deeds of Valour', 'Episodes in the Lives of the Great' and 'Forgotten Sports'. He particularly liked drawing animals: 'Nobody could put so wistful an expression into the faces of lions, elephants, dragons and pterodactyls, whose artless ways he seemed to consider rather more deserving of compassion than human foibles' (Knox). Not a great draughtsman, his strength lay in his comic ideas. He was 'an artistic descendant of his compatriot Doyle, and used a gentler and quieter version of the same artistic brogue' (Fougasse). Price relates that he once drew a cartoon (23 November 1921) in which a factory worker was seen rolling a single oat. The blockmakers thought it was blemish and removed it, whereupon Morrow insisted that it should be stamped on every copy of the magazine by hand. He usually signed his drawings 'Geo. M.'. In addition he painted watercolours. George Morrow died on 18 January 1955.
PUB: *George Morrow, His Book* (1920), *Podgy and I* (1926), *Some More* (1928)
ILL: E. V. Lucas and C. L. Graves, *England Day by Day* (1903), *Signs of the Times* (1906), *If* (1908); M. R. Mitford, *Country Stories* (1896); H. Graham, *Familiar Faces* (1907); C. L. Graves, *Musical Monstrosities* (1909); E. V. Lucas, *Swollen-Headed William* (1914), *In Gentlest Germany* (1915); Marcus, *Morals for the Young* (1915); A. P. Herbert, *The Wherefore and the Why* (1921), *Tinker Tailor* (1922); E. V. Knox, *Parodies Regained* (1921), *Fiction as She is Wrote* (1927); A. Marshall, *Simple Stories* (1927), *Simple People* (1928); A. P. Herbert, *Wisdom for the Wise* (1930); A. Herbertson, *Hurrah for the O-Pom-Pom* (1931); J. B. Morton, *The Death of the Dragon* (1934); I. Plunkett and R. Mitchell, *Ye Goode Old Days* (*c.* 1936)

EXHIB: RA; RBA
COLL: BM

MORROW, Norman (fl. 1890s–after 1914). Caricaturist. One of eight sons of George Morrow, a decorator, Norman Morrow was the brother of ALBERT, GEORGE, Harry (who helped found the Ulster Literary Theatre) and EDWIN MORROW. Little is known of his life, but as four of the five artist brothers studied at Belfast School of Art and the South Kensington Schools it is probable that he did. He worked for the *Bystander* and other journals and was 'an outstanding caricaturist' (BRADSHAW) but died young during World War I.

'Mr Fullerjoy' – *see* Walker, J. C.

'Mr Therm' – *see* Fraser, Eric George

MURRAY, Webster (fl. 1930s–d.1952). Joke cartoonist and illustrator. Webster Murray was born in Toronto, Canada, the son of a clergyman. He left school at 17 to join the Maclean Publishing Company as a junior artist while studying art in the evenings under a nephew of George Cruikshank who had also taught Charles Dana Gibson. Four years later he came to London and studied at St John's Wood Art School, the Slade and the Regent Street Polytechnic. During World War I he served in the infantry, attaining the rank of captain. After the war he started working for the new weekly, *Pan*, with GILBERT WILKINSON and others and then produced double-page drawings for *Tatler*. He then went to live in Paris for two years before returning to London to work for the *Sketch, Bystander, Men Only, Eagle* and others. In addition he designed advertisements for Erasmic, Schweppes, Amami Toilet Preparations, etc. In World War II he joined the RAF but later became an Air Raid Warden. He married the children's book illustrator Joan Kiddell-Monroe. Murray was also well-known for his portraits of leading society figures of the time. He died in February 1952.
PUB: [with A. St H. Brock] *Fireworks and Fêtes* (1946)
ILL: Apuleius, *The Golden Ass* (1946); Longinus, *Daphnis and Chloe* (1947); R. S. Young, *Cricket on the Green* (1947)

MUSGRAVE-WOOD, John Bertram 'Emmwood' (1915–99). Political cartoonist, caricaturist and painter. John Musgrave-Wood was born in Leeds, Yorkshire, on 22 February 1915 the son of Gerald Musgrave-Wood, a landscape painter, and one of three brothers, all artists. Educated at Leeds Modern School and Leeds College of Art, he worked at first in his father's studio. He then served as a steward on a cruise liner and began drawing the passengers. During World War II he joined the Duke of Cornwall's Light Infantry as a PT instructor. He was later commissioned in the Sherwood Foresters and while in India in 1941 volunteered to join Orde Wingate's Chindits, serving in Burma and China and attaining the rank of major. Demobilized in 1946 he produced a book (with Patrick Boyle, later 13th Earl of Cork and Orrery) about his experiences with the Chindits, signing himself 'JON'. He also studied painting at Goldsmith's (c. 1948) while contributing illustrations ('Emmwood's Aviary') and theatre caricatures to *Tatler & Bystander* (1948–54), taking over from TOM TITT. He also drew TV illustrations for *Punch*, showbusiness illustrations for the *Sun-*

day Express (from 1953) and political cartoons for the *Evening Standard* (1955–7), being succeeded by FRIELL. He was in addition Editor of the *Junior Express* newspaper and contributed to *Life* magazine. In 1957 he joined the *Daily Mail* as Political Cartoonist with ILLINGWORTH, taking over from him when he retired in 1969 and alternating with TROG. When Trog left after the paper merged with the *Daily Sketch* and went tabloid in 1971 he began to alternate his drawings with those of the *Sketch*'s former cartoonist, MAC. Emmwood worked mostly in pen, brush and ink. He was one of the founder members of the British Cartoonists' Association in 1966. John Musgrave-Wood retired in 1975 (being succeeded by MAC) and moved to France. He died in Vallabrix, near Uzes, on 30 August 1999.

PUB: [with P. Boyle] *Jungle, Jungle, Little Chindit* (1946)
COLL: UKCC; NPG
EXHIB: FR

'Didn't he invent the deckchair?'

David Myers, n.d.

MYERS, David (b. 1925). Editorial, joke and pocket cartoonist, illustrator and greetings card designer. David Myers was born in London on 8 December 1925, the son of Sidney Myers, a civil engineer, and served in the Royal Fusiliers (1944–7). After demobilization he attended the Sir John Cass Art School (1947–8) and St Martin's School of Art (1949–51). Then, when his fiancée moved to Australia, he followed and became Pocket Cartoonist on the *Melbourne Argus* (1951–2). Returning to London he got a job as OSBERT LANCASTER's holiday understudy on the *Daily Express* and later became Editorial Cartoonist on the *Evening News* (1965–8), tak-

ing over from LEE. He resigned when they refused to publish an anti-Enoch Powell cartoon and turned freelance, contributing cartoons to *Punch* (including covers), *People*, *Daily Mail*, *Daily Sketch*, *Daily Mirror* and *Star*, and also producing greetings cards and advertising work. He later devised and wrote the BBC TV children's series *Sebastian the Incredible Drawing Dog*. Voted CCGB Social and Political Cartoonist of the Year in 1966, he is also a former Treasurer of the Club. He uses Rexel Script pen nibs and Winsor & Newton indian ink on paper.
PUB: 'Sebastian the Incredible Drawing Dog' series (four titles, 1987)

N

NASH, John Northcote CBE RA SWE (1893–1977). Painter, illustrator, wood-engraver, art teacher, commercial artist and advertising cartoonist. John Nash was born in Kensington, London, on 11 April 1893, the son of William Harry Nash, a barrister, and the younger brother of the painter Paul Nash. Educated at Wellington College, he was self-taught as an artist. In 1913 he exhibited with his brother at the Dorien Leigh Galleries in London and was elected to the newly formed London Group (1914). During World War I he served with the Artists' Rifles in France (1916–18), being appointed an Official War Artist in 1918. After the war he contributed to *Land & Water* (theatrical cartoons), *Art & Letters*, *Owl* and others. He also produced comic illustrations for books, his first efforts – for L. de G. Sieveking's *Dressing Gowns and Glue* (1919) – being praised by MAX BEERBOHM. He later taught at the Ruskin School of Art (1922–7) and the RCA (1934–40, 1945–57). During World War II he was again appointed an Official War Artist (for the Admiralty) but later joined the Royal Marines. He is perhaps best known as a cartoonist for his comic advertisements for Shell, Guinness and others. Influenced by Edward Lear (who had been in love with his aunt Augusta Bethell), he worked mostly in line for his cartoon work. Primarily a landscape painter in oil and watercolour, he was also a wood-engraver (a founder member of the Society of Wood Engravers), botanical artist and

book illustrator. He was elected SWE (1921), ARA (1940) and RA (1951), and was created CBE in 1964. John Nash died on 23 September 1977.
ILL: More than 50 books including L. de G. Sieveking, *Dressing Gowns and Glue* (1919), *Bats in the Belfry* (1926); 'Belinda Blinders' [D. Coke], *The Nouveau Poor* (1921); W. Cobbett, *Rural Rides* (1930); *One Hundred and One Ballades* (1931); G. White, *The Natural History of Selborne* (1951); *Happy New Lear* (Guinness, 1959); R. Nett, *Thorntree Meadows* (1960)
EXHIB: Dorien Leigh Galleries (1913); GOU (1921), RA (retrospective 1967); NGG (Memorial 1978); MIN (1986)
COLL: T; V&A; MIN; many provincial galleries
LIT: J. Lewis, *John Nash, the Painter as Illustrator* (1978); Sir John Rothenstein, *John Nash* (1983): A. Freer, *John Nash: 'The Delighted Eye'* (1993); R. Blythe, *First Friends* (1999)

NB – *see* Bennett, David Neil and Bentley, Nicolas Clerihew

NEB – *see* Niebour, Ronald

NERMAN, Einar (1888–1980). Caricaturist, portrait painter, illustrator, ballet dancer and theatre designer. Einar Nerman was born in Norrköping, Sweden, and studied art in Stockholm (1905–8), in Paris with Matisse (1909–10) and under C. Wilhelmson (1911), but was mainly influenced by Beardsley. His first drawings were published in a Swedish magazine when he was aged 19 and he first visited London in 1919 as a ballet dancer at the London Coliseum. In 1921, after encouragement by Ivor Novello who had seen his décor for Rolf's Cabaret nightclub in Stockholm in 1918, he returned and produced striking black-and-white and black-and-red weekly theatre caricatures for the *Tatler* (later published as the collection *Darlings of the Gods*), monthly caricatures of singers and musicians for *Eve*, and sundry contributions to *Pearson's* and *London Life* until 1930. While in London he also painted murals for the Fifty-Fifty Club. He then went back to Sweden to work as a portrait painter (1930–39) before moving to New York to work for the *New Yorker* and to draw Hollywood stars for *Journal American*. His work was also published in *Thalia*, *Figaro*, *Pan* and *Söndags-Nisse*. He finally returned to Sweden in 1950 to concentrate on portrait painting, illustration and theatre design. In addition he drew advertisements for Abdulla

Einar Nerman, [Greta Garbo], *Caught in the Act*, 1976

Cigarettes (in black and red) and others. His wife was the daughter of the sculptor Christian Eriksson.

PUB: *Gosta Berlings-bilder* (1916), *30 Brekfort* (1920), *Bland Vackra Barn Och Fula Gubbar* (1929), *Darlings of the Gods* (1930), *Gubbar Med Rim* (1931), *Den Lustige Langdansen* (1947), *Middagen på Traneholm* (1968), *Divor Och Divaner* (1974), *Caught in the Act* (1976)
ILL: H. C. Anderson, *The Swineherd* (1924); E. M. Besly, *The Second Minuet* (1929); E. M. E. Wagner, *Den Namnlosa* (1929)
EXHIB: TM (1976)

NEWMAN, Nicholas Anthony (b. 1958). Joke, pocket and strip cartoonist, illustrator, journalist and scriptwriter. Nick Newman was born in Kuala Lumpur, Malaya, on 17 July 1958, the son of Tony Newman, an RAF officer. He read history at Oxford (1976–9), where he founded *Passing Wind* magazine (1976), and was a business journalist on *Management Today* (1979–83) before becoming a cartoonist. A self-taught artist, his first cartoon was published in *Yachting Monthly*. Pocket cartoonist on the *Sunday Times* (since 1989) he has also worked regularly for *Private Eye* (since 1981), drawing single cartoons and strips such as 'Battle for Britain', 'Dan Dire' and 'Snipcock & Tweed'. He also produced (with Ben Woolley) 'Megalomedia' for the *Guardian* and has contributed to the *Spectator*, *Independent Magazine*, *Yachting Monthly*, *Marxism Today*, *Wisden Cricket Monthly*, *Observer*, *Today*, *Times* Supplements and *Punch*. A scriptwriter for Central TV's SPITTING IMAGE (1983–8), he has co-written (with Ian Hislop) four *Murder Most Horrid* BBC TV shows for Dawn French, contributed sketches to ITV's *The Harry Enfield Show*, and written a Screen 1 film, *Gobble*, and scripts for *Clive Anderson Talks Back* and Channel 5's *The Jack Docherty Show* as well as a radio series, *Gush*. He was voted CAT Pocket Cartoonist of the Year (1997) and CAT Gag Cartoonist of the Year (1998). In addition *Murder Most Horrid* was voted People's Choice Comedy of the Year in 1996. Newman works in pen, ink, felt-tip, biro and 'anything else within arm's reach'.
PUB: *Newmanship* (1985), [with I. Hislop] *The Battle for Britain* (1987), *The Best of Nick Newman* (1990), [with D. AUSTIN and K. WILLIAMS] *Far from the Madding Cow!* (1990), (ed.) *Spitting Image: The Giant Komic Book* (1985), [with T. Davies] *Wallace and Gromit and the Lost Slipper* (1997), *Anoraknophobia* (1998), *Crackers in Space* (1999)

Nick Newman, *Spectator*, *c.* 1990

ILL: Private Eye, *The Thrid* [sic] *Book of Boobs* (1985); T. Dalrymple, *If Symptoms Persist* (1995), *If Symptoms Still Persist* (1996); S. Parke, *The Church-English Dictionary* (1991); *101 Things Jesus Never Said* (1992); C. Douglas and A. Nickolds, *Pod Almighty* (1996); R. Moore, *Behold the Front Page* (1993)
EXHIB: CG; BC; (with HECTOR BREEZE) JDG

NIBLETT, Frederick Drummond 'Nibs' RSA (fl. 1880s–after 1924). Caricaturist, illustrator, political cartoonist and painter. Nibs was born in Edinburgh and had an English father and an Irish mother. His uncle was Rear-Admiral Niblett. He attended Fettes College and, intended for the sea, then studied architecture and later designed posters before becoming a political cartoonist and caricaturist. He drew seven caricatures for *Vanity Fair* (notably an oft-reprinted portrait of Winston Churchill, 1911) and also contributed to *Crown* (1906–7), *Throne, Bystander, Printer's Pie, St Stephen's Review, Tatler, Evening News, Illustrated Sporting & Dramatic News, Sketchy Bits, Globe, Blighty, Penny Budget, Sunday Express, Daily Sketch* and *London Attractions*. He also painted portraits in oils. His black-and-red illustrated version of the poem by

Thomas Hood, 'The Dream of Eugene Aram', featuring the famous actor Henry Irving, was dedicated to John Lawrence Toole, of Toole's Theatre.
ILL: T. Hood, *The Henry Irving Dream of Eugene Aram* (1887); N. H. Willis, *Dulcima's Doom and Other Tales* (1890); C. Rae-Brown, *The Henry Irving Souvenir* (1905)
EXHIB: RSA (1882–4); RA
COLL: NPG (Duke of Windsor, 1st Earl of Birkenhead, 1911)

NIBS – *see* Niblett, Frederick Drummond

NICHOLSON, J. C. 'Nix' (1896–1937). Joke cartoonist. Nix began work as a cartoonist on the *Newcastle Evening Chronicle* and then the *Leeds Evening News* before joining the *News Chronicle*. He died on 18 September 1937 following a motor accident.

NICK – *see* Hobart, Nicholas

NIEBOUR, Ronald 'Neb' (*c.* 1902–72). Pocket, strip and sports cartoonist and art teacher. Ronald Niebour was educated at Barry County School with LESLIE ILLINGWORTH, but instead of following Illingworth to the local Cardiff Art School he went to sea and spent two years in the Merchant Navy. Encouraged by an uncle who was a Superintendent of Handicraft Teaching he then studied metalwork and woodwork and became a teacher of handicrafts at schools in Birmingham, Weymouth and Kendal for three years. Self-taught as an artist, he then drew football cartoons for the *Barry Dock News* and *Cardiff Evening Express*, became Sports Cartoonist on the *Oxford Mail* (drawing in the style of TOM WEBSTER), and was later staff artist on the *Birmingham Evening Dispatch & Gazette*. He joined the *Daily Mail* in 1938, working at first as an illustrator for features such as the Women's Page and Gardening Notes. However, he is best known for the regular pocket cartoons he began to draw for the paper during World War II, continuing until his retirement on 1 December 1960. He also drew advertisements for Winsor & Newton amongst others and wrote articles. Neb worked with a brush and drew his pocket cartoons about a foot square. He specialized in characters with large bulbous noses. Cartoons by Neb and Illingworth were found in a file in Hitler's Chancellery after the war. Ronald Niebour died at his home in Benajaràfe, near Malaga, Spain, on 18 July 1972.

PUB: [with ILLINGWORTH, MOON, LEE and GITTINS] *400 Famous Cartoons* (1944)
COLL: UKCC

NIX – *see* Nicholson, J. C.

NOBODY, A – *see* Browne, Gordon Frederick

NORFIELD, Edgar George 'EN' FRSA (fl. 1930s–d. 1977). Joke and strip cartoonist, painter, illustrator and writer. Edgar Norfield studied at the Cambridge School of Art, and in London and Paris. He drew cartoons for *Night & Day, Strand, Men Only, London Opinion* (including covers) and *Punch*. In addition he wrote articles for *London Opinion* and contributed a glamour art series, 'Great Moments in a Girl's Life', to the magazine. He also drew strips for children's comics in the 1930s, such as 'Charlie Chick' for *Boys' and Girls' Daily Mail*, and painted in oils and watercolour. An admirer of C. E. BROCK, he owned Brock's desk easel. Elected FRSA, he was a member of the Savage Club and the London Sketch Club.
PUB: *Hic, Haec, Hock!* (1934), *Steady, Boys, Steady* (1943), [with C. R. Benstead] *Alma Mater* (1944), *Beautiful You* (c. 1947), *Mother of Parliaments* (1948), *Gyp's Hour of Bliss* (n.d.)
ILL: L. Dutton, *Rags, M.D.* (1933); J. Gibbons, *Roll On, Next War!* (1935); 'Globetrotter', *Tips and Gratuities* (1938); R. Arkell, *War Rumours* (1939), *Green Fingers Again* (1942), *And a Green Thumb* (1950); P. Gallico, *The Small Miracle* (1951); L. Carroll, *Alice in Wonderland* (n.d.)
EXHIB: RI

O

'Oddentifications' – *see* Wren, Ernest Alfred

'Old Bill' – *see* Bairnsfather, Charles Bruce

OLLIE – *see* Collins, Clive Hugh Austin

ORPEN, Sir William Newenham Montague RA RWS RHA RI NEAC (1878–1931). Painter and caricaturist. William Orpen was born in Stillorgan, Co. Dublin, on 27 November 1878, the son of Arthur Herbert Orpen, a Protestant solicitor and amateur watercolourist. He was the younger brother of Richard Caulfield Orpen RHA, architect and watercolourist, President of the Architectural Association of Ireland and Governor of the National Gallery of Ireland, and was the brother-in-law of Sir William Rothenstein NEAC (Principal of the Royal College of Art). Leaving school at the age of 12 he studied at the Metropolitan School of Art, Dublin (1890–97), and the Slade (1897–9), where fellow students included Augustus John and Wyndham Lewis. Intending to work as a caricaturist but failing to be accepted by *Punch* he returned to Dublin to teach part-time at the Dublin School of Art (1902–14) while also exhibiting paintings at NEAC (1900), the Royal Academy (from 1908) and elsewhere. He then ran a short-lived art school in Chelsea with Augustus John (1903–7), helped set up the Chenil Gallery (1906) and was a founder member of the National Portrait Society (1911). In World War I he served in the army (1916) and was later appointed an Official War Artist (1917–19). The caricatures he drew at the Paris Peace Conference in 1919 were widely admired. However, though he was financially very successful in his main occupation as a portrait painter (reputedly earning more than £54,000 in 1929 alone) his technique of using photographs as an aid did not meet with universal approval. Indeed, he was himself caricatured 'working in his own way' by MAX BEERBOHM (Orpen is depicted painting a portrait of a man seated with his back to the artist and reading a newspaper). Knighted in 1918, he was elected ARA (1910), RA (1919), was President of the Society of Sculptors, Painters & Gravers (1921) and declined the Presidency of the Royal Academy. A member of the Athenaeum, Garrick, Savile and Arts Clubs, he was Chairman of the Chelsea Arts Club (1929). He married Grace Knewstub, the daughter of Rossetti's secretary. Sir William Orpen died, probably of alcohol poisoning, in London on 29 September 1931 aged 53.

PUB: *An Onlooker in France 1917–1919* (1921), *Stories of Old Ireland and Myself* (1924)
EXHIB: Agnew's (1918); RA, B; M (Memorial 1933); Knoedler Gallery, New York (Memorial 1932); ROI; NEAC; RSA
COLL: T; NPG; IWM; NGI; provincial museums
LIT: R. Pickle, *Sir William Orpen* (1923); P. G. Konody and S. Dark, *Sir William Orpen, Artist and Man* (1952)

ORR, Cecil Edward Parker (1909–65). Joke, political and strip cartoonist, poster artist, caricaturist, illustrator and writer. Cecil Orr was born in Glasgow on 29 September 1909, the son of a fish and poultry merchant. He was educated at Gourock and Greenock High Schools. At the age of 11 he drew posters for local cinemas and shops in Gourock and produced and illustrated the school magazine. After studying at Glasgow School of Art for two years he began drawing illustrations for Collins' boys' annuals and for Osborne, Peacock & Co., and turned professional at the age of 18, joining Associated Scottish Newspapers (1928–41) as illustrator and cartoonist. During World War II he served in the RAF (enlisting in 1941). Orr was a prolific artist working for *Radio Times*, *Sunday Mail*, *Red Poppy*, *Sketch*, *Glasgow Daily Record* (political cartoons) and numerous children's comics (e.g. *June*, *Swift*). He also produced posters for the theatre and the Scottish Department of Agriculture, designed stage scenery, drew advertisements and caricatures, and illustrated children's books. Orr worked in line, wash and colour and used Gillott 290 and 170 pens with ball-pointed writing nibs such as Waverley or Ruby for lettering and Drawlet for anything larger. He died on 23 August 1965.
ILL: L. Lane, *How to become a Comedian* (1945)
COLL: BFI

OSPOVAT, Henry (1877–1909). Illustrator, caricaturist and painter. Born in Russia, the son of a Jewish Talmudist, Henry Ospovat emigrated with his family to Manchester. He studied at Manchester School of Art and in 1897 won a scholarship to study lithography at the South Kensington Schools. His first commissions were for book illustration and for magazines such as the *Idler*. In *Books and Persons*, Arnold Bennett said that he was 'among the few who can illustrate a serious author without insulting him'. He later developed a distinctive style of caricature and his drawings were published in the *Man-chester Guardian* (e.g. one of Harry Lauder, 1909) and elsewhere. He also drew in chalk and painted. A planned book of caricatures, 'Stars of the Music Hall Stage', remained incomplete when he died in London, aged 32, on 2 January 1909.
ILL: W. Shakespeare, *Sonnets* (1899), *Songs* (1901); M. Arnold, *Poems* (1900); C. E. Maud, *Heroines of Poetry* (1903); R. Browning, *Men and Women* (1903); *The Song of Songs* (1906)
EXHIB: BG; NEAC
COLL: BM; V&A
LIT: O. Onions, *The Work of Henry Ospovat* (1911)

'Our Dumb Blonde' – *see* Ferrier, Arthur

OWEN, William (1869–1957). Political and joke cartoonist, illustrator, commercial artist, journalist and broadcaster. Will Owen was born in Malta, the son of Thomas Owen, a British naval officer (later an Engineer Commander), and returned to England in 1870. He was educated at the Mathematical School in Rochester, Kent, and studied at the Lambeth School of Art under Thomas McKeggie and at Heatherley's. He began work at the Post Office Savings Bank's headquarters in London (*c.* 1885–*c.* 1912), where a fellow clerk was the future novelist W. W. Jacobs. They became lifelong friends and after their first joint efforts in the *Idler*, Owen illustrated (from 1899) many of Jacobs' stories in the *Strand* magazine in a partnership that lasted more than 40 years (their last joint work was in 1939). He moved to France *c.* 1912 but returned to the UK when war broke out. Owen also contributed (from 1890) cartoons and illustrations to *Bystander*, *Girl's Realm*, *Grand*, *Graphic*, *Passing Show*, *Holly Leaves*, *Humorist*, *London Magazine*, *London Opinion*, *Pears Annual*, *Pearson's*, *Sketch*, *Pick-Me-Up*, *Printer's Pie*, *Punch*, *Temple*, *Windsor Magazine*, *Sketch* and *Tatler*, amongst others. In addition he drew the character 'Ally Sloper' in *Ally Sloper's Half Holiday* for a while after the death of its most famous artist, W. G. Baxter before W. F. THOMAS took over. Influenced by PHIL MAY and JOHN HASSALL, he also designed postcards and posters, his most famous creations being the (originally ragged and barefooted) Bisto Kids in the gravy advertisement 'Ah, Bisto!' (1919) and 'Bovril puts BEEF into you' (1925). He also produced advertisements for Kodak, Nestlé, Oxo, Sunlight Soap, Vim, Erasmic, Lux, Brown & Poulson Cornflour, Watson's No. 10 Whisky and others, designed wallpaper (especially nursery friezes), drew

colour covers for Woolworth's 'Readers Library' and designed comic postcards for Tuck, Davidson Bros, Meissner & Buch, Wrench and David Allen (postcard versions of his theatre posters). In addition he was a broadcaster on radio, notably as 'Father William' on the BBC's *Children's Hour*. He was a member of the Yorick Club. Will Owen died on 14 April 1957.
PUB: *Alleged Humour* (1917), *Three Jolly Sailors and Me* (1919), *Old London Town* (1921), *Potted London* (1934), *Mr Peppercorn* (1940)

ILL: W. W. Jacobs, *A Master of Craft* (1900), *At Sunwich Port* (1902), *Odd Crafts* (1903), *Dialstone Lane* (1904), *Short Cruises* (1907), *Salthaven* (1908), *Sailors' Knots* (1909); A. E. Copping, *Jolly in Germany* (1910); J. K. Jerome, *A Miscellany of Sense and Nonsense* (1923); D. McCulloch [Children's Hour's 'Uncle Mac'], *Gardening Guyed* (1931); B. S. Jones, *What's the Buzz?* (1943), *What's the Dope?* (1944)
EXHIB: BSG; Royal Cambrian Academy
COLL: BM; V&A

P

PAL – *see* Paléologue, Jean de

PALÉOLOGUE, Jean de 'PAL' (1860–1942). Caricaturist, illustrator and poster artist. Jean de Paléologue was born in Bucharest, Romania, and studied in England. His drawings appeared in the *Strand Magazine* (e.g. the series 'Pal's Puzzle Page') in the early 1890s and a number of his caricatures were published in *Vanity Fair* (including a watercolour of the magazine's leading artist, SIR LESLIE WARD, published on 23 November 1889). He then moved to France and was a poster artist and humorous illustrator working for *La République* before moving to the USA where he began working for the film industry *c.* 1900. PAL also contributed to *Le Rire* (1896–8), *La Bicyclette* (1894), *Le Petit Bleu* (1898), *Le Frou-Frou* (1902), *Sans Gêne* (1902), *Au Quartier Latin* and others. Jean de Paléologue died in Miami, Florida.
COLL: NPG

PAPAS, William (b. 1927). Political and strip cartoonist, illustrator and painter. Bill Papas was born on 15 July 1927 in Ermelo in the Transvaal, South Africa, the son of Kostas Papas, a baker and restaurant owner. After World War II he studied art in Johannesburg, at Beckenham Art School, Kent, and at St Martin's (1947–9). He then returned to South Africa to work as an artist and reporter on the *Cape Times* (in which his first cartoon was published in 1951), *Johannesburg Star* and *Drum Magazine* (1952–8), leaving to become a farmer and timber trucker. Papas came back to the UK in 1959, succeeding

Low drawing political cartoons for the *Guardian* (1963–9, being succeeded in turn by LES GIBBARD) as well as a strip cartoon about a mouse, Theodore. He also contributed to the *Sunday Times* (1960–65) and *Punch* (1959–70, including covers). Banned from South Africa in 1980 because of his cartoons on apartheid, he went to Greece on a sabbatical from the *Guardian* in 1969 and stayed till 1983, producing book illustrations and exhibiting his artwork. He then moved to Geneva and thence to Portland, Oregon, in 1984 and has since produced illustrations and pen-and-ink and watercolour pictures of American cities. In 1992 he began a self-syndication service and intermittently supplies political cartoons to *Los Angeles Times*, *Newsday*, *Kansas City Star* and other US and Canadian papers. He was one of the founder members of the British Cartoonists' Association in 1966. He works with pen and indian ink and for his watercolours uses Arches cold-pressed watercolour paper.
PUB: [with A. Sussens] *Under the Tablecloth* (1952), *The Press* (1964), [with G. Moorhouse] *The Church* (1965), [with N. Shrapnel] *Parliament* (1966), *Tasso* (1967), *No Mules* (1967), *A Letter from India* (1968), *A Letter from Israel* (1968), *Taresh the Tea Planter* (1968), *Theodore, or the Mouse Who Wanted to Fly* (1969), *Elias the Fisherman* (1970), *The Monk and the Goat* (1971), *The Long-Haired Donkey* (1972), *The Most Beautiful Child* (1973), *The Zoo* (1974), *People of Old Jerusalem* (1980)
ILL: Many books including G. Mikes, *Jamaica* (1965), *How to Be Affluent* (1966); T. Papas, *Mr*

Nero (1966); J. Stone, *The Law* (1966); M. Muggeridge, *In the Valley of the Restless Mind* (1977); C. S. Lewis, *The Screwtape Letters* (1979); A. Oz, *Soumchi* (1980); T. Papas, *Papas' Greece* (1997)

EXHIB: Greek Centre; Indian Tea Centre; Dowmunt Gallery; BCO, Athens; Gallerie Kourd, Athens; Old City Museum, Jerusalem; Galerie Weber, Geneva; O'Grady Galleries, Chicago; Senate Office Building, Washington DC; Gusman Cultural Center, Miami; Plaza of the Americas, Dallas; C. G. Rein Galleries, Houston; Calgary Stampede, Canada; LA 90 Art Fair, Los Angeles; Oregon Historical Society, Oregon

COLL: UKCC; NPG; V&A; Vorres Museum, Athens; Old City Museum, Jerusalem

PARKES, Terence 'Larry' (b. 1927). Joke cartoonist and illustrator. Born in Birmingham on 19 November 1927, the son of a welding foreman in a motor-car factory, Larry studied at the College of Arts & Crafts in Birmingham. He spent his National Service in the Royal Artillery (1946–8) and taught art at Lincoln Road Secondary Modern School in Peterborough, Lincolnshire (1951–4), before turning freelance in 1957, working for *Punch, Birmingham Evening Mail, Soldier, Private Eye, Oldie, Guardian* and *Daily Telegraph* as well as working in advertising promoting Double Diamond, Newcastle Brown and Heineken beers amongst others. He has also produced cartoons and commentary for Granada TV's *Afternoon Edition* (1963–4) and for a short while (1973–4) was a scenery painter in Joan Littlewood's Theatre Royal in London. His pseudonym derives from Larry Parks, star of the film *The Al Jolson Story*, which was shown in Peterborough when he was teaching there in 1954 – the pupils' nickname for their art master stuck. Elected an Honorary Fellow of Birmingham Polytechnic (now the University of the West Midlands) in 1991, he began experimenting with sculptured clay cartoons on art themes in 1992. Larry's cartoons never have captions and he draws without roughs on 10 × 8-in. typing paper using a Rolinx dip pen and Rotring black ink (sometimes also watercolour). An admirer of Daumier, Lautrec and Van Gogh, his own work has been praised by Charles Schulz and Harpo Marx. 'His work demonstrates that perfect marriage between style of idea and style of drawing' (HEWISON). He is perhaps best known for his art (particularly

Larry (Terence Parkes), *Punch, c.* 1978

'Rodin' sculpture) jokes and those featuring his 'Man' character.

PUB: *Man in Apron* (1959), *More Man in Apron* (1960), *Man in Office* (1961), *Man at Work* (1962), *Man at Large* (1964), *Man and Wife* (1965), *Man's Best Friend* (1966), *Man in Garden* (1966), *More Man in Garden* (1967), *The Larry Omnibus* (1967), *Man in Motor Car* (1968), *Man in School* (1972), *Man on Holiday* (1973), *Larry* (1974), *Larry's Art Collection* (1977), *Larry on Art* (1978), *Best of Larry* (1983), *Larry's Garden Lot* (1988), *Larry's DIY Man* (1989), *Larry at War* (1995)

ILL: Many books including J. Herriot, *Vets Might Fly* (1976); E. Harlow (ed.), *101 Instant Games* (1977); G. Mikes, *How to be Poor* (1983); K. W. Parsons, *The Way of the Wally* (1984); S. Pile, *The Return of Heroic Failures* (1988); *Private Eye* 'Colemanballs' series (8 books 1982–96); J. Robertson, *Any Fool Can Keep a Secret* (1989)

EXHIB: L; CBG; CG

COLL: V&A; BM; EU; UKCC

LIT: [with M. Bryant] *Larry on Larry* (1994)

PARKINSON, William (fl. 1890–1900) – *see* Bryant & Heneage

PARTRIDGE, Sir John Bernard RI NEAC (1861–1945). Political and joke cartoonist, caricaturist, illustrator and painter. Bernard Partridge was born in London on 11 October 1861, the youngest son of Professor Richard Partridge FRS, President of the Royal College of Surgeons and Professor of Anatomy at the Royal Academy, and Fanny Turner. His uncle was John Partridge, Portrait Painter Extraordinary to Queen Victoria. Educated at Stonyhurst College (with Sir Arthur Conan Doyle), he worked for six months in the offices of the architect H. Hansom (son of the inventor of the Hansom cab) and then spent two years with Lavers, Barraud & Westlake, Ecclesiastical Designers, producing altar-pieces, stained glass, etc. He then studied decorative painting under Philip Westlake (the brother of one of the company's partners), before attending Heatherley's (briefly) and the West London School of Art. He worked at first as a decorator of church interiors and then as a professional actor (under the pseudonym 'Bernard Gould'), appearing in the first production of George Bernard Shaw's *Arms and the Man* amongst others. His first cartoon was published in *Moonshine* and he also contributed cartoons and illustrations to *Judy* (from 1885), *Playgoer, Black & White, Illustrated Bits, Illustrated London News, Lika Joko, Society, Vanity Fair* (caricatures as 'JBP'), *Illustrated Sporting & Dramatic News, Lady's Pictorial, New Budget, Pick-Me-Up, Quiver* and the *Sketch*. Recommended by George du Maurier, he began drawing for *Punch* in February 1891, and subsequently worked for the magazine for over 50 years, producing political and joke cartoons as well as theatre caricatures. He joined the staff in 1891, becoming Second Cartoonist in 1899, and succeeded LINLEY SAMBOURNE as Cartoonist (1910–45), being himself followed by E. H. SHEPARD. In addition he drew advertisements for Lever Brothers, Selfridges and others, designed postcards for Blue Cross Quarantine Kennels during World War I (for soldiers bringing their pet dogs home) and some of his political cartoons were issued as postcards by Wrench. He also exhibited oil paintings, watercolours and pastels and was elected NEAC (1893) and RI (1896). A fine draughtsman in the tradition of Tenniel, he was also influenced by Du Maurier and the book illustrator Hugh Thomson. Ellwood saw him as being, with TOWNSEND and PEGRAM, 'one of a great trio of pen draughtsmen whose work is peculiarly English'. He disliked using more than two figures in a cartoon and tended to draw grandiose, statuesque figures in classical poses: 'His cartoons were theatrical, whereas Sambourne's, and still more RAVEN HILL's, were dramatic' (Price). He mostly worked in pen and ink on Smith's Board covered in 'O.W.' paper (usually 10 × 13 in.). His ideas were often supplied for him and, though always a reliable artist (he never got uniforms wrong), he always felt his work was rushed to meet deadlines. A member of the Chelsea Arts Club and the Athenaeum Club, he was knighted in 1925. Bernard Partridge died in London on 9 August 1945.

PUB: *Punch Drawings* (1921), *Fifty Years with Punch* (1946)

ILL: J. K. Jerome, *Stageland* (1899); F. Anstey, *Voces Populi* (1890), *The Travelling Companions* (1899), *Mr Punch's Pocket Ibsen* (1893), *Under the Rose* (1894), *Lyre and Lancet* (1895), *Puppets at Large* (1897), *A Bayard from Bengal* (1902); M. Wyman, *My Flirtations* (1892); A. Dobson, *Proverbs in Porcelain* (1893); J. M. Barrie, *Tommy and Grizel* (1901); R. Browning, *Rabbi Ben Ezra and Other Poems* (1915)

EXHIB: RA; RI; NEAC; FAS (1902, Memorial 1946)

COLL: BM; V&A; NPG; UKCC; IWM; Stonyhurst School

LIT: D. P. Whiteley, *Bernard Partridge and Punch* (1952)

PAV – *see* Minet, Francis

PAYNE, Charlie Johnson 'Snaffles' (1884–1967). Sporting artist, caricaturist, writer and journalist. Charlie Payne was born in Leamington Spa, Warwickshire, on 17 January 1884, the son of a bootmaker. A self-taught artist, he began selling hunting and horseracing drawings after spending three years as a gunner in the Royal Garrison Artillery (1902–5). Caricatures drawn by him under the pseudonym 'Snaffles' (from the character in Surtees' comic hunting books) first appeared in the *Bystander* in 1907 and the following year prints of his drawing were issued by Fores. He also contributed to *Illustrated Sporting & Dramatic News* (from 'Hunting Types', 1910), *Graphic* (signing himself 'Charlie Payne'), *Punch* and others. In World War I he served as a mechanic in the Royal Naval Auxiliary Service and the RNVR, becoming a lieutenant in the Camouflage Department (1917), and was European Correspondent for the *Graphic*. After the war he worked mostly for

Illustrated Sporting & Dramatic News until 1932. During World War II he designed aerodrome camouflage and then served in the Home Guard. He was influenced by his friend CECIL ALDIN and H. M. BATEMAN, and was a member of the Fine Art Trade Guild. Snaffles died in Wiltshire on 30 December 1967. He is not to be confused with 'Snaffle', the writer Robert Dunkin.

PUB: *My Sketchbook in the Shiny* (1930), *'Osses and Obstacles* (1935), *More Bandobast* (1936), *A Half Century of Memories* (1949), *Four Legged Friends and Acquaintances* (1951), *I've Heard the Revelly* (1953)

ILL: G. Brooke, *Horse Lovers* (1928); M. J. Farrell, *Red Letter Days* (1933); J. K. Stanford, *Mixed Bagmen* (1947)

EXHIB: Court Gallery; Malcolm Innes Gallery; McDonald Booth Gallery; Alpine Club Gallery

COLL: British Sporting Art Trust; IWM

LIT: J. Welcome and R. Collins, *Snaffles: The Life and Work of Charlie Johnson Payne* (1987)

PEAKE, Mervyn Lawrence (1911–68) – *see* Bryant & Heneage

PEARS, Charles ROI RSMA (1873–1958). Marine painter, joke cartoonist, caricaturist, illustrator and author. Charles Pears was born in Pontefract, Yorkshire, on 9 September 1873, the son of G. W. Pears, an amateur painter and musician. He was educated at East Hardwick & Pontefract College and in 1895 contributed his first theatrical sketches to the local weekly, the *Yorkshireman*. After having some drawings published in the *Idler* and *Judy* he won a competition organized by the *Studio* magazine and illustrated a book by the actor Albert Chevalier (best known for singing 'My Old Dutch'). Moving to London in 1897, he was introduced into the art world by Chevalier and in 1898 succeeded S. H. SIME as theatrical caricaturist for *Pick-Me-Up*. A collection of his drawings from the journal, featuring 20 famous men (e.g. Balfour, W. G. Grace, Mark Twain) and 100 theatre figures, was published in 1902. He also contributed to *Punch* (from 1897), *Dome, Butterfly, Bystander, Cassell's, Girl's Realm, Rions, Illustrated London News, London, London Opinion, Longbow, Ludgate Magazine, Nash's, Gentlewoman, Yellow Book, Odd Volume, Pears Annual, Pearson's, Printer's Pie, Quartier Latin, Sketch, Strand, Tatler* and the *Windsor Magazine*. Pears also designed post-

ers for Cunard Steamship Co., London Underground, Empire Marketing Board and others, and drew advertisements for Fry's Chocolate (e.g. 'Far Too Good to Share'), etc. In addition he painted maritime scenes, later founding the Society of Marine Artists and becoming its President. A member of the Royal Cruising Club, he was elected ROI in 1913. During World War I he served in the Royal Marines and was Official War Artist to the Admiralty (1915–18) and again in World War II (1940–45). Charles Pears died on 28 January 1958.

PUB: *'Men': Drawn and Rhymed About* (1902), *Mr Punch's Book for Children* (1902), *Mr Punch's New Book for Children* (1903), *From the Thames to the Seine* (1910), *From the Thames to the Netherlands* (1914), *South Coast Cruising* (1931), *Yachting on the Sunshine Coast* (1932)

ILL: G. James, *Toby and His Little Dog Tan* (1903); W. M. Thackeray, *Some Round-About Papers* (1908); R. H. Dana, *Two Years Before the Mast* (1911); J. Masefield, *Salt-Water Poems and Ballads* (1911); C. Dickens, *Works* (1913); R. P. Gossop, *In the Press and Out Again* (1913); P. F. Westerman, *Sea-Scouts All* (1920); L. Carroll, *Alice's Adventures in Wonderland* (1922)

EXHIB: RA; ROI; FAS; NEAC; RI; L

COLL: V&A; IWM; THG

LIT: J. A. Hammerton, *Humorists of the Pencil* (1905)

PEATTIE, Charles William Davidson (b. 1958). Strip cartoonist and painter. Charles Peattie was born in Manchester on 3 May 1958 and attended St Martin's School of Art. After a successful period as a portrait painter he became a full-time cartoonist creating (with Mark Warren) the strips 'Ad Nauseam' for *Direction* (1986–8), 'Dick' for *Melody Maker* (1985–8) and 'Celeb', a sympathetic depiction of an unashamed and unrepentant has-been rock star, for *Private Eye* (since 1987). However, he is perhaps best known as the creator (with Russell Taylor) of the 'Alex' strip about Alex Masterley, who first appeared in 1987 as a 25-year-old merchant-banker whizz kid notable for an impressive degree of self-confidence, intolerance and gadget-obsession and who has slowly metamorphosed over the years. The series began in the *London Daily News* (February–July 1987), moved to the *Independent* (1987–91) and has been running in the *Daily Telegraph* since 1991. Peattie uses a dip-pen and ink on white marker-pad paper and describes his influences as 'too numerous to mention, but

they include MICHAEL HEATH, Robert Crumb, RONALD SEARLE, CARL GILES, Clare Brétecher, Parker and Hart'.
PUB: [with M. Warren] *The Pocketsized Dick* (1987), *Celeb* (1991); [with R. Taylor] 'Alex' series (from 1987), *The Full Alex: Collected Strips 1987–98*
EXHIB: CG; BC
COLL: V&A; IWM

PEGRAM, Frederick RI (1870–1937). Illustrator, joke cartoonist and painter. Fred Pegram was born at 22 Cardington St, Somers Town, London, on 19 December 1870, the son of Alfred Pegram, a cabinet maker, and Alice Freeman. He was the first cousin of C. E. BROCK and H. M. BROCK (who later married Pegram's sister Doris). He may also have been related to Henry Alfred Pegram RA. At the age of 15 he studied at the Westminster School of Art (fellow students included Henry Tonks, Aubrey Beardsley and MAURICE GREIFFENHAGEN) and after contributing theatrical sketches to the *Pall Mall Gazette* (1886) became a staff artist for the *Gazette* and *Queen* at the age of 16. In 1890 he spent three months at the Académie Julian in Paris, returning to draw cartoons and illustrations for *Pictorial World, Illustrated London News, Gentlewoman, Black & White, Cassell's, Daily Chronicle, Fun, Harmsworth, Holly Leaves, Idler, Illustrated Sporting & Dramatic News, Judy, Lady's Pictorial, Minster, New Budget, Printer's Pie, Queen, Quiver, Tatler* and *Punch* (1894–1937). In addition he designed advertisements for Mackintosh's Toffee, Player's, Ronuk Polish, Selfridges, etc., and created the famous stripy-dressed 'Kodak Girl'. During World War I he served as a Special Constable at Buckingham Palace. Influenced by Edwin Abbey, he admired BATEMAN and was himself greatly admired by BRADSHAW ('He never did a slipshod drawing') and was later one of the Advisory Staff for Bradshaw's Press Art School. 'Even if his jokes and his milieu became increasingly stereotyped, his draughtsmanship as late as the early Thirties was still capable of giving a thrill of pleasure' (Price). He used a Brandaner 515w nib and also painted, drew portraits in pencil, watercolour, chalk and pastel, and etched. A founder member of the Chelsea Arts Club and later its President (1904), he was elected RI (1925). He married Jane Gray, sister of the artist Ronald Gray RWS NEAC, who modelled for his women. He was also an extremely good fencer and was invited to represent England in Paris. Fred Pegram died of lung cancer at his home at 65 Earls Court Square, London, on 23 August 1937 aged 66.
PUB: *The Man Who Wishes He Had Not Married* (1888)
ILL: Many books including B. Disraeli, *Sybil* (1895); F. Marryat, *Mr Midshipman Easy* (1896), *Masterman Ready* (1897); F. Mathew, *The Rising of the Moon* (1898); Sir W. Scott, *The Bride of Lammermoor* (1898); Sir W. Besant, *The Orange Girl* (1899); M. Edgeworth, *Ormond* (1900); C. Dickens, *Martin Chuzzlewit* (1900)
EXHIB: RA; RI; FAS (Memorial 1938)
COLL: V&A; BM; THG

PETERSON, Ian (fl. 1930s–40s). Joke cartoonist and illustrator. Ian Peterson was born in the north of England and studied organic chemistry at the Faculty of Technology, Manchester University, and worked briefly at first as a research chemist. He then joined the advertising department of an engineering firm and ran his own agency for a short time before moving to London as a freelance advertising and editorial illustrator. He next moved to Paris where he remained for nine years, working for *Ric-et-Rac, Candide, Intransigeant, Le Rire, Continental Daily Mail* and other publications. He returned to Britain on the outbreak of World War II and, deemed unfit for military service, continued to draw cartoons for *Men Only, London Opinion, Punch, Sunday Chronicle, Razzle* (including covers), etc., and to illustrate children's books. BRADSHAW has said of him: 'he works with a very sure line, and . . . varies delicacy with strength in a most attractive way. The precision with which he draws background details is almost scientific in its accuracy, although he cheerfully disguises this integrity when he has a broadly humorous message to put over.'

PETT, William Norman (1891–1960). Joke and strip cartoonist. Norman Pett was born in Birmingham on 12 April 1891, the son of John Ernest Pett, a jeweller. He studied with the Press Art School run by PERCY BRADSHAW and later taught art at Moseley Road Junior Art School in Birmingham, where one of his pupils was PETER MADDOCKS, and the Birmingham Central School of Art. He also contributed cartoons to *Punch, Passing Show* and others and drew strips for children's comics such as *Comet, Knockout* and *Girl*. However, he is best known as the creator of 'Jane' for the *Daily Mirror*. Jane was originally based on Pett's wife Mary, who in real life had actually received a telegram asking her to look after a distinguished visitor who spoke no English, 'Count Fritz von Pumpernickel' – who turned out to be a red dachshund. At first a single-panel weekly series, 'Jane's Journal' began on 5 December 1932 and featured a Bright Young Thing and her dog. It later became a daily multi-panel strip. When writer Don Freeman was engaged in December 1938 – introducing the idea of the character playfully shedding clothing during her adventures – and professional model Christabel Drewry (whom Pett met at the Birmingham Central School of Art) took over as Jane (1940), the feature became immensely popular. During World War II Jane's appeal was such that Hannen Swaffer, talking of her influence on the RAF in 1943, commented: 'The morale of the RAF depended on how much clothing she had left on in the *Daily Mirror* that morning. A legend grew up that Jane always stripped for victory. She was the anti-Gremlin.' She even appeared emblazoned on aircraft, tanks and submarines, and specially drawn whole-page 'Jane' cartoons appeared as educational features in the Combined Operations magazine *Bulldozer*. She was also published in *Union Jack* and *Stars & Stripes*. Always accompanied by her faithful dachshund, Fritz (named after one of Pett's own dachshunds which he used to breed), she was in love with Secret Service officer Georgie Porgie. When Pett retired, his assistant Mike Hubbard took over the drawing (1 May 1948) until the strip's final episode on 10 October 1959 (*see also* GAMMIDGE). Pett himself went on to create a similar striptease character, 'Susie' (who had a white poodle), for the *Sunday Dispatch* in 1948 and continued to draw for children's comics until his death. 'Jane' calendars were also produced (1947–9) as well as merchandise such as belts and ties, and in addition she appeared on stage, in an Eros film, *The Adventures of Jane* (1949), starring Christabel Drewry, and more recently in *Jane and the Lost City* (1988) and the BBC South TV documentary *Jane* (1989). Pett was the brother-in-law of advertising artist John E. Keay. He worked in pen, ink and watercolour, was an accomplished draughtsman and preferred drawing from life. He was a member of the Bullfrogs Club. Norman Pett died in Keymer, near Brighton, on 16 February 1960.

PUB: *Pett's Annual* (1944), *Jane's Summer Idle* (1946), *Jane's Journal* (1946), *Jane on the Sawdust Trail* (1947), *Another Journal by Pett* (1948), *Susie of the Sunday Dispatch* (1956), *Farewell to Jane* (1960), *Jane at War* (1976)
EXHIB: CAT
COLL: NAAFI Museum, Camberwell (Jane watercolour)

PETTIWARD, Daniel (b. 1913). Painter, writer, broadcaster, illustrator and joke cartoonist. Daniel Pettiward was born in Polzeath, Cornwall, on 7 November 1913, the third child of a well-to-do landowning father who was a gifted amateur draughtsman, and the younger brother of ROGER PETTIWARD ('Paul Crum'). He was educated at Eton and University College, Oxford, where he was President of his college Athletic Club. During World War II he served in the RASC (1940–46) and later attended Salisbury School of Art. In the 1950s he invented 'Non-Art' ('a guide to becoming a successful cartoonist without actually being able to draw') and wrote and illustrated a number of articles on the subject for *Punch* (to which he contributed in several disciplines from 1937 to 1970) and *Young Elizabethan*, which were later collected into a book, *Money for Jam*. Described by FOUGASSE (rather to his annoyance) as being 'of the tribe of Thurber', he has worked in pen, pen and wash, watercolour and gouache, and admires Crum, HOFFNUNG and Rowlandson. In the late 1960s he gave up drawing for publication – mainly out of pique as *Punch* and others considered his 'non-art' cartoons funnier than his properly drawn ones. In 1970, though continuing as Drama Critic for the *Southern Evening Echo*, he abandoned writing as well, in favour of painting, cartooning and caricaturing for sale to the general public. Several combined and solo exhibitions of his work have been held and for 10 years he was a regular contributor to the Royal Institute of Painters in Watercolours exhibitions at the Mall Galleries.
PUB: [illustrated by P. Crum] *Truly Rural* (1939), *Money For Jam* (1956)
ILL: V. Graham, *A Cockney in the Country* (1958)
EXHIB: RSW; Salisbury Playhouse; Heron Gallery; The North Canonry, Salisbury; Hemyngsby, Salisbury

PETTIWARD, Roger 'Paul Crum' (1906–42). Joke cartoonist, caricaturist and painter. Roger Pettiward was born on 25 November 1906 in

'I don't know what to do with Catchpole, sir: he just keeps smiling through.'

Paul Crum (Roger Pettiward), *c.* 1940

Suffolk, the second child of a well-to-do land-owning father who was a gifted amateur draughtsman, and the elder brother of the *Punch* writer and illustrator DANIEL PETTIWARD. He went to Eton, where he won all the drawing prizes as well as the middleweight boxing cup (he was 6 ft 5¹/₂ in. at school), leaving in 1925 to study agriculture at Christ Church, Oxford, where he was captain of the college rowing club and drew caricatures for *Isis, Sunday Express* and *Bystander*. He then studied art at the Vienna Academy and in Munich, the Slade and Paris, and accompanied Peter Fleming on his 1932 expedition to Brazil (recounted in Fleming's *Brazilian Adventure*). He also drew illustrations of restaurant scenes for *London Week* (1935–60) and Fortnum & Mason's catalogues. A contributor to *Punch* (1936–40) and *Night & Day* (1937), he signed sometimes with an anticlockwise spiral whorl. One of his most famous cartoons was of two hippos in a pool with the caption 'I keep thinking it's Tuesday'. Very influential, he was 'a most individual humorist whose magnificent inconsequences had equally magnificent solidity of foundation . . . these two, PONT and Pettiward, probably did more during this period to carry the development of modern pictorial humour a whole stage further than any two, or ten, or twenty others put together' (FOUGASSE). He usually drew in line or line and wash as well as colour, but occasionally used scraperboard. In Pettiward's view, every line in a cartoon, not just faces and noses, should be witty and the people should be recognizable types, not non-existent grotesques. He introduced 'a new style of bleak, fantastic humour, in which drawing and idea formed a unity. He created a world of precise insanity . . . He led the way to a humorous art that could be responded to without complete cognition' (Price). HEWISON has compared his near-surreal sense of humour with that developed much later in *The Goon Show* and *Monty Python's Flying Circus*. A member of the Euston Road Group, Crum admired Topolski, BERT THOMAS, FRANK REYNOLDS and George Grosz. Captain Roger Pettiward was killed on 19 August 1942 while leading 'F' troop of No. 4 Commando in the raid on Dieppe. A collection of his work, edited by Ruari McLean, was published after his death.

PUB: [ed. R. McLean] *The Last Cream Bun* (1984)

ILL: P. Fleming, *Variety* (*c.* 1933); D. Pettiward, *Truly Rural* (1939)
EXHIB: Eton College; CG; LG; M; NEAC; RP; RBA

PETTY, Bruce Leslie (b. 1929). Joke and strip cartoonist, illustrator and filmmaker. Bruce Petty was born in Doncaster, Melbourne, on 23 November 1929. He attended Box Hill High School and studied art and design at Royal Melbourne Technical College (1945). In 1946 he joined Owen Bros advertising agency, Melbourne, working on animation, and in 1950 joined Colorgravure Publications, Melbourne, as an illustrator. Moving to London in 1953, he worked as a freelance illustrator for ABC TV, the *Sunday Pictorial*, AEI, the International Wool Secretariat and contributed cartoons to *Punch* (including covers), *Lilliput, Spectator, Esquire, Graphis, This Week, New Yorker* and *Saturday Review*. After six months in New York (1958) he returned to Melbourne in 1959 and worked for World Records, British Nylon Spinners, Volkswagen and Briggs & James advertising agency before joining the *Sydney Daily Mirror* and the newly formed *Australian* in 1965, moving to the *Melbourne Age* in 1976. He won an Academy Award for his animated short film *Leisure* (1976). HEWISON has observed that 'Bruce Petty's ideas are nearly always placed in the centre of some violent action; action as it is happening or just after it has stopped happening.'
PUB: *Australian Artist in South East Asia* (1962), *Petty's Australia* (1967), *The Best of Petty* (1968), *The Penguin Petty* (1972), *The Petty Age* (1978)
ILL: K. F. Barnsley, *Mr Paley* (1957); P. Solsona, *Casa Pepe Book of Spanish Cooking* (1957)
COLL: UKCC

PEYTON, Michael (b. 1921). Sports cartoonist and illustrator. Michael Peyton was born in Houghton-le-Springs, Co. Durham, on 8 January 1921, the son of Jerimiah Peyton, a coalminer. In World War II he served in a reconnaissance battalion and started drawing cartoons while a prisoner of war in Germany. He later escaped and joined the Russian Army. After the war he attended Manchester School of Art and the Central School of Art and after having his first cartoon published by *Soldier* magazine in 1949 became a full-time freelance cartoonist. He was Art Editor of *New Scientist* from 1972 to 1973. Mike Peyton specializes in sailing/boating car-

toons though he also draws a regular feature for *Horse & Hound* and has drawn on skiiing. His work has appeared in *Yachting Monthly, Die Yacht, Voile et Voiliers, Practical Boat Owner* and most yachting magazines worldwide. He is married to the author Kathleen Peyton. He works in pen and wash.
PUB: 18 books including *Come Sailing* (1975), *Hurricane Zoe* (1977), *The Pick of Peyton* (1983), *Home and Dry* (1989), *Why Do We Do It?* (1995), *On the Ebb* (1998)
ILL: More than 20 titles
EXHIB: Six exhibitions, e.g. Aldeburgh Regatta

PHB – *see* Bellew, Hon. Patrick Herbert

PHELIX – *see* Burnett, Hugh

PHILPIN, William – *see* Jones, William John Philpin

PHIPPS, Julian Vandeleur (1907–91). Joke and strip cartoonist, illustrator, journalist and cartoon editor. After attending Lancing School Julian Phipps studied law at Trinity College, Oxford (contemporaries included OSBERT LANCASTER, Graham Greene and Quintin Hogg) and while there drew cartoons for *Isis* and *Cherwell*. A self-taught artist, with the help of his friend Buzz Burrows ('The Obstinate Artist') of the *Daily Sketch* he began work as a freelance illustrator and cartoonist before joining the *Daily Mail* (1929), with which he stayed for more than eleven years as a journalist (illustrating his own articles) and cartoonist, drawing such features as 'Laugh with Phipps' and 'Crazy News Reel' (1937–8). He also gave broadcasts on the art of cartooning on BBC Radio. During World War II he served in the Royal Engineers and with an anti-aircraft regiment in East Anglia before being commissioned as an RAF photo-interpreter, attaining the rank of flight lieutenant. He returned to the *Daily Mail* after the war, succeeding Francis Marshall as fashion artist (1947–8), and then drew a strip, 'Judy', for the *Evening News* with Derek Tangye. He then left Associated Newspapers to become Art Editor of the *Daily Mirror* (1949–53), succeeding ZEC, where he took on some of the first joke cartoon work of REG SMYTHE, later to create 'Andy Capp'. Returning to Associated Newspapers in 1953 he became Art Editor of all strip and panel cartoons and began the 'Cartoon Sketch' feature in the *Daily Sketch* in 1954. He helped launch such famous strips as 'Tug Transom',

'Carol Day', 'Matt Marriott', 'Tiffany Jones', 'Wack', 'Focus on Fact' and ALEX GRAHAM's 'Fred Basset'. Known as 'Phipps the Strips', he retired to Malta in October 1970, being succeeded by KEITH MACKENZIE. He mostly worked in pen and ink and wash but also painted in oil and watercolours.
PUB: *Phipps' Annual* (1933)

PIERROT – *see* Weisz, Victor

PILBROW, Giles (b. 1967) Joke and strip cartoonist and TV scriptwriter and producer. Giles Pilbrow was born in Romsey, Hampshire, on 5 July 1967, the son of Peter Pilbrow, a farmer. He studied maths and philosophy at New College, Oxford (1986–9), but is self-taught as an artist. He worked at first as an advertising account manager before becoming a scriptwriter and producer for TV programmes such as BBC2's *Have I Got News for You* (from 1998), Channel 4's *The Big Breakfast* (1995) and Central TV's SPITTING IMAGE (1991–6). His first cartoon was published in the *Guardian* in 1990 and he has also contributed to *The Times, Sunday Times, Spectator, Punch, Private Eye, New Statesman, Financial Times, Maxim, TV Times* and others. He works in indian ink and watercolours on cartridge paper. He cites his early influences as being Uderzo (creator of 'Asterix') and RALPH STEADMAN.
PUB: *The Chockablock Book* (1995), *Fetch* (1996), *Pilbrow's Puzzle Adventures* (1997), *The Little Guide to Pets* (1999), *The Little Guide to Mums* (1999), *The Little Guide to Dads* (1999), *The Little Guide to Babies* (1999)
ILL: B. Moses, *While Shepherds Washed their Socks by Night* (1997), *We Three Kings* (1998); P. Ham and N. Gardner, *The Sunday Times' 50 Essential Questions on Money* (1997)

'Pilot Officer Prune' – *see* Hooper, William John

PIP – *see* Mendoza, Philip

POELSMA, Dominic (b. 1936). Political, joke and strip cartoonist and caricaturist. Dominic Poelsma was born in Leeuwarden, Holland, on 14 January 1936, the son of Johan Poelsma, a sports instructor. A largely self-taught artist, he has worked in advertising in Holland (where his first cartoon was published in 1951), Australia and London, and attended Melbourne Technical College part-time in the 1950s. Political Cartoonist for the Australian publication

Newsweekly (1957–9), he produced a series of 'English Worthies' caricatures for the *Evening Standard*'s 'Londoner's Diary' in 1971 with humorous verse by Angus McGill. In addition he has drawn theatre cartoons for the *Evening Standard* (1973–5) and caricatures ('The Chairman Says . . .') for the *Spectator* (1973–5). However, he is perhaps best known for his collaboration with McGill on the *Standard*'s 'Augusta' strip (originally entitled 'Clive') which has run in the paper since January 1968 and in the *Mail on Sunday* since 1988. Influenced by Doeve, Hergé, Schultz and Low, he works in pen and ink, watercolours and felt-tip markers.
PUB: [with A. McGill] *Clive* (1968), *Clive in Love* (1970), *Clive and Augusta* (1971), *Augusta the Great* (1977), *I, Augusta* (1978), *Augusta* (1989)
ILL: M. Markham, *Old is Great* (1978), *A Chauvinist is . . .* (1979); P. Brown, *Beware of the Teenager!* (1986); J. Morrison, 'Reading Games' series (four books, 1988); D. Gillett, *Rescuing the Nation's Health* (1993)
COLL: BM

PONT – *see* Laidler, Gavin Graham

'Ponty an' Pop' – *see* Jones, Grenfell

'Pop' – *see* Watt, John Millar and Hogg, Gordon

POSY – *see* Simmonds, Rosemary Elizabeth

POTT, Charles L. (1865–after 1907). Joke cartoonist, illustrator and painter. Charles Pott was born in Hampstead, London, on 9 January 1865, the son of Laslett John Pott, a painter of historical subjects. He was educated in Germany and elsewhere and, after working for a short while in the City, studied at Calderon's Art School in St John's Wood. He then set out as a professional landscape painter, but having had some illustrations accepted by *Illustrated Sporting & Dramatic News* in 1887 began contributing joke cartoons and illustrations to magazines such as *Cassell's Saturday Journal, Illustrated Bits, Graphic* and *Punch* (1900–1907). He also worked for *Chums* from its very beginning, notably the series 'Ye Revysed Hystory of England'. A member of the Volunteer Army, many of his cartoons were on military subjects. He had a simple outline style influenced by Richard Doyle.
EXHIB: RBA; ROI
COLL: THG
LIT: J. A. Hammerton, *Humorists of the Pencil* (1905)

POY – *see* Fearon, Percy Hutton

PRANCE, Bertram (1889–after 1944). Illustrator, joke cartoonist and painter. Bertram Prance was born in Bideford, Devon, on 5 December 1889, the son of Captain F. W. Prance, a shipping merchant. He studied with PERCY BRADSHAW's Press Art School and contributed cartoons to *Humorist* (1924–40), *Punch*, *Passing Show*, *London Opinion*, *Strand Magazine*, *Nash's* and others. A friend of W. HEATH ROBINSON, he was a member of the Savage Club and President of the London Sketch Club (1948).
ILL: A. Armstrong, *We Like the Country* (1940), *Village at War* (1941), *Cottage into House* (1944)
EXHIB: RA; Arlington Gallery

'Prehistoric Peeps' – *see* Reed, Edward Tennyson

PRIESTLEY, Christopher (b. 1958). Political and strip cartoonist, caricaturist and illustrator. Chris Priestley was born in Hull on 25 August 1958 and studied at Manchester Polytechnic (1976–80). He worked at first as a caricaturist for *Record Mirror* (1981–5) and as an illustrator for the *Listener*, *Radio Times*, *The Times* (from 1983) and *Independent* (from 1983). He was then an illustrator for the *Economist* (1990–96, including covers) and was Political Cartoonist on the *Independent* (1995–8). He also drew a strip ('7.30 for 8') for the paper (1997–8). In addition he has contributed to the *Financial Times*, *Observer* (including the 'Babel' strip), *Guardian*, *Sunday Times*, *Daily Telegraph*, *Sunday Telegraph*, *Independent on Sunday* (including the 'Bestiary' strip illustrated by CHRIS RIDDELL) and others. He works mostly in dip-pen, brush and ink but also paints. He admires the work of Jules Feiffer, Tomi Ungerer, ANDRÉ FRANÇOIS and the early drawings of RONALD SEARLE. His wife is the textile designer Sally Coombes.

PRITCHETT, Matthew 'Matt' (b. 1964). Joke and pocket cartoonist. Matt Pritchett was born on 14 July 1964, the son of journalist Oliver Pritchett and grandson of novelist Sir Victor (V. S.) Pritchett. He studied graphics at St Martin's School of Art and, unable to get work as a film cameraman, was for a time a waiter in a pizza restaurant, drawing cartoons in his spare time. He had his first drawings published in *New Statesman*. His work has also appeared in *Punch*, *Spectator* and other publications and he has been Pocket Cartoonist on the *Daily Tele-*

graph and *Sunday Telegraph* since 1988, succeeding MARK BOXER. His awards have included Granada TV's *What the Papers Say* Cartoonist of the Year (1992), *UK Press Gazette*'s Cartoonist of the Year (1996, 1998) and CAT Pocket Cartoonist of the Year (1995, 1996). Matt's drawing style has been influenced by that of BRYAN McALLISTER and Sempé, and he admires the cartoonists of the *New Yorker*. He uses a fine Profipen felt-tip and occasionally watercolour (up to 1994 also sometimes Letratone). He is married to the fashion designer Pascale Smets.
PUB: *The Best of Matt* (annuals from 1991)
EXHIB: JDG
COLL: BM

PRO – *see* Probyn, Peter Clive

PROBYN, Peter Clive (1915–91). Joke and strip cartoonist, animator and arts administrator. Born on 18 November 1915, the son of Frank Probyn, Professor of the Horn at the Royal College of Music and a member of the London Philharmonic Orchestra, Peter Probyn went to Rudyard Kipling's and BRUCE BAIRNSFATHER's old school, the United Services College. He left at 16 and worked in Highams advertising agency until bad health (TB) forced him to recuperate in Midhurst, Sussex, where he decided to become a humorous artist. At the age of 19 he sold six sketches to *Men Only* on the day the magazine first appeared, submitting the drawings under the pseudonym 'PRO' (he didn't use his full name until he was 21). He also contributed to *Night & Day*, *Punch*, *Men Only*, *Illustrated London News*, *Current Affairs*, *Passing Show*, *Homes & Gardens*, *Lilliput* and *Tatler & Bystander*. During World War II he served in the Home Guard and was later a teacher before returning to work as a freelance artist and designer, mainly in advertising for companies such as Electrolux, Gibbs Shaving Cream, Stewart & Lloyds Steel, BOAC, Royal Insurance and especially Ind Coope for whom he created the popular Double Diamond 'Little Man' with his bowler hat and Scottie dog who appeared on hoardings in the 1950s. He also designed greetings cards for Royles and Book Tokens, drew strip cartoons for *Eagle* (e.g. 'Grandpa'), and produced animated films for NATO. In 1962 he became County Art Advisor to East Sussex Education Authority and was a governor of Brighton College of Art, chairman of the Art Advisers Association and a committee member

Peter Probyn, [Little Man], (Double Diamond advertisement), *c.* 1950

of the South East Arts Council. In addition, as a lifelong wine enthusiast and expert, he was for 25 years a member of the publications committee of the Co-operative Wine Society, for which he drew many illustrations. He married the artist Kissane Keane in 1946. Probyn worked mostly in line or line and wash and was particularly influenced by the work of *New Yorker* cartoonists. He died on 2 November 1991.

PUB: (ed.) *The Complete Drawing Book* (1970)
ILL: Novels by F. Clifford, E. Fearon and others
COLL: Wine Society, Stevenage

PUGH, Jonathan Mervyn Sebastian (b. 1962). Pocket and strip cartoonist. Jonathan Pugh was born in Worcester on 17 February 1962, the son of John Mervyn Cullwick Pugh, a solicitor. He was educated at Dragon School, Oxford, Downside (near Bath) and Oxford Polytechnic. Self-taught as an artist, his first cartoon was published in the *Literary Review* in 1988. He began drawing *The Times*' Diary cartoon in 1995 and has been the paper's front-page Pocket Cartoonist since 1996 and Business Cartoonist since 1997. His work has also appeared in *Punch*, *Spectator*, *Private Eye* and the *Tablet*, and his advertising clients include Visa and Barclaycard. He was voted CAT Pocket Cartoonist of the Year in 1998. Influenced by Sempé, QUENTIN BLAKE and GILES, he works mostly in pen and ink on paper.

ILL: T. Deary, *The Joke Factory* (1991); R. Stannard, *Here I Am* (1992); A. Woodham, *Get Up and Go!* (1994); P. Clayton, *Stop Counting Sheep!* (1994); Pastor Ignotus, *A Parish Year* (1998)

PVB – *see* Bradshaw, Percy Venner

PYNE, Kenneth John (b. 1951). Joke and strip cartoonist, caricaturist and illustrator. Ken Pyne

'I've just heard the first cuckoo of spring cough.'

Ken Pyne, *Punch*, 13 April 1990

was born in London on 30 April 1951, the son of John Ernest Pyne, a boot-repairer. Self-taught, he had his first cartoon published in *Punch* at the age of 16 – the youngest artist in the magazine in the 20th century. However, he worked in a number of jobs, including layout artist on *Scrap & Waste Reclamation & Disposal Weekly*, before becoming a full-time freelance cartoonist at the age of 20. As well as *Punch* he has contributed to *Private Eye* (since 1976, notably the 'Corporation Street' strip since October 1986), *Today, The Times, Independent, Guardian, Evening Standard, Hampstead & Highgate Express, Oldie, New Statesman, People, Observer* and *Which?* Voted CCGB Joke Cartoonist of the Year (1981) he has also done a considerable amount of advertising work and has illustrated three guidebooks for English Heritage and six edi-

tions of the *Good Beer Guide* (1985–9, 1992). He uses a mapping pen with a Gillott nib.
PUB: *The Relationship* (1981), *Martin Minton* (1982), *Silly Mid-Off* (1985), *This Sporting Life* (1986), *In the Bleak Mid-Winter* (1987)
ILL: A. Miall, *Musical Bumps* (1981); P. Freedman, *Glad to be Grey* (1985); A. Hunter, *Swim, Bike, Run* (1985); B. Pearson, *Business Strategy* (1987), *Time Management* (1988); M. Van Mesdag, *Think Marketing* (1988); S. Rose, *The Shareholder* (1989); J. L. Spencer, *Getting Paid* (1991), *How to Make the Most of Your Accountant* (1992); P. Wood, *If the Sun Doesn't Kill You, the Washing-Machine Will* (1993); C. Donnellan 'Issues for the Nineties' series (more than 30 books, from 1990)
EXHIB: BC; CG; [with Kevin Woodcock] JDG
COLL: V&A; BM; UKCC; Salon International du Dessin et d'Humour, Switzerland

Q

QUIZ – *see* Evans, Powys Arthur Lenthall

R

R – *see* Rushton, William George

RAEMAEKERS, Louis (1869–1956). Political cartoonist and painter. Louis Raemaekers was born in Roermond, Holland, on 6 April 1869. He studied in Amsterdam, at the Brussels Academy under De Kruyf and with Blanc-Garin in Paris. Influenced by Forain, he first began to concentrate on political cartoons in 1912 and became famous while working as a cartoonist and illustrator on *De Telegraaf* during World War I. Indeed, his vicious, often bloodthirsty, anti-German cartoons led to his prosecution by the Dutch authorities for endangering their neutrality in the conflict. His drawings were none the less widely exhibited and published in magazines and newspapers in France and the UK such as the *Daily Mail, Bystander, L'Illustration, La Grande Guerre, Le Matin, Le Jour-*

nal, L'Humanité, La Baïonnette and others. Some were also produced as postcards by George Pulman & Sons and (in French and English) by Imprimerie Elsevier (Amsterdam). In 1915 an exhibition of more than 500 of his hard-hitting drawings at the Fine Art Society in London caused a sensation, and when he came to Britain the following year to seek asylum Prime Minister Lloyd George was so impressed by his work that he persuaded him to go to the USA, where his drawings were syndicated by Hearst Publications, in an effort to enlist American help in the war. 'He drew with astonishing freedom and vigour, and exposed the bestial treachery of the German War-lord and his fellow criminals with a flaming indignation which no other wartime artist surpassed' (BRADSHAW). *The Times'* famous war correspondent, Sir Percy Robinson, held that he was one of the six great men – including statesmen and military commanders – whose effort and influence were most decisive during World War I. After the war he concentrated on illustration work but drew anti-Nazi cartoons in *De Telegraaf* in the 1930s. Later director of a drawing school in Holland, he also painted portraits. Awarded the Légion d'Honneur (1916), he was made an Honorary member of the Royal Society of Miniature Painters (1916). The Savage Club held a dinner in his honour chaired by LANCE THACKERAY, and the Institute of Journalists also fêted him at a lunch at the Royal Hotel, London, on 8 December 1915. Louis Raemaekers died in Scheveningen, Holland, on 26 July 1956.

PUB: Many books including *The Great War: A Neutral's Indictment* (1916), *Raemaekers' Cartoons* (1916), *America in the War* (1918), *Raemaekers' Cartoon History of the War* (1919), *The Caxton Edition of Raemaekers' Cartoons* (1923)
ILL: Many books including E. Cammaerts, *The Adoration of the Soldiers* (1916), *Through the Iron Bars* (1917); J. van A. Kueller, *A Young Lion of Flanders* (1916); J. W. R. Scott, *The Ignoble Warrior* (1916); W. Dowsing, *War Cartoon Sonnets* (1917)
EXHIB: FAS (1915, 1916, 1917, 1918, 1920)
COLL: V&A; IWM

RAFF – *see* Hooper, William John

RALSTON, William (1848–1911) – *see* Bryant & Heneage

RAUSCH – *see* Whitford, Francis Peter

RAVEN HILL – *see* Hill, Leonard Raven

RAY – *see* Chesterton, Raymond Wilson

RAYMONDE, Roy Stuart (b. 1929). Joke cartoonist, comic painter and illustrator. Roy Raymonde was born on 26 December 1929 in Grantham, Lincolnshire, and attended Harrow School of Art (1944–6) where one of his teachers was GERARD HOFFNUNG. After National Service in Malaya (1948–50), he joined the studio of a Fleet Street advertising agency as an illustrator (1950–60), during which time he began freelancing as a cartoonist for such publications as the *Daily Mirror, Daily Sketch, Star, Men Only* and *Fashion Weekly*. Around 1960, after selling his first cartoon to *Punch*, he be-

came a full-time cartoonist, contributing regularly to the *Sunday Telegraph, Mayfair, Punch* (including covers and illustrations for 'Doc Brief' 1985–8), *Reader's Digest* and, since 1971, *Playboy* (USA and Germany). Regular features for the *Sunday Telegraph* (1969–72) have included 'Patsy & John' 'The Bergs', 'Them', 'Boffins at Bay', 'Raymonde's Blooming Wonders' and 'Raymonde's Rancid Rhymes'. In addition, he drew covers and illustrations for the short-lived revival of *Time & Tide* (1988–91) and has given lectures and talks in Korea and Japan (1990, 1991, 1992). Voted CCGB Feature Cartoonist of the Year in 1966, he was awarded the Gold Prize at the Kyoto International Cartoon Exhibition in 1996. Raymonde works in many media, including watercolour, gouache, pen and brush, and admires Tomi Ungerer, QUENTIN BLAKE and Adolf Born. His son, Paul, is also a professional cartoonist and muralist.

PUB: *The Constant Minx* (1961), *More Constant Minx* (1961), *Starters Russia* (1972), [with R. Holles] *The Guide to Real Village Cricket* (1983), *The Guide to Real Subversive Soldiering* (1985)
EXHIB: Marunie Gallery, Kyoto
COLL: SIM; Ritsumeikan Peace Museum, Kyoto; Kyoto Seika Universty, Kyoto; V&A; UKCC

READING, Bryan Lawrence (b. 1935). Joke and strip cartoonist, illustrator and animator. Bryan Reading was born in London on 24 February 1935, and after serving an apprenticeship in printing worked in advertising studios, producing cutaway technical drawings for Jaguar and Austin Motors as well as exhibition and leaflet designs. His first published cartoons appeared in *Argosy* in 1953. A contributor to *Punch, Private Eye, Spectator, New Statesman, Oldie* and other magazines, his first strip, 'The Belchers' (at first written by BRYAN McALLISTER), appeared in Richard Boston's monthly *Vole* (1977–81). He has also drawn strips for the *Evening Standard* (1976–80), *Building Design* (1978–92), *Traditional Homes* (1985–92) and the *Law Society's Gazette* (1991–4). Political Cartoonist on the *Sunday Mirror* (1996) he has also drawn for *Daily Mail* (1978–86), *Rolls-Royce News, Sun, London Daily News* (1987), *Guardian* (1980–88), *Construction News* (since 1988), *Rotary Magazine* (since 1992), *Countryman* (1992–6), *Classic & Sportscar Magazine* (1995–6) and *Classic Car Mart* (since 1997). In addition, he has produced film animation for BP (1957) and artwork for film and TV productions (Euston Films, 1989–91). His 'Con-

'Good news, sir – someone's stolen the Hockney.'

Bryan Reading, *Oldie*, April 1994

sumer Counsel' strip in the *Evening Standard* won the Argos Consumer Award in 1980 and, a former committee member of the CCGB, he has been voted CCGB Feature Cartoonist of the Year three times (1983, 1987, 1988). He has also been a jury member of the *Hürriyet* International Cartoon Competition in Istanbul (1988, 1995). A meticulous worker, especially with regard to architectural detail, he usually works in line without tints or wash using a Pilot fine liner pen.

PUB: *The Belchers* (1983), *Drawing Cartoons and Caricatures* (1987), *Cruel Britannia* (1993), *Morgan Mania* (1993), *More Morgan Mania* (1997)

ILL: More than 60 books including M. Danby, *The Awful Joke Book* (1979), *The Armada Funny Story Book* (1980), *The Even More Awful Joke Book* (1982), *The Most Awful Joke Book Ever* (1984), *The Batty Cartoon Book* (1989), *Fun for Six Year Olds* (1989)

EXHIB: Building Centre; BC

COLL: V&A; UKCC

REED, Edward Tennyson (1860–1933). Political and joke cartoonist, caricaturist and illustrator. Born on 27 March 1860 in Greenwich, London, E. T. Reed was the only son of Sir Edward James Reed KCB FRS, Chief Constructor of the Royal Navy (he also designed Japan's first battleship, the *Foo Soo*), Liberal MP for Cardiff, and Lord of the Treasury in Gladstone's 1886 administration. His mother was Rosetta Barnaby, sister of Sir Nathaniel Barnaby who succeeded his father as Chief Constructor. He was educated at Harrow School and began to read for the Bar, but ill-health cut short his studies and instead he accompanied his father to Egypt and the Far East (1879–80). On his return he studied at Calderon's Art School for 18 months and under Burne-Jones but, failing to get into the RA Schools, began work as a portrait painter. When this failed he turned to illustration and cartoons. His first published works were drawings for his father's book *Japan: Its History, Religion and Traditions* (1880)

181

followed by a sketch in the weekly *Society* (1888), in which some of the early drawings of PHIL MAY had also appeared. Then, with the help of LINLEY SAMBOURNE who introduced him to the Editor Sir Francis Burnand, he began to contribute to *Punch* (June 1889) and joined the staff the following year. The first of his popular anachronistic 'Prehistoric Peeps' series ('The First Hansom') appeared in the *Punch Almanack* for 1893 and some of these were also reproduced as postcards by Wrench. He later succeeded HARRY FURNISS as the magazine's parliamentary caricaturist, illustrating the 'Essence of Parliament' feature (1894–1912) and himself handing over to A. W. LLOYD when he moved to the *Bystander* in 1912. He also drew political and legal cartoons for the *Sketch* (from 1893) and contributed to *Idler*, *English Illustrated Magazine*, *Passing Show* and others. In addition, he wrote a course for the London School of Cartooning (as did FRED BUCHANAN and ARTHUR FERRIER). Though he also drew in pen, ink and wash, he preferred pencil, and usually worked quite small (sometimes even the same size as reproduction). 'His solid shapes, his dark foregrounds against lighter backgrounds, springing out of the paper like a silhouette, pointed towards the hard poster-techniques of early twentieth-century comic art, towards the methods of TOM BROWNE and the hunting artist CECIL ALDIN' (Price). Of his political drawings Reed said: 'I go for a man's <u>expression</u>, and I try and caricature that more than his features . . . I go down to the House. I carefully study a man. Next morning I sketch him from memory or from very rough notes which I may have made in the House in my sketchbook' (*Strand*, Vol. 8). He owned a chest of drawers that once belonged to John Leech. E. T. Reed died in London on 12 July 1933.

PUB: *Mr Punch's Prehistoric Peeps* (1896), *Mr Punch's Animal Land* (1898), *Mr Punch's Book of Arms* (1899)
ILL: Lord Alfred Douglas, *Tails with a Twist* (1898); H. W. Lucy, *A Diary of the Unionist Parliament 1895–1900* (1901); *The Balfourian Parliament 1900–1905* (1906); R. C. Lehmann, *The Adventures of Picklock Holes* (1901); E. de la Pasture, *The Unlucky Family* (1907); M. Pigott, *The Beauties of Home Rule!* (1914); E. E. Spicer and E. C. Pegler, *De Mortuis Nil Nisi Bona* (1914); W. H. Burnet, *Quite So Stories* (1918)
EXHIB: FAS (1899); LG; ROI; New Gallery
COLL: V&A; BM; NPG

LIT: Sir Shane Leslie (ed.), *Edward Tennyson Reed* (1957)

REID, Arthur [ARThur or ART REID] (b. 1936). Joke cartoonist, caricaturist, illustrator, sculptor and writer. Born in Inverurie, Aberdeenshire, on 24 April 1936, the son of Duncan Reid, a crofter, Arthur Reid attended Aberdeen College of Commerce (1967–71) before studying sculpture and ceramics at Gray's School of Art, Aberdeen (1971–6), and art and design education at Aberdeen College of Education (1976–7). His first cartoon was published in *Blighty* in 1957 and his work has appeared in *Punch*, *Spectator*, *Doctors' Post*, *Private Eye*, *Playboy*, *Penthouse*, *Mayfair* and in various advertising campaigns. Co-organizer of the FECO Edinburgh International Cartoon Festival from 1986 to 1993, he is the founder and President of the Cartoon Art Society and the founder of the School of Cartoon Sculptors. The winner of numerous awards, including the Golden Plaquette of the City of Ostend (1992), he has also served as a judge at international cartoon festivals at Knokke-Heist, Belgium (1981) and Margate, Kent (1989). His main influence has been the work of Thomas Rowlandson. He uses a McDougall's Shoulder Pen F and Rotring Rapidoliner on Frisk CS10 paper. For roughs he works on Executive typing paper and uses Bristol Board for colour.
EXHIB: Artspace, Aberdeen
COLL: KN; UKCC

REYNOLDS, Frank RI (1876–1953). Joke cartoonist and illustrator. Frank Reynolds was born in London on 13 February 1876, the son of the artist William George Reynolds, and the brother of the actor Tom Reynolds. He studied at Heatherley's with JAMES THORPE and contributed to *Judy*, *Longbow*, *Pick-Me-Up*, *Playgoer*, *Cassell's*, *Illustrated London News*, *Sketchy Bits* (including covers) and *Sketch* (full-page comic drawings). He was a staff artist on the *Illustrated London News* and *Sketch* in the early years of the century and also painted watercolours, being elected RI in 1903. In 1906 he began contributing to *Punch*, joining the staff in 1919 and succeeding his brother-in-law F. H. TOWNSEND as Art Editor (1920–30). He also worked as a book illustrator, establishing his reputation with a Gift Book edition of *Pickwick Papers* (1910), and many of his Dickensian characters were

WHAT OUR WAGS HAVE TO PUT UP WITH
WIFE OF HUMORIST: *'No, dear, that's not funny.'*

Frank Reynolds, *Punch*, 23 May 1928

published as postcards by A. V. N. Jones & Co. Though he drew many varieties of cartoon he is particularly remembered for his anti-Kaiser pictures in *Punch* during World War I, notably the famous 'Study of a Prussian Household Having its Morning Hate' (1915), and for his colour work in the Almanacks and Summer Numbers. Left-handed like Townsend (and hence of the 'north-east school of shading' rather than the more normal north-west), he worked in pen, pencil (preferably Venus or Koh-i-Noor), conté crayon, chalk, gouache and watercolour and rarely used models. He used Whatman Hot-Pressed Watercolour Sketching Board, drawing roughs on cartridge paper. Reynolds was admired by Thorpe, who dedicated *English Illustrators in the Nineties* to him, and by Ellwood who called him a 'worthy successor of Townsend'. FOUGASSE once described him as 'a latter-day John Leech with the added fluidity and linear expression that "process" allowed'. BRADSHAW also noted that 'He seems to have been the first illustrator to realize the character in backs.' His style was very influential and 'in the Twenties and Thirties he, perhaps, contributed more than any other artist to giving an issue of *Punch* its character' (Price). President of the London Sketch Club (1909) he was also a

183

member of the Garrick Club and the Arts Club. Frank Reynolds died on 18 April 1953. His son John Patrick Reynolds (1909–35), who committed suicide, was also a cartoonist and comic illustrator (notably of W. C. Sellar and R. J. Yeatman's books *1066 and All That* and *And Now all This*) and created the famous twin-headed figures for Shell advertisements.

PUB: *'Punch' Pictures by Frank Reynolds RI* (1922), *The Frank Reynolds Golf Book* (1932), *Hamish McDuff* (1937), *Off to the Pictures* (1937), *Humorous Drawing for the Press* (1947)

ILL: W. Sapte, *By the Way Ballads* (1901); K. Howard, *The Smiths of Surbiton* (1906); J. N. Raphael, *Pictures of Paris and Some Parisians* (1908); C. Dickens, *The Adventures of Mr Pickwick* (1910), *David Copperfield* (1911), *The Old Curiosity Shop* (1913)

EXHIB: RI; WG

COLL: V&A; F; IWM; THG

LIT: A. E. Johnson, *Frank Reynolds RI* (1907); P. V. Bradshaw, *The Art of the Illustrator 8* (1918)

RIDDELL, Christopher (b. 1962). Political and strip cartoonist, illustrator and writer. Chris Riddell was born on 13 April 1962 in Cape Town, South Africa, and came to the UK in 1963. Educated at Archbishop Tenison's Grammar School, he attended Epsom School of Art & Design and studied illustration at Brighton Polytechnic Art School. He was Political Cartoonist on the *Economist* (1988–97) and the *Independent* and *Independent on Sunday* (1991–5) and has been Political Cartoonist on the *Observer* since 1995. In addition he has drawn political cartoons for *Sunday Correspondent* (1989–90), was business cartoonist on the *Observer* (1990–91) – for which he has also produced a strip, 'Antrobus' – and has drawn covers for *Punch, Economist, New Statesman* and *Literary Review*. He has also written and illustrated a number of children's books such as *The Wish Factory* ('Magical and inventive – like Heath Robinson with a few drinks inside him . . .' [*Independent*]). Voted Caricaturist of the Year by CAT in 1996, he also won the

Chris Riddell, [John Bull, German stereotype (having exchanged hats)], *Economist*, 9 March 1991

'Pardon me, is that corner seat occupied?'
'Obviously!'

W. L. Ridgewell, *Punch*, 16 May 1934

Macallan Award for the best Labour election cartoon (1997). Riddell cites his influences as being E. H. SHEPARD, Tenniel and WILLIAM HEATH ROBINSON, as well as book illustrators of the 19th and early 20th centuries. He prefers to work in ink or ink and watercolour, using a brush and steel nib pen.

PUB: *Ben and the Bear* (1986), *The Fibbs* (1987), *Bird's New Shoes* (1987), *Mr Underbed* (1986), *When the Walrus Comes* (1989), *The Wish Factory* (1990), *The Bear Dance* (1991), *Buddhism for Sheep* (1996), *Feng Shui for Cats* (1997), *Feng Shui for Dogs* (1997), [with P. Stewart] *Beyond the Deepwoods* (1998)

ILL: Many books including T. Hughes, *Ffangs the Vampire Bat and the Kiss of Death* (1986); M. Hoffman, *Beware, Princess!* (1986); R. McCrum, *The Dream Boat Brontosaurus* (1987); A. Gibson, *The Abradizil* (1990); K. Cave, *Something Else* (1995); A. Durrant, *Angus Rides the Goods Train* (1996); R. McGough, *Until I Met Dudley* (1997); H. C. Anderson, *The Swan's Stories* (1997)
EXHIB: JDG; LCG
COLL: UKCC; IWM; NPG; BM

RIDGEWELL, William Leigh (1881–1937). Joke and strip cartoonist, illustrator, lithographer and commercial artist. W. L. Ridgewell was born at 53 Buckingham Place, Brighton, on 8 September 1881, the son of Frederic William Ridgewell, a commercial traveller and talented amateur illustrator, and Helen Leigh Riches. Educated at Brighton Grammar School, he was then apprenticed to an engraver, from whom he learned seal engraving, heraldic art and lithographic drawing. He also studied at Brighton School of Art in his spare time and took a correspondence course in black-and-white illustration. His first published drawings were six postcard designs when he was aged 17 and he continued to work as a freelance commercial artist, producing advertisements, posters and postcards, until 1914. During World War I he served in India (1914–19), teaching lithography to Sepoys and drawing posters for the Indian War Loan and for recruitment, while also contributing cartoons and sketches to *Indian Ink* and *The Looker-On*. He later contributed to *Punch* ('the harbinger of a complete change of style in the paper', Price), *Humorist, London Opinion, Fragments* ('The Adventures of Plum and Apple' strip), *Tit-Bits, Bystander, Passing Show* and others. He also drew advertisements for Stone's Ginger Wine, Pratt's Petrol, etc. W. L. Ridgewell died on 7 November 1937 in Cassell Hospital, Penshurst, Sevenoaks, Kent, after jumping from a window while the 'balance of his mind was disturbed'. He was aged 56.
PUB: *Line and Laughter, a Book of Drawings by Ridgewell* (1934)
ILL: H. Graham, *More Ruthless Rhymes for Heartless Homes* (1930)
COLL: Brighton Museum

RIGBY, Paul Crispin (b. 1924). Political cartoonist, painter and illustrator. Paul Rigby was born in Sandringham, Melbourne, on 25 October 1924 and studied art at Brighton Technical School in Melbourne, leaving aged 15 to work in a commercial art studio and then as a freelance commercial artist and book and magazine illustrator (1940–42). After serving in the Royal Australian Air Force in World War II (1942–6), he joined Western Australian Newspapers (1948–52) as an illustrator and in 1952 became Political Cartoonist on the *Perth Daily News*. He was then recruited by Rupert Murdoch to be the first Political Cartoonist (with CLIVE COLLINS) on the newly launched *Sun* (1969–74) in London (being succeeded by FRANKLIN), while also working for the Springer Group in Germany and the *National Star* in the USA. Rigby returned to Australia and the *Sydney Daily Telegraph* in 1975 and moved to the USA to work for the *New York Post* in 1977, then for the *New York News* (his son Bay took over his job on the *Post*). His cartoons have won five Australian Walkely Awards (1960, 1961, 1963, 1966, 1969), the New York Press Club Award (1981) and the US Newspaper Guild's Page One Award (1982). Sir Larry Lamb (Editor of the *Sun*), has called him 'a superb draughtsman, and a complete professional'. He works in pen and ink on Bristol board (Grafix or Craftint).
PUB: 20 books including [with B. K. Ward] *Willow Pattern Walkabout* (1959), *Rigby* (1970), *Paul Rigby's Course of Drawing and Cartooning* (1976), *New York and Beyond* (1984)
ILL: B. K. Ward, *Perth Sketchbook* (1966); A. Linkletter, *Linkletter Down Under* (1968)
EXHIB: Melbourne Gallery

RILETTE – *see* Sykes, Charles

RILEY, Henry Arthur RI (1895–1966). Editorial and joke cartoonist, commercial artist and painter. Harry Riley was born in Chelsea on 6 July 1895, the son of John Riley, a hansom cab driver and amateur artist, but was brought up on his uncle's small farm in Leicestershire. He left school at 15 and studied at Hammersmith School of Art before becoming a junior artist at Norfolk Studios, a commercial art studio in Fleet Street, while studying in the evenings at Bolt Court School of Art (1910–15) under Walter Bayes RWS. In World War I he served in the 3rd County of London Yeomanry in Salonica, Palestine and France and while abroad had cartoons published in *London Opinion, Blighty* and the *Humorist*. He returned to Norfolk Studios

in 1919, but later turned freelance and set up his own commercial studio in New Court, Lincoln's Inn, specializing in men's fashion drawings. He was Editorial Cartoonist for the *Sunday Chronicle* in World War II and in the late 1940s and '50s was a cartoonist entertainer on TV, appearing in such programmes as *Owen Brannigan's Music Room* and *Flotsam's Follies*. He also studied at St Martin's School of Art (1931) and drew railway posters and advertisements for Reeves & Sons amongst others. Elected RI in 1939, he was a member of the Ridley Art Club. He was also elected President of the London Sketch Club (1934), President of the Chelsea Arts Club (1955) and Chairman of the Savage Club (1958), designing the latter's centenary dinner menu card in 1957. In addition to his work as a cartoonist he was an accomplished painter in oils and watercolours, and designed his own house in Dunstall Road, Wimbledon. For his watercolour work he used David Cox paper and sable brushes and according to BRADSHAW worked very fast (Bradshaw claimed to have seen him complete a portrait in oils, and frame it, in under four minutes!). Harry Riley died in Mile End Hospital, London, on 19 May 1966.
ILL: L. Carroll, *Alice in Wonderland* (1945)
EXHIB: RI; RA; RBA; ROI; Arlington Gallery

RIRE – *see* Gardner, Norman Gouldney Rodway

RITCHIE, Alick P. F. 'APFR' (1869–1918). Political cartoonist, caricaturist, illustrator, poster artist and writer. Alick Ritchie was born in Dundee, Scotland, and began work in the shipbuilding industry. He then sold jute before coming to London. After two years studying art in Antwerp he returned to London and, encouraged by John Latey, Editor of the *Penny Illustrated Paper*, began to contribute to periodicals in the 1890s. Apart from *Penny Illustrated* itself, his work appeared in the *Illustrated Mail* (political caricatures), *Eureka*, *Bystander*, *London Mail*, *Strand*, *Ludgate Magazine*, *King*, *Evening News*, *Pall Mall Budget*, *Sketch*, *St Paul's*, *Sketchy Bits*, *Pick-Me-Up* (1894) and *Vanity Fair* (15 caricatures, 1911–13: he thought his portrait of George Bernard Shaw was his best-ever caricature) amongst others. He also drew sporting caricatures for Player's Cigarettes ('Straight Line Caricatures') and a great many posters, earning him the nickname 'Poster Fame' Ritchie. His book *Y? Studies in Zoo-all-awry* is an illustrated col-

lection of humorous verses (all beginning with 'Why . . .') about imaginary composite animals (e.g. the Buffalocust, the Rhinoscerostrich).
PUB: *Y? Studies in Zoo-all-awry* (1912)
COLL: NPG

ROBB, Brian (1913–79). Illustrator, joke cartoonist, teacher and painter. Brian Robb was born on 7 May 1913 in Scarborough, Yorkshire, and educated at Malvern College. He studied at Chelsea School of Art (1930–34) and the Slade (1935–6) before turning freelance artist and illustrator, contributing cartoons to *Night & Day* (1937), *Strand* and *Punch* (1936–9) while also drawing advertisements for Shell, Windsmoor (posters), Dictaphone and others. During World War II he served in the army in the Middle East and the cartoons he drew for *Crusader* and *Parade* were collected into a book. From 1945 he concentrated on book illustration (ARDIZZONE called him 'a born illustrator in the great tradition of the nineteenth century') and after lecturing at Chelsea Art School, where his pupils included children's book writer and illustrator Marjorie-Ann Watts, daughter of ARTHUR WATTS, he became head of the Illustration Department at the RCA (1963–78), being succeeded by QUENTIN BLAKE. He worked mostly in pen and ink in a style similar to

'It says "Beat the eggs until stiff". I've been beating for two hours and I'm still as fresh as a daisy.'

Brian Robb, *Night & Day*, 8 July 1937

Pont's, but also painted in oils and water-colour, notably views of Venice. Brian Robb died in August 1979.
PUB: *My Middle East Campaigns* (1944), *My Grandmother's Djinn* (1976), *The Last of the Centaurs* (1978)
ILL: Many books including Aywos, *Hints on Etiquette* (1946); L. N. Andreyev, *Judas Iscariot* (1947); R. Raspe, *Twelve Adventures of the Cele-brated Baron Munchhausen* (1947); Apuleius, *The Golden Ass* (1947); L. Sterne, *A Sentimental Jour-ney* (1948), *Tristram Shandy* (1949); H. Fielding, *Tom Jones* (1953); Aesop, *Fables* (1954); J. Roose Evans, *The Adventures of Odd and Elsewhere* (1971), *The Secret of the Seven Bright Shiners* (1972), *Odd and the Great Bear* (1973), *Elsewhere and The Gathering of the Clowns* (1974), *The Re-turn of the Great Bear* (1975)
EXHIB: LON; Prospect Gallery; Heffer's Gal-lery, Cambridge
LIT: E. Ardizzone, 'Brian Robb' in *Signature* (1950)

ROBERTS, Donald (b. 1936). Joke, strip and political cartoonist, illustrator and animator. Don Roberts was born in Devon on 17 April 1936, the son of a hotelier, and spent 7 ½ years in RAF Fighter Command and the Air Minis-try. He then worked as a propaganda artist for the Foreign Office (1960–63) before joining the *Daily Sketch* as a staff artist (1964–5). Art Direc-tor of the *Daily Express* (1965–71), he turned free-lance in 1972. Since then his work has appeared in more than 50 US and European publications including the *Daily Express* (notably the strip 'Spare Ribs' with FRANK DICKENS), *Punch*, *Daily Mail*, *New Yorker*, *Paris-Match*, *Scottish Daily Record* ('Small World' strip, 1982–91), *Sunday Mirror* (political cartoons, 1986), *Daily Mirror*, *Reader's Digest*, *Farming News*, (1982–91), *Wales on Sunday* (caricatures), *Today* (political and sports cartoons, 1988) and elsewhere. In addi-tion he has drawn for advertising (e.g. the 1975 Guinness calendar), produced cartoons for Channel 4's *A Week in Politics* (1988–93), and illustrated and designed books. Since 1992 his work has mainly consisted of character origina-tion for animation studios such as Treehouse Productions. He was one of the founder mem-bers of the British Cartoonists' Association in 1966 and is an admirer of HOFFNUNG, GOETZ and Sempé. Don Roberts works with a 1290 Gillott nib, brush, wax pencil, and watercolour.
PUB: *The Captive: An Opera* (1960)

ILL: J. Rydon, *Oysters With Love* (1968); J. Banks, *What Goes Up Must Come Down* (1964); P. Ayres, *Poems* (1971); C. Gardner, *The Great Trog Con-spiracy* (1972)

ROBERTS, R. J. Lunt (fl. 1913–after 1964). Joke cartoonist and illustrator. Lunt Roberts was a regular contributor to *Punch, Cassell's Children's Annual, Daily Mail Annual, Humorist, London Opinion, Knockout, Passing Show, TV Comic, Rocket* and other publications. He also worked as a staff artist and illustrator for *Evening News* (1930s–60s) and illustrated many children's books. Lunt Roberts usually worked in pen, brush and ink and crayon. He was elected Presi-dent of the London Sketch Club in 1939.
PUB: [with J. B. Lowke] *A Book of Swimming* (1945)
ILL: Many books including J. N. More, *Dugout Doggerels from Palestine* (1922); M. England, *Warne's Happy Book for Girls* (1938); T. Henley, *Let's Find Hidden Treasure* (1947); M. Saville, *The Riddle of the Painted Box* (1947), *Redshanks Warn-ing* (1948), *Two Fair Plaits* (1948), *The Flying Fish Adventure* (1950); A. MacVicar, *Stubby Sees it Through* (1950); K. Fidler, *Pete, Pam and Jim* (1954); R. L. Stevenson, *Two Stories* (1964)

ROBINSON, Charles RI (1870–1937). Illustra-tor and joke cartoonist. Born on 22 October 1870 in Islington, London, Charles Robinson was the second son of Thomas Robinson, wood-engraver and principal illustrator for *Penny Illustrated Paper*, and Eliza Ann Heath. His grandfather, Thomas Robinson, was a book-binder and wood-engraver, his uncle Charles was an engraver and artist for *Illustrated Lon-don News*, his elder brother was the illustrator Thomas Heath Robinson and his younger brother was WILLIAM HEATH ROBINSON. Edu-cated at Islington High School, he was appren-ticed to the lithographic printers Waterlow (1887–94), where he designed posters, etc., and studied in the evenings at the West London School of Art (c. 1892) and Heatherley's (where he later taught black-and-white drawing). Pri-marily a book illustrator (beginning in 1895 with Aesop's *Fables* and R. L. Stevenson's *A Child's Garden of Verses*), his first cartoon was published in the *Bystander* in November 1911 and he also contributed to *Tatler* and others. Influenced at first by Art Nouveau and Aubrey Beardsley, he also excelled at parodying Beardsley, using the pseudonym 'Awfly Weirdly'. Elected RI in 1932, he was a member of the London Sketch Club and became its President in 1926. The children in his version of Frances Hodgson Burnett's *The Secret Garden* were modelled on his own. He usually drew his cartoons in ink and wash, but also painted in watercolours and exhibited at the Royal Academy. Charles Robinson died in Botley, Buckinghamshire, on 13 June 1937.

PUB: *Christmas Dreams* (1896), *The Ten Little Babies* (1905), *Fanciful Fowls* (1906), *Peculiar Piggies* (1906), *Black Bunnies* (1907), *Black Doggies* (1907), *Black Sambos* (1907)

ILL: More than 100 books including R. L. Stevenson, *A Child's Garden of Verses* (1895); H. D. Lowry, *Make Believe* (1896); E. Field, *Lullaby Land* (1897); *Fairy Tales from Hans Christian Andersen* (1899); W. Canton (ed.), *The True Annals of Fairyland* (1900); W. Jerrold, *Nonsense! Nonsense!* (1902); I. H. Wallis, *The Cloud Kingdom* (1905); L. Carroll, *Alice's Adventures in Wonderland* (1907); P. B. Shelley, *The Sensitive Plant* (1911); F. Hodgson Burnett, *The Secret Garden* (1911); O. Wilde, *The Happy Prince* (1913); A. A. Milne, *Once On a Time* (1925)

EXHIB: RA; RI; L

COLL: V&A; THG

LIT: L. de Freitas, *Charles Robinson* (1976)

ROBINSON, William Heath (1872–1944). Joke cartoonist, illustrator and commercial artist. Heath Robinson was born on 31 May 1872 in Islington, London, the third son of Thomas Robinson, wood-engraver and principal illustrator for the *Penny Illustrated Paper*, and Eliza Ann Heath. His grandfather, Thomas Robinson, was a bookbinder and wood-engraver, his uncle Charles was an engraver and artist for *Illustrated London News*, and his elder brothers were the illustrators Thomas Heath Robinson and CHARLES ROBINSON. Educated at Islington High School, he studied at Islington School of Art (aged 15) and the RA Schools (1892–5), selling a drawing to *Sunday* magazine while still a student (1896). He then worked briefly as a landscape painter but, unsuccessful, turned to illustration. His first sale was of a drawing to the children's journal *Little Folks*, his first commission was for *Sunday* magazine, and his first book illustrations were published in 1897. He wrote and illustrated his first book, the fairy story *The Adventures of Uncle Lubin*, in 1902, and in March 1905 had his first cartoon published in the *Tatler*. The same year he began working for the *Bystander* (drawing its 21st birthday cover in 1924) and later produced whole-page comic features in the *Sketch* (from 1906). He also contributed to *Strand*, *Good Housekeeping*, *Good Words*, *Humorist*, *Nash's Magazine*, *Pearson's*, *London Magazine*, *Radio Times*, *London Opinion*, *Graphic*, *Rions*, *Lectures Pour Tous*, *Fantasio* (1915–16), *Le Pays de France* and *Holly Leaves*. During World War I his three anti-German cartoon collections were greatly admired and he repeated the success in World War II with *Heath Robinson at War* (1941). In addition he drew advertisements for Hovis, Johnnie Walker, Chairman Tobacco, Connolly Leather, Smith's Sectric Clocks, Standard Fireworks, Oxo, Mackintosh's Toffee, Moss Bros, Comfort Soap, High Duty Alloys, Eno's, Hector Powe, etc., and the 96-page book *Railway Ribaldry* (1935) was actually commissioned as a centenary celebration for Great Western Railways. He also drew comic postcards for Valentines (e.g. the series 'The Gentle Art of Catching Things', 1909) and designed theatre sets and the cocktail bar of the luxury liner *The Empress of Britain*. Heath Robinson is best known for creating bizarre cartoon contraptions which caused his name to enter the language to describe an 'absurdly ingenious device' (*OED*). However, unlike ROWLAND EMETT'S, his drawings could rarely be turned into reality. At first influenced by SIME, 'his drawings were composed with a care and ingenuity which reminds one . . . of Doré; at other times in the bold yet subtle disposition of blacks and whites, they are reminiscent of Beardsley' (NICOLAS BENTLEY). He was a member of the Savage Club and the Chelsea Arts Club and was President of the London Sketch Club (1920). William Heath Robinson died in Highgate, London, on 13 September 1944.

PUB: Many books including *The Adventures of Uncle Lubin* (1902), *Bill the Minder* (1912), *Some Frightful War Pictures* (1915), *Hunlikely!* (1916), *The Saintly Hun: A Book of German Virtues* (1917), *Flypapers* (1919), *Get On With It* (1920), *The Home Made Car* (1921), *Quaint and Selected Pictures* (1922), *Humours of Golf* (1923), *Absurdities* (1934), *Railway Ribaldry* (1935), [with K. R. G. Browne] *How to Live in a Flat* (1936), [with C. Hunt] *How to Make the Best of Things* (1940), *Heath Robinson at War* (1941), *The Penguin Heath Robinson* (1966)

ILL: R. Johnson and T. O'Cluny, *The Merry Multifleet and the Mounting Multicorps* (1904); *The Works of Rabelais* (1904); R. Carse, *The Monarchs of Merry England* (1907–8); N. Hunter, *The Incredible Adventures of Professor Branestawm* (1933); R. F. Patterson, *Mein Rant* (1940)

JAZZ BAGPIPES

W. Heath Robinson, *Inventions*, 1973

EXHIB: FAS (1924, Memorial 1945); Medici Galleries (1972); Mappin Art Gallery, Sheffield (1977); CBG (1987, 1992); RFH (1992); CG
COLL: BM; V&A; CAT
LIT: W. Heath Robinson, *My Line of Life* (1938); L. Day, *The Life and Art of William Heath Robinson* (1947); J. Lewis, *Heath Robinson, Artist and Comic Genius* (1973); J. Hamilton, *William Heath Robinson* (1992); G. Beare, *The Illustrations of W. Heath Robinson* (1983), *Heath Robinson Advertising* (1992)

ROBINSON, Wyndham (*c.* 1883–after 1951). Political cartoonist, caricaturist, fashion artist and illustrator. Wyndham Robinson was born in London, the son of a journalist. Intending to become a fashion artist and encouraged by 'Albert', the leading artist in this field at the time, he studied at Lambeth Art School under Philip Connard and at Chelsea School of Art. However, on seeing DYSON's drawings when a student he decided to become a cartoonist. In World War I he served in the Artists' Rifles and Royal Field Artillery, attaining the rank of captain, and after the war spent a year in Germany with the Army of Occupation. He then (with his army friend the BBC broadcaster Lewis Hastings) became a tobacco-farmer in Southern Rhodesia for seven years, but failed in the slump of 1928 and turned to drawing once more. He moved to Cape Town after being offered a job managing an advertising agent's studio and later worked as caricaturist and cartoonist on the *Cape Times* for five years. Returning to London, he became Political Cartoonist on the *Morning Post* from 1932 until it was absorbed by the *Daily Telegraph* in 1937 and later succeeded his friend GRIMES as Political Cartoonist of the *Star*, leaving Grimes to concentrate on his hugely successful 'All My Own Work' series for the paper. He also contributed illustrations to *Strand Magazine*, fashion drawings to *Queen* and cartoons to *Night & Day*, *Punch*, *Men Only*, *Tatler*, *London Opinion* (including covers, e.g. April 1951) and *Lilliput*. In addition, he was one of the Advisory Staff at PERCY BRADSHAW's Press Art School. His style was greatly influenced by the work of DAVID LOW.
PUB: *Cartoons from the Morning Post* (1937)
ILL: W. H. Horder, *Petrol Fumes* (1937); R. C. Robertson Glasgow, *I Was Himmler's Aunt* (1940), *No Other Land* (1942), *Rain Stopped Play* (1948)

ROSS – *see* Thomson, Harry Ross

ROSCISZEWSKI, Jan Stanislaw de Junosza 'Tom Titt' (1885–1956). Caricaturist and illustrator. Tom Titt was born in Warsaw and came to England in 1907 to study art at the Regent Street Polytechnic. He published his first caricature in 1910 in a Polish newspaper for which a friend of his was London correspondent, but his first drawing for a British journal was for the weekly *New Age*. He later produced regular illustrations for a gossip page in the *Daily Sketch*, worked for *Reynolds News* and in 1930 succeeded NERMAN as theatre caricaturist on *Tatler*, being succeeded in 1948 by EMMWOOD. He also contributed to *Everybody's*, *Daily Telegraph*, *Westminster Review*, *Spectator*, *Yorkshire Post*, *Glasgow Herald*, *John Bull*, *Sphere*, *Evening Standard*, *Daily Chronicle*, *Daily Express* ('Talk of London'), produced a series of caricature cards for Brownlee, and had his work animated by Joe Noble for Broda-Jenkins Ltd. 'His style, in which exact observation mingled with a rich strain of elfin fantasy, was unique, and remained so in spite of being prophetic of a school of caricature which flourishes today . . . a brilliant yet always kindly delineator of a generation of London's actors and actresses' (*Tatler* obituary). He sketched in pencil and then used a medium pointed writing nib. Tom Titt died in December 1956.
PUB: *Caricatures* (1913)
ILL: C. P. R. Graves, – *And the Greeks* (1930); A. E. Wilson, *Theatre Guyed* (1935)
COLL: IWM
EXHIB: Doré Galleries (1913)

ROTH, Arnold (b. 1929). Joke and strip cartoonist and illustrator. Arnold Roth was born in Philadelphia, USA, on 25 February 1929, the second of six children of a wholesale cut-flower salesman. He studied at the Central High School, the University of the Arts and the Philadelphia Museum College of Art and has been a freelance artist since 1951. His work has appeared in *Holiday*, *Saturday Evening Post*, *Nation*, *Playboy*, *Punch*, *Esquire*, *Time*, *Fortune*, *New York Times*, *Washington Post*, *Newsweek*, *New Yorker* and many other publications. A Past President of the National Cartoonists' Society, he has also been elected a member of the *Punch* Table and is currently on the board of the Museum of Cartoon Art (USA). In addition he has lectured widely on cartoon art and received numerous awards for his work, including the NCS's Reuben Award (1984) and Best Illustrator Cartoonist Award. He draws with a Higgins Boldstroke nylon-point pen or a Gillott 404 nib and indian ink, and also uses watercolour.

ILL: Many books including *Grimms' Fairy Tales* (1963)

ROTH, Stephen (1911–after 1944). Political, sports and joke cartoonist and illustrator. Czech by birth, Stephen Roth, who signed his work 'Stephen', moved to Prague in 1931 and drew sports cartoons, joke illustrations and portraits for various papers and magazines before becoming Political Cartoonist on the anti-Nazi weekly *Demokraticky Stred* edited by Dr H. Ripka (later head of the Czechoslovak Propaganda Department in London during World War II). Forced to leave Czechoslovakia in 1938, he went to Poland, then Sweden before arriving in London only days before war broke out in September 1939. By 1941 he was contributing political cartoons to the Ministry of Information, *Central European Observer* and the Free Norwegian newpaper *Norsk Tidend*. His popular series 'Acid Drops' began to appear in the *Sunday Pictorial* in 1942. He also contributed to the *Star*, *Lilliput*, *Daily Mirror*, *Central Press*, *Courier*, *Daily Mail* (sports cartoons) and others, and the Czech premier Jan Masaryk wrote a Foreword to his book *My Patience is Exhausted* (1944).

PUB: *Divided They Fall* (1943), *My Patience is Exhausted* (1944), *Finale* (1944)

EXHIB: [with TRIER, Hoffmeister, Pelc and Z. K.] Czechoslovak Institute, London (1943)

ROUNTREE, Harry (1878–1950). Joke and strip cartoonist and illustrator. Harry Rountree was born in Auckland, New Zealand, the son of

'Heil Hitler! Let me present V4 – our best secret weapon yet.'

Stephen Roth, [Hitler, Goebbels *et al.*], *Finale*, 1944

Stephen Gilbert Rountree, an accountant. He was educated at Queen's College, Auckland, and began work in the lithographic department of Wilson & Horton Printers in the city, designing showcards, labels for jam tins, and advertisements for the *New Zealand Herald* and *Weekly News*, which were printed by the company. Moving to London in 1901, he studied with Percival Gaskell RBA at the Regent Street Polytechnic, and got his first big break when S. H. Hamer, Editor of *Little Folks*, asked him to illustrate his book on animals. He later contributed to *Punch* (1905–39), *Tatler, King, Daily Mail, Cassell's Magazine, Graphic, Strand Magazine* (including stories by Wodehouse and Conan Doyle), *Humorist, Playtime* (from 1919, including covers), *Boy's Own Paper, Radio Times, L'Universel, Comica* (1908–9), *Sketch, Little Folks* and others. In addition, he drew illustrations for travel books and children's annuals, designed greetings cards, calendars and postcards (e.g. 'The Sporting Duckling' series for the British Showcard & Poster Co.), and worked in advertising for Dexter Weatherproofs, Bobby & Co. Department Stores (posters), Derry & Toms (posters), Mansion Polish and others – notably a long-running series featuring mice for Cherry Blossom Shoe Polish (for which he did more than 1000 drawings). During World War I he served as a captain and adjutant in the Royal Engineers. He was later on the Advisory Staff of BRADSHAW's Press Art School and produced a watercolour course ('Birds, Beasts and Fishes') for it. Best known for his drawings of animals, he was 'essentially a maker of funny pictures, neither a satirist nor a caricaturist, but a genial humorist, with a large, free style in line and colour' (*Times* obituary). He worked in ink (using No. 598 Perryan Art Pens), wash and watercolour on Imperial Quarto-size ($14 \times 10^5/8$ in.) Whatman 'Cambridge' hot-pressed board and did not leave a margin around his drawings. 'The chief characteristics of his work are its whimsical, fantastic, often eerie humour, its sense of movement and vitality, and its unique technical distinction' (Bradshaw). President of the London Sketch Club in 1914, he was also a member of the Savage Club and was a committee member of the St Ives Society of Artists, Cornwall. In addition, he served as a Town Councillor in St Ives (1945–8), and was Chairman of the Publicity Committee. He was a great friend of Harold Earnshaw, illustrator husband of MABEL LUCY ATTWELL. His motto was 'If you want to be happy – Draw animals!' There is a commemorative bronze plaque to him, designed by W. C. H. King of the Royal Society of British Sculptors, near the Sloop Inn, St Ives. Harry Rountree died in West Cornwall Hospital, Penzance, Cornwall, on 26 September 1950.

PUB: Many books including *The Child's Book of Knowledge* (1903), *Harry Rountree's Annual* (from 1907), *Rountree's Ridiculous Rabbits* (1916), *Birds, Beasts and Fishes* (1929), *Jungle Tales* (1934), *Rabbit Rhymes* (1934)

ILL: Many books including E. Nesbit, *Pug Peter* (1905); L. Carroll, *Alice's Adventures in Wonderland* (1908), *Through the Looking Glass* (1928); A. Conan Doyle, *The Poison Belt* (1913); A. Dumas, *The Dumas Fairy Tale Book* (1924); L. Rountree, *Me and Jimmy* (1929), *Ronald, Rupert and Reg* (1930), *Dirty Duck and Wonderful Walter* (1931); E. Blyton, *The Children of Cherry-Tree Farm* (1940), *The Children of Willow Farm* (1942)

EXHIB: RA; New Gallery, St Ives

COLL: Auckland Art Gallery; THG

LIT: P. V. Bradshaw, *The Art of the Illustrator 4* (1918)

ROWLEY, Hon. Hugh (1833–1908) – *see* Bryant & Heneage

ROWSON, Martin George Edmund (b. 1959). Political and strip cartoonist, caricaturist and illustrator. Martin Rowson was born on 15 February 1959 in London, the son of Dr K. E. K. Rowson, a virologist, and is a self-taught artist. While reading English at Pembroke College, Cambridge (1978–82), he contributed cartoons and illustrations to *Broadsheet*. After Cambridge his first published cartoon series was 'Scenes from the Lives of the Great Socialists' in the *New Statesman* (1982–3). He has also contributed to *Financial Weekly* (1984–9), *Sunday Today* (1986–7), *Today* (pocket and editorial cartoons, 1986–93), *Sunday Correspondent* (caricatures and strips, 1989–90), *Independent on Sunday* ('Logorrhoea' strip since 1991 [renamed 'Pantheon' 1994]), *Independent Magazine* (1993–4), *Guardian* (1987–8, and editorial cartoons since 1994), *Weekend Guardian* (1991–3), *Time Out* (since 1990), *Dublin Sunday Tribune* (since 1991), *Daily Mirror* (illustrations since 1996), *Observer* (financial cartoons 1996–8), *Tribune* (political cartoons and 'Blair's Babies' strip since 1994), *Daily Express* (illustrations since 1998), *The Scotsman* (editorial cartoons since 1998) and the *Times Educational Supplement* (editorial cartoons since 1998). In addition, he has worked as an occasional book reviewer for *Sunday Correspondent* (1989–90), *Independent on Sunday* (since 1990) and *Guardian*, writes a column in *Tribune* and has been a council member of the Zoological Society of London since 1992.

PUB: [with K. Killane] *Scenes from the Lives of the Great Socialists* (1983), *Lower Than Vermin: An Anatomy of Thatcher's Britain* (1986); *The Waste Land* (1990)

ILL: J. Cicatrix, *Imperial Exits* (1995); A. Clarke, *The Nodland Express* (1995); W. Self, *The Sweet Smell of Psychosis* (1996); L. Sterne, *The Life and Opinions of Tristram Shandy* (1996); J. Sweeney, *Purple Homicide* (1997)

EXHIB: Ravensdale Gallery; Rogues Gallery, Edinburgh; Politico's Bookshop

COLL: BM

RUAN – *see* Angrave, Bruce

RUSHTON, William George (1937–96). Actor, author, caricaturist, illustrator, broadcaster and political, strip and joke cartoonist. Born in Kensington, London, on 18 August 1937, the son of John Rushton, a publisher, Willie Rushton was educated at Shrewsbury School (from 1950) where he was a contemporary of Richard Ingrams and with him co-edited and drew cartoons for *The Salopian*. He later drew cartoons for the Oxford University magazine *Mesopotamia*, though not a student at the university himself. After National Service in the army he worked at first in a solicitor's office for a year (1959) before turning freelance, drawing cartoons for *Tribune* and illustrating children's books for Harrap. He was then appointed Political Cartoonist for *Liberal News* (where he also created a strip, 'Brimstone Belcher') and in 1961 was a co-founder, with Richard Ingrams, Christopher Booker and Paul Foot, of the satirical magazine *Private Eye*, for which he also designed the 'Little Gnittie' masthead (a portrait of fellow satirist John Wells in a spoof of the Crusader logo on the *Daily Express*). In 1963 he stood for election as an Independent against Prime Minister Sir Alec Douglas-Home in the Kinross and Perthshire by-election but lost his deposit. A self-taught artist, he produced cartoons, caricatures and illustrations for many newpapers and magazines including *Private Eye* (taking over the illustrations for 'Auberon Waugh's Diary' when NICOLAS BENTLEY died in 1978 and contributing countless cartoons, in-

cluding covers), *Oldie, Literary Review* (including colour covers), *Daily Telegraph* (notably illustrations to Auberon Waugh's 'Way of the World' column), *Daily Express* and *Punch*. His stage debut was in Spike Milligan's *The Bedsitting Room* (1962) and he also acted in films (e.g. *Those Magnificent Men in Their Flying Machines*, 1964), and regularly appeared on TV and radio shows such as *That Was the Week That Was* (1962), *Jackanory* (for which he also wrote scripts) and *I'm Sorry I Haven't a Clue* (from 1976). Influenced by SEARLE, PONT, FOUGASSE, BENTLEY, GILES, Saul Steinberg and B. Kliban, he worked with pen and ink, roughing out faces in pencil first (he often signed his drawings simply 'R'). 'His drawings were distinguished by their clean line and bold use of black and white. His caricatures were always recognizable' (*Daily Telegraph* obituary). John Wells said of him: 'He seemed like G. K. CHESTERTON and Fred Astaire and STRUBE and GILES all in one.' Willie Rushton died in London on 11 December 1996 aged 59. His son Toby is also a cartoonist.

PUB: *William Rushton's Dirty Book* (1964), *The 'I didn't know the way to King's Cross when I first came here but look at me now' Book* (1966), *How to Play Football* (1968), *The Day of the Grocer* (1971), *Sassenach's Scotland* (1975), *The Geranium of Flüt* (1975), *Superpig* (1976), *Pigsticking, A Joy for Life* (1977), [with F. Ward] *Unarmed Gardening* (1979), *The Reluctant Euro* (1980), *The Filth Amendment* (1981), *W. G. Grace's Last Case* (1984), *Willie Rushton's Great Moments in History* (1985), *The Alternative Gardener* (1986), *Marylebone Versus the World* (1987), (ed.) *Spy Thatcher* (1987), *Every Cat in the Book* (1995)

ILL: Many books including J. Talbot, *Elephant on the Line!* (1979); J. Needle, *Wild Wood* (1981); M. Rosen, *A Cat and Mouse Story* (1982); R. Mash, *How to Keep Dinosaurs* (1983); D. Rushton, *The Queen's English* (1985)

EXHIB: CG

COLL: V&A; BM

RUSLING, Albert (b. 1944). Joke and strip cartoonist, illustrator and writer. Albert Rusling was born in Liverpool on 27 October 1944 and left school at 15 to work in an advertising agency. A self-taught artist, he turned full-time professional cartoonist in 1968 and has contributed to many magazines and newspapers such as *Punch* (including covers), *Private Eye* (including the strip 'Old Macdonald' since May

1992), *Guardian* and *Financial Times*, and has written and illustrated a number of books.
PUB: *The Mouse and Mrs Proudfoot* (1984), [with M. WILLIAMS] *The Very, Very, Very Last Book Ever: Part One* (1986), *The Criminals' Bumper Fun Book* (1990)

RUTH – *see* Beerbohm, Sir Henry Maximilian

RW – *see* Winnington, Richard

RYAN, John Gerald Christopher (b. 1921). Author, illustrator, animator and cartoonist. John Ryan was born in Edinburgh on 4 March 1921, the son of Sir Andrew Ryan KBE CMG, a diplomat. Educated at Ampleforth College, York (where he was taught by the cartoonist Father Sylvester), he studied at the Regent Street Polytechnic (1946–8). During World War II he served in the Lincolnshire Regiment in Burma and India (1942–5). After the war he was Assistant Art Master at Harrow School (1948–55) during which period he began contributing strips to children's comics such as *Eagle* and *Girl*. His best-known creation, 'Captain Pugwash' – 'the bravest, most handsome pirate of the Seven Seas' – first appeared in *Eagle* comic on 14 April 1950, was screened on BBC TV from *c.* 1958 and later appeared in *Radio Times* for eight years. Pugwash's red-and-black striped shirt was inspired by Ampleforth College's football team's colours. Other memorable cartoon series include 'Harris Tweed – Extra Special Agent', 'Sir Prancelot', 'Mary, Mungo and Midge' and 'Lettice Leefe', many of which have also appeared in animated versions for BBC TV. In addition he has worked as a cartoonist on the *Catholic Herald* since 1966 and has written

John Ryan, [Captain Pugwash], n.d.

and illustrated a number of children's books. Influenced by H. M. BATEMAN, John Ryan works in pen and indian ink with watercolour or wash.
PUB: *Rolling in the Aisles* (1975) plus more than 40 children's books including the 'Captain Pugwash' series (18 titles from 1956), 'The Ark Stories' series (12 titles from 1980), 'Crockle' series, *Dodo's Delight* (1977), *Doodle's Homework* (1978), *Mabel and the Tower of Babel* (1990), *Jonah, a Whale of a Tale* (1992)
EXHIB: RA; Trafford Gallery; Royal Pavilion, Brighton; travelling exhibition shown in schools, libraries, museums, etc., all over UK
COLL: UKCC; MOMI

S

SALLON, Ralph David [real name Rachmiel David Zelon] MBE (1899–1999). Caricaturist. Ralph Sallon was born on 9 December 1899 in Sheps, Poland, the son of Isaac Meyer Zelon, a women's tailor. He came to England at the age of four and was brought up in the East End. He later attended Crouch End School and (briefly) Hornsey School of Art (1914). He served in the army in World War I and in 1922 moved to South Africa where his first caricature was published in the *Natal Mercury* in 1923. After two years he returned to England, studied at St Martin's School of Art and joined *Everybody's Weekly* (1925–45), while also contributing caricatures to *East Africa* (1930–39). Resident caricaturist on the *Jewish Chronicle* (*c.* 1930–91)

Ralph Sallon, [Herbert Morrison], *Sallon's War*, 1994

he has worked freelance for *Tatler, Bystander, Vanity Fair, Illustrated Sporting & Dramatic News, Daily Herald* (1943–8), *Daily Mail, Blighty, Artist, Sunday Empire News, Daily Sketch, Reader's Digest, Observer, British Digest* and *Daily Express*. During World War II he produced propaganda cartoons for aerial leaflets, etc., including *Message*, the Free Belgium newsletter produced in London. Staff caricaturist on the *Daily Mirror* (1948–91), he has also produced *Vanity Fair*-style full-colour caricature prints of 12 distinguished lawyers (1962) and five Lord Chancellors (1989) for Butterworths publishers. In addition he has worked in advertising for BP, the GPO and others and drawn covers for *Time* and *Life*. An admirer of the work of SPY, Caran D'Ache, Low and BATEMAN, he was awarded an MBE in 1977 and was honoured as the CCGB's first Master Cartoonist in 1995. He prefers to draw from life and works first in pencil and then indian ink with a pen or brush (and sometimes watercolour) on Whatman Board or paper. Ralph Sallon died in Barnet General Hospital on 29 October 1999.

PUB: *Sallon's War* (1995)

EXHIB: Cabinet War Rooms
COLL: Wig & Pen Club; BFI

SAMBOURNE, Edward Linley (1844–1910). Political and joke cartoonist, caricaturist and illustrator. Linley Sambourne was born at 15 Lloyd Square, Pentonville, London, on 4 January 1844, the son of Edward Mott Sambourne, an American-born wholesale furrier. His mother, Frances Linley, was a distant relative of the composer Thomas Linley and his daughter Elizabeth Anne Linley, the wife of R. B. Sheridan. Educated at the City of London School (1855–6) and Chester College Training School (1857–60), at the age of 16 he was apprenticed as a draughtsman to John Penn & Sons, marine engineers, in Greenwich. Self-taught as an artist (apart from two weeks at the South Kensington Schools), he began working for *Punch* after a work colleague showed one of his drawings to his father, a friend of the magazine's Editor, Mark Lemon. His first contribution (an initial letter 'T') appeared on 27 April 1867 and he joined the staff in 1871, remaining with the magazine for more than 40 years until his death in 1910. He later illustrated the 'Essence of Parliament' feature (taking over from C. H. Bennett and being himself succeeded by HARRY FURNISS), drew caricatures for 'Punch's Fancy Portraits' and on 1 January 1901 succeeded Tenniel as Cartoonist (being himself succeeded by BERNARD PARTRIDGE). He also contributed to *Black & White, Sketch* (including covers), *Good Words, Pall Mall Magazine* (including its first-ever cover, 1893), *Minster, Daily Chronicle, Illustrated London News* (including its Jubilee cover, 1892). In addition he was an accomplished book illustrator. Influenced at first by Charles Bennett, Keene, Leech and Tenniel he also admired the *Fliegender Blätter* artist Wilhelm Busch ('To me, personally, some of the designs of the late Wilhelm Busch, of Munich, seem to have more humour, if by that is meant fun, than anything I can remember having seen' (*Strand*, Vol. 27). He paid great attention to details and developed a style 'which for sheer purity of line and solid correctness of draughtsmanship has not been excelled among British artists' (Low). Veth thought him the greatest English caricaturist since Rowlandson and for THORPE he was 'after Keene, the greatest of the *Punch* artists'. His strength was in the classical, the formal, the decorative and 'the contrived grotesque' (Price). Amongst his best known cartoons are 'Vivat

Imperator' (7 January 1903) depicting Edward VII as Emperor of India, and 'The Mahogany Tree' for the Jubilee issue of *Punch* (18 July 1891), showing all the members of the *Punch* Table (which is in fact made of deal). As well as a library of 10,000 photographs, he used models, preferring to draw figures in the nude at first and then adding clothes afterwards. Known as Sammy to his friends, he greatly influenced PHIL MAY ('Everything I know I learnt from Sammy') and was himself caricatured by SPY for *Vanity Fair* (1882). He was a member of the Two Pins Riding Club (named after Gilpin and Turpin). He married Marion Herapath, daughter of Spencer Herapath FRS, and their daughter Maud (Mrs Messel) was also an illustrator and one of the earliest female artists on *Punch* (contributing from 1893, at the age of 16, as 'M. S.'). Her descendants include the designer Oliver Messel and Princess Margaret's former husband, the Earl of Snowdon, and their son, Viscount Linley. Edward Linley Sambourne died at his home, 18 Stafford Terrace, Kensington (now Linley Sambourne House) on 3 August 1910.
ILL: F. C. Burnand, *The New History of Sandford and Merton* (1872), *The Real Adventures of Robinson Crusoe* (1893); J. C. Molloy, *Our Autumn Holiday on the French Rivers* (1874), *Our Holiday in the Scottish Highlands* (1875); J. E. Jenkins, *The Blot on the Queen's Head* (1876); *Ben Changes the Motto* (1880); Lord Byron, *Venice from Childe Harold* (1878); C. Kingsley, *The Water Babies* (1885); Lord Brabourne, *Friends and Foes from Fairyland* (1886); M. Noel, *Buz or the Life and Adventures of a Honey Bee* (1889); W. M. Thackeray, *The Four Georges* (1894); *Papers from Punch* (1898); *Three Tales from Hans Andersen* (1910)
EXHIB: RA; FAS (1893)
COLL: V&A; Linley Sambourne House; NPG
LIT: C. Veth, *Comic Art in England* (1930)

SANDFORD, Matthew 'Matt' (1875–1943). Caricaturist, political cartoonist and painter. Matt Sandford was born in Ulster. He worked at first in Manchester as a caricaturist for the *Manchester Evening Chronicle* and the Hulton Press Group before moving to London to work for the *Daily Sketch* when it was launched (in 1909). He also contributed to *Daily Graphic*, *Evening Standard* and others. A. S. Mellor said of Matt: 'after E. T. REED of *Punch* I considered him the greatest political caricaturist'. He used a brush and wash, working usually 8 × 9 in., and also painted in oils. A member of the

London Press Club, a number of his drawings adorned its walls. Matt Sandford died in London on 30 December 1943 aged 68.
ILL: S. Stokes, *Personal Glimpses* (1924); F. E. Smith, *Contemporary Personalities* (1924)
COLL: NPG (caricature of 1st Viscount Runciman, 1924)

SAVA – *see* Botzaritch, Anastas Sava

SCARFE, Gerald (b. 1936). Joke cartoonist, caricaturist, illustrator, animator and film-producer. Gerald Scarfe was born on 1 June 1936 in St John's Wood, London, the son of a banker. Bedridden with asthma until the age of 11, he won a prize for an Ingersoll watch advertisement in *Eagle* (beating David Hockney) and began drawing regularly for the comic while still at school. He started work in his uncle's commercial art studio while studying at St Martin's School of Art in the evenings and then turned freelance, his first cartoons being published in the *Daily Sketch* (1957), *Evening Standard* and *Punch* (1960). But it was at *Private Eye* (from 1961, including 11 covers) that he really found his style, and his cover for the 1963 annual caused it to be banned by the four largest book wholesalers (including W. H. Smith). He also produced giant puppets of Harold Wilson, Ian Smith and President Johnson for a CND rally in London (1966) and later joined the *Daily Mail* as a war artist (1967–8). He then moved to the *Sunday Times* and made papier-mâché caricature models for *Time* magazine covers (1967) while also contributing to *Esquire* and *Fortune*. A commission from the COI led to the construction of a 30ft-high scrap-metal Gulliver figure for Expo 70 in Japan (1970). At this time he also directed a film, *Hogarth*, for BBC TV's *Omnibus*, followed by the animated film, *A Long Drawn-out Trip* (1973). This brought him to the attention of pop group Pink Floyd and work on another film, *The Wall* (1982), for MGM, which he art-directed and for which he produced puppets, inflatables and animation sequences. He has also designed for the theatre, including sets for the English National Opera. As well as drawing and painting, Scarfe has worked in papier-mâché, metal, plaster and chicken wire, leather and a wide variety of other media. He is an admirer of SEARLE (who later admired him) and John Berger has described him as 'a natural satirical draughtsman. Gillray was one, Rowlandson wasn't. George Grosz was one, but Low isn't. The supreme examples are Goya and Daumier.' Scarfe's

THE THREE PRIME MINISTERS

Gerald Scarfe, [Thatcher, Wilson, Heath], n.d.

distinctively violent and grotesquely distorted images reflect his own attitudes to his subjects: 'I can only express good by a comparison between evil and greater evil.' He was the winner of the CCGB Special Award (1966). Scarfe is married to the actress and author Jane Asher.

PUB: *Gerald Scarfe's People* (1966), *Indecent Exposure* (1973), *Expletive Deleted* (1974), *Gerald Scarfe* (1982), [with B. Mooney] *Father Kissmass and Mother Claws* (1985), *Scarfe by Scarfe* (1986), *Seven Deadly Sins* (1987), *Lines of Attack* (1988), *Scarfeland* (1989)

ILL: R. West, *Sketches from Vietnam* (1968); J. Asher, *Moppy is Happy* (1987), *Moppy is Angry* (1987); T. Jones, *Attacks of Opinion* (1988)

EXHIB: Tib Lane Gallery, Manchester; Waddell Gallery, New York; GG; CG; Chester Arts Centre (Retrospective, 1978); MAN; Vincent Price Gallery, Chicago; Bradford Art Gallery; Graves Art Gallery, Sheffield; NPG; RFH and York, Cleveland, Bristol, etc., tour (1983–4); CBG

COLL: NPG; [poster] BM; UKCC

LIT: *Scarfe by Scarfe* (1986)

SCHLEGEL – *see* Mallet, Harcourt Dennis

'Schmidt the Spy' – *see* Leete, Alfred Chew

SCHRANK, Peter (b. 1952). Political cartoonist and caricaturist. Peter Schrank was born in St Gallen, Switzerland, on 23 September 1952. He was educated at Basel Art School (1973–7) and came to the UK in 1981. His first cartoon was published in *Time Out* in October 1981 and he has since worked for *Sunday Business Post* (since 1989), *Basler Zeitung* (since 1993), *Independent* and *Independent on Sunday* (since 1995). He has also contributed to *New Statesman*, *Times* Supplements and other publications, and was a resident commentator on the week's cartoons for the cable and satellite TV station European Business News (1995–6). He cites his influences as Saul Steinberg and Tomi Ungerer. His favoured medium is pen, brush and ink 'with a little bit of help from an airbrush'.

COLL: International Museum of Cartoon Art (IMCA), Boca Raton, Florida

SCHWADRON, Harley Lawrence (b. 1942). Joke cartoonist and illustrator. Harley Schwadron was born on 23 November 1942 in

Harley Schwadron, *Boston Globe*, 1998

New York City, the son of Allen Schwadron, a tax lawyer, and was educated at Bowdoin College, Brunswick, Maine (graduating in philosophy in 1964) and the University of California at Berkeley (MA in journalism, 1967). He worked as a newspaper reporter in Connecticut and as a public information officer at the University of Michigan before becoming a full-time cartoonist. A self-taught artist, his work has appeared in *Punch*, *Wall Street Journal*, *Washington Times*, *Playboy*, *Penthouse*, *Omni*, *Barron's*, *Reader's Digest* and others. He received the Scripps Howard Foundation's Charles Schulz Award for his work in 1983.
ILL: More than 20 books as well as University of Michigan campus guides (1985–93)
EXHIB: University of Michigan School of Art, Ann Arbor, Michigan
COLL: Gerald Ford Library, University of Michigan

SCOTT, Ian James ARCA (b. 1914). Political cartoonist and cartoonists' agent. Born in London on 30 July 1914, Ian Scott attended St Martin's School of Art (1928–32) and the Royal College of Art (1932–5). During World War II he served with the Royal Engineers in the Middle East and subsequently ran the Drawing Office of RE Base depot in Ismailia, where he edited a wall newspaper and wrote and produced shows for the troops. After the war he was Political Cartoonist on the *Daily Sketch* (1954–6), resigning to join the *News Chronicle* (1956–7). He then left to set up a specialist art agency for cartoonists, Kingleo Studios (1954–87), which represented more than 100 artists. He was also the founder and first Chairman of the Cartoonists' Club of Great Britain in 1960 and is now its Honorary Life President.
PUB: (ed.) *British Cartoonists' Album* (1962), (ed.) *British Cartoonists' Year Book* (1964), (ed.) *From Russia With Laughter* (1965)

SCULLY, William (b. 1917). Joke cartoonist. Bill Scully was born in Ilkeston, Derbyshire, on 12 June 1917, the son of a builder and an amateur artist, and studied at Nottingham School of Art. He worked for four years as a pipe-tester in an ironworks and spent seven years in an artificial silk factory before having his first cartoons accepted by the *Bystander*. During World War II he served in the Army Ordnance Corps and became Art Editor of *AIM*, an army magazine

(1943–5), and then worked on the staff of JAMES FRIELL's *Soldier* (1945–6) under Art Editor PETER ENDER. His work has appeared in *Punch* (including covers), *Bystander*, *Sunday Telegraph*, *Spectator*, *Sketch*, *New Yorker*, *London Opinion*, *Men Only*, *Lilliput*, *Tatler* and other publications. An admirer of American artists such as Charles Dana Gibson, James Montgomery Flagg (*see* LEETE), Peter Arno, James Thurber and the artists of *Judge* and *Life*, Scully's cartoons also show the influence of *New Yorker* cartoonists. HEWISON has described his work as 'marvellously free and autographic but with a tight control over the use of tone. You are always aware of *space* in a Scully drawing.' Scully himself holds that a humorous drawing should never be realistic or photographic: 'Even in serious art, the impression of labour should not be obvious. In comic art it is fatal.'
COLL: UKCC

'Sculptoons' – *see* Davien, Geoffrey

SEARLE, Ronald William Fordham RDI AGI (b. 1920). Caricaturist, cartoonist, illustrator, designer and publisher. Ronald Searle was born in Cambridge on 3 March 1920, the son of William James Searle, a railway engineer, and educated at the Boys' Central School, Cambridge. He started work as a solicitor's clerk, then joined the hire-purchase department of the Co-op, studying in the evenings and later full-time at Cambridge Technical College and School of Art (1935–9) where contemporaries included Joan Brock, daughter of H. M. BROCK. His first cartoons, published in the *Cambridge Daily News* (October 1935–9) – where his predecessor was SIDNEY MOON – and *Granta* (1936–9), were signed 'R. W. F. Searle'. During World War II he served with 287 Field Co. Royal Engineers from 1939, contributing to the *Daily Express* (1939), *Discovery*, *London Opinion* (1940) and *Lilliput* (1941) until captured by the Japanese at the fall of Singapore. From 1942 to 1945 he was a prisoner of war in Siam (labouring on the infamous Burma–Siam railway for seven months in 1943) and in Changi, Singapore, where he met GEORGE SPROD. Returning to England, he began work for *Illustrated*, *Strand Magazine*, *John Bull*, *Daily Herald*, *Pie*, *Tatler & Bystander*, *Men Only*, *Radio Times*, *The Studio* and *Lilliput*. He was cartoonist on *Tribune* (1949–51) and the *Sunday Express* (1950–51), Special Feature Artist on the *News Chronicle* (1951–3) and cartoonist for the same paper (1954), and cartoonist and theatre artist for *Punch* (1949–62), succeeding STAMPA and introducing caricatures to the page for the first time for many years. During the Suez crisis in 1956 he served in the headquarters of the Department of Psychological Warfare. He has also contributed cartoons to *New Yorker, Life, Sketch, Der Spiegel, Men Only, Le Canard Enchaîné, London Opinion, Time & Tide, Holiday, Saturday Evening Post, Young Elizabethan, Figaro Littéraire, Sports Illustrated, Forward, Graphis* and others, and has drawn regularly for *Le Monde* since 1995. His extensive advertising work has included Lemon Hart Rum, Guinness, American Express, Cadbury's, British Telecom and others. In addition he has designed medals for the French Mint (from 1974) and the British Art Medal Society (from 1983) and been a designer and/or drawn animation sequences for a number of films including *John Gilpin* (1951), *On the Twelfth Day* (1954) – which was nominated for an Academy Award – *Energetically Yours* (1957), *Those Magnificent Men in Their Flying Machines* (1965), *Monte Carlo or Bust* (1969), *Scrooge* (1970) and *Dick Deadeye* (1975). A one-time member of the Chelsea Arts Club, he also designed the Chelsea Arts Ball in 1954. Founder of the Perpetua Press with his first wife, Kaye Webb (the publisher, children's author and former Assistant Editor of *Lilliput*), he has received many international awards for his work, including National Cartoonists' Society of America Awards (1959, 1960, 1966) and the CAT Lifetime Achievement Award (1995). Particularly memorable characters created by Searle include the devilish schoolgirls of St Trinian's (featured in five films) and Nigel Molesworth in the books written by Geoffrey Willans. Left-handed (his right hand was crushed while working on the Burma–Siam railway in World War II), he works in a variety of media, but mostly pen and ink with wash, gouache or watercolour. He sketches in fountain pen but uses dip pen for final artwork. For many years he used woodstain instead of ink (Stephens Liquid Stains: Ebony) but has since worked with Super Yang-tse Encre de Chine. A very influential artist, HEWISON has described him as 'arguably the foremost graphic artist this century'. In 1967 he married his second wife, the theatre designer Monica Koenig.

PUB: More than 40 books including *Forty Drawings* (1946), *Hurrah for St Trinian's* (1948), *The Female Approach* (1949), *Back to the Slaughterhouse* (1951), [with G. Willans] six books from *Down With Skool!* (1953); *Souls in Torment* (1953), *The Rake's Progress* (1955), [with A. Atkinson] four books from *The Big City* (1958); *Searle in the Sixties* (1964), *Searle's Cats* (1967), *The Square Egg* (1968), *The King of Beasts* (1980), *The Illustrated Winespeak* (1983), *Ronald Searle's Golden Oldies* (1985), *To the Kwai – and Back* (1986), *Something in the Cellar* (1986), *Ah Yes, I Remember it Well* (1987), *Slightly Foxed – But Still Desirable* (1989), *The Curse of St Trinian's* (1993), *Marquis de Sade Meet Goody Two-Shoes* (1994), *Ronald Searle dans le Monde* (1998)

ILL: More than 40 books including P. Campbell, *A Long Drink of Cold Water* (1949), *A Short Trot with a Cultured Mind* (1950), *Life in Thin Slices* (1951); R. Braddon, *The Piddingtons* (1950), *The Naked Island* (1952); W. Cowper, *The Diverting History of John Gilpin* (1954); C. Fry, *An Experience of Critics* (1952), *A Phoenix Too Frequent* (1959); C. Dickens, *A Christmas Carol* (1961), *Great Expectations* (1962), *Oliver Twist* (1962); J. Thurber, *The Thirteen Clocks and the Wonderful O* (1962); S. Kortum, *The Hatless Man* (1995)

EXHIB: Batsford Gallery; LG; New York; Hanover; La Pochade, Paris; Galerie Gurlitt, Munich; GG; Cooper-Hewitt Museum, New York; Neue Galerie Wien, Vienna; IWM; BM; F; BIB (1973); Museum of Fine Arts, San Francisco and others

COLL: CAT; V&A; BM; IWM; BIB; Kunsthalle, Bremen; WBM; Stadtmuseum, Munich; Art Museum, Dallas; Staatliches Museum, Berlin; Cooper-Hewitt Museum, New York; University of Texas, Austin

LIT: *Ronald Searle* (1978); *Ronald Searle in Perspective* (1984); R. Davies, *Ronald Searle* (1990); G. Vetter-Liebenow, *Ronald Searle* (1996)

SEM – *see* Goursat, Georges

SHAW, John Byam Liston RI ROI ARWS (1872–1919). Painter, illustrator, art teacher and joke cartoonist. John Byam Shaw was born on 13 November 1872 in Madras, the son of John Shaw, Registrar of the Madras High Court, and Sophia Alicia Byam Gunthorpe. He returned to England in 1878, moving to London the following year. He studied at the St John's Wood School of Art (1887) and RA Schools (1890–93) with HEATH ROBINSON, STAMPA and LEWIS BAUMER and while still a student had drawings accepted by *Comic Cuts, Illustrated Bits* and *Moonshine*. He first exhibited at the Royal Academy in 1893 and later also contributed cartoons and illustrations to *Punch, Cartoon, Strand, Graphic, Dome, Cassell's, Connoisseur, Daily Call, Daily Chronicle, Daily Express, Evening Standard* and the *Sunday Times*. In 1904 he began teaching art at King's College, University of London, and in 1910 was a joint founder (with Rex Vicat Cole ROI RBC RBA) of the Byam Shaw and Vicat Cole School of Art in Kensington. His book of satirical drawings, *Life's Ironies*, was published in 1912. A distinguished painter in oils, watercolours and pastels, he also designed tapestry, stained glass, and theatre sets and THORPE thought him 'one of the best of the decorative illustrators' of books. In addition he drew advertisements for Selfridges and others. His cartoon work is mostly in pen and ink. He was elected RI (1898), ROI (1899) and ARWS (1913). John Byam Shaw died in London on 26 January 1919, aged 46.

PUB: *Life's Ironies* (1912)

ILL: More than 25 books including R. Browning, *Poems* (1897); J. Jacobs (ed.), *Tales from Boccaccio* (1899); *The Chiswick Shakespeare* (1899); *Old King Cole's Nursery Rhymes* (1902); J. C. Hadden, *The Operas of Wagner* (1908); F. Sedgwick (ed.), *Ballads and Lyrics of Love* (1908), *Legendary Ballads* (1908); F. A. Steel, *The Adventures of Akbar* (1913); L. Hope, *The Garden of Kama* (1914)

EXHIB: RA; RI; RWS; ROI; DOW

COLL: V&A; B; BR; LE; L; NEW; Ashmolean; IWM; THG

LIT: R. Vicat Cole, *The Art and Life of Byam Shaw* (1932)

SHEPARD, Ernest Howard OBE MC (1879–1976). Joke and political cartoonist, illustrator and painter. E. H. Shepard was born on 10 December 1879 in St John's Wood, London, the son of Henry Dunkin Shepard, an architect and amateur painter. His mother, Jessie Harriet Lee, was the daughter of the watercolour artist William Lee, and as a child Ernest modelled for Sir Francis Dicksee (later President of the Royal Academy), a family friend. Educated at St John's Wood Preparatory School, Colet Court School (with the future Archbishop William Temple) and St Paul's School (with G. K. CHESTERTON and Compton Mackenzie), he studied art at Heatherley's in 1896 aged 16 (with STAMPA) and then won a scholarship to the RA Schools (1897–1902). He worked at first as a painter (first exhibiting at the RA in 1901) and also contributed joke cartoons and illustrations to *Graphic, Illustrated London News, Printer's Pie, London Opinion, Nash's, Odd Volume, Pears Annual* and the *Sketch*. The illustrator Edwin Abbey introduced him to LINLEY SAMBOURNE, who helped him get his first cartoons published in *Punch* (1907), and he subsequently worked for the magazine for nearly 50 years (until 1954), joining the *Punch* Table in 1921 and contributing jokes, political cartoons and covers. He eventually succeeded RAVEN HILL as Second Cartoonist (1935–45) and PARTRIDGE as Cartoonist (1945–9), himself handing over to ILLINGWORTH. In World War I he served in the Royal Artillery (1915–18) in France, Belgium and Italy, achieving the rank of major and being awarded the Military Cross at Ypres (1917). However, though he worked as a political cartoonist he was ill-suited to the job: 'He never found it easy to get a likeness . . . Nor could he manage the sheer indignation which gives political satire its weight' (Penelope Fitzgerald). He is far better known as a book illustrator, notably for *When We Were Very Young* and the subsequent 'Pooh' volumes written by the Assistant Editor of *Punch*, A. A. Milne, and which first appeared in the magazine in January 1924. Though Piglet, Eeyore the donkey (Shepard's own favourite) and Tigger are all fictional, Christopher Robin was actually A. A. Milne's son and the original drawing of Pooh bear was based on Shepard's son's bear 'Growler'. Immensely popular, the books spawned a wide range of spin-offs (though Shepard dismissed the 1966 Disney animated film as 'a travesty'). However, the critics were not unanimous: reviewing *The House at Pooh Corner* for the New Yorker (as 'Constant Reader'), Dorothy Parker wrote 'Tonstant Weader fwowed up'. As a book illustrator Hodnett thought Shepard was the 'only follower of Hugh Thomson who equalled him in lightness of spirit and mastery of that obstinate instrument, the pen' and considered his *Everybody's Pepys* 'one of the few almost perfect English illustrated books'. FOUGASSE also saw him as 'one of the great line draughtsmen, artistic descendant, like Gibson, of the American Edwin Abbey'. His *Wind in the Willows* characters were also more popular than Rackham's originals, but he refused to work on *Peter Pan* because he felt it could not be illustrated. An admirer of PHIL MAY and Charles Keene, he liked using small stubs of pencil and worked in ink, pen and occasional black crayon on smooth art

board or watercolour paper. He rarely used solid blacks, preferring cross-hatching and fine line or crayon for shadows. He also painted in oils. Shepard had a very dynamic style: 'He was preoccupied by the frieze rather than the group. Above all he was thinking in terms of the dance. With Shepard the rest of *Punch* began to look static' (Price). Known to his family and friends as Kipper, he married Florence Chaplin, granddaughter of the engraver Ebenezer Landells (one of the founders of *Punch*). Their daughter Mary Shepard (who married *Punch*'s editor E. V. Knox) was also an illustrator (notably of *Mary Poppins*). His step-granddaughter is the novelist Penelope Fitzgerald. A member of the Savage Club, he was appointed OBE in 1972. E. H. Shepard died in Midhurst, Sussex, on 24 March 1976 aged 96.
PUB: *Fun and Fantasy* (1927), *Ben and Brock* (1965), *Betsy and Joe* (1966)
ILL: Nearly 100 books including A. A. Milne, *When We Were Very Young* (1924), *Winnie the Pooh* (1926), *Now We Are Six* (1927), *The House at Pooh Corner* (1928); G. Agnew, *Let's Pretend* (1927); K. Grahame, *The Golden Age* (1928), *Dream Days* (1930), *The Wind in the Willows* (1931); Jan Struther, *Sycamore Square* (1932); R. Jefferies, *Bevis* (1932); L. Housman, *Victoria Regina* (1934), *The Golden Sovereign* (1937); Sir J. C. Squire, *Cheddar Gorge* (1937)
EXHIB: RA; UKCC (1974); V&A (Memorial, 1969); [retrospective] Sally Hunter Fine Art (1988)
COLL: BM; V&A; US; UKCC; IWM
LIT: E. H. Shepard, *Drawn from Memory* (1957), *Drawn from Life* (1961); R. Knox (ed.), *The Work of E. H. Shepard* (1979)

SHEPHERD, William James Affleck 'JAS' FZS (1867–1946). Animal cartoonist and illustrator. J. A. Shepherd was born in London on 29 November 1867, the son of William Shepherd, a cigar importer. A self-taught artist, his first published drawing was of a bulldog's head for a catalogue of a bulldog show in Hackney (1883) at the age of 16 (he later bred bulldogs). The following year he became a pupil of Alfred Bryan (political cartoonist and theatrical caricaturist on *Judy* and *Moonshine*) and worked with him for three years, spending much of his free time studying and drawing animals at London Zoo (he was later elected a Fellow of the Zoological Society). He then began drawing for *Judy* (1886–9) and later joined the staff of *Moonshine* (1890–93) and the *Illustrated London News*.

Influenced by the anthropomorphic style of the French cartoonists Grandville and Griset, he contributed cartoons of animals dressed as humans to *Black & White, Boy's Own Paper, Cassell's, Chums, Good Words, Illustrated Sporting & Dramatic News, Sketch* and *Tatler*. He also drew a number of popular series for the newly launched *Strand* magazine, notably 'Zig-Zags at the Zoo' (1891–4) which was later produced as a sequence of animated films by Phillips Philm Phables (1919), and contributed to *Punch* for 46 years from July 1893, his last drawing appearing in the *Almanack* for 1939. In addition he drew advertisements for *Femina* magazine and others, and in 1911 he was awarded a gold medal at the International Exhibition of Humorous Art in Rivoli, Italy. He said he preferred to draw 'character – not caricature', and worked mainly in outline but also used wash or colour (and occasionally painted on silk). Animals were a lifelong passion for Shepherd who, as well as bulldogs, had a pet raven called 'Elijah'. 'He had a remarkable gift for registering human expressions and emotions on their faces and in their poses without blurring or overdistorting their animal characteristics; and he did it all with an amazing mastery and economy of line' (*Punch* obituary). THORPE greatly admired his work: 'Shepherd's drawings of animals are the best and funniest that have ever been made.' He was a member of the Savage Club. J. A. Shepherd died at his home, Woodmancote Manor, Cirencester, Gloucestershire, on 11 May 1946.
PUB: *Zig-Zags at the Zoo* (1895), *Tommy at the Zoo* (1895), *Zig-Zag Fables* (1897), *The Frog Who Would A-Wooing Go* (1900), *Who Killed Cock Robin?* (1900), *A Thoroughbred Mongrel* (1900), *The Donkey Book* (1903), *Funny Animals and Stories About Them* (1904), *Old Dedick's Tales* (1904), *The Life of a Foxhound* (1910), *A Frolic Round the Zoo* (1926), *Animal Caricature* (1936)
ILL: A. Morrison, *Zig-Zags at the Zoo* (1895); A. Chester, *Tommy at the Zoo* (1895); J. C. Harris, *Uncle Remus* (1901), *Nights With Uncle Remus* (1925); E. W. D. Cuming, *Wonders in Monsterland* (1901), *Three Jovial Puppies* (1907), *Idlings in Arcadia* (1934), *The Arcadian Calendar* (1943); E. Selous, *Jack's Insects* (1910), *The Zoo Conversation Book* (1911), *Jack's Other Insects* (1920); E. Rostand, *The Story of Chanticleer* (1911); *The Bodley Head Natural History* (1913); W. Garstang, *Songs of the Birds* (1922)
EXHIB: PAG (1928)
COLL: BM

SHEPPERSON, Claude Allin ARA ARWS RI ARE RMS (1867–1921). Painter, illustrator and joke cartoonist. Claude Shepperson was born in Beckenham, Kent, on 25 October 1867. He studied law at first then changed to art, spending two years in Paris at the Atelier Humbert & Gervex and at Heatherley's. He then worked as book illustrator and painter, exhibiting landscapes and social scenes, while also contributing cartoons and illustrations to *Black & White*, *Cassell's*, *English Illustrated Magazine*, *Graphic*, *Harmsworth*, *Idler*, *Illustrated Bits*, *Illustrated London News*, *Pall Mall*, *Pears Annual*, *Queen*, *St Paul's*, *Sketch*, *Strand* (e.g. illustrations to Kipling's 'Puck of Pook's Hill' and H. G. Wells's 'The First Men in the Moon'), *Tatler*, *Pick-Me-Up*, *Wide World*, *Windsor Magazine* and *Punch* (c. 1905–20). In addition he drew advertisements for Erasmic, British Commercial Gas Association, Pears Soap, Kodak and others. His drawings usually featured high society figures, often with Kensington Gardens as a background, and his *Punch* cartoons were 'classic examples of the ultimate in patrician atmosphere' (Ellwood). In his book illustration work he was influenced by Edwin Abbey. He worked in a variety of media including oil, watercolour, chalk, charcoal, pastel, ink and pencil and also practised etching and lithography. However, for his line work he would first sketch nudes in charcoal on very thin banknote paper and draw clothes in ink over this, usually at near-reproduction size. He was also 'the greatest master of placing or composition in English pen drawing' (Ellwood), a view emphasized by BRADSHAW: 'One notices over and over again the diagonal treatment, in which a line drawn from one of the top corners of the drawing to the bottom corner on the opposite side almost evenly divides the light and tone of the picture; and against this broad arrangement of the background, the figures are placed with the utmost sureness and success. In the disposition of the figures, the "S" shape is used frequently.' A member of the Chelsea Arts Club, Langham Sketch Club and London Sketch Club, he was elected RI (1900), RMS (1900), ARWS (1910), ARE (1919) and ARA (1919). Claude Shepperson died in Chelsea, London, on 30 December 1921. ILL: S. Weyman, *Shrewsbury* (1898); W. Shakespeare, *The Merchant of Venice* (1899), *As You Like It* (1900); G. Borrow, *Lavengro* (1899); B. Disraeli, *Coningsby* (1900); Sir W. Scott, *The Heart of Midlothian* (1900); E. Philpotts, *Up-Along and*

Down-Along (1905); E. V. Lucas, *The Open Road* (1913); J. Keats, *Poetical Works* (1916)
EXHIB: RA; RI; RWS; LG (Memorial, 1922); AG; FAS; GG; G; L; M; RMS; RSA
COLL: V&A; B; LE; BM; THG
LIT: P. V. Bradshaw, *The Art of the Illustrator 5, C. A. Shepperson* (1918)

SHERRIFFS, Robert Stewart (1908–60). Caricaturist and illustrator. R. S. Sherriffs was born in Arbroath on 13 February 1906. An arts medallist at Arbroath High School, he studied art and heraldic design at Edinburgh College of Arts. His first published caricature (of actor John Barrymore) was spotted in the *Bystander* by Beverley Nichols, who asked him to illustrate the 'Woad' series of celebrity profiles he was writing for the *Sketch*. This led to Sherriffs producing regular full-page theatre and film drawings for the magazine. He also drew caricatures for *Nash's Magazine* in the 1930s. A contributor to *Radio Times* from 1927, he took over the illustration of the series 'Both Sides of the Microphone' when the magazine's cartoonist ARTHUR WATTS was killed in an air crash in 1935, and occasionally drew covers. During World War II

Robert Sherriffs, [Joan Crawford], *Punch*, 1952

he served in the Tank Regiment, Royal Armoured Corps, making drawings for education and aircraft recognition. He succeeded JAMES DOWD as film caricaturist on *Punch* (1948–60) and was one of the contenders (with VICKY, HYNES and others) considered for DYSON's spot on the *Daily Herald* (GEORGE WHITELAW was eventually chosen, Sherriffs not being considered 'sharp' enough). In addition, he illustrated stories for the *Evening News* and *Strand*, drew advertisements for Four Square Tobacco and others, designed menus (Masonic dinners, Savage Club – of which he was a member) and covers for *Men Only* (succeeding Hynes), and wrote a comic novel, *Salute If You Must* (1944), but never achieved his ambition to draw a wordless novel in 300 pictures. Influenced by the linear quality of DULAC (with whom he had once worked) and Beardsley, he developed a decorative calligraphic approach to caricature and preferred working in brush to pen, using Chinese inks for colour illustrations. Price has described his caricatures as 'sculptural, the face built up in rocky planes on a base of firmly apprehended character', and the artist himself as 'a bitter fantastic with a whirling imagination'. Sherriffs also said that he was a disciple of DERRICK but as Price has pointed out, 'this must be a psychological influence as nobody else can see it in his work'. He had a photographic memory and once stated: 'I regarded caricatures as designs and the expressions on faces merely as changes in a basic pattern.' He died on 26 December 1960.

PUB: [S. Bond ed.] *Sherriffs at the Cinema* (1985)
ILL: C. Marlowe, *The Life and Death of Tamburlaine the Great* (1930); R. Arkell, *Playing the Games* (1935); [aircraft sketches and cartoons] G. B. S. Ransford, *The Recognition of Operational Aircraft* (1944); E. Fitzgerald, *The Rubaiyat of Omar Khayyam* (1947); C. Dickens, *Captain Boldheart* (1947) and *Mrs Orange* (1948); H. S. Deighton (ed.), 'A Portrait of Britain' series (from 1951)
EXHIB: Times Bookshop; NFT; NT; CG
COLL: NPG; BFI; UKCC; V&A

SHERWOOD, G. S. (fl. 1925–d.1958). Joke cartoonist and illustrator. G. S. Sherwood contributed social cartoons to the *Humorist* (1925–40), *Men Only*, *London Opinion*, *Tit-Bits*, *Passing Show* and others. Regarding his *Punch* work (1930–38), Price described him as 'one of the more consistently successful amusers . . . [whose

style] stemmed from the later developments of RIDGEWELL, with an occasional backward glance to W. BIRD'. He had the same agent (Owen Aves) as ILLINGWORTH and A. C. Barrett. G. S. Sherwood died in June 1958.
ILL: H. F. Ellis, *The Pleasure's Yours* (1993), *Much Ado* (1934), *Mr Punch's Limerick Book* (1923); L. Carroll, *Verses from Alice* (1944)

SHORT – *see* Mackay, Wallis

SIC – *see* Sickert, Walter Richard

SICKERT, Walter Richard 'SIC' RA PRBA NEAC ARE (1860–1942). Painter, etcher, art teacher, actor, illustrator and caricaturist. Walter Sickert was born on 31 May 1860 in Munich, the eldest son of the Danish painter, illustrator, and graphic artist Oswald Adalbert Sickert (who was also on the staff of the German satirical magazine *Fliegende Blätter*) and an Anglo-Irish mother, Eleanor Louisa Moravia Henry. He was the elder brother of the landscape painter Bernard Sickert NEAC. The family came to London in 1868 and he was educated at Bayswater Collegiate School and at King's College School (1870–71). He then worked as an actor with Sir Henry Irving and at Sadler's Wells, etc. (1877–81). At the age of 19 he met Whistler, who encouraged him to study art at the Slade under Alphonse Legros (1881–2), at Heatherley's (1881) and in Paris. He first exhibited at the RBA in 1884 and spent six years working under Whistler as his studio assistant (from 1882) before starting up on his own, frequently travelling to Dieppe in France to work with Degas, POWYS EVANS and others. Primarily a painter (he later tutored Sir Winston Churchill), Sickert was an admirer of the *Punch* cartoonist Charles Keene and contributed to the *Idler, Cambridge Gazette, Yellow Book, Savoy, Pall Mall Budget, Whirlwind, Gil Blas* and others. In addition he drew (as 'SIC') caricatures of George Moore, Israel Zangwill and MAX BEERBOHM for *Vanity Fair* (1897) and others for the *New Age* (1911). He also taught at Westminster School of Art (1908–12, 1915–18). One of the early members of the Chelsea Arts Club, he was elected ARA (1924) and RA (1934) and was President of the RBA (1928). His first wife was the daughter of the calico printer and statesman Richard Cobden MP, and his third wife was the painter Thérèse Lessore, daughter of the watercolourist Jules Lessore. Walter Sickert died on 22 January 1942 in Bathampton, Somerset.

EXHIB: NG (1941); T (1960); FAS (1973); NEAC; RBA; RE; RI: ROI: RSA; RA (1992)
COLL: V&A; BM; Tate; NPG; National Liberal Club (portrait); various provincial galleries
LIT: L. Browse, *Sickert* (1960); W. Barron, *Sickert* (1973); D. Sutton, *Walter Sickert* (1976); RA Catalogue (1992)

SIGGS, Lawrence Hector (1900–72). Joke cartoonist, commercial artist and illustrator. Lawrie Siggs was born in Wolverton, Buckinghamshire, on 30 March 1900. His father owned a men's outfitters. Deeply interested in country life, he started drawing animals and birds as a child, modelling in candle-grease until his parents bought him Plasticine. Appendicitis interrupted his wireless studies at the London Telegraph Training College and he was greatly influenced while convalescing by the illustrator ALBERT MORROW, who was in the same ward with a broken jaw. He became a wireless operator with Marconi at the age of 18 and went to sea, serving on five ships. He later left Marconi and began to work as a freelance commercial artist and cartoonist. As well as designing posters, drawing advertisements (for Bovril, Meridian Knitwear, etc.) he also contributed to *Lilliput*, *Men Only*, *Punch* (35 years), *Bystander*, *Daily Telegraph*, *John Bull*, *Daily Express* (illustrating Middleton's gardening column), *Evening Standard*, *Saturday Evening Post*, *New Yorker* and *Poppy Annual*. Ideas for his cartoons were often inspired by domestic situations, with particular emphasis on children and animals. The humour was gentle and never sarcastic or satirical. He once said that 'A joke is only good if an editor picks it.' Siggs worked mostly in pen and ink but occasionally also used colour wash or watercolour. Price has described him as 'the most careful delineator of the suburban background, and also the most poetic and fantastic in humour'. In HEWISON's view his finely balanced cartoons have a strange, lingering resonance: 'he does not take us directly to the target but sends us through a series of ricochets until we reach the bull's eye from an oblique angle'. He died in Wyatt's Green, near Brentwood, Essex, on 1 July 1972.
COLL: Natural History Museum; V&A; HM the Queen Mother; UKCC

SILENUS – *see* Sillince, William Augustus

SILLINCE, William Augustus RWS FSIA RBA SGA (1906–74). Joke and political cartoonist, illus-

trator, painter and writer. William Sillince was born on 16 November 1906 in Battersea, London, the son of William Patrick Sillince, a Royal Navy marine engineer. He was educated at Osborne House, Romsey, and studied at the Regent Street Polytechnic School of Art and the Central School of Arts & Crafts (1923–8). Sillince began as a designer in advertising (1928–36), working for Haddons agency and clients such as Player's Cigarettes, Esso and Guinness, before turning freelance, contributing to *Punch* (1936–74, including whole-page political cartoons [from 1936] as deputy to ILLINGWORTH), *Bystander*, *Christmas Pie* and other magazines as well as illustrating books. He also taught part-time at Brighton College of Art (1949–52), was lecturer in graphic design at Hull Regional College of Art (1952–71) and designed the Alice in Wonderland Room at Burton Constable Hall (1967). In addition he created the series *John Bull's Other Region* for BBC TV (North), contributed to *Yorkshire Post* (1964–74) and wrote on cartooning in *The Artist*. An accomplished watercolourist, he was elected associate (1949), then full member (1958), of the Royal Society of Painters in Watercolour and elected RBA (1949) and FRSA (1971). His cartoon work is very distinctive for its textured look. He first sketched with a soft (2B) pencil on thin typewriting paper, then, using another thin sheet of paper (one side of which had been rubbed all over with 4B pencil) he transferred his sketch (using a 3H pencil) on to canvas-grained paper which he had previously burnished to smooth it down. Finally, he would use a Hardtmuth Negro pencil for the finished drawing. (However, he also used pen and ink in his earlier work and for his political cartoons.) FOUGASSE has described him as 'a humorist-stylist and, technically, a most excellently equipped artist, with an enthusiasm for experiment'. At first he used an ideas man for his jokes but later thought them up himself. Influenced by Daumier, Gillray and Rowlandson he also worked as 'Silenus'. William Sillince died on 10 January 1974.
PUB: About 20 books including *We're All in It* (1941), *We're Still All in It* (1942), *United Notions* (1943), *Combined Observations* (1944), *Minor Relaxations* (1945), *Comic Drawing* (1950), *Yorkshire Life* [poems] (1966)
ILL: G. K. Chesterton, *Wine, Water and Song* (1943); D. L. Sayers, *Euen the Parrot* (1944); A. Armstrong, *My Friend Serafin* (1949); R. Rangemoore, *This Merrie English* (1954); E. Hartwood,

It Don't Cost You a Penny (1955); L. Berg, *The Story of the Little Car* (1955); V. Ross, *Basic British* (1956); Sir John Leal, *The Saint and the Boy* (1957); H. Treece, *The Jet Beads* (1961); E. Fraser, *Before Jesus Came* (1963), and others

EXHIB: HU; RA; RBA; RWS; RSA; NEAC

COLL: BM; IWM; SM; NG New Zealand; Sunderland; Worthing; Hull

SIME, Sidney Herbert RBA (1865–1941) Painter, illustrator, theatre designer, magazine editor, caricaturist and fantasy cartoonist. Sidney Sime was born in Manchester but was brought up in Liverpool. After school he worked at first as a pit-boy in a colliery and then as a signwriter. Having studied at Liverpool School of Art (1883–9), where he won prizes for drawing, he moved to London *c.* 1890 and began work as a painter, exhibiting at the Royal Society of British Artists and being elected RBA in 1896. His first drawings were published in *Ludgate Magazine* (1891), *Illustrated London News* (1892) and *Boy's Own Paper* (1893), but his reputation as an (often macabre) cartoonist began in earnest in 1895 with a series of 'after-life' jokes (usually full-page in monochrome) for *Pick-Me-Up* which were deemed blasphemous in some quarters. He also drew theatre caricatures for the magazine until 1898 (when he was succeeded by CHARLES PEARS) and contributed to *Idler, Eureka, Black & White, Unicorn, Strand, Queen, Pall Mall Magazine, Windsor, Minster, Illustrated London News, Holly Leaves, Illustrated Sporting & Dramatic News, Butterfly, Sketch, Tatler* and other magazines ('those God-forsaken sponge-cakes of the suburban soul!'). Briefly Editor of *Eureka*, he bought Jerome K. Jerome's *Idler* in 1898 (having been left £14,000 by an uncle, a wealthy Edinburgh solicitor) and was Co-Editor of the magazine (1899–1901) until it folded. In 1905 he began to illustrate the first of ten books for the fantasy writer Lord Dunsany, and then went to the USA for six months to work for the Hearst newspaper group (1905–6). He also designed theatre sets and costumes for plays written or produced by Lord Howard de Walden (1909–14) and drew caricatures of actors. 'One of the ablest pen-and-ink draftsmen of the early years of the twentieth century . . . Sime was a master of the fantastic' (Hodnett). His highly inventive and often disturbing fantasy drawings owe something in style to Beardsley and William Blake. Randolph Hearst called him 'the Greatest Living Imaginative Artist' and DAVID LOW described him as 'a beautifully imaginative artist with a mordant fancy that sometimes overlaid his observation of character, but whose studies of people neverthless are full of true and well-balanced caricature'. Sidney Sime died in Worplesdon, Surrey, on 22 May 1941.

PUB: *Bogey Beasts* (1923)

ILL: Lord Dunsany, *The Gods of Pegana* (1905), *Time and the Gods* (1906), *The Sword of Welleran* (1908), *A Dreamer's Tales* (1910), *The Book of Wonder* (1912), *Tales of Wonder* (1916), *Chronicles of Rodriguez* (1922), *The King of Elfland's Daughter* (1924), *The Blessing of Pan* (1927), *My Talks with Dean Spanley* (1936); A. Machen, *The House of Souls* (1906), *The Hill of Dreams* (1907); W. H. Hodgson, *The Ghost Pirates* (1909)

EXHIB: Baillie Gallery (1907); RBA (1924, 1927); SGG; Sime Memorial Art Gallery, Worplesdon, Surrey

COLL: V&A; Worplesdon Memorial Hall; THG

LIT: G. Locke, *From an Ultimate Dim Thule* (1973), *The Land of Dreams* (1975); S. Heneage and H. Ford, *Sidney Sime* (1980)

SIMMONDS, Rosemary Elizabeth 'Posy' (b. 1945). Joke and strip cartoonist, illustrator and writer. Posy Simmonds was born on 9 August 1945 in Cookham Dene near Maidenhead, Berkshire, the daughter of a farmer. She attended Queen Anne's School, Caversham, and studied fine art and French at the Sorbonne in Paris and graphic design at the Central School of Art, London (1964–8). Her first cartoon was published on *The Times*' women's page in 1968 and her first regular daily cartoon feature was 'Bear', which began in the *Sun* on 17 November 1969, the day of the relaunch of the paper by Rupert Murdoch. However, she is perhaps best known for her work on the *Guardian* since 1972, first as an illustrator, then with her celebrated weekly strip about the polytechnic sociology lecturer George Weber and his family which began in May 1977 (originally entitled 'The Silent Three'). She has also contributed to the *Sunday Times, Observer, Spectator, Radio Times, Punch, New Society, Cosmopolitan, Country Living* and *Harpers*. In addition she has produced a number of books – including children's books – and a cartoon documentary, *Tresoddit for Easter* (1991) for BBC TV (Tresoddit in Cornwall was the regular fictional holiday resort of the Webers). She has also lectured at literary festivals and broadcast on BBC radio. Posy Simmonds was voted Cartoonist of the Year in Granada TV's

Posy Simmonds, *Pure Posy* (title page), 1987

What the Papers Say Awards (1980) and in the British Press Awards (1981) and she has also been a committee member of the Cartoonists' Club of Great Britain. Ambidextrous, she drew the Webers strip on semi-transparent A2 layout paper using 0.2–0.4 Rapidographs with Rotring ink using a dip pen for white lettering and a fat pen for spoken text and narrative – the bastardized typeface used she has christened 'Anal Retentive'. She admires the work of SEARLE, GILES and Steinberg. The sister of Richard Simmonds MEP, she is married to de-signer and typographer Richard Hollis.
PUB: *Bear Book* (1969), *Bear* (1974), *More Bear* (1975), *Mrs Weber's Diary* (1979), *True Love* (1981), *Pick of Posy* (1982), *Very Posy* (1985), *Pure Posy* (1987), *Fred* (1987), *Lulu and the Flying Babies* (1988), *The Chocolate Wedding* (1990)

ILL: K. Wright, *Rabbiting On and Other Poems* (1978), *Hot Dog and Other Poems* (1981), *Cat Among Pigeons* (1989); H. Carpenter, *The Captain Hook Affair* (1979); D. Ashford, *The Young Visiters* (1984); A. Rusbridger, *A Concise History of the Sex Manual* (1986); H. Belloc, *Matilda* (1991)
EXHIB: CG; MOMA; Manor House Museum & Art Gallery, Ilkley; RFH; Cheltenham Museum & Art Gallery
COLL: V&A; BM

SIMONDS, David Thomas (b. 1960). Editorial/political cartoonist and illustrator. David Simonds was born in Pinner, Middlesex, on 18 May 1961 and after taking a one-year Foundation Course at St Albans School of Art studied graphic design at North Staffordshire Polytechnic (1980–83). He began work as a children's

book illustrator (his first commission being for Gyles Brandreth's *Big Book of Ghosts* in 1984) before drawing caricatures and illustrations for magazines such as *Radio Times* (1985–90), *New Civil Engineer* (1985–8) and *Which?* He now works regularly as a cartoonist and illustrator for the *Economist* (since 1989), *Guardian* (since 1991) and *New Statesman* (since 1996). In addition he drew cartoons on Channel 4 for Will Hutton's TV series *False Economy* (*c.* 1995). Influenced by STEADMAN, SEARLE, Tomi Ungerer and Heinrich Kley, he works mostly in pen and ink.
ILL: G. Brandreth, *Big Book of Ghosts* (1984); R. Leeson, *Never Kiss Frogs* (1988), *One Frog Too Many* (1990)

SMILBY – *see* Wilford-Smith, Francis

'Smiling Through' – *see* Lee, Joseph Booth

SMITH – *see* Weisz, Victor

SMITH, Albert Talbot (1877–1968). Joke cartoonist and illustrator. A. T. Smith was born in Canton, China, on 20 July 1877, the son of Frederick Burgess Smith, a merchant. He was educated at Whitgift School and studied at Croydon School of Art. Some of his earliest drawings were published in *Fun* (1899) and he later contributed to *Punch* (1902–47), *Bystander*, *Odd Volume*, *Sketch*, *Humorist*, *Passing Show*, *Strand*, *London Opinion* and others. His military service (1914–19) earned him the rank of major. He worked mostly in pen and ink in a style which echoed that of WALLIS MILLS. A shooting enthusiast, he joined his local rifle club in Chipstead, Surrey, before World War I and was for many years its President (from 1926), writing the club's history in 1950.
PUB: *Chipstead & District Rifle Club: 1906–1950* (1950)
EXHIB: J. Collins & Son Gallery, Bideford, Devon (1986)

SMITH, David Edward (b. 1943). Caricaturist and illustrator. David Smith was born on 7 September 1943 in King's Lynn, Norfolk. He studied at St Martin's School of Art and the Central School of Arts & Crafts (1962–6), later taking a BA in the history of art at the Courtauld Institute (1977–80) and an MA at Birkbeck College, University of London. He began producing caricatures for the *Guardian*'s book page in 1981, contributed a weekly caricature to the *Frank-*

furter Allgemeine Magazin (1981–5) and was the *Independent*'s first caricaturist in 1986. In addition, his drawings have been published regularly in the *Observer*, *Daily Telegraph*, *Daily Mail* (sports profiles), *Times Literary Supplement* (including covers), *Literary Review*, *Punch*, *Listener*, *Musical Times*, *Toronto Star*, *Paris-Match*, *Libération*, *Le Point*, *Aamulehti*, *Etela-Suomen Sanomat* and *Investors Chronicle* amongst others. Using strictly black pen-and-ink, he employs a tight cross-hatching technique using a crow-quill nib; for his colour work he generally uses the same technique with added wash. He is an admirer of André Gill, DAVID LEVINE and TROG (especially his colour work).
ILL: S. Barnes, *A la Recherche du Cricket Perdu* (1989); E. Abelson, *Misalliance* (1989); S. Hoggart, *America, A User's Guide* (1990)
COLL: A; UKCC

SMITH, Gary James 'Gary' (b. 1963). Caricaturist and illustrator. Gary Smith was born in

Gary Smith, [Pope John Paul II], *Sunday Times*, 1997

Portsmouth on 5 December 1963 and is self-taught. Concentrating on arts (especially theatre and film) caricature and illustrations for book reviews, his work has appeared in the *Daily Mirror* (1982–7), *London Daily News* (1987), *International Herald-Tribune* (1989–91), *Sunday Times* (from 1983), *Daily Mail* (from 1987) and *Radio Times* (from 1989). He also contributed to *Vogue, Tatler, Elle, Today* and *Punch* and designed covers for books by Keith Waterhouse and others. Influenced by Hirschfeld, Covarrubias, Don Bevan, NERMAN and SHERRIFFS, he works with brush and ink or (for colour) brush and gouache on paper.
EXHIB: LAN; Rebecca Hossack Gallery

SMITH, George William 'Gus' (1915–99). Joke and pocket cartoonist and illustrator. Born in Upney, Essex, on 8 December 1915, George Smith left school at 16 to work as a clerk in the Russian Oil Company. He then trained as an architect at Exeter University and began to draw cartoons in 1939. After World War II, in which he served with the RASC (achieving the rank of captain), he worked as a surveyor for Shell-Mex while still freelancing as a cartoonist for such publications as *Punch, Radio Times, Everybody's, Sketch, Bystander, John Bull, Lilliput* and *Men Only*. He then joined the BBC's overseas service (1946) before becoming staff Pocket Cartoonist on the *Evening News* (1953–72). He also designed posters for the Royal Society for the Prevention of Accidents and illustrated more than 200 textbooks for teaching English as a foreign language for publishers in Germany, Sweden, Denmark and Norway. Gus Smith died in Fleet, Hampshire, on 19 June 1999.
ILL: B. Lampitt, *Trogs in the Suburbs* (1973); plus more than 200 EFL textbooks
COLL: UKCC; BM

SMITH, William Douglas (1916–73). Sports, strip and pocket cartoonist and lecturer. Doug Smith was born in South Shields, Tyne and Wear, on 29 October 1916, the son of Allison Hart Smith, an employee of the fruit wholesalers Gilroy's (whose family included JOHN GILROY), and the brother of Allison Smith, journalist. After attending Westoe Secondary School, South Shields, he joined the Merchant Navy aged 16. A self-taught artist, he sold his first cartoon to the *Shipbuilding & Shipping Record* in 1936. After serving in the Merchant Navy during World War II he joined the *Shields Gazette*

as a staff artist and cartoonist (1945–50), creating 'Brassie', a daily strip about a naval cadet. He then moved to the *Newcastle Evening Chronicle* (1950–60) – where colleagues included Angus McGill (*see* POELSMA), broadcaster Harold Williamson and film critic Tom Bergman – drawing the front-page pocket cartoon 'Smile with Smith' before moving to London to join the *Evening News* as Sports Cartoonist (1960–73). He also contributed to *Saturday Evening Post* and others. In addition, he travelled widely in the UK and USA with his 'Quick on the Draw' illustrated lecture tours (1950–73). Most of his work was in pen and ink on card or paper. He was the father of the journalist Valerie Grove. Doug Smith died of a heart attack in Harefield Hospital, London, on 22 August 1973 aged 56.
PUB: Three volumes of 'Brassie' cartoons (1946–50)
LIT: V. Grove, *On the Death of a Parent* (1994)

SMYTHE [real name SMYTH], Reginald (1917–98). Joke and strip cartoonist. Reg Smythe was born on 10 July 1917 in Hartlepool, Cleveland (then Yorkshire), the son of Richard Smyth, a boat-builder in the Teesside shipyards. He attended Galleys Field School and left at 14 to work as an errand boy for a butcher. In 1936 he joined the Royal Northumberland Fusiliers and during World War II served as a machine-gunner in North Africa, achieving the rank of sergeant (1945), while also submitting cartoons to Cairo magazines. After the war he worked as a telephone clerk for the GPO in London (1946) and later began designing posters for the company's amateur dramatic group and contributing occasional cartoons to specialist journals such as *Fishtrader's Gazette* and *Draper's Record*. He turned full-time freelance in 1950, selling his first drawing to *Everybody's*, and contributing to *Speedway World* ('Smythe's Speedway World'), *Monthly Speedway World* ('Skid Sprocket'), *Evening Standard, Punch* (once only) and the Mirror Group's *Reveille* amongst others. He joined the *Daily Mirror* in 1954, producing the regular feature 'Laughter at Work' before creating the daily 'Andy Capp' cartoon for the newly launched northern edition of the paper on 5 August 1957. It quickly turned into a strip, spread to the other editions and from 6 May 1960 also featured in the *Sunday Pictorial* (later renamed the *Sunday Mirror*). At the time of Smythe's death the strip had been syndicated to 1700 newspapers in 51 countries outside the

Reg Smythe, [Andy Capp], *The World of Andy Capp*, 1990

UK, had been translated into 14 languages and was read by 250 million people. It became the subject of a stage musical (starring Tom Courtenay with music by Alan Price) and in 1988 an ITV series based on the character, adapted by Keith Waterhouse and starring James Bolam in the title role, was screened in the UK. In addition, Andy Capp was used to advertise beer, Post Office bonds, etc., and the strip was voted CCGB Best Strip Cartoon of the Year five years running (1961–5). The flat-capped, pigeon-fancying, beer-swilling, work-shy northerner Andy was created when Smythe was on holiday. As the artist himself said: 'Andy Capp was born on the A1. The trip was seven hours, and the name took three – the pun on "handicap" was irresistible. He's a horrible little man, but he's been very good to Reg.' Capp's wife, Florrie, was named after Smythe's mother, Florence, but though Andy was supposedly based on a real person, Smythe never revealed who (it is now widely held to have been his father). Andy always wore his cap and the only time he was ever pictured without it was in his bed, with Florrie shouting 'You can get up now, your cap's been handed in.' The strip also spawned (28 May 1960) a junior version, 'Buster, son of Andy Capp' (complete with flat cap), which later developed into the children's comic *Buster*, and a female spin-off, 'Mandy Capp', but neither was written or drawn by Smythe. He was left-handed and worked with an Osmiroid left-handed pen using a broad nib for lettering and Daler Trimline board. He was one of the founder members of the British Cartoonists' Association in 1966. Reg Smythe returned to Hartlepool in 1976 after 40 years' absence and died there of cancer on 13 June 1998.
PUB: *Smythe's Speedway World* (1952), 'Andy Capp' series (annuals from 1959)
EXHIB: Dash Gallery ('40 Years of Andy Capp'); Williamson Art Gallery, Birkenhead
COLL: UKCC; BM
LIT: [with L. Lilley] *The World of Andy Capp* (1990)

SNAFFLES – *see* Payne, Charles Johnson

SNARK, THE – *see* Wood, Starr

SPEED, Lancelot (1860–1931). Joke cartoonist, illustrator and pioneer animator. Lancelot Speed was born in London on 13 June 1860, the son of William Speed QC, a barrister. He was educated at Rugby School and his contemporaries at Clare College, Cambridge, included the illustrators J. D. Batten and H. J. Ford. A self-taught artist, he contributed to *Illustrated London News*, *Graphic*, *Sphere*, *Punch*, *Illustrated Sporting & Dramatic News*, *Good Words*, *English Illustrated Magazine*, *Windsor*, *Portfolio* and *Young England* amongst others. In addition, he was an important pioneer animator. Having experimented on his own since 1912, he was hired by Neptune Picture Co. as an artistic adviser on settings and costumes and later produced eight 10-minute 'Bully Boy' films for the company (1914–15) before it collapsed. He then moved to Imperial Pictures and produced a number of animated war films such as *Tank Pranks* (1917), *Tommy Atkins* (1918), *Britain's Effort* (1918) and *Britain's Honour* (1919). After the war he was technical adviser for Astra Films' *The Adventures of Pip, Squeak and Wilfred* (1921), based on the *Daily Mirror* cartoon strip by A. B. Payne. He also illustrated numerous books. He worked mainly in black and white with a fine line. Thorpe described him as 'another of many competent craftsmen whose work was adequate without being brilliant'. Lancelot Speed died in High Barnet, Hertfordshire, on 31 December 1931.
PUB: *The Limbersnigs* (1896)
ILL: Many books including H. F. Wilson, *Carmen Pooleviense* (1886); H. Rider Haggard, *Eric Brighteyes* (1895); E. Bulwer Lytton, *The Last Days of Pompeii* (1897); W. J. Courthope, *The Paradise of Birds* (1889); A. and E. Castle, *If Youth But Knew!* (1906); T. Hughes, *Tom Brown's Schooldays* (1911); [with H. J. Ford] A. Lang, *The Red Fairy Book* (1890), *The Blue Poetry Book* (1891)

SPENCER, William (b. 1921). Pocket cartoonist. Will Spencer was born in London's East End on 23 April 1921. He trained at his local art school in West Ham (1935–7) and his first cartoon was published in the *News Chronicle* in 1954. During World War II he served in the RAF's Transport Command. He is best known for his 'Animal Crackers' animal pocket cartoon which ran for over 20 years, at first in the *News Chronicle* (1954–60) then the *Daily Mail* (1960–71) when it took over the *Chronicle*. Another series, 'Moments with Mama', appeared in *Woman's Own* (from 1965). Spencer also worked in advertising and created the slogan 'Don't say brown, say "Hovis"' (for Aldridges). In addition he ran the Orchard Studio gallery in Chichester (from 1970) selling his own silk-screen printed, framed cartoons.
PUB: *Animal Crackers* (1969), *Animal Antics* (1985)
EXHIB: Orchard Studio, Chichester

SPI (fl. 1920s). Political cartoonist. Spi succeeded FRANK REYNOLDS as Political Cartoonist on *Reynolds News* and was working regularly for the paper by 1926, at first signing his name in capitals in a circle. He was later (1937) succeeded by GILES.

SPIKE – *see* Gibbard, Leslie David and Mendoza, Philip

SPITTING IMAGE – *see* Law, Roger; Fluck, Peter and Stoten, David Alan

SPRINGS, John (b. 1962). Caricaturist and painter. John Springs was born in Chapeltown, Leeds, on 6 February 1962, the son of a Latvian garage owner. After school in Yorkshire, he studied art and drama at Park Lane College, Leeds, before becoming a full-time caricaturist and painter. His first drawing was published in *Arab Times* (1978), and he has contributed to the *Spectator* since 1980 (including covers). His work has also appeared in *Literary Review, Tatler, Sunday Times Magazine, Melbourne Age, Listener, Harpers & Queen, Daily Telegraph, Sunday Telegraph, New Yorker, Independent Magazine, GQ, Times Saturday Review, Esquire, Observer Magazine, Women's Quarterly, New Republic* and other publications. He has also illustrated 'Man in the News' for the *Financial Times* since 1989 and was resident caricaturist on BBC TV's *Newsnight* (1992–7). Springs uses a fine-nib pen with elaborate cross-hatching and sometimes also works

John Springs, [Anthony Burgess], *Sunday Times, c.* 1980

in watercolour, gouache and oil paint. His painting – portraits and landscapes – includes a mural of Margaret Thatcher in Rules Restaurant, Covent Garden. He lists his influences as being US illustrator Steve Ditko, William Coldstream, LEVINE, Rowlandson and MAX BEERBOHM.
ILL: F. Maclean, *The Isles of the Sea* (1985); P. J. O'Rourke, *The New Enemies List* (1996)
EXHIB: NT; Sally Hunter Gallery; JDG; Rebecca Hossack Gallery (paintings)
COLL: V&A; BM

SPROD, George Napier (b. 1919). Joke and political cartoonist, illustrator and writer. George Sprod was born in Adelaide, South Australia, on 16 September 1919 and attended Norwood High School and Urbrae Agricultural High School. During World War II he served as a gunner in 2/15 Field Regiment, Australian Artillery, but was taken prisoner at the fall of Singapore. He then spent three and half years working on the Burma railway and in Changi, Singapore, where he met RONALD SEARLE. After the war he worked as a political cartoonist for Frank Packer in Sydney (1945–9) and later came to London to work for various Fleet Street publications, including *Punch*, before returning to his home country. Malcolm Muggeridge's favourite cartoonist, he works mostly in pen and ink. Price linked him with the other 'decorators' EMETT and FFOLKES, but says he is 'less light and whimsical than ffolkes, often macabre. He liked caryatids, urns, madness and the frenzy behind the cairngorm.'

PUB: *Chips off a Shoulder* (1956), *Bamboo Round My Shoulder* (1982), *Sprod's View of Sydney* (1984), *When I Survey the Wondrous Cross* (1990)

ILL: Many books including G. Ashe, *The Tale of a Tub* (1950); J. B. Boothroyd, *The House About a Man* (1959); C. L. Woolley, *As I Seem to Remember* (1962); V. B. Holland, *An Explosion of Limericks* (1967)

EXHIB: (Various 1949–69) London; New York; Sydney; Amsterdam

COLL: Australian War Memorial, Canberra; UKCC

LIT: [autobiography] *Life on a Square-Wheeled Bike* (1987)

SPY – *see* Ward, Sir Leslie Matthew

SPY Junior – *see* Unvardy, Imre Laszlo

STAMPA, Giorgio [later George] Loraine (1875–1951). Joke cartoonist and illustrator. G. L. Stampa was born in Constantinople (now Istanbul) on 29 November 1875, the second son of the architect Giorgio Domenico Stampa – who designed Manchester Free Trade Hall, the British Embassy in Therapia near Constantinople, and the Sultan's Palace in Constantinople amongst other buildings – and a descendant of the Italian Renaissance poet Gaspara Stampa (1520–54). After his father's projects in Turkey were completed, the family returned to Britain in 1877 and G. L. Stampa was educated at Appleby Grammar School, Bedford Modern School, Heatherley's School of Art (1892–3) and the RA Schools (1893–5), where fellow students included HEATH ROBINSON and LEWIS BAUMER. Stampa shared a studio with SAVILE LUMLEY. His first published drawing appeared in *Punch* in March 1894 and in 1900 he became a full-time illustrator and cartoonist working mainly for *Punch* (he drew nearly 2500 illustrations, in-

cluding initial letters, for this magazine alone) but also contributing to *Bystander, Humorist, Graphic, Strand Magazine, London Opinion, Moonshine, Pall Mall Magazine, Sketch, Tatler, Windsor Magazine, Cassell's Magazine, Rions, Lectures Pour Tous, Comica* (1908–9) and others. He also produced Christmas cards for clubs and societies, illustrated programmes for charity events and drew advertisements for Comfort Soap and others. Greatly influenced by Charles Keene and PHIL MAY (particularly in his subject matter) in his early work, Stampa gradually found his own style and is best remembered for his drawings of Cockneys and street urchins, his book illustrations and his theatre cartoons for *Punch* (sometimes signed 'Harris Brooks'), which he produced for 56 years (1894–1949) along with WHITELAW and HASELDEN, being succeeded by RONALD SEARLE. He was deemed unfit for service in World War I and too old for service in World War II. A member of the Savage Club, in 1927 he cashed a cheque made out to him by A. P. Herbert on a napkin at a Club dinner. Stampa was a genial eccentric and his *Punch* obituary described him as 'the last of the Bohemians'. He always carried a drawing pad and a pencil stub (new pencils were cut into four pieces) and worked in ink, oil, pastel and watercolour on Velum paper and board at a drawing board tilted at 45 degrees. Described as 'a master of black and white . . . But a humorist in the great Leech tradition' (*Daily Chronicle*), his last drawing for *Punch* was an 'Impressions of Parliament' decoration in 1949. He was a director of Johnson's Sporting Gallery, Covent Garden. His first cousin, Willie Heelis, married the children's writer Beatrix Potter. G. L. Stampa died in London on 26 May 1951.

PUB: *Loud Laughter* (1907), *Easy French Exercises* (1907), *Ragamuffins* (1916), *Humours of the Street* (1921), (ed.) *In Praise of Dogs* (1948)

ILL: 14 books including E. V. Lucas, *Specially Selected* (1920), *Urbanites* (1921); A. Armstrong, *Easy Warriors* (1923); R. Kipling, *Supplications of the Black Aberdeen* (1929), *Thy Servant a Dog* (1930), *Collected Dog Stories* (1934)

EXHIB: RA; WG; WAC tour (1986); CG; Italian Cultural Institute; Salisbury Festival; BC; NT; Abbott Hall, Kendal; Hatton Gallery, Hereford; Nelson Museum, Monmouth; RFH; Oriel Gallery, Cardiff and others

COLL: UKCC; A; CAT; V&A; BM; TM; THG

LIT: F. Stampa Gruss, *The Last Bohemian: G. L. Stampa of Punch* (1991)

STANIFORTH, Joseph Morewood (1863–1921). Political cartoonist, illustrator and painter. J. M. Staniforth, who often signed his work 'JMS', was born in Cardiff on 16 May 1863 and educated at St John's School, Cardiff. He was then apprenticed to the Lithographic Department of the *Western Mail* (1878) and ten years later joined the editorial staff as an illustrator, drawing daily cartoons from 1893. In addition, he drew regularly for the *Cardiff Evening Express* and the *News of the World*, contributed to *Punch* and, a member of the South Wales Art Society, painted in oils and watercolours. Succeeded on the *Western Mail* by ILLINGWORTH, he died in Lynton, Devon, on 17 December 1921. He usually drew in fine pen and ink in black and white.
PUB: *The General Election 1895* (1895), *Cartoons of the Boer War* (1900), *Cartoons of the Welsh Revolt* (1905), *Cartoons by J. M. Staniforth* (1909), *Cartoons of the War* (1914)
COLL: National Library of Wales, Aberystwyth

STARKE, Leslie Hugh (1905–74). Joke cartoonist, caricaturist, commercial artist and illustrator. Leslie Starke was born in Cupar, Fife, on 25 November 1905 and was badly mauled by a sheepdog at the age of three. He worked in a solicitor's office in Cupar for ten years and was a self-taught artist drawing caricatures of local cricketers on the *Fife Herald* (1928–9) before coming to London as a songwriter (he was an accomplished pianist). He then worked in the theatre and for a firm of automatic machine contractors. During World War II he served in the RAF (1941–5) but continued to draw cartoons and began producing advertisements for the Ministry of Food, including one claimed as the largest in the world displayed across the face of County Hall and proclaiming 'Food is a Munition of War – Don't Waste It'. He became a full-time freelance in 1946, working for *Punch*, *New Yorker*, *Lilliput* (including covers), *John Bull*, *Men Only*, *Sketch*, *London Opinion*, *World's Press News*, *New Elizabethan*, *Illustrated*, *Esquire*, *Saturday Evening Post* and *Collier's*, as well as producing a considerable amount of advertising work, including calendars for the Royal Society for the Prevention of Accidents. In addition he drew illustrations to handbooks for the Rheumatism and Arthritis Council and children's puzzle books published by Starfish Books. Starke always used a brush and was a firm believer that the best jokes don't need captions.

Price has said that 'with ANTON and TAYLOR, he represented the first generation of crazy humorists at their best'. Leslie Starke died on 16 November 1974.
PUB: *Starke and Unashamed* (1953), *Stark Staring* (1955), *Starke Parade* (1958)
ILL: 'J.P.C', *Poetic Justice* (1947); T. Berkeley, *We Keep a Pub* (c. 1955); N. R. Smith, *Things to Collect* (1971); L. Hurley, *Shamus and the Green Cat* (1972)
EXHIB: CG
COLL: V&A; CAT; UKCC; BM

STEAD – *see* Steadman, Ralph Idris

STEADMAN, Ralph Idris (b. 1936). Political and joke cartoonist, caricaturist, illustrator, printmaker and writer. Ralph Steadman was born on 15 March 1936 in Wallasey, Cheshire, the son of Lionel Raphael Steadman, a commercial traveller. He was educated at Abergele Grammar School and worked at first as a trainee manager with F. W. Woolworth, Colwyn Bay, before becoming an apprentice aircraft engineer with De Havillands in Chester (1952). He spent his National Service in the RAF (1954–6) and his first cartoon (about Nasser and the Suez crisis) was published in the *Manchester Evening Chronicle* in 1956. He then joined the Kemsley Newspaper Group as a cartoonist (1959–61). While studying art part-time at East Ham Technical College (1959–66), the London College of Printing (1961–5) and with PERCY BRADSHAW, he also freelanced cartoons for *Punch* (including covers), *Daily Sketch*, *Private Eye* (from May 1962) and the *Daily Telegraph* – signing himself at first 'STEAD' – until he became Artist-in-Residence at Sussex University (1967). He later worked for the National Theatre (1977), *The Times* (three months, 1970–71) and the *New Statesman* (1976–80) and has contributed cartoons to *Rolling Stone*, *Radio Times*, *Black Dwarf*, *New York Times*, *Times Higher Education Supplement*, *New Scientist*, *Guardian*, *Observer*, *Sunday Times* and *Independent*. He has won numerous awards for his work including the V&A's Francis Williams Book Illustration Award (1973), Designers' & Art Directors' Association Gold Award (1977), American Institute of Graphic Arts Illustrator of the Year (1979), W. H. Smith Illustration Award (1987), BBC Design Award (1987), CAT Advertising Cartoonist of the Year Award (1995, 1996, 1998), and received an Honorary D.Litt. from the University of Kent in 1995.

In addition, he has directed a film for TVS (1992), designed for the stage, written libretti, designed stamps for the GPO (1986), given lectures and designed Oddbins catalogues (since 1987). Steadman uses pens, brushes, inks, acrylics, oils, etching, silkscreen and collage, and has also produced sculptures in iron and steel. He has an often brutal, savage style and Lucie-Smith has referred to him as 'a moralist in the tradition of Hogarth'. He greatly admired GILES. Ralph Steadman is a member of the Chelsea Arts Club.

PUB: *Two Cats in America* (1964), *The Little Prince and the Tiger Cat* (1965), *Ralph Steadman's Jelly Book* (1967), *The Yellow Flowers* (1968), *Still Life with Raspberry* (1969), *Dogs' Bodies* (1970), *Little Red Computer* (1970), *Ralph Steadman's Bumper to Bumper Book for Children* (1973), *Flowers for the Moon* (1974), *Two Donkeys and the Bridge* (1974), *America* (1974), *Cherry Wood Cannon* (1978), *Sigmund Freud* (1979), *No Good Dogs* (1982), *I, Leonardo* (1983), *Between the Eyes* (1984), *Paranoids* (1986), *Scar Strangled Banner* (1987), *That's My Dad* (1986), *The Big I Am* (1988), *No Room to Swing a Cat* (1989), *Near the Bone* (1990), *Tales of the Weirrd* (1990), *The Grapes of Ralph* (1992), *Teddy, Where Are You* (1994), *Still Life with Bottle* (1994), *Gonzo: The Art* (1998), *The Book of Jones* (1995)

ILL: More than 50 books including M. Damjan, *The Big Squirrel and the Little Rhinoceros* (1965); H. Wilson, *The Thoughts of Chairman Harold* (1967); L. Carroll, *Alice in Wonderland* (1967), *Through the Looking Glass* (1972), *The Hunting of the Snark* (1975); J. Deveson, *Night Edge* (1972); H. S. Thompson, *Fear and Loathing in Las Vegas* (1972), *Fear and Loathing on the Campaign Trail* (1975), *The Curse of Lono* (1981); B. Stone, *Emergency Mouse* (1978), *Inspector Mouse* (1980), *Quasimodo Mouse* (1984); T. Hughes, *The Threshold* (1979); R. L. Stevenson, *Treasure Island* (1985); F. O'Brien, *The Poor Mouth* (1971); G. Orwell, *Animal Farm* (1995)

EXHIB: NT (1977); RFH (1984, 1986); WBM; October Gallery; Tricycle Theatre; Exeter Arts Festival; Canterbury Festival; CG and others

COLL: UKCC; V&A; CAT; Smithsonian; BM

STEPHEN – *see* Roth, Stephen

STEVENS, G. A. 'GAS' (fl. 1910s). Political cartoonist and illustrator. G. A. Stevens was Political Cartoonist on the *Star* (evening sister paper of the *Daily News*, once edited by Charles Dickens) during World War I, being succeeded in 1919 by DAVID Low. Drawing mostly in line, he also contributed to *Strand Magazine* and others, and produced two collections of anti-Kaiser cartoons. He may have been related to, but chronologically cannot be the same person as, George Alexander Stevens, who was born in London on 28 June 1901 and studied at Ruskin College, Oxford, under Sydney Carline (1921–5) and at the Slade, was Advisory Officer on Arts and Crafts to the National Council of Social Service and was author of the British Institute for Adult Education's book *Painting For Fun* (1940).

ILL: S. Lupton, *An English ABC for Little Willie and Others* (n.d.); Anon., *Nursery Rhymes for Fighting Times* (1915)

STOTEN, David Alan (b. 1962). Caricaturist, sculptor, designer and TV director. Born in Barton-le-Cley, Bedfordshire, on 28 April 1962, David Stoten attended Icknield High School, Luton, where he was a contemporary of comic artist Steve Dillon, and studied graphic design and illustration at St Martin's School of Art (1981–4). A regular contributor to *Mad* magazine (1981–5), he began work for SPITTING IMAGE Productions in 1984 as a caricaturist, designing and modelling the puppets. Since he studied film direction at the National Film & Television School his work at Spitting Image has also included directing animation and title sequences for the programme. In addition, he has freelanced for the *Economist*, *Guardian*, *Sunday Express* and *New Yorker* and lectured at the RCA and Royal College of Surgeons. He works mostly in pencil, then models in clay followed by a plaster (or fibreglass) mould filled with latex (or foam).

PUB: contributor to all Spitting Image books (*see* ROGER LAW entry)

EXHIB: [as Spitting Image] CG

STOTT, William Ronald (b. 1944). Joke cartoonist and illustrator. Bill Stott was born in Preston, Lancashire, on 20 May 1944, the son of Ronald Stott, a policeman, and studied painting and lithography at Harris College of Art, Preston (1962–6), and Liverpool Art School (1966–7). Formerly a teacher for 30 years, he has been a regular contributor to *Times Educational Supplement* since 1987 and he has also done freelance work for other *Times* Supplements, *Punch*, *Private Eye*, *Daily Express*, *Amateur Photographer*,

Yachting World, Education, Automobile, Insider, Practical Caravan, and numerous specialist magazines. In addition he has produced drawings for advertising (e.g. National Breakdown) and is a popular after-dinner speaker. Stott prefers to work with a steel nib pen in ink with wash or watercolour. However, he also likes painting in oils and acrylics and cites his influences as BILL TIDY and MIKE WILLIAMS.
PUB: 21 titles in 'The Crazy World of . . .' series (from 1988), 13 titles in 'Jokes' series (from 1990)
ILL: D. Shiach, *Steps to Spelling* (1984); educational books for William Collins Ltd
EXHIB: BAG; Everyman Theatre, Liverpool
COLL: Open University

STOWELL, Gordon (b. 1928). Joke cartoonist, illustrator and model-maker. Gordon Stowell was born on 3 November 1928 in Worsley, Manchester, and apart from training with the Press Art School correspondence course run by PERCY BRADSHAW is self-taught. His first cartoons were published in Manchester local papers (1942–50). Freelance since 1955, his cartoons have appeared in *Punch, Private Eye, New Statesman, Stamp News, What Mortgage, What Finance, Maintenance & Equipment News* (40 years), *What Investment, Prep School, Civil Service Opinion, Oldie* and others. He has also designed greetings cards and produced 3D models out of clay and other materials of characters from Edward Lear's nonsense rhymes and other subjects. Stowell works in pen and ink and watercolour and cites his influences as being Osborn, Steig, HOFFNUNG and SEARLE. His wife Janet is also an illustrator and printmaker.
PUB: *Going with the Crowd* (1962), 'Glow-Worm Books' series (1967–71), 'Little Fish Books' series (1975–84), *Bats in the Belfry* (1985)
ILL: Many books including A. Knowles, 'Hippity Dog' series (from 1979); C. Matthews, *Dimitra of the Greek Islands* (1980); J. Piggott, *Kiku of Japan* (1980); P. Seymour, *Our Wonderful World* (1981); H. Davies, *The Joy of Stamps* (1983)

STRUBE, Sidney Conrad (1892–1956). Political cartoonist. Sidney Strube was born in Bishopsgate, London, on 30 December 1892, the son of Frederick Strube, a wine merchant who kept the Coach and Horses pub in Charing Cross Road. He studied at St Martin's School of Art and began work as a junior draughtsman designing overmantels for a furnishing company. Then, after working in an advertising

Sidney Strube, [Little Man], n.d.

agency, he attended the JOHN HASSALL School of Art (1910), where Hassall encouraged him to submit caricatures to the *Conservative & Unionist* (later renamed *Our Flag*) during the 1910 election. After four were accepted he had work published in *Bystander, Evening Times* and *Throne & Country*. When the latter publication refused a drawing he took it to the *Daily Express* who published it and by 1912 he had an exclusive freelance contract with the paper. After service as a PT and bayonet instructor in the Artists' Rifles in World War I he joined the staff of the *Express* as Political Cartoonist (1918–48) and created the immortal 'Little Man' with his umbrella, bow-tie and bowler hat, who became a national symbol of the long-suffering man-in-the-street 'with his everyday grumbles and problems, trying to keep his ear to the ground, his nose to the grindstone, his eye to the future and his chin up – all at the same time', in Strube's own description. An immensely popular artist, he was also one of the highest paid, earning £10,000 a year in 1931 (this figure had been offered by the *Daily Herald* to lure him away but the *Express* matched it and the *Herald* settled for DYSON instead). However, in 1948 (the day before his 56th birthday) he was suddenly sacked after a disagreement with the Editor, being succeeded by CUMMINGS (as Political Cartoonist) and GILES. He then freelanced for the *Sunday Times, Time & Tide, Everybody's* and *Tatler*. During World War II he produced a number of memorable poster campaigns including 'Yield Not an Inch! Waste Not a Minute' and 'The Three Salvageers'. In addition he drew advertisements for Guinness and others. He was made a Freeman of the City of London and was a member of the London Sketch Club and the Savage. In 1927 he married the *Daily Express* fashion artist Marie Allright. Strube (whose name rhymes with 'Ruby') never allowed malice to enter his cartoons and, a fastidious worker, his motto was 'Never let it go until you are satisfied – and never be satisfied!' An admirer of PARTRIDGE, FRANK REYNOLDS and Low, he worked on Whatman board with indian ink after sketching preliminary outlines in pencil. He was known familiarly as 'George' from his habit of addressing others by this name (his son really was called George). Sydney Strube died at his home in Hampstead on 4 March 1956.

PUB: [with W. F. Blood] *The Kaiser's Kalendar for 1915* (1914), 12 volumes of cartoons (1927–47) including *Cartoons from the Daily Express* (1927–8), *Strube's Annual* (1929–30), *100 Cartoons* (1931–5), *Strube's War Cartoons* (1944)

COLL: V&A; UKCC

STUDDY, George Ernest (1878–1948). Joke and strip cartoonist, illustrator and animator. G. E. Studdy was born on 23 June 1878 in Devonport, Plymouth, Devon, the son of Ernest Holdsworth Studdy, a lieutenant in the Argyll and Sutherland Highlanders. He was educated at Clifton College, Bristol, and Dulwich College, London (left 1896), and would have gone into the Army but for a childhood accident when a pitchfork went through his foot. He attended evening classes at Heatherley's and spent a term at Calderon's School of Animal Painting, but worked as an apprentice engineer for Thames Iron Works and then as a stockbroker before becoming a cartoonist. His first contributions were strips to boys' story papers like *Big Budget*, *Boys' Weekly* and *Comic Cuts* during the 1890s, but by World War I he was working regularly for the *Sketch* (full-page wash plates), *Tatler* ('New Illustrations for Old German Fairy Tales' series, 1915), *Bystander*, *Graphic* and *Illustrated London News*. He also produced animation shorts for Gaumont, the films appearing monthly under the title 'Studdy's War Studies' (1915–16), and contributed to *The Field*, *Punch* (only once, 24 December 1902), *Little Folks*, *Windsor Magazine*, *Rions*, *Lectures Pour Tous* (1909–

11), *Fantasio* (1922–5), *Le Rire* (1927–8), *Passing Show*, *Humorist*, etc. In addition he worked in advertising (e.g. Pan Yan Pickle, Swan Ink) and produced postcards for Mansell, R.P.S., Inter-Art and Valentine's of Dundee, some of them in the style of McGILL under the pseudonym 'Cheero'. Perhaps his most famous creation was 'Bonzo', a white bull terrier pup with black spots who began life as an incidental dog in illustrations and first appeared with this name (christened by *Sketch* Editor Bruce Ingram) in the *Sketch* on 8 November 1922 (the 'Studdy Dog' had appeared in the magazine since 1918). Enormously popular, the sleepy-eyed Bonzo – who walked on two feet, smoked cigarettes and often wore a bow-tie – featured widely in merchandising from clocks and cigarette cards to bronze car mascots. He also appeared on stage (e.g. at the Lyceum in *Sleeping Beauty* in 1924), as a miniature in Queen Mary's Doll's House (1922), and was used to advertise D. W. Griffith's film, *One Exciting Night*, as well as Eclipse Razors, Pan Yan Pickle, Wolsey Ten cars, Pascall Butter Almonds and – in the first neon-light advertisement in Piccadilly Circus in 1924 – Pinnace Cigarettes. In the pre-Disney era his only serious rival was Felix the Cat, and by 1926 he had become the star of 26 silent animated short films (e.g. *Bonzolino* and *Bonzo Broadcasted*) produced by New Era Films (the first of which was the occasion of the first-ever royal film premiere on 14 October 1924), supported by a weekly strip in *Tit-Bits* which was later syndicated in the USA. Bonzo last appeared in the *Sketch* in July 1927 and was replaced by a Bonzo-like cat ('Ooloo') in 1929. (He also drew a donkey, 'Yop', in the *Sunday Graphic* in the 1930s.) Studdy's own dogs were a succession of cocker spaniels always called Ben. A member of the Savage Club, he was elected President of the London Sketch Club in 1921. His motto was 'Work while others play.' He rarely worked on paper, preferring to draw in pen and indian ink on board. G. E. Studdy died of lung cancer on 25 July 1948 at his home, 75 Philbeach Gardens, London SW5. Zelda Westmead, 'agony aunt' on the *Mail on Sunday*, is his granddaughter.

PUB: *The Studdy Dogs Portfolio* (1922), *Uncle's Animal Book* (1923), plus nearly 30 Bonzo books including *The Bonzo Book* (1925) and nine *Bonzo Annuals* (1930–52)

ILL: H. T. Sheringham, *Fishing – A Diagnosis* (1914), *Fishing – Its Cause, Treatment and Cure*

(1925); F. Rayle, *Dopey and Dotty* (n.d.), *A Day with Dopey* (n.d.)
EXHIB: BSG; L
COLL: US National Film Archive (Bonzo animation); IWM
LIT: P. Babb and G. Owen, *Bonzo: The Life and Work of George Studdy* (1988)

STYX – *see* Harding, Leslie Clifford

SULLIVAN, Edmund Joseph RWS RE (1869–1933). Political and joke cartoonist, illustrator, painter and art teacher. E. J. Sullivan was born in London on 6 September 1869, the son of the artist Michael Sullivan ARCA. He was the younger brother of J. F. SULLIVAN and older brother of the architect Leo Sullivan FRIBA (later Vice-President of the Architectural Association). The family moved north when he was one and he was educated at Mount St Mary's College, Chesterfield, and then, when they moved south again when he was six, in Hastings. He studied at first under his father and had his first drawing published in *Scraps c.* 1884. Joining the *Graphic* (1889) as a staff artist aged 19, he then worked for the newly launched *Daily Graphic* (1890–93) with CLEAVER, CORBOULD, PHIL MAY and the future influential art teacher A. S. Hartrick OBE NEAC RWS (with whom he shared a studio at one point). He next moved to the *Penny Illustrated* as writer and artist and later joined the staff of the *Pall Mall Budget*. He also contributed to many other publications including *Good Words, English Illustrated, Gentlewoman, New Budget, Ludgate, Pall Mall Magazine, Pearson's, Black & White, Windsor, Yellow Book* and *Punch*. In addition he illustrated many books (from 1896), amongst them Carlyle's *French Revolution* which BRADSHAW thought was his masterpiece (THORPE preferred the earlier *Sartor Resartus*, 'one of the greatest triumphs of illustration of the nineties'). During World War I he drew powerful anti-German cartoons, many of which were reproduced in *The Kaiser's Garland* (1915). Though Thorpe admired his 'fascinating, excellent drawings', he described the book as a 'whole-hearted hymn of hate . . . the venom is often overdone and one feels sometimes more disposed to laugh than to share the hatred and anger'. He later taught book illustration and lithography at Goldsmiths' College, London (notable pupils included D. L. MAYS, ERIC FRASER, Graham Sutherland and Rowland

Hilder OBE, President of the Royal Institute of Painters in Watercolour), and designed a watercolour course 'Still Life and Flower Painting' for the Press Art School. In addition he drew advertisements for John Dewar Whisky, Lever Bros, Shell-Mex, Selfridges (announcing its opening in 1909) and others. He worked in pen and ink, chalk and wash, and also painted watercolours and etched. 'One of the great masters in pen-and-ink illustration' (Thorpe), he was influenced by Dürer, von Menzel and Vierge, and worked at first in the style of the illustrators Edwin Abbey and Hugh Thomson but later developed his own style. He usually used models, drew close to production size and had a habit of continuing to work on parts of his pencil sketch while inking in the rest of the drawing. President of the Art Workers' Guild (1931), he was elected RWS (1929) and RE (1931). E. J. Sullivan died in London on 17 April 1933.
PUB: *The Kaiser's Garland* (1915), *The Art of Illustration* (1921), *Line* (1922)
ILL: More than 30 books including G. Borrow, *Lavengro* (1896); I. Walton, *The Compleat Angler* (1896); T. Carlyle, *Sartor Resartus* (1898), *The French Revolution* (1910); A. Tennyson, *A Dream of Fair Women* (1900), *Maud* (1922); H. G. Wells, *A Modern Utopia* (1905); F. de la Motte Fouqué, *Sintram and his Companions* (1908); E. Fitzgerald, *The Rubaiyat of Omar Khayyam* (1913); G. Outram, *Legal and Other Lyrics* (1916)
EXHIB: RA; RWS; RE
COLL: BM; V&A; CAT; National Gallery, Melbourne; IWM; THG; NPG
LIT: J. Thorpe, *Edmund J. Sullivan* (1948)

SULLIVAN, James Francis 'Jassef' (1853–1936). Joke and strip cartoonist, caricaturist, author and illustrator. J. F. Sullivan was the son of the artist Michael Sullivan ARCA. He was the elder brother of E. J. SULLIVAN and the architect Leo Sullivan FRIBA (later Vice-President of the Architectural Association). While studying at the South Kensington Schools he started to contribute strip cartoons to *Fun* (Tom Hood's rival to *Punch*, published by the Dalziel brothers), continuing to work for the magazine for nearly 30 years (*c.* 1871–1901). His most famous series, 'The British Working Man, by Someone Who Does Not Believe in Him', in which he satirized the working class, began on 14 August 1875 and was later published in book form. He also drew 'The Queer Side of Things' for the *Strand* magazine and contributed strips, single-

MARIAGE DE CONVENANCE

E. J. Sullivan, [Kaiser Wilhelm II], *The Kaiser's Garland*, 1915

SYKES

panel cartoons and caricatures to *Black & White*, *Cassell's*, *Cassell's Saturday Journal*, *Lady's Pictorial*, *Lika Joko*, *Ludgate*, *Butterfly*, *Minster*, *Idler*, *New Budget*, *Pearson's*, *Pick-Me-Up*, *Punch* (1893), *St Paul's*, and the *Sketch*. In addition he wrote and illustrated a number of children's books and was a member of the Savage Club. He often worked from models and preferred a sable brush to a pen, drawing in lampblack, and usually signed his work 'J. F. S', 'Jas F.' or 'Jassef'. J. F. Sullivan died in London on 5 May 1936.
PUB: *The British Working Man* (1878), *The British Tradesman* (1880), *Among the Freaks* (1896), *Flameflower and Other Stories* (1896), *Here They Are* (1897), *Here They Are Again* (1899), *The Great Water Joke* (1899), *Queer Side Stories* (1900)
EXHIB: FAS (1898); RBA
LIT: D. Kunzle, *The Early Comic Strip* (1973)

'**Supermac**' – *see* Weisz, Victor

SYKES, Charles 'Rilette' (1875–1952). Illustrator, sculptor, caricaturist and commercial artist. Charles Sykes is probably best known for his advertisements for De Reske cigarettes under the pseudonym 'Rilette'. Perhaps less well known is the fact that he designed the original Rolls-Royce 'Spirit of Ecstasy' mascot in 1911 and race cups for Ascot from 1926. He was also a poster designer and magazine illustrator and his drawings and cartoons appeared in the *Sunday Dispatch*, *Woman*, *Printers Pie* and others. In addition he drew caricatures, two of which (featuring the pianist Cernikoff) were published in *Drawing & Design* in July 1923.
EXHIB: G; L: RA: RI
COLL: V&A; THG

T

TALBERT – *see* McLean, Talbert

TAYLOR, John Whitfield 'JWT' MSIAD (1908–85). Joke and strip cartoonist. J. W. Taylor was born in Stoke-on-Trent, Staffordshire, on 11 May 1908 and first showed interest in cartoons when he received a collection of FRANK REYNOLDS' drawings for a Christmas present at the age of 14. Educated at the Orme Boys' School, Newcastle-under-Lyme, and at Manchester University (where he read French and drew for *Rag Bag*), he was a schoolteacher in the Potteries when he began to take art lessons from PERCY BRADSHAW's course. His first cartoons were accepted by *Punch* (1935) quickly followed by *Men Only*, *London Opinion*, *Lilliput* and others. He also contributed to *Eagle* ('Educating Archie' strip), *Staffordshire Evening Sentinel* and (as Headmaster of Holden Lane High School, Stoke-on-Trent) *The Teacher*. Greatly admired by his contemporaries ('one of the greatest cartoonists of the 20th century' – BUD HANDELSMAN), he worked at first in pen and ink or charcoal and wash but later concentrated on brushwork and excelled at producing very witty ideas with a spare, uncluttered line. Price has described him as 'the most consistent of the crazy artists . . . He was, perhaps, best when barest, nothing distracting attention from the purity of his nonsense.' He was a member of the Savage Club and the Society of Staffordshire Artists. J. W. Taylor died on 12 December 1985. His son, David, was Editor of *Punch* from 1986 to 1989.
COLL: BM; UKCC

TERRY, Herbert Stanley (1890–after 1950). Joke cartoonist. Stan Terry was born in Birmingham on 13 March 1890, the son of F. Herbert Terry, a manufacturer. Educated at Bede College, Northumberland, he studied at Wolverhampton School of Art and with PERCY BRADSHAW's Press Art School. He contributed to *London Opinion*, *Punch*, *Sketch*, *Bystander*, *Humorist*, *Passing Show*, *Windsor Magazine*, *Tatler*, *Illustrated Sporting & Dramatic News*, *Magpie*, *Strand*, *Blighty* and others. A member of the London Sketch Club, he retired to South Wales.

THACKER, Cecil Fox (b. 1915). Joke and strip cartoonist. Bill Thacker was born on 16 June 1915 in Denbighshire, North Wales, and is self-taught. He sold his first cartoons to *Motor Cycle* in 1939 and later contributed regularly to the magazine (1954–71). In World War II he flew with the Air Transport Auxiliary Service and after the war worked as a technical artist for

BOAC before turning freelance cartoonist. His work has appeared in various publications but especially *Autocar* (1958–72), *Aeroplane, Tit-Bits, Everybody's, Reveille, Daily Mirror, BOAC Review* (c. 1952–75), *Amateur Photographer* and *Do It Yourself* (1968–83). He also drew a captionless strip featuring a character called Battersby in *Practical Gardener* for 12 years. Bill Thacker works in pen and ink.

PUB: *The Taming of the Screw* (1984)

THACKERAY, Lance RBA (c. 1870s–d.1916). Joke cartoonist, illustrator, painter and postcard designer. Lance Thackeray was born probably in the 1870s in Yorkshire. He contributed to the *Sketch* and *Sketchy Bits* in the 1890s and his work later appeared in the *Graphic, Punch* (1905–8), *Strand* and others. He designed his first postcards for Raphael Tuck in 1900 during the Boer War and in all produced about 950 for Raphael Tuck, A. & C. Black, David Allen and other companies, notably in the incomplete sentence 'write away' style ('I trust this will reach . . .'), with appropriate picture, created originally by CYNICUS. Other popular series were those featuring women, e.g. 'In the Smart Set' and 'Popular Plays', both for Tuck. In addition he drew advertisements for Nestlé's Swiss Milk and others and produced several series of humorous prints, like his friend CECIL ALDIN, a neighbour in Bedford Park, Chiswick. Elected RBA (1899), he was a member of the Savage Club and Langham Sketch Club and was one of the founders, with PHIL MAY, Cecil Aldin, TOM BROWNE and DUDLEY HARDY, of the London Sketch Club (1898), becoming its President in 1910. He also painted pictures (notably of Egypt in watercolour) and exhibited at the Royal Academy and elsewhere. During World War I he served in the Artists' Rifles, but died in Brighton on 11 August 1916.

PUB: *The Light Side of Egypt* (1908), *The People of Egypt* (1910)
ILL: G. Frankau, *The XYZ of Bridge* (1906)
EXHIB: LG (1908); FAS (1910); WG (1913); RI; RA; RBA
LIT: T. Warr and K. Lawson, *The Postcards of Lance Thackeray* (1979)

THELWELL, Norman (b. 1923). Joke cartoonist, illustrator and landscape painter. Norman Thelwell was born on 3 May 1923 in Birkenhead,

Norman Thelwell, *Angels on Horseback*, 1957

Cheshire, the son of a machinist, and was educated at Rock Ferry High School, Birkenhead. In World War II he served in the East Yorkshire Regiment, Royal Electrical and Mechanical Engineers (1942–6). While Art Editor of an army publication in New Delhi, he had his first cartoons published in *London Opinion*. After the war he studied under H. P. Huggill ARCA ARE and G. H. Wedgwood ARCA at Liverpool College of Art (1947–50) and lectured on design and illustration at Wolverhampton College of Art (1950–57). He sold his first drawing to *Punch* in 1950 and contributed more than 1600 cartoons – including 60 covers – to the magazine (1952–77) as well as working for the *News Chronicle* (1956–60), *Sunday Dispatch* (1960–61), *Sunday Express* (1963–71) and *Tatler* (1971–6). His freelance work has included *London Opinion*, *Lilliput*, *Daily Express*, *John Bull*, *Illustrated*, *Picture Post*, *Eagle*, *New Review*, *Farming Express*, *Farmer's Weekly*, *Countryman* and *Esquire*. He has also produced book jackets and worked in advertising (Guinness, W. H. Smith, GPO, etc.) and for TV. A fine draughtsman, Thelwell has a realistic style, placing 'cartoon' figures in naturalistic settings and with great attention paid to detail. He is particularly well known for his cartoons on fishing, sailing, motoring and English country life – especially those (from 1953) featuring young girls and ponies. His cartoons are signed 'thelwell' written with blob serifs in a wavy line while his landscapes and other paintings have the signature 'NORMAN THELWELL'. 'His jokes belonged to the tradition, not of TOWNSEND, but of the poetic, fantastic humorists who usually had their vision with completely unnaturalistic drawing' (Price). He was one of the founder members of the British Cartoonists' Association in 1966.

PUB: More than 30 books, including *Angels on Horseback* (1957), *Thelwell Country* (1959), *The Penguin Thelwell* (1963), *The Compleat Tangler* (1967), *A Plank Bridge by a Pool* (1978), *Thelwell Annual* (1980), *Some Damn Fool's Signed the Rubens Again* (1982), *How to Draw Ponies* (1982) ILL: M. J. Baker, *Away Went Galloper* (1962); C. Ramsden, *Racing Without Tears* (1964) EXHIB: TRY; CBG
COLL: V&A; CAT; UKCC
LIT: [autobiography] *A Millstone Around My Neck* (1981), *Wrestling with a Pencil* (1986)

THOMAS, Herbert Samuel MBE (1883–1966). Joke and political cartoonist, caricaturist and illustrator. Bert Thomas was born in Newport, Monmouthshire, on 13 October 1883, the son of Job Thomas, a monumental sculptor who had helped decorate the Houses of Parliament. Apprenticed at first to an engraver in Swansea at the age of 14 (designing brass doorplates), he began selling music-hall cartoons to the *Swansea Daily Leader*, *Daily Post*, *News* and *Echo*. When he was 17 Sir George Newnes, MP for Swansea and founder of the *Strand Magazine*, saw some of his drawings and published them. Then, on the recommendation of Albert Chevalier, a popular music-hall comedian of the time, he joined a London advertising agency (1902). After freelancing for *Pick-Me-Up* and *Ally Sloper's Half Holiday* he began a long association with *Punch* (1905–48) and *London Opinion* (1909–54), contributing political and social cartoons and latterly the popular 'Child's Guide' to celebrities series. He also contributed to *Humorist*, *Men Only*, *Sketch*, *Passing Show*, *Radio Times*, *Bystander*, *Fun*, *Graphic* and the *World*. Thomas served as a private in the Artists' Rifles in World War I (1916–18) and was official artist for the War Bonds campaign, producing for it Britain's largest poster, which covered the face of the National Gallery (1918). Painted in oils, it was 75 feet long and depicted Drake facing the Spanish Armada. He also produced posters for the Royal Exchange and in Cardiff and Glasgow. His most famous cartoon was "Arf a Mo', Kaiser!' featuring a grinning Cockney Tommy lighting a pipe before engaging the enemy. It was drawn (supposedly in ten minutes) for the *Weekly Dispatch* on 11 November 1914 as part of the paper's tobacco-for-troops fund. This and other contributions to the war effort earned him an MBE (1918). After the war he produced a red-and-black series for the *Sketch* and drew illustrations to the 'Cockney War Stories' letters column in *Evening News* (a collection of which was published in 1930). In World War II he again produced memorable posters, including the 'Is Your Journey Really Necessary?' series for the Railway Executive Committee (1942). In addition he drew advertisements for Oxo, Player's Navy Cut Cigarettes, Eno's, Hector Powe, Comfort Soap and others, designed postcards for Gale & Polden, and was on the Advisory Staff of BRADSHAW's Press Art School. 'His very individual line, broken as if he had dashed the idea down while it was white-hot in his mind, was rather like BAIRNSFATHER's, though he was a far more varied artist and his jokes were generally better. He had some of the attack and speed of RAVEN HILL' (Price). For his *Punch* work he usually drew in pen and ink but elsewhere used mostly a brush, a favourite technique being to use an old matted brush on Whatman or Clifford Milburn board to get a chalk-like line. He also worked in charcoal and wash, pencil, chalk-grain scraperboard, litho chalk and 'splatter' (tint obtained by splattering a toothbrush dipped in ink). An admirer of Keene, Ospovat, Eduard Thöny and PHIL MAY, he never used models or made on-the-spot sketches. He was a member of the Savage Club and the Chelsea Arts Club. Bert Thomas died on 6 September 1966.

PUB: *One Hundred War Cartoons from London Opinion* (1919), *In Red and Black* (1928), *500 of the Best Cockney War Stories* (1930), *Cartoons and Character Drawing* (1936), *Fun at the Seaside* (1944), *Fun on the Farm* (1944), *A Mixed Bag* (1945), *Fun in the Country* (1946), *Fun in Town* (1946), *Playtime* (1947), *Toy Land* (1947), *A Trip on a Barge* (1947), *Railways By Day* (1947), *Railways by Night* (1947), *Close-ups Through a Child's Eye* (n.d.)

ILL: Many books including W. W. Jacobs, *Sea Whispers* (1926); T. R. Arkell, *Meet These People* (1928); C. P. R. Graves, *Candid Caddies* (1935); H. Simpson, *Nazty Nursery Rhymes* (1940), P. Bradshaw, *Marching On* (1943); A. Reubens, *Podgy the Pup* (1945)

EXHIB: London Salon; Boston Public Library (1965)

COLL: BM; V&A; IWM; UKCC; NPG

LIT: P. V. Bradshaw, *The Art of the Illustrator 6* (1918)

THOMAS, Paul Michael (b. 1961). Political/editorial, pocket, joke and strip cartoonist and illustrator. Paul Thomas was born in Radlett, Hertfordshire, on 3 November 1961. He studied at Camberwell School of Arts & Crafts (1981–4) and began contributing cartoons freelance to various newspapers and magazines soon after. He had his first strip ('Wold Affairs') published in 1987 in the *Spectator* (for which he has also drawn covers) and drew the main political cartoon for *Punch* from 1989 to 1992, as well as a strip 'The Safeways' (1990–92). He was also the magazine's Cartoon Editor from January 1992 until it closed later the same year. In 1998 he succeeded GRIFFIN as Editorial/Political Cartoonist on the *Daily Express* and began drawing pocket cartoons for the paper at

the same time. He has also contributed to the *Independent on Sunday* (front-page pocket cartoons since 1989), *Evening Standard* (business cartoons, 1990–97), *Sunday Telegraph* (political cartoons, 1996), *Tablet, Private Eye, Independent* and others. In addition, he has taught graphic design and illustration on a Foundation Course at the University of Hertfordshire (1988–96). Paul Thomas works in pen and ink and Letratone and lists his influences as being MICHAEL HEATH, GARLAND, PETER BROOKES, H. M. BATEMAN and Aubrey Beardsley.

ILL: H. Davies, *Snotty Bumstead* (1991), *Snotty and the Rent-a-Mum* (1993), *Snotty Bumstead the Hostage* (1995)

THOMAS, William Fletcher (1862–after 1922). Joke cartoonist, illustrator and painter. W. F. Thomas was born in Salford, near Manchester. He was educated in Halifax and worked at first for a calico print designer while studying part-time at an art school and then briefly in Paris. His first drawings appeared in the children's comic, *Random Readings* and *Toby*, and after having some cartoons published in *Judy* he came to London (c. 1884) to join the newly founded *Ally Sloper's Half Holiday*, at first as a general comic illustrator and then as Chief Cartoonist (1888) on the death aged 31 of W. G. Baxter. He continued to draw the character until the magazine ceased in September 1916 and then returned once more when it was revived in 1922 (*see also* WILL OWEN). In addition, he contributed to *New Budget, Captain* (including covers), *Punch* and HARRY FURNISS' *Lika Joko* amongst others. Thomas worked mostly in pen and ink but also painted landscapes and exhibited at the Royal Academy.

EXHIB: RA

LIT: J. G. Reid, *At the Sign of the Brush and Pen* (1898)

COLL: BM

THOMPSON, Harold Underwood 'Anton' (1911–96). Joke cartoonist, illustrator and writer. Harold Underwood Thompson was born in West Kirby, Cheshire, on 9 April 1911, the son of Arthur Henry Thompson, an English rancher in Australia whose family were merchant shippers trading with Australia out of Liverpool. His father died in June 1911 while on a visit to relations in England. Harold's elder sister was ANTONIA YEOMAN. He studied life drawing at Heatherley's (1931–2), lettering at St Martin's

School of Art (1934) and printing at Bolt Court. He also took private classes in illustration at Stephen Spurrier's school (1935) and, after applying for a permit, spent two years drawing antique furniture in the V&A from 1936. Self-taught as a cartoonist, he began submitting drawings under the pseudonym 'H. Botterill' to *Bystander* (1935–7) and *Night & Day* (1937). In 1937 he formed a partnership with his sister, and together they produced cartoons for *Punch* as 'Anton' (though the weekly 'Antons' in the *Evening Standard* [1939] were entirely his). Twice mentioned in dispatches in World War II, his service commanding minesweepers and convoy escort vessels in the Royal Navy interrupted his work during this period, though Antonia continued to submit 'Anton' cartoons. After the war they teamed up again and produced numerous 'Anton' cartoons for *Punch, Lilliput, London Opinion, Men Only* and others. Antonia eventually took over the job completely in 1949 when he became too busy with other work (he later became a senior director of Lonsdales international advertising and marketing organization). A former member of the Artworkers' Guild, Harold Underwood Thompson also wrote a number of short stories for London dailies, *Punch*, etc., designed posters and show-cards for Orient Shipping Line and others, and drew advertisements for Northern Aluminium, etc. An admirer of the artists of the *New Yorker*, he worked mostly in black and white with a very flexible Gillott 290 nib and indian ink, using colour occasionally for Christmas issues and other special numbers. Harold Underwood Thompson died in Wells, Somerset, on 21 November 1996.

PUB: [both with A. Yeoman] *Anton's Amusement Arcade* (1947), *Low Life & High Life* (1952), [marketing] *Product Strategy* (1962)
COLL: V&A; UKCC

THOMPSON, Robert (b. 1960). Joke and strip cartoonist, and greetings card designer. Robert Thompson was born in Burton Pidsea, Yorkshire, on 21 July 1960, the son of Wildon Thompson, a groundsman. Educated at Withernsea High School, Yorkshire, he studied illustration at Leeds Polytechnic (1979–82) and while still a student had his first cartoon published in the *Hull Star* (1979). Since then he has contributed to *The Times, Spectator, Observer, Guardian, Daily Telegraph, New Statesman, Oldie, Private Eye, Punch* and others. In addition he was Art Editor and then Art Director of Camden Graphics (1983–95), producing greeting cards and paper products. He usually draws in pen and ink.
PUB: *Pointless Things to Do* (1995)

'Mark my words, it won't last.'

Robert Thompson, in M. Heath (ed.), *The Spectator Cartoons*, 1997

ILL: I. Hislop (ed.), *Cutting Humour* (1993); S. Greenberg (ed.), *Hate Thy Neighbour* (1998)
COLL: BM

THOMSON, Harry Ross (b. 1938). Joke and strip cartoonist, illustrator and designer. Born in Hawick, Roxburghshire, on 5 October 1938, Ross Thomson (who signs his work 'roSS') attended George Watson College, Edinburgh, and studied graphic design at Edinburgh College of Art (1957–61). He moved to London in 1962 and began contributing cartoons to *Punch* (including covers from 1968), *Private Eye, Daily Express, The Times* (a strip, 'Hoff'), *Oui, Reader's Digest* and *Playboy* (Germany). In addition he has done considerable work in advertising for companies such as BOAC, Midland Bank, London Transport, Dulux and the Royal Bank of Scotland, and devised and animated a CD Interactive title *Whizzo Goes on Holiday* for Philips. He has won cartoon awards at the Skopje International Cartoon Exhibition, Yugoslavia (1971, 1972, 1973), Knokke-Heist, Belgium, and Kyoto, Japan. His early influences were ANDRÉ FRANÇOIS, QUENTIN BLAKE and Tomi Ungerer. He started drawing using the top of a Pelikan ink bottle but now uses size 0 paintbrushes for black and white and Dr Martin's watercolour, coloured inks, gouache and occasionally coloured felt-tip pens.
PUB: *A Noisy Book* (1973), *Ross's Guide to Motor-Racing* (1975), *Ross's Guide to Airports* (1977), [with B. Hewison] *How to Draw and Sell Cartoons* (1985), *The Blow-up Doll Companion* (1987), *Doggy Tales* (1989), *Moggy Books* (1991), *Are We There Yet?* (1992), *Captain Jones and the Ghost Ship* (1996)
ILL: B. Green, *Swingtime in Tottenham* (1976); E. Holt and M. Perham, *Historic Transport* (1979), *Customs and Ceremonies* (1980); L. and J. Cooper, *Leo & Jilly Cooper on Cricket* (1985)
COLL: UKCC

THORPE, James H. (1876–1949). Joke cartoonist, illustrator and author. James Thorpe was born in Homerton, London, on 13 March 1876 and was educated at Bancroft's School. He left school aged 17 and trained as a civil servant, later teaching at King's College Civil Service Department, London (1894–1902). He studied art in the evenings at Lambeth School of Art, North London School of Art and Heatherley's (1897) – where he was a contemporary and friend of FRANK REYNOLDS – and with FRANCIS CARRUTHERS GOULD's son, Alec. He won a prize for a cartoon of Sir William Harcourt in *Picture Politics* in July 1894 and his first published drawing was for the *Morning Leader* (September 1898). Thorpe eventually became a full-time cartoonist and illustrator, working at first for music publishers, *The Troubador, Table Talk* and the *Windmill* (from its first issue, 1898). He won a silver medal for poster design at the International Advertisers' Exhibition (1900), designed advertisements for the London Press Exchange (1902–22), produced posters for Bell's Three Nuns Tobacco and contributed theatrical drawings to *Bystander*. In addition he worked for *Graphic, London Opinion, Sketch, Nash's, Tatler, Windsor Magazine, Yorkshire Post, Printer's Pie* and *Punch* (1909–40), and was a member of the London Sketch Club and Chelsea Arts Club. During World War I he served in the Artists' Rifles and later the RFC (1914–19). He also wrote monographs and a pioneering book on the illustrators of the 1890s. When Frank Reynolds was commissioned by the *Sketch* to go to Paris in 1904, Thorpe and their mutual friend, STARR WOOD, accompanied him. In 1929 he visited the USA and contributed to *Life*. Influenced by PHIL MAY (they even used the same model, George Riches), his drawings were admired by RAVEN HILL. 'He will be remembered for his faithful renderings of sunlit outdoor scenes and for the clean economical lines of the cricketers, fishermen and other "open air" characters he loved to portray' (*Punch* obituary). James Thorpe died on 22 February 1949.
PUB: *The Cricket Bag* (1929), *Phil May* (1932), *English Illustration – the Nineties* (1935), *Come for a Walk* (1940), *Edmund J. Sullivan* (1948)
ILL: I. Walton, *The Compleat Angler* (1911); E. E. Foot, *Jane Hollybrand* (1932); H. de Selincourt, *Over!* (1932), *Moreover* (1934), *The Saturday Match* (1937); A. Clitheroe, *Silly Point* (1939)
EXHIB: RI; LG
COLL: V&A
LIT: [autobiography] *Happy Days: Recollections of an Unrepentant Victorian* (1933)

TIDY, William Edward (b. 1933). Joke and strip cartoonist, illustrator, writer and broadcaster. Bill Tidy was born in Tranmere, Cheshire, on 9 October 1933, the son of William Edward Tidy. Educated at St Margaret's School, Anfield, Liverpool, he worked at first for R. P. Houston, a shipping office in the city (1950–51). He then joined the Royal Engineers as a regular soldier

(1952–5), serving in Germany, Korea and Japan where he sold his first cartoon to *Mainichi*, an English-speaking newspaper, in 1955. Returning to Liverpool, he worked as a layout artist at the Pagan Smith advertising agency (1956–8) and drew advertisements for *Radio Times* (1956). He became a professional cartoonist in 1957. Perhaps his best-known strips have been 'The Cloggies' for *Private Eye* (1967–81) and the *Listener* (1985–6), and 'The Fosdyke Saga' in the *Daily Mirror* (1971–85) – later broadcast as a 42-part series on BBC Radio 4. He has also produced work for *Punch* (including covers), *Oldie*, *New Scientist* ('Grimbledon Down'), *Camra* ('Keg Buster'), *Datalink* ('Red Spanner'), *Today*, *Mail on Sunday*, *Sunday Dispatch* ('Nero'), *Yorkshire Post*, *Picturegoer*, *Daily Sketch* ('Sir Griswold'), *Everybody's*, *John Bull*, *General Practitioner* ('Dr Whittle'), *Tit-Bits* and others. In addition he has contributed single cartoons to a wide variety of publications, has designed board games, ventriloquists' dummies, stage sets and trophies, is a frequent after-dinner speaker, has written and presented BBC TV programmes such as *Tidy Up Walsall*, *Tidy Up Naples* and *Three Days Last Summer* and has regularly appeared on Channel 4's *Countdown* and BBC Radio 4's *I'm Sorry I Haven't a Clue*. His advertising work has included drawings for Batchelors, Bass Breweries, Dale Farm and Evans Halshaw amongst others. He won Granada TV's *What the Papers Say* Cartoonist of the Year Award (1973) and was CCGB Humorous Cartoonist of the Year (1966). Bill Tidy's style has been influenced by ERIC BURGIN and the early work of RONALD SEARLE. Like JAK, he draws hands in the Disney style, with only three fingers and a thumb. He works on A4 Croxley Script paper and uses a dip pen with a Gillott 303 nib and Pelikan ink. He was one of the founder members of the British Cartoonists' Association in 1966.

PUB: More than 30 titles including *Sporting Chance* (1961), *Oh, Cleo!* (1962), *Tidy's World* (1969), *The Cloggies* (1969), *Tidy Again* (1970), 15 volumes of 'The Fosdyke Saga' series (from 1971), *Robbie and the Blobbies* (1982), *A Day at Cringemound School* (1984), *The World's Worst Golf Club* (1987), *The Incredible Bed* (1990), *Draw me 387 Baked Beans* (1991), *The Tidy Book of Quotations* (1998)
ILL: More than 70 titles including J. Wells, *The Exploding Present* (1971); S. Pile, *The Book of Heroic Failures* (1979); P. Alliss, *Bedside Golf* (1980); M. Pyke, *Food for All the Family* (1980); C. Freud,

Hangovers (1981); G. Melly, *This Curious Game of Cricket* (1982)
EXHIB: L and UK tour (1986–8); CG
COLL: UKCC
LIT: [with F. Milner] *Bill Tidy – Drawings 1957–86* (1986); [autobiography] *Is There Any News of the Iceberg?* (1996)

TIM – *see* Timyn, William

TIMYN, William 'Tim' MBE (1902–90). Joke, political and strip cartoonist, animator and sculptor. William Timyn was born in Vienna on 5 October 1902 and studied painting, drawing and sculpture at the Vienna Academy of Arts. He worked at first as Political Cartoonist and animal artist before emigrating to England in 1938. Here he began work as a Political Cartoonist on *John Bull* and *World's Press News* and contributed to *Punch* and *Lilliput*. During the war years he undertook commissions for the Ministry of Information and other departments, and produced portraits of famous British personalities. He also created a number of strips – 'Wuff, Snuff and Tuff' (*Woman Magazine*), 'Caesar' (*Sunday Graphic*), 'Oh Johnny' (*John Bull*) and 'Mimi' (*Weltwoche*, Switzerland) – which were syndicated internationally. Perhaps his best-known character was Bengo the Boxer puppy (based on his own dog of that name) for BBC TV, which he first presented on camera himself as a picture sequence narrated by Sylvia Peters. It later became an animated feature on *Blue Peter* (1962) and led to widespread merchandising and syndication. He also created for the same children's programme the adventures of Bleep the Spaceboy and his human friend Booster. In addition he was a successful sculptor and produced portrait busts of Sir Malcolm Sargent (Royal Albert Hall), Guy the gorilla (London Zoo), Petra the Blue Peter dog (BBC Television Centre, 1978), Sir Francis Chichester, Sir Bertrand Russell and others. He received the MBE in 1988 and died on 31 May 1990.
EXHIB: Vienna, Cologne (1930s); Moorland Gallery; TRY; Keyser Gallery, Cirencester; Wildlife Art Gallery, Hollywood; RA; Game Coin, San Antonio; World Wildlife Convention, Las Vegas
COLL: [sculptures] RAH; BBC Television Centre; London Zoo; UM; Riverside Foundation, Calgary, Canada

TIMOTHY – *see* Birdsall, Timothy

'Tishy' – *see* Webster, Gilbert Tom

TOM TITT – *see* Rosciszewski, Jan Stanislaw de Junosza

TOUT, The – *see* Buchanan, P. R. G.

TOWNSEND, Frederick Henry Linton Jehne ARE (1868–1920). Joke and political cartoonist, illustrator and etcher. F. H. Townsend was born in London on 26 February 1868. He attended the Lambeth School of Art (1885–9) with RAVEN HILL and Arthur Rackham and also studied wood-engraving at the City & Guilds of London Institute. While still a student he contributed to *Sunlight* magazine and some of his first illustrations were for the original publication of two of Oscar Wilde's earliest stories, 'Lord Arthur Savile's Crime' and 'The Canterville Ghost' in the *Court & Society Review*. He then began working regularly for the *Illustrated London News* and drew theatre sketches for *Lady's Pictorial*. He also contributed to *Ariel, Black & White, Cassell's, Daily Chronicle, Fun, Gentlewoman, Good Words, Idler, Longbow, New Budget, Pall Mall, Strand, Pall Mall Gazette, Graphic, Pearson's, Pick-Me-Up* (as 'Findeville'), *Printer's Pie, Queen, Quiver, Royal Magazine, Sketch, Sphere, Judy, Tatler, Unicorn* and *Windsor*. He began drawing for *Punch* in 1896 (joining the Table in 1905) and later became its first-ever Art Editor (1905–20), being succeeded on his death by his brother-in-law FRANK REYNOLDS. He mostly contributed social cartoons to the magazine, as well as illustrating the 'Parliamentary Sketches' feature (which PARTRIDGE called 'in some ways his most interesting achievement . . . he rollicks among the politicians in the festal spirit of some roguish puppy'), but sometimes also deputized for Raven Hill to draw the big whole-page political cartoon. In addition he illustrated many books and drew advertisements for British Commercial Gas Association and others. He later studied etching uder Sir Frank Short RA RI PRE (*c.* 1913) and was elected ARE in 1915. During World War I he served in the Special Constabulary. Influenced by Edwin Abbey in his book illustration work, he was an admirer of Keene, and FOUGASSE saw echoes of Du Maurier in his cartoons, saying 'he took advantage of process to produce a thin, energetic, vital line, while keeping du Maurier's fullness of tone'. Townsend was admired by THORPE as 'another of the great illustrators of the nineties', and Ellwood added that 'he was certainly our greatest master of facial expression'. Left-handed, he used models and drew roughs in pencil on chalk-surface paper, then transferred these in pen and ink on to Bristol Board (usually 12 × 10 in.). He worked mostly in pen and ink but also used wash. One of the founder members of the Chelsea Arts Club, he was also an expert fencer and illustrated the English version of Baron de Bazancourt's classic, *Secrets de l'Epée*. Townsend died suddenly on a golf course in Hampstead, London, on 11 December 1920 aged 52. He was buried in Highgate Cemetery.
PUB: *'Punch' Drawings by F. H. Townsend* (1921)
ILL: More than 30 books including S. J. Duncan, *A Social Departure* (1890), *An American Girl in London* (1891), *The Simple Adventures of a Memsahib* (1893); T. L. Peacock, *Maid Marian* (1895), *Gryll Grange* (1896), *Melincourt* (1896); F. Marryat, *The King's Own* (1896); C. Brontë, *Shirley* (1897), *Jane Eyre* (1897); C. Dickens, *A Tale of Two Cities* (1902); R. Kipling, *The Brushwood Boy* (1907); F. Barclay, *The Following of the Star* (1911)
EXHIB: RA; RE; FAS (Memorial, 1921); NEA; RBA; RSA
COLL: BM; V&A; THG
LIT: P. V. Bradshaw, *The Art of the Illustrator 2: F. H. Townsend* (1918)

TOY, William Harry (1885–1915). Political cartoonist and caricaturist. W. H. Toy was born in Exeter, Devon. He worked at first as a clerk in the Devonshire local education authority's office and then came to London to work for the Kent County Council Education Authority, for which he continued to work until his sudden death aged 30. A student of PERCY BRADSHAW's correspondence art school, he was otherwise self-taught and later set up an art school of his own in partnership with Clifford Turner. His first published drawings were theatrical caricatures for *Play Pictorial* and *Throne*. However, he is best known as the Political Cartoonist on the *Daily Sketch*. He also drew a satirical war cartoon series, 'Nursery Rhymes for the Times', for the paper and often included portraits of his office colleagues in his cartoons. In addition he drew theatrical caricatures for *Punch* and *Tatler*, and contributed to the *Daily Mirror*. He worked on Bristol Board, largely in pen and

ink. Toy died of heart failure in Teignmouth, Devon, on 26 July 1915.
ILL: M. F. Drew, *Notions About Nations* (1914)
COLL: UKCC

TRIER, Walter (1890–1951). Joke and political cartoonist, caricaturist and illustrator. Walter Trier was born in Prague on 25 June 1890, the son of a German-speaking leather-glove manufacturer. He attended the Nikolander Realschule in Prague, the Industrial School of Fine & Applied Arts and the Prague Academy (1905–6) before moving to the Munich Academy (1909) to study under Franz von Stuck, a former cartoonist. The same year (when he was 19) his first drawings were published in *Simplicissimus* and *Jugend*. In 1910 he joined the staff of *Lustige Blätter* and moved to Berlin, also contributing to the *Berliner Illustrierte Zeitung* (1910), *Die Dame* (1923) and *Uhu* (1924). He then designed costumes and stage settings for Max Reinhardt's *Das Gross Schauspielhaus* (1924), became a member of the Berliner Sezession group (1926) and began to illustrate Erich Kästner's children's books (15 titles 1929–51), the first of which – *Emil and the Detectives* – quickly became a classic. In 1929 he was elected Vice-Chairman of the Association of Illustrators of Germany. After the burning of 'subversive' literature in Berlin, including books illustrated by Trier, he moved to London (1936), drawing title cartoons for Pinewood Film Studios and beginning his long association as cover artist and cartoonist for *Lilliput* (1937–49). Starting with the very first issue he produced 147 cover designs for the monthly featuring his familar couple and their black Scottie dog, explaining: 'The couple was the embodiment of something eternally amusing – youth, love . . . Sometimes they are young, sometimes older, sometimes naturalistic and sometimes stylized, in all possible costumes of all sorts of periods, not even of flesh and blood, but as chopped trees or fruit or often as toys . . .' During World War II he produced political cartoons for the London-based German weekly *Die Zeitung*, *Life* and *New York Times*, and in 1944 illustrated John Betjeman's books column in the *Daily Herald*. After the war he was commissioned to produce egg-shell caricatures of delegates to the United Nations Organization (1945) and contributed to *Illustrated*. He emigrated to Toronto, Canada, in 1947 and worked for Canada Packers Ltd (one of Canada's larg-

est food processors) designing advertisements for Klik & Kam (tinned meats), Maple Leaf Cheese, Domestic Shortening, Quix Soap, York Peanut Butter, etc., as well as for Imperial Life Insurance and others. He also contributed caricatures to *Saturday Night Magazine*, covers for *New Liberty* and designed Christmas cards for William Coutts. He died on 8 July 1951.
PUB: *Toys* (1923), [with F. A. Colman] *Artisten* (1928), *10 Little Negroes* (1944), *8192 Quite Crazy People* (1949), *8192 Crazy Costumes* (1949), *Dandy in the Circus* (1950)
ILL: Numerous books including P. Benndorf, *Till Eulenspiegel* (1920); A. Roda Roda, *Die Verfolgte Unschuld* (1920); E. Kästner, *Emil und die Detektive* (1929) [and 14 others]; E. Mordaunt, *Blitz Kids* (1941); D. Seth-Smith, *Jolly Families* (n.d.)
EXHIB: Berliner Sezession, Berlin; Galerie Andre, Prague; Stern House, Brno; Czechoslovak Institute, London (1943); Nicholson Gallery; University of Toronto; International Youth Library, Munich; Archivarion Gallery, Berlin
LIT: Art Gallery of Ontario, *Humorist Walter Trier* (catalogue, 1980)

TROG – *see* Fawkes, Walter Ernest

TURNER, Martyn (b. 1948). Political cartoonist, caricaturist and writer. Martyn Turner was born on 24 June 1948 in Wanstead, Essex, the son of Ernest Turner, a general dealer, and attended Bancroft's School, Woodford Green, and The Queen's University of Belfast (1967–71). A self-taught artist, his first cartoons were published in *The Irish Times* and *Belfast Sunday News* in June 1971. Political Cartoonist on the *Belfast Sunday News* (1971–4), he was also Editor of *Fortnight* magazine, Belfast (1972–6), and was Political Cartoonist of the *Sunday Express* (1996–8). He has been Political Cartoonist on the *Irish Times* since 1976. His work is reprinted weekly in the *Belfast Telegraph* and is syndicated by the Cartoonists' & Writers' Syndicate, New York. He has also contributed to the *Guardian* and various foreign journals and has written occasional columns for the *Irish Times*, *Christian Science Monitor*, *The Australian* and the *Belfast Telegraph*. Winner of the Hibernia Press Award for writing and cartooning in 1975, he was named Commentator of the Year in the Irish Media Awards (1995) and was awarded an Honorary Doctorate from the University of

Ulster (1998) for his work 'as a gifted and influential cartoonist'. Turner works in brush and ink and uses acrylic and gouache for colour cartoons. He cites his influences as being HEWISON, EMMWOOD and SEARLE.

PUB: *The Book* (1983), *Illuminations* (1985), *Not Viking Likely* (1986), *A Fistful of Dailers* (1987), (ed.) *Thin Black Lines* (1987), *Heavy Weather* (1989), *The Guy Who Won the Tour de France* (1991), *The Long Goodbye* (1992), *Politics et Al* (1992), (ed.) *Columba!* (1993), *The Odd Couple* (1994), (ed.) *Thin Black Lines Rides Again* (1994), *Pack up Your Troubles* (1995), *The Noble Art of Politics* (1996), *Brace Yourself, Bridge It!* (1998)

ILL: More than 12 books
EXHIB: More than 20 in Ireland
COLL: National Library of Ireland; Presidential Election Collection, University of Hartford, Connecticut; SAM; International Museum of Cartoon Art, Florida; UKCC; University of Ulster; University of Ohio

'**Two Types, The**' – *see* Jones, William John Philpin

TWYM – *see* Boyd, Alexander Stuart

U

ULLYETT, Royden Herbert Frederick (b. 1914). Sports cartoonist. Roy Ullyett was born in Leytonstone, Essex, on 16 March 1914, the son of Henry John Emerson Ullyett, Secretary-Manager of Slazengers sports equipment manufacturers. A self-taught artist, his first cartoon was published in the *Southend Times* (*c.* 1932). His first job was working for a colour printing firm but at the age of 19 he joined the *Star* as sports cartoonist. After serving as a pilot in the RAF in World War II, he returned to the paper while also drawing as 'Berryman' for the *Sunday Pictorial* until 1953. Influenced by TOM WEBSTER, he was sports cartoonist at the *Daily Express* from 1953 to 1998. He draws with a No. 6 brush and indian ink on Bristol or Whatman board and often includes a sparrow in his drawings to comment on the main action. Roy Ullyett was one of the founder members of the British Cartoonists' Association in 1966.

PUB: 19 annuals (1956–74), [with JON] *'I'm the Greatest!'* (1975), *Cue for a Laugh* (1984)
ILL: T. H. Cotton, *Henry Cotton Says . . .* (1962); T. E. Bailey, *The Greatest of my Time* (1968); J. Greaves and N. Giller, *Stop the Game: I Want to Get On!* (1983)
COLL: Royal & Ancient Golf Club, St Andrews
LIT: [autobiography] R. Ullyett and N. Giller, *While There's Still Lead in my Pencil* (1998)

'**Uncle Oojah**' – *see* Webb, Hector Thomas Maybank

UNVARDY, Imre Laszlo 'Spy Junior' (1885–after 1922). Caricaturist. Imre Unvardy was born in Budapest, Hungary, on 20 March 1885, the son of Julius Unvardy, a portrait painter. He studied art at Budapest Academy and assisted LESLIE WARD from 1918 until Ward's death in 1922, after which he worked as 'Spy Junior', contributing caricatures to *Vanity Fair*, *Mayfair* and others. He also worked as an illustrator and portrait painter. His wife was the illustrator Mabel Sims.

ILL: A. A. Milne, *The Bookman of Augustine Birrell*
EXHIB: Grafton Gallery; AG

UPTTON, Clive (b. 1911). Political cartoonist, illustrator, caricaturist, poster artist and painter. Clive Upton was born in Highbury Barn, London, on 12 March 1911, the son of Clive William Upton [*sic*], a touch-up artist for Swain's engravers who later worked for the *Daily Mail*. Educated at Brentwood Grammar School, Essex, at the age of 16 he studied at Southend Art School and (at 19) Central School of Art, but turned professional illustrator before completing his studies. He later also studied at Heatherley's. An illustrator for *Strand Magazine* (notably of stories by Margery Allingham and Valentine Williams in the 1930s and '40s), *Good Housekeeping*, *Woman's Illustrated* (e.g. stories by Barbara Cartland), *Tit-Bits*, *Nash's*, *Tatler*, *Radio Times*, *Look & Learn*, *Sphere* (including covers), *John Bull* (including covers) and others, he has also produced advertisements for GEC, Johnnie Walker Whisky, Mars, Bovril, Guinness, Horlicks, Kelloggs, Nestlé's, the 'Beer is Best' campaign and numerous other clients via the Clement Danes and Owen Aves press agencies. In addition he has designed book jackets and drawn illustrations for UK and US publishers and was sent by the Colonial Office to Ghana to produce instructional booklets about how to grow better cocoa beans. In 1939 he unsuccessfully applied for Poy's old job as Political Cartoonist on the *Daily Mail* (Uptton's friend ILLINGWORTH was taken on instead). During World War II, he was Political Cartoonist on the *Daily Sketch* and *Sunday Graphic* (1939–42) and later worked for the Ministry of Information producing propaganda drawings and painting. Perhaps his best-known wartime work was 'This is the Year' (*Sunday Chronicle*) and 'We Kneel only to Thee' (*Sunday Graphic*), both of

which were reproduced widely as posters. He later won prizes for his posters in the National Outdoor Advertising Awards (1958, 1959) and continued to work as a landscape and portrait painter (commissions included portraits of Harold Macmillan and Anthony Eden) and illustrator until 1987 when his eyesight began to fail. Clive Uptton is a left-handed artist but writes with his right hand. As well as his pen and ink line drawings he also likes to work in oils, watercolours and acrylics. He added an extra 't' to his name in the 1930s to differentiate himself from another illustrator called Upton. A former committee member of the Chelsea Arts Club, he is also a member of the Savage Club.
ILL: Several titles for Warner Press (USA)
COLL: IWM

'Useless Eustace' – *see* Greenall, Jack

V

'Varoomshka' – *see* Kent, Capel John

VICTORIA – *see* Davidson, Lilli Ursula Barbara Victoria

VICKY – *see* Weisz, Victor

W

WADLOW, Geoffrey Arthur (b. 1912). Joke cartoonist, illustrator and commercial artist. Geoffrey Wadlow was born in London on 3 November 1912, the son of an amateur black-and-white artist and oil painter, but spent his youth in what is now Merseyside. He attended Birkenhead Institute Grammar School and worked at first in business, taking the exams for the Chartered Institute of Secretaries before moving to his company's advertising department. Here he worked on layouts and took the Advertising Association's exams while also studying life drawing, anatomy and composition at Camberwell School of Art. His first car-

toon was accepted by *Night & Day* in 1937 but the magazine folded before it was published. His first *Punch* cartoon appeared in 1938. During World War II he served in the National Fire Service and the RAF (1939–46). For many years he worked as art director of an advertising agency and in 1955 won the National Outdoor Advertising Award for his poster illustrations. As a cartoonist he has contributed to *London Opinion, Lilliput, Men Only, Tatler & Bystander, Everybody's, John Bull, Tit-Bits, Evening Standard* and other publications. Influenced by TOM WEBSTER and the *New Yorker* cartoonist Robert Day, he works in pen and ink or pen and wash

(monochrome and full colour). FOUGASSE has described his work as 'pleasing confused-thought subjects treated in a pleasingly confused-thought style of drawing' and BRADSHAW saw him as the creator of 'an odd world of pop-eyed, spindle-legged puppets'.
ILL: Unilever, *Marketing* (n.d.), *Market Research* (n.d.) and various staff handbooks, etc.

WAIN, Louis William (1860–1939). Joke and strip cartoonist, illustrator and animator. Louis Wain was born in Clerkenwell, London, on 5 August 1860, the son of Louis Matthew Wain, an embroiderer and textile salesman. His French mother, Felicia Marie Boiteux, designed carpets and church fabrics. Educated at the Orchard Street Foundation, Hackney, and at St Joseph's Academy, Kennington, he intended at first to become a musician but later studied at the West London School of Art (1877–80). He began work there as an assistant teacher (1880–82) and his first drawing, 'Robin's Breakfast' (featuring two bullfinches and signed 'L. Wain'), appeared in the Christmas 1881 issue of *Illustrated Sporting & Dramatic News*. He joined the staff of the paper the following year. His first cat drawing was published in 1883 and after the success of his book illustrations for Kari's *Madame Tabethy's Establishment* (1886) and his double-page drawing 'The Kitten's Christmas Party' (featuring more than 150 cats) in the Christmas issue of the *Illustrated London News* the same year, he concentrated on anthopomorphic cats, often dressed in human clothes. He joined the staff of the *Illustrated London News* in 1886 and also contributed jokes, strips and illustrations to *Boy's Own Paper*, *Chums*, *Playbox* (e.g. the strip 'Purry Pusskin', 1904), *Father Tuck's Annual*, *Moonshine*, *Captain*, *English Illustrated Magazine*, *Gentlewoman*, *Lloyds Weekly News*, *Windsor*, *Pearson's*, *Sketch*, *Little Folks*, *Pall Mall Budget*, *Judy* and others. In addition, he illustrated numerous books (11 in 1903 alone), began his own annual which ran for over 20 years (1901–22) and drew cat postcards for Raphael Tuck and many others. He moved to the USA in 1907 and drew two cat strip cartoons for *New York American* (1907–10). On his return to England he fell from a bus (1914) and was badly concussed, which, combined with other factors, may have led to his future mental illness. He experimented with animated films in 1917 but by 1924 was declared insane. Not a good businessman (he had been sued for debt in 1907),

he had failed to retain reproduction rights in his works and was thus confined in a pauper's ward in Tooting Hospital, suffering from schizophrenia. However, after a public appeal, backed by figures such as Princess Alexandra, Prime Minister Ramsay Macdonald and H. G. Wells, he was transferred to a private room at the Royal Bethlehem Hospital (now the Imperial War Museum) in 1925 where he continued to work: an exhibition of his drawings appearing at the Twenty One Gallery that year. He was later moved to Napsbury Hospital near St Albans (1930–39). Described by *Punch* as 'the Hogarth of Cat Life' he worked at great speed, at one time producing up to 600 drawings a year. Influenced by the great 19th-century anthropomorphic humorous illustrators such as Grandville and Griset, he was a near contemporary of the animal cartoonists J. A. SHEPHERD, G. E. STUDDY and CECIL ALDIN, but at the height of his fame eclipsed all other comic cat artists: 'He has made the cat his own, he invented a cat style, a cat society, a whole cat world. English cats that do not look and live like Louis Wain's cats are ashamed of themselves' (H. G. Wells). He was elected President of the National Cat Club in 1891. Louis Wain died in Napsbury Hospital near St Albans, Hertfordshire, on 4 July 1939.
PUB: Many books including *Puppy Dog's Tales* (1896), *Pussies and Puppies* (1899), *Louis Wain's Annual* (1901–21), *Nursery Book* (1902), *Baby's Picture Book* (1903), *Big Dogs, Little Dogs, Cats and Kittens* (1903), *Kitten Book* (1903), *In Animal Land* (1904), *Animal Show* (1905), *Cats About Town* (1907–10), *A Cat Alphabet* (1914), *Daddy Cat* (1915), *Pussy Land* (1920), *Animal Book* (1928)
ILL: More than 90 books including Kari, *Madame Tabethy's Establishment* (1886); F. W. Pattenden, *Our Farm* (1888); R. Leander, *Dreams of French Firesides* (1890); C. Morley, *Peter, A Cat o' One Tail* (1892); M. A. Owen, *The Old Rabbit and the Voodoo* (1893); G. C. Bingham, *The Dandy Lion* (1900), *Fun and Frolic* (1902), *Kittenland* (1903), *Claws and Paws* (1908); S. C. Woodhouse, *Cats at Large* (1910); *Cinderella and Other Fairy Tales* (1917); C. M. Rutley, *Valentine's Rocker Books* (1920–21)
EXHIB: XXI Gallery (1925); Clarendon House Gallery (1937); V&A (1972–3); Parkin Gallery; CBG (1983, 1989); RBA
COLL: BM; V&A; Institute of Psychiatry; THG
LIT: R. Dale, *Louis Wain, the Man Who Drew Cats* (1968); B. Reade, *Louis Wain* (1972); M. Parkin, *Louis Wain's Cats* (1983)

WAITE, Keith (b. 1927). Editorial/political and joke cartoonist, and illustrator. Keith Waite was born in New Plymouth, New Zealand, on 19 March 1927, the son of Albert Waite, the owner of a coalmine, and attended Elam School of Art in Auckland (1948–9). He began as a cartoonist on the *Taranaki Daily News* and *Auckland Weekly News* and then *Otago Daily Times* (1949–51). Arriving in the UK in 1951, he joined Kemsley Newspapers, working for the *Glasgow Daily Record* and *Glasgow Daily News* (1952–3), then freelanced for *Punch* (from 1953), *Men Only* and others before becoming Editorial/Political Cartoonist on the *Daily Sketch* (1956–64, taking over from IAN SCOTT), the pre-Murdoch *Sun* (1964–9), *Sunday Mirror* (1970–80) and *Daily Mirror* (1969–85). He was business-page cartoonist on *The Times* from 1987 to 1997. Voted CCGB Cartoonist of the Year in 1963, Keith Waite has also won several international awards for his work. He was one of the founder members of the British Cartoonists' Association in 1966 and its first-ever Treasurer.
PUB: *Waite Up to Date* (1951), *The Worlds of Waite* (1981)
COLL: UKCC; IWM; NZCAT; Alexander Turnbull Library, Wellington, New Zealand

WAL – *see* Coop, J. Wallace

WALKER, Jack (fl. 1914–21). Political cartoonist. Jack Walker was Political Cartoonist of the *Daily Graphic* and also contributed to *Bystander*.
PUB: *The Daily Graphic Special War Cartoons* (Vols 1–7, 1914–15)

WALKER, J. C. (1892–1981). Political and sports cartoonist, and caricaturist. J. C. Walker was born in Cardiff in September 1892 and was an apprentice in a marine engineering firm at Barry Dock before giving it up aged 19 to join the army. In World War I he served on searchlight duty and won competitions for advertisements for Cherry Blossom Shoe Polish and Swan Pens and also contributed to *Royal Magazine* and *Blighty*. After the war he returned to marine engineering as a draughtsman and advertisement designer (1919–24) while freelancing sports cartoons for the *South Wales Evening Express*. He joined the paper as Sports and Political Cartoonist in 1926 and began contributing to the *News of the World* in 1939. As 'Marksman' (he was a Bisley champion) he drew the front-page political cartoon of the latter paper from 1941 but though Fleet Street beckoned, he preferred working from Wales and so opted for an exclusive freelance contract with Kemsley Newspapers rather than moving to London. Other papers he contributed to include *Sheffield Telegraph*, *North-Eastern Gazette* and *Glasgow Record*. At one time he shared an office with the young LESLIE ILLINGWORTH (then working on the *Evening Express*'s sister paper, the *Western Mail*) and he also contributed to *South Wales Echo* in later life. During World War II he was an Instructor of Musketry in the Home Guard. One of Walker's more enduring characters was the jovial 'Mr Fullerjoy', a typical man in the street who wore spectacles through which you couldn't see the eyes. A supporter of the view that 'ridicule is often more deadly than dynamite', he could draw with either hand and would use pencil for roughs and a fine sable brush with ink for the finished artwork, as it helped the ink dry quicker. He drew 18 × 12 in. for 6 × 4 in. reproduction on Winsor & Newton Fashion Plate Drawing Board and indicated tone with blue pencil or transparent blue watercolour paint. He also sometimes signed his work 'JCW'. BRADSHAW said of him: 'Walker is not only a genuinely comic draughtsman, but his bold, live work is associated with an intuitive news sense, a wide knowledge of world affairs, and an uncanny ability to see, from a humorous angle, the very essence of a topical situation . . . He always worked boldly and cleanly, simplifying his message in strong line and dead black; but since he substituted a brush for his pen his work has gained in breadth, spirit and urgency, his portraits seem more lively and spontaneous . . .' In the 1940s he wrote a series of articles for the *Artist* entitled 'How I Became a Successful Cartoonist' which were later turned into a book. J. C. Walker retired to Barley in Hertfordshire in 1966 and died there on 26 October 1981.
PUB: Three collections of his cartoons, [autobiography] *A Cartoonist at Work* (1949)

WALTER – *see* Goetz, Walter

WALTER, John Gardner (1913–99). Joke cartoonist. John G. Walter was born in Congresbury, Bristol, on 6 June 1913. He trained in the drawing office of an aircraft company and had his first cartoon published in *Punch* on 28 December 1932. He also contributed to *Radio Times*, *Everybody's*, *Illustrated* and various motoring magazines. During World War II he produced pamphlets and illustrated booklets. After the war his work in local government took over from his other activities. He was influenced by HEATH ROBINSON.

ILL: *ROTOL: The History of an Airscrew Company* (n.d.)

WARD, Sir Leslie Matthew 'Spy' RP (1851–1922). Caricaturist and portrait painter. Leslie Ward was born in Harewood Square, London on 21 November 1851, the eldest son of Edward Matthew Ward RA and Henrietta Mary Ada Ward (painter of royalty and art teacher to Princess Alice of Albany and others). He was also (on his mother's side) the grandson of the engraver George Raphael Ward, great-nephew of the portrait painter John Jackson RA, and great-grandson of the famous animal painter James Ward RA. His great-great uncle was the landscape and animal painter George Morland, who married the sister of James and William Ward, the engraver. Educated at Salt Hill Preparatory School near Slough and at Eton, he exhibited a bust of his brother and a painting at the Royal Academy when he was 16 (1867) before studying architecture under Sydney Smirke RA and Sir Edward Barry at the RA Schools (1871). He was then apprenticed to W. P. Frith RA (who painted the hugely popular 'Brighton Beach') and began to exhibit portraits in oil and watercolour. After seeing his caricature of the eminent (anti-Darwin) zoologist Professor Richard Owen, the painter Sir John Everett Millais (a close friend of Ward's father) introduced him to Thomas Gibson Bowles, editor and proprietor of *Vanity Fair*. This (unsigned) portrait (published on 1 March 1873 when Ward was 22) subsequently became the first of more than 1000 of his drawings (nearly half the magazine's entire output) that Bowles published over the next 36 years (1873–1909) under the pseudonym 'Spy' (chosen after discussion with Bowles to match that of the magazine's great contributor Carlo Pellegrini, 'Ape'). He also worked for the *Graphic, Strand* and the weekly *Newspaper World* (alternating with SEM from 1910 when his age began to tell, and being assisted by UNVARDY from 1918). He never drew women (the one exception being Georgina Weldon for *Vanity Fair*), greatly angered Trollope with his portrait of the novelist (1873), and thought his best caricature was of Lord Haldon ('I laugh myself when I look at it'). Elected RP (1891), he was

knighted in 1918. The first English artist to draw the portrait-chargé popularized in France by André Gill in the 1850s (Pellegrini was Italian), he worked in watercolours. In describing his method he said: 'I catch hold of the leading feature and slightly, very slightly, exaggerate. I don't mean facial or physical features exactly, so much as that characteristic by which each man is known best to friend and foe alike.' He also sometimes signed his work 'L. Ward' or reversed this as 'Drawl'. His two sisters were also artists. Leslie Ward died in London on 15 May 1922.

EXHIB: RA; RP; DOW; NPG 'Vanity Fair' (1976)
COLL: NPG; V&A; NGI; L; THG; BM
LIT: Sir L. Ward, *Forty Years of 'Spy'* (1915); R. T. Mathews and P. Mellini, *In 'Vanity Fair'* (1982)

WATSON, Alex Noel (b. 1929). Joke cartoonist and journalist. Alex Noel Watson was born in Airdrie, Lanarkshire, on 2 December 1929 and was brought up in Coatbridge. The son of Alex Grant Watson, a journalist, photographer and crossword compiler, and his wife Isa, also a journalist, he studied graphic and commercial art at the Glasgow School of Art (1948–52) and at Jordanhill Training College (1952–3). His first cartoon was published in the *Glasgow Sunday Mail* in 1947. He spent his National Service in the Royal Army Educational Corps (1954–6) and began work as a freelance cartoonist for the *Hereford Times* ('Watson's Wisecracks', 1955–70). An art teacher in Croydon (1956–63), he joined the *Croydon Advertiser* group of newspapers as a staff cartoonist (1965–78) while continuing to contribute freelance cartoons to other publications, specializing in religious and business jokes. His work has appeared in the *Evening Standard, Daily Sketch, Weekend, Tit-Bits, Sunday Citizen, John O' London's, Time & Tide, Spectator, Daily Telegraph, Punch, New Society, Life & Work* (20 years), *Methodist Recorder* (since 1965), *Daily Express, Daily Star, Financial Weekly, Sunday Times, Private Eye, Presbyterian Record* (Canada, 20 years), *New Yorker, New York Times, Toronto Star, Croc* and elsewhere. He has also lectured on cartoon art to various societies and on CBC Radio in Canada. In 1997 he created a beaver character, Tobik, which has been used as a logo and featured in animated promotional material for a Czech company. He has also designed book covers, worked as a film critic and feature writer and has written travel articles for the

Toronto Star (since 1965). Noel Watson works mostly on Ivrex Board in pen and ink, sometimes also with wash or watercolour, and cites his influences as being the artists of the *New Yorker*, notably its former Art Editor Lee Lorenz.
ILL: C. S. Elston, *La Colonie de Vacances* (1961); H. W. Tame, *Peter and Pamela Grow Up* (1960); R. Stephenson, *Un-Christmas Characters* (1993); J. A. Simpson, *All About Christmas* (1994); N. W. Goodacre, *Making Marriage Work* (1996)
EXHIB: St Andrews University; [travel drawing] RA
COLL: Thurber House, Columbus, Ohio; National Museum of Canada; Princeton University, New Jersey

WATT, John Millar (1895–1975). Strip cartoonist, illustrator, commercial artist and painter. Millar Watt was born in Greenock, Scotland, on 14 October 1895. He studied art at the Sir John Cass Institute under Harold Stabler and in 1912 was apprenticed to the Mather & Crowther advertising agency (eventually becoming chief poster artist) while attending evening classes at Westminster School of Art under Walter Bayes. During World War I he served as a second lieutenant in the Essex Regiment, Artists' Rifles (1915–18) but was later reposted to the Highland Regiment and produced technical drawings for instructional lectures in the field. After the war he studied sculpture briefly at the Slade under Harvard Thomas (1919) but left complaining it was 'full of Russian princesses filling in time'. Returning to Mather & Crowther, he found additional work drawing newspaper sports cartoons and illustrations for the *Sphere* while attending evening classes at St Martin's School of Art. On 20 May 1921 he created his most enduring character, Pop, star of Britain's first comic strip for adults, which originally appeared in the *Daily Sketch* as 'Reggie Breaks it Gently', intended as a rival to W. K. HASELDEN's box cartoon in the *Daily Mirror*. At first a typical paterfamilias businessman – whose mouth is rarely seen except when emitting a cry or shout – the balding Pop worked in the City and wore a top hat, striped trousers, spats, cravat and umbrella (originally he also sported a moustache and pince-nez). Gradually, however, he developed into an Everyman figure and appeared in many guises, from artist to boxer and medieval knight to caveman. FOUGASSE described him as 'a direct descendant of Falstaff and Mr Pickwick,

of Jorrocks and Old Bill – like all of them he is a cheerful mixture of opposites and contradictions, of realist and idealist: he is the happy warrior, the hopeful pessimist, the matter-of-fact romantic . . . He is, as it were, the average Briton's idea of the average Briton, he is Mr Everyman as seen by himself – he is, in fact, Mr Everypop.' Very popular (syndicated worldwide and admired by Sir Alfred Munnings, Low, FRANK REYNOLDS and STRUBE amongst others), the strip started as four panels, then became three and, when Watt left to concentrate on advertising work in 1949 and GORDON HOGG ('Gog') took over, finally appeared as a single frame. The original design of the strip was quite unique, ignoring as it did the confines of the box frame and allowing words (which never appeared in balloons) and the drawing to spill across the panels in the manner of oriental screen paintings. After he handed over the strip to Gog, it continued in the *Graphic* and then the *Daily Mail* until its final episode on 23 January 1960. Watt, meanwhile, returned to advertising and freelance illustration for clients such as the *Graphic*, *Sphere* (including covers), *Illustrated London News* (including covers), *Everybody's* (in black and orange), *Reader's Digest* (including covers), *Look & Learn*, *Princess*, *Beano*, *Beezer*, and *Robin Hood* annuals. He also created advertising campaigns for Ben Truman ('More Hops in Ben Truman'), Shell, Cherry Blossom and Rowntree's Fruit Gums and designed the first Sunblest Bread trademark. During World War II Watt served in the Home Guard in St Ives, Cornwall. Married to the flower and landscape painter, Amy Millar Watt (née Maulby Biggs), he was a member of the Ipswich Art Club and the St Ives Society of Artists. John Millar Watt died in Lavenham, Suffolk, on 13 December 1975.
PUB: 'Pop' annuals (1924–49)
ILL: *Robin Hood*, *Beezer*, etc., annuals
EXHIB: RA (1936, 1937); [retrospective] Church Street Gallery, Lavenham, Suffolk (1989, 1991)

WATTS, Arthur George DSO (and bar) ARBA (1883–1935). Joke cartoonist, illustrator and painter. Arthur Watts was born on 28 April 1883 in Chatham, Kent, the son of Joseph Watts, a Deputy Surgeon-General in the Indian Medical Service. Educated at Dulwich College, London, he sold his first published drawings (illustrations for *Boy's Champion*) when he was still at school (he was paid 1s. 6d for each). He then studied art at Goldsmiths' College (two years) and the Slade and took classes in book illustration at the Regent Street Polytechnic. After that he studied in Antwerp, Paris, Moscow and Madrid before returning to the Slade. In 1904 (at the age of 21) he had his first cartoon published in *London Opinion* and he subsequently began contributing regularly to the *Strand, Pearson's, London Magazine, Tatler* and *Bystander*. During World War I he served in the RNVR (1914–19), took part in the Zeebrugge raid and was twice awarded the DSO. He later also worked for *Humorist, Life, Nash's, Punch, Radio Times* (including covers and illustrations for 'Both Sides of the Microphone', 1928–35) and the *Sketch* amongst others. In addition he designed posters for London Underground, Great Western Railway, etc., and drew advertisements for Comfort Soap, Ronuk Polish and others. Watts was elected ARBA in 1923. A characteristic of his art was the use of overhead angles and drawing as if from above the scene. He claimed that he drew bird's-eye views because he always wanted his cartoons to appear on a full page and that this was the best means of achieving this (*Artist*, December 1934). In humour and style he was part of 'the RIDGEWELL–SHERWOOD–Watts school' (Price) influenced by H. M. BATEMAN, which in turn influenced the work of NICOLAS BENTLEY and others. Watts never used Bristol Board, preferring instead thick hot-pressed paper, and worked in pen and brush using Higgins ink or Stephens' Ebony Water Stain. He also used scraperboard and painted. He was a member of the Savage Club. The children's book writer and illustrator Marjorie-Ann Watts is his daughter. Arthur Watts died in an air crash in Switzerland on 20 July 1935.

PUB: *A Painter's Anthology* (1924)
ILL: A. R. Thorndike and R. Arkell, *The Tragedy of Mr Punch* (1923), *A Little Pilgrim's Peeps at Parnassus* (1927); E. G. V. Knox, *Poems of Impudence* (1926); G. B. Hartford, *Commander, R.N.* (1927); E. M. Delafield, *Diary of a Provincial Lady* (1930), *The Provincial Lady Goes Further* (1932); H. F. Ellis, *So This is Science!* (1932) and others
EXHIB: FAS (1936); RA; RBA; CAC
COLL: V&A; UKCC; BM

WAY, Steven (b. 1959). Joke cartoonist and editor. Steve Way was born in Plymouth on 1 January 1959, the son of Colin F. Way, an electrical engineer, and studied graphic design at Leeds Polytechnic. His first cartoon was published in *National Student* in 1990. He has been Cartoon Editor of *Punch* (1989–92, being succeeded by PAUL THOMAS, and again from 1997), Editor and co-founder (with John Sorrell) of the shortlived 'cartoon newspaper' *The Cartoonist* (1993) and Cartoon Editor of *Maxim* (1995–8). His drawings have appeared in *Punch, Private Eye* (from 1992), *Spectator, Listener, Independent, Sunday Correspondent* and the *Observer*. He works with a Gillott 303 dip pen and indian ink – usually Dr Martin's Blackstar waterproof variety. The many artists he cites as having influenced his work include QUENTIN BLAKE, RALPH STEADMAN, FRANK DICKENS, Johnny Hart, George Herriman and Edward Sorel.

'Weary Willy and Tired Tim' – *see* Browne, Thomas Arthur

WEBB, Hector Thomas Maybank 'Thomas Maybank' (1869–1929). Joke and strip cartoonist, illustrator and painter. Thomas Maybank was born in Beckenham, Kent. At the age of eight he was thrown from a horse and, injuring his hip, spent two years in St Thomas's Hospital, London. He later became an architect and surveyor and was Assistant Road Surveyor for the Borough of Croydon. Some of his earliest work was for *Pick-Me-Up* (1900, comic decorations) and he began drawing full-time in 1902, notably humorous fairy illustrations and cartoons in *Punch* (1902–9) which show the influence of Richard Doyle. He also contributed to *Bystander, Graphic, Pearson's, Printer's Pie, Passing Show, Tatler* and the *Windsor Magazine*. In addition, he drew illustrations for Ward Lock children's books (notably their 'Wonder Book' series, including the celebrated end-papers which were later published in a single volume, *Mirth by Maybank*). However, he is perhaps best known for his creation of the character 'Uncle Oojah' (originally 'Flip-Flap the Great Oojah'), a huge elephant in striped pyjamas, which first appeared as a single-panel cartoon in the *Daily Sketch* on 18 February 1919 with text by Flo Lancaster (Florence Wallis). A great success, it became a strip in 1921 and the children's supplement to the paper was later renamed the *Oojah Sketch*. The other characters in the series were Oojah's nephew, Jerrywangle, a black cat called Snooker and a boy, Don. After Webb's death it was drawn by H. M. Talintyre and continued into the 1950s when it was renamed

'Jerry, Don and Snooker'. In addition, Maybank produced comic postcards for H. Munk and was a painter and exhibited at the Royal Academy. He died in Esher, Surrey.

PUB: [with F. Lancaster] 10 'Uncle Oojah' books including *Oojah House* (1922), *Oojah Annual* (1922), *Oojah's Treasure Trunk* (1926), *Mirth for Young and Old Alike* (1937)
ILL: M. Drayton, *Nymphedia* (1906); T. Lodge, *Rosalynde* (1907); R. C. Lehmann, *The Sun-Child* (*c.* 1907); L. Carroll, *Alice's Adventures in Wonderland* (1910); A. Herbertson, *Teddy and Trots in Wonderland* (1910); W. H. Prescott, *The Conquest of Peru* (1913)
EXHIB: RA; RBA; ROI; RHA
COLL: V&A

WEBSTER, Gilbert Tom (1886–1962). Sports and political cartoonist, journalist and caricaturist. Tom Webster was born in Bilston, Staffordshire, on 17 July 1886, the son of an ironmonger, and educated at Royal Wolverhampton School. His first job (aged 14) was as a booking-office clerk for the Great Western Railway in Handsworth, Staffordshire. Self-taught as an artist, he won prizes for humorous drawing offered by the *Birmingham Weekly Post* and *Athletics News*. He then got a job as cartoonist on the *Birmingham Sports Argus* and in 1912 joined the *Daily Citizen* in London as Political Cartoonist, while also freelancing for *Star* and *Golf Illustrated*. In World War I he served with the Royal Fusiliers but was invalided out with rheumatic fever in 1916. He then made animated films such as *The History of a German Regiment* (1917), *Charlie at the Front* (1918) and *Charlie Joins the Navy* (1918). He joined the *Evening News* as Sports Cartoonist in 1918, later moving to the *Daily Mail* (1919–40). In 1924 (a year in which he was reputed to be the highest paid cartoonist in the world – earning £20,000) he helped organize the revue *Cartoons* at the Criterion Theatre, London, and in the 1929 General Election his cartoons were projected on to a huge screen in Trafalgar Square which gave the results. He also produced 14 oil panels of sports figures for the gymnasium of the *Queen Mary* (1936). During World War II he was a war correspondent and participated (with Gracie Fields) in concert parties in France and Belgium as cartoonist and comedian. On his return he worked first for Kemsley Newspapers (1944–53) and later *News Chronicle* (1953–6). He also drew caricatures for *Courier*. His most famous creation was Tishy, the racehorse which was reputed to cross its forelegs when running. Tishy also featured in two animated films – one by Joe Noble had a royal premiere at the Hippodrome, London, on 12 December 1922 and another appeared in 1926. Other characters included the Bloated Bookmaker, the Hori-zontal Heavyweight and George, the walrus-moustached sports devotee. His caricatures were also very idiosyncratic, perhaps the most famous being of the billiards champion, Melbourne Inman. Webster sketched in charcoal, chalk or pencil, worked on Bristol Board or cardboard with a Waverley pen and drew approximately 1½ times published size. Able to draw from life without looking at the paper, he had a Daimler fitted with an easel in the back seat so that he could start his drawings en route to the office after an event. He created a new style of multi-subject sports panel (but *see also* CHARLES GRAVE) which incorporated a running commentary or storyline within the frame, described by Low as 'comic pictorial gossip reporting . . . He disdains draughtsmanship and banks on un-diluted verve and raciness almost entirely.' He was a member of the Savage Club. Tom Webster died in London on 21 June 1962.

PUB: 20 annuals (1920–39) beginning with *Tom Webster of the 'Daily Mail' Among the Sportsmen* (1920), *The Humours of Sport* (1936)
EXHIB: UKCC
COLL: UKCC

WEISZ, Victor 'Vicky' FSIA (1913–66). Political, pocket and strip cartoonist, caricaturist and illustrator. Victor Weisz was born at 14 Regensburgerstrasse, Berlin, on 25 April 1913, the son of Dezso Weisz, a Hungarian Jewish jeweller and goldsmith, and Isabella Seitenbach. At the age of 11 he studied with the painter Tennstedt, and on the death by suicide of his father in 1928 began drawing caricatures freelance (his first sale, aged 15, was of a German boxer) until he joined the graphics department of the radical anti-Hitler journal *12 Uhr Blatt*. By 1929 he was sports and theatre cartoonist on the paper, signing his work 'V. Weiß'. In 1933 the paper was taken over by the Nazis and by 1935 Vicky had arrived in the UK (becoming a British citizen in 1947). His first work was drawing caricatures and cartoons for various publications including the *Evening Standard*, the *Daily Telegraph*'s 'Peterborough ' column, *World Film News* ('Cockalorum' series), *Sunday Chronicle*

'One man in his time plays many parts.' – *As You Like It*

Vicky (Victor Weisz), [Churchill], *Daily Mirror*, 30 November 1954 (strip 'Vicky by Vicky'), *Punch, Sunday Dispatch, Daily Mail* ('Funny Figures' series), *Headway, Courier, Daily Mirror* ('Nazi Nuggets' series), *Sketch, Lilliput, New Statesman, Men Only, Tatler, Time & Tide* (1936–43) and *Daily Express.* After a trial to replace WILL DYSON on the *Daily Herald* (WHITELAW got the job), he joined the staff of the pro-Liberal *News Chronicle* (1939) as Political Cartoonist, also drawing strips such as 'Weekend Fantasia' and 'Young Vicky's Almanack' and sharing an office with RICHARD WINNINGTON. After the departure of Editor Gerald Barry he moved to the *Daily Mirror* (1954), succeeding ZEC. He joined the *Evening Standard* under Editor Charles Wintour four years later (his first cartoon appeared on 3 November 1958), taking over the daily cartoon (except Wednesdays and Saturdays), from 'Gabriel' (JAMES FRIELL). He also worked as 'Pierrot' for *L'Express* (1958–9) and as 'Smith' contributed pocket cartoons to the *News Chronicle.* In addition he drew advertisements for Simpson's Services Club and others. Perhaps his most memorable creation was 'Supermac' (first published in the *Evening Standard* on 6 November 1958), intended to ridicule PM Harold Macmillan but which somehow developed into an endearing image. A passionate Socialist, he was, with DAVID LOW and ILLINGWORTH, perhaps the most influential political cartoonist of recent times ('Vicky is a genius' – Randolph Churchill; 'the best cartoonist in the world' – Michael Foot). His scratchy, brittle pen line has also had considerable impact on the later work of NICHOLAS GARLAND. Himself influenced by Low and Käthe Kollwitz (especially in his bleak 'Oxfam' style), Vicky worked mostly in ink and brush on board, and as a caricaturist once said 'I don't make fun of a face. I make fun of what is behind that face.' He sometimes drew a small version of himself in his cartoons, commenting on the main character's actions. He was voted Cartoonist of the Year (1960) by Granada TV's *What the Papers Say* but refused to accept the CCGB's Political Cartoonist of the Year Award in 1965. In addition he is credited with designing the logo for the Campaign for Nuclear Disarmament. A stage version of Vicky's life, *No End of Blame*, was produced by Howard Barker at the Oxford Playhouse on 5 February 1982. Suffering from depression, Victor Weisz committed suicide by an overdose of sleeping pills at his home in London on 23 February 1966 at the age of 52.

PUB: *Drawn by Vicky* (1944), *Aftermath* (1946), *The Editor Regrets* (1947), [with 'Sagittarius'] *Up the Poll!* (1950), *Stabs in the Back* (1952), *Meet the Russians* (1953), *New Statesman Profiles* (1957), *Vicky's World* (1959), *Vicky Must Go!* (1960), *Twists* (1962), *Home and Abroad* (1964)
ILL: R. Nurnberg, *Schmeling* (1932); G. W. L. Day, *Outrageous Rhapsodies* (1938), *We Are Not Amused* (1940), *Sigh No More, Ladies* (1948); W. Douglas-Home, *Home Truths* (1939); P. Noble, *Profiles and Personalities* (1946); 'Sagittarius', *Let Cowards Flinch* (1947); M. Shulman, *How to be a Celebrity* (1950); I. Mackay, *The Real Mackay* (1953); E. Hughes, *Pilgrim's Progress in Russia* (1959)
EXHIB: Lefevre Galleries; RFH (Memorial, 1967); CG; NPG and tour; CBG
COLL: UKCC; NPG; BFI; CAT
LIT: *Vicky: A Memorial Volume* (1967); R. Davies and L. Ottaway, *Vicky* (1987); M. Bryant (ed.), *Vicky's Supermac* (1996)

'What a Life!' – *see* Wilkinson, Gilbert

WHEELER, Colin (b. 1938). Pocket and editorial cartoonist, journalist and painter. Born in Hindhead, Surrey, on 23 February 1938, Colin Wheeler studied at Farnham School of Art (1954–8), and the RA Schools (1958–61). A teacher for 20 years he had his first cartoon published in the *Times Educational Supplement.* He has also worked freelance for *Private Eye, Guardian, Daily Telegraph, New Statesman, New Scientist* and others and has contributed editorial cartoons to the *Independent on Sunday.* In addition he has produced the daily front-page pocket cartoon for the *Independent* since 1986 and has written a number of articles, reviews, etc., for the paper (as well as for the *Daily Telegraph* and others) on architecture, painting and sculpture. He has an 'artfully spare, almost doodled style' (FRANK WHITFORD) and in his pocket cartoons never uses pencil. His larger political drawings use a lot of cross-hatching and graphite pencil rather than mechanical tints.
PUB: *A Thousand Lines* (1979), *Off the Record* (1980)
EXHIB: CG; GG [paintings]

WHISTLER, Reginald John (1905–44). Painter, illustrator, stage designer, commercial artist and advertising cartoonist. Rex Whistler was born in Eltham, Kent, on 24 June 1905, the second son of Henry Whistler, an architect and estate agent. His younger brother was the writer and glass-engraver Laurence Whistler, and his maternal great-great-grandfather was the silversmith Paul Storr. Educated at Haileybury School, he won prizes from the Royal Drawing Society every year from 1912 to 1923. He studied at the RA Schools for one term (1922) and then under Henry Tonks at the Slade (1922–6). While still a student he was commissioned to paint a strip-cartoon mural for the Tate Gallery's restaurant ('The Pursuit of Rare Meats'). He also drew comic illustrations for *Nash's Magazine, London Mercury, Radio Times* (1931, including covers), *Tatler* (1935–37) and others, and designed cartoon advertisements for Fortnum & Mason, Guinness ('Songs of our Grandfathers', 1936), Rothmans, Shell ('Reversible Faces' series later published in *!OHO!*, 1946), etc. In World War II he was commissioned into the Welsh Guards (1939) and was killed near Le Mesnil, Normandy, on 18 July 1944. In addition to his other work he illustrated books, designed sets and costumes for the theatre (including curtain designs for C. B. Cochran's comic revues), painted murals (e.g. for Sir Philip Sassoon, Lady Louis Mountbatten, the Marquess of Anglesey and others) and in 1944 produced 'HRH the Prince Regent Awakening the Spirit of Brighton' (now in the Brighton Pavilion).

PUB: *The Königsmark Drawings* (1952)
ILL: Sir F. Swettenham, *Arabella in Africa* (1925); W. de la Mare, *Desert Islands* (1930), *The Lord Fish* (1933); L. Whistler, *Armed October* (1932), *The Emperor Heart* (1936), *!AHA!* (1978); B. Nichols, *Down the Garden Path* (1932), *A Thatched Roof* (1933), *The New Forget-Me-Not* (1934); S. Harcourt-Smith, *The Last of Uptake* (1942); E. Oliver, *Night Thoughts of a Country Landlady* (1943); C. Aberconway, *The Story of Mr Korah* (1954)
EXHIB: V&A (AC Memorial Exhibition, 1960)
COLL: T; V&A; BM; BN; NPG
LIT: L. Whistler and R. Fuller, *The Work of Rex Whistler* (1960); L. Whistler, *The Laughter and the Urn* (1985)

WHITELAW, George Alexander (1887–1957). Political cartoonist, illustrator and caricaturist. George Whitelaw was born on 22 June 1887 in Kirkintilloch, Dumbartonshire, the son of Dr William Whitelaw, Medical Officer of Health for the Kirkintilloch District. He attended Lenzie Adademy and Glasgow High School and stud-

ied under MAURICE GREIFFENHAGEN RA for a year at Glasgow School of Art. He first contributed drawings to *Boy's Own Paper, Chums* and *Captain* before beginning work as artist / cartoonist on the *Glasgow Evening News* at the age of 17. In 1915 he came to London as Political Cartoonist for the *Passing Show* and after service in World War I (working on camouflage in the Tank Corps) returned there in 1919. He began regularly producing theatre drawings for *Punch* c. 1930 with G. L. STAMPA, contributed celebrity caricatures to the *London Mail* and later succeeded WILL DYSON as Political Cartoonist on the *Daily Herald* (1938–49) – VICKY, HYNES and SHERRIFFS having failed to get the job – and was himself succeeded by DAVID LOW. He also contributed to *John Bull* (including covers, caricatures and political cartoons), *Christmas Pie, London Opinion* and *Bystander* (colour caricature series 'George Whitelaw's Who's Zoo' comparing celebrities with animals). In addition he produced advertisements for J. Lyons and others. He admired Tenniel (it was seeing Tenniel's *Punch* drawing of John Bull as a boy that inspired Whitelaw to become a cartoonist), SAMBOURNE, PHIL MAY and TOM BROWNE and used to work exclusively with a pen, but later preferred the spontaneity of the brush technique. BRADSHAW has called him 'a first-class draughtsman . . . [with a] splendid sense of character and unerring feeling for composition'. In addition he exhibited portrait etchings of celebrities and was a former Chairman of the Savage Club. He died on 19 September 1957.

ILL: R. Arkell, *Bridge Without Sighs* (1934)
EXHIB: G; L

WHITFORD, Francis Peter 'Rausch' PhD (b. 1941). Pocket cartoonist, illustrator, lecturer and writer. Frank Whitford was born in Bishopstoke, Hampshire, on 11 August 1941 and is a self-taught artist. He was cartoonist and illustrator on the *Sunday Mirror* (1965–6), Pocket Cartoonist on the *Evening Standard* (1966–7), and has been Pocket Cartoonist on the *Sunday Mirror* since 1969. In addition, he has been Lecturer on the History of Art at University College, London (1970–74) and Cambridge University (1974–86), Tutor in the History of Art at the RCA (1986–91), art critic of the *Sunday Times* (since 1991) and gave two series of broadcasts about cartoonists on BBC Radio 4. He draws in pen and ink. He was one of the founder members of the British Cartoonists' Association in 1966.

PUB: *Trog: 40 Graphic Years* (1987) and numerous books about aspects of European art

WHITTOCK, Colin John (b. 1940). Editorial and joke cartoonist, comic artist, illustrator and writer. Colin Whittock was born in Birmingham on 25 February 1940 and is a self-taught artist. Having failed 'O' level art at the Central Grammar School, Birmingham, he worked as a shopfitter before turning full-time freelance. Editorial Cartoonist on the *Birmingham Evening Mail* since 1969, his principal freelance work has been for *Punch, Daily Mirror, Sun, Daily Sketch, Tit-Bits, Weekend, Reveille, Oldie* and *Private Eye*, and advertising clients have included TNT, British Telecom, Jaguar, Powergen and Tubes Ltd. He has also produced greetings cards for Rainbow Cards and drew 'Champ', 'Lazy Bones' and 'Miss Marple' for *Whizzer & Chips* (1971–89). He works mostly in pen, ink and wash but sometimes also uses watercolour.
PUB: *The Perils of Pushing Forty* (1986), *The Perils of Moving House* (1987), *The Perils of Parenthood* (1987), *The Perils of Getting Married* (1988), *The Perils of Motoring* (1989)
ILL: P. Allis, *More Bedside Golf* (1982); R. Reardon, *Bedside Snooker* (1983); S. Waddell, *Bedside Darts* (1984); E. Straiton, *Positively Vetted* (1984), *A Vet on the Set* (1985); T. Blackburn, *The Very Best of Tony Blackburn* (1989); D. Lloyd, *G'Day Ya Pommie B . . .!* (1992); J. Slim, *Rotten Haystacks* (1998)
COLL: B

'Wicked Willie' – *see* Jolliffe, Gray

WILES, Alec E. 'Alec' LSIA (b. 1924). Joke cartoonist, illustrator and painter. Alec Wiles, who signs himself 'Alec', was born in Southampton on 1 January 1924, the son of Harry Cecil Wiles, an electrician, and elder brother of ARNOLD WILES. He was educated at St Mark's School, Southampton, and studied at Southampton School of Art (1937–9). His work has appeared in *Punch, Daily Sketch, Soldier, Lilliput, John Bull, Everybody's* and elsewhere. He is also a sculptor and a marine, landscape and portrait painter.
EXHIB: RA; RP; RBA; SGA

WILES, Arnold Frederick (b. 1926). Joke cartoonist and illustrator. Arnold Wiles was born in Southampton on 1 June 1926, the son of Harry Cecil Wiles, an electrician, and younger brother of ALEC WILES. Educated at St Mark's School,

Southampton, as a child he won several newspaper colouring competitions, including a BBC Radio *Children's Hour* painting competition (1938). He then worked in Cunliffe-Owen's aircraft factory (1942–4), making tools for Spitfires, before joining the Royal Signals as a wireless operator (1945–8). Self-taught as an artist, he sold his first cartoon to *Punch* in 1943 and regularly contributed cartoons and cover designs to *Soldier* and joke cartoons to *Blighty, Lilliput, Men Only, John Bull, Everybody's* and *London Opinion*. Since the war he has freelanced mostly for *Punch* (including covers), *Private Eye, Countryman, Daily Sketch, Daily Mirror, People, Sun, Daily Star, Marine Pollution Bulletin* (8 years), *Farming News, Chat, Angling Times* and numerous other angling, business and medical journals in the UK and Europe. A specialist in angling cartoons (he has sold more than 1000 drawings on this subject alone), he has also designed humorous greetings cards for Royle, Classic and Raphael Tuck and produced photographic angling calendars for Jarrolds (1978, 1979). Arnold Wiles works in pen and ink, scraperboard and watercolour and cites his influences as Charles Keene, PHIL MAY and DAVID LANGDON.
PUB: *Dog in the House* (1961), *A Pretty Kettle of Fish* (1966), [with H. Stoker] *Fishing for Bass with Bill and Bob* (1966), *Everything in the Garden* (1967), *Away from it All* (1968), *Motorist at Large* (1969), *Start Fishing – A Guide for Beginners* (1983), *Wiles on the Water* (1994)
ILL: J. Anthony, *Hark! Hark! The Ark!* (1960); M. Boyce Drew, *The Little Dogs Laughed* (1961); J. Eilts, *Ungewöhnliche Tage* (1981)
EXHIB: Copperhouse Gallery, Hayle, Cornwall; Cartoon Corner, Butterfly World, Fraddam, Cornwall
COLL: V&A

WILFORD-SMITH, Francis 'Smilby' (b. 1927). Joke cartoonist. Francis Wilford-Smith was born in Rugby on 12 March 1927, the son of a pharmaceutical chemist and businessman. He enlisted in the Merchant Navy at the age of 16, and served as a radio officer in World War II (1943–6), while also working as an undercover agent for US Naval Intelligence. After the war he attended Camberwell School of Art (1946–50) where a romantic attachment to a fellow student Pamela Kilby (later to become his wife), led to their collective nickname 'The Smilbys' which gave rise to his *nom de plume*. (Fellow students at Camberwell included TROG and

'. . . and after all, the cord and tassel must have been revolutionary in its day.'

Smilby (Francis Wilford-Smith), *Nebelspalter*, 4 February 1986

HUMPHREY LYTTELTON.) He then did various jobs, including film animator for Halas & Bachelor, assistant display manager for Richard Shops and assistant to the industrial designer Ian Bradbery FSIA. His first drawings appeared in *British Farmer, Melody Maker* and *News Chronicle* (1949–59) before he was awarded a *Punch* scholarship, offered in 1951 to encourage young cartoonists. Within six months his work appeared in *Punch, Lilliput, London Opinion* and *Men Only* and he turned full-time cartoonist. His work has also appeared in *Picture Post, Illustrated, John Bull, Courier, Spectator, Paris-Match, Lui, Pardon, Playboy* (France and Germany), *Diners Club Magazin* (Austria), *Nebelspalter, Autosport, Vi Menn* (Norway) and elsewhere. For some years he was relief artist for MICHAEL FFOLKES on the *Daily Telegraph*'s 'Peter Simple' column. In addition, he has illustrated many advertising campaigns from Guinness to ICI and

Boots and has been a freelance ideas consultant to a number of agencies (e.g. KMP, J. Walter Thompson). In 1960 he began a very successful relationship with *Playboy* magazine, for which he has so far produced more than 350 full-page colour cartoons in nearly four decades. At about the same time he abandoned the UK market to concentrate on the USA and has had cartoons published in the *New Yorker, Esquire, Saturday Evening Post, New York Times, Saturday Review, DAC News* and *Look*. An expert on and major collector of blues and gospel music, he owns the world's most important collection of 78 rpm recorded piano blues, and has written and broadcast on the subject on TV and radio (having been twice nominated for Sony Music Awards). Influenced at first by FRANÇOIS (Price said he 'married the tradition of CRUM with the new tradition of François'), Steinberg, ILLINGWORTH, ARTHUR WATTS and French Art Deco artists Marty, LePape, Charles Martin and Barbier, Smilby works in indian ink and Winsor & Newton Artists' Watercolour on Sanders board or Arches watercolour paper. He was forced to retire in 1998 due to failing eyesight (glaucoma) and Parkinson's Disease. His wife is a former teacher at Guildford School of Art and designer of *Good Housekeeping*.
PUB: *Stolen Sweets* (1981)
EXHIB: CG; Los Angeles, London, Munich, Switzerland; Meisel Gallery, New York
COLL: SAM

WILKINSON, Gilbert (1891–1965). Joke cartoonist, illustrator and watercolourist. Gilbert Wilkinson was born in Liverpool in October 1891 and nearly drowned in the Mersey at the age of five. He studied at Liverpool Art School (under Robert Fowler) for a year, then moved with his family to London and studied at the Bolt Court Art School and in the evenings at Camberwell (under A. S. Hartrick) and the City & Guilds Art School. He then won a scholarship which enabled him to be apprenticed to colour printers Nathaniel Lloyd for seven years. At the time greatly influenced by the work of ARTHUR MORELAND, then working at the *Morning Leader*, Wilkinson had his first drawings accepted by the paper when he was still at Lloyd's and later deputized for Moreland when he was ill. He also began contributing cartoons to *London Opinion* and others. In World War I he served in the London Scottish Regiment (1915–19), attaining the rank of lance-corporal, and

after the war returned to *London Opinion* and drew colour covers for *Passing Show* for 13 years (1921–34) until it merged with *Illustrated*. He also contributed to *Strand Magazine, Good Housekeeping, Punch, Pan, London Mail, John Bull* (including covers), *Drawing & Design* (including covers), *Judge, Cosmopolitan, Nash's, Saturday Evening Post* and *College Humor* (Chicago) and even turned down a staff job on *Life* magazine. In addition he drew advertisements for Kodak, J. Lyons and others. Perhaps his most memorable creation was the daily topical sequence 'What a War!', featuring characters such as Panicky Perce, Ruby Rumour and Gertie Gestapo, which appeared in the *Daily Herald* during World War II, continued in peacetime as 'What a Life!' and later transferred to the *Sun* on the *Herald*'s demise in 1964. In all he drew nearly 8000 cartoons for these two papers alone. 'He had a highly developed comic gift which was seen at its best in social commentary. Like the late J. R. HORRABIN he knew how to depict the humours of City offices and he had a masterly understanding of life in suburbia' (*Times* obituary). He worked mostly in line and wash using a Mitchell 0299 pen and Winsor & Newton No. 2 ink on paper (he disliked Bristol Board). In addition he painted in oils and watercolour and worked in charcoal and crayon. His signature was, famously, almost indecipherable. He was a member of the London Sketch Club. Gilbert Wilkinson died of a heart attack at his home in Pinner, Middlesex, on 10 June 1965.
PUB: *What a War!* (1942, 1944), *What a Life!* (1946, 1948)
ILL: C. Dickens, *A Christmas Carol* (c. 1930); various titles by P. G. Wodehouse
EXHIB: Arlington Gallery

WILLIAMS, Christopher Charles 'Kipper' (b. 1951). Joke and strip cartoonist and illustrator. Kipper Williams was born on 30 December 1951, the son of Aubrey Williams, a local government officer, in the Wirral, Cheshire, and attended Ellesmere Port Grammar School. He studied fine art at Leeds University (1970–74), where he drew cartoons for *Leeds Student* magazine, publishing his first collection of cartoons in 1973 and winning a *New Statesman*/NUS Student Journalist Competition in 1974. He then went to the Royal College of Art (1974–6) and became a full-time cartoonist immediately afterwards. He has contributed to *New Society, New Statesman, Private Eye, Radio Times, European, Top*

of the Pops Magazine, Punch, Euromoney, Spectator, Smash Hits* and *Nursing Times*. In addition he created the strips 'The Lady and the Wimp' for *Time Out* (1983), 'Pile 'em High' for the *Sunday Times* (1992) and 'Eurocats' for the *Guardian* (1992), and since 1991 has drawn a daily cartoon for the *Guardian*'s finance pages. He prefers to work with a Goode steel-nib pen and black Rotring ink, using Dr Martin's inks for colour work.
PUB: *Warning! This Computer Bytes!* (1986), *The Lady and the Wimp* (1986), [with D. AUSTIN and N. NEWMAN] *Far From the Madding Cow!* (1990), *No Peas for the Wicked* (1996)
ILL: Many books including T. McGuinness, *So You Want to be a Rock 'n Roll Star?* (1986); M. Walsh, *Models in Clinical Nursing* (1991); P. Ford and M. Walsh, *New Rituals for Old*; M. Radcliffe, *Seven Ages of Nursing* (1998)
EXHIB: CG; Cheshire Arts Touring Exhibition (1996–7)
COLL: BM; UKCC

WILLIAMS, Glan (1911–after 1977). Political cartoonist, caricaturist and painter. Glan Williams was born in Pentrechwyth, Swansea. He came to London in 1930 to work on the *Daily Express* while also contributing to other publications. In World War II he served in the Welch Regiment attached to a camouflage unit. After the war he worked in advertising and regularly contributed political cartoons to *Time & Tide* and *Reynolds News* and theatre drawings to *Tatler & Bystander*. He drew caricatures for *Evening News* in the 1970s and painted murals. He usually signed his work 'GLAN'.

WILLIAMS, Michael Charles (b. 1940). Joke cartoonist and illustrator. Mike Williams was born on 24 February 1940 in Liverpool, the younger brother of PETE WILLIAMS, and attended Quarry Bank High School. A self-taught artist, he started work in Henry Pybus and Littlewoods commercial art studios in the city (1957–66) before turning freelance cartoonist, selling his first drawing to *Punch* in 1967. His cartoons have also appeared in *Private Eye, Spectator, Playboy, Daily Sketch, Oldie* and *The Times*. Advertising work has played an important part in his career and his clients have ranged from BMW and Guinness to the Julius Baer Bank for which he created the polar-bear image. In addition, he has produced greetings cards for Valentine's of Edinburgh and the Ink Group

'OK, who forgot the jacket potatoes?'

Mike Williams, *Squib*, December 1992

(Australia). Briefly Cartoon Editor of *Punch* (1997), he is an admirer of Mankoff, Grosz and Michael Maslin. Mike Williams works in pencil, pen and watercolour.

PUB: *Oh No! Not the '23* (1987), *You Can't Still Be Hungry* (1988), [with A. RUSLING] *The Very, Very, Very Last Book Ever: Part One* (1986)
EXHIB: Albert Dock Gallery, Liverpool; Chester Town Hall; Chester Library; BC
COLL: BM

WILLIAMS, Peter George (b. 1937). Joke cartoonist. Pete Williams was born in Liverpool on 27 January 1937, the elder brother of MIKE WILLIAMS. Self-taught, he is a part-time art teacher at the Alice Elliott and Watergate Schools in Liverpool. His cartoons have appeared in *Punch*, *Private Eye*, *Daily Mail*, *Spectator*, *Daily Mirror*, *Daily Express*, *Daily Star*, *People*, *Men Only* and *Mayfair*. Voted Berol Cartoonist of the Year (1987) and a prizewinner in the Waddingtons International Cartoon Awards (1988), he has also won international awards in Belgium and Japan.
EXHIB: BAG; Colchester Gallery, Essex; Bury St Edmunds, Suffolk; Library Theatre, Manchester

WILLSON, Richard David (b. 1939). Caricaturist and illustrator. Richard Willson was born in London on 15 May 1939 and studied architecture at Kingston School of Art and graphic design at Epsom School of Art. Caricaturist on the *Observer* (1968–71) and *The Times* (since 1971), he has also worked freelance for the *Spectator*, *Washington Post*, *New Statesman*, *New Scientist*, *Tablet*, *Business Traveller*, *Euromoney*, *Investors Chronicle*, *Punch*, *Financial Weekly*, *Accountancy Age*, *Computing*, *Lloyds Log*, *Ecologist*, *New Internationalist*, *United Nations* and *Racing Post*. In addition, he has produced a considerable amount of advertising work. Richard Willson has a fine, cross-hatched style with big heads on small bodies that show the influence of DAVID LEVINE. He also admires the work of Daumier and Saul Steinberg.
PUB: *The Doomsday Fun-book* (1977), [with P. Rogers] *As Lambs to the Slaughter* (1981), *The Green Alternative* (1985)
ILL: M. Ivens, *Born Early* (1975); R. Stilgoe, *The Richard Stilgoe Letters* (1981); J. Tarbuck, *Tarbuck on Golf* (1983), *Tarbuck on Showbiz* (1984)

WILSON, David RI RBA (1873–1935). Political and joke cartoonist, illustrator, caricaturist,

painter and art teacher. David Wilson was born on 4 July 1873 at Minterburn Manse, Co. Tyrone, the son of a clergyman. He was educated at the National School and at Royal Belfast Academical Institution and began work for North Bank, Belfast, while attending the local art school in the evenings. He later came to London, drawing political and joke cartoons for the *Daily Chronicle* (from 1895) and other publications before becoming chief cartoonist on the *Graphic* (1910–16). He also contributed to *Punch* (1900–14), *Bystander*, *Fun*, *Sketch*, *Temple Magazine*, *Kinematograph Weekly* (caricatures), *Strand*, *New Clarion*, *The Artist* (caricatures for 'Round the Studios' feature), *Play Pictorial* and *Passing Show*. In addition he produced propaganda posters during World War I and in the 1930s taught commercial art at St John's Wood Art School and flower painting in watercolour by correspondence course from his home at 22 Downton Avenue, Tulse Hill, London.
PUB: *Through a Peer Glass* (1908)
ILL: A. A. Braun, *Wilhelm the Ruthless* (1917)
EXHIB: RA; Paris Salon; FAS (1935); BN; BEL; RI; RBA
COLL: IWM; V&A

WILSON, Mervyn (1905–59). Joke and strip cartoonist and illustrator. Mervyn Wilson, whose mother was a talented amateur artist, was born in London and studied part-time at HASSALL's Correspondence School while working in the family business. He then attended St John's Wood Art School and the Royal Academy Schools and after working in a commercial studio began contributing serious drawings to *Radio Times* (from 1929), before developing a talent for humour in the magazine, notably in amusing little marginal sketches illustrating the BBC's programmes. In his *Radio Times* drawings he often included a portrait of the magazine's Art Editor (later Editor), Douglas Graeme Williams. Before World War II he worked for the Department of Ancient Monuments for 14 months, helping to restore frescoes, decorated ceilings, etc., at Windsor Castle, the Houses of Parliament and other historic buildings. During the conflict he served in the Home Guard and ARP, leaving in May 1945. He then drew a strip cartoon for the *Daily Express* recording the adventures of 'Mike', a radio character, and produced strips for children's periodicals. He also contributed to *Punch* (from 1935), *Men Only*, *Night & Day*, *London Opinion*, *Lilliput*, *Tatler*, *New*

Yorker and other publications. In addition he designed advertisements for Manfield Shoes, Bovril, Guinness, etc. Wilson rarely used pencil and preferred to draw directly on to paper in pen and ink. His chubby little figures appear to be drawn with primitive simplicity, the lines 'slashed on to the paper with no concern for any quality but boldness . . . where shading is called for, it appears to be stabbed in spasmodically with a worn nib; but the final ragged result is extraordinarily arresting' (BRADSHAW). R. D. Usherwood (Art Director of the *Radio Times* 1950–60) described him as 'One of the most distinguished comic artists in the country. His highly individual style was admired by artists for its expert control of line and texture, and his humour, based on a kindly observation of life around him, was easily acceptable to the layman.' Mervyn Wilson died in July 1959, aged 54.
EXHIB: AG; RBA

WILSON, Oscar RMS ARBA (1867–1930). Painter, illustrator and joke cartoonist. Oscar Wilson was born in London and studied art at the South Kensington Schools and at the Antwerp Academy under Charles Verlat and Beaufaux. He contributed to *Black & White*, *Cassell's*, *Illustrated London News*, *London Opinion*, *Madame*, *New Budget*, *Sketch* and *Pick-Me-Up* (from the 1890s). He also painted in oils and watercolour and was elected RMS (1896) and ARBA (1926). Oscar Wilson died on 13 July 1930.
ILL: G. I. Witham, *The Last of the Whitecoats* (1906), *The Adventures of a Cavalier* (1914); E. Grierson, *Bishop Patteson of the Cannibal Islands* (1927)
EXHIB: RA; RBA; RI; RMS; L
COLL: LE

WINNINGTON, Richard (1905–53). Film critic, caricaturist, strip cartoonist, illustrator and writer. Richard Winnington was born in Edmonton, London, on 10 September 1905, the son of an accountant. He was the brother of a reporter for the *Sunday Chronicle* and of Alan Winnington, Chief Sub-Editor on the *Daily Worker*. Educated at Bancroft's School, he received no formal art training. Working first as a salesman, then as a clerk for Thomas Cook Ltd, he was employed by Heinz canned foods when he sold his first comic strip, about two pigeons called Bib and Bob, to the *Daily Express* in 1936. The same year he joined the *News*

Chronicle as an illustrator and later became the paper's celebrated film critic, illustrating his own column (1943–53) and sharing an office with VICKY. In addition he wrote film criticism for the *Daily Worker* under the pseudonym 'John Ross' (1943–8). He was described by Augustus John as 'a brilliant draughtsman and true critic', and NICOLAS BENTLEY said of him: 'No other artist of his *genre* could bite out the character of his victims with a more shrewd or more economical wit.' Winnington always drew his illustrations *after* he had written the film review and seldom produced a caricature for a film he liked. 'His skill lay not just in his devastating caricatures of the main players in a film but in an exposure of their roles. He could sum up the whole *sense* of a film in a single drawing without text. The scenic background to his characters was often as important as they were' (Rotha). An admirer of Gillray and Hogarth, his fine, scratchy style was strengthened by a bold use of indian ink applied with a brush. He worked on layout paper and often pasted on new heads if he wasn't happy with a caricature. In his own words: 'The only way of making a caricature is from the inward exposure of the eye and mind. Else it is a mere exaggeration distorting physical peculiarities, or representational romantic likeness. The comment that bites home is between the two and cannot be defined.' NICHOLAS GARLAND has admired his 'ability to catch likenesses in reckless, flying lines that break every rule of perspective and proportion'. He signed his drawings 'RW'. Richard Winnington was married to PEARL FALCONER from 1938 to 1947. He died on 17 September 1953.
PUB: *Drawn and Quartered* (1948); [with N. Davenport] *The Future of British Films* (1951)
EXHIB: NFT (1975)
COLL: BM; V&A: CAT; BFI
LIT: P. Rotha (ed.), *Richard Winnington* (1975)

WOOD, Clarence Lawson RI FZS (1878–1957). Painter, illustrator and joke cartoonist. Lawson Wood was born on 23 August 1878 in Highgate, London, the grandson of the architectural artist Lewis John Wood RI and son of landscape painter Pinhorn Wood RI. At the age of 16 he studied art at the Slade and Heatherley's and also took evening classes at Frank Calderon's School of Animal Painting. He joined the staff of magazine publisher C. Arthur Pearson (a friend of his father) at the age of 18 and soon became its chief artist, leaving after six years to turn freelance. In World War I he served in France for nearly three years as an officer in the Kite Balloon Wing of the RFC and at GHQ. An accomplished poster designer, Lawson Wood also drew cartoons for *Graphic* (1907–11) and *Punch* (notably a 'Stone Age' series), *Bystander*, *Strand Magazine*, *Nash's* (including covers), *Sketch*, *Boy's Own Paper*, *Fry's Magazine* (including covers), *Illustrated London News*, *Puck*, *Royal Magazine*, *Collier's* (covers) and *London Opinion*, and as 'Hustlebuck' with the sporting artist Keith Sholto Douglas MC (1882–1963), who married his daughter Phoebe. In addition, he produced work for advertising (e.g. Fry's, Alwetha Raincoats, Segment Motor Rims), designed three-colour decorative household prints for Lawrence & Jellicoe, drew postcards for Carlton, Dobson-Molle, David Allen (also theatre posters), Davidson Brothers, Henderson, Inter-Art, Tuck, Valentine and others, and designed and made wooden toys, 'The Lawson Woodies', featuring animals, birds and human figures. He is perhaps best remembered for his humorous animal subjects, especially Gran'pop the artful ginger ape which first appeared in the *Sketch* in 1932 and led to considerable merchandising, including pottery, calendars, postcards and Kensitas cigarette cards (1935) and, but for the outbreak of World War II, would have been turned into an animated film by Ub Iwerks' studio. Lawson Wood had a specially made enamel palette more than a foot square and worked on Milburn Drawing Board at an architect's desk. He married the fashion artist Charlotte Forge in 1902. A member of the London Sketch Club and Savage Club, he was elected a Fellow of the Zoological Society. Lawson Wood died on 26 October 1957.

PUB: Many books including *The Book of Lawson Wood* (1907), [with J. B. Kernahan] *The Bow Wow Book* (1912), *Splinters!* (1916), *The Noo-Zoo Tales* (1922), *Lawson Wood's Fun Fair* (1931) and Gran'pop annuals (from 1935)

ILL: Many books including J. Finnemore, *The Redmen of the Dusk* (1899); H. Caine, *The White Prophet* (1909); R. Waylett, *A Basket of Plums* (1916), *A Box of Crackers* (1916); *Old Nursery Rhymes* (1931)

EXHIB: D; L; RA; RI; Sunderland; BSG; DG; London Salon; WG

COLL: V&A; THG

LIT: A. E. Johnson, *Lawson Wood* (1910); P. V. Bradshaw, *The Art of the Illustrator 1* (1918)

WOOD, Starr 'The Snark' (1870–1944). Caricaturist, joke cartoonist and journalist. Starr Wood was born in London on 1 February 1870, the eldest son of a customs officer and great-grandson of Captain Starr Wood, King's Pilot. He was educated at the Stoke Newington Collegiate School where he won several prizes for drawing. A self-taught artist, he worked at first as a chartered accountant in a debt-collecting business in the City from the age of 17 (1887–92). After his first drawing was published in Israel Zangwill's *Ariel* in 1892, he turned freelance cartoonist, contributing to many publications including *Chums*, *Fun*, *Sketch*, *Judy*, *Pick-Me-Up*, *Idler*, *Chips*, *Parade*, *John Bull*, *English Illustrated Magazine*, *Bystander*, *Humorist*, *Passing Show*, *Tatler*, *Moonshine*, *Strand*, *St Paul's*, *Sketch*, *Le Pêle-Mêle*, *Rions*, *Lectures Pour Tous* (1910–12), *London Opinion*, *Printer's Pie* and *Punch* (from August 1898 until at least 1935). He was one of the founders and first Art Editor of *The Windmill* quarterly and later (with publisher Harry Angold) ran *The Snark* or *Starr Wood's Annual*, a twice-yearly illustrated magazine (1910–after 1934) with covers of stylish women drawn by him. Starr Wood was a member of the London Sketch Club and the Savage Club. Influenced by PHIL MAY, he was colour blind and worked chiefly in line 'using a thin and moderately economical style which had zest and flow. His subjects were generally in the field of marital *contretemps*, domestic quirks, and various kinds of incongruity, and he did a good deal on the humours of golf' (*Times* obituary). Starr Wood died in Rickmansworth, Hertfordshire, on 2 September 1944.

PUB: *Rhymes of the Regiments* (1896), *Cocktail Time* (1896), *The Snark's Annual* (1910), *Dances You Have Never Seen* (1921), *PTO: A Collection of 94 Humorous Drawings* (1934), [with H. Simpson] *Woman en Casserole* (1936); *Starr Wood's Winter Annual* (1935)

ILL: L. Hillier, *The Potterers' Club* (1900); A. Armstrong, *The After-Breakfast Book* (1937); H. I. MacCourt, *Women as Pets* (1938)

EXHIB: L; Meadrow Gallery, Surrey (1982)

COLL: V&A

WOODCOCK, Kevin Robert (b. 1942). Joke cartoonist. Born in Leicester on 2 September 1942, Kevin Woodcock attended Leicester College of Art (1961–4) and has contributed cartoons to *Private Eye*, *Daily Sketch*, *Spectator*, *Knave*, *Fiesta*, *Punch* and *Brain Damage*. Influ-

Kevin Woodcock, *City Rules OK*, 1983

enced by ROWLAND EMETT, ANDRÉ FRANÇOIS and RONALD SEARLE, he works in pen and ink straight onto A4 art or thick typing paper and for colour uses watercolour and gouache. He also uses collage.
PUB: *Private Eye Kevin Woodcock* (1978), *City Rules OK* (1983), *You Are Here* (1987)
EXHIB: CG

WREN, Ernest Alfred 'Chris' ARAeS (1908–82). Joke cartoonist, illustrator, commercial artist, writer and editor. Chris Wren ('Chris' was a nickname that stuck) was born in Hampstead, London, on 5 July 1908. He was a descendant of the architect Sir Christopher Wren. After studying at St Martin's School of Art (1922) he worked as a commercial artist with G. S. Royds advertising agency (1926–39). His first aeroplane caricatures were published in *Aeroplane* magazine (1932) and he also contributed illustrations and cartoons to W. E. Johns' *Popular Flying* ('Did You Know?' series) and *Flight* (signing them 'Christopher'). In 1934 he joined 604 Squadron Royal Auxiliary Air Force as successively a rigger, armourer and (when the RAAF merged with the RAF in 1941) Aircraft Recognition Instructor. He was then Air Recognition Training Officer, Combined Operations (1943–4) and later served in Technical Intelligence (1944–5), achieving the rank of flight-lieutenant. He is best known for the creation of the 'Oddentifications' series of aeroplane caricatures (with accom-

panying verses) which were published in *Aeroplane* at the suggestion of Sir Peter Masefield, then Technical Editor of the magazine. The first drawing (of a Handley Page Hampden) appeared on 14 March 1941 and the last in August 1947. The series was such a success that similar cartoons were drawn by the German and Japanese forces. He also drew more than 100 caricatures of aircraft for Masefield's *The Aeroplane Spotter* (from 3 April 1941). After the war he was Editor of the *Inter-Services Aircraft Recognition Journal* (1945–8), Press Relations Officer of the Society of British Aircraft Constructors (1946–8) and Editor of *Esso Air World* (1963–78). However, he also continued to draw cartoon series for *Aeroplane* such as 'Wrenderings' (from 25 September 1947) and 'Wroundabouts' (from 1948). In addition he was a prolific designer of Christmas and anniversary cards in ink, wash and watercolour for aviation bodies, including the Red Arrows aerial display team. He was greatly respected by the flying community: 'The aviation business looks on Chris Wren as being to aviation what DAVID LOW was to politics' (Sir Peter Masefield). Awarded the C. P. Robertson Memorial Trophy of the Air Public Relations Association in 1978, he was a founder member of the Tiger Club, a member of the RAF Club, Vice-President of the Guild of Aviation Artists and an Associate Member of the Royal Aeronautical Society. He died on 9 December 1982.
PUB: *Oddentifications* (1942), [with S. E. Veale] *How Planes Fly* (1953)

WYSARD, Antony (1907–84). Caricaturist and illustrator. Tony Wysard was born in Pangbourne, Berkshire, and educated at Harrow School. He worked at first as an accountant in the City before moving into advertising. He later became Advertising Manager for Alexander Korda's film studios and began contributing caricatures to *Tatler* (1929–39), *Bystander, Sphere, Strand* (illustrations and 'The Uncommon Man' title-page caricature series, August 1948 until the magazine's penultimate issue, February 1950), *Harper's Bazaar, World's Press News* ('Like Father Like Son' series in the 1930s), the *Daily* and *Sunday Express* and *Daily Dispatch*. He drew in line and full colour. After World War II, during which he was commissioned into the Queen's Westminster Regiment, he returned to Korda's studios before becoming Associate Editor of *Harper's Bazaar*.

He then founded his own advertising consultancy, specializing in print design (an example being a promotional booklet for the 40th anniversary of London wholesale butchers Woodhouse Hume), and was Editor of *Wheeler's Review*.

PUB: (ed.) *Woodhouse Hume Ltd, 1958* (1958)
ILL: T. Kavanagh, *Colonel Chinstrap* (1952); St John Cooper (ed.), *Gilbert Harding's Treasury of Insult* (1953)
EXHIB: WG (1936)
COLL: NPG

Y

YEATS, Jack Butler 'W. Bird' RHA (1871–1957). Painter, illustrator, writer and strip and joke cartoonist. Jack B. Yeats was born in London on 29 August 1871, the son of the Irish painter John Butler Yeats RHA and the younger brother of the poet William Butler Yeats. He spent his childhood in Sligo, Ireland, then came with his family to London in 1887 and studied at the South Kensington Schools, Chiswick Art School and the Westminster School of Art under Frederick Brown (one of the founders of the New English Art Club). His first drawings were published in the *Vegetarian* (1888–94), *Ariel* (1891–2) and *Paddock Life* (1891–4) while he was still a student. He also contributed joke and strip cartoons as well as illustrations to *Chums*, *Fun* (1901), *Illustrated Bits*, *Judy*, *Lika Joko*, *New Budget*, *Quartier Latin*, *Sketch*, *Funny Wonder*, *Big Budget* (where he created the first-ever comic animal hero, Signor McCoy the Wonderful Circus Hoss), *Comic Cuts* (including the first-ever Sherlock Holmes parody 'The Adventures of Chubblock Homes', 1893, which later moved to *Funny Wonder*), *Longbow*, *Cassell's Saturday Journal*, *Comic Home Journal*, *Halfpenny Comic*, *Illustrated London News*, *Jester & Wonder*, *Puck* and *Punch* (1896–1941). He returned to Ireland in 1902 and thereafter, apart from his contributions to *Punch*, occasional book illustrations and (until 1925) designs for the Cuala Press (run by his sisters), devoted himself to painting and writing. Elected RHA (1915), he was awarded the Légion d'Honneur (1950) and became a governor of the National Gallery of Ireland (1939). He was an admirer of the work of children's book illustrators such as Randolph Caldecott and Walter Crane. As to his cartoon work, Price has written of the 'mad uncertainty of his line' when it came to drawing for *Punch*: 'his humour was irrational, wild and precise, his draw-

ing much criticized as incompetent. He broke all the rules and his genius still draws readers back to volumes in which nothing much else appeals to them.' His contributions to *Punch* were signed 'W. Bird' (KENNETH BIRD later deliberately adopted the pseudonym 'Fougasse' to avoid any confusion with his predecessor). He died in Dublin on 28 March 1957.

PUB: *James Flaunty* (1901), *A Broadsheet* (1902–3), *A Broadside* (1908–15), *The Scourge of the Gulph* (1903), *The Bosun and the Bob-Tailed Comet* (1904), *A Little Fleet* (1909), *Life in the West of Ireland* (1912), *Sligo* (1930)
ILL: E. Rhys, *The Great Cockney Tragedy* (1891); W. B. Yeats, *Irish Fairy Tales* (1892), *Reveries over Childhood and Youth* (1911); J. H. Reynolds, *The Fancy* (1905); J. M. Synge, *The Aran Islands* (1907), *In Wicklow, West Kerry and Connemara* (1911); P. Colum, *A Boy in Erinn* (1913), *The Big Tree of Bunlahy* (1933); G. Birmingham, *Irishmen All* (1913)
EXHIB: Clifford Gallery (1897): NG (1942); NGI (1945, 1971); T (1948); Boston, USA (1951); AR & W (1991)
COLL: T; NGI; E; BR; LE; Y and galleries abroad
LIT: H. Pyle, *Jack B. Yeats: A Biography* (1970), *A Catalogue Raisonné of the Work of Jack B. Yeats* (1991); R. Skelton (ed.), *The Selected Writings of Jack B. Yeats* (1991)

YEOMAN, Beryl Antonia Botterill [née Thompson] 'Anton' FSIA (1907–70). Joke cartoonist, commercial artist and illustrator. Beryl Thompson was born on 24 July 1907 in Esk, Queensland, Australia, the daughter of Arthur Henry Thompson, an English rancher whose family were merchant shippers trading with Australia out of Liverpool. The family visited England in 1911, staying with relatives in West Kirby, Cheshire, where her brother, HAROLD

'. . . and this is my wife's little den.'

Anton (Antonia Yeoman and Harold Underwood Thomson), *Anton's Amusement Arcade*, 1947

UNDERWOOD THOMPSON, was born in April the same year and her father died in June. The family decided to stay in the UK and eventually settled in Brighton. Confined to bed with TB of the spine as a child, Beryl lost two fingers of her right hand in her teens and learned to write and draw with her left. She attended the Royal Academy Schools (1928) and studied art under Stephen Spurrier for a year before becoming a freelance commercial artist. She took the name 'Antonia' when she became a Roman Catholic in her early twenties. She also produced advertising posters and showcards with her brother (then working as the cartoonist 'H. Botterill') and in 1937 they formed a partnership producing cartoons as 'Anton' (though the 'Antons' in

the *Evening Standard*, 1939, were entirely his). When, after the war, Harold's work as director of an advertising agency left him less time for drawing, Antonia took over the name herself (from 1949 the cartoons were entirely hers). The drawings of spivs, forgers, dukes and duchesses were very popular and appeared in *Tatler*, *Lilliput*, *Men Only*, *New Yorker*, *Evening Standard*, *Private Eye* and *Punch*. She also drew a series of popular advertisements for Moss Bros, and others for Simpson's Services Club, Morley Outfitters, Saxone Shoes, etc. The only female member of *Punch*'s Toby Club, she was also the first woman elected to the Chelsea Arts Club (her husband John Yeoman, Mayor of Chelsea and Secretary of the Council for the Preservation of

Rural England, was already a member). She died in Chelsea on 30 June 1970. Price wrote of the *Punch* cartoons 'the jokes stayed good volume after volume. The drawing was decorative and the massed blacks showed up well on the page . . . the world . . . was calmly, courteously, mad.'
PUB: [both with H. Underwood Thompson] *Anton's Amusement Arcade* (1947), *Low Life and High Life* (1952)
ILL: 17 books including V. Mollo, *Streamlined Bridge* (1947); V. Grahame, *Here's How* (1951);

D. Parsons, *Can it be True?* (1953), *Many a True Word* (1958); M. Laski, *Apologies* (1955); S. Mead, *How to Live Like a Lord Without Really Trying* (1964); D. Briggs, *Entertaining Single-Handed* (1968)
EXHIB: LAN (1984); RSA, SGA; Upper Grosvenor Galleries; CG
COLL: V&A; UKCC
LIT: J. Yeoman (ed.), *Anton* (1971)

'Yobs, The' – *see* Husband, William Anthony

Z

ZEC, Philip (1909–83). Political cartoonist, illustrator, commercial artist and editor. Philip Zec was born on 25 December 1909 in London, the son of Simon Zec, a Russian émigré tailor, and his wife Leah Oistrakh. One of eleven children, he was the brother of Donald Zec (later to become film journalist on the *Daily Mirror*). He attended Stanhope Elementary School and St Martin's School of Art and at 19 set up his own commercial and photographic studio, working for J. Walter Thompson and other agencies. When Basil Nicholson (creator of the 'night starvation' campaign for Horlicks) joined the *Daily Mirror* as Features Editor he invited

A FROG HE WOULD A-WOOING GO

Philip Zec, [Laval], *Daily Mirror*, 30 October 1941

Zec to be Political Cartoonist for the paper (1939–54), being succeeded eventually by VICKY. Zec's most notorious cartoon, 'The Price of Petrol Has Been Increased by One Penny – Official' (5 March 1942), depicted a torpedoed sailor clinging to a raft and led to a storm of controversy. His original caption, changed by 'Cassandra' (William Connor, who often wrote his captions), had been 'Petrol is Dearer Now' and the drawing was one of a series attacking profiteers. However, to the Government it appeared as subversive, unpatriotic and 'Worthy of Goebbels at his best' (Herbert Morrison, then Home Secretary). Questions were raised in the House of Commons and for a time the *Mirror* was under threat of closure. After the war Zec became head of the strip-cartoon department and a director of the paper, succeeding Hugh Cudlipp as editor of the *Sunday Pictorial* (1950–52). He later moved to the *Daily Herald* as Political Cartoonist (1958–61). In addition he was a director of the *Jewish Chronicle* for 25 years and Editor of *New Europe*. His style differed from that of Low and others in that he put more venom into his drawings, preferring in World War II to depict Nazis as snakes, vultures, toads or monkeys rather than strutting buffoons. And like those of Low, NEB, BUTTERWORTH and many others, his name was on Hitler's death-list. Philip Zec died in Middlesex Hospital, London, on 14 July 1983.
ILL: E. F. Herbert, *Blossom the Brave Balloon* (1941), *Wimpy the Wellington* (1942)
COLL: UKCC

ZOKE – *see* Attwell, Michael

Bibliography

General works relating to artists listed in this dictionary. Works relating to individual artists appear under the appropriate entries (LIT)

All books were published in London unless indicated otherwise. The dates are those of first publication.

Amstutz, W., *Who's Who in Graphic Art* (Amstutz & Herdeg/De Clivo Press, Zürich/ Dübendendorf, 1962/1982)

Ashbee, C. R., *Caricature* (Chapman & Hall, 1928)

Bahnsen, S. P. and Fogelström, P. A. (eds), *Verdensdramaet i Karikaturer, 1939–1945* (Commodore, Copenhagen, 1945)

Baker, K., *The Prime Ministers: An Irreverent Political History in Cartoons* (Thames & Hudson, 1995)

—— *The Kings and Queens: An Irreverent History of the British Monarchy* (Thames & Hudson, 1996)

Bateman, M., *Funny Way to Earn a Living* (Leslie Frewin, 1966)

Beare, G., *Index to the Strand Magazine 1891–1950* (Greenwood Press, Westport/London, 1982)

Beetles, C. et al., *The Illustrators* (Chris Beetles Gallery, catalogues 1991–8)

Bénézit, E., *Dictionnaire des peintres, sculpteurs, dessinateurs et graveurs* (Librairie Gründ, Paris, 1976)

Bradshaw, P. V., *The Art of the Illustrator* (Press Art School, 1918)

—— *They Make Us Smile* (Chapman & Hall, 1942)

—— *Lines of Laughter* (Chapman & Hall, 1946)

—— *Brother Savages and Guests: A History of the Savage Club 1857–1957* (W. H. Allen, 1958)

Bryant, M., *World War II in Cartoons* (W. H. Smith, 1989)

Bryant, M. and Heneage, S., *Dictionary of British Cartoonists and Caricaturists 1730–1980* (Scolar Press, Aldershot, 1994)

Clark, A., *Dictionary of British Comic Artists, Writers and Editors* (British Library, 1998)

Coysh, A. W., *Dictionary of Picture Postcards in Britain 1894–1939* (Antique Collectors Club, Woodbridge, 1984)

Cross, T., *Artists & Bohemians: 100 Years with the Chelsea Arts Club* (Quiller, 1992)

Cuppleditch, D., *The London Sketch Club* (Dilke Press, 1978/Alan Sutton Publishing, Stroud, 1994)

Dalby, R., *The Golden Age of Children's Book Illustration* (O'Mara Books, 1991)

Darracott, J., *A Cartoon War* (Leo Cooper, 1989)

Davies, R., *Caricature of To-Day* (Studio, 1928)

Demm, E. (ed.), *Der erste Weltkrieg in der Internationalen Karikatur* (Fackelträger, Hanover, 1988)

Dictionary of National Biography (Smith Elder, 1885–1912/OUP, 1927–71 plus supplements)

Douglas, R., *The World War 1939–1945, the Cartoonists' Vision* (Routledge, 1991)

—— *Between the Wars 1919–1939, the Caroonists' Vision* (Routledge, 1992)

—— *Great Nations Still Enchained, the Cartoonists' Vision of Empire 1848–1914* (Routledge, 1993)

—— *The Great War 1914–1918, the Cartoonists' Vision* (Routledge, 1995)

Doyle, B. (ed.), *Who's Who of Boys' Writers and Illustrators* (Brian Doyle, 1964)

Driver, D., *The Art of Radio Times* (BBC, 1981)

Edwards, R. (ed.), *A Sense of Permanence? Essays on the Art of the Cartoon* (University of Kent, Canterbury, 1997)

Ellwood, G. M., *The Art of Pen Drawing* (Batsford, 1927)

Feaver, W., *Masters of Caricature from Hogarth and Gillray to Scarfe and Levine* (Weidenfeld & Nicolson, 1981)

Felmington, M., *The Illustrated Gift Book, 1880–1930* (Scolar, Aldershot, 1988)

Fougasse [K. Bird], *The Good-tempered Pencil* (Max Reinhardt, 1956)

Gale, S. H., *Encyclopedia of British Humorists* (Garland Publishing, New York/London, 1996)

Geipel, J., *The Cartoon: A Short History of Graphic Comedy and Satire* (David & Charles, 1972)

George, M. D., *English Political Caricature: A Study of Opinion and Propaganda* (Clarendon Press, Oxford, 1959)

Gifford, D., *The British Comic Catalogue 1874–1974* (Mansell, 1975)

—— *Victorian Comics* (Allen & Unwin, 1976)

—— *The International Book of Comics* (Hamlyn, 1990)

Gombrich, E. H., *Art and Illusion* (Phaidon, 1960)

—— *Meditations on a Hobby Horse* (Phaidon, 1963)

Gombrich, E. H. and Kris, E., *Caricature* (Penguin, 1940)

Grant, I. F., *The Unauthorized Version: A Cartoon History of New Zealand 1840–1987* (David Bateman, Auckland/Fraser Books, Masterton, 1980/1987)

Grayland, E., *More Famous New Zealanders* (Whitcomb & Tombs, Christchurch, 1972)

Greenwall, R., *Artists & Illustrators of the Anglo-Boer War* (Fernwood Press, Vlaeberg, 1992)

Griffiths, D., *Encyclopedia of the British Press* (Macmillan, Basingstoke, 1993)

Grosvenor, P. (ed.), *We Are Amused: The Cartoonists' View of Royalty* (Bodley Head, 1978)

Guichard, K. M., *British Etchers 1850–1940* (Robin Garton, 1977)

Hadley, P. (ed.), *The History of Bovril Advertising* (1972)

Hammerton, J. R., *Humorists of the Pencil* (Hurst & Blackett, 1905)

Hardie, M., *Water-colour Painting in Britain* (Batsford, 1966–8)

Harper, C. G., *English Pen Artists of To-Day* (Macmillan, 1892)

Heller, S., *Man Bites Man: Two Decades of Satiric Art* (Hutchinson, 1981)

Herbert, W. A. S., *Caricatures and How to Draw Them* (Pitman, 1951)

Hewison, W., *The Cartoon Connection* (Elm Tree Books, 1977)

Hillier, B., *Posters* (Weidenfeld & Nicolson, 1969)

—— *Cartoons and Caricatures* (Studio Vista/Dutton, 1970)

Hodnett, E., *Five Centuries of English Book Illustration* (Scolar Press, Aldershot, 1988)

Hofmann, W., *Caricature from Leonardo to Picasso* (John Calder, 1957)

Holme, C. (ed.), *Modern Pen Drawings in Europe and America* (The Studio, London/Paris/New York, 1901)

—— (ed.), *Pen, Pencil and Chalk* (The Studio, London/Paris/New York, 1911)

Horn, M. (ed.), *The World Encyclopedia of Comics* (Chelsea House, New York, 1976)

—— *The World Encyclopedia of Cartoons* (Chelsea House, New York, 1980)

Horne, A., *The Dictionary of 20th Century British Book Illustrators* (Antique Collectors Club, Woodbridge, 1994)

Houfe, S., *The Dictionary of British Book Illustrators and Caricaturists 1800–1914* (Antique Collectors Club, Woodbridge, 1978)
—— *Fin de Siècle: The Illustrators of the Nineties* (Barrie & Jenkins, 1992)
—— *The Dictionary of 19th Century British Book Illustrators and Caricaturists* (Antique Collectors Club, Woodbridge, 1996)
Huggett, F. E., *Cartoonists at War* (Windward, 1981)
Johnson, J. and Greutzner, A., *The Dictionary of British Artists 1800–1940* (Antique Collectors Club, Woodbridge, 1976)
Kingman, M. L., Hogarth, G. A. and Quimby, H., *Illustrators of Children's Books 1957–66* (Horn Book, Boston, 1968)
Kunzle, D., *The History of the Comic Strip: The Nineteenth Century* (University of California Press, Los Angeles, 1990)
Laffin, J., *World War I in Postcards* (Alan Sutton, 1988)
Lambourne, L., *An Introduction to Caricature* (HMSO, 1983)
Lambourne, L. and Hamilton, J., *British Watercolours in the Victoria and Albert Museum* (Sotheby Parke Bernet, 1980)
Lofts, W. O. G. and Adley, D. J., *The Men Behind Boys' Fiction* (Howard Baker, 1970)
Low, D., *British Cartoonists, Caricaturists and Comic Artists* (Collins, 1942)
Lucie-Smith, E., *The Art of Caricature* (Orbis, 1981)
Lynch, B., *A History of Caricature* (Faber & Gwyer, 1926)
Lynx, J. (ed.), *The Pen Is Mightier: The Story of the War in Cartoons* (Lindsay Drummond, 1946)
McDonald, I., *Vindication! A Postcard History of the Women's Movement* (Deirdre McDonald/Bellew, 1989)
—— (ed.), *The Boer War in Postcards* (Alan Sutton, Stroud, 1990)
Maddocks, P., *How to Be a Cartoonist/How to Be a Super Cartoonist* (Elm Tree Books, 1986)
—— *Caricature and the Cartoonist* (Elm Tree Books, 1989)
Mahoney, B. E., Latimer, L. P. and Folmsbee, B. (eds), *Illustrators of Children's Books 1744–1945* (Horn Book, Boston, 1947)
Mallalieu, H., *Dictionary of British Watercolour Artists* (Antique Collectors Club, Woodbridge, 1976/1990)
Mathews, R. T. and Mellini, P., *In 'Vanity Fair'* (Scolar Press, Aldershot, 1982)
Meglin, N., *The Art of Humorous Illustration* (Watson-Guptill, New York, 1973)
Meissner, Gunther, *Allgemeines Künstler-Lexikon der bildenden Künstler aller Zeiten und Volker* (Seeman, Leipzig, 1983; K. G. Saur, Munich/New Providence, 1992)
Muir, P. H., *Victorian Illustrated Books* (Batsford, 1971)
Muster, H. P., *Who's Who in Satire and Humour* (Wiese Verlag, Basel, 1989–1990, 3 vols)
Norgate, M. and Wykes, A., *Not So Savage* (Jupiter Books, 1976)
Ormond, R. and Rogers, M. (eds), *Dictionary of British Portraiture: Vol. 4 The 20th Century* (Batsford/NPG, 1981)
Osterwalder, M., *Dictionnaire des illustrateurs 1800–1914* (Editions Ides et Calendes, Neuchâtel, 1989)
Pennell, J., *Pen Drawing and Pen Draughtsmen* (Macmillan, 1889)
—— *Modern Illustration* (Bell, 1895)
Peppin, B., *Fantasy Book Illustration 1860–1920* (Studio Vista, 1975)
Peppin, B. and Micklethwaite, L., *Dictionary of British Book Illustrators: The Twentieth Century* (John Murray, 1983)
Perry, G. and Aldridge, A., *The Penguin Book of Comics* (Penguin, 1967)
Philippe, R., *Political Graphics: Art as a Weapon* (Phaidon, Oxford, 1982)
Pound, R., *The Strand Magazine 1891–1950* (Heinemann, 1966)

Price, R. G. G., *A History of Punch* (Collins, 1957)

Reid, J. G., *At the Sign of the Brush and Pen* (Simpkin Marshall, 1898)

Russell, L. and Bentley, N., *The English Comic Album* (Michael Joseph, 1948)

Saint-Martin, C. and Bertin, J.-M., *5000 Dessinateurs de Presse et Quelques Supports en France de Daumier à Nos Jours* (Solo/Té. Arte, Paris, 1996)

Savory, J. J., *The Vanity Fair Gallery: A Collector's Guide to the Caricatures* (Barnes, New York, 1979)

Shikes, R. E. and Heller, S., *The Art of Satire: Painters as Caricaturists and Cartoonists from Delacroix to Picasso* (Pratt Graphics Center/Horizon Press, New York, 1984)

Sketchley, R. E. D., *English Book Illustration of To-Day* (Kegan Paul, Trench, Trubner, 1903)

Spalding, F., *Dictionary of 20th Century Painters & Sculptors* (Antique Collectors Club, Woodbridge, 1990)

Spielmann, M. H., *The History of Punch* (Cassell, 1895)

Stephens, F. G. and George, M. D., *Catalogue of Political and Personal Satires in the British Museum* (British Museum, 1870–1954)

Stephenson, R., *The Animated Film* (Tantivy Press, 1973)

Thames & Hudson Encyclopedia of Graphic Design & Designers (Thames & Hudson, 1992)

Thieme, U. and Becker, F., *Allgemeines Lexikon der bildenden Künstler von der Antike bis zur Gegenwart* (Engelman, Leipzig, 1907–50; Seeman, Leipzig, 1951–78)

Thomas, P. D. G., *The American Revolution* (Chadwyck-Healey, Cambridge, 1986)

Thomson, R. and Hewison, W., *How to Draw and Sell Cartoons* (Quarto, 1985)

Thorpe, J., *English Illustration: The Nineties* (Faber & Faber, 1935)

Turner, J. (ed.), *The Dictionary of Art* (Macmillan, 1996)

Usherwood, R. D., *Drawing for Radio Times* (Bodley Head, 1961)

Veth, C., *Comic Art in England* (Hertzberger, 1929)

Viguers, R. H., Dalphin, M. and Miller, B. M. (eds), *Illustrators of Children's Books 1946–56* (Horn Book, Boston, 1958)

Vollmer, H., *Allgemeines Lexikon der bildenden Künstler des XX Jahrhunderts* (Seemann, Leipzig, 1953–62)

Walker, M., *Daily Sketches: A Cartoon History of Twentieth-century Britain* (Muller, 1978)

Waters, G. M., *Dictionary of British Artists Working 1900–1950* (Eastbourne Fine Art, Eastbourne, 1975)

Westwood, H. R., *Modern Caricaturists* (Lovat Dickson, 1932)

Whalley, J. L. and Chester, T. R., *A History of Children's Book Illustration* (John Murray/V&A, 1988)

Who Was Who in the Theatre 1912–1976 (Gale Research, Detroit, 1978)

Who's Who in Art (Art Trade Press, 1927–)

Windsor, A. (ed.), *Handbook of Modern British Painting 1900–1980* (Scolar Press, Aldershot, 1992)

—— (ed.), *Handbook of Modern British Painting & Printmaking 1900–1990* (Ashgate, 1998)

Wingfield, M. A., *A Dictionary of Sporting Artists, 1650–1990* (Antique Collectors Club, Woodbridge, 1992)

Wood, C., *Dictionary of Victorian Painters* (Antique Collectors Club, Woodbridge, 1971)

Wood, J., *Hidden Talents: A Dictionary of Neglected Artists Working 1880–1950* (Jeremy Wood Fine Art, Billingshurst, 1994)

Wynn Jones, M., *The Cartoon History of Britain* (Tom Stacey, 1971)

—— *A Cartoon History of the Monarchy* (Macmillan, 1978)

Zeman, Z., *Heckling Hitler, Caricatures of the Third Reich* (Orbis, 1984)